See p. 195
41?
5+5

Ecology of Cities and Towns

A Comparative Approach

The unprecedented growth of cities and towns around the world, coupled with the unknown future effects of global change, has created an urgent need to increase ecological understanding of human settlements, in order to develop inhabitable, sustainable cities and towns in the future. Although there is a wealth of knowledge regarding the understanding of human organisation and behaviour, there is comparatively little information available regarding the ecology of cities and towns. This book brings together leading scientists, landscape designers and planners from developed and developing countries around the world, to explore how urban ecological research has been undertaken to date, what has been learnt, where there are gaps in knowledge, and what the future challenges and opportunities are.

MARK J. MCDONNELL is the Director of the Australian Research Centre for Urban Ecology at the Royal Botanic Garderns in Melbourne, and an Associate Professor in the School of Botany at the University of Melbourne.

AMY K. HAHS is a GIS ecologist at the Australian Research Centre for Urban Ecology at the Royal Botanic Gardens in Melbourne, and a Research Fellow in the School of Botany at the University of Melbourne.

JÜRGEN H. BREUSTE is a Professor of Geography in the Department of Geography and Geology at the University of Salzburg in Austria.

Ecology of Cities and Towns

A Comparative Approach

Edited by

MARK J. McDONNELL
Australian Research Centre for Urban
Ecology, Royal Botanic Gardens
Melbourne, c/o School of Botany,
The University of Melbourne,
VIC 3010, Australia

AMY K. HAHS
Australian Research Centre for Urban
Ecology, Royal Botanic Gardens
Melbourne, c/o School of Botany,
The University of Melbourne,
VIC 3010, Australia

JÜRGEN H. BREUSTE
Research Group Urban Ecology,
Department of Geography and Geology,
University of Salzburg, A–5020 Salzburg,
Austria

CAMBRIDGE
UNIVERSITY PRESS

CAMBRIDGE UNIVERSITY PRESS
Cambridge, New York, Melbourne, Madrid, Cape Town, Singapore, São Paulo, Delhi

Cambridge University Press
The Edinburgh Building, Cambridge CB2 8RU, UK

Published in the United States of America by Cambridge University Press, New York

www.cambridge.org
Information on this title: www.cambridge.org/9780521861120

First published 2009

Printed in the United Kingdom at the University Press, Cambridge

A catalogue record for this publication is available from the British Library

Library of Congress Cataloging-in-Publication Data

Ecology of cities and towns : a comparative approach / edited by Mark J. McDonnell,
Amy K. Hahs, Jürgen H. Breuste.
   p.   cm.
   Includes bibliographical references and index.
   ISBN 978-0-521-86112-0 (hardback) – ISBN 978-0-521-67833-9 (pbk.)   1. Urban ecology (Biology)   2. Nature–Effect of human beings on.   3. Urban ecology.   4. Human
ecology.   I. McDonnell, Mark J.   II. Hahs, Amy K.   III. Breuste, Jürgen.   IV. Title.
   QH541.5.C6E278 2009
   577.5'6072–dc22

                                                                          2008049147

ISBN 978-0-521-86112-0 hardback
ISBN 978-0-521-67833-9 paperback

This book is dedicated to the memory of Katarina (Nina) Löfvenhaft, colleague and friend.

Contents

List of contributors

Andrew H. Baldwin
Department of Environmental Science and Technology, University of Maryland, College Park, MD 20742 USA

Stella Belliss
Landcare Research, PO Box 40, Lincoln 7640, New Zealand

David Blockley
Centre for Research on Ecological Impacts of Coastal Cities, University of Sydney, NSW 2006, Australia

Henk Bouwman
School of Environmental Sciences and Development, North-West University (Potchefstroom Campus), Private Bag X6001, Potchefstroom, 2520 South Africa

Jürgen H. Breuste
Research Group Urban Ecology, Department for Geography and Geology, University of Salzburg, A-5020 Salzburg, Austria

William R. Burch, Jr
Yale School of Forestry & Environmental Studies, New Haven, CT 06511, USA

Mary L. Cadenasso
Department of Plant Sciences, University of California, Davis, CA 95616, USA

Margaret M. Carreiro
Department of Biology, University of Louisville, Louisville, KY 40292, USA

Carla P. Catterall
Environmental Sciences, Griffith University, Nathan, Qld 4111, Australia

M. G. Chapman
Centre for Research on Ecological Impacts of Coastal Cities, University of Sydney, NSW 2006, Australia

Fiona J. Christie
School of Forest and Ecosystem Science, The University of Melbourne, Creswick, VIC 3363, Australia

Sarel Cilliers
School of Environmental Sciences and Development, North-West University (Potchefstroom Campus), Private Bag X6001, Potchefstroom, 2520 South Africa

Brianna Clynick
Centre for Research on Ecological Impacts of Coastal Cities, University of Sydney, NSW 2006, Australia

Jerry Cooper
Landcare Research, PO Box 40, Lincoln 7640, New Zealand

Jennifer E. Dixon
School of Architecture and Planning, The University of Auckland, Auckland, New Zealand

Ernst Drewes
School of Environmental Sciences and Development, North-West University (Potchefstroom Campus), Private Bag X6001, Potchefstroom, 2520 South Africa

Charles T. Eason
CE Research Associates Limited, 4 Arkely Avenue, Pakuranga, Auckland, New Zealand

Gerhard Eisenbeis
Department of Biology, The Johannes Gutenberg-University Mainz, Mainz, 55099 Germany

Clas Florgård
Department of Urban and Rural Development, Unit of Landscape Architecture, Swedish University of Agricultural Sciences, SE-75007 Uppsala, Sweden

Guy Forrester
Landcare Research, PO Box 40, Lincoln 7640, New Zealand

Rhys O. Gardner
178 Cliff View Dr., Green Bay, Auckland, New Zealand

Peter M. Groffman

Institute of Ecosystem Studies, Box AB, Millbrook NY 12545 USA

Glenn R. Guntenspergen

US Geological Survey, Patuxent Wildlife Research Center, Superior, WI, USA

Amy K. Hahs

Australian Research Centre for Urban Ecology, Royal Botanic Gardens Melbourne, c/o School of Botany, The University of Melbourne, VIC 3010, Australia

Graeme Hall

315 Madras St, Christchurch, New Zealand

Andreas Hänel

Museum am Schölerberg, Am Schölerberg 8, D-49082 Osnabrück, Germany

Hiroshi Hashimoto

Meijo University, Faculty of Agriculture, Department of Environmental Bioscience, Kitashirakawaoiwakecho, Kakyo-ku, Kyoto 606-8502, Japan

Dieter F. Hochuli

School of Biological Sciences, University of Sydney, Sydney, NSW 2006, Australia

Dianna M. Hogan

US Geological Survey, Reston, VA 20192, USA

Maria E. Ignatieva

Environment, Society and Design, Lincoln University, Lincoln 7647, New Zealand

D. Johan Kotze

Department of Biological and Environmental Sciences, University of Helsinki, FI-00014 Helsinki, Finland

Robert G. M. Kwak

Landscape Centre, Alterra, PO Box 47, 6700 AA Wageningen, The Netherlands

Susanna Lehvävirta

Department of Biological and Environmental Sciences, University of Helsinki, FI-00014 Helsinki, Finland

Katarina Löfvenhaft

Department of Physical Geography and Quaternary Geology, Stockholm University, 106 91 Stockholm, Sweden (Deceased)

Boris Lomov
School of Biological Sciences, University of Sydney, Sydney, NSW 2006, Australia

Orie L. Loucks
Department of Zoology, Miami University, Oxford, OH 45056, USA

Michael McCarthy
School of Botany, The University of Melbourne, VIC 3010, Australia

Mark J. McDonnell
Australian Research Centre for Urban Ecology, Royal Botanic Gardens Melbourne, c/o School of Botany, The University of Melbourne, VIC 3010, Australia

Nancy E. McIntyre
Department of Biological Sciences, Texas Tech University, Lubbock, TX 79409-3131, USA

Colin D. Meurk
Landcare Research, PO Box 40, Lincoln 7647, New Zealand

Ulla Mörtberg
Department of Land and Water Resources Engineering, Royal Institute of Technology, SE-10044 Stockholm, Sweden

Laura R. Musacchio
Department of Landscape Architecture, University of Minnesota, 89 Church St SE, Minneapolis, MN 55455, USA

Yosihiro Natuhara
Graduate School of Agriculture and Biological Sciences, Osaka Prefecture University, Sakai 599-8531, Japan

Hilary A. Neckles
USGS Patuxent Wildlife Research Center, 196 Whitten Road, Augusta, ME 04330, USA

Martha G. Nielsen
US Geological Survey, Water Science Center, Augusta, ME 04330, USA

Jari Niemelä
Department of Biological and Environmental Sciences, PO Box 65, FIN-00014 University of Helsinki, Finland

Charles Nilon
Department of Fisheries and Wildlife Sciences, University of Missouri-Columbia, Columbia, MO 65211-7240, USA

Kristina L. Nilsson
Department of Urban and Rural Development, Unit of Landscape Architecture, Swedish University of Agricultural Sciences, SE-75007 Uppsala, Sweden

Heather North
Landcare Research, PO Box 40, Lincoln 7640, New Zealand

Kathryn O'Halloran
Landcare Research, PO Box 40, Lincoln 7640, New Zealand

Kirsten M. Parris
School of Botany, The University of Melbourne, VIC 3010, Australia

Mitchell A. Pavao-Zuckerman
Institute of Ecology, University of Georgia, Athens, GA 30602, USA

Julie People
Centre for Research on Ecological Impacts of Coastal Cities, University of Sydney, NSW 2006, Australia

Steward T. A. Pickett
Institute of Ecosystem Studies, Box AB, Millbrook, NY 12545, USA

Richard V. Pouyat
USDA Forest Service, Northern Research Station, c/o Center for Urban and Environmental Research and Education, University of Maryland Baltimore County, Baltimore, MD 21227, USA

Jessamy J. Rango
Department of Biology, Anne Arundel Community College, Arnold, MD 21012-1895, USA

Robbert Snep
Landscape Centre, Alterra, PO Box 47, 6700 AA Wageningen, The Netherlands

Glenn H. Stewart
Bio-protection and Ecology, Lincoln University, Lincoln 7647, New Zealand

Bill Sykes
Landcare Research, PO Box 40, Lincoln 7640, New Zealand

Wim Timmermans
Landscape Centre, Alterra, PO Box 47, 6700 AA Wageningen, The Netherlands

Christopher E. Tripler
School of Arts and Sciences, Endicott College, Beverly, MA 01915, USA

Anthony J. Underwood
Centre for Research on Ecological Impacts of Coastal Cities, University of Sydney, NSW 2006, Australia

Rodney van der Ree
Australian Research Centre for Urban Ecology, Royal Botanic Gardens Melbourne, c/o School of Botany, The University of Melbourne, VIC 3010, Australia

Marjorie R. van Roon
School of Architecture and Planning, The University of Auckland, Auckland, New Zealand

Kathryn Whaley
Queen Elizabeth II National Trust, PO Box 3341, Wellington, New Zealand

Mike Wilcox
9 Scott Avenue, Mangere Bridge, Auckland, New Zealand

Rüdiger Wittig
Institute of Ecology, Evolution and Diversity, Johann Wolfgang Goethe University, 60323 Frankfurt/Main, Germany

Jun Yang
Department of Landscape Architecture and Horticulture, Temple University – Ambler, 580 Meetinghouse Road, Ambler, PA 19002, USA

Vesa Yli-Pelkonen
Department of Biological and Environmental Sciences, PO Box 65, FIN-00014 University of Helsinki, Finland

Zhou Jinxing
Institute of Forestry, Chinese Academy of Forests, Beijing 100091, China

Wei-Xing Zhu
Biological Sciences Department, Binghamton University, Binghamton, NY 13902, USA

Wayne C. Zipperer
USDA Forest Service, Southern Research Station, PO Box 110806, Bldg 164
Morwy Rd, Gainesville, FL 32611-0806, USA

Nadya Zvyagna
Landcare Research, PO Box 40, Lincoln 7640, New Zealand

Preface

Calls to study the ecology of urban areas were first made in the early twentieth century by both social scientists and traditional ecologists (i.e. plant and animal ecologists) (Adams, 1935, 1938). Some 40 years later, the Ecological Society of Australia held a symposium and published a follow-up book entitled *The City as a Life System* (Nix, 1972) which aimed to stimulate public and professional interest in the ecology of cities. At about the same time, a workshop was convened in the USA by The Institute of Ecology (TIE), now defunct, which brought together ecologists from a diversity of disciplines to identify national and regional urban needs. The proceedings of this workshop were published in a book entitled *The Urban Ecosystem: A Holistic Approach* (Stearns and Montag, 1974). Unfortunately, these books were not widely distributed and thus these early workshop efforts did not stimulate new North American or Australian ecological studies of human settlements. In contrast, European and some Australasian researchers have embraced the ecological study of urban ecosystems for over 30 years (e.g. Numata, 1976, 1977; Newcombe *et al.*, 1978; Boyden *et al.*, 1981; Bornkamm *et al.*, 1982; Natuhara and Imai, 1996, 1999; Breuste *et al.*, 1998; Sukopp, 1998, 2002).

Over the past 10 years there has been a growing call to increase our knowledge of the physical, biological and social components of cities and towns in order to develop a greater understanding of their ecology and to help mitigate some of the impacts that human settlements are having at local, regional and global scales (Grimm *et al.*, 2000; Collins *et al.*, 2000; Pickett *et al.*, 2001; Alberti *et al.*, 2003). These efforts are understandable and laudable given the increasing realisation that the growth of cities lies at the core of many environmental and social problems facing the world today. With the unparalleled growth of human settlements around the world, coupled with the unknown effects of global change, there is now an urgent need to increase our ecological understanding of cities and towns.

The inspiration for this book came from a symposium held at the International Association for Landscape Ecology (IALE) World Congress in Darwin, Australia, in 2003 and a workshop held in Melbourne the same year. Leading ecologists, landscape architects and planners met to discuss and assess the current state of the field of urban ecology. One modest goal of these meetings and this book was to bring together researchers from around the world. Although studies in North America, Europe and Asia have produced excellent advances in the field of urban ecology, there have been relatively few interactions between the different groups. This book is intended to build on our current level of ecological understanding of cities and towns, which was last summarised by McDonnell and Pickett (1993b) and Breuste *et al.* (1998), and to promote the use of the comparative ecological approach in the study of human settlements.

A book such as this could not be put together without the help of many different people. We would like to thank our fellow members of the Steering Committee from the original workshop in 2003: Margaret Carreiro, Glenn Guntenspergen and Jari Niemelä, who provided valuable input and feedback regarding the structure of the workshop, and hence this book. Thanks also to Kirsten Parris and Jari Niemelä who organised the follow-up symposium at the 2004 Conservation Biology meeting at Columbia University, New York City. M. J. M. and A. K. H. would like to thank Phil Moors and Pauline Ladiges for their support of the 2003 workshop and the subsequent efforts in compiling this book. The many staff and students at the Australian Research Centre for Urban Ecology (ARCUE) were also instrumental both during the workshop and the compilation of this book.

We are indebted to the Baker Foundation for their generous ongoing financial support for ARCUE, without which we could not have undertaken this project. We would also like to acknowledge their financial assistance for the 2003 workshop and symposium and subsequent preparation of this book. Generous financial and in-kind support for the workshop was also provided by the US Geological Survey, the School of Botany at the University of Melbourne, and the Royal Botanic Gardens Melbourne.

We would also like to thank all of the scientists who participated in the 2003 symposium and workshop and the follow-up symposium in 2004, as their involvement helped to shape the ideas presented here. We would like to express our gratitude to Alan Crowden for encouraging us to produce a book and for facilitating its publication with Cambridge University Press. We are grateful to all of the contributors for their enthusiasm in preparing their chapters, and their efforts in reviewing and providing feedback on chapters submitted by their peers.

The overall quality and content of the book was greatly enhanced by several groups of people. We would like to thank Maggie McDonnell and Adam, Barbara, and Kelly Hahs for their assistance in compiling the index. We are grateful to Lily McDonnell for creating the cover illustration. Julia Stammers has provided invaluable assistance during the editing, proof-reading and indexing stages. Finally, we acknowledge and appreciate the efforts of the Cambridge University Press production team including Dominic Lewis, Alison Evans, Charlotte Broom and Lindsay Nightingale in creating the book. In particular, Lindsay's sharp eye and remarkable editiorial skills significantly improved its quality and readability.

1

Introduction: Scope of the book and need for developing a comparative approach to the ecological study of cities and towns

MARK J. MCDONNELL, JÜRGEN H. BREUSTE AND AMY K. HAHS

Introduction

The growth of cities and towns together with the associated increase in their ecological 'footprint' is one of the most serious ecological problems facing the world today. The increase in the number of people living in cities and towns, coupled with the magnitude and intensity of human activities, has resulted in what Likens (1991) refers to as human-accelerated environmental change. This includes changes in land use, toxification of the biosphere, invasion of exotic species and loss of biotic diversity. These changes are most evident in major cities, but significant changes are also occurring in peri-urban areas, in small towns and especially in coastal settlements. The rate of change associated with the expansion and creation of cities and towns is particularly high in developing countries (Lee, 2007). Human-accelerated environmental change is occurring at small and large spatial scales throughout the world, but the true magnitude of the impact of these changes is difficult to envisage because of uncertainties in the predicted effects of global climate change (IPCC, 2001).

We face many challenges and potential conflicts if we are to manage current day-to-day problems and attempt the bigger task of creating sustainable cities and towns in the future. Although cities and towns are dominated by human-built structures and activities (buildings, vehicles, impermeable surfaces, parks,

Ecology of Cities and Towns: A Comparative Approach, ed. Mark J. McDonnell, Amy K. Hahs and Jürgen H. Breuste. Published by Cambridge University Press. © Cambridge University Press 2009.

etc.), they are functioning ecosystems that possess many of the same components (plants, animals, water, soil, etc.) and processes (i.e. nutrient and water cycling) as less human-dominated natural systems (McDonnell and Pickett, 1993b; Grimm *et al.*, 2003). If we are to succeed in creating sustainable cities and towns, we need a more comprehensive understanding of how these ecosystems are structured and how they function. It is equally important that everyone associated with human-dominated environments, including planners, builders, economists, policy makers, academics and the public, use this understanding when making decisions that affect the physical, socio-economic and ecological vigour of these ecosystems (Nilon *et al.*, 2003). Attempts have been made to incorporate ecological principles into urban planning but more efforts will be needed (Sukopp *et al.*, 1995; Niemelä, 1999a; Felson and Pickett, 2005).

Historically, there has been a plethora of information available on the physical and socio-economic condition of cities and towns. Unfortunately, our current ecological understanding of cities and towns is poor by comparison because traditional ecological studies, especially in the New World and Oceania, have focused on areas with low human population densities (McDonnell and Pickett, 1993b). Over the past 20 years there has been a growing body of research on the ecology of cities and towns (Gilbert, 1989; Sukopp *et al.*, 1990; McDonnell and Pickett, 1993b; Breuste *et al.*, 1998; Pickett *et al.*, 2001; Paul and Meyer, 2001; Sukopp, 2002), but the demand for additional information and for the development of 'general principles' by policy makers, management and public stakeholders has been difficult to fulfil with the available state of our knowledge.

The bulk of our current understanding comes from research that can be described as 'ecology in cities' (Grimm *et al.*, 2000). These studies are focused on the effect of human settlements on populations, communities and ecosystems and, for example, would involve the study of the distribution and abundance of native and exotic organisms within a city or the rate of decomposition within remnant patches of vegetation in a city versus patches outside a city. Relatively few studies have focused on the 'ecology of cities', which involves developing an integrated understanding of the ecology of the collective parts of cities and towns (Grimm *et al.*, 2000). These studies would involve assessments of the flux of nutrients, water, energy and organisms throughout entire cities and towns (Newcombe *et al.*, 1978), or the effects of land-use change over time on the distribution and abundance of organisms within a city (Wu *et al.*, 2003). It seems reasonable to deduce that the most appropriate and productive questions that can be addressed using this integrated approach are at the scale of whole cities and towns. Focusing research questions at this scale requires multidisciplinary teams of researchers and large amounts of resources (time, money and energy) that are difficult for individual research groups to acquire, and thus, understandably, relatively little progress has been made. The result is that there have been few basic ecological studies focused on the ecology 'of' cities.

Over the past five years there has been a growing call to integrate the physical, biological/ecological and social components of urban environments in order to develop a holistic ecology of urban areas which has been identified as the crucial first step in creating sustainable cities (Collins *et al.*, 2000; Grimm *et al.*, 2000; Pickett *et al.*, 2001; Alberti *et al.*, 2003). Historically, ecologists have been criticised for using very coarse measures to represent the human and economic components of urban ecosystems. However, in many cases we are still trying to understand even these coarse-scale ecological patterns. To some extent, the level of integration between the social, physical and ecological sciences is limited by our least developed level of understanding. In most cases, this is the ecological information. As illustrated by several chapters in this book, this ecological understanding is now reaching the point at which we can start to incorporate finer-scale understandings of the social and political systems, and move towards a more sophisticated understanding of the ecology 'of' cities. However, studies of ecology 'in' cities will continue to play an important role in the short term, as we attempt to bring our ecological understanding up to a level that matches our understanding of social and physical patterns and processes within cities and towns.

Today, interest in the ecology of cities and towns around the world is growing in leaps and bounds. Not surprisingly, concurrent with this recent interest there has been a significant growth in the number of new academic and government programmes, and in research dollars spent on studying the ecology of human settlements. The resulting increase in published research certainly assists in filling the ecological information gaps mentioned earlier (Theobald, 2004). Cities vary enormously in their human population, history of development, cultural make-up, spatial extent and physical location, but there is still a remarkable similarity throughout the world in both their structure and dynamics. Ecological studies of urban and suburban ecosystems are loosely based on existing principles from such fields as geography and landscape ecology. Many of these studies already use a comparative approach (McDonnell and Hahs, Chapter 5), although the comparative aspect is not explicitly acknowledged and the studies involve primarily local or regional comparisons (e.g. urban–rural gradients). At present there has been little attempt to compare the ecology of different cities and towns at continental and global scales in order to construct a more comprehensive conceptual framework for creating comparable methodologies and general principles (i.e. confirmed generalisations).

The purpose of this book is (1) to evaluate the current state of understanding of the ecology of cities and towns around the world, and the methodologies used to obtain this information; (2) to provide examples of how ecological information has been effectively integrated into urban management and planning schemes; and (3) to explore the opportunities and challenges of developing a comparative approach to the ecological study of cities and towns.

The book is separated into four sections, each of which contains contributions from leading scientists, landscape architects and planners in the field. Part I provides a foundation for evaluating the merits of challenges of conducting comparative studies of cities and towns. Several chapters also explore the theoretical underpinning of the science and provide examples of conceptual frameworks for conducting the research. Most of the chapters provide an assessment of the current urban ecology literature, but this collection of reviews is unique in that it includes research conducted not only on terrestrial habitats but also freshwater, estuarine and marine environments. Chapter 5 explicitly investigates the past, present and future uses of comparative ecology, and presents some suggestions about how to expand the scope of comparative studies of cities and towns to continental and global scales. Historically, the study of urban and suburban environments has been conducted in developed countries; Chapter 6 explores the application of the existing urban ecology conceptual frameworks to the study of urban environments in South Africa. The final chapter in this section explores the use of models as tools for conducting comparative studies of cities and towns.

Part II provides an up-to-date assessment of the research questions, hypotheses, methodologies and statistical analyses currently used by leading urban ecologists to understand the ecology of animals, insects, plants and ecosystem dynamics of cities and towns located in both the Northern and Southern Hemispheres. The chapters in this section broaden the current level of understanding of the ecology of urban environments by investigating not only the typical urban and suburban terrestrial environments, but also marine habitats, roadsides and front yards. It is impossible in a book of this size to cover every current research topic, but our goal is to highlight some of the seminal studies that are currently being conducted in the hope of stimulating new research on cities and towns.

Part III includes a collection of chapters by ecologists, landscape architects and planners that provide concrete examples of how the integration of ecological understanding and design principles can be used to create more sustainable cities and towns. They describe techniques for analysing the structure of urban and suburban landscapes and methods of conducting ecological assessments. Chapter 23 explores the similarity of garden and park forms around the world and suggests how new designs and plantings can help maintain biodiversity and ecological processes in human settlements. There are several chapters that provide unique insights into preserving biodiversity in cities and towns as well as preserving and managing specific habitats such as remnant patches of vegetation, parkland, streams and wetlands. One of the major impacts of cities and towns is the creation of new developments. Chapter 27 explores how the integration of research from several fields into design and building practices can assist in preserving biodiversity and improving the quality of life for city dwellers.

There are five chapters in Part IV which include three different types of commentaries. Chapters 30 to 32 provide specific opinions on topics related to the ecological study of cities and towns, and the integration of scientific information into urban and landscape planning. Chapters 33 and 34 are summaries of the proceedings of the original Melbourne workshop. They provide some insights into the flavour of the meeting and an indication of future opportunities in the field, especially those related to conducting comparative studies. Finally, Chapter 35 provides an overall synthesis of the themes that have arisen from the book and also outlines some directions for future opportunities for research and integration of scientific understanding into landscape and urban design.

Most chapters were originally presented as papers at the two meetings. However, a few additional chapters have been included to provide greater coverage of the current scope of knowledge related to the ecology of cities and towns. During the original meetings and in the preparation of this book, all the participants/contributors were challenged to think more broadly about the state of our knowledge and identify the gaps as well as the effectiveness of our current methodologies and tools. They were also asked to consider ways to improve the integration of ecological, physical and socio-economic data into our studies in order to achieve better conservation and design outcomes. Finally, we encouraged them to assess whether there are general principles about the components of the systems they study and their interactions, and the opportunities that exist to conduct further comparative studies. These general themes are woven throughout the book and will be evident to the reader by the number of cross chapter references. We hope that this volume will provide a useful collection of conceptual frameworks, research results, methodologies, designs and outcomes which will stimulate new integrated research in the field and assist in developing general principles for creating sustainable cities and towns in the future.

Part I OPPORTUNITIES AND CHALLENGES OF
CONDUCTING COMPARATIVE STUDIES

2

Comparative urban ecology: challenges and possibilities

JARI NIEMELÄ, D. JOHAN KOTZE AND VESA YLI-PELKONEN

Introduction

Our research has been inspired by the views of Dennis and Ruggiero (1996) who emphasised that even simple inventories, if done with quality and consistency and repeated over large geographical areas, can provide valuable understanding about ecology and the impacts of humans across the world. Approximately 75% of the human population in industrialised countries lived in cities in 2003 and it is projected that half of the world's population will be urban by 2007 (United Nations, 2004). In order to ensure that urban areas are planned for the well-being of both city dwellers and urban biodiversity, knowledge of the responses of the urban ecosystem – including ecological and human components – to the influence of urbanisation is pivotal (McDonnell and Pickett, 1990; Niemelä, 1999a).

Urbanisation creates patchworks of modified land types that exhibit similar patterns throughout the world. Nonetheless, little is known about whether these changes affect biodiversity in similar ways across the globe, or depend more on local conditions (Samways, 1992). Thus, there is a need for comparative, international research to assess the effects of these activities on native biodiversity, and, where possible, to minimise adverse effects (Dennis and Ruggiero, 1996; Andersen, 1999). Such research could potentially distinguish globally recurring patterns and convergence from more local phenomena. The new knowledge could enhance the development of urban ecology as a scientific discipline and

Ecology of Cities and Towns: A Comparative Approach, ed. Mark J. McDonnell, Amy K. Hahs and Jürgen H. Breuste. Published by Cambridge University Press. © Cambridge University Press 2009.

foster international collaboration among researchers and managers in finding ways to mitigate the adverse effects of human-caused landscape change.

A useful framework in which to investigate the biotic and abiotic effects of urbanisation is the urban–rural gradient approach (McDonnell and Pickett, 1990; Blair and Launer, 1997; McDonnell et al., 1997; Niemelä, 1999a; Niemelä et al., 2002; Pickett et al., Chapter 3). Such gradients, from densely built city cores to increasingly rural surroundings, reflect diminishing intensities of human intervention on originally similar land bases. Although types of ecosystems and human impacts differ across the world, making global comparisons difficult, urban landscapes are relatively comparable around the world and provide a useful framework for comparative work on a global scale (Niemelä, 1999b).

This kind of research on ecology in cities forms the necessary basis for ecology of cities, which integrates ecological and human systems in the urban setting. However, we still lack a firm understanding of ecology in cities, partly because ecologists have been reluctant to pay attention to urban areas and partly because of a lack of a theoretical framework within which to conduct such research. This is particularly true for marine and coastal habitats (as discussed by Chapman and Underwood, Chapter 4; Chapman et al., Chapter 9). It appears that theories developed in and for other environments do not always do justice to the special features of urban ecological systems (Niemelä, 1999a).

The aim of this chapter is, first, to discuss the theoretical and conceptual basis of urban ecology. In particular, we examine whether theories developed for other environments are useful in studying ecological questions in cities. Second, we use examples from across the world in a comparative manner to highlight the special features of urban ecological systems and to show how such studies can contribute to the development of theory in urban ecology. To deepen the comparative aspect, we discuss two different cases of comparative work: one dealing with a conceptual framework of urban ecosystems developed in the United States and applied in Finland, another based on a common methodology for examining biotic responses to urbanisation in visually similar urban land-mosaics in different parts of the world.

What is urban ecology?

In order to define the concept 'urban ecology', the constituent words 'urban' and 'ecology' need to be discussed. 'Urban' refers to a human community with a high density of people, their dwellings and other constructions. Numerical definitions of urban do exist (based, for example, on population density), but a general definition is more practical for research purposes. A useful way to define 'urban' is to consider gradients of land use. According to Forman and Godron (1986), the intensity of human influence divides landscapes into five broad types spanning the continuum from pristine natural environments to urban centres highly modified by people. At the pristine end of the gradient, natural landscapes support mostly unmanaged native biota, while the managed landscape consists of planted and/or managed native or non-native species. In the middle of the gradient, cultivated landscapes consist of a matrix of agricultural lands that can be either crops or grazing land. The suburban landscapes include low- to moderate-density housing, yards and roads. The urban end of the gradient represents landscapes of the most intense human influence dominated by high-density residential and commercial buildings, roads and other paved surfaces. Despite obvious differences, all these land-use types may include patches of other types (Forman and Godron, 1986). This urban-to-rural gradient forms a fruitful concept for examining ecological effects of the intensity of human influence on the biota (McDonnell *et al.*, 1997). Although this approach has been shown to be successful in terrestrial habitats, the usefulness of the urban–rural gradient (or its equivalent) has not been extensively explored for identifying human impacts on coastal habitats extending out from centres of the human population.

The meaning of the word 'ecology' has expanded during recent decades (Egerton, 1993). More specifically, Haila and Levins (1992) recognise four different meanings of the term. Ecology the science investigates nature's 'economy' (flows of matter and energy or the distribution and abundance of organisms), while ecology as nature is seen as the resource base for humans. Ecology the idea is a concept that views human existence in relation to ecology the science ('human ecology') and ecology the movement refers to political activities related to ecological and environmental issues (the 'green' movement).

As a consequence, 'urban ecology' is a complex concept with different dimensions. However, here we define 'ecology' as natural science but keep in mind its other definitions. The different approaches to urban ecological research indicate that urban ecology is a broad discipline which can be defined as ecological research in the urban setting (Rebele, 1994). In addition to the scientific component, urban ecological studies usually aim at applications of research in the planning and management of urban green areas (Wittig and Sukopp, 1993). Thus, urban ecology is by nature an applied science.

It is useful to distinguish between two complementary approaches to the study of urban ecology. Research into ecology *in* cities refers to studies on the physical environment, soils, fauna and flora, and differences between urban and other environments (Grimm *et al.*, 2000; Pickett *et al.*, Chapter 3). This kind of research forms the necessary foundation for understanding ecological processes and patterns in urban ecosystems. Research into the ecology *of* cities builds on the foundation formed by research into ecology in cities and may use partly similar methods. The ecology of cities approach, however, uses the ecosystem framework and studies the urban area as an interactive system including both human and ecological components. Clearly, a framework for studies in ecology of cities should include both ecological and human systems.

Thus, it is evident that as well as being of applied nature, urban ecology is multidisciplinary. Both urban research and its applications would gain from increased collaboration between ecologists, sociologists and urban planners (see Blood, 1994). Ecological research and its applications would benefit from the input of knowledge of human actions in urban areas, while the development of residential areas that maintain and improve the quality of life, the health and the well-being of urban residents would benefit from a better ecological understanding.

Urban ecology: a neglected field of ecological studies?

Traditionally, mainstream ecological research has neglected urban areas. Ecologists have focused on pristine or rural nature, and have considered urban nature as less 'worthy', owing to strong human influences in cities (Gilbert, 1989; McDonnell and Pickett, 1993a; McDonnell, 1997). For example, although 80% of the Finnish population is urban (and increasing), urban studies have not been appreciated by ecologists in the country. As a consequence, urban ecological research is not well developed in Finland, biodiversity of urban habitats is poorly documented in many cities, and thus baseline information about urban ecology is scarce. As a result, the possibilities of applying ecological knowledge in urban planning are limited. This unsatisfactory situation has been recognised by planners, managers and concerned citizens, many of whom regard the use of scientifically gathered ecological information an integral tool in urban planning (Haila, 1995; Yli-Pelkonen and Niemelä, 2005).

Luckily, this state of affairs appears to be changing for several reasons. First, profound changes in ecological understanding are taking place (Pickett *et al.*, 1992; McDonnell, 1997; Pickett *et al.*, 1997c). The traditional view of ecology has been that of a balanced nature (see Pimm, 1991), i.e. that ecological systems are in equilibrium. Disturbed systems are in disequilibrium, and, therefore, not 'good' nature according to the equilibrial view. This view of ecological systems is giving way to dynamism and the recognition that systems are often not in equilibrium.

Second, urban green space is becoming increasingly important for residents in a socio-cultural respect – for recreation, or as a source of peace and inspiration (Tyrväinen *et al.*, 2003). Visiting urban green areas and particularly 'favourite places' provides urban residents with an important opportunity for self-restoration and relaxation (Korpela *et al.*, 2001). Furthermore, urban residents increasingly choose their area of residence based on the existence of green areas and easy access to such environments (Grahn and Stigsdotter, 2003).

Third, in Finland, new legislation states that biodiversity must be considered and citizen participation must be secured in urban planning. This new legislation combined with the changing views and attitudes of the increasing number of urbanites contributes to increasing the value of urban biodiversity.

Fourth, and related to the previous points, the laws of 'market economy' operate here. Because of urbanisation, urban green space is decreasing and people are willing to pay more for houses close to green areas (supply versus demand) (Tyrväinen, 1997, 2001). This increases the value (both monetary and appreciation) of urban green and encourages urban planners to take biodiversity into consideration in urban land-use planning.

Why are urban ecosystems special?

Many ecological processes, such as predation, competition and decomposition, are the same in urban and rural nature (Sukopp and Numata, 1995; Walbridge, 1997). Urban nature has, however, special features that are caused by the strong influence of humans. These effects can be viewed as negative or positive for the ecosystem. For instance, rates of certain ecosystem processes appear to be higher in urban than in rural sites (Carreiro *et al.*, Chapter 19; and Pouyat *et al.*, Chapter 20). Pouyat *et al.* (1997) reported that both mass loss and nitrogen release from litterbags placed in oak stands along an urban–rural gradient in southeastern New York reached their maximum in urban stands, and net nitrogen mineralisation rates were much higher in urban than in rural stands. Litter fragmentation by earthworms and higher soil temperatures in urban sites are potential causes of these differences (McDonnell *et al.*, 1997). In addition to providing insight into the functioning of ecosystems, this kind of information is of vital importance for planning and management purposes.

Three main properties that distinguish urban landscapes from natural ones may help explain patterns and processes in urban settings (Trepl, 1995; Niemelä, 1999a). These are: integration (organisation, connectivity) among urban habitat patches and communities in them; high degree of invasion by alien species; and succession as determined by humans ('arrested succession'; Bradshaw 2003) and changes to the abiotic environment. To these, a high diversity of urban nature can be added. This biodiversity relates both to species diversity and diversity of habitat types. In the following we briefly discuss each of these properties.

Integration among urban habitat patches

Integration (connectivity) among habitat patches and their respective species communities is often low in cities. Patches are isolated from each other by a matrix of built environment and non-native vegetation, making dispersal difficult and risky, at least for poorly dispersing organisms (Gilbert, 1989). For instance, Davis (1978) noted that the best predictor of species richness of ground arthropods in gardens in London was the proportion of green areas within a 1-km radius of the sampling site.

The degree to which urban habitat patches are isolated from each other varies from species to species. For birds, the built environment between green patches within a city is not a dispersal barrier, while for less mobile species such an environment may be an insuperable obstacle. In addition to dispersal ability, the habitat requirements of species affect their distribution in urban environments. Thus, a combination of good dispersal ability and wide habitat requirements may be an advantage in urban environments (Gilbert, 1989).

The general landscape ecological approach (Forman and Godron, 1986) could be successfully used in urban environments to address issues related to size, connectivity and isolation of habitat patches (Duhme and Pauleit, 1992a). Some more specific theories have also been used in urban studies. For example, in accordance with island biogeography theory, Klausnitzer (1993) provided several examples of the positive relationship between species richness and the area of the habitat patch as would be predicted from classical island biogeography theory. Similarly, Weigmann (1982) noted that species richness of several groups of arthropods correlated positively with the size of the habitat patch, and Brown and Freitas (2003) reported a positive correlation between species richness of butterflies and size of urban forest patches in Sao Paulo, Brazil.

Although the theory of island biogeography is appealing for planning purposes owing to the clarity of its basic principles, the theory deals with species richness and neglects species identities. However, species composition is an important consideration in any planning situation. Furthermore, urban habitats are quite different from true islands because, in the urban setting, there is usually no evident mainland to serve as a source area. On the other hand, the matrix in cities may not be as hostile for some species as water surrounding oceanic islands because there are networks of habitat patches that may enhance species dispersal through an urban area (Duhme and Pauleit, 1992a). Despite these shortcomings, the theory of island biogeography may serve as an exploration of the relationship between species richness and characteristics of urban habitat patches. Useful ecological information for planners and managers must, however, include more precise knowledge about species composition and population sizes.

Another application of landscape ecology and the island biogeography theory has been the recommendation that habitat patches should be connected by movement conduits (corridors, greenways) to enhance dispersal of individuals and thereby increase population persistence in the connected patches (Simberloff *et al.*, 1992; Niemelä, 1999b). According to recommendations by Noss (1993), such greenways should be designed and managed for native species. This will require consideration of the needs of species sensitive to fragmentation and human disturbance over the needs of introduced and opportunistic species that tolerate or thrive in urban landscapes (see also Dawson, 1994). Furthermore, the cost-effectiveness of designing and setting aside corridors should be carefully compared with other means of maintaining urban biodiversity (Dawson, 1994). Noss (1993) also emphasised that the planning unit should be the minimal area necessary to ensure demographic and genetic survival of the species. Naturally, the spatial scale will vary depending on the area requirements of the focal species. However, greenways and corridors should not be a substitute for the protection of large, intact nature reserves in the urban or suburban landscape (see also Dawson, 1994; Mörtberg and Wallentinus, 2000). For instance, it was demonstrated by Halme and Niemelä (1993) that only large, continuous forest tracts can maintain populations of the most sensitive forest carabid beetles.

These corridor issues are all ecological, but there may be other justifications for establishing ecological greenways, such as aesthetic values or wind barriers. Part of the controversy of movement corridors is that professionals with different disciplinary backgrounds may understand the concept of 'corridor' differently, which may lead to confusion about the goals or implied functions of corridors (Hess and Fischer, 2001).

Although the establishment of movement conduits in the landscape appears appealing, there is inconclusive information about their significance for biota (Simberloff *et al.*, 1992; Bennett, 1999; Niemelä, 1999b), in particular in urban environments (Adams and Dove, 1989). Making management suggestions based on such incomplete knowledge is a typical situation where scientists are concerned about making a Type II error by accepting a false null-hypothesis (that corridors have no effect). Therefore, scientists tend to favour the 'precautionary' principle and suggest that, despite gaps in our understanding of the usefulness of corridors, it is better to retain corridors and then assess their role than to lose them and find out afterwards that they were important (Saunders and Hobbs, 1991; Harrison and Voller, 1998).

Invasion of urban habitats by species

Increased human travel and cultivation of exotic species, for example in gardens, have increased the frequency of introductions of non-native species, especially in cities (Rebele, 1994). For instance, in Berlin, the proportion of alien plant species increased from 28% in the outer suburbs to 50% in the built-up centre of the city (Sukopp *et al.*, 1979a). Studies along a 140-km urban–rural environmental gradient starting in New York City showed a considerably higher exotic earthworm biomass (2.16 g worms/m^2) and abundance (25.1 worms/m^2) in urban forests than in rural forests (0.05 g worms/m^2, 2.1 worms/m^2; McDonnell *et al.*, 1997; Steinberg *et al.*, 1997). Another example of successful urban invaders is insects. For instance, in western Canada, the 20 ground beetle (Carabidae) species of European origin are synanthropic (Spence and Spence, 1988) and make up the majority of carabids in cities (Niemelä and Spence, 1991; Niemelä *et al.*, 2002). Although introduced species, including domestic animals, add to the diversity of urban environments, they may depress populations of native species (McDonnell *et al.*, 1993; Lepczyk *et al.*, 2003).

Succession and abiotic conditions in urban habitats

Many urban habitats are kept at an early successional stage by regular disturbance, such as mowing and woodland thinning. This 'arrested succession' (Bradshaw, 2003) may create successional stages that are rich in species, as shown by Small *et al.* (2003) for carabids in derelict sites in England. Furthermore, the patchy distribution of urban habitats, combined with varying degrees of management and disturbance (such as trampling) and stochastic events, results in a number of successional pathways across habitat patches. Even adjacent patches may show very different successional patterns depending on the colonisation history of plants, which is to a great extent determined by chance events (Gilbert, 1989). This historical uniqueness and overwhelming external control of succession is an important feature distinguishing urban habitats from more natural ones (Trepl, 1995).

Also, several abiotic factors differ between urban and rural areas, temperature being one of the most obvious ones. Many species requiring high temperatures thrive in cities owing to increased temperatures compared to the surroundings (Gilbert, 1989). This 'heat island effect' can be considerable (see Kalnay and Cai, 2003). For instance, compared with rural areas, average temperatures in cities are approximately 1–2 °C higher during winter, and 0.5–1.0 °C higher during summer in the mid-latitudinal United States (Botkin and Beveridge, 1997). However, the heat island effect may be unfavourable to some native species, such as snails, that cannot tolerate the increased temperatures (Baur, 1994).

High alpha- and beta-diversity in urban landscapes

The high total species richness of an urban landscape is a result of high richness in individual habitat patches (alpha-diversity) and variation in species communities between patches (beta-diversity) (see Rebele, 1994). Numerous studies document high alpha-diversity in urban habitat patches from various parts of the world. A contributing factor is that many species of different origins find suitable conditions in anthropogenic habitats. For instance, the area of wastelands and of semi-natural grass–herb forests is approximately the same in Vantaa, southern Finland, but the number of vascular plant species is much higher in wastelands (412 species) than in the grass–herb forests (262 species). The reason is that, in addition to slightly higher numbers of native species, wastelands harbour more immigrant species than do grass–herb forests (Ranta et al., 1997). Similarly, Gödde et al. (1995) reported from Düsseldorf, Germany, that highly disturbed sites, such as wastelands and gravel pits, had greater species richness of vascular plants, butterflies, grasshoppers, landsnails and woodlice than did more natural habitats.

Some groups of organisms do not, however, thrive in cities. Lawrynowicz (1982) reported that in the parks of the Polish city Lodz, species richness of macro-fungi decreased from 185 species in the suburban zone to 38 species in the urban core of the city. Also, Pouyat et al. (1994) reported that the abundance of fungi in forest patches increased with distance from New York City towards its rural surroundings along a 140 km long transect. Ranta (2001) showed that even though lichen species richness increased more than 10-fold in the Finnish city of Tampere from 1980 to 2000 (a possible consequence of the virtual elimination of sulphur dioxide emissions), mean species richness of lichens in the city was still lower (7.60 species) than in the surrounding rural environment (13.83 species).

In addition to high alpha-diversity, variation between patches (beta-diversity) is often high in urban landscapes. For instance, in the Helsinki metropolitan area (Finland), variation in community structure of plants was higher among urban habitats (various kinds of parks and wastelands) than among semi-natural forest sites outside the city (Tonteri and Haila, 1990). Similarly, Czechowski (1982) noted that variation in carabid communities was high among urban forest patches (average value of similarity index 46%), probably because of the poor dispersal ability of the species.

In addition to invasion, local extinctions maintain variation in species composition among urban habitats (Rebele, 1994). Extinctions occur because of habitat destruction or slow disappearance of species from patches that have been fragmented into small and isolated remnants. While there is ample evidence of species becoming locally extinct through habitat destruction and degradation (e.g. Gilbert, 1989), extinctions due to isolation and/or decreased size of the habitat patch are more difficult to show. Application of the metapopulation theory (Hanski, 1998) might shed light on the dynamism of populations in the urban setting.

Ecology in cities and ecology of cities

As was indicated in the previous section, ecology in cities across the world has been studied using ecological theories and concepts developed for environments other than urban. For instance, the biotic effects of isolation of green areas have been studied using the theory of island biogeography, and effects of disturbance have been compared to expectations from the intermediate disturbance hypothesis.

Studies using these theories have produced variable results. For instance, the expectation of increasing species richness with increasing patch size derived from island biogeography theory does not necessarily hold for urban green areas. An example is the relationship between the number of mammal species and size of urban habitat patches in Oxford, England (Dickman, 1987). When only undisturbed patches were considered, there was a statistically significant positive correlation between mammalian species richness and patch size. However, when disturbed patches were also included, the correlation disappeared, indicating that features of urban environments may confound 'normal' community patterns, and may complicate the use of theories developed in other environments.

Also, expectations derived from the intermediate disturbance hypothesis do not always hold for urban areas, sometimes because of the dominance of introduced species (Niemelä et al., 2002). Such discrepancies between expectations derived from theories and urban reality prompt one to question whether we can successfully use ecological theories and approaches developed for other environments in the urban setting. Do we need theories and approaches designed specifically for urban areas?

Trepl (1995) felt that what was needed was a new theory of urban ecology, or at least a framework within which urban ecological research could be conducted. Such a framework could be based on the general landscape ecological approach adapted to urban environments (Duhme and Pauleit, 1992a). The framework would need to deal with the structure and functioning of urban ecosystems: that is, the theory would have to identify and be adapted to the specific features (such as invasion or disturbance) of urban ecosystems that distinguish them from other ecosystems. Although there are differences between urban and rural ecosystems, the basic ecological processes are similar. The main difference is the strong human presence and impact on urban landscapes. Thus, it appears that the existing ecological theories can be applied when studying ecology in the urban setting, but the human impact needs to be considered by adapting the theories to urban conditions. It would be worth studying which assumptions of ecological theories are inappropriate or fail in urban situations in order to modify the theories for urban use.

Although a completely distinct theory of urban ecology may not be needed for ecology in cities, such a theory is needed for ecology of cities, which studies the urban area as an interactive system of human and ecological components. Pickett *et al.* (1997b) proposed that the urban-to-rural land-use gradient could serve as a model system for the study of the responses of biotic communities to human disturbance (see also McDonnell *et al.*, 1997; Niemelä *et al.*, 2002; Pickett *et al.*, Chapter 3). The idea is to compare sites with the same original physical environment (e.g. forest patches), but differing in measurable features of urbanisation from city centres to their rural surroundings. Until now, gradient analysis has been mainly applied in purely ecological research, but the inclusion of social, economic and cultural components would produce a more holistic view as emphasised by the 'human ecosystem model' (Pickett *et al.*, 1997b). The combination of the 'human ecosystem model' and gradient analysis to studies of the special properties of urban ecosystems (isolation, invasion and succession) would seem to form a fruitful approach to urban ecological research. Specific ecological hypotheses to be tested could, for instance, include metapopulation theory.

Comparative research in ecology in cities

To discuss challenges of international, comparative research in urban ecology we present two case studies. The first deals with the use of the 'human ecosystem model' developed in the United States and in Europe (Finland), and the second presents an international initiative with a standardised methodology to study the ecological effects of urbanisation.

Adapted model for research on Finnish urban land-use planning

To study integrated approaches of urban ecological and social systems, Pickett *et al.* (1997b) introduced the 'human ecosystem model', while Grimm *et al.* (2000) presented a modified scheme where they developed further the dynamic structure of the model. As the scheme draws attention to important variables, interactions and feedbacks around land-use change, we wanted to test its generality by examining whether it was applicable in another urban ecosystem and planning setting, i.e. in Finland.

In adapting the model to Finnish conditions, we emphasise the role of land-use planning as a major driver of changes in urban areas (Fig. 2.1). The boxes

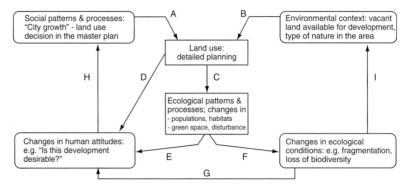

Fig. 2.1. A model for addressing the system dynamics of a detailed planning process in an urban setting in Finland. Different variables (boxes), interactions and feedbacks (arrows) are explained in the text (adapted from Grimm *et al.*, 2000, and Yli-Pelkonen and Niemelä, 2005).

include the main variables, such as 'land use' and some examples related to detailed planning in Finland (Fig. 2.1). Arrows indicating determinants and their impacts and feedbacks are marked by letters (A to I). For instance, A and B are the principal determinants of the 'land use' variable. In the model of Grimm *et al.* (2000), social patterns and processes, such as societal decisions and human behaviour, were the direct drivers of the change in land use.

In Finland, the municipality has the planning authority, and therefore we emphasise the role of planners in our modified model. Adapted to Finnish urban planning, the main policy driver is the 'inevitable' city growth through area reservations in the master plan. Determinant (B) in the Finnish planning context is the availability of vacant and suitable land for new residential areas. In Finland, there are still reasonable amounts of non-protected green areas left in cities, but there are increasingly contradictory views about their use.

Grimm *et al.* (2000) stated that the first central variable, land use, is the determinant of the second central variable, ecological patterns and processes (C). In the Finnish setting, land use is the result of a detailed planning process, which affects ecological patterns and processes in the area. As Grimm *et al.* (2000) noted, humans may react to perceived change in land use through changes in environmental views and attitudes (D), even if ecological changes have not taken place. On the other hand, Grimm *et al.* (2000) stated that the residents may respond when changes in ecological patterns and processes become visible (E). For instance, changes in floral and faunal populations, their habitats and vegetation patterns or reduction of green areas potentially make people concerned about the benefits of development. Participatory planning in Finland may provide residents with more opportunities to react and contribute during the planning process or during the implementation phase of the plan.

Changes in ecological conditions may result from changed ecological patterns and processes (F) (Grimm *et al.*, 2000). Such changes in ecological conditions can be, for example, loss of biological diversity, habitat fragmentation or less viable populations. Furthermore, changes in ecological conditions may affect humans and result in changes in their attitudes (G) (Grimm *et al.*, 2000). This can occur even if previous changes through D or E were unnoticed or ignored. For instance, if a city plan results in further fragmentation of natural habitats and local residents perceive this as a negative change, it may alter their attitudes toward the plan or to urban development in general.

Changes in human attitudes may feed back to decision-making and other societal patterns (H) (Grimm *et al.*, 2000). In the Finnish case, questions such as 'Does our city need to grow?' and 'If it has to, in what ways?', or 'How does the new master plan take green areas into account?' have been asked by the public. In such cases, the depicted cycle in Fig. 2.1 begins again, resulting in modified detailed plans. The pace of the cycle depends on the pace of ecological and human responses. It may be faster if society and people have an interactive impact on the plan or slower if they react to changes in ecological conditions after the implementation of the plan. According to Grimm *et al.* (2000), changes in ecological conditions can also affect the whole environmental context (I). For instance, if changes in ecological conditions are considered too severe, more green areas may be set aside in the following planning round.

This comparative research showed that the 'human ecosystem model', with its modifications, is applicable also in Finland. The model can help to understand the dynamics of specific detailed urban plans. If we are able to predict the potential changes in ecological conditions caused by planned land-use change, we may be able to predict the reactions of the residents who, in turn, have the potential to influence the planning process in order to modify the plan before irreversible ecological changes have taken place.

Comparative research on ecological effects of urbanisation

Our second example illustrates how comparative, international research can contribute to our understanding of urban ecological systems and to the development of theory. We present the framework, rationale, some results and future challenges of an international initiative to examine how general the ecological effects of urbanisation are around the world (GLOBENET project, http://www.helsinki.fi/science/globenet).

The background of the GLOBENET project is that urbanisation creates patchworks of modified land types that exhibit similar patterns around the world. Nonetheless, little is known about whether these changes affect biodiversity in similar ways across the globe, or depend more on the unique aspects of local conditions (Samways, 1992). A multi-regional programme could potentially distinguish globally recurring patterns and convergence from more local phenomena. Such knowledge could foster international collaboration among researchers and managers in finding ways to mitigate the adverse effects of human-caused landscape change. Thus, there is a need to develop simple protocols to assess the effects of these activities on native biodiversity and, where possible, to minimise adverse effects.

To assess changes in anthropogenic landscapes we have developed a global programme that uses a common field methodology (pitfall trapping), and the same taxonomic group (carabid beetles, which form definable assemblages) in urban landscapes in different parts of the world. Carabids are sufficiently varied taxonomically and ecologically, as well as being abundant and sensitive enough to human-caused disturbances to be a reliable monitoring group. They have been widely studied in relation to land use throughout the world (see Lövei and Sunderland, 1996; Niemelä, 1996; Rainio and Niemelä, 2003). Recent studies, spanning several countries, have shown that although species identities differed, the general patterns of community response to anthropogenic disturbance were surprisingly similar (e.g. Niemelä *et al.*, 2002). Such results clearly illustrate the possible significance of a multi-regional approach and foster confidence in the feasibility of a general theory for landscape planning and design.

A problem in assessing general human impacts on ecosystems across the world is that the types of ecosystems and human impacts differ considerably. Urban landscapes typically consist of densely built and highly developed cores surrounded by decreasing intensity of development and increasing 'naturalness'. Urban–rural gradients have this appearance all over the world, although the exact patterns and types of ecosystems differ. Thus, these gradients can provide a framework in which ecologists can examine human-induced landscape changes and compare the findings across the world to unravel generalities in community structure in relation to these changes. Through consistent monitoring efforts, these landscapes can be treated as field experiments for addressing basic ecological questions and issues related to the impact of humans on their environment (McDonnell and Pickett, 1990; Pickett *et al.*, Chapter 3). It is important to note that in the GLOBENET project we do not compare cities per se, but patterns along the gradients between cities.

An advantage of the gradient approach is that specific hypotheses can be derived from previous work. For instance, one can ask whether the intermediate disturbance hypothesis (Connell, 1978; Wootton, 1998) applies to urban–rural gradients, whether habitat homogenisation through urbanisation always leads to faunal similarities, or whether habitat homogenisation and species introductions lead to more convergence than homogenisation alone. One might also ask whether there is a temporal dimension (i.e. whether older cities show more faunal effects) or a spatial dimension (i.e. whether cities with more and better connected green areas show less marked faunal effects).

To date the GLOBENET protocol has been used in five cities; Sofia, Bulgaria; Edmonton, Canada; Helsinki, Finland; Debrecen, Hungary; and Hiroshima, Japan (Alaruikka *et al.*, 2002; Niemelä *et al.*, 2002; Ishitani *et al.*, 2003; Venn *et al.*, 2003; Magura *et al.*, 2004). The carabid beetles collected in woodlands in these cities showed some evidence of an increase in overall abundance and species richness from city centres to the rural surroundings, but no evidence of elevated diversity at suburban sites, as predicted by the intermediate disturbance hypothesis. When carabid species were classified into forest and open habitat species, a clear picture emerged; the proportion of forest species decreased significantly from the surrounding rural environments to the city centres, while the proportion of open habitat species increased significantly towards the city centres. Furthermore, as predicted, the proportion of large carabid beetles decreased towards the city centres (see Blake *et al.*, 1994; Ribera *et al.*, 2001), as did the proportion of short-winged species.

These results are encouraging as they show that carabid beetles respond in a similar and predictable manner to urbanisation in different cities across the globe. The challenge here is to infer process from these observed patterns. For example, forest carabids may be negatively influenced in cities because of small forest patch size, strong edge effects, patch isolation and/or disturbance intensity and frequency. In particular, edge effects and disturbance need to be quantified – and at the appropriate scale – in order to determine their effects on the urban biota. Lehvävirta and Kotze (Chapter 31) discuss quantification in urban environments in more detail.

Conclusions: challenges and contribution of comparative work

Several conclusions and challenges emerge from the comparative work reviewed here. First, it is evident that if we are to make significant contributions toward the study and understanding of urban ecosystems as integrated ecological and human systems, appreciation of urban ecology needs to be enhanced among citizens and especially among scientists. As reported here, new directions in ecological thinking and changing views in society indicate that urban ecology is slowly gaining importance and appreciation. Interestingly, it seems that society at large, and urban residents in particular, are responding more rapidly to the threats facing urban green environments than are ecologists.

Second, comparative, international research is vital in increasing our understanding of the biotic effects of urbanisation across the globe, as the GLOBENET project has shown. Furthermore, the knowledge generated from this comparison could enhance the development of urban ecology as a scientific discipline and foster international collaboration among researchers and managers in finding ways to mitigate the adverse effects of human-caused landscape change. However, because the structure of the ecosystems and the size of cities differ, we face difficulties in defining what we are actually comparing. It is evident that studies are needed for distinguishing generalities from local patterns ('local spices') and for creating concepts and frameworks for urban ecology, but what are the methods to be used? For instance, is the gradient approach used in the GLOBENET project the most appropriate method for distinguishing between general and local patterns?

Third, it is imperative to understand the effects of urbanisation on ecosystem function, but measuring ecosystem function is difficult and it may be that surrogates are needed. The level of biodiversity has been suggested as an indicator for assessing whether or not natural systems are being maintained in a 'functionally integrated state' (Probst and Crow, 1991), but is this approach useful in cities? Clearly, research into the relationship between ecosystem function and level of biodiversity is needed in cities.

Fourth, we may ask whether theories developed for other environments are useful in urban habitats. Or do we need to develop distinct theories for the study of ecology in cities? As the basic ecological processes are similar between urban and rural ecosystems, it appears that the existing ecological theories can be applied when studying ecology in the urban setting, but the effects of the strong human impact (such as management, invasive species and pollution) need to be considered. For instance, strong disturbance may complicate and confound correlations between species richness and patch size.

Fifth, progress has been made in developing frameworks for studying ecology of cities, i.e. integrating ecological and human systems in cities (e.g. the human ecosystem model, Pickett et al., 1997b; Pickett et al., Chapter 3). However, progress on the ecological part of such an integrated framework is hampered by the lack of a firm ecological foundation due to the lack of research on ecology in cities. Linking ecology and social sciences is vital if we are to influence urban planning processes in such a way that our future cities are able to provide healthy and pleasant environments for the residents, as well as maintain (urban) biodiversity.

Acknowledgements

A small portion of this chapter previously appeared in Niemelä (1999a). We thank the Academy of Finland for research funds (to the ECOPLAN project) and the GLOBENET contributors for conducting comparative research across the world (S. Venn, L. Penev, I. Stoyanov, J. Spence, D. Hartley, E. Montes de Oca, M. Ishitani, T. Magura, B. Tóthmérész and T. Molnár). The paper was improved by comments from Mark McDonnell and anonymous referees.

3

Frameworks for urban ecosystem studies: gradients, patch dynamics and the human ecosystem in the New York metropolitan area and Baltimore, USA

STEWARD T. A. PICKETT, MARY L. CADENASSO, MARK
J. MCDONNELL AND WILLIAM R. BURCH JR

Introduction

This chapter addresses the conceptual frameworks that have been used in urban ecological studies in two US metropolises, and the theoretical challenges for urban ecology that flow from these experiences. The two topics relate well because frameworks lay out the structure of knowledge in a subject area, and the theoretical assessment addresses the applicability of frameworks beyond the two cities used here. The frameworks began to be articulated with the establishment of the Urban–Rural Gradient Ecology (URGE) programme in the New York City metropolitan region in the early 1980s (McDonnell and Pickett, 1990). That programme continued until the relocation of its leader, Mark McDonnell, to Australia in 1998.

Although the urban–rural gradient framework has been effective in studying the biological components of human-dominated ecosystems, there has been an increasing call to better integrate the biological, physical and socio-economic components of urban systems (Niemelä *et al.*, 2000; Grimm *et al.*, 2000; Collins *et al.*, 2000; Pickett *et al.*, 2001; Alberti *et al.*, 2003). In the Baltimore Ecosystem Study, a Long-Term Ecological Research project (LTER) funded by the National Science Foundation, which is part of a network of 26 long-term studies in various ecosystem types located throughout North America and its territories (http://

Ecology of Cities and Towns: A Comparative Approach, ed. Mark J. McDonnell, Amy K. Hahs and Jürgen H. Breuste. Published by Cambridge University Press. © Cambridge University Press 2009.

www.lternet.edu), the urban–rural gradient framework has been extended to include social sciences (Grimm *et al.*, 2000). Because the Baltimore Ecosystem Study (BES) builds closely upon the New York URGE study, they encompass a wide range of approaches to urban ecological studies and present an excellent opportunity to examine conceptual frameworks that can be used to promote and integrate urban ecological studies.

The chapter follows four steps: first, it presents the utility and nature of conceptual frameworks. It then presents the framework used by the URGE project in New York. Following that, the additions to the New York framework to support the integrated work in Baltimore are presented. The chapter finally examines important questions about the nature of theory as it applies to urban ecosystems, and identifies the problems and opportunities that exist for development of a more comprehensive theory for urban ecological studies in the future.

What good are conceptual frameworks?

A framework is a conceptual tool to tie together and organise a broad area of investigation (Cadenasso *et al.*, 2003b). It is different from either a model or a theory (Pickett *et al.*, 1994b). Models represent the structure or function of a system, conceptually, graphically, quantitatively or physically. Models also specify the parts of a system, the relationships between them, and the range of dynamics that are possible in the relationships and the states of the system. Importantly, models also specify the boundaries and spatial and temporal scale of a system. A theory is a larger, more inclusive structure, constituting a system of conceptual constructs in the specific domain of a subject area. Theories permit causal explanation of observations within that domain (Pickett *et al.*, 1994b). Models of various sorts are one of the many parts of theory. For example, theories also include assumptions, facts, generalisations and hypotheses.

In contrast to both models and theories, a framework is a hierarchical structure that embodies a repertoire of causes for multiple kinds of systems across multiple scales. Frameworks suggest the structure models can take, and lay out the variables that might be included in them. Frameworks also articulate the gradients of contrast across which comparisons and syntheses can be accomplished in a subject. That is, the variables within a framework can represent continua. For example, a framework might point to 'population density' as a causal component. Such a variable can range from low to high values.

Frameworks exist within all important theoretical areas in science. For example, in physics, a very large framework links quantum electrodynamics, weak interactions, strong interactions and electro-weak interactions (Rohrlich, 1987). Ultimately this framework might represent a unified, grand theory of modern physics, and the relationship of the four theories within a single large framework points to new research questions. Note that because each of the four theories has its own framework, the larger unified framework would contain the more specific frameworks. In other words, frameworks themselves can be nested within still larger frameworks. Comprehensive frameworks include such elements as causal repertoires arranged in a hierarchical structure. Frameworks provide opportunities to address multiple scales, generate model templates, integrate and synthesise information, identify information gaps and aid communication (Cadenasso *et al.*, 2003b).

Causal repertoire

A causal repertoire is a complete roster of the causes, factors, constraints and interactions that may operate in a domain of interest. From this complete roster, which is more than an arbitrary or convenient shopping list, the components of specific models will be drawn (Salmon, 1994). For example, the framework for vegetation dynamics, or succession (Pickett and McDonnell, 1989) contains three components, which suggests that successional models must consider three broad kinds of process: differential availability of open sites in which succession can occur, differential species availability at a site, and differential species performance (Fig. 3.1). The components of a causal repertoire can be combined with one another to suggest hypotheses about structure–function relationships. For example, the effect of differential species performance may be conditioned by the structure or resources that exist within a site at the start of succession. Large differentials in species resource demand may result in faster rates of succession due to increased competition compared with less distinct species differences. Furthermore, because the various factors included in a framework will span contrasting conditions, they suggest gradients for comparison. Again, using plant succession as a general example, differential site availability may range from conditions that have very low resource availability to those that have a high degree of residual resources. Thus, frameworks identify relevant causes, and suggest how those causes might relate to one another.

Hierarchical structure

Because of their hierarchical structure, frameworks provide the means to translate from the abstraction of general definitions to the specifics of operational models (Jax, 1998). At the higher levels in a hierarchical framework, general processes and relationships are identified. Nested within these large processes are several finer levels of more specific interactions, mechanisms and processes (Pickett and Kolasa, 1989). In other words, each of the higher level processes can be decomposed into one or several levels of more specific processes

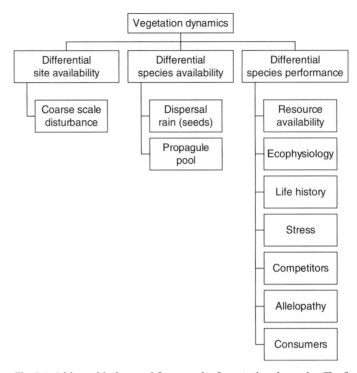

Fig. 3.1. A hierarchical, causal framework of vegetation dynamics. The framework identifies the phenomenon of interest as the highest, most general level of the hierarchy. Major process areas appear as the next level, and each of those processes is composed of or affected by subsets of other processes, mechanisms or causes. Based on Pickett and McDonnell (1989).

that are the particular mechanisms by which the phenomenon occurs. The lower level processes included in a framework illuminate the detailed interactions that occur on fine scales or in very specific situations. For example, differential species performance in the vegetation dynamics framework encompasses more specific processes such as herbivory, competition and predation. Each of these more specific processes will in turn be divisible into even more specific processes (Fig. 3.1). For example, in the succession framework, herbivory will be divided into processes that affect it, such as presence of various herbivore populations, constraints on the herbivores by physical factors, plant defensive mechanisms and so on. Thus, a framework is a tool that relates the abstract components of theory to the particularities of the real world. It is such hierarchical structure that allows general processes to be operationalised into useful models.

Addressing multiple scales

In addition to addressing different degrees of generality, frameworks can address coarse- and fine-scale situations. For example, a framework for the structure and function of ecological boundaries identifies the subject matter to

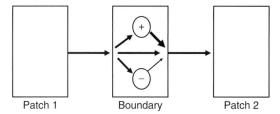

Fig. 3.2. A general template for models examining the structure and function of ecological boundaries. Any model of boundary function would minimally have to identify the contrasting areas or patches separated by the boundary, the kind of flux across the boundary, and the ability of the boundary to control the flow. Modified from Cadenasso *et al.* (2003b).

be a flux of matter, energy, organisms or information across heterogeneous space (Cadenasso *et al.*, 2003b). To understand the chosen flux, specific contrasts in heterogeneity, say patches, must be identified, along with the nature of the boundary separating the patches. However, such specification can be made on any spatial scale an investigator is interested in. The framework can apply to transitions across soil horizons or movements of animals across the ecotone between biomes (Belnap *et al.*, 2003; Cadenasso *et al.*, 2003a).

Generating model templates

In illustrating the ability of a framework to apply to multiple scales, we used boundary function as an example (Cadenasso *et al.*, 2003a). Arranging the component processes specified by a framework into a form that exposes the relationships between them establishes a model template (Cadenasso *et al.*, 2003b). Such a template can be used in many kinds of system within the domain, as well as across scales. For example, a boundary model template has been derived from a hierarchical framework for the control of fluxes across heterogeneous mosaics. The model template states that the flux across a boundary is determined by the contrast between elements (patches) adjoining the boundary and by the structure of the boundary (Fig. 3.2). This kind of relationship can be expressed in many ways, including as an equation, or as box and arrow diagrams (Fagan *et al.*, 2003).

Integration and synthesis

Because frameworks identify causes and relationships, and because they apply to many systems and scales, they can show the relationships between seemingly disparate systems. The general plant successional or vegetation dynamics framework suggests that studies of invasive species may profitably examine differentials in site conditions, species availability and species performance. Vegetation management can be informed by those same phenomena (Luken, 1990). Likewise, the boundary framework can apply to natural or human-dominated landscapes. Hence, integrating different kinds of subject matter can be facilitated by a framework (Pickett *et al.*, 1994a).

Identification of information gaps

Closely related to the potential for synthesis is the ability of frameworks to help identify gaps in the data on a subject. Laying out the causes in an explicitly hierarchical way may also point to concepts that are needed to link the general with the specific. Alternatively, individual kinds of observations, or models to link different observations, or generalisations to apply to different systems may be conspicuous by their absence when a framework is articulated.

Communication

Finally, a framework can enhance communication between specialists in different disciplines, and with non-specialists (Pickett *et al.*, 1999a). A framework reminds researchers which phenomena represent general processes, and which ones represent disciplinary detail. If scientists can tune the degree of generality or specificity of their message appropriately, they may have a better chance of engaging people from other disciplines or from the public in an understanding of their subject matter (Cadwallader, 1988). Communication with specialists in other disciplines is of course the first step in interdisciplinary research. Communicating successfully with the public has many benefits, ranging from public support of science to correct use of scientific information in policy decisions (Pickett, 2003).

The discussion to this point has laid out what a framework is, and what it does. We now present the two general frameworks that have supported our urban ecological research in New York and in Baltimore. Each of these general frameworks, like the one from modern physics mentioned earlier, contains within it more focused or specific frameworks.

New York metropolitan area: URGE

The general research framework for the programme on Urban–Rural Gradient Ecology (URGE) in the New York metropolitan region drew on existing concepts in ecology and applied them to a new system. Leaders in this project included Mark McDonnell, Steward Pickett, Richard Pouyat and Margaret Carreiro. The first component of the framework was the concept of the ecological gradient and the second component involved humans as part of the ecosystem. Each of these more specific conceptual areas itself possesses a framework.

Ecological gradients

Gradients have been important to ecology since the work of such pioneers as H.A. Gleason (1917) who used the concept to explain the distribution of vegetation and its component species. In spite of its long history, the concept still remains unclear to many. This is because it can refer to a concrete or literal transect in space or time, or to a conceptual ordering of assemblages or conditions (Whittaker, 1967; Margules and Austin, 1994). In the concrete case, a gradual change in physical conditions or in vegetation structure is observed across a transect. Change in vegetation with elevation along a mountainside is one example. In the abstract or conceptual case, sites representing different physical conditions or vegetation structure are arrayed along a constructed or model gradient (Austin and Gaywood, 1994). Ordination of vegetation from spatially distributed sites onto an axis that represents their quantitative rank in an abstract space is an example. Ordinations, for instance, commonly represent successional trajectories abstracted from spatial observation, or differing degrees of moisture or nutrient requirements in a plant assemblage. This distinction between literal and ordinated gradients is important to bear in mind, since urban–rural gradients, like those used in non-urban ecological studies, can be concrete or abstract. Both concrete and abstract gradients were used in the URGE project (McDonnell et al., 1993). Of course, the underlying sampling transect was a literal ordering of sample stands with distance from Manhattan, New York (Fig. 3.3).

No gradient in the field will represent a single environmental or biotic contrast. Rather, gradients are often complex (Allen and Wyleto, 1983). That means that they comprise multiple environmental contrasts. Moisture and light availability often vary inversely with one another in the field, and a gradient of one necessarily entails a gradient of the other (Tilman, 1982). Such complexity often makes it difficult to discern causation along gradients. Indeed, there may be multiple causes of change along gradients. However, mechanism can be inferred by relying on a suite of methods. Ordination techniques that separate environmental variation into orthogonal axes, studies that span time periods over which the covariation in factors changes, and experimental studies of the hypothesised mechanisms can all contribute to disentangling complex causation on gradients. For example Niemelä et al. (2000, Chapter 2) hypothesised that the average size of organisms should decrease with increasing stress related to urbanisation. Their data on carabid beetle assemblages across urban–rural gradients in Bulgaria, Canada, and Finland confirmed this hypothesis (Niemelä et al., 2002).

To summarise, the gradient component of the URGE framework originated in ecology, and suggests that changes occur in three kinds of parameters: (1) physical or chemical conditions; (2) biotic assemblages and organisms; and (3) ecosystem processes.

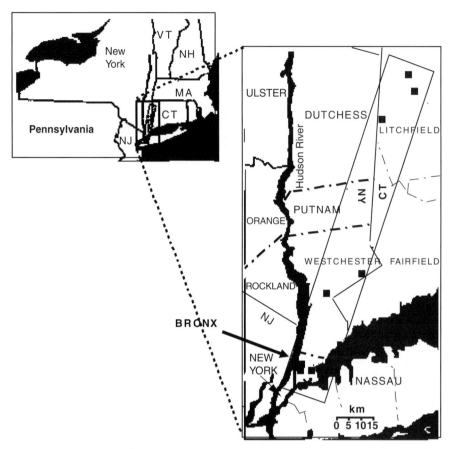

Fig. 3.3. A map of the sites used in the New York City URGE programme. Adapted from McDonnell and Pickett (1990). The transect runs for 140 km from New York City, encompassing a series of oak-dominated forest stands on soils derived from the same bedrock. The transect trends slightly northeastward to maintain its position on that bedrock.

Urban–rural gradient framework

McDonnell and Pickett (1990) proposed that urbanisation produces a complex environmental gradient that provides ecologists with the opportunity to answer questions vital to understanding the impacts of urbanisation, while also providing a context for addressing ecological questions of general importance and applicability. The exploitation of this new opportunity required the development of an urban–rural gradient framework. This framework, like those described earlier, is hierarchical in structure and contains a causal repertoire that identifies a comprehensive list of the causes, factors, constraints and interactions that need to be considered when conducting research along urban–rural gradients (Fig. 3.4). The urban–rural gradient framework is composed of four

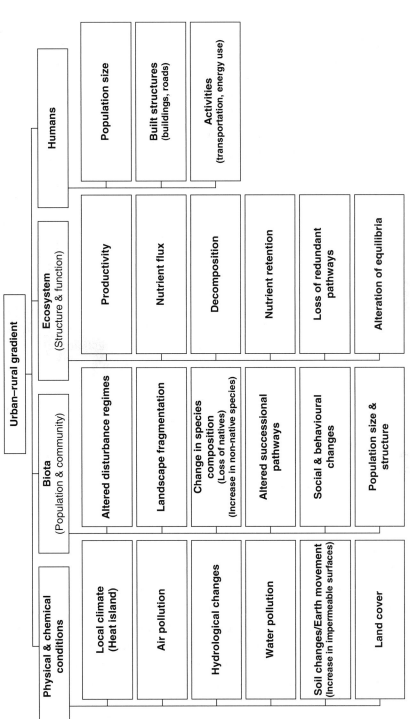

Fig. 3.4. A hierarchical, causal framework used in the New York URGE programme. Similar to the vegetation framework (Fig. 3.1) this framework identifies the phenomenon of interest as the highest, most general level of the hierarchy. Major process areas appear as the next level, and each of those processes is composed of or affected by subsets of other processes.

categories of processes or subsystems: physical and chemical, biota, ecosystem and humans (Fig. 3.4). The first three come from the ecological tradition, and the fourth is virtually new to mainstream ecology. At the initial creation of the URGE framework the human component of ecosystems was identified as an important element, but because the real focus of the effort was on the more traditional ecological questions, the treatment of the human factors was relatively simplistic, including assessments of only population size, built structures and human activities such as transportation and energy use (McDonnell and Pickett, 1990; McDonnell *et al.*, 1993). See further discussion of this component below. The other three categories of processes were divided into several subcomponents to provide a richness of detail that is required to identify the environmental gradient and the biotic and ecosystem responses. An urban–rural gradient may also be defined by physical and chemical changes such as climate, pollution, soil modification and land-cover type, but these in turn could affect both biotic and ecosystem responses along the gradient. For example, the biotic response to the urban environmental gradient may manifest itself in changes in species composition, altered disturbance regimes, habitat fragmentation and altered successional pathways. Correspondingly, the ecosystem changes along the gradient could be measured in levels of productivity or the rate and nature of nutrient cycles. Which processes are included in any urban–rural gradient study depends on the questions being addressed.

Ecological research along urban–rural gradients

Recent work has emphasised the need to quantify the specific factors that define a gradient of urbanisation, since there are so many potential ecological, social and physical aspects of urbanisation (McIntyre *et al.*, 2000). The urban–rural gradient framework includes many of these factors under physical and chemical processes (Fig. 3.4). Quantifying such a wide range of interacting, potentially causal factors remains a challenge for research. This is especially important since different disciplines, different agencies in a country, and different nations may have different official definitions of urbanisation (McIntyre *et al.*, 2000). For example, the definition of urbanisation by the US Bureau of Census is based primarily on population density within municipalities. This definition has evolved through time as the nature of urban areas in the United States has changed. Note, however, that the definition does not explicitly deal with the nature of the built environment, which is of course a major factor of the urban ecosystem (Weeks *et al.*, 2003).

Several examples of variation along the urban–rural transect were discovered in the New York metropolitan area. Hydrophobicity of urban soils was greater than in rural soils (White and McDonnell, 1988). Nitrogen deposition as throughfall was found to be higher in urban and suburban forest stands than in rural sites (Lovett *et al.*, 2000). This is echoed in the higher rates of nitrogen mineralisation toward the urban end of the gradient (Pouyat *et al.*, 1997). Corresponding differences were discovered in litter quality, the presence of earthworms, and shifts in soil fungal composition (Pouyat *et al.*, 1994; Steinberg *et al.*, 1997; Carreiro *et al.*, 1999). Ozone concentrations followed a different spatial pattern, being greater outside the metropolitan core toward the east, reflecting the prevailing wind patterns (Gregg *et al.*, 2003). Taken together, these changes represent major changes in the function of forest stands embedded in a matrix of increasingly urbanised land.

Humans as components of ecosystems

As previously described, the second component of the framework used in the New York Metropolitan URGE project was the concept of humans as components of ecosystems. Whether and how to incorporate humans in conceptions and studies of the ecological world have been matters of controversy for a long time (Marsh, 1864; Williams, 1993). Marsh (1864) stated the conundrum of whether humans were to be considered a part of nature or not. The classical ecological view of systems places humans outside ecosystems (Botkin, 1990; Pickett *et al.*, 1992; Botkin and Beveridge, 1997). In this capacity they have most often been viewed as negative impacts. While this captures some of the major effects of humans, the approach seems less likely to encourage understanding of the full richness of interactions between the human and the biogeophysical components of ecosystems. During the course of the URGE project, we were able to work with a social geographer, Kimberly Medley, who helped us to document population density, road densities and traffic volumes in the $16 \, km^2$ blocks surrounding the forest stands we were studying. These data fall into several compartments of the urban–rural gradient framework, including land cover, air pollution and humans (Fig. 3.4). While all of these human parameters were significantly correlated with the nitrogen dynamics we had studied in these forests, traffic volume explained slightly more of the variation than the other variables (Medley *et al.*, 1995; Pouyat *et al.*, 1995a). This is probably related to the origin of local nitrogen deposition in automobile exhaust. It was significant that a functional or process variable – traffic volume – rather than a static parameter such as density of roads or automobiles, or the more distal variable of human population density, had the greatest explanatory power.

The inclusion of humans as components of the ecosystem takes advantage of the ecosystem concept as originally presented by Tansley (1935). Most ecosystem research ignored humans, or considered them to be external drivers of ecosystem structure and function. However, Tansley noted that humans were indeed components of ecosystems as he defined the term. He went further, and encouraged ecologists to study humans as well as the plants and animals they were used to studying.

The URGE framework, comprising the urban–rural gradient framework and the explicit inclusion of humans as components of ecosystems, was aimed at similar oak forest stands on similar substrates, but arrayed along a transect from dense urban, through suburban, to highly forested landscapes (McDonnell *et al.*, 1993). Therefore, the focus might be said to be on ecology in the city (Pickett *et al.*, 1997a; Grimm *et al.*, 2000; Niemelä *et al.*, Chapter 2). A familiar kind of ecosystem – closed canopy forest stands – was chosen to test the effects of urbanisation on familiar ecological processes – soil and plant nitrogen dynamics. This was, for the URGE team of traditionally trained ecologists, a reasonable way to start the exploration of urban systems. We were able to learn a great deal about the patterns and mechanisms of biogeophysical processes under different degrees of urbanisation. The urban–rural gradient framework has been successfully applied to the study of a variety of organisms throughout the world (cf. Theobald, 2004; Hahs and McDonnell, 2006; and see Carreiro *et al.*, Chapter 19, and Zipperer and Guntenspergen, Chapter 17). Of particular note is the use of this framework in the Global Network for Monitoring Landscape Change (GLOBENET) project which is assessing human impacts on biodiversity in different cities (Niemelä *et al.*, 2000, Chapter 2). In the following sections we explore the conceptual framework and challenges of another approach which has been termed the ecology of the city (Pickett *et al.*, 1997b; Grimm *et al.*, 2000) using the case of the Baltimore Ecosystem Study (BES) Long-Term Ecological Research project.

Conceptual frameworks in the Baltimore Ecosystem Study

The BES builds on the framework used in the New York City URGE project. In Baltimore, study sites are scattered throughout the metropolis, representing different degrees of urbanisation (Pickett *et al.*, 1997a; Fig. 3.5). Hence, an urban–rural gradient can be exploited. More specifically, one of the large study watersheds, the Gwynns Falls (17 150 ha), represents a transect ranging from industrial and commercial sites on the banks of the Chesapeake Bay, through old residential, to early twentieth-century suburbs, to old villages now being swallowed by the rapid conversion of agricultural land to suburbs (Fig. 3.5). Embedded in this watershed are agricultural tracts and large forested urban parks. The urban–rural gradient in Baltimore is completed by comparison with a reference forested watershed, Pond Branch, which is not contiguous with Gwynns Falls (Fig. 3.5). Additional watershed sites are used to focus atmospheric flux tower studies, stream valley restoration and different treatments of storm

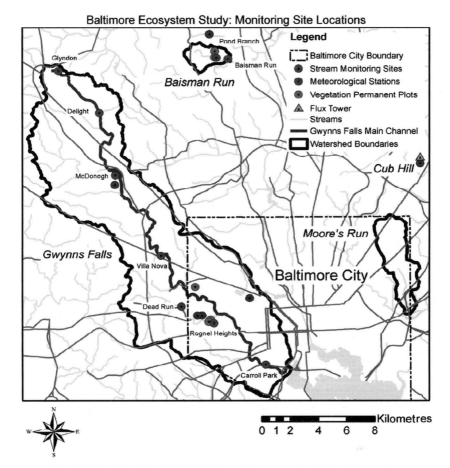

Fig. 3.5. Sampling sites for the Baltimore Ecosystem Study, based on major watersheds. Watersheds are used as integrators, and reflect different degrees of urbanisation. The Baisman Run watershed contains Pond Branch, which serves as a forested reference for the project. Different kinds of sampling plots or facilities are identified across the urban landscape. See also colour plate.

water management. Thus the entire gradient in Baltimore is not a literal transect, although some of the study sites are arrayed on a transect (Fig. 3.5).

Because BES is an LTER project, more resources and a larger range of expertise are available than we could bring to bear on our work in New York. While the New York study linked a handful of researchers, including plant ecologists, landscape ecologists, soil scientists, microbial ecologists, invertebrate ecologists and ultimately a geographer, the BES roster was larger from the start. It added many disciplines, including hydrologists, atmospheric scientists, stream geomorphologists, palaeoecologists, wildlife ecologists, historical geographers, demographers, historians, social scientists, ecological economists, spatial statisticians, modellers, educators, urban designers and experts in community development. This, of course, means that the complexity of the urban–rural gradient in Baltimore is being examined by a group representing a diversity of disciplines that can tease apart more of its complexity than our small team could examine in New York. But the ordination approach is the same, as is the use of a variety of research approaches, including mechanistic studies, extensive sampling, comparison and time series research.

The ecosystem approach is also being used in Baltimore, and humans continue to be considered a component of the system. However, there are some refinements in the use of the ecosystem concept. For example, we have come to realise that the term 'ecosystem' connotes three different things (Pickett and Cadenasso, 2002). First is the basic definition, an organismal complex and an abiotic complex, and the interactions between the two in a bounded area (Tansley, 1935). Second is the suite of models that must be specified in order to apply the concept to the material world (Jax, 1998). These models add details that apply the general, scale-independent concept of ecosystem to specific places and contexts, as was discussed when presenting frameworks. Ecosystem models range from budgetary summaries of nutrient and energy transformations between biotic and abiotic components, to simulation algorithms (Sala *et al.*, 2000; Chapin *et al.*, 2002). Finally, the term has metaphorical uses. Depending on whether the metaphor is being used in informal, specialist or interdisciplinary contexts, the images invoked will be different. Metaphorically, ecosystem can simply mean a place, or it can imply connectedness, or it can imply richness of composition. Specifically in the public realm, it often is taken to imply diversity, stability or some other socially valued attribute of the world. It is important to know what kind of connotation is being attached to the term ecosystem in a particular dialogue. We have found this refinement to be helpful in using the ecosystem concept in a large, interdisciplinary project.

New frameworks applied to BES

The urban–rural gradient framework, and the ecosystem inclusive of humans (Fig. 3.4), have provided a firm foundation for the work in Baltimore. However, the richness of new disciplines that have been brought to bear in BES has permitted and required us to extend the conceptual scope of the project beyond that of URGE in New York. In addition to responding to the broadening of disciplines contributing to the project, BES examines not only the 'green' components of the metropolis, but the entire range of habitat types. This has required us to deal explicitly with the whole scope of heterogeneity that urban areas encompass – from remnant or newly emerged green patches, to almost entirely engineered locations, and everything in between (Neville *et al.*, 1995). The notorious heterogeneity of cities (Clay, 1973) thus itself becomes a subject of study, rather than a characteristic of the external environment of green spaces of ecological interest.

Patch dynamics

Patch dynamics is a specific framework that recognises the spatial heterogeneity of ecological systems (Wu and Loucks, 1995; Pickett *et al.*, 1999b). Although heterogeneity can exist as discrete, spatially delimited units like patches, it can also exist as continua. We use patch dynamics to represent both of these ways to perceive heterogeneity. In its discrete form, patch dynamics resolves heterogeneity into bounded units that differ in structure, composition or process from adjacent units. Each unit may change through time, and so the entire mosaic of patches may also change. The mosaic can change in composition, frequency of types, sizes, shapes or configurations of different patch types. The changes may be stimulated by interactions within each unit, by fluxes between units, or by events that originate from outside the system (Pickett *et al.*, 2000). The same things can be said about continuous spatial variation, or fields, as can be said about patches: different parts of the field change in composition or frequency of representation; spatial contiguity of similar and contrasting points shifts through time; and fluxes will respond to the topology of the surface.

Patch dynamics may apply to any scale on which spatial heterogeneity can be mapped. In an urban situation patches may be defined by a combination of biogeophysical, built, and social elements (Grove and Burch, 1997; Zipperer *et al.*, 2000; Grove and Burch, 2003). In fact, patches at a particular scale can often be divided into constituent patches. For example, neighbourhoods are one sort of patch delimited in cities. Such patches can be recognised by building type, density of occupancy, type of use, demographic or ethnic composition, vegetation, topographic breaks and so on. Within each neighbourhood, finer-scale elements of heterogeneity can be recognised, including such things as yards and gardens with their vegetation, street plantings, commercial and residential buildings, types of paved areas, households and so on. Likewise, at coarser scales, neighbourhoods can be aggregated into zoning blocks, census block groups, districts, etc.

Hydrological patchiness

In hydrology, the concept of variable source area (VSA; Black, 1991) plays much the same role that patch dynamics plays in ecology (Black, 1991). Because hydrology is unified by the flow of a single substance – water – the role of spatial heterogeneity focuses on explaining the runoff, storage or influx of water. Hydrological characteristics discriminate patches in terms of surface permeability, porosity, hydrological conductivity and so on (Band *et al.*, 1993; Brun and Band, 2000). Therefore, vegetation cover, soil type, soil and other surface covers, temperatures and saturation are important characteristics of hydrological patches. Furthermore, the spatial arrangement of patches that function to differing degrees as sources or sinks may affect the landscape dynamics. Whether absorptive or impervious surfaces are located upslope or downslope matters a great deal for the hydrological function of a slope and of a watershed. Integrated watershed function thus reflects patch structure and configuration of the watershed.

The socio-spatial component

Social science has also recognised the importance of spatial heterogeneity in urban systems (Logan and Molotch, 1987). Social heterogeneity is expressed in demographic and ethnic terms, in income, education, and access to services and public resources, in real estate prices and desirability, and in terms of investment and disinvestment. Temporal cycles in economic investment are important drivers of the system as well (Krugman, 1996). Again, the approach is very reminiscent of patch dynamics, although a leading synthesis of this approach cites ecological principles that are rather out of date (Gottdiener and Hutchison, 2000). Thus the connection between patch dynamics and the socio-spatial component of the framework is not yet well developed.

Human ecosystem framework

A final new component framework has been used by the BES. Machlis and co-workers (Machlis *et al.*, 1997; Force and Machlis, 1997) recognised that if humans are truly to be considered part of ecosystems, it will be necessary to specify the kinds of structures and processes that humans contribute to in ecosystems. This includes not only the obvious infrastructure and buildings that people construct, but also the social structures, such as cultural features, institutions and social networks. The variety of these social and cultural components of ecosystems is scarcely recognised by ecologists. A causal repertoire laying out the social structures is therefore needed. Such a framework can suggest the great potential for connections between ecological patterns and processes and social patterns and processes. Machlis *et al.* (1997) identify this as the human ecosystem framework.

The human ecosystem is composed of two major subsystems (Fig. 3.6). One is the resource system, and the other is the human social system. Resources are further divided into those supplied by spatially explicit biogeophysical

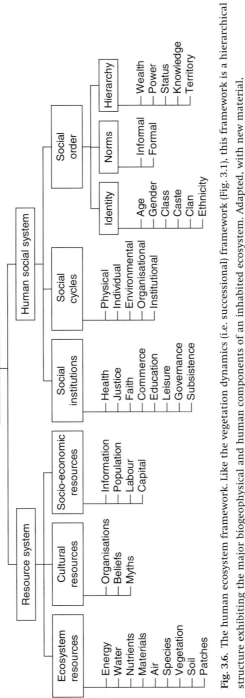

Fig. 3.6. The human ecosystem framework. Like the vegetation dynamics (i.e. successional) framework (Fig. 3.1), this framework is a hierarchical structure exhibiting the major biogeophysical and human components of an inhabited ecosystem. Adapted, with new material, from Machlis *et al.* (1997).

ecosystem services (Pickett *et al.*, 1997b), and those supplied by culture and socio-economic processes. There are still more specific resources in each of these realms (Machlis *et al.*, 1997). The framework, as expected, is hierarchical as indicated by the different levels of detail in Fig. 3.6. The human social system is made up of social institutions, social cycles and social order. Institutions are social devices that accomplish specific tasks, such as to provide for health, express faith, facilitate commerce, educate the populace, fill leisure time, govern and feed people. Social order is enforced by rank hierarchies, social identity and norms of behaviour. Each of these components of social order has its own contributing factors. Members of a society are ranked by wealth, power, status, knowledge and control of territory. Social identity is based on gender, ethnicity, age, class, caste and clan. Finally we note that all of the expressions of institutions, and forms of social order, can change as individuals, organisations, environments and institutions change through time.

This component framework is extremely important in guiding interdisciplinary work. Without such an exhaustive accounting of the social and biogeophysical components of an inhabited, built or highly managed system, ecologists are unlikely to recognise the richness of social phenomena they must relate to their variables and models. The framework reminds ecologists that the relatively straightforward demographic variables that they might rely on to describe humans as components of ecosystems are only part of the story. Of course, numbers and age distributions of humans matter. However, a great deal else matters as well. We need to know what kinds of social structures and constraints guide people in making decisions that affect ecological structures and processes in metropolitan areas (Grove *et al.*, 2006a). How households gather and use information that affects their environmental impact, and how institutions relate to one another in managing resources, are crucially important. Furthermore, the framework firmly embeds humans and their institutions in ecosystems. Marsh's (1864) conundrum of whether humans are part of ecosystems is solved by this framework that explicitly includes humans. The use of this framework in studying the ecology of cities and towns does not require every study to incorporate all of its components; instead it provides researchers with a tool to evaluate what components need to be assessed to address the research questions being asked.

Research in BES exemplifying use of the frameworks

Nitrate is an important groundwater and stream pollutant. How much nitrogen in the form of nitrate is generated in different patches along the metropolitan gradient, and how much flows into streams, are research interests of BES. Ultimately, policy makers wish to know how much nitrogen is released into the Chesapeake Bay estuary, since they have a mandate to reduce the nitrogen loading of the bay. Patches in riparian zones, based on work in non-urban ecosystems, are expected to convert nitrate into N_2 gas and so reduce the nitrate loading of streams. Work in BES has discovered the drying of urban riparian soils, caused by structural modifications upstream of the riparian areas, as well as isolation of the floodplains due to extreme downcutting by urban streams that are prone to flash flooding. This disconnection of riparian soils from the hydrological regime of ground water and the streams has robbed riparian zones of their denitrification function (Groffman *et al.*, 2003). Practically, this result suggests that restoration of stream form must be coupled with restoration of hydrological function of riparian zones to reap the service of denitrification in urban streamside soils. In order to assess the input of nitrogen from lawn fertiliser, residential lawn management practices were surveyed in suburban neighbourhoods. Law *et al.* (2004) discovered that households occupying lower and higher value homes applied less fertiliser (in kg per ha of lawn area in the watershed) than those in houses of intermediate value. This research uses the three contributing frameworks for urban research. It uses the gradient framework and patch dynamics or variable source area frameworks, in examining the nitrogen dynamics of specific patches, and the human ecosystem framework in examining hydrological processes outside the riparian zone and adding an assessment of fertiliser use.

Ecologists often relate data on ecosystem processes to gradients of land-use change. Attempts to relate land use/land cover to stream nitrogen loading in the Gwynns Falls drainage in Baltimore found poor correlations (Groffman *et al.*, 2003). This has reinforced ongoing work to establish a new land-cover classification scheme that can account for greater structural heterogeneity than the usual division of urban land into transportation and commercial, residential areas of low, medium and high density, industrial, barren and water, for example. Cadenasso *et al.* (2007) have developed a new classification, aimed specifically at urban areas, which uses not only built features but also the type and proportion of woody and herbaceous vegetation to discriminate patches. Built features include paved areas, the nature and density of buildings, and their complexity based on size and footprint. The classification thus focuses on patch structure, but combines natural and anthropogenic elements. This new classification links patch dynamics and the human ecosystem frameworks in the context of the entire urban–rural gradient.

Other research in BES combines these same frameworks. Space prevents us from describing all these projects here. Examples include study of the spatial distribution of household environmental decision-making, social structure in small catchments, carbon flux and sequestration in the changing residential matrix, and modelling of ecosystem services on a watershed basis.

Combining these frameworks can promote a new synthesis that describes the ecology of the metropolis. This contrasts with the examination of ecology in the city, which was exemplified in the URGE work. Rather than remaining focused on the ecology of green areas in the metropolitan matrix, as important as that is, the approach of ecology of the city seeks to understand the entire urban matrix as an ecological system (Collins *et al.*, 2000). This same perspective motivated the ecosystem budget approach which was famously used in Hong Kong (Boyden *et al.*, 1981; Warren-Rhodes and Koenig, 2001). However, the contemporary use of the budgetary approach also aims at understanding the fine-scale heterogeneity of budgets, and the matter and energy transformations that control them (Chapin *et al.*, 2002). For example, a current question is: how do different neighbourhoods and land management practices contribute to the nutrient and energy budgets of the metropolis? This question complements the question asked in Hong Kong: what is the material and energy budget of the metropolis? When finer-scale heterogeneity is the focus, it becomes more important to use sophisticated social variables that can be spatially partitioned. It is not only the net demography of the metropolis, but the migrations within it, the sizes and behaviours of households in different locations, and the investment and disinvestment from place to place in the central city, old suburbs, new suburbs, industrial zones and exurbs, for example. In all of these approaches the gradient of urbanisation is important. Researchers can make many choices: what parameters of the many legitimate and possible ones are chosen to characterise urbanness? How much of the gradient is covered by the comparisons, and what position along the complex gradient does each sample site represent? What socio-economic boundaries should be recognised?

The combination of frameworks may seem to present an impossibly contingent and idiosyncratic model of urban ecosystems. Each of the many components of urban ecosystems can vary. The history and environmental constraints of each metropolis combine to make a unique trajectory. However, as scientists, ecologists wish to generalise and compare, and determine whether there are universal patterns or processes in urban ecosystem structure and dynamics. This desire leads to the theoretical challenges that urban ecology faces.

Theoretical challenges

Theory is the tool that allows scientists to generalise across disparate cases and to combine different processes. Theory is a conceptual system that allows explanation in a specified domain of inquiry (Pickett *et al.*, 1994b). It is founded on assumptions about the structure of the system, and assumptions about what processes act, and what governs those interactions. It articulates concepts to organise its approach to the subject, and to synthesise simple observations into coherent patterns. Theory confirms observations as facts that can be checked by independent observers and observed in different systems. It makes generalisations that abstract and idealise core processes from the many facts available. It articulates laws, which are a particularly strong and reliable form of generalisation. Theory generates models, or representations of the parts, interactions and dynamics of major components of the system or of the entire system of interest. Through models, or through uncertainty about its basic assumptions, it proposes hypotheses to test using observation, comparison and experiment. Finally, it erects a framework to tie the various components together. The frameworks we have discussed to this point are, we believe, important ones to combine in structuring a theory of urban ecosystems. However, because that theory does not yet exist, anything more than a sketch is impossible. There are several issues we identify that require attention in the attempt to build an urban ecosystem theory.

The problem with 'urban'

The idea of urban is so familiar that great care must be taken in building a theory on that foundation. Because some 80% of people in most fossil-fuel subsidised countries live in areas officially designated as urban, and an increasing proportion of the total global population is migrating in that same direction, most researchers are familiar with urban systems. However, there is a danger that idiosyncratic personal experience might substitute for rigorous understanding. Idiosyncrasy is permitted by a metaphorical rather than a systematic use of the term urban, even in research papers (McIntyre *et al.*, 2000). It becomes impossible to compare among systems if the model of urban that is being used in a study is not clear. Since urban can be defined on the basis of population density, activities of economic production, structure and density of the built environment and infrastructure, absence of a particular kind of vegetation cover and presence of another, and so on, specificity is required. Often surrogate variables are used, as was the case in laying out the New York urban–rural gradient. Distance was the initially hypothesised defining variable. As the research progressed, other variables were measured across the sites to give a quantitative basis for the comparison (McDonnell *et al.*, 1995). However, that project did not have the resources to examine many social, demographic and structural variables that might have been appropriate. Because of the complex layering of biogeophysical, social, economic and institutional factors, urban gradients with a large number of sample sites must be used and the variables must be quantified.

An additional aspect of the idiosyncrasy of urban definitions may be the values that different researchers and cultures bring to the idea of urban. These are only a problem when they are unstated, but still influence the structure and interpretation of research. If subsumed values are not assessed, their subtle influence on the assumptions that scientists make about the structure, function, sustainability and desirability of various ecosystems that differ in degree of urban expression will be invisible. Knowing the reason for assumptions helps propel them toward evaluation.

Some values may emerge as biases

In the United States, for example, there is a deep strain of romantic anti-urbanism (Nash, 1982). This may arise from the American colonial penchant to devalue urbanity in order to differentiate itself from its originally European parentage. The Jeffersonian ideal of the independent farmer, and the gridded frontier to be divided and settled, further retreats from the urban. More recently, as many US cities have become a conspicuous home of groups with little access to resources, power or education, other negative biases have become attached to city living. Such prejudices harm the social groups so labelled, and harm cities through the scientific, social and economic neglect that may result. The paucity of information on ecological processes in urban settings hampers people who need to make environmental decisions for urban households, neighbourhoods, institutions and governments.

One major barrier to an integrated theory of urban systems is the fact that different legitimate definitions of urban are possible. For example, different disciplines may have different definitions of the urban subject matter. Human demography has a numerical approach, social geography a spatial approach, and urban design focuses on figure and ground or the density and massing of buildings and their associated landscapes. Definitions may also be specific to the mission of a government agency that makes or follows official policy. For example, the US Bureau of the Census carries out a constitutional mandate to enumerate the population of the country every 10 years. They define urban to track the movements of people and livelihoods. The definition has changed over time to reflect the way people use land, travel and commute, and allocate time between production and leisure. The United Nations Food and Agriculture Organization (FAO) defines urban to promote its mission of tracking the world's agricultural activity and output. Furthermore, specific models may use the term urban quite differently. Many ecologists will use the term to refer to the dense, built-up part of a city, as for example when they refer to 'urban versus suburban'. This contrast is used even by some members of BES. Others, as we have done throughout this paper, use the term to refer to the entire range of environments that a metropolis may include, extending from telecommuter exurbs, to old village centres on the fringe of suburbia, through new subdivisions, to old 'streetcar suburbs' that are often now within city limits, to the dense neighbourhoods built in the era before the dominance of motorised transport. Within such an urban mix there are also industrial and commercial areas, wilderness parks, manicured pleasure grounds and golf courses, malls, commercial strips, and the rest of the familiar range of architectural and land-use types (Clay, 1994). To avoid leaving out any of this complexity, we often use the word 'metropolitan' for this complete diversity of sites.

Science in the system

An additional issue to be addressed by urban ecological theory is that of participation in the system being studied. Because scientists have a responsibility to report their findings to the public, and especially to share their insights with residents of areas where scientific research takes place, the information gathered may change the behaviour of the system. One view of scientific objectivity suggests that researchers try not to affect the focal system. This is essentially impossible if scientists honour the hospitality of urban dwellers and managers. In fact, because humans and institutions have the capacity to learn and to alter their behaviour based on new knowledge, sharing information may well alter the system. Instead of trying to avoid such alteration, it may be possible to learn how new scientific information has affected the behaviour of decision leaders, institutions, and jurisdictions in the metropolis. Such studies may appropriately be carried out by education researchers, or by social scientists who have the tools and training to conduct assessments.

Interdisciplinary research

One theoretical challenge facing urban ecosystem research is interdisciplinarity. Clearly, the perspectives of multiple disciplines must be brought together to understand the metropolitan ecosystem. One can hardly understand the structure and function of cities and suburbs without calling on the knowledge of physical scientists, biological ecologists and social scientists of various kinds. However, truly interdisciplinary research that generates shared questions, common analyses, and consensus on conclusions is difficult and slow to mature. Besides the simple time and open-mindedness that are required of practitioners from different disciplines, integrators must be aware of the differences in the theories of the different disciplines, which may be more or less well articulated or developed. For instance, theory in hydrology is very well developed, while that in ecology is more unevenly developed.

In spite of the difficulties in developing a theory for urban ecological studies, there are heartening signs of progress (Zipperer *et al.*, 1995; Collins *et al.*, 2000;

Pickett *et al.*, 2001; Yli-Pelkonen and Niemelä, 2005). The increase of interdisciplinary effort in urban systems around the world suggests that these issues can be overcome. Indeed, in discussing the challenges, we have noted some solutions. These include: (1) recognising the nature of theory, and realising that theory takes time to develop in a new area; (2) recognising the need to counter the familiar but vague and provocative nature of the term 'urban' in most discussions; (3) recognising the different legitimate perspectives that different disciplines bring to urban studies, and seeking commonality among them. Beyond these needs, we note two additional steps.

An inclusive framework for urban ecological theory

The conceptual complexity discussed above suggests two general needs as urban ecological theory is developed: a neutral concept of 'urban', and the development of a common meaning. Following the example of the ecosystem as an important ecological definition (Pickett and Cadenasso, 2002), we suggest that a comprehensive, neutral concept of urban be adopted. The ecosystem definition is neutral in the sense that it can be applied to any scale, and any biotic and abiotic complex. Specific ecosystem models based on this definition then identify the scales, components, interactions and dynamics of interest. Perhaps a similar, general definition of urban might be useful. Such a definition would highlight human population density and the associated social institutions, and the predominance of built and infrastructural elements. Of course, biotic elements other than people exist in urban systems, and at least some biogeophysical ecosystem processes persist in built and engineered sites. The definition would apply to city centres and to exurbs, just as the ecosystem definition can apply to wild and managed ecosystems. Specific urban models would say how much density is present, how it is distributed, within what borders it exists, what institutions are present, and what remnant ecological processes persist. Models would go on to specify the interactions within and between these components, and how they might change through time. A neutral definition of urban would also aid the development of a comparative ecology of cities and towns as has been done in ecosystem science (Cole *et al.*, 1991).

The combination of the frameworks, discussed above, would guide the construction of the models. The human ecosystem framework (Fig. 3.6) includes the general social and bioecological phenomena from which to select those for particular models. The remaining frameworks address the distribution of different factors contained in the human ecosystem framework through space. Some factors may exist in different intensities or magnitudes over space. The urban–rural gradient framework (Fig. 3.4) places these factors and intensities in

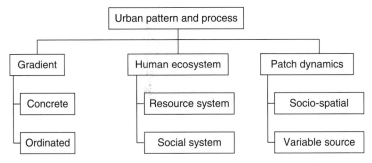

Fig. 3.7. Components of a general, integrated framework for urban ecological research combining major frameworks that have been used successfully in specific urban ecological studies. Gradients are represented either by concrete transects, or by quantitative ordinations in abstract space. The human ecosystem is represented by its two major subsystems (cf. Fig. 3.6 for details). Spatial heterogeneity as a driver and result of system structure and function is generalised by patch dynamics, which can incorporate the more specific hydrological spatial analysis of variable source area, and the socio-spatial approach to urban systems.

coarse-scale arrangement through the metropolis and beyond. The three remaining frameworks – patch dynamics, the variable source area approach and the socio-spatial approach – place several of the ecosystem factors explicitly in space. These spatial frameworks may apply to differences from parcel to parcel, or to the scale of the entire metropolis. Putting these two families of frameworks together suggests a general framework for urban ecological theory (Fig. 3.7).

Even the form of urban ecological theory is in a rudimentary state (Niemelä, 1999b). We believe the framework pieced together from the biophysical and human perspective on ecosystems, and the spatially explicit approach now recognised by bioecological, physical and social sciences, has great promise to promote and link diverse research on urban ecosystems. However, this framework goes beyond the desire to develop a common language, which is often stated as a crucial step in achieving interdisciplinary synthesis. Because terminology can be used in common by a group, but can still refer to different concepts, assumptions and theoretical structures, the more appropriate goal is to develop a common meaning (Bohm, 1996). Such meaning delves beneath the surface of the terminology, to examine the frameworks the terminology implies. This paper has attempted to combine several recognised frameworks used by different disciplines that contribute to understanding urban systems. The combined framework (Fig. 3.7) may serve as a tool to develop common meaning. Continuous and open-minded dialogue is required to fully exploit the common foundation the framework represents.

Acknowledgements

We thank Jari Niemelä for helpful comments on an earlier draft of the manu-script. We thank the Cary Institute of Ecosystem Studies for early support of the Urban–Rural Gradient Ecology research project, and the Lila Wallace Fund for supporting the research in the primary forest of the New York Botanical Garden where the project began. The Australian Research Centre for Urban Ecology is grateful for support provided by the Baker Foundation. The work of the Baltimore Ecosystem Study was supported by grants DEB 9714835 and DEB 0423476, with substantial in-kind support from the US Department of Agriculture Forest Service, and administrative support and research partnership from the Center for Urban Environmental Research and Education at the University of Maryland, Baltimore County. We thank our many colleagues in ARCUE and BES for sharing their insights, and for their intellectual support.

4

Comparative effects of urbanisation
in marine and terrestrial habitats

M. G. CHAPMAN AND A. J. UNDERWOOD

Introduction

Urbanisation and agriculture are likely to be the most extensive environmental impacts that humans impose on the natural world. In 1997, it was
estimated that across developed and undeveloped countries, 50% of people
would live in urbanised environments by 2000, with 400 million of them in only
25 cities (Botkin and Beveridge, 1997). These are not particularly new figures and
are probably already out of date, but there is no doubt that the trend worldwide
is for people to crowd into smaller and smaller areas as populations grow. The
density of people in urbanised environments is very large (in excess of 2000
people/km^2) and, because of limits to the heights of buildings, cultural impera-
tives for home ownership and so on, urban centres are spreading rapidly.

What is less often thought about is where the large cities are. An aerial view of
the planet at night clearly shows the lights of the large urbanised centres. Apart
from those in the eastern part of the USA and western Europe, these lights
clearly outline the coasts and large river systems of the continents (Earth's city
lights, courtesy NASA; http://earthobservatory.nasa.gov). Most large and small
cities, especially those that developed prior to extensive road and rail transport,
are on the coast or along waterways because of reliance on water for transport
and travel. Eleven of the 15 largest cities in the world are coastal. More than half
of the world's population lives within 100 km of the coast (Vitousek *et al.*, 1997b),
and coastal populations and cities are growing faster than those elsewhere.

Ecology of Cities and Towns: A Comparative Approach, ed. Mark J. McDonnell, Amy K. Hahs
and Jürgen H. Breuste. Published by Cambridge University Press. © Cambridge University
Press 2009.

Cities cause a continuous array of environmental perturbations. These include so-called pulse, press (Bender *et al.*, 1984) and ramp disturbances (Lake, 2001), to which ecological assemblages may show either pulse or press responses (Glasby and Underwood, 1996). Pulse disturbances may occur, for example, when a new structure such as a pier is being constructed. There may be a lot of boat movement, noise, dredging, etc. associated with construction of the structure, but, once it has been built, those particular disturbances cease. This is a pulse disturbance – it is relatively short term and then that particular disturbance reduces to background levels. The structure itself may remain as a press disturbance – it is there for a long period, during which it may continue to have impacts on the environment. A ramp disturbance occurs when there are repeated small disturbances, with incomplete recovery between them. Conditions gradually decline to a crucial level, after which there is permanent change to the system. Disturbances such as these may be extremely important in urbanised environments, e.g. gradual accumulation of contaminants from urban runoff, but they have not yet been widely investigated or considered.

For obvious reasons, studies of the ecological impacts of cities have a long history (Botkin and Beveridge, 1997). Most of these have had a terrestrial focus because of large changes in land use caused by urbanisation. Despite the proximity of many cities to the coastline and the likelihood that many of the impacts identified for terrestrial habitats may also apply to nearshore coastal habitats, there have been relatively few empirical studies that have examined specific effects of cities on marine or estuarine habitats. Studies of mangrove forests and similar wetlands are notable exceptions (Zedler, 1988). These semi-aquatic habitats superficially resemble terrestrial habitats because of their visual domination by large plants. The list of interesting ecological questions that have been addressed in urban settings include, for example, physiological responses of plants and animals, effects of pollution on productivity and nutrients, structure and function of fragments of habitat, truncated food webs, edge effects, biodiversity and genetic isolation, as summarised by McDonnell *et al.* (1997).

A cursory look through the literature suggests large differences between the approach taken by ecologists investigating urban impacts, according to whether they are dealing with terrestrial or aquatic habitats. Terrestrial ecologists appear to focus on changes to habitat or diversity of species, usually with respect to plants and/or vertebrates. Aquatic ecologists seem to be concerned primarily with issues of contamination of water and estuarine (coastal) sediments; most studies are about specific aspects of fauna in relation to contamination. Effects of cities on aquatic plants are seldom considered, except for wetlands (as mentioned previously) and seagrasses (e.g. Hauxwell *et al.*, 2003).

In addition, it appears that terrestrial or aquatic ecologists who examine urban problems tend to publish in different journals, with very few aquatic papers in those journals dedicated to urban studies. This suggests that, if ecologists primarily publish in the sorts of journal they are most likely to read (which seems probable), then terrestrial and aquatic ecologists looking at effects of cities may well be reading a different set of literature. This is likely, first, to create an artificial separation of perceptions of the ecological impacts of cities into terrestrial and aquatic components as if these do not interact. Second, it will minimise 'cross-cultural exchanges' of ideas, approaches, analytical techniques, and so forth. For one example, the 'urban–rural gradient' (McDonnell and Pickett, 1990) as a sampling approach is widely represented in terrestrial studies, but is not generally used in a similar way in aquatic studies, where BACI techniques (comparisons from Before to After a potential impact in Control and potentially Impacted locations) are more often used (Green, 1979; Underwood, 1992). Therefore, making comparisons across habitats is fraught with difficulties because spatial and temporal scales of measurement and the measurements made are not comparable (see also Underwood and Petraitis, 1993).

Therefore, the first part of this study is a literature review to determine the extent to which these perceptions were true and widespread. This is followed by an evaluation of some important ecological effects of urbanisation on coastal habitats.

Literature survey

To examine the focus of studies of ecological effects of urbanisation, relevant literature was surveyed. All papers in the journals *Urban Ecosystems* (1997–2002) and *Landscape and Urban Planning* (1995–2000) were examined. Because of the dearth of papers addressing aquatic issues in this search (Table 4.1), it was also extended to *Estuaries* (2000–2003) and *Estuarine, Coastal and Shelf Science* (1995–2000). All reviews and all papers predominantly about planning, modelling, mapping of land use, Geographical Information Systems, routine monitoring and social issues were ignored and only empirical studies that directly addressed ecological questions were included. In addition, *Ecology* (1985–1998) and *Ecological Applications* (1991–1998) were searched for the words urban or urbanisation (urbanization) in the abstract or as keywords.

Although many papers covered more than one aspect of urbanisation, in order to draw comparisons between marine and terrestrial studies, all papers were put into one or more of four broad categories of environmental impacts. These were studies:

(1)   predominantly associated with changes to habitat, including loss, alteration and fragmentation of natural habitats and the provision of new 'habitat' by built structures, e.g. buildings, docks, piers;

Table 4.1. *The proportion of ecological papers in different journals that have examined ecological effects of urbanisation in terrestrial, marine or freshwater habitats, for plants, vertebrates or invertebrates and examining changes in habitat, species or other ecological processes.*

Journal	UE	LUP	ECSS	Es	EA/Ec
Dates	(1997–2002)	(1995–2000)	(1993–2003)	(2000–2003)	Issues on Web
No. papers surveyed	47	43	91	17	10
Prop. of total papers	45%	10%	8%	5%	?
Terrestrial	94%	93%	1%	0%	50%
Freshwater (wetland)	4%	5%	0%	6%	0%
Freshwater (other)	0%	2%	8%	12%	20%
Marine (wetland)	2%	2%	14%	12%	0%
Marine (other)	2%	0%	79%	88%	30%
Plants	51%	74%	20%	18%	30%
Mammals	17%	7%	0%	0%	10%
Other vertebrates	21%	35%	4%	24%	40%
Invertebrates	9%	9%	27%	41%	20%
Habitat loss/ change/ fragmentation	55%	41%	17%	0%	10%
Species loss/ change/ diversity	44%	93%	28%	47%	90%
Introduced or invasive species	5%	7%	2%	12%	40%
Contamination/ pollution	11%	17%	81%	98%	20%
Ecological processes/ functions	38%	21%	12%	18%	40%
Direct human disturbance	17%	0%	1%	0%	0%

Notes:

UE – *Urban Ecosystems;* LUP – *Landscape and Urban Planning;* ECSS – *Estuarine, Coastal and Shelf Science;* Es – *Estuaries;* EA – *Ecological Applications;* Ec – *Ecology.*

(2)   predominantly associated with changes to species diversity and composition of assemblages, due to loss or introduction of species and/or changes in relative abundances, e.g. species becoming pests;

(3)   associated with effects of contaminants and pollution;

(4)   on direct effects of human activities and behaviour, e.g. traffic, walking, noise, fishing.

In addition, papers were categorised as dealing with terrestrial, freshwater (including wetlands) and/or marine (including mangrove forests) habitats and covering ecology of plants, vertebrates and/or invertebrates.

Results of literature survey

The results of the literature survey are summarised in Table 4.1. More than 2000 papers were first examined, with 208 selected for categorisation because they met the criteria for selection. Over all the journals examined, there was not a large difference in the percentage of papers that addressed urban issues from a terrestrial (48% of papers averaged over all journals) or marine viewpoint (46%), whereas studies in freshwater habitats were less represented (11%). Note that some papers covered more than one type of habitat. There was, however, a strong tendency for terrestrial and aquatic papers to be published in different journals. Journals aimed primarily at urban ecological studies (*Urban Ecosystems* and *Landscape and Urban Planning*) predominantly published papers dealing with terrestrial topics. Effects of cities on aquatic habitats were predominantly in journals that dealt with aquatic habitats, although they formed only a small proportion of papers in those journals.

The second clear difference is that studies of invertebrates were found in only a small proportion of papers in terrestrial habitats, where the majority of papers were about plants, followed closely by birds and mammals. Note that not all papers, about contamination for example, addressed specific taxa and, therefore, these categories do not necessarily sum to 100%. Similarly, some papers addressed more than one taxon and the percentages in the different categories may sum to more than 100%. A much larger proportion of papers in aquatic habitats were studies of invertebrates. Recently, more attention has been paid to effects of urbanisation on invertebrates as their crucial contribution to biodiversity is more widely recognised (see also Natuhara and Hashimoto, Chapter 12; Hochuli *et al.*, Chapter 13; McIntyre and Rango, Chapter 14; and Eisenbeis and Hänel, Chapter 15).

Changes to habitat, through loss, fragmentation and changes to spatial pattern, were far more common in the terrestrial literature, whereas studies of changes in abundances and diversity of species were relatively widespread among terrestrial and marine habitats. This is probably due to changes to habitats on land being very visual as cities spread and replace natural habitats with built structures. At first glance, apart from wetlands and mangroves, intertidal habitats that are also dominated by trees, marine habitats in and around cities appear little altered. In contrast, a very large proportion of the marine literature dealt with issues of contamination and pollution, whereas little of the terrestrial literature surveyed dealt with contamination of soil or air, specifically from an ecological (rather than human health) point of view. Fewer than half of the papers dealt with ecological processes (such as breeding, growth and predation), rather than descriptive measures of diversity, habitat-size and so on.

This survey did raise some important issues about the holistic effects of cities. It appears that aquatic and terrestrial impacts are viewed differently with respect to the taxa of most interest and the type of impact considered most important. Terrestrial and aquatic ecologists investigating effects of cities are largely publishing in journals with very different foci. In addition, until recently, most studies were about ecology in cities, where the city was merely a site for an ecological study (Grimm et al., 2000). Now, terrestrial researchers are recognising the concept of the ecology of cities, where ecological processes may be fundamentally different from natural areas because human behaviour is intimately incorporated into ecological patterns and processes in cities (Collins et al., 2000; Pickett et al., 2001; Alberti et al., 2003; Niemelä et al., Chapter 2; Pickett et al., Chapter 3). This approach is not yet widely used in marine ecological research in cities.

As a further part of this study, therefore, Reports on the State of the Environment were examined for councils along the coast of Australia. Local governments (through municipal and shire councils) are important end-users of ecological knowledge (e.g. Sydney Coastal Councils Group, 1998). They are obliged to report regularly on the 'state' of their local environment, although they do not generally collect good quantitative data, nor do they usually access the scientific literature for current areas of concern. State of Environment Reports were examined for fourteen councils, one each from South Australia, Queensland, South Australia, Tasmania and Western Australia, with the remaining nine from New South Wales. All councils were coastal and therefore contained estuarine or marine habitats. These were a mix of city (municipal) councils from large urbanised centres and shire councils, from outside the large cities, but with rapidly developing populations. Although all fourteen listed concerns about water quality, five of them (36%) listed direct concern with aspects of change to marine habitats and six (43%) with changes to marine species. These included issues such as fish kills, intertidal foraging and changes to mangroves. Therefore, although in comparison with terrestrial habitats there has been relatively little research on changes to marine/estuarine habitats and native marine species as a consequence of expanding urbanisation, there is public concern about these issues.

In general, loss and fragmentation of habitat, with subsequent flow-ons to maintenance of diversity of species, are widely seen as urban problems in terrestrial habitats, but not in nearshore marine habitats associated with cities. Is this because cities do not fragment or destroy adjacent marine habitats, because fragmentation is not such a major problem for many marine biota, or simply because this is not a topic that has attracted the attention of marine ecologists working in urban environments? Similarly, although there are widespread concerns about overfishing worldwide (Ludwig, 1993), loss of marine species due to expanding cities does not appear to be of concern. This is clearly not the case for many terrestrial species affected by expanding urbanisation. Again, is this because diversity of marine species does not change much in response to urban expansion?

In contrast, contamination of water and sediments around harbours and urbanised estuaries is a widespread concern. Is this because contamination is often clearly visible (Harms, 1990; Ryan and Moloney, 1993)? Or is it because of issues of human health, which are a greater problem where people swim in, drink or eat food from water, than in similarly contaminated terrestrial areas?

It is therefore relevant to examine some of these issues in more detail, in order to evaluate whether the apparent paucity of research about loss, fragmentation or change of marine habitats and changes to species diversity in association with cities does reflect a probable lack of impact to these habitats and the species living in them. This may tell us whether the ideas and approaches being developed with respect to terrestrial habitats will be useful for marine habitats, or whether the terrestrial and marine environments are so different (in structure, taxa and problems) that separate agenda are inevitable.

Changes to habitat

Changes to habitat imposed by urbanisation vary from the extreme, where there is complete loss of natural habitat and replacement by built structures in the centre of a city, through more suburban areas, where built structures are interspersed with patches of natural habitat or 'constructed parklands', to the outskirts of the city, where either agricultural land or natural landscapes may predominate. This is commonly referred to as the urban–rural gradient (McDonnell and Pickett, 1990). Changes to coastal habitat in and around cities are less clear-cut and more patchy, although, as for terrestrial habitats, there are also important issues of loss, fragmentation and replacement.

Loss and fragmentation

Although it is difficult to separate the effects of loss of habitat from those of fragmentation, because the latter generally leads to loss of the total amount of habitat, these topics were one of the most frequently considered questions in terrestrial studies of urbanisation (Table 4.1). Conversion of 'green' to 'brown' space gives rise to much concern about the sustainability of remaining green areas as patches become smaller and more isolated (e.g. Metzger, 1997; Schiller and Horn, 1997). Apart from loss of wetlands, which have in the past been seen as wastelands and 'reclaimed' for development (Zedler, 1988), loss or

Fig. 4.1. Building of walls, piers, marinas and wharves strongly affects the shoreline along urbanised estuaries. These examples are from shores around Sydney, Australia.

fragmentation of marine habitats adjacent to coastal cities is less obvious (Manson *et al.*, 2003). Dredging the sea bottom for shipping or fishing can alter areas (e.g. Iannuzzi *et al.*, 1996), but, unless reefs or seagrass beds are affected directly (Walker *et al.*, 1989), these have received relatively little attention.

Yet there is large-scale alteration of the shoreline along shores of all coastal cities, with replacement of natural habitat by constructed walls, piers, etc. These lead to direct loss of intertidal and subtidal natural habitat, with fragmentation of that remaining. For example, in Sydney Harbour (recognised worldwide for its 'natural' appeal), more than 90% of some areas of the shoreline is constructed, replacing natural habitat of one form or another (Fig. 4.1).

The extent to which replacement of natural by constructed shores does represent loss depends on the extent to which species can use these artificial structures in lieu of natural habitat. Where walls replace soft sediments (e.g. beaches or mudflats), which is often done to stabilise shorelines (Walker, 1988), loss is obvious – a vertical concrete wall will not support the assemblage that lives naturally on a gently sloping beach. Where the original natural shores were hard, rocky surfaces, the suite of species supported by the two forms of structure may (e.g. Chapman and Bulleri, 2003) or may not (e.g. Connell and Glasby, 1999) be different. Indeed, it has been suggested that artificial shores can augment intertidal assemblages by supplying additional habitat (Thompson *et al.*, 2002).

The literature survey focused on another major difference between studies of fragmentation and loss of habitat due to cities in terrestrial and marine environments. Most papers are about terrestrial plants (Danielson *et al.*, 1997) or vertebrates, particularly birds (e.g. Jokimäki, 1999) and mammals (Riley *et al.*, 2003). Because invertebrates are a major (albeit rather ignored; New, 1993) component of biodiversity in marine and terrestrial habitats, it is surprising that there have been relatively few studies on how the change of habitat associated with cities affects terrestrial invertebrate species (but see Niemelä *et al.*, 2000, 2002 and Chapter 2). Plants, vertebrates and invertebrates living in the same habitat can show very different responses to loss or fragmentation of habitat. For example, Olff and Ritchie (2002) showed that diversity of birds in the Netherlands decreased with habitat-loss and fragmentation, whereas diversity of butterflies was affected only by loss, not by fragmentation.

It is not likely that these studies will have great relevance to marine habitats for a number of reasons. First, it is less clear that the size of a patch of habitat is important for maintaining diversity in marine habitats. Patch size is clearly very important in maintaining diversity of birds (e.g. Jokimäki, 1999) and plants (e.g. Bastin and Thomas, 1999), with smaller patches generally supporting less diversity because of edge effects or loss of habitats (e.g. Danielson *et al.*, 1997). Much of the diversity in marine systems is composed of algae (seaweeds) and invertebrates. Many of these species rapidly colonise disturbed or cleared patches of habitat (Dayton, 1971; Sutherland, 1980; Connell, 1983), even when these are relatively small. Algae and many invertebrates are sessile and the scales over which mobile animals move and use resources are usually very small. In addition, many important resources (e.g. nutrients, food or potential prey items) are repeatedly supplied, even to very small patches of habitat, via the water column. Biological and physical factors frequently clear new space, preventing long-term monopolisation of patches of habitat by few species (Levin and Paine, 1974; Paine, 1979; Sousa, 1979a).

Because of connectivity via the water column, the population structure of marine organisms is generally considered very open, with physically isolated patches connected by larval flow (Thorson, 1950; Scheltema, 1971) and/or movement of adults (Martel and Chia, 1991; Wang and Xu, 1997), which tends to lead to rapid recovery and resilient populations (Holling, 1973). There is, however, a great lack of knowledge of the true connectedness of populations of marine organisms near or away from urban centres. There is generally no information about which populations are sources of propagules and which are sinks (Pulliam, 1988). Recent genetic evidence suggests relatively little variation in some pools of larvae (Hedgecock, 1994) or relatively little genetic exchange among widespread populations (Palumbi, 2003), although there is good evidence for dispersal of some species over very large distances (Scheltema, 1971). Many marine larvae may only disperse very short distances and populations may be connected by a series of relatively close 'stepping-stones' rather than widespread larval interconnection (Shanks *et al.*, 2003). If this situation is common, populations of adult marine invertebrates in highly fragmented and disturbed environments may be more vulnerable than traditionally thought.

This also implies that marine habitats are likely to be more susceptible to fragmentation of the 'supply lines' connecting patches of habitat, rather than to fragmentation of the patches themselves (Fig. 4.2). The range of artificial structures built along shorelines, especially those that protrude into the waterway (e.g. bridges, runways, piers) rather than those that run along the shore (e.g. retaining walls), can cause strong changes to water currents and flow (e.g. Gomez-Gasteira *et al.*, 2002). These can alter conditions for persistence of native species or promote the expansion of invasive species (Floerl and Inglis, 2003). There does not appear to be a similar scenario for the terrestrial environment, where connectivity between patches is generally enhanced by corridors of vegetation similar to that in the patches.

Provision of new habitat

New habitat is also provided by urbanisation by the building of new structures, which can be used directly by some biota, or strongly alter nearby 'natural' habitat. In terrestrial systems, the built structure itself (e.g. a new building or road) is seldom seen directly as providing habitat, although some species do use and benefit from buildings. For example, Crucitti *et al.* (1998) showed that scorpions in Rome were commonly found inside buildings, and Eversham *et al.* (1996) compared various constructed sites as habitat for carabid beetles. Slip and Shine (1988) showed that large diamond pythons used buildings for shelter, and bats are commonly reported to use bridges, buildings and other constructed habitat as roost sites (e.g. Bruijn, 1990).

Some species have become extremely successful in surviving and thriving in the habitats closely associated with housing, roads, urban gardens and parks. McKinney (2002) referred to these species as urban exploiters. For example, many birds find abundant nesting sites in managed parklands and gardens (Soh *et al.*, 2002). Common rodents have done particularly well in many urban settings (e.g. Zhu *et al.*, 1986), and even rural species, such as the harvest mouse, may be more common in urban environments than once thought (Dickman, 1986). The ecological value of many of these newly created habitats appears to depend on how

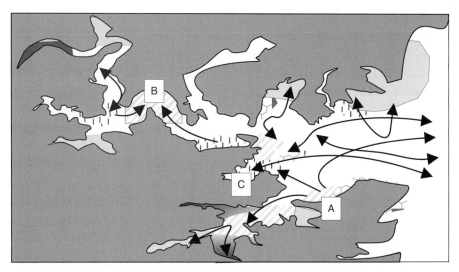

Fig. 4.2. Marine habitats in estuaries are typically patchy. Some patches (e.g. 'A') act as sources of propagules, others (e.g. 'B') act as sinks, whereas others export and import individuals (e.g. 'C') (upper figure). Therefore, if a patch which acts as a sink (i.e. 'B') is destroyed, there is little effect elsewhere (lower figure). If a patch that acts as a source (i.e. 'A') is destroyed, there may be failure of recruitment in other patches, which may then not be sustainable in the long term. In addition, structures that disrupt connectivity via the movement of water ('D' in the lower figure) may have serious effects on maintenance of patches elsewhere by diverting the flow of water, which carries nutrients and propagules.

well they mimic natural habitats and, therefore, other biotic components (e.g. vegetation) are frequently important.

This is in contrast to many marine artificial structures, where the physical structure itself appears very important in providing habitat, e.g. structures in marinas for fish (Rilov and Benayahu, 1998) or seawalls for intertidal invertebrates (e.g. Chapman and Bulleri, 2003). There are also, however, examples of research into indirect effects of constructed structures in marine habitats. For example, in the West Indies, sea urchins have been shown to play an important role in controlling abundance of aquatic plants, although a major artefact in these studies may affect the generality of the reported results. Most of the relevant work was done around jetties and wharves, i.e. where there was relatively easy access, so the results may not be applicable to natural areas (Hay, 1984).

Although large areas of a freshwater or estuarine water-body adjacent to a city are unlikely to be altered by intrusive built habitats, this is usually not true of the habitat formed by the interface between the water and the land. In many coastal cities, the natural shoreline has been replaced by walls, port developments, piers and pilings (e.g. Walker, 1988; Glasby and Connell, 1999). This usually goes hand-in-hand with straightening of the shoreline, thus replacing complex, variable habitat (e.g. alternating rocky and soft-sedimentary habitats) with a homogeneous habitat, whose surface complexity, aspect, slope, etc. are often different from those of natural hard shores (see Chapman et al., Chapter 9). Such habitats are very rapidly colonised by a wide range of organisms. Numerous studies have, however, shown that the assemblages associated with artificial habitats differ from those living in natural habitats (e.g. fish associated with marinas (Rilov and Benayahu, 1998), subtidal epibiota on pier pilings (Glasby, 1998) and pontoons (Connell, 2000), and epibiota on intertidal seawalls (Chapman, 2003; Chapman and Bulleri, 2003)).

Similar patterns are found in freshwater environments affected by changes to shorelines. For example, Wolter (2001) showed reduced diversity of fishes living in stretches of rivers which had been canalised and straightened with riprap or sheet pile walls.

New habitat provided by artificial structures can also be considered in the framework of Type I and Type II patches (Connell and Keough, 1985; Sousa, 1985) with respect to which types of taxa will colonise these patches, from where and, at what rates and, therefore, the potential for built structures to act as surrogates of natural habitats. Type I patches were defined as patches of one habitat embedded in a matrix of another habitat – often because a disturbance to the original matrix created a cleared patch. An example is a patch in a mussel-bed cleared by storms. The cleared area is a Type I patch surrounded by mussels

(Levin and Paine, 1974). Type II patches, in contrast, are areas of new habitat inserted or created in another habitat (Connell and Keough, 1985).

Many built structures associated with urbanisation are typically Type II patches. For example, bridges, marinas and docks are often built on soft sediments in order to embed the supporting structures into the substratum. Therefore, the habitats associated with these structures are surrounded by soft sediments and physically isolated from natural hard substrata. New structures, such as seawalls, which might connect patches of natural rocky shore (Thompson et al., 2002), might be considered Type I patches – equivalent to areas cleared by disturbance within a natural matrix. The reality of this analogy depends on how well such structures represent natural habitats cleared of biota (see Chapman et al., Chapter 9). There is considerable ecological theory about colonisation and persistence of biota in Type I or Type II patches (Connell and Keough, 1985; Sousa, 1985), but the applicability of this theory to urban structures, of different sizes and surrounded by different habitats, has not yet been explored.

Alternatively, artificial structures may influence biota in adjacent habitat by: (1) degrading those habitats (e.g. McAllister et al., 1996; Lindegarth and Hoskin, 2001), or (2) disrupting patterns of connectiveness among natural patches, e.g. by disrupting water movement and, hence, the supply of propagules (Gomez-Gesteira et al., 2002). Similar processes may operate in the terrestrial components of cities. For example, in Oula in Finland, the proximity of buildings to urban parks directly affected densities of particular species of birds in the park, independently of the sizes of the parks and diversity of plants growing in them (Jokimäki, 1999).

Effects of cities on species

In addition to indirect effects on species via changes to habitat, urbanisation can affect species directly by exploitation, introduction of competitors or predators, etc. Many of these changes are well documented for terrestrial species, especially for the larger or more charismatic fauna and flora. Little, in contrast, has been documented for marine species living in and around cities, largely because such a large component of marine biodiversity is small, cryptic and not well described.

Loss of species

Species diversity in and around cities is often reduced indirectly, by loss and fragmentation of their habitats (discussed above). Most terrestrial studies have examined loss of plants or vertebrates (e.g. Nilon and Pais, 1997), with little emphasis on changes to invertebrate assemblages, although McIntyre et al. (2001)

showed differences in species composition (but not in number of species) of ground-dwelling arthropods among urban and natural habitats in Phoenix (Arizona), probably related to decreasing structural complexity in increasingly urbanised habitats. For some species, direct mortality may be due to other factors occurring around cities, e.g. from road traffic (Shuttleworth, 2001) or hunting (Kilpatrick *et al.*, 2002). See van der Ree (Chapter 11), Natuhara and Hashimoto (Chapter 12), Hochuli *et al.* (Chapter 13) and Eisenbeis and Hänel, (Chapter 15) for additional insights into this topic.

Many marine species, especially fish and invertebrates, are directly exploited for food or bait, much of which still continues in and around large cities (e.g. Fairweather, 1991; Kingsford *et al.*, 1991). Where this has been extremely prevalent, there are severe reductions and localised extinctions of populations of some species (e.g. the barnacle *Pollicipes pollicipes* in Spain and Portugal; personal observation). Large assemblages of species can be eliminated or destroyed, such as occurs with the destruction of oyster reefs (McKenzie, 1996) or where subtidal reefs are 'mined' for boring bivalves along the coast of Italy (Fanalli *et al.*, 1994). Even in relatively sparsely occupied areas, exploitation of easily accessible areas, such as intertidal seashores, has been shown to cause extremely complex changes to natural biota (Castilla and Duran, 1985; Lasiak, 1991).

Although fishing pressure can be managed to prevent environmental degradation and severe reduction in populations, there is often not the political will to do this, so exploitation of marine species continues to increase with increasing human population size. In addition, laws to control further loss of species, e.g. the Convention on International Trade in Endangered Species of Wild Flora and Fauna 1973 (CITES), seldom discuss marine species and those for which there is concern are mainly 'higher' vertebrates, such as whales. In 2003, only five species of marine fish and six species of corals were listed under CITES (Tsamenyi *et al.*, 2003). One reason is that there have been very few recent marine extinctions compared with terrestrial species, especially for invertebrates (Carlton, 1993). Nevertheless, hundreds of species of invertebrates that have been described in the past have never been redescribed (Carlton, 1993). Whether these are extinct or naturally very rare and therefore probably still extant somewhere is not known. It is difficult to measure the absence of small, cryptic species in most marine habitats (Chapman, 1999).

Introduced and pest species

In contrast to the loss of many species in and around cities, others can become very abundant. These include species introduced from elsewhere, either intentionally or otherwise. Such changes may be gradual or relatively sudden. For example, Godefroid (2001) showed gradual changes in plant assemblages in

Brussels in the past half century, owing to replacement of sensitive species by nitrophilous and shade-tolerant species. Vuorisalo *et al.* (2003), in contrast, showed rapid increases in populations of hooded crows (*Corvus corone cornix*) in two cities in Finland in recent years, despite a long association of relatively small populations of this species with the cities. The reasons for the sudden increases were complex and were not simply related to an increase in food, as had been shown for this species elsewhere.

Some species are intentionally introduced into areas, but then may rapidly disperse into and through other nearby environments. For example, the house crow was introduced into Malaysia as a house pet, but then rapidly spread through many parts of Asia (Ward, 1968). Native species can also spread in urban areas, taking advantage of additional food, shelter, lack of predators and so forth, greatly increasing in densities and often becoming a severe pest species to human and other native flora and fauna (see Low, 2002, for examples in Australia).

Although the economic and ecological problems associated with the spread (intentionally or accidentally) of introduced species have been long recognised (e.g. Elton, 1958), it has been relatively ignored in inshore marine and estuarine systems compared with terrestrial and freshwater habitats (Ruiz *et al.*, 1997). Unless there are human health issues (Hallegraeffe *et al.*, 1988) or commercial implications to fisheries (e.g. Ross *et al.*, 2002), or the species has spread widely and visibly into marine habitats that are readily accessed by people (e.g. Sanderson, 1990; Holloway and Keough, 2002), many introductions have probably not been recorded. Local effects on biodiversity can be large and devastating (Simberloff, 1981), but in other cases, biodiversity appears to persist in association with extremely abundant introduced or invasive species. Even when the introduced species has complex, structural effects on habitat, effects on biodiversity may be spatially very variable (e.g. Holloway and Keough, 2002). Introduced species are often readily incorporated into marine assemblages and, in effect, form part of the natural assemblage (Crisp and Southward, 1959; Ruiz *et al.*, 1997).

There have been a number of intentional introductions to marine environments near cities, particularly for aquaculture. For example, both the Atlantic oyster, *Crassostrea virginica*, and the Pacific oyster, *Crassostrea gigas*, were introduced into San Francisco Bay to establish commercial fisheries, although the former did not persist and *C. gigas* became an important species locally. Along with these species came a large number of unintentionally introduced species, many of which still persist and have become incorporated into natural assemblages in the bay (Ruiz *et al.*, 1997).

Because so many cities are on the coast and all early travel between cities was by boat, most marine invasions have been the result of accidental introductions, e.g. on the hulls of boats (Floerl and Inglis, 2003) or in ballast water (Carlton and

Geller, 1993). Rates of invasion via ballast water are increasing, owing to the quantities of water carried by the large ships of today and the speed with which they move over the oceans, which allows survival of propagules and adults between the time of loading and discharge of water. Areas around major coastal cities on all continents have recorded introductions (Ruiz *et al.*, 1997), with 70 introduced species reported from inshore Australian waters. In fact, recently, of the three most abundant species found in sediments in Port Philip Bay in 1998, two were introduced bivalves and one an introduced polychaete, each of which probably arrived via ballast water (Wilson *et al.*, 1998).

Because most marine invertebrates and many seaweeds are relatively sparse, small and cryptic, measures of their presence/absence in a habitat in most ecological/monitoring studies are rather 'hit-and-miss' (Chapman, 1999). Even in relatively large sampling programmes of benthic marine invertebrates, a large proportion of species are found as single individuals, indicating a sparse and patchy distribution (Gray, 2002). There is therefore great uncertainty around measures of presence or absence, resulting in the inability to distinguish between true absence of a species in a habitat and 'absence' due to lack of finding that species in a set of samples (Gaston, 1994). Therefore, the disappearance of a species cannot always be distinguished from its decline to densities so small that it is not sampled during most routine monitoring programmes. Neither is it clear whether the apparent appearance or spread of a species is due to natural change in distribution or abundance of native biota that were previously under-sampled, or the introduction of new species (see Phillips and Price (2002) for discussion of spread of the weed *Caulerpa*).

The real numbers of introduced invertebrates in urbanised coastal waters are, therefore, likely to be severely underestimated because of the cryptic nature of many coastal marine organisms and the difficulties of distinguishing among introduced and native species, particularly in the field (Wilson *et al.*, 1998). With the current increase in global transport and travel, it is difficult to see how such widescale movement of marine organisms among areas can be stopped. The same is true of many introduced plants, which are planted in large numbers in urban areas. Many hybridise with and alter the genetic populations of native species. It may simply be a case of learning to live with 'The New Nature' (Low, 2002), however unattractive a proposition that may be.

Contamination versus pollution

The review of literature showed that pollution was perceived to be the most important effect (with respect to the number of published papers) that cities have on adjacent marine habitats. These were generally effects of nutrients (from sewage and urban/agricultural runoff), heavy metals and similar toxins. Terrestrial studies of pollution concentrate on air pollution, particularly effects on human health (Moore *et al.*, 2003) and effects of, for example, acid rain on biota (Izuta, 1998; Fyson, 2000) or habitats (Bard, 1999). There are also increasing problems of the disposal of solid waste produced by cities in very large amounts. This can be unsightly, smell, use up lots of land and, more importantly from an ecological point of view, lead to very large numbers of pest species, e.g. rats, gulls, crows (Gabrey, 1997; Belant *et al.*, 1998; Vuorisalo *et al.*, 2003), which thrive on the increased source of food. These species can, in turn, affect the abundance of non-pest, native species.

A complete review of effects of contamination on biota is too large to cover in detail in this chapter and is, in any case, dealt with in great detail in the specialist literature, but there are a few points worth making with respect to marine pollution in urban environments. The first is to distinguish between contamination (the amount of a particular component in the water or marine sediments) and pollution (the ecological effect of that contaminant; GESAMP, 1994). Many published studies and most routine monitoring measure the former, i.e. the quality of water. This is quite appropriate for issues of human health, where maximal allowable levels of contaminant are determined by legislation (Underwood, 2000), but that cannot automatically be taken to mean there is pollution, i.e. a measurable effect of that contaminant on a species, assemblage or ecological process (Underwood, 1996).

Although very large concentrations of some contaminants can be found in coastal waters (Birch, 1996), their effects on inshore ecology are not generally well documented (but see Underwood, 2000). In fact, many marine assemblages appear to be resilient to many environmental contaminants. For example, when the disposal of sewage from the city of Sydney, Australia (a city of more than 4 million people), was moved offshore, a study was commissioned to examine the recovery of subtidal epibiota in areas that had been subjected to disposal of raw sewage and then primary-treated sewage for over 70 years. This biota was measured within a few metres of the outfall pipe and also many kilometres away. Sampling showed no change consistent with recovery, because there were no measurable effects of sewage on the existing assemblage in the first place (Chapman *et al.*, 1995).

This does not, of course, mean that sewage never has an effect on coastal habitats. Increased tidal flushing and water movement are likely to ameliorate impacts by rapidly dispersing contaminants. Changes to nutrients in poorly flushed waters of estuaries and coastal lakes, have, in contrast, been strongly correlated with blooms of opportunistic macro-algae (e.g. Sfriso *et al.*, 1992; Fong and Zedler, 2000). The above discussion does, however, show that measures of contamination cannot automatically be taken to mean that there is, or there should be expected to be, ecological change (Underwood, 1989, 1995b).

With respect to disposal of solid waste at sea, that is an ongoing and vexed issue. There is considerable community effort to clear up waste, such as plastic, glass and tyres (e.g. Clean-up Australia Day, during which thousands of individuals remove discarded rubbish from the sea). There is also no doubt that a lot of rubbish, especially plastics and discarded fishing gear, entangles and kills marine vertebrates (Derraik, 2002). But, at the same time, waste produces habitat for many species. Therefore, disposal of large amounts of waste at sea is frequently portrayed as the 'provision of artificial reefs' and viewed as a 'positive' impact. This is not the forum to go into the lack of logic of 'positive' versus 'negative' impacts. Suffice to say, the introduction (or increase in abundances) of any species in an area where it would not normally live (or would be kept at small abundances by restricted availability of habitat) must affect other components of the environment – those species that normally live in the area.

Ultimately, the ecological effects of pollutants will only be really understood when a large proportion of the vast resources that go into measuring contamination is spent trying to understand the effects of that contamination on biota. This is best done using field experimentation (Underwood and Peterson, 1988) and, fortunately, inshore marine habitats are very amenable to manipulation of species (Connell, 1972; Paine, 1994) and habitats (Sousa, 1979b) to address such questions. Thus, Morrisey *et al.* (1996), in a well-controlled and replicated field experiment, conclusively demonstrated the effects of copper on subtidal benthic fauna. Using similar procedures, Lindegarth and Underwood (2002) found that intertidal assemblages showed no responses to the same manipulative treatments, indicating an important problem with simply extrapolating experiments from one habitat to another, even in the same part of the world (see also Crowe, 1996).

Final comment

In addition to the direct effects on species and habitats caused by building large cities, large numbers of people may have strong environmental impacts, simply by their use of natural habitat. Noise might affect breeding birds, traffic can kill large numbers of animals on and off the road, the use of boats can add contaminants and rubbish, propellors and anchors can damage seabeds and associated flora and fauna. Even an activity as apparently harmless as walking can affect vegetation and associated fauna. For example, the physical impact of walking has been shown to affect carabid beetles (Grandchamp *et al.*, 2000), seagrasses (Eckrich and Holmquist, 2000), reefs (Hawkins and Roberts, 1993) and intertidal rocky shores (Povey and Keough, 1991; Brosnan and Crumrine, 1994). Often this activity is viewed as harmless and may occur because areas are perceived as natural and therefore visited frequently. The use of boardwalks, or other similar structures, to attempt to solve one perceived problem may cause a different form of impact (e.g. Kelaher *et al.*, 1998; Weis and Weis, 2002).

Nevertheless, cities are here to stay. Coastal development will increase faster than any other forms of urbanisation, at least while there is any accessible undeveloped coast left to develop. This review has attempted to show that the effects of people in cities extend seaward in addition to landward, but, although many of the problems in the marine habitats adjacent to cities are similar to those on land, it is not at all clear that the ecology in these two broad environments responds to the same problems in the same way. Priorities do (and to some extent probably should) differ between terrestrial and marine habitats.

Terrestrial concerns focus on large habitat-forming vegetation and charismatic fauna, such as mammals and birds – species that are very vulnerable to changes to and loss of habitat, particularly fragmentation. Similar changes in habitat are not of great concern in the marine environment, although we suggest that they should receive much more attention. Marine vertebrates other than fish are not common around many cities, and fish are largely viewed as an extractable resource, rather than a concern for conservation. Invertebrates – the backbone of biodiversity – are more visible in some marine habitats, such as reefs and rocky shores, than in many terrestrial habitats. Yet the open population structure, with presumed strong connectivity among populations, suggests that recovery from disturbance is rapid and frequent, and the populations are considered quite resilient. How much change to habitat and invasion by feral species these populations can tolerate is, however, a great unknown.

Nevertheless, despite these large differences in perceived effects of cities between terrestrial and marine habitats, there are points of similarity in the sorts of changes that are occurring in the city environment, e.g. loss, fragmentation and replacement of habitat, exploitation of species, introduction of pests and contamination. Until more ecologists working in urban environments start interacting across the land–water interface, in addition to across the ecological–sociological interface (Pickett *et al.*, 2001, Chapter 3), it is unlikely that we will develop a full, or even a realistic understanding of the ecological effects of cities. It is up to individual researchers to develop new research programmes that will bridge this gulf between the land and the sea.

Acknowledgements

The University of Sydney and Australian Research Council through its Special Research Centres Program funded this research. We thank innumerable students, colleagues and friends for lively discussion, debate, enlightenment and ideas, which have made our research into the effects of urbanisation in marine habitats such an exciting and rewarding venture. Mark McDonnell and two anonymous reviewers made many helpful comments on an earlier draft of this chapter.

5

Comparative ecology of cities and towns: past, present and future

MARK J. MCDONNELL AND AMY K. HAHS

Introduction

Comparative studies can be simply described as the systematic assessment of similarities and differences between diverse entities, philosophies and styles. To conduct such studies requires similar data that can be compared and an appropriate method or scheme of comparison. For example, comparisons can range from a simple assessment of the morphological traits of different species of plants to a comparison of the political and economic systems of different cities. Such studies have provided important new understandings about the evolutionary relationships between plants as well as the factors that influence the creation and dynamics of political and economic systems around the world. Comparative studies are a valued and well tested method of developing new understandings in a diversity of subjects and are especially well suited to studies of literature, religion, linguistics, medicine, biology and sociology. In the field of sociology, the comparative approach has been vital to understanding the structure and dynamics of human societies (Bollen *et al.*, 1993). This chapter focuses on the less studied role of comparative studies in understanding the ecology of cities and towns.

In the field of biology, comparative methods have been successfully applied in the traditional subdisciplines of evolution, behaviour and ecology (Gittleman and Luh, 1992) and indeed in new fields such as comparative phylogeography (Bermingham and Moritz, 1998). Comparative studies of plant and animal traits

Ecology of Cities and Towns: A Comparative Approach, ed. Mark J. McDonnell, Amy K. Hahs and Jürgen H. Breuste. Published by Cambridge University Press. © Cambridge University Press 2009.

have provided the foundations for the well developed classification and phylogenic systems currently used to understand the taxonomic and phylogenic relationships between organisms. The creation of these classification and phylogenic systems provides tremendous opportunities for additional comparative studies designed to provide a more detailed understanding of evolutionary and ecological relationships between organisms and the environments in which they occur. For example, plant biologists have effectively used comparative studies to understand the distribution of plants and elucidate the response of the world's flora to a wide range of environmental conditions (Bradshaw, 1987; Heal and Grime, 1991).

Traditional ecologists (those who study primarily non-human organisms and systems) have also used comparative studies to develop a greater understanding of the structure and composition of communities and ecosystems (Peters, 1986; Odum, 1988; Kilham and Hecky, 1988; Cole *et al.*, 1991). Comparative studies can take several forms depending upon the objective of the study. Heal and Grime (1991) identified three major forms of comparative studies: (1) comparisons across ecosystems of the same class (comparative analysis of ecosystems); (2) across ecosystems of different classes (cross-system comparison of components); or (3) across disciplines (cross-system comparison of ecosystems). The different types of information that can be investigated when comparing ecosystems include: (1) a measure of similarity between ecosystems; (2) the way that special characteristics vary among ecosystems; and (3) identifying causal relationships and mechanical functions and how they vary among ecosystems (Downing, 1991). There are also several approaches that can be used to undertake comparative studies, including evaluating research outcomes against other published studies, meta-analysis, or designing a study that sets out a priori to be comparative (Lehvävirta and Kotze, Chapter 31).

Peters *et al.* (1991), in their assessment of the role of comparative ecology with respect to the larger field of ecology, conclude that this approach has been fundamental to the development of the science, and yet, because of its utility and pervasive use, it is difficult to distinguish it from the other approaches that make up the science of ecology. They go on to advise practitioners of comparative ecology to identify the goals of their studies clearly in order to make their work relevant to a broader audience of researchers (Peters *et al.*, 1991). An especially provocative use of comparative studies has been the development of the field of predictive limnology which, in contrast to the more common species-specific approach to the science, uses very basic models and regressions to predict simple, operational and commonly studied characteristics of aquatic systems (Peters, 1986).

Social scientists also conduct ecological research on cities, but unlike the traditional ecologists, they primarily focus on humans. Ecological terms were first applied to describe the structure and function of cities by the 'Chicago School' (Hawley, 1944; Park and Burgess, 1967) and are still used to some degree in the field of human ecology (Schwirian, 1974; Hawley, 1986). Humans are the main focus of the social scientists' study systems (i.e. urban ecosystem). They also promote the need to bring together physical, socio-economic and traditional ecological data in order to create a holistic understanding of the structure, composition and dynamics of cities. Social scientists, human ecologists and urban geographers have continued to debate the usefulness of the early applications of traditional ecological theory to the study of cities (Alihan, 1964; Catton and Dunlap, 1978; Cousins and Nagpaul, 1979), but the documentation of the physical features of cities followed by an investigation of how structural patterns may influence social processes is still a useful concept today (Dunlap and Catton, 1994). Indeed, these studies have created an abundance of socio-economic and geographical data for cities around the globe and much of the research is focused on comparative studies (Schwirian, 1974). The development of a more robust comparative ecology of cities would involve the integration of the traditional ecological and social approaches to the study of cities and towns.

McDonnell *et al.* (Chapter 1) propose that the effective creation of sustainable cities in the future requires the development of a significant knowledge base on the ecology of urban environments. This could provide important generalities about the structure and function of urban systems which are critical for developing ecologically and socially sensitive planning and building schemes as well as mitigation measures. Social scientists studying the ecology of cities have a well-developed understanding of the structure of cities as well as human organisation, activities and behaviours. Owing to the reluctance of traditional ecologists to study human-dominated ecosystems, there is comparably little information available on the ecology of the non-human components of cities (McDonnell and Pickett, 1993b; McDonnell *et al.*, 1993).

To help the development and expansion of our ecological knowledge base, we propose that there needs to be a concerted effort to facilitate the application of the comparative approach to the ecological study of cities and towns. As described above, comparative studies are an important tool for scientists and can reveal general principles, identify system properties, aid the formation of new hypotheses, uncover potential causal factors and reveal undiscovered public knowledge (Bradshaw, 1987; Peters *et al.*, 1991; Strayer, 1991). The aims of this chapter are: (1) to describe the ecological consequences of urbanisation; (2) to discuss the utility of the comparative approach to the ecological study of cities and towns; (3) to explore the development of classification systems that will assist in comparative ecological studies of urban environments; and (4) to discuss the challenges and opportunities of using local, regional and global comparative studies to advance our understanding of the ecology of cities and towns.

Ecological consequences of urbanisation

Human-modified urban landscapes differ from more natural areas in many respects. The environmental conditions of human settlements can be considered to fall into four categories: (1) the creation of new land cover; (2) alteration to the physical and chemical environment; (3) the creation of new biotic assemblages of plants and animals; and (4) changes to the disturbance regime (Sukopp, 1998; Kinzig and Grove, 2001).

Urban development alters the physical and abiotic environment by increasing the amount of impervious surfaces and decreasing local water-holding facilities. This changes patterns of runoff and drainage by redirecting stormwater out of the system via networks of drains and channels. The increase in impervious surfaces also leads to changes to the heat budget associated with increased heat retention of built surfaces, higher albedo with multiple absorption points, and the generation of waste heat produced within the urban area (Gilbert, 1989; Oke, 1989). These two factors combine to produce warmer day- and night-time temperatures in urban areas (Brazel et al., 2000; Baker et al., 2002). This effect is regional, however, as supplemental watering can lower maximum day-time temperatures for cities (e.g. Phoenix, AZ) that are situated in arid regions (Brazel et al., 2000; Pickett et al., 2001). The widespread use of automobiles and the proximity of industrial centres to the urban work-force also provide numerous point sources of pollution that lead to higher concentrations of CO_2 (Ziska et al., 2004), NO_x (Bridgman et al., 1995), metals such as lead, copper, zinc, chromium and vanadium (Watmough et al., 1998; Callender and Rice, 2000), polycyclic aromatic hydrocarbons (PAHs) (Gingrich and Diamond, 2001; Wong et al., 2004) and higher particulate dust deposition in urban areas (Lovett et al., 2000).

New forms of land cover occur where the indigenous vegetation of an area is replaced by agriculture, buildings, paving, gardens and parks, and the remaining relicts of indigenous vegetation are progressively modified. Recreational activities may create a network of paths through the patch, where the soil becomes compacted and seedlings are unable to germinate or establish. New plant species may be introduced to the remnant patch, through deliberate plantings or accidental introductions from the surrounding landscape. These newly introduced species may eventually replace the more sensitive indigenous species and displace other indigenous species from large areas of the remnant patch.

The introduction of new plant and animal species contributes to the formation of new biotic interactions (Atkinson and Cameron, 1993). These new interactions may be further influenced by changes to disturbance regimes associated with recreational use and management activities. Changes include the suppression or regulation of fires, increases in trampling, dumped rubbish, mechanical damage, weed removal, construction of park infrastructure, and altered grazing practices (Matlack, 1993b).

The characteristics of the landscape are also altered by increasing urbanisation. Transects across three different cities in the USA found that the diversity of land-cover types was higher in the urban areas than in the surrounding landscape (Medley *et al.*, 1995; Alberti *et al.*, 2001; Luck and Wu, 2002). The increased land-cover diversity was accompanied by a reduction in mean patch size and a corresponding increase in the density of patches. These patterns highlight the heterogeneous nature of urban areas, where there are many different land-cover elements that change over a very fine spatial scale.

The current scope of comparative studies of urban environments

Previous ecological studies of urban environments have used a variety of comparative approaches ranging from case studies of a single habitat or biotope to studies of complex urbanisation gradients extending over 100 km (Fig. 5.1). By their definition, urban–rural gradient studies compare the ecological conditions at the urban end of the gradient to those at the more rural end. However, the comparative aspect of these studies has been more implicit rather than explicit.

In general, the approaches used to study the ecology of cities can be grouped into five different categories (Fig. 5.1): (1) case study of ecological conditions within a single study site in an urban environment (Cwikowa *et al.*, 1984; Bhuju and Ohsawa, 1998, 1999, 2001; Godefroid and Koedam, 2003); (2) patterns of change amongst numerous study sites where the local context is treated categorically as 'urban' (Hobbs, 1988a); (3) patterns of change amongst numerous study sites representing the more urban end of an urbanisation gradient, such as within a single urban area (Lehvävirta and Rita, 2002; Malmivaara *et al.*, 2002; Hope *et al.*, 2005); (4) patterns of change amongst numerous study sites located along an urban–rural gradient (Guntenspergen and Levenson, 1997; McDonnell *et al.*, 1997); (5) patterns of change in a study site over time (Florgård, 2000; Kirkpatrick, 1986, 2004; Lunt, 1998; Rudnicky and McDonnell, 1989). These five approaches have been used to study a diversity of questions focused on different levels of biological organisation including populations, communities and ecosystems.

To date, most of the research has been conducted at local and regional scales. We use the term local to describe comparative studies conducted within single cities or metropolitan areas (e.g. Song *et al.*, 2005). By regional studies we refer to those that have been conducted along gradients (transects) of over 100 km

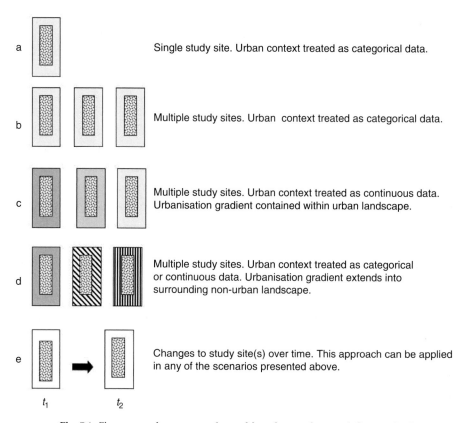

a   Single study site. Urban context treated as categorical data.

b   Multiple study sites. Urban context treated as categorical data.

c   Multiple study sites. Urban context treated as continuous data. Urbanisation gradient contained within urban landscape.

d   Multiple study sites. Urban context treated as categorical or continuous data. Urbanisation gradient extends into surrounding non-urban landscape.

e   Changes to study site(s) over time. This approach can be applied in any of the scenarios presented above.

t_1 t_2

Fig. 5.1. Five approaches commonly used in urban ecology to define study sites.

(e.g. McDonnell *et al.*, 1997; Carreiro *et al.*, Chapter 19), or studies of geographically separated cities and towns within the same state or territory (e.g. Schwartz *et al.*, 2006). However, these approaches can also be applied to comparative studies at the continental and global scale. The main difference in this case would be the scale of the study site. For example, a study comparing the ecological footprint of cities might use the approach of Fig. 5.1c, where the study site is the city itself, and each city has been characterised in terms of the human population density or the area taken up by the city's urban development.

The approach researchers take to selecting their research sites and how much they quantify the landscape context depends on the questions being asked (see Catterall, Chapter 8). Case studies that examine single habitats or populations (Fig. 5.1a) provide little or no opportunity for comparisons in space owing to the lack of a contextual reference, but they do allow for comparisons over time (Fig. 5.1e). Studies that treat measures of urban as categorical (Fig. 5.1b), or explicitly quantify the level of urbanisation within cities (Fig. 5.1c) or along urbanisation gradients (urban–rural gradients) that extend beyond city centres to peri-urban and rural areas (Fig. 5.1d), all provide opportunities for productive comparative studies within cities and between cities and non-urban environments. They all lend themselves to investigations of change over time (Fig. 5.1e), albeit with different levels of sophistication. It is important to note that comparing the categorical, continuous and gradient data between cities will require the use of standardised, quantitative measures for classifying both the independent (predictor) and dependent (response) variables.

In Table 5.1, we group published ecological studies of cities and towns according to the approach they use (e.g. the use of a single case study, all the way to the study of several sites along an urban–rural gradient) and the level of biological organisation that the research addresses (e.g. population, community, ecosystem and landscape). The studies listed in the table are illustrative rather than comprehensive, owing to space limitations. From our analysis of the existing studies it appears that many of the early European studies of the ecology of cities examine species, populations and communities at one site or several sites ordered categorically (Sukopp, 2002). In the past decade there has been a multitude of urban–rural gradient studies focused on communities and ecosystems. Our analysis has revealed that many of them use simple land-use classifications to quantify urbanisation gradients. There are relatively few studies focused on how best to quantify or classify the urban landscape. The need for these latter studies will be addressed in more detail below.

As described above, there are numerous comparative ecological studies of cities conducted at local and a few at regional scales, but the same is not true of continental and global scales. Most of the global or continental environmental comparative studies of cities relate to air and water pollution (see Singh et al., 2007; Viana et al., 2007). Brazel et al. (2000) compared the climates of Baltimore and Phoenix (US LTER sites) and found a pronounced relationship between the minimum temperatures in the urban versus the rural sites as a function of population increase in both cities. As population size increased, the minimum temperatures increased. Kasanko et al. (2006) conducted a comparative study of the changes in land use and population in 15 European cities. They found that the greatest population growth and urban expansion occurred in the 1950s and 1960s. They also found that the structure of European cities has become less compact and has begun to resemble urban sprawl which is a characteristic of US cities. Clergeau et al. (1998) studied the abundance and diversity of birds along urban–rural gradients in two cities on different continents (Quebec, Canada, and Renees, France) and found that species richness decreased with increasing urbanisation, but that breeding bird abundance had a distinct bimodal pattern in both cities. This pattern was attributed to the contribution of the larger number of native birds at the rural end of the gradient and the larger number of introduced species at the urban end.

Table 5.1. *The range of published research as a function of research approach (e.g. from case study to urban–rural gradients) and the level of biological organisation reported in the study.*

Study approach	(1) One site (case study)	(2) Several sites: urban categorical	(3) Several sites: urban quantified	(4) Several sites: urban–rural gradient	(5) Change over time
Species/ Populations	Tigas *et al.*, 2002; Williams *et al.*, 2006; Jim, 1998	Nowak, 1996; Blair, 1996	Slabbekoorn and Peet, 2003; Millsap and Bear, 2000; Shukuroglou and McCarthy, 2006	Nowak and McBride, 1991; Boal and Mannan, 1999	
Community	Odgers, 1994; Bhuju and Ohsawa, 1998; Landolt, 2000; Godefroid and Koedam, 2003; Zanette *et al.*, 2005	Hobbs, 1988a, 1988b; Jokimäki and Suhonen, 1998; Jim and Lie, 2001; Thompson *et al.*, 2003	Melles *et al.*, 2003; Mörtberg, 2001; White *et al.*, 2005	Guntenspergen and Levenson, 1997; Niemelä *et al.*, 2002; Parris, 2006; Williams *et al.*, 2005	Rudnicky and McDonnell, 1989; Lunt, 1998; Florgård, 2000; Chocholousková and Pysek, 2003; Kirkpatrick, 2004
Ecosystem	Lorenz *et al.*, 2004; McPherson, 1998; Bidwell *et al.*, 2006	Brazel *et al.*, 2000		Pouyat *et al.*, 1994; McDonnell *et al.*, 1997; Carreiro *et al.*, 1999; Pouyat and Carreiro, 2003	
Spatial landscape	Young and Jarvis, 2001	Batty, 1995	Kasanko *et al.*, 2006	Luck and Wu, 2002; Hahs and McDonnell, 2006	Jenerette and Wu, 2001; Nowak, 1993

One of the few truly global ecological comparisons of cities was the GLOBENET project done by Niemelä *et al.* (2002). They studied Carabid beetle assemblages in forest patches along urban–rural gradients in Helsinki, Finland, Sofia, Bulgaria and Edmonton, Canada. They found similar communities of Carabid beetles along each of the gradients for the cities they studied. This suggests that the assemblages were not affected by the associated changes in the environment due to urbanisation. The GLOBENET project (Niemelä *et al.*, Chapter 2) has been expanded to include Debrecen, Hungary (Magura *et al.*, 2004), and Hiroshima City, Japan (Ishitani *et al.*, 2003). The GLOBENET project is described in more detail by Niemelä *et al.* (Chapter 2). Their approach should serve as a model for future global comparative studies of cities and towns.

The development of a classification system for urban environments

As previously described, the use of comparative studies in the fields of biology and ecology has been possible because of the existence of systems of classification for both the independent (predictor) and dependent (response) variables involved in the comparisons. In biology, the widely accepted taxonomic and phylogenic classification of the Earth's flora and fauna has provided for a diverse array of comparative studies ranging from the comparative study of leaf morphology (Givnish, 1987) to the comparative study of the ecology of tidal freshwater salt marshes (Odum, 1988). In the broad field of ecology, the dependent (response) variables investigated by comparative studies have included species distributions (Nilon, Chapter 10), nutrient cycling, trophic structures of ecosystems, productivity rates and biomass accumulation, to name a few. These variables have been compared between systems where the independent (predictor) variable has been a function of soil classification, land use, climate, elevation and latitude, as well as within and between biomes. In addition, many comparative ecological studies have been carried out along gradients of resources, pollution and disturbance (Vitousek and Matson, 1991). In all of these studies, the independent (predictor) variables can be readily identified and measured, providing an explicit and useful basis for comparison.

Creating a more comprehensive understanding of cities and towns requires the development of new hypotheses and confirmed generalisations which are critical to the development of any field of science (Pickett *et al.*, Chapter 3). To achieve this requires the explicit development and adoption of a variety of systems or schemes that are capable of characterising urban environments and can form the foundation for future comparative studies. This is especially important for the establishment of global comparisons (e.g. between cities around the world). To be effective, standardised measures of human settlements

Table 5.2. *Potential variables that can be used to develop a system to classify urban environments.*

Demographic variables
  Human population density
  Economic characteristics
  Governance types
Physical variables
  Area
  Growth pattern
  Distance to other urban areas
  Description of urban morphology
  Study scale

Source: Modified from McIntyre *et al.*, 2000.

should include both physical and demographic components and variables that are: (1) relatively easy to quantify; (2) able to discriminate between different conditions within and between cities; (3) useful in identifying potential causal factors; and (4) repeatable in time and space by different researchers.

McIntyre *et al.* (2000) have made a very useful contribution toward developing a standard set of measures to characterise urbanisation in their review of how urban has been defined within the social and natural sciences. They present a number of potential indices for urbanisation based on demographic and physical features and rates of ecological processes (Table 5.2). Many of the potential variables listed in Table 5.2 are relatively easy to quantify for cities around the world. Theobald (2004) has reviewed the concept of defining urbanisation using ecological patterns and processes and has developed a human-modification framework based on the regularity and heterogeneity of land-cover patches, and the degree to which natural processes, such as wildfire, are controlled. Although land-cover data are relatively easy to obtain, this framework has not been widely adopted by researchers.

McDonnell and Pickett (1990) proposed the use of the gradient approach to study the ecology of cities and towns. Gradient studies are extensively used in the field of ecology to explore how organisms, populations, communities and ecosystems respond to environmental factors that vary in space (e.g. elevation and pollution). They proposed that in the formation of cities and towns measurable changes occur in the physical, biological and social structures across the landscape creating what they refer to as urban–rural gradients (i.e. urbanisation gradients) (McDonnell *et al.*, 1993, 1997). This approach provided a useful framework for conducting some of the first studies to compare the ecology of extensively modified urban environments with less modified suburban and rural environments (McDonnell *et al.*, 1997). Over the past 15 years, the approach has been widely used throughout the world to study the impact of human settlements on a variety of organisms and ecosystems (McKinney, 2006; McDonnell and Hahs, 2008). Thus, urban–rural gradient studies have been especially useful in providing a method for conducting comparative studies at local and regional scales.

Urbanisation gradient studies have been criticised for presenting gradients that were too simplistic (McKinney, 2006). This is primarily due to the common practice of taking a transect approach to represent the urbanisation gradient (McDonnell *et al.*, 1993, 1997; Luck and Wu, 2002; Weng, 2007). As we have learned more about urbanisation gradients, the importance of capturing the characteristics of the landscape at different locations has become more apparent. The increased use of Geographic Information Systems, and the greater accessibility of satellite imagery, have also aided the move away from the use of transects to define gradients, to using direct measures of urbanisation at a location to characterise the local landscape context.

The large body of work that has been conducted using the urbanisation gradient approach has provided several insights into how urbanisation affects the ecology 'in' and 'of' cities; where ecology 'in' cities refers to small-scale, usually single discipline studies within a city; and the ecology 'of' cities incorporates socio-economic and human ecosystem elements to form an understanding of ecology at a broader, multi-disciplinary scale (Grimm *et al.*, 2000; Pickett *et al.*, 2001, Niemelä *et al.*, Chapter 2) . Currently most urbanisation gradient studies and ecological studies of cities in general would be considered to address the ecology 'in' cities.

Previous studies of the ecology 'in' cities have provided much useful information as well as insights into creating functional classification systems for use in urban environments. From this work we have learned: (1) it is important to define explicitly the urban environments and urbanisation gradients using quantitative measures, as this allows studies to be compared with equivalent conditions, as well as ensuring that the status of the study site is captured for the period of the study (Hahs and McDonnell, 2006); (2) we need to move beyond viewing the urbanisation gradient as a linear transect, and begin to recognise that gradients also exist within cities, as this will allow us to take a more sophisticated approach to defining the location of our study site within the landscape; and (3) we need to improve our understanding of the measures used to define urban and urbanisation gradients, as well as the measures used for the response variable, as the selection of specific measures can influence the findings of the study.

With respect to point (3) above, there are five major considerations to address when selecting or comparing measures that represent urban environments and urbanisation gradients. These considerations are: (1) the use of a broad measure versus a specific measure of urbanisation; (2) whether the measure represents a demographic or physical aspect of the landscape, or a quantitative landscape metric; (3) redundancy or correlation between selected measures; (4) how the characteristics (scale, typology) of the landscape classification system used will interact to influence the outcomes of the study; and (5) the ability to attach a biological or ecological interpretation to the selected measure. These considerations are briefly discussed below.

Broad versus specific measures of urbanisation

The measures used to quantify gradients can be defined with differing levels of precision. For example, elevation can be used to capture the broad gradient of changes with increasing altitude on mountains. This broad gradient is composed of a complex range of conditions, but can be easily quantified using a coarse, quickly obtained measure (i.e. elevation). More sophisticated measures of temperature, rainfall, light intensity, etc. can be obtained to provide a more precise measure of a specific gradient.

Urban environments and urbanisation gradients can be thought of in a similar way. There are broad measures of urbanisation, such as human population density, or proportion of impermeable surfaces, which are relatively easy to measure and common to all cities (Table 5.2; McIntyre et al., 2000). These measures can be used to define some basic conditions or gradients, and results can be compared between studies and between cities. However, these measures often represent a diversity of conditions forming a complex gradient, and may not be as useful in defining causal mechanisms behind ecological patterns (Catterall, Chapter 8). Therefore, specific measures may also be required to help elucidate the observed patterns. For example, Blewett and Marzluff (2005) found a correlation between the density of tree snags along an urbanisation gradient and the abundance of cavity nesting birds. Such measures would be specific to each individual study, and might not be captured as easily by existing data.

The combination of broad and specific measures of urbanisation used to define the gradient would be determined by the study being undertaken and the level of preceding information that is available. For example, an initial study may only be interested in whether there is an observable pattern in an urban environment or along an urbanisation gradient, and therefore require only a broad measure of urbanisation to define the context. However, a study may already have established that there is a pattern, and now be working to determine which mechanisms are acting to influence the observed pattern, in which case there would be a call to investigate more specific aspects of urbanisation, such as the magnitude, duration, frequency and timing of activities such as mowing or vehicular traffic. In this case, the cost of quantifying these additional measurements would be justified.

The use of broad measures of urbanisation also has an important role to play in advancing our understanding of ecology 'in' and 'of' cities. They provide a general definition of the urban context which can be used to establish some basic ecological research in urban areas, and they provide a common element that allows for a greater integration between studies conducted on different systems, or at different points in time or space (McIntyre *et al.*, 2000). For these reasons, and because of the limited ability of specific measures to integrate diverse research efforts, the remainder of this chapter will focus on the more general broad measures of urbanisation.

Different types of measures: demographic, physical and spatial

Broad measures of urbanisation generally fall into three groups: (1) demographic measures related to the human population, such as population density or median income; (2) physical or chemical measures, such as the density of roads, or concentration of pollutants (McIntyre *et al.*, 2000); or (3) quantitative landscape metrics, such as the number of patches, or their configuration in the landscape. The type of measure used may be determined by the nature of the study, or the nature of the most accessible data. However, the outcome of the study and the opportunities to compare between studies will be partly determined by the type of measure selected to represent the urban context. While the values of these measures are all likely to be related, they do represent different aspects of the urban environment, and thus provide different insights into the ecology 'in' and 'of' cities.

Redundancy or correlation between measures

The objective of quantifying a broad measure of urbanisation is to provide an urban context or a gradient of increasing urban intensity, so it is reasonable to expect a high degree of correlation between metrics. However, some metrics may be more highly correlated than others and thus using both measures to represent urbanisation may result in a lot of redundant information. This is particularly likely where the measures capture the same component of urbanisation using slightly different methods (for example, the extent of the road network can be represented as the area covered by the road network, or as a linear length of roads). This is a particularly important consideration for quantitative landscape metrics, as most metrics are calculated using information about the edge and area of polygons in the landscape. However, there is also a degree of complementary information that can be gained by using measures that capture different aspects of the urban environment. The key is identifying measures that are complementary but relatively independent (relatively low correlation) and that have minimal redundant information. One example of how this might be achieved is to use Principal Components Analysis on a group of measures, as was demonstrated for Melbourne by Hahs and McDonnell (2006).

The land-cover and land-use classification systems

According to a recent review by Herzog and Lausch (2001), the number of land-cover types used in landscape studies ranged from 2 to 29. This led to difficulties when comparing the results from the different studies, particularly as the presence of linear features, such as roads, influenced the spatial patterns observed in the study. Forman (1995) distinguished between coarse-grained and fine-grained landscapes. Sophisticated typologies generally produce more complex (fine-grained) landscapes, whereas landscapes with a more simplified topology are likely to produce simpler (coarse-grained) landscapes. The choice of the land-cover typology will generally be determined by the objective of the study. Studies investigating broad-scale questions, such as comparing residential and commercial landscapes, can use a simplified classification whereas studies investigating fine-scale patterns within the landscape, such as comparing the nature of front gardens with back gardens, require a more complex land-cover classification (Kirkpatrick et al., 2007).

This consideration is particularly important when the urban context or gradient of urbanisation is being represented by quantitative landscape metrics. Most of the landscape metrics related to composition and configuration are influenced by the number and typology of the landscape classification. Many are also influenced by the grain size and extent used when mapping the different landscape elements (Wu et al., 2002; Wu, 2004). Therefore, when using landscape metrics to define landscape context or gradients, it is important to state explicitly the grain size, extent and classification used to represent the landscape elements, and to compare outcomes from studies that used comparable methodologies to represent the landscape. This is particularly true for fine-scale landscapes, as the sensitivity of the metrics to the classification is likely to increase as the number of classes increases.

Attaching a biological or ecological interpretation to classification systems

For a classification scheme to be effective and useful, we need to be able to attach a biological or ecological interpretation to the selected measures. There may be a discrepancy between how well a measure can capture different levels of urbanisation, and how useful it is in investigating ecological patterns and processes. This is due to the difference between spatial patterns and ecological patterns (Watt, 1947). The relationship between these two types of pattern can be unidirectional: for instance, the extent of impermeable surfaces in a catchment (spatial pattern) influences the quality of the water in the stream (ecological pattern) (Hunsaker and Levine, 1995). Alternatively, it can be reciprocal: for instance, the distribution of fruit trees in a landscape (spatial pattern) influences the distribution of frugivorous birds (ecological pattern), which in turn can influence the distribution of fruit trees (McDonnell and Stiles, 1983). Therefore it is important to determine that the assumed relationships between the urbanisation measure and the ecological response are realistic (Li and Wu, 2004). One tool available for determining the nature of the relationship between the variables is the hierarchical patch dynamics approach, which predicts that the relationship between variables will only be interactive when the spatial and temporal scales of the spatial pattern and the ecological response are similar (Wu and David, 2002; Wu et al., 2003).

Once again, this consideration is particularly relevant to quantitative landscape metrics, as one of their conceptual flaws is that while the meaning of a metric may be easily understood mathematically, it may be difficult to interpret biologically (Li and Wu, 2004). However, there are aspects of this consideration that are equally applicable to the other two groups of urbanisation measures.

Selecting a standard group of measures to represent an urban context or gradient

In light of these considerations, it should be possible to identify a standard set of broad measures of urbanisation. These measures would be useful for determining generalities about the ecology 'in' and 'of' cities, and could help to integrate the growing body of research in this field. By providing a common measure of urbanisation for studies on ecology 'in' cities, it may be possible to combine the outcomes of these studies to begin developing a better understanding of the ecology 'of' a city. Insights into the mechanisms behind particular ecological responses would then require a finer-scale investigation, using more specific measures of urbanisation.

Our understanding of these broad measures is still developing. We still need a better understanding of which measures are being used most frequently, although the investigation by McIntyre et al. (2000) is a great starting point. We need to investigate how useful the different measures are for predicting the outcomes of particular studies, and for integrating different studies. We also need to understand how sensitive they are to the classification typology, and their compatibility with other regularly used metrics.

Beginning to address these issues requires a new area of research for urbanisation gradient studies: studies that examine the measures themselves and investigate which would be the most useful common measures for comparative research and the integration of ecological studies on various temporal and spatial scales.

Future challenges and opportunities

To develop sustainable cities in the future will require more use of ecological principles in the design, planning, construction and management of cities. As described in this chapter, and as apparent from all the chapters in this book, over the past few years there has been a significant increase in our understanding of the ecology of cities and towns, but more is required. Much of this understanding comes from local or regional studies that use research conducted along gradients of urbanisation. We have also developed sophisticated methods of characterising human settlements using newly available satellite imagery and Geographical Information Systems. One of the major challenges ahead for researchers is to develop and use appropriate independent (predictor) and dependent (response) variables that can be compared from local to global scales.

Pickett *et al.* (1994b) state that the development of confirmed generalisations is critical to the advancement of ecological theory. Such generalisations or principles are formed when a body of tested facts results in condensations and abstractions of our understanding (Pickett *et al.*, 1994b). On a landscape scale, one of the best examples in the field of urban ecology is the relationship between the amount of impermeable surfaces in a watershed and the health of streams. Researchers studying the ecology of streams in urban environments over the past 20 years consistently found that if the surrounding watershed was covered by more than 20% impermeable surfaces there was a significant reduction in stream biota and health (Paul and Meyer, 2001). The knowledge of this confirmed impact on aquatic ecosystems contributes to our basic understanding of the ecology of streams, and it has also been adopted as an important ecological principle in urban planning and design, and in the development of stream management strategies.

Another important generalisation related to aquatic systems was developed by Peierls *et al.* (1991) and Cole *et al.* (1993) by comparing the human population of 41 major cities located around the world with the export of nitrogen into nearby rivers and oceans. They found that as the human population of cities increases there is a significant increase in nitrate export as described by their equation:

$$\text{Log (NO}_3 \text{ export)} = 0.64 \times \log(\text{population density}) + 1.5 \qquad (5.1)$$

Table 5.3. *Schematic table to illustrate what most of the comparative studies conducted in terrestrial urban ecology have been focused on to date. Cells with a higher number of + indicate a greater relative body of work.*

Focus of study	Scale of comparative studies			
	Local	Regional	Continental	Global
Pattern	++++	+++	++	+
Process	++	+		
Mechanistic	+			

The use of this relationship (i.e. generalisation) is critical to effectively reducing the negative impacts of cities on urban rivers and marine environments by controlling population density or implementing mitigation strategies.

With regards to terrestrial environments in cities and towns, we could find few if any confirmed generalisations in the literature. The work of Niemelä *et al.* (2002, Chapter 2) and the other GLOBENET researchers has provided a strong foundation for identifying generalisations about the effect of cities and towns on Carabid beetle populations at a global scale. Another example, described by Eisenbeis and Hanël (Chapter 15), demonstrates a growing concurrence of data that indicate that light pollution in cities has a significant and measurable negative impact on night-flying insects.

Recently, there has been growing interest in the confirmation of the phenomenon of biotic homogenisation in cities, but additional planned continental and global comparisons need to be done to create more robust generalisations (Clergeau *et al.*, 2006; McKinney, 2006; Schwartz *et al.*, 2006). At the ecosystem scale, Kaye *et al.* (2006) have suggested that cities and towns have a distinct biogeochemistry. Again, more comparative biogeochemistry studies such as those by Carreiro *et al.* (Chapter 19) and Pouyat *et al.* (Chapter 20) would aid in developing new generalisations and principles in regard to the flux of nutrients in urban ecosystems.

An assessment of the nature of comparative studies conducted on the ecology of cities and towns suggests that most studies have focused on terrestrial systems at local or regional scales and studied patterns (e.g. distribution of species) (Table 5.3). There are relatively few studies that have examined non-terrestrial systems (Chapman and Underwood, Chapter 4) or that have focused on continental and global scales. There are also relatively few studies that have examined processes (e.g. species performance) and mechanisms (e.g. competition, predation).

The paucity of some of these study areas is no doubt due to time, money and energy constraints. Process and mechanistic studies are usually harder to conduct than determining the distribution of species (i.e. pattern studies) for they require more detailed information over longer periods of time. To develop comparative studies that span continents and the globe requires extraordinary efforts on behalf of the researchers. With these limitations declared, it is important to highlight the fact that there are many exciting and fruitful opportunities for ecologists working in cities and towns around the globe to develop new confirmed generalities in order to increase our ecological understanding of human settlements. Below are 12 examples of questions that we feel could provide significant information if they were investigated using a comparative approach at regional to global scales:

(1)   How does species diversity change with different levels of urbanisation?
(2)   What are the traits of plants and animals that allow them to flourish in urban environments or result in their demise?
(3)   How are ecosystem productivity and biomass accumulation affected by increasing levels of urbanisation?
(4)   What is the minimum size of a functional remnant habitat?
(5)   How are plant community assembly rules affected by different levels of urbanisation?
(6)   How are symbiotic, mutualistic and parasitic relationships between organisms affected by different levels of urbanisation?
(7)   How do fluxes of heat, CO_2 and other greenhouse gases change with different levels of urbanisation?
(8)   How do trophic web structures change with varying levels of urbanisation?
(9)   How do limits on successional change and community regeneration vary with different levels of urbanisation?
(10) How does the level of urbanisation influence an organism's susceptibility and resistance to pests and pathogens?
(11) How do different levels of urbanisation affect the ability of exotic species of plants/animals to provide similar ecosystem services to native organisms in cities?
(12) What effect do different levels of urbanisation have on predator–prey relationships?

Certain questions, such as those examining species diversity, are more easily conducted at continental and regional scales as opposed to questions involving species performance or trophic structures because the larger the scale the greater the likelihood of including different species. Thus, a productive exercise would be to assess the nature of the questions that could be addressed and compared within cities and between cities at regional to global scales. Independent of the questions being addressed or the scale of the study, maximising research outcomes from comparative studies will require: (1) clear identification of the goals of the studies so they can be applicable to a wider audience; (2) use of the widest spatial scales possible ranging from local to global; and (3) use of the most appropriate predictor and response variables available.

In conclusion, the challenge for scientists studying the ecology of cities and towns is the development of a set of confirmed generalisations or principles which will motivate basic research while also informing practitioners who design, build and manage cities and towns. One of the most efficient ways of developing these generalisations or principles will require the explicit uptake of well-designed comparative studies conducted at local to global scales.

6

Comparative urban ecological research in developing countries

SAREL CILLIERS, HENK BOUWMAN AND ERNST DREWES

Introduction

As of 2003 more of the world's population lives in urban than in rural settings, and this provides us with immense challenges in the planning, management and conservation of urban areas. Cities in sub-Saharan Africa are growing faster than in any other region as a result of migration, reflecting people's hopes of escaping rural privation more than actual opportunity in the cities (United Nations Population Fund, 1996). This sociological phenomenon is also backed by statistical reason: in South Africa a new resident moving into a city has a 60% chance of securing a work opportunity, while the general chances for someone remaining in a rural area are about 40% (Policy Co-ordination and Advisory Services, 2003). In our view, this increase in urbanisation provides enough reason to study the ecology of cities, towns and settlements.

According to Niemelä (1999a) an important reason for the study of urban ecosystems is that the creation of healthy and pleasing urban settings should be based on ecological knowledge of human impacts on urban ecosystems. Detailed ecological information is needed for better urban spatial planning (Niemelä, 1999a). Certain ecological processes in cities are the same as in rural areas, but aspects such as invasions by alien species and external control of succession are more prevalent in urban areas (Trepl, 1995). In South Africa, another justification for studies of urban environments is to conserve the high biodiversity of the area, because the process of urbanisation has resulted in the fragmentation of

Ecology of Cities and Towns: A Comparative Approach, ed. Mark J. McDonnell, Amy K. Hahs and Jürgen H. Breuste. Published by Cambridge University Press. © Cambridge University Press 2009.

previously intact natural environments. In the Cape Metropolitan Area it was estimated in 1990 that fragmentation due to urbanisation has caused the total extinction of at least five plant species and the local extinction of more than 15 species (Wood et al., 1994). With over 18 000 species of vascular plants of which at least 80% are endemic, the flora of South Africa is exceptionally rich (Huntley, 1996) and needs to be considered in any type of urban development.

As clearly shown throughout this book, comparative studies of the ecology of cities, towns and settlements can enhance our knowledge of the structure and dynamics of urban ecosystems, including addressing the lack of information on indigenous plant and animal communities (Niemelä et al., Chapter 2; McDonnell and Hahs, Chapter 5). According to McDonnell and Hahs (Chapter 5), the question remains whether ecological generalisations can be developed from these comparative studies. Amongst other issues, important questions need to be asked regarding indigenous plant and animal communities, such as the ability of these communities to persist in cities, the major ecological causes of the demise of these communities in cities, and alterations to the structure and the composition of cities to maintain these communities (McDonnell and Hahs, Chapter 5).

Most of the contributions in this book are from the general perspective of a developed country. An inevitable question is to what extent these discussions also apply to developing countries. This question is even more complicated in a country like South Africa with its dualistic development characterised by a predominantly 'Third World' sector backed by a relatively strong 'First World' infrastructure. There is a general perspective that biophysical issues such as conservation, biodiversity, energy efficiency and rehabilitation of damaged landscapes do not get enough emphasis in settled areas in developing countries, because socio-economic issues such as poverty, equity, health, redistribution of wealth, and wealth creation are bigger concerns (Hindson, 1994). According to Osibanjo et al. (2002), an important issue in developing countries remains the close linkage between industrial activities that lack effective pollution control measures and the surrounding human communities that provide the labour.

Pickett et al. (1997b, 2001, Chapter 3) proposed that an integrated framework which includes physical, ecological and socio-economic components should be followed to advance knowledge of urban areas as ecological systems. Following the ecosystem approach is a relatively new idea in urban ecology, referred to as the 'ecology of cities' in which all the different components are combined to, for example, determine how cities process energy or matter relative to their surroundings (Grimm et al., 2000; Pickett et al., 2001). The integrated framework also forms the basis of the long-term ecological research (LTER) projects in Baltimore and Phoenix in the United States (Grimm et al., 2000; Pickett et al., Chapter 3). Testing of this framework in the LTER projects is based on prior studies in which extensive hypotheses were developed. Both LTER projects in the USA are doing 'ecology in cities' but are framing their work within the context of a city as an ecosystem (Grimm *et al.*, 2000). The main research questions in these projects were to determine how the spatial structures of socio-economic, physical and ecological factors in an urban area related to each other, to determine the fluxes of energy, matter, capital and population in urban systems and how they change over time, and to determine how people can develop and use an understanding of urban areas as an ecological system to improve the quality of their environment (Pickett *et al.*, 1997b; Grimm *et al.*, 2000). Although these questions are also important in South Africa, the lack of prior knowledge on urban ecosystems, an enormous increase in urbanisation, and complex social issues conferred by an immense cultural heterogeneity will probably lead us to follow a slightly different approach.

The main objective of this chapter is to assess the use of an integrated approach involving physical, ecological and socio-economic components to address urban ecological issues in developing countries using the North-West Province in South Africa as a case study. Additionally, a brief overview of the application and advantages of urban agriculture will be given.

The current situation in the North-West Province, South Africa

The North-West Province (Fig. 6.1) is regarded as a rural province, because only 34% of the population lives in urban areas (Tladi *et al.*, 2002a). The urbanisation rate is, however, increasing fast, mainly because of the lack of employment opportunities in rural areas. According to Tladi *et al.* (2002b), one should not lose sight of the extensive patterns of settled areas other than cities and towns, namely rural settlements, informal settlements and traditional villages with few if any basic services. Many of these are concentrated in large communal areas. All these settlements make up the spectrum of urban areas in the province. The siting and development of urban areas (including the settlements) in the North-West Province has been based on factors such as proximity to mining activities, proximity to the industrial centres of Johannesburg and Pretoria (Fig. 6.1), the availability of water, and historical colonial, homeland and apartheid policies (Tladi *et al.*, 2002b).

Socio-economic issues

Walmsley and Mangold (2002) recommended that social aspects which are associated with illiteracy, increasing urbanisation, youth development, rural communities and health services particularly for HIV and AIDS need to be urgently addressed in the North-West Province. With the exception of three municipal districts, all had a poverty rate of over 40% (Fig. 6.2). Those areas with

Republic of South Africa

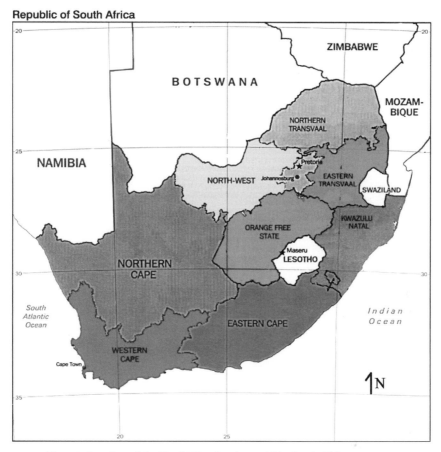

Fig. 6.1. Location of the North-West Province within South Africa.

poverty rates just under or over 80% are situated in the western parts of the province (Fig. 6.1) which are less developed and have lower rainfall. The province has a potential labour force of 1.2 million of which only 62% are employed. This is the second highest provincial figure for South Africa (Tladi *et al.*, 2002a). Some municipal areas have unemployment rates of close to 70% (Fig. 6.3). Based on the United Nations Human Development Index (HDI), the North-West Province is the third lowest of South Africa's nine provinces in terms of quality of life (Tladi *et al.*, 2002a). The HDI measures the overall achievements in an area in three dimensions of human development, namely life expectancy, knowledge (including literacy) and standard of living (Schwabe *et al.*, 2001). The illiteracy rate of the province is 30%, which is significantly higher than in the rest of the country (17%), making environmental awareness raising difficult to address (Tladi *et al.*, 2002a). Based on the HDI of the province, the western and central parts show the greatest deprivation – at around 40% (Fig. 6.4).

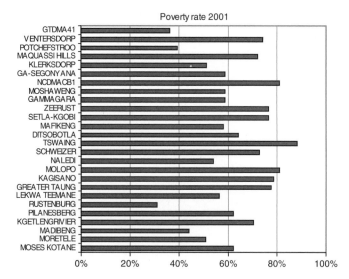

Fig. 6.2. Poverty rate of the different municipal districts of the North-West Province in 2001.

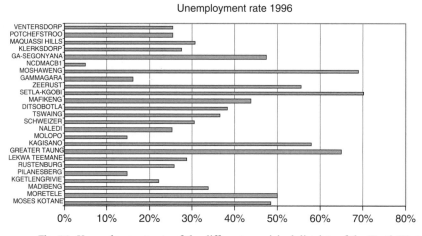

Fig. 6.3. Unemployment rate of the different municipal districts of the North-West Province in 1996.

To illustrate pressures on housing, the cities of Potchefstroom and Klerksdorp and the towns of Orkney, Stilfontein and Hartbeesfontein will be presented as examples (Metroplan, 2000). With an accumulated population of about 700000, the area containing these towns is the closest to a metropole in the province. A total of 30% of all the formal houses represent dwellings for people with low income (less than US$150 per month) while 30% of houses are informal. Formal houses are permanent structures with basic facilities such as water and electricity, and a 'life span' of 20 years or more, while informal houses are temporary structures, mostly without basic facilities. The fact that 55% of all informal

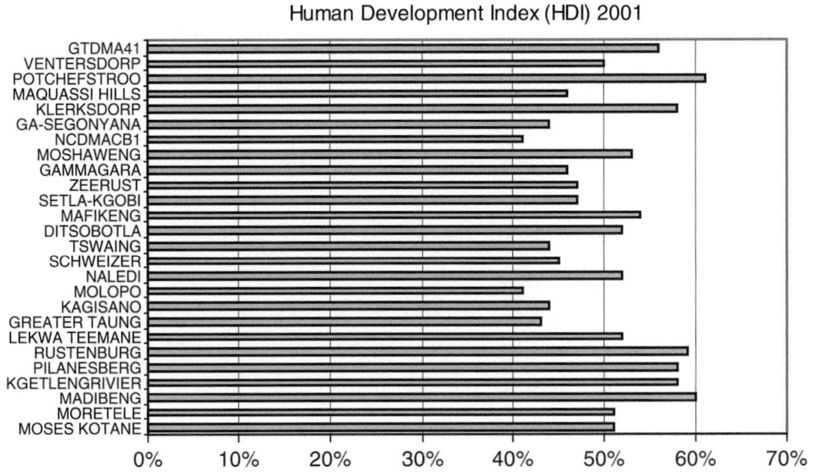

Human Development Index (HDI) 2001

Fig. 6.4. Human Development Index (HDI) of the different municipal districts of the North-West Province in 2001 based on three dimensions of human development, namely life expectancy, knowledge (including literacy) and standard of living.

houses are not on designated plots (Metroplan, 2000) but in natural and semi-natural areas is quite disturbing. Increasing urbanisation places an extreme pressure on the natural environment around cities as was clearly indicated by extensive vegetation studies in the cities of Potchefstroom (Cilliers *et al.*, 1998, 1999; Cilliers, 1999) and Klerksdorp (Van Wyk *et al.*, 1997, 2000). To complicate this matter of environmental degradation, there is an immediate need for more housing in these areas (Metroplan, 2000).

Environmental issues

The North-West Province has a wide array of species, ecosystem and habitat diversity, both in terrestrial and aquatic environments, a result of the diverse nature of the biophysical environment (Mangold *et al.*, 2002a). Fifty terrestrial vegetation types exist in the province and can be classified into four distinct major vegetation types: Kalahari savanna, grasslands, plains bushveld and mountain bushveld. In some of these vegetation types up to 66% of the total surface area is transformed, mainly by agricultural, industrial and urban activities (Strategic Environmental Focus, 2003). The aquatic ecosystems in the province are also diverse and productive and include rivers, streams, dams, lakes and other wetlands such as marshes, bogs, mires, endorheic pans (shallow depressions with no drainage outlet) and dolomitic eyes (Mangold *et al.*, 2002a). Dolomitic eyes are fed by ground water originating from fractures in the underlying dolomite. These wetlands are influenced by factors affecting surface and ground water and are, therefore, extremely sensitive and often possess unique, highly endemic ecosystems (Strategic Environmental Focus, 2003). In terrestrial ecosystems there are also several plant species in the Red Data Book for South Africa which are considered to be 'rare', with one succulent species (*Euphorbia perangusta*) which has been accorded 'endangered' conservation status (Mangold *et al.*, 2002a). Succulents such as the Turk's cap (*Aloe peglerae*) and fairy elephant's foot (*Frithia pulchra*) are regarded as endemic to the Magaliesberg Mountain Range in the province (Mangold *et al.*, 2002a). A total of 36 bird species in the province are listed in the Red Data Book and some of these species are found nowhere else, including the blue crane (*Anthropoideus paradiseus*), the national bird of South Africa. The black harrier (*Circus maurus*) and jackal buzzard (*Buteo rufofuscus*), regional raptor endemics, also have their northern South African distribution limit in this province, to name but a few. Several mammal species are also listed in the Red Data Book, one of which (wild dog) is listed as 'endangered', while eight are considered to be 'vulnerable' and nine are 'rare' (Mangold *et al.*, 2002a).

This province falls, however, within what is described by the United Nations as 'affected drylands' which are perceived to be ecologically sensitive as they are more vulnerable to major ecological disturbances (Mangold *et al.*, 2002a). Several environmental issues in South Africa can be regarded as environmental security risks: in other words, environmental changes that are so extensive, rapid and sustained that they interact negatively with other structural or political weaknesses (Van Wyk, 2003). The most important such risk in South Africa is water scarcity, and North-West is classified as a water-scarce province as there is a substantial import of water from outside the province (Howard *et al.*, 2002).

The entire province also shows high land and soil degradation indices, in comparison with the rest of the country, owing to losses of vegetation cover and changes in plant species composition. Most of the degradation is the result of overgrazing and trampling, bush encroachment, alien plant invasions and deforestation, especially in communally managed areas (Meyer *et al.*, 2002). Because of the 'apartheid' policies of the past, millions of South Africans were concentrated in some of the least productive and most ecologically sensitive areas, and population densities were worsened by high birth rates (Van Wyk, 2003). One-third of South Africa's population relies on wood for fuel and each person burns an average of 3 kg of wood per day, contributing significantly to the rate of deforestation (Van Wyk, 2003). According to Van Wyk (2003), inefficient agricultural and town planning practices contributed to the problem of soil erosion, as South Africa loses about 3000 tonnes of topsoil annually through drainage into rivers and oceans. Soil is lost at 30 times the rate at which it was formed and costs about US$120 million a year to replace. In the North-West Province, soils of communal areas are more degraded than those of commercial areas. Soil and air pollution are also important environmental problems. Solid waste and effluents from industry, manufacturing and households, as well as

Table 6.1. *Legislative issues developed and implemented to assist in sustainable development in the North-West Province, South Africa.*

	International level	National level	Provincial level	Municipal level
Directive	Agenda 21	National Strategy for Sustainable Development	Spatial Development Framework (SDF)	Spatial Development Framework (SDF)
		White Paper on Spatial Planning	Industrial Strategy	
			Rural Strategy	
Prescriptive		Municipal Systems Act (IDP)	Biodiversity Database	Land-Use Management System (LUMS)
		State of Environment Report	Zoning Plan	

ammonium-based fertilizers and chemicals (mainly from agricultural activities) are the most important pollutants.

Planning, management and legislative issues

Several projects have been initiated recently in the North-West Province to address the issues of sustainability. These projects can be regarded as either directive or prescriptive on international, national, provincial and municipal (local government) levels (Table 6.1). All these projects form an integral part of South Africa's commitment to Local Agenda 21, through the development of a National Strategy for Sustainable Development (NSSD) for South Africa by the Department of Environmental Affairs and Tourism (DEAT, 2001). Agenda 21 is a global action plan for achieving environmentally, socially and economically sustainable development endorsed at the United Nation's Earth Summit held in 1992 (Agenda 21: United Nations, 1992). One of the most important projects is the State of the Environment Report (SoER) which followed a 'systems analysis' view of the relationship between the environment and humans on a provincial level, but formed a solid basis for detailed research on different scales (Mangold *et al.*, 2002b). The SoER followed a framework referred to as DPSIR where the major components are driving forces (D), pressures (P), state (S), impacts (I) and responses (R) (Mangold *et al.*, 2002b). Other important contributions included a rural development strategy (Potchefstroom University, 2000), a long-term strategy for industrial and economic development (K2M Technologies, 2002), a site inventory and database for biodiversity (Strategic Environmental Focus, 2003) and a Provincial Spatial Development Framework (PSDF; Maxim Planning Solutions, 2003).

On the national level, a number of other policy initiatives and legislative frameworks have also been formulated. Probably the most important of these refer to a shift in emphasis from national or regional spatial planning to the concept of 'Developmental Local Government' (South Africa, 2001). Accordingly, national and international development guidelines must be facilitated and interpreted in what are referred to as Integrated Development Plans (IDPs) at the local and district municipal levels (South Africa, 2000).

In terms of the objectives of this chapter, it is also important to relate the application of IDPs in terms of their application and future comparative research possibilities. Socio-economic and environmental issues are dealt with at these levels mainly in terms of Spatial Development Frameworks (SDF) and Land-Use Management Systems (LUMS) on a municipal level (Table 6.1). The former provides guidance (directive) with regard to future spatial development, while the latter controls new and existing development (prescriptive) (South Africa, 2002). For any environmental or biophysical concerns to be effectively addressed in future, SDF and LUMS must be included and adapted to guide physical development or conservation as an integral part of the abovementioned IDP. The IDP is a legal document once accepted by the provincial government, and must be updated at least every five years. Although the guiding principles from these policy and legislative documents mostly reflect global best practice, they lack guidance with regard to their application in towns and cities in different stages of development. Another limiting factor in implementing sustainable development practices in South Africa is the different approaches emphasised by environmental and spatial planning policies (Drewes and Cilliers, 2004). On the one hand, this leads to duplication in certain components of spatial development and significant paradigm differences in others. For example, spatial planning policies are based on, and support, the South African Government's vision of 'developmental local government' which strongly encourages new development. On the other hand, the latter development initiatives are heavily restricted by numerous complicated environmental policies and legislation.

The way forward

Although certain social and environmental issues are dealt with in spatial planning processes in the province, emphasis should be placed in the future on approaches in which an integration between socio-economic and environmental issues is promoted, with a focus on environmental quality. According to Van Kamp *et al.* (2003), it is difficult to establish a generally accepted framework or a coherent system to evaluate aspects of and trends in environmental quality in relation to well-being. The phrase 'environmental quality', as used in the literature, refers either to conditions of the environment in which people live (air or water pollution, poor housing or soil retention, to give a few examples), or to some attribute of people themselves (such as health or educational achievement; Pacione, 2003). In his approach, Mitchell (2000) regarded environmental quality to consist of aspects such as physical and mental health; physical environment including climate and pollution; natural resources, goods and services, community and personal development and security. In this chapter we will highlight the use of urban agriculture as a vehicle for integrated urban ecological research working towards increasing environmental quality and the establishment of a sustainable development index to determine environmental quality.

The role of urban agriculture in the ecology of cities and towns

Urban agriculture is defined in different ways in the literature (Ellis and Sumberg, 1998), but according to Smith and Nasr (1992) it refers to the activities linked to food production in cities. Although urban agriculture is not restricted to developing countries, it has increasingly been seen as a major means of supplementing incomes in South Africa and even as a new element to manage poverty in cities (May and Rogerson, 1995). No poverty alleviation will happen, however, if urban agriculture is not regarded as a major land use by city managers and if a range of policy interventions is not included (Dewar, 1994). These prerequisites clearly emerged from social studies conducted in settlements in South Africa, where access to land with secure title and the accompanying threat of competitive pressures on land use for purposes of shelter are regarded as the major problems with respect to the establishment of urban agriculture (May and Rogerson, 1995). Lynch *et al.* (2001) also described land tenure as a major problem and emphasised that it should be looked at holistically in terms of how it fits in with urban structure, urban problems and the livelihoods of individuals and communities.

Extensive debates are being held on the ability of urban agriculture to solve the problems of poverty, job creation and other important social issues (Ellis and Sumberg, 1998; Madaleno, 2000). May and Rogerson (1995) suggested that we need to evaluate the benefits of urban agriculture in comparison to alternative economic opportunities. In our view, however, overemphasising the economic benefits of urban agriculture could obscure the social, nutritional and ecological values of urban cultivation. Olivier (1999) regarded urban agriculture as a socio-economic survival strategy and emphasised that it can form the basis of a range of local industries that uses special skills of people, promotes skill training, and develops a sense of community through stimulating participation and a sense of responsibility.

From an ecological point of view, urban agriculture can improve the environmental quality of cities through the reduction and transformation of waste, reduction of food-related transport, saving of natural resources, prevention of soil erosion and reduction in pollution, and through city beautification by converting vacant lots and degraded land into healthy green areas (Olivier, 1999; Madaleno, 2000). In South Africa, vacant land in urban areas is often illegally occupied by land-hungry people. Allowing crop production in these vacant areas may be a sustainable way of keeping the land earmarked for further development but not for conservation purposes, away from dubious land uses until further development can take place. This approach of making unused land available to urban farmers for a restricted period is also followed in other African countries and is described as the 'accommodative' approach (Lynch *et al.*, 2001).

The contribution of urban agriculture towards conservation of biodiversity should also not be neglected. Olivier (1999) mentioned that organically managed food-growing gardens could create dispersal corridors to draw wildlife such as birds, small mammals and reptiles into the city since natural predators are essential to controlling pests. Additionally, Trowbridge (1998) argued that retaining the natural or spontaneous vegetation around cultivated fields may have several ecological advantages such as reduction of the overall soil temperature and evaporation rate, and certain plants including 'weeds' may act as natural deterrents to pests.

Integrative approach to the study of South African urban areas

The issues discussed so far clearly indicate the need to develop management principles for urban areas in which ecosystem principles and constraints are integrated with development and public management decisions, an approach proposed in the human ecosystem model (Pickett *et al.*, 1997b, Chapter 3). May and Rogerson (1995) suggested, however, that locally generated solutions to ecosystem problems that are supported through the development of informal and grassroots innovations such as specific methods of urban cultivation should be emphasised. It is important to ensure that social and ecological systems interact in the planning and implementation of urban agriculture practices. Grimm *et al.* (2000) proposed a conceptual framework that could be followed to ensure that ecological processes are addressed, testable predictions are made and tools are provided that decision makers can use to create a more ecologically sound policy. An application of this framework is also illustrated by Niemelä *et al.* (Chapter 2). It would be a challenge to address the environmental constraints (e.g. lack of suitable land, water scarcity and soil erosion) and societal constraints (e.g. lack of knowledge and infrastructure, land tenure problems, financial limitations and perceptions of economic and political benefit) associated with drastic land-use change towards urban agricultural practices in urban open spaces. It would be equally difficult to determine what the effect would be on the various ecological and social patterns and processes in the urban areas. It is critical that we follow an integrated approach to the study of urban areas in South Africa, for Coovadia *et al.* (1993) concluded that environmental concerns are clearly linked to issues of poverty and social justice. Thus it is important to develop programmes such as urban agriculture that have both ecological integrity and social empowerment as interactive and mutually dependent goals. Page (2002) described the interest in urban agriculture, by both practitioners and the government, as the result of the crossing of categorical boundaries between what is economic, ecological, political and cultural.

Potchefstroom urban agriculture project: a case study

An urban vegetable cultivation project following an integrated approach was initiated in the city of Potchefstroom, North-West Province, as part of community development. The main objectives of this project were to: (1) create jobs; (2) counter malnutrition with minimum environmental impact, minimum water consumption and maximum community involvement – including women and youth; (3) spend less effort and expense on vegetable cultivation; and (4) use a method that was more in balance with nature and its processes. The method of vegetable cultivation used by Ecocircle Holdings (http://www.ecocircle.com) was followed in this project, but adaptations were made to several aspects such as the layout of the circles and the method of irrigation (Fig. 6.5). In this method, vegetables were cultivated in circles with a diameter of 1m, forming clusters of seven circles, which are referred to as an agro-ecosystem. Each circle should be surrounded by ruderal (wasteland species) or natural vegetation. The advantages of this approach include conservation of water, reduction in rain runoff, less desertification and erosion, conservation of existing vegetation, cost-effectiveness, planned and maintained production and less labour use. Other key factors about the ecocircle growing method are that: (1) minimum tillage is needed, once the area is established; (2) no machinery is required and standardised garden tools reduce implementation costs; (3) continuous year-round production ensures food security; (4) organic methods ensure soil fertility improvement; (5) there are no input costs for pesticides and herbicides; and (6) seed saving programmes contribute to sustainability and reduced running costs. For additional information on the ecocircle method of urban agriculture see: http://www.ecocircle.com.

Fig. 6.5. Ecocircle development in South Africa. (a) A cluster of seven ecocircles in a previously disadvantaged community in Ikageng, South Africa. (b) The irrigation system used in an ecocircle cluster. Materials were produced from recycled car tyres and plastic bags. (c) An example of one circle. Note the existing vegetation surrounding the circle. (d) School children participating in agricultural practices as part of extra-curricular activities.

Fig. 6.5. (*cont.*)

Several urban agricultural studies have been conducted in Africa (Coovadia *et al.*, 1993; May and Rogerson, 1995; Ellis and Sumberg, 1998; Lynch *et al.*, 2001; Asomani-Boateng, 2002; Page, 2002), but more empirical research is needed to answer the expressed concerns about the impact of urban agriculture on environmental and health issues (Lynch *et al.*, 2001). Although the ecocircle method used in Potchefstroom is regarded as ecologically friendly and sustainable there are no quantitative data available that can prove these statements. It is therefore imperative to introduce various projects in ecocircles focusing on specific environmental issues such as sustainable water use. Another important aspect of agriculture using organic methods that should be further investigated is the use of companion and trap plants for integrated pest management following 'stimulo-deterrent' diversion strategies (push–pull system). These strategies have been extensively used in other agricultural sectors in Africa (Khan *et al.*, 1997; Van den Berg *et al.*, 2001). Lack of suitable land in urban areas for agricultural practices places a huge pressure on the conservation of natural and semi-natural grasslands in urban fringes and fragmented areas inside the city, which is, in itself, a difficult process to manage (Cilliers *et al.*, 2004). The introduction of small-scale vegetable cultivation practices in some of these natural and semi-natural areas is a possibility, but it should be based on vegetation dynamics studies to determine the effect on the composition and abundance of plant species and communities in between the circles. Pilot studies by Putter (2004) on the dynamics of several urban open spaces in the city of Potchefstroom over a three-year period indicated that a highly invasive but native grass species, *Cynodon dactylon*, became more abundant in between ecocircles owing to an increase in trampling. More studies in this regard are necessary. Soil ecological processes in terms of organic matter breakdown are extremely important in the functioning of terrestrial ecosystems. The process of breakdown has been investigated extensively in soil ecology and it is generally accepted that disturbance of this highly complex process may influence nutrient information and cycling and eventually soil fertility (Knacker *et al.*, 2003). A pilot study by Smith *et al.* (2004) on organic matter breakdown and feeding activities in grasslands in Potchefstroom indicated increased rates of biological activities following anthropogenic activities in urban environments.

Additionally, it is important to determine people's general view of the ecocircle approach and how it influences socio-cultural hierarchies such as wealth, power, status, knowledge and territory, which are regarded by Pickett *et al.* (2001) as critical to patterns and processes of human ecological systems. From preliminary studies, it is clear that the cultural heterogeneity of Potchefstroom will have a huge impact on the success of the ecocircle approach. The poorer communities in which the ecocircles are established are dominated by the Batswana ethnic group, but Xhosas and South-Sothos also live in the area. Some ecological advantages of ecocircles are neutralised by the strong belief of some of the ethnic groups that the area around their houses should be open and devoid of any vegetation, indicating the tidiness of the household ('lebala concept'), which results in large amounts of bare ground in some communities. Another perceived advantage of ecocircles, namely that selling vegetables would add to their meagre income, is hugely challenged by the philosophy of 'ubuntu' or sharing between fellow countrymen and women (http://www.shikanda.net/general/gen3/research_page/ubuntu.htm) Many urban farmers will not sell any of their vegetables, but rather share with neighbours. To deal with these cultural beliefs will require well-structured environmental education programmes. These programmes should aim at a more holistic understanding of urban ecosystems and the achievement of global sustainable development through local action (Roberts, 2001). In a study on the municipal area of Durban, South Africa, Roberts (2001) discussed the development of an environmental management system and proposed a number of practical principles that should be followed in advancing a more holistic understanding of urban ecosystems. In future, in our own studies on urban agricultural practices, we should focus on educating women about sustainable practices because they have to cook and, in many cases, provide for their families day to day, as their husbands may live and work away from home, often in mines. Common slogans amongst the women of some ethnic groups, such as 'a woman holds a knife at its sharp edge' and 'if you teach a woman, you teach a nation' emphasise this approach.

Sustainable Development Index

The terms 'sustainability' or 'sustainable development' have been mentioned several times in this chapter. There are several definitions and different interpretations of these terms, as indicated by Van Kamp *et al.* (2003) and Chiesura (2004). Agenda 21, discussed earlier, urged the development of indicators for sustainable development (SD) and several examples of these indicators exist. Barrera-Roldán and Saldívar-Valdés (2002) developed indicators addressing various economic, social and natural aspects, Pacione (2003) focused more on human sociological aspects, while other authors emphasised aspects of biodiversity. Oliver (2002) distinguished between compositional, structural and functional indicators of vegetation condition within the context of biodiversity conservation, while Scholes and Biggs (2005) developed a Biodiversity Intactness Index (BII) for southern Africa as an indicator of the overall state of biodiversity in a given area, which can be used together with other indicators such as the IUCN (International Union for Conservation of Nature and Natural Resources) Red List of threatened species (IUCN, 2007). Chiesura (2004), on the other hand, suggested that sustainability indicators for urban development should include more parameters about public spaces and green open areas, as well as indexes reflecting citizens' satisfaction and perception of their living environments.

To develop indicators for sustainable development for urban areas it could be a useful exercise to draw information from existing sets of indicators such as those mentioned above, if the relevant data are available for cities. Another approach would be to evaluate a set of indicators developed specifically for urban areas, for example by UN-HABITAT (http://www.unhabitat.org) and add certain extra indicators. The existence of established socio-economic criteria with which to describe the urban habitats, such as the criteria used by UN-HABITAT, allows the description in broad terms of the urban conditions, using economic and social information. The Global Urban Observatory (GUO) of UN-HABITAT addresses the urgent need to improve the worldwide base of urban knowledge, and thereby assist governments, local authorities and civil society to develop and apply policy-orientated urban indicators, statistics and other urban information. The GUO was established by UN-HABITAT in response to a decision of the United Nations Commission on Human Settlements, which called for means to monitor global progress in implementing the Habitat Agenda (Istanbul Declaration on Human Settlements) and to monitor and evaluate global urban conditions and trends. In particular, Chapter 4 (Global Plan of Action), Section C (Sustainable human settlements development in an urbanizing world) calls for 'Environmentally sustainable, healthy and liveable human settlements'. Paragraph 139 contains a whole set of objectives that promotes a healthy environment, adequate shelter and sustainable human settlements. In order to achieve this, governments are asked to:

- Promote the sustainable use and conservation of urban and peri-urban biodiversity such as forests, habitats and species, and this should be incorporated within the local development planning activities;
- Protect existing forests and encourage afforestation;
- Encourage the establishment of productive and recreational green belts around urban and rural agglomerations;
- Reduce the degradation of the marine environment due to land-based activities;
- Ensure that children, through play, have daily access to natural areas, and this should be supported by educational activities; and
- Ensure that the public can participate at all levels of environmental decision-making.

The GUO concentrates on building local capacity to select, collect, manage and apply indicators and statistics in policy analysis. It sees this as fundamental, both to tracking progress in implementing the Habitat Agenda and to monitoring urban conditions and trends as input to participatory decision-making. Current activities are based on the development of an integrated network of

National and Local Urban Observatories. The beneficiaries are policy makers at all levels and organisations of the civil society participating in sustainable urban development. The main area of work is the generation, analysis and dissemination of global, regional and national urban indicators and statistics (http://www.unhabitat.org).

Based on the Habitat Agenda, the United Nations Commission on Human Settlements, UNCHS (Habitat), has developed an indicators system that contains a set of 30 key indicators and nine qualitative data. These are regarded as the minimum data required for reporting on urban development. The indicators measure performances, trends and progress in the implementation of the Habitat Agenda. Indicators therefore provide a comprehensive picture of cities, which will provide a quantitative, comparative base for the condition of cities and show progress towards achieving urban objectives.

Two different types of data are included in the minimum set (http://www.unhabitat.org). The first are Key Indicators: indicators which are both important for policy and relatively easy to collect. They are quantitative (numbers, percentages and ratios) and cover aspects such as shelter (seven indicators such as pricing, evictions and access to water), social development and eradication of poverty (four indicators including under-five mortality, crime and gender gaps), environmental management (eight indicators – to be discussed later), governance (no indicators but qualitative information), and international cooperation (again only qualitative information). The second type of data is Qualitative Information, which gives an assessment of aspects that cannot easily be measured quantitatively but should also be included.

The UNCHS environmental management criteria cover the following aspects: population growth, water consumption, price of water, air pollution, waste water treatment, solid waste disposal, disaster prevention and mitigation, travel time, transport modes and local environmental plans in support of Agenda 21.

The above information shows the existence of established indicators that can be derived mostly from generally available information or information that, in some instances, can be easily obtained. Given the scope of the GUO, these indicators are also restricted to the scale of a city as such, and not its sub-units. It is also obvious that very few of these indicators concern non-human biology or ecology, but they do cover pollution in various ways. The ecological functioning of a city as such is not included. Barrera-Roldán and Saldívar-Valdés (2002) have done much better in including 11 natural indicators in their proposed set of 21 indicators for sustainable planning and development, such as hydrological balance, water quality, air quality, vegetation cover changes, soil use, erosion, oxygen contribution by vegetation, habitat destruction and protected areas. However, a variety of ecological aspects are not dealt with. A general goal in urban ecological studies should be to fill this current gap in information needed to derive statements about the ecological integrity of urban areas. Not only will this enrich the currently scarce set of information on cities as a whole, it will also be applicable to smaller habitat units (residential, industrial and commercial areas) and could provide managers of urban areas with management options and measurement tools with which to improve these areas, in conjunction with all the other criteria already available. We therefore propose to call this set of indicators (to be developed and defined) the Urban Ecological Integrity Index (UEII).

Indexes have been successfully developed for a number of ecosystem types, with particular reference to rivers and streams. The experience embedded in these successful and applicable management tools (which exist in different forms across the world) should be considered when embarking on such a scheme for urban areas. The current initiative by the US-EPA to develop methods for evaluating wetland condition could prove particularly helpful (http://www.epa.gov/waterscience/criteria/wetlands). Although quite a number of specific documents have been produced, it is document no. 6, 'Developing metrics and indexes of biological integrity', that we could consider as a basis for developing UEII (http://www.epa.gov/waterscience/criteria/wetlands/6Metrics.pdf). In this document, a specific framework is proposed for how attributes can be derived, evaluated and incorporated, based on the work of Karr *et al.* (1986). Based on the overall aim of the framework, it acknowledges existing work and also defines new work.

In short, this method proposes an initial two-pronged approach. On the one hand are the steps that need to be taken to establish a gradient of human disturbance, and on the other, the steps that are required to identify the ecological attributes that will respond to this gradient. The selection of the ecological attributes that can be used is open to debate and depends on the availability of data for a specific city, but aspects such as the degree of 'urbanness' (as used by Weeks, 2003); vegetation diversity; vegetation structure; diversity indices of birds, ants, butterflies and small mammals; soil biota and other soil criteria such as organic matter breakdown; plant stress measurements; corridor connectivity and many other aspects also dealt with in this book could be used. Then follows a process whereby the dose–response relationships are analysed and scored, and the best of these selected as constituents of (in the wetlands case) the Indexes of Biological Integrity (IBI), or, in our case, the UEII.

Although developing the UEII (or any other comparable set of interrelated indices) is easier said than done, it must also be realised that the available ecological/biological data and body of knowledge on which river, stream or even wetland indicators can be based are much more comprehensive than those available to ecologists working in the urban environment. Ecological/biological studies are often non-existent in cities in developing countries because more emphasis is placed on socio-economic issues such as poverty and health, both mentioned earlier in this chapter. So the UEII also needs to recognise, and eventually become integrated into, the existing sets of social and economic indicators already in use, such as those of GUO. It will also need to recognise that a wide range of urban ecological conditions exists, especially when comparing urban areas from developed and developing regions, and that these conditions are regionally (not globally) specific. Even within cities, major ecological differences exist, based on the population, historical and economic settlement patterns. Since urban ecology is (and has been) based on these gradients, we have the opportunity to address and take on board these differences, and link the social, economic and ecological parameters into a body of useful understanding, and eventually a toolbox for planners and managers to identify additional interventions with which to improve the conditions of the people in their care. In this way, the 'green issues' that are normally low on the agendas of developing countries can achieve a higher level of recognition with policy makers and implementers, if the supportive linkages between ecology, economy and society can be shown.

Conclusions

The importance of urban ecological studies which place the emphasis on integration between physical, ecological and socio-economic aspects is discussed in this chapter against the backdrop of the North-West Province, South Africa, which has some serious socio-economic and environmental limitations. Although not enough emphasis is placed on issues such as biodiversity and conservation in developing countries, these are important issues that need to be addressed without neglecting important socio-economic issues such as poverty, health and unemployment, to mention a few. Many authors have indicated that urban agriculture can contribute immensely in addressing these socio-economic issues (Dewar, 1994; May and Rogerson, 1995; Ellis and Sumberg, 1998).

We also indicate the importance of policies and legislation regarding sustainable development in urban areas as part and parcel of South Africa's commitment to Local Agenda 21. There is quite an elaborate system of directive and prescriptive projects addressing the issues of sustainable development in the North-West Province of South Africa. Cilliers *et al.* (2004) indicated, however, that the application and interpretation of these legislative policies are often left to local government which neglects many of the requirements. Roberts (2001) mentioned the need to empower all stakeholders, from politicians and heads of industry to individuals and community-based organisations. Individuals need to understand the extent and importance of urban areas as human ecosystems, and we propose urban agricultural practices as a means to establish this awareness in developing countries. Sustainable agricultural practices, like the ecocircle approach we have followed, aim to address socio-economic and ecological issues and strive towards integration of these issues. Furthermore, social context and day-to-day needs will improve the way that individuals relate to their environments (Roberts, 2001). Empowerment of planners, managers and policy makers could be aided by sustainable development indexes for urban areas. It is important to realise that once an Urban Ecological Integrity Index (UEII) has been developed it will give a specific number for sustainability to a specific city, which could be extremely useful in comparing different cities with each other. Although we propose the development of an UEII, we acknowledge the fact that there is an immense lack of ecological data in urban ecosystems, compared with other ecosystems, especially in developing countries.

There are several issues concerning developing countries (which are mainly development orientated) that would hamper comparative studies in the urban environment. First, the concept of 'settled areas' reflects the whole urban spectrum or system, including secondary cities, towns, service centres and rural villages. The latter can refer to a communal system whereby land is owned by the tribal head or simply to informal squatter areas in rural zones with little or no access to services. The question that must first be asked in a developing country like South Africa is whether these types of 'settled areas' should be evaluated in terms of future research and development at all, as they are clearly unsustainable (Tladi *et al.*, 2002b). Ideally, the development-orientated approach, which differs drastically from that of developed countries, must be resolved before proposals for the expansion of urban agriculture to these areas are contemplated.

Second, as mentioned, the integration of environmental management with spatial planning and management must be evaluated. At the moment, interactions between these spheres of government is increasing rapidly in South Africa, but basic departure points and administrative practices must be refined for all three levels of government. A third issue that also relates to integrating the socio-economic components of settled areas with the environmental or biophysical components is the lack of sufficient spatially explicit data (i.e. Geographical Information System (GIS) databases). The President's Office (Policy Coordination and Advisory Services, 2003) has formally acknowledged the use of GIS for sustainable spatial development practices, but again, the effective implementation on local and district municipal level across the country is hampered by the enormous lack of appropriate data.

The ecological issues of urban ecosystems and approaches towards urban ecological research discussed in this book, which are mainly focused on developed countries, are also important for developing countries. It could be that developing countries do not realise this and often hide behind aspects such as lack of data and lack of funds. Although these issues are real, researchers in urban environments in developing countries have much to offer with regards to comparative urban ecological research following an integrated approach. Because of the immense ecological and social heterogeneity in developing countries, empirical studies on issues such as the effect of poverty (direct and indirect) on biodiversity and ecological processes and services in urban ecosystems will contribute immensely to our knowledge of the functioning of urban ecosystems. Urban agricultural studies and the development of a sustainability index are only two approaches that could be followed in addressing our needs for more information on urban ecosystems.

7

Using models to compare the ecology of cities

MICHAEL MCCARTHY

Introduction

Models are ubiquitous in ecology. By providing simplified representations of reality, models help ecologists to grapple with ecological systems that are inherently complex. From the theoretician who might construct models of the persistence of a species in patches through to a person collecting field data on a plant or animal, all ecologists think of ecological systems in the presence of incomplete information. Because our understanding of how ecological systems operate is based on a simplified representation of reality, all ecologists (in fact all people), whether they like to admit it or not, are modellers. The models may be written explicitly or simply contained within our minds; regardless, people make predictions using simplified versions of what they believe to be true, so all people construct and use models.

In this chapter, I will examine the role of models in ecology, and in particular how they can be used to compare the ecology of cities. I will briefly examine the range of models that are used in ecology, and argue that quantitative models are most useful for comparative ecology. I will then conclude by discussing some statistical issues associated with reporting analyses of quantitative models. But before I do this, I would first like to introduce you to mountain ash (*Eucalyptus regnans*) forests, an ecological system with which I am at least partly familiar, and one that I will use as an example throughout this chapter.

Ecology of Cities and Towns: A Comparative Approach, ed. Mark J. McDonnell, Amy K. Hahs and Jürgen H. Breuste. Published by Cambridge University Press. © Cambridge University Press 2009.

A narrative about mountain ash forests

Mountain ash forests dominate many of the high rainfall areas of south central Victoria and areas of Tasmania. Their most common occurrence in Victoria is to the east of Melbourne in the Dandenong Ranges and the southern slopes of the Great Dividing Range, in the Otway Ranges to the southwest of Melbourne and to the southeast in South Gippsland (Costermans, 1983). Mountain ash trees tend to occur as the only species in the overstorey and with a range of smaller trees, shrubs and herbaceous plants in the understorey.

Mountain ash are some of the fastest growing trees in the world, and are the tallest flowering plant. The outer layer of bark is shed annually in long ribbons. The bark and other material that is shed as the trees grow lead to the accumulation of large quantities of flammable material (Ashton, 1975). Mountain ash forests occur in areas of high rainfall, although they usually experience an annual summer drought. The combination of dry conditions in late summer and early autumn and high fuel loads mean that these forests burn with an average interval of approximately 100 years (McCarthy et al., 1999). If the fire is of sufficient intensity, the trees will be killed, although not all fires kill all trees (Smith and Woodgate, 1985; McCarthy and Lindenmayer, 1998; Mackey et al., 2002). Following fire, seeds that are released from the canopy-borne capsules germinate in an ash bed. Regeneration is usually rapid, with tree height reaching approximately 50 m in 40 years (Mackey et al., 2002). In the presence of the overstorey and dense understorey vegetation, seeds that do germinate rarely survive for more than a few years because of the low light levels. Therefore, while fires cause the death of individual trees, disturbance is necessary for the persistence of the species, provided that the minimum fire intervals are long enough (more than about 20 years) to allow sufficient seed to develop (Ashton and Attiwill, 1994).

The high growth rate of the trees and their usually straight form make mountain ash forests an attractive resource for timber harvesting. The wood is used for producing pulp for paper and timber for various uses. During timber harvesting operations, trees are clearfelled in areas of up to 40 ha, with vigorous regeneration from seed being common.

The other main value of mountain ash forests relates to their effect on water production. It is this feature that makes these forests particularly relevant to urban ecology. Because of the high rainfall in mountain ash forests and their extensive occurrence to the east of Melbourne, they provide a majority of the water supply of Melbourne (Ashton and Attiwill, 1994), a city of more than 3 million people. The ecology and management of these forests has a large influence on the quantity and quality of the water that flows from the forest.

Following intense fires or timber harvesting, the regenerating forest transpires a much greater amount of water, reducing streamflow by approximately 50% below the yield from an old-growth forest (Kuczera, 1987).

Mountain ash forests also play an important role in wildlife conservation. Of particular note is Leadbeater's possum (*Gymnobelideus leadbeateri*), an endangered arboreal marsupial that is largely restricted to the mountain ash forests to the east of Melbourne (Lindenmayer, 1996). Acacia shrubs and large trees with hollows are two of the most important habitat elements for Leadbeater's possum, with the former providing food and acting as a foraging substrate and the latter providing nesting and denning sites. Hollow-bearing trees are a critical resource in many parts of Australia, with 350 species of vertebrates known to use holes in trees (Gibbons and Lindenmayer, 2002). For many of the arboreal marsupials of mountain ash forest, the absence of appropriate hollows will make the forest unsuitable habitat (Lindenmayer, 1996). Hollows that can be occupied by vertebrates take well over 100 years to develop in eucalypts because Australia lacks primary hollow excavators such as woodpeckers. Hollows form by the slow process of decay by fungi and subsequent excavation usually by termites.

Because of the importance of timber, water supply and conservation values of mountain ash forests, there has been considerable debate about the proper management of these forests (see Creedy and Wurzbacher, 2001). Timber harvesting reduces the abundance of large old trees that provide important habitat for a range of species (Lindenmayer, 1996). The streamflow from a forest harvested on a rotation of 50–100 years will be less than the streamflow in the absence of timber harvesting and other disturbances. Therefore, timber harvesting reduces, at least to some extent, the wildlife and water values derived from mountain ash forests. While this trade-off is relatively well understood, management of mountain ash forests is complicated by the relatively rare occurrence of intense unplanned fires, which are difficult to control and impossible to eliminate. Managers of mountain ash forests and Melbourne's water supply corporation are forced to plan with the prospect of rare events that may have profound effects on the production of timber, water and wildlife habitat.

Types of models

Mental models

The above description of mountain ash ecology and management is a model. It ignores many of the features of mountain ash ecology that are known (Ashton and Attiwill, 1994), and the vast array of detail that is completely unknown. It is an incomplete description of my own mental model of mountain ash ecology and management, because I neglected to mention invertebrates, other vertebrates, additional information of forest structure and other attributes with which I am familiar. My mental model is likely to be similar to that of some of my colleagues (e.g. Lindenmayer, 1996), but somewhat different from some other ecologists although clearly influenced by them (e.g. Ashton and Attiwill, 1994). It is also likely to differ from that of forest managers and people who use the forest for its timber, water or recreational opportunities.

Mental models play a critical role in ecology. Our understanding of ecological systems forms the basis of our opinions and beliefs that influence the research questions and topics that we explore. Our mental models of ecological systems drive these research topics because we tend to pursue the ones that we expect to yield interesting information. Few ecologists would be happy to pursue research questions that they predicted to be irrelevant. Our mental models form the basis of expert judgement, which we may provide to decision-makers or use to design and plan research programmes. These models constantly change with our ecological experience and provide the foundation for flashes of inspiration that may lead to new research questions and opportunities.

Despite the importance of mental models in ecology, they are not directly helpful for the task of comparing the ecology of cities because they are contained within each person, and cannot be communicated fully to others. As Lehvävirta and Kotze (Chapter 31) state, undeclared theoretical background or mental models hamper comparisons. Instead, to use the information that is in these models it is necessary to make them more concrete. One approach to do this is to develop qualitative models.

Qualitative models

Qualitative models are simply a form of description, whether that is a narrative, such as that presented above for mountain ash forests, or a diagram. One qualitative model of water supply from mountain ash forests may be represented as a diagram (Fig. 7.1). In this model, rainfall either becomes streamflow or is returned to the atmosphere via evapotranspiration, the rate of which depends on the successional stage of the forest. The subsequent streamflow is either stored for later use or is released downstream. Clearly, this model is a simplification of reality, with several causes of water loss and many attributes referred to in the above narrative being ignored. Further, I have neglected to include any detail of meteorology, the influence of rainfall variability and subsurface water flow, to mention but a few things. Despite its obvious limitations, it remains a reasonable model and goes some way towards communicating my mental model of the ecology of mountain ash forests and their importance for supplying water to Melbourne. It would be relatively easy to add further detail to the diagrammatic model to describe more fully my mental model. This

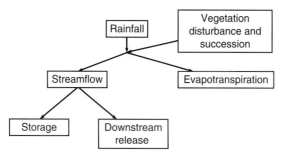

Fig. 7.1. A diagrammatic model of water supply from mountain ash forest, in which rainfall either becomes streamflow or is lost to evapotranspiration. The rate of evapotranspiration depends on the successional stage of the forest, a consequence of previous disturbance. The subsequent streamflow is either stored or released downstream. Other losses of water from the system, such as evaporation from the stream or water storage and seepage into the ground water, have been ignored in this diagram.

is perhaps the most important role of qualitative models, which is assisting communication of mental models.

The main drawback of using qualitative models for comparing the ecology of cities is that these models mainly represent matters of opinion or may only include elements that are convenient rather than sufficient. One might try to compare cities by examining the inclusion or exclusion of different attributes or processes in qualitative models. However, differences between qualitative models may not represent substantive ecological differences. The most useful models for comparing cities are quantitative, which will allow numerical comparison (see Lehvävirta and Kotze, Chapter 31).

Quantitative models

Some quantitative models may simply provide an estimate of a quantity, such as biomass of a forest, or describe a relationship. For example, Kuczera (1987) estimated the relationship between annual streamflow and the age of mountain ash forests (Fig. 7.2). He derived this relationship by analysing changes in streamflow over time for a number of catchments (watersheds) that contain mountain ash forest. The analysis demonstrates the predicted decline in water yield as the forest first regenerates. Water yield reaches a minimum at 25–30 years of age, before increasing over the next century. The dot on the yield curve represents forest that is 65 years old (Fig. 7.2). Much of the mountain ash forest is currently in this state after large and devastating fires in 1939 burnt approximately 20% of Victoria's public forest (Gill, 1981; Griffiths, 2001). In the absence of further fires, a substantial increase in water yield is expected.

Although based on a statistical analysis of data, Kuczera's water yield curve is a model. If we use this to predict water yield, we are forced to ignore the fact that

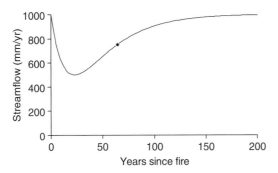

Fig. 7.2. Predicted streamflow per year from mountain ash forest as a function of forest age (based on Kuczera, 1987). The dot represents the age in 2004 of much of the mountain ash forest that was burnt in 1939.

rainfall varies from year to year and from place to place, with subsequent influences on streamflow. Indeed, some mountain ash forest occurs in areas where the annual rainfall is less than 1000 mm, for which the yield in Fig. 7.2 is clearly inappropriate because streamflow should be less than rainfall. Nevertheless, the Kuczera curve represents an average relationship that is useful for approximating streamflow from catchments. This sort of model prompts questions about the appropriation of streamflow by different cities and the ecological consequences. For example, we could examine how stream environments and biodiversity are influenced by reduced flow, and the interactions between these two. The model of water yield allows us to consider the additional impacts of water diversion in addition to variation in flow arising from the occurrence of fire.

To obtain more precise predictions of streamflow from different mountain ash forests, Watson *et al.* (1999) developed a hydrological model that represented the landscape as a series of cells. Flow was modelled on a daily basis by moving water between the cells and extracting water from cells as a function of the vegetation. Such a model attempts to simulate some of the physical hydrological processes rather than simply describing a statistical relationship. In some ways it is similar to models with which ecologists are familiar, such as those of population dynamics and dispersal of animals (e.g. Snep *et al.*, Chapter 26).

Integrating physical and ecological models

It is not for a single ecologist to decide on the ecological attributes of cities that are most useful for comparison. The actual structure and features of models that should be used for comparing cities are a matter of discussion among all ecologists. However, one aspect of modelling that I believe is particularly conducive to comparing the ecology of cities is the integration of physical and social models with ecological models. I will focus on the integration of physical and ecological models because I am more familiar with these, but there is considerable scope for also integrating social models (Niemelä *et al.*, Chapter 2; Nilon, Chapter 10). In general, a broad range of physical models are applicable to the ecology of cities. For example, models are used in the study of pollution, climate, hydrology and urban development. The ecological influence of these processes can be explored by modelling their interaction with ecological systems. For example, models of the response of tree growth to ozone (Gregg *et al.*, 2003) and models of the production and distribution of ozone in a range of cities could help to examine the relative influence of this form of pollution in different cities.

An important aspect of the integration of physical and ecological models is that relevant physical models may not be developed at the same temporal and spatial scales as ecological models. The immediate reaction of ecologists might be to change the scale of the physical models. However, we could also attempt to change the scale at which we model ecological processes. Regardless of the approach used, such integration is rarely trivial. As an example of integrating physical and ecological models, I will return to the mountain ash forests.

Because of the trade-off between timber harvesting and the supply of water, some of Melbourne's water catchments are protected from timber harvesting. Ongoing economic analyses investigate the question of optimal management of these water catchments to determine whether timber harvesting is warranted (see Creedy and Wurzbacher, 2001). The main conclusion of these analyses is that the optimal management strategy (whether to log, and the optimal rotation length if logging does occur) depends on the relative benefits of the timber, water and non-extractive values such as wildlife habitat or carbon sequestration (Creedy and Wurzbacher, 2001). However, most of these analyses have ignored the occurrence of fire, which is the main ecological process in these forests. By ignoring fire, it is likely that the supply of timber, water and wildlife habitat will be overestimated.

Disturbance ecology is one area with which ecologists are familiar and for which we have a range of models. One of these suites of models describes how the age structure of a landscape is expected to change as a function of the disturbance interval (van Wagner, 1978; Johnson and Gutsell, 1994; McCarthy and Burgman, 1995; McCarthy *et al.*, 2001). For example, these models can be used to demonstrate that if disturbances occur systematically (e.g. logging a forest on a fixed rotation), then the age structure will approach a uniform distribution, and no forest will exceed the rotation age (McCarthy and Burgman, 1995). In contrast, if disturbances occur completely at random, the expected proportion of the landscape of different ages will be described by a geometric

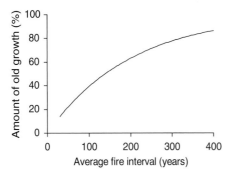

Fig. 7.3. Expected percentage of the forest older than 100 years (old growth) as a function of the average fire interval, assuming that fires occur completely at random.

distribution (van Wagner, 1978; McCarthy and Burgman, 1995). In this case, the proportion of forest that is expected to be older than x years of age will approximately equal $\exp(-x/m)$ (for large mean disturbance intervals), where m is the mean disturbance interval. Therefore, the proportion of the forest expected to exceed the average disturbance interval under random disturbance is 37% ($\exp[-1]$). More generally, we can define old-growth forest as being older than 100 years, for example, and plot the amount of old-growth forest as a function of the mean fire interval (Fig. 7.3). Even with average fire intervals that are considerably longer than 100 years, a noticeable proportion of the forest is expected to be young. This emphasises the influence that rare events can have on the dynamics of ecological systems.

These models of disturbance can be used to investigate how streamflow is predicted to change as a function of mean fire interval. This can be achieved by determining the amount of forest predicted to be of each particular age, calculating the yield expected from each part of the forest as a function of its age, and then summing these amounts. Mathematically, this is a weighted average of the water yield curve, with the weights determined by the age structure of the forest. Thus, assuming a geometric distribution of forest age, the expected yield (Y) will be

$$Y = \sum_{i=1}^{\infty} p(1-p)^{i-1} y(i) \qquad (7.1)$$

where p is the annual risk of fire and equal to the inverse of the mean fire interval ($1/m$), and $y(i)$ is the water yield curve, describing water yield as a function of forest age (i). If the Kuczera (1987) curve given in Fig. 7.2 is used for $y(i)$, then we can plot the expected water yield as a function of the mean fire interval in the absence of any other disturbances (Fig. 7.4). When the mean fire interval is 100 years, which is the approximate interval in mountain ash forests

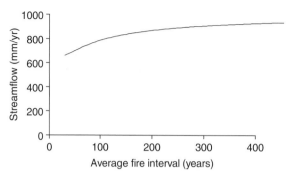

Fig. 7.4. Expected long-term average water yield from mountain ash forest as a function of the average fire interval, assuming that fires occur completely at random.

(McCarthy *et al.*, 1999), the water yield is expected to be more than 20% below the old-growth yield. This prediction represents a long-term average that is expected over the course of a century or more. It is approximately equal to the water yield that is currently being achieved from the extensive areas of forest that were burnt in 1939. It is possible to make similar predictions about the sustainable timber yield under different mean fire intervals.

These analyses demonstrate how physical models can be integrated with ecological models, and that such models are important for understanding the ecology and management of these systems. They can also contribute to comparisons of the ecology of cities by allowing us to examine common questions, for example in this case how protection of cities' water supplies can contribute to conservation of biodiversity. More generally, they provide a common framework for defining the relationships to be examined and the attributes to be measured.

The remainder of this chapter focuses on how ecologists should undertake such tasks in a way that will facilitate comparison.

Quantification

Ecologists are well versed in quantifying ecological relationships. Most ecologists know accepted methods for measuring the environment and are at least moderately conversant with the details of statistical analyses. Despite this, some ecologists may be surprised to learn that there is more than one possible approach to conducting statistics. With an average of approximately 30 null hypothesis tests reported in each article in the journal *Ecology* (Anderson *et al.*, 2000), it is reasonable to conclude that null hypothesis testing is the dominant statistical school of ecologists. While the rationale of null hypothesis testing is sound for its intended purpose (Chow, 1996), the way null hypothesis testing is used by most ecologists can lead to difficulties. The primary difficulty involves problems of reporting statistics, and four aspects in particular are relevant to comparative ecology. These are that mostly trivial (false) null hypotheses are tested, *p*-values are routinely misinterpreted, biological importance is usually ignored, and the size of the effect being studied and precision are often not reported (Anderson *et al.*, 2000).

Trivial null hypotheses

Most null hypotheses tested by ecologists are trivial; a reasonable person would conclude that they are false without collecting any data (Anderson *et al.*, 2000). Most of these trivial null hypotheses can be described as nil nulls, for example when the null hypothesis is that there is no difference between the means of two groups. If we already know the null hypothesis is wrong (for example, if we know that the two groups differ), the decision about whether we reject the null hypothesis should be of no interest. Nevertheless, ecology journals are replete with examples of tests of trivial null hypotheses.

Of course, not all null hypotheses are trivial. Careful thought about the problem, the range of possible explanations for the data that are to be collected, and the corresponding logical hypotheses (as distinct from statistical null hypotheses) should ensure that sensible null hypotheses are used (Underwood, 1997; Lehvävirta and Kotze, Chapter 31). Unfortunately, it seems that many ecologists do not follow such a process (Anderson *et al.*, 2000).

Misinterpretation of p-values

The *p*-value of a statistical test is the basis for deciding whether or not to reject a null hypothesis. If the *p*-value is less than the nominated Type I error rate (usually set without thinking at 0.05), then we conclude that the data are unusual for the given null hypothesis, and consequently the null hypothesis is rejected. If the *p*-value is not sufficiently small, then we fail to reject the null hypothesis. This logic leads many ecologists to assume that the *p*-value provides information about the truth of the null hypothesis. If the *p*-value is small, the null hypothesis is disproven, and if it is large the null hypothesis is confirmed. This is flawed logic, because significance testing is only designed to reject null hypotheses; it can never confirm that a null hypothesis is true. Despite this, ecologists often report results using language such as 'Variable X did not influence variable Y ($P = 0.2$)', and conclude incorrectly that they have evidence that X and Y are unrelated (Anderson *et al.*, 2000).

Biological importance is usually ignored

To interpret null hypothesis tests usefully, one needs to know the biological importance of any differences and the chance of rejecting the null hypothesis if a biologically important difference actually exists. For example, assume we are interested in whether the annual survival rate of foxes differs between two cities. The trivial null hypothesis that most ecologists would use would be that there is no difference. However, we may decide that a difference of 10% would be sufficient to explain an observed difference in fox abundance. In this case, a 10% difference is biologically important and we could calculate the probability of obtaining a statistically significant result if the difference really was of this magnitude. This is a statistical power calculation, something that is rarely conducted in ecology (Peterman, 1990). If we had little chance of obtaining a statistically significant result with the available research budget, a non-statistically significant result would not be particularly helpful.

In contrast, if we did obtain a statistically significant result, it does not mean that the difference is biologically important. With sufficient resources, even the smallest and most inconsequential difference can lead to a statistically significant result. The main question when one obtains a statistically significant result is whether it is biologically important. 'Statistically significant' does not mean 'important'. Similarly, 'not statistically significant' is not the same as 'not important'.

Despite the necessity of considering biological importance when conducting null hypothesis tests (when interpreting both significant and non-significant results), it is ignored by most ecologists (Anderson *et al.*, 2000). Part of the reason for this is that we cannot determine the size of differences that are likely to be important because we have insufficient knowledge of ecological systems. It could be argued that in such circumstances we have no business conducting null hypothesis tests because the importance of the result is not interpretable.

Effect size and precision not reported

The failure to report the size of the estimated effects and the precision of these estimates is in some ways a consequence of the preceding problems in reporting statistics in ecology. For example, assume that we failed to reject the null hypothesis of no difference in survival rate of foxes between cities. Further, assume that we interpreted that outcome as evidence for no difference and did not consider the possibility that we would fail to identify a biologically important effect. In such circumstances, we would rarely report the estimated size of the difference and the precision of the estimate because we believe, at least implicitly, that the difference is zero. However, the effect size and measure of precision are crucial for comparative ecology by providing suitable data for meta-analysis (Gurevitch and Hedges, 1993). We cannot conduct meaningful quantitative comparisons without them (see also Lehvävirta and Kotze, Chapter 31).

Even in cases where statistically significant results are obtained, effect sizes are often not reported in ecological studies (Anderson *et al.*, 2000). In some cases, even the direction of the relationship is ignored. Again, comparative studies require this information. For example, consider the recent study by Hope *et al.* (2003) as a case in point in which relationships between plant diversity and various geographic and socio-economic factors were examined. This paper was chosen arbitrarily as an example; there are an enormous number of possible papers that could have served the same purpose. In urban areas, Hope *et al.* (2003) found statistically significant relationships to explain plant diversity (the number of genera in 30 m × 30 m plots) for three variables; these were family income, median age of housing and whether the area had been used for agriculture at some time in the past. The results of the statistical analyses were reported in terms of the magnitude of the test statistic and the *p*-value. Neither of these values tells us the size of the effect or the precision of the estimate, but at least the direction of the effect was indicated. A graph of the relationship between plant diversity and income was presented, indicating approximately the size of the effect for this variable. However, the precision of the estimated relationship and the partial effect of income (while holding the other terms in the model constant) cannot be determined from the information in the paper. The possible magnitude of the non-significant effects was ignored completely (Hope *et al.*, 2003) probably because of the implicit assumption that non-significant effects are not important (the effect size is assumed to be close to zero). If we had equivalent studies in other cities, we would not be able to determine whether similar relationships between socio-economic variables and plant diversity exist without obtaining the original data.

The way ahead

Because of the misuse of null hypothesis testing, there have been suggestions in other disciplines that it be abandoned (e.g. Schmidt, 1996). It is debatable whether banning null hypothesis significance testing would improve the use of statistics in ecology. Whether null hypothesis testing is used or not, it is important to place a greater emphasis on estimating the size of effects and their precision (Fidler *et al.*, 2006), and also thinking more clearly about the logic of null hypothesis testing when it is used (Underwood, 1997). There are a range of methods for estimating effect sizes and determining the precision of estimates, including those based on information theoretic and Bayesian methods, which are becoming more commonly used in ecology and related disciplines (e.g. Anderson *et al.*, 2000; Wade, 2000; McCarthy, 2007).

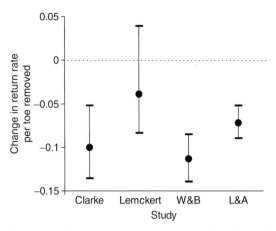

Fig. 7.5. Predicted change in return rate of frogs for each toe removed for four different studies (Clarke, 1972; Lemckert, 1996; Williamson and Bull, 1996; Lüddecke and Amézquita, 1999). The circle is the best estimate of the effect and the bars represent 95% confidence intervals. Negative values represent an adverse effect of toe clipping. Reproduced from McCarthy and Parris (2004).

The advantage of placing a greater emphasis on estimating the size of the effect and its precision in comparative studies can be seen in Fig. 7.5, which illustrates the effect of toe clipping in frogs (McCarthy and Parris, 2004). In three of the four studies, there is clearly a negative effect of toe clipping, with the 95% confidence intervals not encompassing zero. This negative effect means that the return rate of frogs declines as more toes are clipped. In the other study, the confidence interval includes zero, indicating that the results are consistent with no effect. However, the width of the confidence interval demonstrates that the effect could be at least approximately as large as the other studies in which a negative effect is clear. While we cannot be sure there is a negative effect in one of the studies, the confidence intervals demonstrate that the results are consistent with at least a similar effect in all four studies being possible.

If null hypothesis testing had focussed on the nil null (that of no effect), we would have obtained a significant effect in three studies, and a non-significant effect in the fourth (Fig. 7.5). Unthinking acceptance of the null in this case might lead us to conclude that the four studies are not consistent with each other. This in fact has happened in the past, with authors concluding that toe clipping has inconsistent effects (e.g. Humphries, 1976; Lemckert, 1996; Reaser and Dexter, 1996). The problem does not lie with null hypothesis testing per se, but rather in the common misinterpretation of the results. A statistically significant result merely states that the data are not consistent with the null hypothesis of no effect; we cannot be confident of an effect in the fourth study where a significant result was not obtained. The individual tests of each study do not provide any information about whether the results are consistent with each other, nor about the possible magnitude of differences. Such information can only be obtained if the results are presented in such a way that a meta-analysis can be conducted by providing estimates of effect sizes and measures of the precision.

We have a range of models that can be used for comparing the ecology of cities. Integration of ecological models with those of physical and socio-economic systems appears to be particularly fruitful for understanding the relative importance of different processes in different cities. However, comparative studies of cities require a greater focus on estimation than is currently done by most ecologists. Comparative studies will be hampered unless we provide estimates of the size of effects we are studying and measure and report the precision of these estimates.

Part II ECOLOGICAL STUDIES OF CITIES AND TOWNS

8

Responses of faunal assemblages to urbanisation: global research paradigms and an avian case study

CARLA P. CATTERALL

Introduction

Urban areas worldwide share many features, including high human population densities, the presence of high levels of chemical input to air, water and soil, and the redirection and/or piping of above-ground water flows. As habitat for fauna, their other distinctive features include planted and maintained lawns and gardens, many simple and impervious surfaces (e.g. buildings, roads), patches of remnant native vegetation, and a liberal supply of human food scraps and wastes (McDonnell and Pickett, 1990; Marzluff *et al.*, 2001; Nilon, Chapter 10; van der Ree, Chapter 11). These features also show characteristic spatial variation. In commercial and industrial domains, built structures dominate the available space, whereas in suburban residential areas, buildings are interspersed with gardens and lawns, which in turn may vary in size and nature. There is often an 'exurban' sprawl (Marzluff, 2001; Miller *et al.*, 2001) containing residential areas which have larger allotment sizes, lower densities of dwellings, and more land occupied by lawns or vegetation. These global similarities are driven by trans-national export of technologies and cultures.

We might expect such similarities in environmental structure and function to produce worldwide similarities in the nature of urban wildlife assemblages. The notion that there are types of ecosystem which occur patchily across different continents ('biomes' sensu Begon *et al.*, 1990) is familiar to ecological science. Examples include rainforests, savanna woodlands, heathlands, deserts

Ecology of Cities and Towns: A Comparative Approach, ed. Mark J. McDonnell, Amy K. Hahs and Jürgen H. Breuste. Published by Cambridge University Press. © Cambridge University Press 2009.

and saltmarshes. While the organisms in a particular biome may differ in taxonomy, phylogeny and diversity between continents, they show parallel or convergent adaptations. For example, rainforests with tall buttressed trees, many vines, many fleshy-fruited plants and large-bodied frugivorous birds occur on many continents. Biomes of a particular type share aspects of ecosystem structure and function, such as physical context, vegetation structure, functional variety of organisms, and key disturbance agents and regimes. For example, periodic burning is an intrinsic part of ecosystem function in many savannas, but not in rainforests. The ecological patterns and processes that characterise particular biomes across continents have been identified through rigorous local ecological research into assemblage composition and ecological processes over many years, with a more general understanding being progressively built through synthesis.

The biomes described above are considered to be 'natural' ecosystems. However, interpretations of ecological processes within these ecosystems have varied, from a more equilibrial world view to a perspective which acknowledges that ongoing climate change and human intervention have had longstanding influences in many ecosystems (Williams, 1993). The former view emphasised temporal stability and fine-tuned sets of interactions between climate and vegetation, or among co-evolved sets of interacting species, whereas the latter considers that areas viewed as 'natural' by European colonists of the past 200 years may have been greatly influenced by the activities of aboriginal people for thousands of years previously (e.g. Williams, 1993; Bowman, 2000). Furthermore, aspects of biodiversity in many biomes may be tied to disturbance regimes, through the existence of spatial habitat mosaics whose elements are differing stages in post-disturbance succession (for example, following localised tree fall in rainforests or fire in Australian heathlands). In some cases, it is likely that humans have been the disturbance agent, for example by regular burning (Bowman, 2000). Many apparently 'undisturbed' ecosystems may in fact be relics of earlier types of land use (Williams, 1993), the nature and extent of which have been forgotten following extirpation of aboriginal peoples by European settlers.

Urban areas, lying at the more human-dominated end of the spectrum, have historically been excluded from widespread recognition by ecologists as a worldwide ecosystem type. Consequently, the urban biome has been largely spurned as an interesting subject for rigorous scientific ecological research (McDonnell and Pickett, 1993a; Niemelä, 1999b; Bowman and Marzluff, 2001). However, neither their relatively recent addition to many bio-regions nor their high human density necessarily means that urban ecosystems, across the globe, cannot share common species assembly rules and ecological processes. Clearly, the relative recency of urban areas means that evolution and co-evolution would be less important determinants of their species assembly than other processes such as colonisation, extinction, habitat selection and environmental filtering. But this does not mean that urban areas are necessarily less amenable to rigorous ecological study, using established principles and methods, than other biomes. In fact there are several reasons why it is important to treat urban biodiversity seriously as a subject of ecological research. Urban areas are typically located in productive (and hence biologically important) places, and they contain the last remaining individuals of some threatened species (Low, 2002). Urban areas also contain novel combinations of environmental factors (Pickett *et al.*, 1997b, Chapter 3), which have the potential to provide new insights into the processes which affect biodiversity. Furthermore, they are becoming spatially significant: the Earth's human population is growing, and an increasing proportion are living in urban areas, whose areal extent is in turn increasing at a faster rate than urban population growth (McDonnell and Pickett, 1990; Pickett *et al.*, 1997b; Alberti *et al.*, 2001; Marzluff *et al.*, 2001).

If ecological research can identify global commonalities in the patterns of terrestrial biodiversity in urban areas, or in the processes which have the most influence on them, then this would provide predictive power for likely future trends in currently undeveloped areas. This understanding would also provide a better basis for planning, management and urban design to achieve better biodiversity outcomes in newly urbanising regions (Pickett *et al.*, 1997b; Niemelä, 1999b; Marzluff *et al.*, 2001; McDonnell and Hahs, Chapter 5). Consequently, there have recently been several calls for researchers to apply the techniques and concepts developed within other ecosystems to reveal the ecological structures of urban populations, communities and ecosystems, and to elucidate the processes which underlie them (McDonnell *et al.*, 1997; Marzluff *et al.*, 2001). A failure to reveal useful information would indicate inadequacies in ecological principles or methods, not limitations to urban areas as a subject of scientific research.

Careful empirical investigations, within an analytical framework which is guided by existing ecological principles and testable hypotheses, should be able to reveal the ecological patterns and processes which characterise species assemblages in urban ecosystems (McDonnell *et al.*, 1997; Bolger, 2001; Bowman and Marzluff, 2001). Here I present an example of such an investigation: a case study of the responses of bird assemblages to urbanisation in subtropical Australia. Then I discuss varying approaches that have been applied to the general question, 'What determines terrestrial biodiversity in urban areas?', and consider issues which are likely to be important in future studies of urban biotas, if we are to develop a global understanding of their ecology.

Responses of bird assemblages to urbanisation in subtropical Australia: a case study

Urbanising southeast Queensland

The urbanising subtropical region of eastern Australia is centred on the rapidly growing city of Brisbane (approximately 27° 30′ S, 153° E), together with the adjacent urban areas of the Sunshine Coast and Gold Coast to its north and south, respectively. These lie mostly within southeast Queensland, although the southern Gold Coast also extends into northern New South Wales. The region's human population size, around two million people in the early 1990s, increased by around 100 000 people per annum during much of the 1990s, making it the continent's fastest growing region (Catterall and Kingston, 1993). As in many Australian cities, housing allotments in most older residential areas are relatively large (typically 0.1 ha or more), and the growing human population is being accommodated in an expanding exurban sprawl, where allotments are often 0.2–10 ha or more.

European settlement of the region is relatively recent, having begun in the mid 1800s. It was rapidly followed by clearing of the formerly continuous forest cover ('bushland') for pasture and agriculture, mainly in lowland areas. From the mid 1900s, suburban development began to expand, in some places on land formerly cleared, and in others replacing remnant forests. Ongoing deforestation rates have become a significant conservation issue in the region (Catterall *et al.*, 1997b). However, because of historical vagaries of landowner inclination and circumstance, coupled with changing town planning approaches, patches of remnant bushland were, at least initially, retained in places. These have become encircled by residential suburbs where the land cover is a mixture of impervious surfaces, built structures and large gardens that are nutrient-rich and well watered (owing to added fertiliser and irrigation), containing mown grassy lawns sprinkled with scattered small trees and shrubs. Many of the component plants are cultivated species introduced from other parts of the world, although since the 1970s there has been an increased use of plants native to Australia (and sometimes to the region), often comprising taller, more densely planted, shrubs and trees. There has also been an increasing frequency of housing developments established beneath scattered original eucalypt trees which were retained when bushland was cleared prior to development.

The style of suburban land cover may be fairly uniform within areas of hectares to tens of hectares, but at broader scales of tens to hundreds of square kilometres, the region is a complex spatial mosaic of different forms of land cover. Some elements of this mosaic are the different types of residential development, each with its characteristic style and size of houses and gardens. Others are business and industrial domains dominated by built structures, grassy parklands and golf courses with scattered trees, patches of cropland or remnant cleared pasture, and remnant native forest of different types. These differing forms of land cover constitute different types of potential fauna habitat, which provide resources of differing quality and quantity. All occur within patches of varying size. Prior to European settlement, the native vegetation cover was also a diverse mosaic of different vegetation types, in which eucalypt forests dominated, and rainforests were well represented. Hence, patches of remnant vegetation also vary in nature.

Analytical design framework for assessing responses of bird assemblages

The case study considers how and why bird species assemblages in the urbanising greater Brisbane region are responding to the land-cover changes which have accompanied human settlement. Birds, both in urban areas and elsewhere, are a flagship group which provides a source of pleasure and fascination to many people who otherwise have no special interest in nature (Catterall, 1991). Many people like to feel that they are building or maintaining gardens that are attractive to native birds, and which help support them. Birds are also functionally diverse, relatively common, easily and cost-effectively surveyed and identified, and taxonomically stable, and the ecology of individual species is relatively well known. Hence they are well suited to this type of study.

A series of research projects has investigated the ways in which birds respond to deforestation and urbanisation in the study region (including Catterall *et al.*, 1989, 1991, 1997a, 1998, 2002, 2004; Park, 1994; Bentley and Catterall, 1997; Green and Catterall, 1998; Sewell and Catterall, 1998; Oertel, 1998; Martin and Catterall, 2001; Piper and Catterall, 2003, 2004). In this paper I both draw upon their findings and present new analyses of data compiled from seven of these studies (Table 8.1). Each project involved a quantitative and controlled comparison of selected attributes of the target biota (in this case the composition, relative frequency and abundance of bird species), across differing forms of land cover (an 'observational experiment' sensu Eberhardt and Thomas, 1991), using the following common design protocol.

First, land-cover types to be compared were chosen (these are the controlling factors of central interest), each defined by criteria relating to both local habitat structure and spatial context. Replicate sites were then located for each land-cover type. As far as possible, replicates were spatially well separated, to allow them to represent independent sets of birds, and sites from different land-cover types were interspersed. Careful site selection was used to achieve experimental control (again, as far as possible) by limiting or stratifying the variation in other factors (e.g. elevation, proximity to water) whose influence on the avifauna might otherwise confound and complicate the results. Standardised sampling

Table 8.1. *Types of land cover compared, and sources of the information used in the case study.*

Type of land cover	No. of sites	No. of cases[a]	Data sources[b, c]	Description[d]
Pasture	5	1	A	Cleared areas of introduced pasture grasses grazed by dairy cattle; some scattered trees and occasional fences.
Bare suburbs	36	2	B,C	Suburbs with houses (15–20 m frontage), roads, and gardens dominated by grassed lawns, and containing very few scattered shrubs, or trees either native or exotic. Negligible trees >8 m.
Treed suburbs	45	3	C(2),D	Suburbs with houses (15–30 m frontage), roads, and gardens with well-developed cover of taller trees and shrubs, either native or introduced. Three subcategories: 'canopy suburbs' (17 sites) where residences and gardens were established beneath thinned original canopy eucalypts; 'planted suburbs' (20) containing gardens with many planted trees and shrubs, a substantial proportion comprising introduced species; 'gardens and parkland' (8) which included some areas of planted suburb and some grassy recreational areas with widely spaced trees.
Eucalypt forest remnants:				See below
10–20 ha	28	2	D,E	
4–10 ha	35	2	C,D	
1–2 ha	8	1	D	
Eucalypt forest tracts ≫100 ha	96	6	C,D,E,F(2),G	Broadly characterised by a 30–70% canopy of tall trees of *Eucalyptus* and allied genera, above a structurally moderately complex understorey of small trees, shrubs and tall grasses.

Table 8.1. (*cont.*)

Type of land cover	No. of sites	No. of cases[a]	Data sources[b, c]	Description[d]
Rainforest	10	1	A	Canopy cover of tall trees generally above 70%, high floristic diversity of characteristic, mainly broad-leaved genera, highly complex multi-layered vegetation structure, ground layer of dense leaf litter.
Total	263	18	7	

Notes:

[a] A case is a land-cover type containing replicate sites within a particular study, usually separated by >1 km. Apart from pasture, the minimum number of sites per case was eight; many were 16–20.

[b] Sources: A, Catterall *et al.*, 2004; B, Catterall *et al.*, 1991; C, Sewell and Catterall, 1998; D, Oertel, 1998; E, Catterall *et al.*, 1998 and unpublished; F, Bentley and Catterall, 1997; G, Park, 1994. Data collection occurred in six different years, between 1985 and 2000.

[c] Birds at each site were sampled with a transect 100 m × 30 m, visited six times on different days (usually in the morning) for 15 minutes (excepting source (D) which used 20 minutes and (A) which used 30 minutes to allow more difficult detection in dense rainforest). Data were from a successive winter (May–August) and summer (October–January), three visits in each, except for source (B) which used two successive winters (suburbs show little seasonal turnover) and source (A) which used two visits in each of February–April, June–July, October–November. All birds known to be on or immediately above the transect were counted.

[d] See Sewell and Catterall (1998) and Catterall *et al.* (2004) for quantitative characterisations of vegetation structure. The minimum patch area of broadly similar habitat around a site was 20 ha, except for eucalypt forest remnants of specified sizes and some rainforest sites. Transects were placed as far as possible from the edges of remnant patches, and >200 m (often much more) from edges.

at each site (in this case, a temporal series of visual transect counts) was then used to measure a number of response variables (aspects of the avifauna). Each study included a subset of the land-cover types listed in Table 8.1; in some cases these were more finely subdivided, and some included additional types not analysed here (e.g. forest edges, regenerating or reforested areas).

The projects compiled for this paper provide data for 18 combinations of land cover and study, spanning a 15-year period (1985–2000) (Table 8.1). Six of the component studies were also summarised in Catterall (2004) and further data (rainforest, pasture) were added from the seventh study (Catterall *et al.*, 2004). All studies used a similar measurement of the avifauna (Table 8.1): a count of individuals of each species by an observer during six visits to a small-scale transect (100 m × 30 m). In the present overview, all avifauna measurements are based on the presence or absence of each bird species at a site (across all visits), in order to minimise the effects of variation between observers (although analysing the data using abundance gave similar results). Across all 263 sites, 144 bird species were recorded.

Selected results and outcomes

Bird species richness was insensitive to most variation in environmental attributes, being similar across most land-cover types (Fig. 8.1). However, pasture and bare suburbs both had site-specific species richness around half of that seen

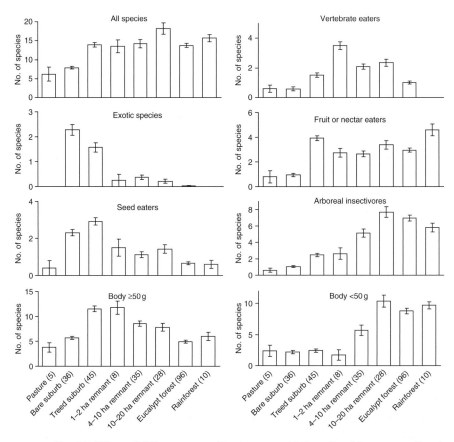

Fig. 8.1. Effects of different types of land cover on bird species richness, overall and within functional groups based on origin, feeding and body mass. Land-cover types are ordered from pasture, through suburbs of increasing vegetation cover, to native forests of increasing canopy extent and density. All remnants were eucalypt forest. Bars are standard errors; sample sizes (numbers of sites) in brackets below axes. Birds were recorded at each site from a plot 100 m × 30 m, surveyed for six visits of mainly 15–20 min (mostly three summer, three winter).

Table 8.2. *Results of pairwise tests of similarity[a] in bird species composition[b] among types of site that vary in land cover (numbers of sites shown in brackets).*

Values in each cell are R dissimilarity statistic above, P-value below. Bold cells show land-cover types whose bird assemblages did not differ significantly. Global $R = 0.44$, $P < 0.001$.

	Bare suburb (36)	Treed suburb (45)	1–2 ha remnant[c] (8)	4–10 ha remnant[c] (35)	10–20 ha remnant[c] (28)	Eucalypt forest (96)	Rain forest (10)
Pasture (5)	0.68 <0.001	0.94 <0.001	0.73 <0.001	0.82 <0.001	0.94 <0.001	0.84 <0.001	0.93 <0.001
Bare suburb		0.40 <0.001	0.47 <0.001	0.58 <0.001	0.79 <0.001	0.73 <0.001	0.93 <0.001
Treed suburb			**0.07** **0.24**	0.39 <0.001	0.79 <0.001	0.56 <0.001	1.00 <0.001
1–2 ha remnant				**−0.16** **0.96**	0.38 <0.001	0.36 <0.001	1.00 <0.001
4–10 ha remnant					0.17 <0.001	0.19 <0.001	0.89 <0.001
10–20 ha remnant						**−0.04** **0.76**	0.90 <0.001
Eucalypt forest							0.57 <0.001

Notes:
[a] ANOSIM (Clarke, 1993), using Bray–Curtis dissimilarities.
[b] Bird data were the presence/absence of all recorded species (total 144) from a plot 100 m × 30 m at each site, surveyed for six visits of mainly 15–20 min (mostly three summer, three winter).
[c] All remnants were eucalypt forest.

in either well-vegetated suburbs or forests. Species richness tended to peak in eucalypt forest remnants of area 10–20 ha, consistent with other recent studies which have reported greatest faunal species richness at intermediate points along urbanisation gradients (Blair and Launer, 1997; Niemelä, 1999b; Blair, 2001; Germaine and Wakeling, 2001; Crooks *et al.*, 2004), probably because the areas contained both 'forest' and 'urban' species. However, this was a minor difference compared with the large reduction in the two simplest habitats. Species richness within eucalypt forest also varied considerably between sites in riparian and upslope areas (Bentley and Catterall, 1997; not shown in Fig. 8.1).

In contrast, the various land-cover types showed much stronger differences in both their species composition and the occurrence of species within particular

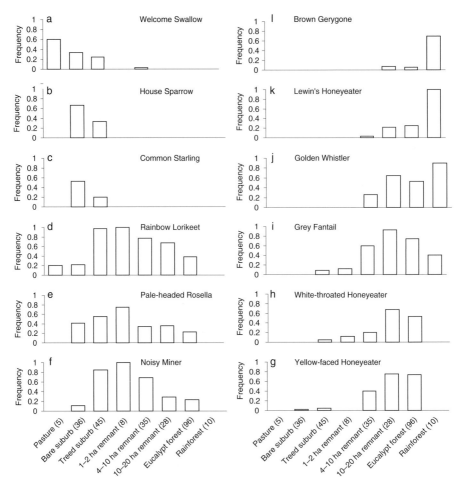

Fig. 8.2. Response patterns in frequency of selected common bird species (graphs a–g), arranged to show progressively differing peak frequencies along the composite gradient of land-cover type, ordered from pasture, through suburbs of increasing vegetation cover, to native forests of increasing canopy extent and density. Frequency is the proportion of sites at which the species was recorded, from a plot 100 m × 30 m, surveyed for six visits of mainly 15–20 min (mostly three summer, three winter); numbers of sites in brackets below axes.

functional groups (Fig. 8.1, Fig. 8.2, Table 8.2). All but 3 of the 28 pairwise comparisons between land-cover types showed a strong difference in species composition ($P < 0.001$, Table 8.2). The exceptions (pairs which did not differ significantly) were: eucalypt forest tracts above 100 ha and eucalypt forest remnants 10–20 ha; eucalypt forest remnants 1–2 ha and those 4–10 ha; and eucalypt forest remnants 1–2 ha and treed (well-vegetated) suburbs.

Sites within suburbs (both bare and well vegetated) contained more exotic species and more seed-eaters than other forms of land cover (Fig. 8.1). These included the ubiquitous house sparrow and common starling (Fig. 8.2), and others (including rock dove, spotted turtle-dove and common mynah). Exotic species were around half of the low overall richness in bare suburbs, but in treed suburbs a similar number of species (1–2 per site) formed only a small proportion of the total avifauna. The relatively small number of native species which commonly occurred in bare suburbs included some which have recently increased in range and/or abundance (such as the willie wagtail and Australian magpie-lark). Catterall (2004) labelled the species which characterised bare suburbs as 'new arrivals'.

The native avifauna of treed suburbs was dominated by a range of different large-bodied species (Fig. 8.1), such as the rainbow lorikeet, pale-headed rosella and noisy miner (Fig. 8.2), and others such as grey butcherbird, scaly-breasted lorikeet, Australian magpie and laughing kookaburra (see also Sewell and Catterall, 1998; Catterall, 2004). This group of species was dubbed 'Aussi icons' by Catterall (2004), because they are widely known and admired by everyday Australians. A number of them feed, at least in part, on other vertebrates.

At the other end of the spectrum, both large areas of intact eucalypt forest and rainforest areas were characterised by a high diversity of small-bodied, foliage-feeding insectivores, especially those which feed in the canopy and mid-storey (Fig. 8.1). These include a number of honeyeaters (Meliphagidae), parda-lotes, thornbills and allies (Pardalotidae), flycatchers (Dicruridae), whistlers (Pachycephalidae), robins (Petroicidae) and fairy-wrens (Maluridae). Eucalypt forest and rainforest had similar numbers of species per site within this functional group, although there was considerable turnover between the two habitats in species identity. For example, the brown gerygone and Lewin's honeyeater occurred mainly in rainforest, the white-throated and yellow-faced honeyeaters were confined to eucalypt forest, and the golden whistler and grey fantail occurred in both (Fig. 8.2). This species group was termed 'neglected foliphiles' by Catterall (2004), since their foliage-feeding habits, small body size and restriction to intact forest have rendered them virtually invisible to most human inhabitants of urban areas, even though many of these species are very common in remnant forest, and well known to bird observers.

Dominance of urban avifaunas by a few, widespread, species has been reported worldwide (Marzluff, 2001). This creates a global biotic homogenisation of urban areas with respect to bird species composition (Blair, 2001; Crooks et al., 2004). However, in the study region this phenomenon was restricted to bare suburbs. In contrast, treed suburbs supported many native species. Also, the occurrence of these birds was not clearly related to whether the suburban vegetation mainly consisted of native plants (see also Catterall et al., 1989;

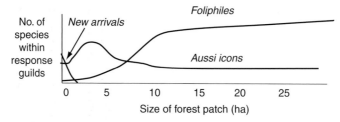

Fig. 8.3. Suggested relationship between the number of species in three simplified response guilds (new arrivals, 'Aussi icons' and foliphiles; see text for explanation; generalist species are ignored) and size of forest fragment, for eucalypt forests in urbanising areas of subtropical eastern Australia.

Parsons *et al.*, 2004); the provision of suitable resources by plant species appears to be of more direct importance than their geographical origin.

Sewell and Catterall (1998) identified four sources of species for assembling urban bird communities in the study region: (1) species which were common prior to any urbanisation and which continue to use only the remaining fragments of the original habitat; (2) species formerly rare or absent for which the urban habitats are suitable (e.g. built areas, grassland or widely spaced trees), including passive colonists imported by humans, active colonists from suitable habitat in nearby regions, or local expanders which formerly occurred only in suitably open patches scattered within the original forested habitat; (3) species which previously used elements of the original habitat (e.g. scattered fleshy-fruited or nectar-bearing trees) in a manner that can also be applied to the urban habitats; and (4) species formerly present which can use urban areas because they have changed their behaviour as a result of learning.

Within the suburban matrix, habitat structure and resource availability must be important determinants of which species use different forms of suburban development. There is some indication that patch size of suburban land-cover types also plays a role. When surveys were conducted within areas where there was 20 ha or more of relatively uniform land cover (either bare or treed suburb) there were clear differences in the avifauna (Figs. 8.1 and 8.2, Table 8.2). However, when sites within the suburban habitat were selected on the basis of habitat immediately around the 0.3-ha transect, there were negligible avifaunal differences between bare and treed areas (Catterall *et al.*, 1991; discussed by Sewell and Catterall, 1998).

For remnant patches of eucalypt forest, the smallest size category (1–2 ha) had a very similar avifauna to that of the treed suburbs, whereas the largest size (10–20 ha) had a very similar avifauna to the large eucalypt forest tracts (Figs. 8.1 and 8.2, Table 8.2). Remnants 4–10 ha in size were transitional. Thus, there appears to be a threshold size for eucalypt forest remnants of around 5–10 ha, at which their bird assemblages become very similar, especially in functional terms, to areas of intact forest (Fig. 8.3; see also Martin and Catterall, 2001; Piper and Catterall, 2003). Furthermore, there is a spatial scaling transition at around 1–2 ha, where the role of a very small forest patch in providing habitat for avifauna is very similar to the role of a liberal supply of scattered individual trees or shrubs, without the consolidated structure of intact forest. In practical terms, this means that creating or retaining very small (<2 ha) patches of eucalypt forest habitat is likely to have similar biodiversity outcomes to planting or retaining individual elements (trees and shrubs) within urban developments, gardens or landscaping projects. It also means that these biodiversity outcomes are different from those which would follow the retention or creation of larger forest patches. The latter will provide habitat for forest avifauna, whereas the former results in a distinctive, non-transitional assemblage of large-bodied, native species. This species mix also resembles that found at the edges of large forest patches in the study region (Catterall *et al.*, 1991, 1997a; Piper and Catterall, 2003).

An important factor contributing to the distinctive differences in the bird species composition of treed suburbs and very small remnants is their occupancy by a particular species, the noisy miner (Catterall *et al.*, 2002; Piper and Catterall, 2003; Catterall, 2004). The noisy miner is a native, large-bodied (63 g), foliage-feeding insectivore which establishes co-operatively breeding colonies. Their group territories are vigorously defended with a uniquely high level of interspecific aggression (Dow, 1977). Experimental removals have confirmed that the noisy miner is responsible for the exclusion of most smaller-bodied bird species, both in the study region (Catterall *et al.*, unpublished data) and elsewhere (Grey *et al.*, 1997, 1998). Across a similar range of sites to that described in this chapter, the abundance of noisy miners showed a strong negative correlation with the number of smaller-bodied birds, and a weaker positive correlation with the number of larger-bodied birds (Catterall, 2004). However, if sites with similar abundances of noisy miners are considered, larger forest patches still support more small-bodied species than small remnants and well-vegetated suburbs, indicating that other factors are also involved (Catterall, 2004).

The factors underlying changes in the bird assemblages of small forest remnants, at least in the greater Brisbane region, appear to be largely a consequence of behavioural processes (habitat selection and interspecific interactions) and resource availability rather than the more commonly cited (Marzluff, 2001) processes of small-population dynamics and top-down predator control. This can be suggested for several reasons. First, many of the small-bodied 'foliphile' species are non-breeding winter immigrants (Catterall *et al.*, 1997a, 1998). Second, behavioural exclusion by noisy miners is clearly important; the threshold remnant size of around 10 ha corresponds with the edge penetration distance of 100–200 m for the noisy miner, suggesting that the small remnants are essentially all 'edge' habitat (Piper and Catterall, 2003). Third, the observed sharp response threshold shared by many species would not be predicted by meta-population dynamics. Fourth, even the non-migratory small-bodied species do not appear to be poor dispersers, and many are considered to be locally nomadic (Catterall *et al.*, 1998). Other possible reasons were discussed by Catterall *et al.* (1997a). Furthermore, the 'foliphiles', although many undertake long-range movements, show finely tuned patterns of local habitat choice. For example, the proximity of a suburban area to remnant forest does not affect its use by these species (Catterall *et al.*, 1991).

I do not mean to suggest that no species show area-sensitivity at larger (>20 ha) patch sizes. Certain species (e.g. eastern yellow robin, white-throated treecreeper and weebill; Catterall *et al.*, 1997 and unpublished data) appear to require larger patches. Furthermore, breeding migrants and year-round residents in the study region show greater area-sensitivity than winter immigrants (Bentley and Catterall, 1997). Apart from exclusion by noisy miners, sensitivity to patch area in some of these species may also occur if a patch is too small for the home range of an individual or breeding group (as suggested by Hostetler, 2001), and for a few of them may involve small-patch population dynamics. Furthermore, we have insufficient information about changes that occur as remnant patches age. Many of the patches surveyed in the case study would be less than 20 years old. In future years, there may be habitat change (perhaps driven by altered fire regimes and/or vegetation recruitment patterns), and further increases in numbers of noisy miners (Catterall *et al.*, 2002). Such changes may alter the area threshold for change in avian assemblage in remnant forest. Within patches close to the current size threshold (5–20 ha), differences in shape, isolation and local habitat may be important, but have not been systematically investigated.

Additionally, population processes may be contributing to changes at broader spatio-temporal scales, since many of the larger-bodied 'Aussi icon' birds of the well-vegetated suburbs, edges and very small remnants are also nest predators, whose presence is associated with a higher predation rate at artificial nests (Piper and Catterall, 2004). This may result in a lowered total breeding output and hence a reduced pool of colonists, which could in turn affect population densities of residents and summer migrants across all remnant bushland areas. However, most species involved are multi-brooded, and not enough is known about the role of re-nesting and early survivorship to make reliable predictions.

The patterns and processes described here must occur widely along coastal eastern Australia. In Sydney (around 700 km to the south of the study region), the avian assemblages show similar patterns of variation in suburbs and forest remnants, similar effects of the noisy miner, and somewhat similar concerns about nest predation rates (Major *et al.*, 1996; Parsons and Major, 2004; Parsons *et al.*, 2004). The entire subtropical Australian coastal zone is becoming rapidly urbanised, and there is a risk that inappropriate development will lead to widespread declines in biodiversity.

Catterall *et al.* (2002) and Catterall (2004) made various management recommendations applicable to this region, including the following. Sustaining avian biodiversity within urban areas requires a diverse habitat mosaic (including sufficiently large areas of different types of native vegetation, and different types of suburban development – a focus on beta diversity). Garden plantings cannot be regarded as a substitute for conserving remnant bushland, but have a distinctive and new set of faunal values. Restored forest patches below 5 ha in area are unlikely to have different biodiversity value (at least for birds) from garden plantings. More public education is needed about the differing roles of the 'Aussi icon' and 'foliphile' species. There would be biodiversity benefits from removing the legislative protection which currently prevents humane culling of the noisy miner. More generally, they concluded that urban design projects need to be conducted at ecologically meaningful spatial scales, and there needs to be more focus on the proportion of the total land area which supports native forest.

Urbanisation and biodiversity: approaches, paradigms, and global syntheses

To obtain answers to the general question, 'What determines terrestrial biodiversity in urban areas?', it is first necessary to establish a framework within which similarities and differences in assemblage structure and causal processes can be assessed, across taxa and across regions. Until recently, studies of urban biodiversity were predominantly descriptive accounts of the biota within a region (Marzluff, 2001), rather than investigations aimed at elucidating factors which underlie the composition, distribution and abundance of the urban biota. Therefore, the study of urban biotas has often lacked a tradition of generalisation, or of building an understanding which could allow predictions of the consequences for biodiversity of different forms of urban design. More recently, there has been a rapidly growing body of quantitative research into spatial patterns of variation in terrestrial biotic assemblages, especially bird assemblages, and environmental parameters (e.g. Blair, 2001; Germaine and Wakeling, 2001; Bolger, 2001, 2002; Niemelä *et al.*, 2002; Hostetler and Knowles-Yanez, 2003; Patten and Bolger, 2003; Crooks, *et al.*, 2004; Hochuli *et al.*, 2004; Parsons *et al.*, 2004; Lim and Sodhi, 2004; this study). Continued growth in this research effort will soon offer opportunities for synthesis and meta-analysis, and hence for an improved global understanding.

However, the success of such syntheses will also depend on the nature and quality of the contributing research projects. Here I discuss four elements of importance to obtaining general insights into the ecology of urban biotas: (1) unifying theoretical approaches; (2) sound analytical designs; (3) comparable forms of response variable; and (4) the definition and selection of meaningful and comparable environmental factors. These approaches are interrelated, and addressing each on its own will be of limited value.

Unifying theoretical approaches

Theoretical paradigms provide a framework which stimulates structured tests of the effects of specific environmental factors on particular aspects of biodiversity. Similar tests that are conducted in different regions, or with different taxa, provide information on whether useful generalisations are possible. During the past two decades, two major ecological paradigms have been widely applied to urban ecosystems: habitat fragmentation and urban–rural gradients.

Theories of habitat fragmentation (e.g. Saunders *et al.*, 1991; Fahrig, 2003) have been applied to many different biomes, whether fragmented by humans or by other agents such as climate or topography (Watson, 2002). They typically view landscapes as binary mosaics in which patches of one type of environment are surrounded by a matrix of a second type. Most frequently, the focus is on the fate of native biota within scattered areas of remnant pre-European vegetation, which remain after much of the landscape has been cleared for human use. However, similar processes would apply to patches of restored habitat. A variety of different ecological processes have been hypothesised as factors which could cause change in species assemblages within such habitat fragments. Specific predictions vary and are still under debate (Harrison and Bruna, 1999; Bolger, 2002; Fahrig, 2003). However, many refer to the same environmental factors: size, shape, age, isolation and aggregated total area of the fragments, and the focus is on understanding or predicting the persistence of species which require only that habitat type. These species are expected to be more likely to persist or be colonisers in fragments which are larger, less linear, less isolated, set within well-vegetated landscapes, and younger (if remnant habitat) or older (if created or restored habitat). However, these factors may show complex interactions, and effects would also depend on a species' dispersal capabilities.

Habitat fragmentation theories can most readily be applied to urban ecosystems by focusing on fragments of native vegetation within the urban matrix, and testing for differences in species and assemblages between fragments of differing size, shape and so on. This approach was incorporated into the case study described here. However, there are serious limitations to its general usefulness in urban ecology. First, fragmentation theory is silent concerning species that might be winners or losers in terms of their ability to survive or thrive within the urban matrix, and on the nature of the ecological processes which might determine this. Hence, it neglects a large part of the urban ecosystem. Second, many applications of the theory falsely assume that the matrix is both inhospitable and non-interactive. Actually, where vegetation remnants are set within suburbs containing planted gardens or parkland, the matrix may variously improve or inhibit dispersal (owing to interactions with species present in the suburbs), contribute new species to the vegetation fragment (from those introduced to the suburbs), contribute to longer-term changes in the quality of the remnant vegetation (e.g. through predation or competition involving dominant plant species), and interact with the fragment to provide distinctive edge habitat.

In contrast, the urban–rural gradient approach (McDonnell and Pickett, 1990; McDonnell et al., 1993) is focused on all environmental attributes of urban ecosystems. Its basic premises are, first, a recognition that within all ecosystems there is measurable quantitative variation in these attributes (which could be abiotic such as temperature or soil nutrient levels, or biotic such as tree cover), which is correlated with measurable variation in biotic responses (such as species' frequencies and ecological processes). Second, these relationships can be scientifically investigated using the gradient analysis techniques pioneered by plant ecologists. Third, such analyses will suggest causal relationships, whose operation can be tested through further, more closely targeted measurements and manipulative experiments (McDonnell et al., 1997; Pickett et al., 1997b).

It was further suggested that spatial distance may often correspond with environmental difference, since cities often have a densely built urban core which is surrounded by concentric rings of diminishing landscape modification (McDonnell et al., 1993, 1997). At the outer extreme lie the 'rural' lands, which define the non-urban end of the gradient. However, there are several potential problems with this. First, owing to the selective placement of many cities along coastlines and at river mouths (Chapman and Underwood, Chapter 4), there are underlying gradients in environmental characteristics which are correlated (and hence confounded) with effects that are a consequence of distance from the urban core. Second, the non-urban spatial extreme can itself show a level of variation in environmental features which exceeds their variation along the urban–rural gradient, thereby greatly reducing its usefulness as a simple reference point. An example of this is the pasture and forest habitats which were both present as non-urban environments in the Brisbane region case study. Third, it may be an unnecessary oversimplification to use spatial distance as an indirect surrogate for environmental gradients. Many cities, especially in rapidly developing areas, show spatial mosaics rather than gradients, with urban patches abutting large areas of native vegetation, along abrupt edges (Blair, 2001; Bolger et al., 2001; this study). Using surrogate spatial gradients assumes that all environmental factors vary in the same way with distance and may prevent discrimination among alternative combinations (Alberti et al., 2001). This can limit the opportunity to develop and experimentally test ideas concerning causal mechanisms, and also limit suggestions for novel urban designs that promote synergies between biodiversity and urbanisation.

As reviewed in the previous section, many authors of recent papers on the responses of faunal assemblages to urbanisation have described their work as studying an urban gradient. Interpretations of the meaning of the gradient have included: (1) sites within remnant vegetation patches located at varying distances from an urban centre (e.g. McDonnell et al., 1993, 1997; Niemelä, 1999b; Niemelä et al., 2002); (2) interior sites within very large remnant vegetation patches, through forest edges to smaller patches of diminishing size (e.g. Patten and Bolger, 2003); (3) sites within suburban areas, through small remnants, to larger forest areas (Crooks et al., 2004); (4) sites whose land cover varies from highly built and poorly vegetated, through residential areas with gardens, recreational areas, to remnant native vegetation (e.g. Blair and Launer, 1997; Blair, 2001); (5) sites within urban areas (excluding remnant forest) that varied in the amount of built structure (Lim and Sodhi, 2004); and (6) sites that were spatially distributed with no clear rationale for their locations (Reynaud and Thiolouse, 2000; Germaine and Wakeling, 2001; Melles et al., 2003). In some cases, authors seem to have regarded studying variation along the urban gradient as an end in itself rather than as the means towards an end of understanding causal relationships. Wide application of such an approach will make comparisons across studies very difficult.

In the Brisbane region case study, there were elements of two gradients: the range of forest patch sizes (1–2 ha through to >100 ha), and the range of local tree canopy cover (from bare suburbs, through treed suburbs to eucalypt forest to rainforest). Both the fragmentation and urban–rural gradient paradigms have stimulated problem-centred scientific research within urban ecosystems, and hence both represent a significant advance over simple descriptions of the biota of urban areas. Clearly, both are useful in stimulating and guiding research into different processes which govern biodiversity in urban ecosystems. However, neither directly provides a predictive tool for urban planning, and there is a risk of perverse outcomes if they are simplistically applied without verification of the underlying causal processes (see also Bolger, 2001, 2002). Research stimulated by these theoretical approaches may ultimately lead to new and different forms of theory or generalisation concerning the ecology of urban areas.

Sound analytical designs

More research effort is needed to reveal the nature of the dominant ecological processes in urban areas. However, to provide useful information, these studies need to be set in a context of rigorous empirical experimental design (McDonnell *et al.*, 1997; Bolger, 2001; Bowman and Marzluff, 2001; Marzluff *et al.*, 2001). Such designs need the capacity to reveal both region-specific patterns and the processes which underlie them. Testing of hypotheses, derived either from theory or from logical reasoning and observation, is an important component of reaching a mechanistic understanding of how urban ecosystems function. Urban areas offer considerable opportunities for mensurative experiments (sensu Eberhardt and Thomas, 1991) which make careful use of the serendipitous occurrence of different patches of a particular type of urban development as the experimental treatments (Pickett *et al.*, 1997b; Marzluff *et al.*, 2001).

This was the approach adopted in the Brisbane region case study. It allows predictions of the outcome of land-use change on local biotas, through the substitution of space for time (e.g. Pickett, 1989). For example, bird species whose abundance is higher in cleared and developed areas than in bushland are frequently also those whose abundance has increased over time following intensifying land use (Catterall *et al.*, 1998). The approach resembles that advocated by Miller *et al.* (2001), except for their differing endpoint of predictive spatial modelling compared with developing a predictive understanding of process (this study). The application of such an approach across a diverse range of taxa was discussed by Catterall *et al.* (2004).

There are several aspects to rigorous empirical design in the study of the responses of biotic assemblages to environmental factors (Eberhardt and Thomas, 1991; Quinn and Keough, 2002; Catterall *et al.*, 2004). It is essential to formulate clear research questions or hypotheses. There must also be clear and appropriate choice of both response (dependent) variables and explanatory (independent; environmental) variables. Environmental variables could be either continuous in nature (as is the case in the simplest interpretation of the urban–rural gradient approach) or discontinuous, in the form of discrete treatments. The former may be either graded levels of a continuous variable or of a set of multiple co-varying factors; the latter are different environments for which intermediate states are rare. There needs to be sufficient replication, to allow the detection of statistically significant effects, to allow valid generalisation, and to allow reliable conclusions to be drawn in cases where there appears to be no effect. Confounding factors (environmental variables which are correlated with a hypothesised explanatory variable, and which would hence complicate the interpretation of apparent relationships) need to be avoided. When this is not possible, they need to be identified and considered. Related to this issue is the need for independence of replicates, which often means sufficient spatial separation. Finally, appropriate measurement regimes are needed for both response and explanatory variables.

A single well-designed study, however, cannot address more than a few aspects of the effects of human settlement within a region (Miller *et al.*, 2001). To gain a useful understanding of the operation of processes which underlie patterns of urban biodiversity will also require serial research projects which, according to the usual pattern of scientific investigation, begin with one set of questions, which may be general and open-ended, and then proceed to more specific questions and tests, as ideas concerning structure and process develop (and others are rejected). This requires a progressive series of studies, typically beginning with the documentation of pattern, and ultimately leading to experimental manipulations, which provide the most conclusive tests of process (McDonnell *et al.*, 1997; Bolger, 2001; Bowman and Marzluff, 2001).

In the case study, progress towards understanding the effects of urbanisation on the regional and local avifauna involved such a series of projects: identification of major forms of land-cover change (e.g. Catterall *et al.*, 1991; Catterall *et al.*, 1997b; Sewell and Catterall, 1998); analytical assessments of the nature of variation in bird assemblages corresponding with these changes (e.g. Bentley and Catterall, 1997; Catterall *et al.*, 1998; Sewell and Catterall, 1998; Martin and Catterall, 2001); formulation of hypotheses concerning mechanisms (e.g. Catterall *et al.*, 1997a); and tests of these hypotheses with either refined and targeted observational comparisons (e.g. Piper and Catterall, 2003) or with field experiments (Catterall *et al.*, unpublished). Understanding the patterns and processes has led to practical suggestions for management (Catterall *et al.*, 2003; Catterall, 2004).

Such a sequence of studies may reveal causal processes that are either inconsistent with, or of a different nature to, those initially hypothesised. For example, the discovery that noisy miners are a major cause of reduced bird diversity in small forest fragments of the Brisbane region would not have been predicted using fragmentation theory (Piper and Catterall, 2003). Likewise, Patten and Bolger (2003), testing ideas developed from previous studies (e.g. Bolger, 2001, 2002; Crooks *et al.*, 2004 and references therein), found that declines in bird species in small coastal sage-scrub remnants in California could not be explained by the expected processes of nest predation. In New York, McDonnell *et al.* (1997) reviewed a series of studies to show that variation in nitrogen mineralisation with distance from the urban core occurred in the opposite direction to that originally predicted, and conducted experiments to reveal the reason for this. In all of these cases, there remained further uncertainties and knowledge gaps to be filled.

Many studies of terrestrial urban biodiversity have been based on designs which do not meet the criteria discussed above. More generally, a high level of scientific rigour has not always been required of research which addresses socially significant ecological issues relating to human impact, compared with that applied to research in basic ecology. In part, this may be associated with the historical rejection of areas of high human impact by ecologists as appropriate subjects for study. There is a need to reverse this perception, because the conclusions from research designs in environmental management issues are used to guide actions which may have significant long-term impacts on human society and the environment. If these conclusions are incorrect as a result of flawed research designs or interpretations, then the cost may also be significant (and much greater than the cost of drawing an incorrect conclusion from a study of, for instance, the evolution of reproductive behaviour). For example, if it was demonstrated that biodiversity had declined in small urban remnants of native vegetation, and an interpretation was then made that the causal process was a lack of immigration to offset stochastic small-population extinctions, then the provision of habitat corridor linkages between remnants could be an effective solution. However, if this interpretation was incorrect, and the declines were caused by habitat degradation or edge effects, then corridor construction would be an ineffective waste of resources (Harrison and Bruna, 1999) unless the corridors had other functions.

Thorough, region-specific, research is essential to inform local planning and management. However, it cannot provide global insights or generalisations. These require the integration of results from different places and taxa. This is only possible where there are some common elements in research design, and in the measurement of both environmental and biotic variables.

Comparable forms of response variable

A major obstacle to making cross-regional comparisons of species-level measurements is the lack of species in common between different regions and different continents. An exception to this is the small set of species which have emerged in literature reviews to be near-universally advantaged by intensive urban development (e.g. among birds, the house sparrow, rock dove and common starling, Blair, 2001; Marzluff, 2001).

To account for the large number of other species, the most common solution has been the use of broad community metrics such as species richness, total abundance and diversity indices. Marzluff's (2001) review found variable and inconsistent patterns in these metrics across urbanisation gradients. Their use involves the loss of significant ecological information. For example, in the Brisbane region case study, most forms of better vegetated land (including both treed suburbs and differently sized forest patches) shared a similar species richness, but their different forms varied greatly in species composition. Furthermore, the loss of species-specific functional information associated with these metrics inhibits the construction of mechanistic hypotheses and the scientific pursuit of processes which underlie the observed patterns.

The use of functional groups of species, if clearly based on ecological characteristics, can overcome this problem. In the case study, measured species richness within functional groupings based on feeding ecology, body size and geographical origin showed clear and differing responses to environmental changes associated with different forms of urbanisation. Marzluff's (2001) review also found more worldwide consistencies when birds' responses were compared at functional group level (e.g. exotic species, predators and parasites, ground nesters, cavity nesters). Other possible bases for grouping include movement patterns and geographical range size. Such classifications are increasingly being used (e.g. Reynaud and Thiolouse, 2000; Melles *et al.*, 2003; Lim and Sodhi, 2004). They are increasingly becoming possible for birds worldwide, as compendia of continental avifaunas, which include information on species' life styles, are becoming available. They provide a common measurement for species on different continents which are taxonomically and phylogenetically distant, but which fill very similar ecological roles as a result of convergent evolution. They also show promise for use in tropical regions, where a high ambient species richness, together with a large number of uncommon species, render it difficult to assess species-specific responses individually.

However, the effective use of functional groupings in cross-regional comparisons requires systems of functional classification that are both ecologically meaningful and applicable in a worldwide context. The most commonly used classification so far has been the dichotomy between 'non-native' and 'native'. However, this has perhaps the least predictive power, and verges on tautology; by showing that urban areas often contain more introduced species, we show that species which live and move successfully with humans do well in cities. The distinction between these two categories will become increasingly complex as more species expand their ranges in response to the availability of anthropogenically modified habitat. It could be more useful to understand what ecological properties enable a species to colonise and live in cities. Classifications based on diet and nesting biology have a clear ecological meaning, but the actual groupings have varied considerably among authors, and the criteria for group membership are rarely stated. For taxa other than birds, there is often insufficient information to allow functional classification of species.

For all taxa, it would also be useful to develop the 'response-guild' concept in a manner which can be consistently applied across regions. Response guilds are empirically based classifications of individually analysed species according to their patterns of response to particular environmental change, such as deforestation or urbanisation (see for example Bentley and Catterall, 1997; Catterall *et al.*, 1998; Sewell and Catterall, 1998; Bolger, 2002; Crooks *et al.*, 2004; Parsons *et al.*, 2004). Terms used for response guilds have included 'forest indicators', 'generalists', 'area-sensitive', 'forest-interior', 'urbanisation-sensitive', 'developed land' and 'urban' species. The criteria for classification and the type of information used as its basis have varied widely, making this another area where comparable classifications would be useful. However, if species can be categorised into both response guilds and functional groups, then the relationship between the two can be assessed using analyses based on cross-tabulation. This approach makes it possible to compare species-level responses across regions, even if there are no species in common.

An alternative approach to the species problem may be through multivariate classification and ordination. During the past decade, there has been a rapid development of computer-based multivariate techniques for efficiently processing large data sets with many species, including methods suited to ecological survey data (e.g. Clarke, 1993; Quinn and Keogh, 2002). These have allowed a greater focus on species composition and its relationships with a wide range of environmental variables (e.g. Reynaud and Thiolouse, 2000; Blair, 2001; Germaine and Wakeling, 2001; Martin and Catterall, 2001; Melles *et al.*, 2003; Lim and Sodhi, 2004; Parsons *et al.*, 2004). Such analyses aim to derive simpler patterns from complex data. But there are many technical issues which may affect their success and interpretation (Quinn and Keogh, 2002). There is also a risk that multivariate ordination will supplant the provision of tabulated summaries of individual species' responses, which are useful in comparative reviews. However, if set in the context of a clear design, these multivariate techniques offer a potential for developing matrices of the relative biotic distance (based on species composition) of environmentally modified sites from reference sites which have been chosen to set the extremes on an urban gradient. Such distance measurements might then be used in cross-regional comparisons.

Definition and selection of meaningful and comparable environmental factors

For effective global comparison, sites also need to have comparable explanatory (environmental) variation in different regions. This is the most difficult current challenge facing comparative research in urban biodiversity. It requires both an explicit recognition and a quantitative description of the environmental differences between experimental treatments, or of the environmental properties of a gradient under study. Furthermore, the measurements need to have ecological meaning.

Marzluff *et al.* (2001) concluded that the lack of environmental measurements was a major deficit in 41% of 101 reviewed studies of the effects of urbanisation on birds. However, many more recent studies of urban biodiversity (e.g. those cited above) have measured a variety of aspects of environmental variation at spatial scales from local (e.g. within-site percentage cover of built structures, trees and grass, at a scale of squared metres) to landscape (e.g. habitat patch size, shape indices, and percentage cover of total and native vegetation, built structures and water, within a radius of hundreds of metres or more). Within the past decade, the increased availability of remotely sensed data and GIS-based metrics have made landscape-scale measurements widely feasible (e.g. Alberti *et al.*, 2001). However, their availability now far exceeds our ability to relate them meaningfully to ecological processes (Miller *et al.*, 2001).

An important feature of urban ecosystems is the hierarchical multi-scale spatial heterogeneity of urban environments (for comprehensive discussions see Alberti *et al.*, 2001; Hostetler, 2001; Miller *et al.*, 2001). One consequence of this is that analyses relating measurements of biota to measurements of environment will be affected by both the spatial scale selected for measurement of the biota (e.g. a 0.1-ha area compared with a 50-ha area) and that selected for measurement of the environment. A species may be sensitive to the presence of a habitat area at a scale which differs from that selected for measurement. For example, if the presence of a 1-ha vegetation patch provides habitat for a species which would otherwise be absent from a built-up area, but the biotic measurements are made over 5 ha (not uncommon in bird census projects), and the land cover is mapped at a scale of 1:100 000 (unlikely to detect habitat patches <10 ha), then no level of numerical or statistical sophistication will be of use in elucidating the processes important to that component of biodiversity. If, in contrast, a species responds to habitat patches only above 10 ha, this could be difficult to detect if measured landscape habitat cover is aggregated over patches above 1 ha. If area-sensitive species are to be assessed by using relatively small sampling units (as in many bird transects), it is important to control the size of the patch of uniform land cover around a sampling site. While area-sensitivity is often considered in relation to forest-dependent species within remnant patches, it would also apply to species from other response guilds. For example, a 'suburban' species may show positive responses to the presence of built structures over several hectares, but be unaffected by a small cluster of houses.

The complexity is increased when surveys of biotic assemblages are conducted across points which vary in terms of many different environmental parameters.

Even multivariate ordination techniques are unlikely to be able to produce clear indications of underlying ecological processes when confronted with the joint complexities of spatial scale/heterogeneity issues and multiple (and potentially interacting) underlying environmental gradients. There is a simple solution to this problem: careful and controlled design and site choice (see above). We need to choose site types to address clear questions and hypotheses. The selection of a limited number of potentially meaningful aspects of environmental variation, control over the remainder, and careful placement of sites within areas of uniform habitat whose minimum size has been carefully considered are all important (see also Miller *et al.*, 2001; Hostetler, 2001).

The outcome also depends on the criteria used for the categories of habitat mapped. It will be extremely difficult to compare the findings of studies in different regions if there is no means of calibrating the magnitude and scale of environmental variation between studies. Ecologically meaningful attributes need to be measured, in a broadly similar manner, across different studies. Local, site-specific measurements of features, such as percentage cover of grass, tree canopy and built structures, are often broadly comparable across studies in different regions. These are measures of, or surrogates for, factors known from autecological studies to be important to individuals and populations of many terrestrial vertebrates. However, the treatment of landscape-scale attributes has been more variable. Measurements have included housing density and the proportion of area within a given radius covered by: buildings, different botanical associations of remnant vegetation, parks and managed green open spaces. A particular problem is the use of culture-specific terms such as 'park' and 'greenspace' which lack objective definitions in terms of the features important to biota. For example, in different places, either of these terms could mean an area of conserved remnant native vegetation, or a grassy mown area with or without scattered trees, even a grassed football field.

It would be useful to develop a global typology of urban land cover, which both recognises major formations which occur worldwide, and provides a quantitative description of decision criteria for these, so that any particular area can be consistently classified by different observers. A typology would deal with the large amount of covariation which occurs in environmental variables in urban areas, and with their spatial patchiness. A successful global typology would need to be operationally useful, provide repeatable measurement values, be not too complex, be relevant to both developed and developing countries, and be referenced to particular spatial scales. It also would need to be anchored in environmental factors which are functionally relevant to living organisms. The criteria of repeatability, global relevance and functional relevance also apply to quantitative measurements of environmental variables along urban gradients.

These considerations rule out a number of commonly used or advocated measures. First, land zoning schemes used by planners are neither globally consistent nor do they capture the critical environmental features that are of functional significance to biota. Second, while surrogate measures such as spatial distance from urban cores, and age of suburb, have region-specific predictive power, they are likely to vary from one region to another in their relationship with the functionally relevant features which they represent. Hence similar values of these surrogates will have different biological meanings in different regions. Measurements of human density share some of the weaknesses of both.

Biologically useful measurements would need to directly incorporate aspects of the land cover contributed by built structures, and by different forms of vegetation. These factors are both important to living organisms in their own right (as places to live, in providing food resources, etc.), and also correlated with other biotically significant factors (e.g. predation risk). Other factors, such as chemical inputs (nutrients, pollutants) and hydrology are also important, but may be more difficult to incorporate. This does not imply that other correlates, such as human density, should not be considered. However, they should not be expected to substitute for the more relevant measurements when comparisons are made across regions or countries with differing culturally determined land-use patterns.

Alberti *et al.* (2001) analysed remotely sensed land-cover measurements in the Seattle region, and obtained six categories of land cover: paved urban, grass/shrub urban, forested urban, grass/shrub/crops, deciduous forest and coniferous forest. It is encouraging that these show a high level of consistency with the types of category used in the Brisbane region case study (in which bare suburbs and treed suburbs correspond with grass/shrub urban and forested urban), which were based on subjective judgment informed by local knowledge, ecological concepts and ground-based visual assessments. Seattle and Brisbane have many socio-economic similarities, which may limit the global applicability of these categories.

Concluding remarks

I have argued that existing ecological principles and methods can be applied to provide understanding of the ecological processes that control changes in biodiversity within the urban biome, in a manner comparable with studies of more 'natural' biomes. Already, a picture is emerging of some of the higher-level ecological characteristics of terrestrial biotic assemblages in urban ecosystems: substantial multi-scale patchiness and beta-diversity; global biotic homogenisation within some urban patch types; non-equilibrial population and community dynamics; an important role for behavioural processes (e.g. dispersal, habitat selection, interspecific aggression); and a special role for relict vegetation patches spared from clearing. There may be unexpected parallels with other ecosystems. For example, in the tropical savannas of northern Australia, there are many scattered small patches of rainforest, considered relicts from an ancient, moister climatic regime. These make an important contribution to regional biodiversity and interact with the surrounding savanna matrix, and their persistence over thousands of years has been dependent on careful management decisions by Aboriginal people (through controlled burning; Bowman, 2000). Future ecological research in urban ecosystems may reveal whether there are shared principles. However, the scientific study of urban ecosystems still faces many challenges. I hope that the comments offered here will contribute to overcoming them.

Acknowledgements

I thank Sven Sewell, Kate Park, Mark Kingston, Anne Oertel, Scott Piper, Joss Bentley, Ronda Green, Darryl Jones, Terry Reis and John Kanowski for their various roles in generating the data sets analysed here. Particular thanks to Scott Piper for help with the data analyses presented here. Discussions with these people, and many others, have contributed to the development of themes and arguments pursued in this chapter. Many other people contributed in various ways to the projects whose data were incorporated. I am grateful to Mark McDonnell, Kirsten Parris and Jari Niemelä for stimulating the production of this chapter, and the conference presentation on which it was based.

9

Effect of urban structures on diversity of marine species

M. G. CHAPMAN, DAVID BLOCKLEY, JULIE PEOPLE
AND BRIANNA CLYNICK

Introduction

As discussed by Chapman and Underwood (Chapter 4), urbanisation is expanding rapidly in estuaries and along the coastlines in all continents across the world. This has led to extremely altered coastal environments, with extensive loss, fragmentation and replacement of natural habitats by built structures (e.g. Mann, 1988; Walker, 1988; Glasby and Connell, 1999). Intertidal habitats, which form the interface between the land and the sea, are most strongly affected by urbanisation, because they are frequently disturbed by commercial and recreational activities (e.g. Iannuzzi et al., 1996), or extremely altered by the desire for 'waterfront' developments and the need to access the water from the land for transport and travel (e.g. Yapp, 1986).

Intertidal mangroves (Young and Harvey, 1996) and saltmarshes (Zedler, 1988) have received most attention with respect to urban development because their loss is immediately obvious and because they can provide habitat for rare or endangered plants or charismatic vertebrates (Zedler, 1993). Intertidal and freshwater wetlands suffered particularly severe loss and fragmentation over many years because they were considered wastelands and, thus, 'reclaimed' for urban development. Fortunately, in some parts of the world, this process is being reversed by active programmes of mitigation and restoration (Zedler et al., 1998).

Similarly, changes to subtidal seagrass meadows have received attention because of their perceived value as nursery grounds for commercially important

Ecology of Cities and Towns: A Comparative Approach, ed. Mark J. McDonnell, Amy K. Hahs and Jürgen H. Breuste. Published by Cambridge University Press. © Cambridge University Press 2009.

fish and crustaceans (Robertson and Duke, 1987; Haywood *et al.*, 1995). In many urbanised estuaries, seagrasses have declined because of overgrowth by algae (Short and Burdick, 1996). This is generally attributed to nutrient enrichment of coastal waters by urbanisation (Hauxwell *et al.*, 2003), although changes to assemblages of fish by fishing may also play a role in controlling algal growth on seagrass (Heck *et al.*, 2000). But apart from mangrove, seagrass and saltmarsh assemblages, there has been very little study of the effects of urban development and associated activities on intertidal habitats, such as beaches, mudflats, boulder fields and rocky shores. Yet, along many developed coastlines, these are common habitats and among those that may be most likely to be affected by urbanisation.

The extensive change to intertidal habitats adjacent to cities is not immediately obvious because most intertidal areas are not simply destroyed and replaced by buildings. Nevertheless, shores in and near cities are frequently 'built over' by seawalls, especially in estuaries with docks, creating artificial intertidal and subtidal structures in the place of natural soft sediments or rocky reefs. In addition, a wide range of other structures are added to shorelines or nearshore waters, including piers, marinas, wharves, floating pontoons and structures for aquaculture. These may add hard surfaces to areas of waterways where hard substrata do not naturally occur, or may simply replace rocky reef with what superficially appears to be similar habitat (e.g. rocky/concrete walls).

In 1999, we mapped the foreshores of Sydney Harbour (New South Wales, Australia) from a boat, to get some idea of the amount of alteration they have sustained. At that time, maps of Sydney Harbour foreshores (which were provided by the then Department of Urban Planning, NSW State Government) stopped at the landward edge of the shore (Underwood and Chapman, 1999). Alteration to intertidal and subtidal areas was scarcely documented. Mapping showed that, in the most built-up areas of the harbour, replacement of natural habitats by urban structures was almost complete. For example, along an approximately 26-km stretch near the centre of Sydney, 96% of the shore was composed of walls, wharves, piers, etc. Even in more natural-looking areas of Middle Harbour, where only 11% of a 17-km stretch of shoreline had been replaced by built structures, 66 smaller structures – piers, private wharves, swimming pool walls, etc. – added to the shoreline (A. J. Underwood, unpublished data). This type of change is probably typical of most urbanised estuaries and no doubt the amount of change in many estuaries is severely underestimated.

The extent to which diversity of marine animals and plants will be conserved in developed coastal areas will depend on a number of factors which are discussed in more detail in Chapman and Underwood (Chapter 4). Although in urban waterways most attention has traditionally been focused on contamination and pollution (see Chapman and Underwood, Chapter 4), many marine animals and plants are quite resilient to reductions in water quality (e.g. Chapman *et al.*, 1995), or can recover from disturbance quickly (Archambault *et al.*, 2001). Similarly, dredged sediments can be quite quickly repopulated (Newell *et al.*, 1998; Roberts and Forrest, 1999), unless dredging removes large areas of vegetated sediment (Hatcher *et al.*, 1989), large sessile animals that provide biogenic habitat (Cranfield *et al.*, 2001) or natural reefs. The assemblage that develops in very disturbed sites may not, however, be the same as the original assemblage (Newell *et al.*, 1998). Urban harbours have been invaded by a large suite of exotic species (Carlton and Geller, 1993; Ruiz *et al.*, 1997), but with few notable exceptions (Ross *et al.*, 2002), many of these co-exist with and do not eliminate native species (Ruiz *et al.*, 1997). Although many marine species are exploited, overfishing is not necessarily extensive in nearshore waters near cities, although there may be much recreational fishing (Kingsford *et al.*, 1991). Finally, human-induced marine extinctions are rare and major changes in numbers of marine organisms are not generally attributed to urbanisation (discussed by Chapman and Underwood, in Chapter 4).

If marine organisms are going to persist in urbanised estuaries, they will need to be able to survive in fragmented and altered habitats. To a large extent, this may depend on the degree to which they are able to use altered and built structures as habitat. This chapter examines the suitability of various built structures (intertidal seawalls, etc.), which are continuously increasing in urbanised environments, as intertidal and subtidal habitat for marine animals and plants.

Intertidal seawalls

The most extensive intertidal habitat along the shores of coastal cities is seawalls. These may be composed of natural rock, or artificial substrata, such as concrete, wood or metal. They can be smooth or complex and vertical or sloping. Of course, if seawalls replace natural soft sediments (such as beach sand), they cannot offer appropriate habitat for the natural fauna and flora and will add new species to the local assemblage. If they replace natural rocky reef, their value as habitat will depend on how well they mimic natural shores (Glasby and Connell, 1999; Chapman and Bulleri, 2003). Despite variability in the ways they may be built, seawalls differ from natural shores in a number of ways.

First, seawalls are generally vertical, or very steeply sloping, whereas many rocky shores can be gently sloping (Fig. 9.1a). Many intertidal and subtidal organisms are strongly influenced by the slope of the substratum (Whorff *et al.*,

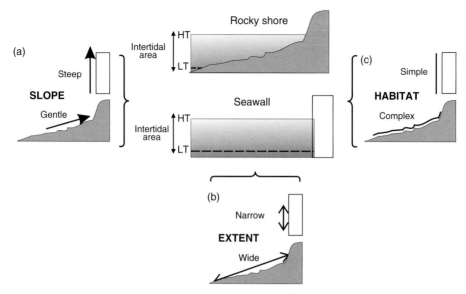

Fig. 9.1. Seawalls differ from natural rocky shores in many ways. First, they generally
have a steeper slope (a). Because of this, they tend to have a much smaller area
(b) and they tend to have more structurally simple surfaces, with fewer of the
microhabitats that may be needed by intertidal organisms (c).

1995; Gabriele *et al.*, 1999; Chapman, 2003). On subtidal reefs, sessile invertebrates tend to be more abundant and diverse on vertical surfaces (e.g. Wendt
et al., 1989; Glasby, 2000). Algae, in contrast, are usually more abundant on
horizontal surfaces (Goldberg and Foster, 2002).

On natural shores, the available intertidal area may be very extensive,
depending on the slope of the shore. Compared with more gently sloping surfaces, the intertidal zone is compressed on vertical walls, reflecting the extent of
the tidal range (Fig. 9.1b). This zone is especially narrow if piers and other urban
structures reduce wave-action. For example, intertidal habitat on many of the
rocky shores in Sydney Harbour can be tens of metres long (from the level of low
to high tide), whereas, on vertical walls, such habitat is compressed to only about
2 m (the tidal range in Sydney). The general positive relationship between the
size of a patch of habitat and the abundance and diversity of species living in it
(species–area curves; e.g. Hawkins and Hartnoll, 1980; McGuinness, 1984) indicates that the reduced available area of intertidal habitat on a seawall alone may
limit the number of species able to live on it. This compression of available space
may potentially bring into proximity species that normally live quite a distance
apart, possibly affecting predator–prey and competitive interactions. This is one
aspect of the ecology of seawalls that has, unfortunately, received little attention
to date.

Finally, on natural intertidal shores, diversity increases with the range and availability of different microhabitats, particularly those that retain moisture or are shaded during low tide (e.g. McGuinness and Underwood, 1986; Astles, 1993; Archambault and Bourget, 1996). Although seawalls may have shallow cracks between adjacent stones, microhabitats such as deep crevices and rockpools are absent from seawalls, therefore potentially diminishing important niches and, in turn, species diversity.

Despite differences in such important features of habitat between rockwalls and natural shores, a wide variety of marine animals and plants do recruit to and live successfully on seawalls and similar structures. These include micro- and macroscopic algae, sessile animals (particularly barnacles, tubeworms, oysters and mussels) and mobile animals, such as limpets, snails and crabs. Differences in the types of organisms found in the different habitats depend on a number of factors, particularly on whether the assemblages are inter- or subtidal.

Therefore, although Connell and Glasby (1999) found that subtidal assemblages in Sydney Harbour differed between natural rocky reefs and a variety of artificial structures, subtidal sandstone rock walls had similar assemblages to those on natural reefs. A similar pattern was found for lowshore intertidal areas of natural shore and seawalls (Chapman and Bulleri, 2003) – assemblages were similar between natural habitats and walls, although patterns varied considerably from one part of Sydney Harbour to another.

Higher on the shore, in contrast, there were differences in intertidal assemblages living on seawalls compared with steeply or gently sloping natural shores. Most species were, however, found in each of the habitats, although again, these patterns varied from one part of the harbour to the other. A species that in one place might be more abundant on seawalls than on shores could show the opposite pattern somewhere else. Variations in directional trends were generally due to differences in abundance or amount of cover from one habitat to the other. This contrasts with research from the Mediterranean, where intertidal assemblages on groynes and breakwaters were very depauperate, dominated primarily by mussels and ephemeral species of algae (Bacchiocchi and Airoldi, 2003).

Most documented studies that have compared assemblages on seawalls to those on natural reefs have measured cover and abundances of taxa in replicate quadrats in a number of sites on the different structures. Such intensity of sampling is necessary to provide precise measures of the numbers, biomass or coverage of the more common species, but may not adequately sample species with sparse distributions. The amount of sampling effort needed to find rare species – especially small, cryptic invertebrates and algae – is generally prohibitively large, in terms of time needed and cost. Nevertheless, these species may be the ones most susceptible to loss of habitat because their populations are naturally small. If they cannot survive in altered habitats, they may decrease below a sustainable level. Therefore, to evaluate whether species that are more sparse in distribution live on seawalls, a survey using 1600 quadrats was done in Sydney Harbour (Chapman, 2003). This survey examined 200 quadrats (over a distance of about 50 m) at each of two intertidal heights in each of four locations. To maximise the number of quadrats in the time available, taxa were recorded in each quadrat as present or absent, and frequencies of occurrence analysed.

Although patterns varied between tidal heights and for each location differently, when all data were combined, a clear pattern emerged. Summed over all quadrats, there were 16% more taxa (mostly identified as species, but with some indistinguishable mixes of species, such as green filamentous algae) on natural, gently sloping shores (126 taxa) than on the seawalls (109 taxa; Fig. 9.2a). In addition, as more area was sampled (more quadrats combined), the species accumulation curves diverged. The number of taxa on the seawall flattened off at a relatively small sample size, as is common for an assemblage where most species are common. Sampling larger areas of seawall did not add many more species to the assemblage than were found in much smaller areas of this habitat. On gently sloping shores, in contrast, the species accumulation curve continued to rise, albeit gently (Fig. 9.2a), indicating an assemblage with a greater proportion of rare taxa (Thompson and Withers, 2003). Further analysis indicated that this pattern was not due to differences in the algae or sessile invertebrates in each habitat, but to differences in mobile invertebrates. Approximately 50% of the mobile invertebrates found on gently sloping seashores were not found on vertical seawalls (Chapman, 2003). On seawalls, the dominant mobile animals were limited to chitons, limpets, gastropods, and some species of crabs (widely foraging species, such as *Pachygrapsus*). Natural rocky shores had a much greater variety of gastropods, whelks, starfish and crabs, but also had sea-urchins and octopuses, which were not found on seawalls.

This small diversity on seawalls may be due to the fact that seawalls are homogeneous structures, without important features within this habitat, such as deep crevices (although there may be small crevices between adjacent blocks of stone). In addition, natural intertidal shores in Sydney Harbour tend to extend into subtidal reef, therefore potentially providing 'corridors' for movement of organisms from subtidal and intertidal regions, although we do not know how much movement there really is. Seawalls are generally bordered by muddy or sandy sediments, which do not support the same sorts of taxa as hard surfaces. These soft sediments may be a barrier to subtidal–intertidal exchange of mobile fauna. Alternatively, many mobile animals may not live on vertical walls because they do not have the tenacity to 'hang' onto a vertical surface in rough water.

(a)

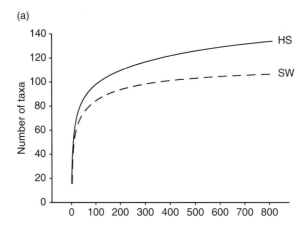

(b)

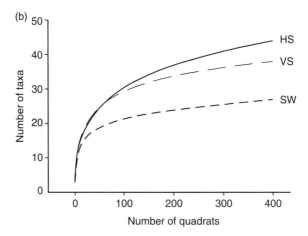

Fig. 9.2. Species accumulation curves for (a) all taxa (algae, sessile and mobile invertebrates) measured in 1600 quadrats in four locations (from Chapman, 2003); (b) mobile species measured from 1200 taxa. HS – 'horizontal' (very gently sloping) shores; VS – 'vertical' (very steeply sloping shores), SW – seawalls.

Some of these questions were explored by identifying and comparing the types of mobile animals found on gently sloping natural shores, with those on steep or vertical natural shores or on seawalls in a second survey based on 1200 replicate quadrats. It was clear that both slope and some other feature of seawalls affected diversity of mobile intertidal animals. There were fewer species on vertical shores and on seawalls than on gently sloping shores, but natural vertical shores supported more species than did walls (Fig. 9.2b). The additional species found in gently sloping or vertical, but natural, shores consisted of a broader range of taxa (e.g. gastropods, anemones, sea-urchins, chitons) than were generally found on seawalls. These data suggest that, although the steep slope of a seawall may directly reduce the number of species living there, differences in habitat quality and not just quantity may account for the greater number of mobile intertidal animals living in natural intertidal areas.

There is also the question of the relative age of seawalls compared with natural shores because older patches of habitat can accumulate species over longer periods of time. Although not as old as natural shores, many of the seawalls in Sydney have been around for decades. Many intertidal species colonise empty patches of habitat readily and rapidly increase in abundance or spread in area. Age of seawalls is therefore unlikely to be a major cause for differences in their assemblages.

Seawalls also, over time, weather and degrade, increasing the habitat complexity and heterogeneity of their surfaces. The rate and degree to which this occurs depends on their construction and environmental conditions. Weathering can result in pits and cracks in the surface, the formation of crevices between adjacent blocks or even greater changes, such as the appearance of large holes or the collapse of entire sections. This creates new habitats in the seawall, which can remain shaded and moist during low tide, or may provide shelter from wave action. These complex additional habitats appear to increase the diversity of animals living on walls: a number of taxa found during low tide in these structures are not found, or are less common, on the faces of the walls (M.G. Chapman, unpublished data).

There is also evidence that changes to urbanised estuaries provide opportunities for exotic and invasive species to establish a foothold. Disturbed habitats may be more susceptible to invasions and, because many estuarine invaders are fouling species (Ruiz et al., 1997), building and/or repairing urban structures may increase greatly the amount of habitat in which they thrive (Floerl and Inglis, 2003). The problem may be exacerbated in urban estuaries because, in addition to supplying a wide range of potentially new habitats, these are the most likely point of entry for exotic species (Ruiz et al., 1997). Nevertheless, there has, to date, been no quantitative and systematic survey on the use of seawalls by exotic species in comparison to their use of natural rocky shores. This should be examined experimentally because generally seawalls are more prolific in parts of harbours that have many additional disturbances, making cause and effect difficult to unconfound.

Finally, the habitats provided by seawalls are potentially affected by other built structures nearby. Thus, the organisms found on seawalls may be altered by nearby marinas changing water flow (Floerl and Inglis, 2003), or by wharves permanently shadowing the walls, changing light regimes and thus altering the assemblage of organisms living on them through bottom-up food-web linkages (Blockley, 2007; Table 9.1). Similarly, walls have the potential to alter flow of

Table 9.1. *Mean percentage cover of the most important components of the sessile assemblage on sections of intertidal seawall in Sydney Harbour.*

	Shaded	Not shaded
Turfing red alga (*Corallina officinalis*)	0.3 (0.3)	**12.9** (4.0)
Ephemeral green algae	0.3 (0.3)	**18.8** (7.5)
Encrusting brown alga (*Ralfsia verrucosa*)	0.5 (0.4)	**16.8** (3.8)
Calcareous tubeworm (*Galeolaria caespitosa*)	0.3 (0.3)	**54.2** (10.1)
Orange sponge (unidentified)	**39.3** (8.5)	0.2 (0.1)
Oyster (*Saccostrea commercialis*)	**32.3** (9.1)	3.4 (1.4)
Mussel *(Mytilus galloprovincialis)*	5.8 (1.7)	0.0 (0.0)

Note:

The areas shaded by a wharf are dominated by oysters and sponges, whereas the unshaded areas are dominated by a calcareous tubeworm and encrusting and turfing seaweeds. Parentheses give standard error, $n = 6$ units.

water or other physical variables, which can alter amount and textural properties of adjacent soft sediments and hence their value as habitat. As in all urban developments, the impacts of urban structures cannot be considered individually, but must be considered within the altered landscape of a city.

Assemblages living on other important urban structures

In addition to seawalls, other types of artificial structures, such as pilings and floating pontoons that are used for the docking and mooring of boats, provide habitat for benthic organisms, including sponges, ascidians, barnacles, crabs and algae. The assemblages inhabiting pilings and pontoons were described many years ago (e.g. Coe, 1932; Karlson, 1978; Caine, 1987), yet these assemblages have only recently been compared with those on natural structures and with other types of artificial structures (e.g. Kay and Keough, 1981; Glasby, 1999a; Connell and Glasby, 1999; Connell, 2000, 2001a; Glasby and Connell, 2001; Holloway and Connell, 2002).

Of the research comparing intertidal and/or subtidal assemblages living on different types of structures, the majority dealt only with the organisms that live directly on the substratum. Generally, researchers have found each type of structure, whether artificial or natural, is inhabited by a different assemblage of organisms. For example, in Sydney, Australia, subtidal assemblages on sandstone natural reefs, sandstone seawalls, fibreglass pontoons, concrete pontoons, concrete pilings and wooden pilings were compared (Connell and Glasby, 1999). Assemblages on seawalls were similar to those on rocky reefs, but differed from those on pilings and pontoons. Those on fibreglass pontoons differed from those on concrete pontoons, concrete pilings and wooden pilings, which were similar to each other. Therefore, differences were complex and could not be simply related to the composition or type of structure.

Other studies have also found that assemblages inhabiting pontoons differ most from those living on many other structures (Glasby, 1999a; Connell, 2001a; Glasby and Connell, 2001). This was due to both the types of taxa present and the amount of space they occupied. For example, coralline algae were more commonly found on natural reefs and seawalls than on pilings or pontoons (Connell and Glasby, 1999), while mussels were very abundant on pontoons, but not on pilings or natural reefs (Connell, 2001a).

Different types of artificial structures vary in a number of ways, all of which are known to affect the abundances and distribution of organisms in natural habitats. For example, the substratum that provides habitat depends on the materials from which a structure is composed, such as natural rock, wood, concrete, fibreglass or plastic. These may also vary in colour, roughness, surface complexity or slope. Age of the structure can also differ; natural structures are generally older than artificial structures and, therefore, they have been available for colonisation for a greater period of time. Nevertheless, as discussed earlier for seawalls, some artificial structures have been around for decades and possibly have the full complement of species that can recruit to and survive on them. Floating pontoons are not attached to the seafloor as are all other types of structures, and therefore rise and fall with the tide. Hence the undersurface and lower part of pontoon sides are always subtidal and the upper part of the sides only wetted by splash and waves. In contrast, nearly all fixed structures, such as seawalls and pilings, provide intertidal and often subtidal habitats, but no area that is continually subjected to swash.

In addition, many features of or conditions in a particular type of natural habitat co-vary as they do for urban structures. So it is not intrinsically obvious which feature(s) are primarily responsible for affecting the developing assemblages. For example, differences in assemblages between pilings and rocky reefs may develop because pilings are usually shaded by wharves and pontoons, while rocky reefs generally are not. Alternatively, organisms on a piling may be near or away from the seafloor, depending on the depth of the water. Organisms on rocky reefs are always near the seafloor, because that is where reefs are found. Therefore, potential predators on the seafloor may more easily find species on a reef than those on a piling. Because several factors that differ among different types of structures may co-vary, field experiments are the only way to separate the effects of such confounding variables, in order to identify the feature(s) of habitat to which the animals are responding.

Hence, Glasby (1999b) used a field experiment to test whether proximity to the seafloor and/or shading caused differences between subtidal sessile assemblages on pilings and natural reefs. Settlement plates were deployed in two positions, close to (deeper in the water) and further from the seafloor (towards the surface of the water). Some plates were shaded with black Perspex roofs, while others were left unshaded. Because artefacts, such as disturbance to water currents, may have been associated with the black roofs, a procedural control of plates with clear roofs was also included. After 12 weeks, there was no artefact associated with the roofs. Assemblages differed between the two depths and according to whether they were shaded or not. For example, spirorbid polychaete worms were more abundant on shaded than on unshaded plates close to the seafloor and were generally more abundant in deeper water.

Sponges also covered larger areas of shaded than unshaded plates, possibly because of larval choice, or enhanced survival in shaded habitats. After 33 weeks, there were still no artefacts associated with the roofs, and shallow and deep assemblages still differed. Now, however, shading only affected deep assemblages. Spirorbids showed no effect of shading, but were more common in deeper water. Shading also no longer affected sponges, but they now occupied more space on shallower plates. Manipulative experiments were therefore able to separate the effects of proximity to the seafloor and shading to show that both factors influenced assemblages and that the effect of shading differed according to proximity to the seafloor. For some taxa, shading alone was sufficient to explain their patterns of abundance between shaded pilings and natural reefs. For others, it was not, and additional (as yet unknown) processes must be operating.

Similarly, a manipulative experiment was used by Holloway and Connell (2002) to separate factors that may affect subtidal assemblages on pontoons and pilings. Pontoons float and thus are not in contact with the seafloor so organisms inhabiting them are constantly exposed to swash. Pilings are fixed into the ground and exposed to swash only for short periods. Pontoons and pilings are also different shapes, sizes and composed of different materials. Six different types of artificial structures were constructed to try to unravel this complexity: (1) floating plastic 'pontoons' (flat vertical sides) exposed to swash; (2) floating wooden pilings (circular, like natural pilings), constantly exposed to wash; (3) fixed pontoons that were not attached to the seafloor, but were only exposed to swash periodically; (4) fixed pilings that were similarly deployed; (5) submerged floating pontoons that were not attached to the seafloor and were exposed to little amounts of swash; and (6) fixed pilings that were attached to the seafloor. Combinations of comparisons among treatments could separate out effects of particular factors. For example, comparisons of treatments 1 and 2 or of 3 and 4 test for differences in assemblages between pilings and pontoons, although they cannot distinguish effects due to the size or shape. That would need a far more complex set of experimental treatments. Similarly, comparisons of treatments 4 and 6 test for differences in assemblages due to connection to the seafloor because they compare assemblages on the same type of structure, with the only difference being connectivity to the seafloor.

The experiment was done in Sydney Harbour and sampled 9 months after the structures were deployed. In general, floating structures had different assemblages of subtidal sessile organisms from those found on fixed structures, with mussels being more abundant on the floating treatments. Swash was also important, because the assemblages that inhabited floating structures exposed to constant swash differed from those on similar structures with little swash. Attached tubeworms, for example, were more sparse on floating structures with constant swash than on those with little swash. Connection to the seafloor, size, shape and composition of the artificial structures did not, however, affect colonisation of the structures.

Other similar experiments have also shown that differences in subtidal assemblages among various artificial and natural structures are not due to predation by fishes (Connell, 2001b), composition of the structure (Connell, 2000), orientation (Glasby and Connell, 2001), or size, shape or age of the substratum (Connell, 2001a; Glasby and Connell, 2001). These different features of habitat may affect patterns of recruitment via larval choice or early mortality, or later changes due to mortality, competition, predation, growth, etc. At this stage, this complexity has not been unravelled.

Provision of secondary habitat for benthic organisms

Many organisms affect abundances of other species by directly providing habitat (e.g. barnacles provide habitat for many small animals; see Reimer (1976); Thompson et al. (1996); many sessile animals and small epiphytic algae grow on the blades of seagrasses, as shown by Borowitska and Lethbridge (1989)) or by acting as ecological engineers and altering availability of resources (e.g. Wright et al., 2002). In marine habitats, mussel-beds (Lintas and Seed, 1994), ascidians (Monteiro et al., 2002) and algal turfs (Kelaher et al., 2001; Olabarria and Chapman, 2001) contain a diverse suite of micro- and macrofauna.

When in large numbers, mussels attach to each other and to the substratum by a series of byssal threads, thus forming extensive beds. These are very complex, three-dimensional matrices that can be made of few or many layers of mussels. Within mussel beds, light, temperature and wave action are reduced, while relative humidity during emersion and sedimentation are increased compared with the outside environment (Nixon et al., 1971; Iwasaki, 1995). Waste-products and shell-debris from the mussels themselves also settle within the matrix (Seed and Suchanek, 1992). These conditions, along with the physical structure of the mussels themselves, provide a wide range of microhabitats for a diverse assemblage of other organisms (Seed and Suchanek, 1992). The shells of the mussels provide additional substratum for sessile organisms (Lohse, 1993) and the sediment and shell-fragments are inhabited by infauna (Seed and Suchanek, 1992). The byssal threads and gaps between the mussels are used by mobile organisms, such as crabs, mobile worms, amphipods and some bivalves.

Habitat-forming species are very common on artificial and natural habitats in urbanised estuaries (Chapman and Bulleri, 2003). Some, particularly mussels, are often dominant parts of sessile assemblages on artificial structures, where they can cover up to 100% of the available substratum (e.g. Dean and Hurd, 1980; Somaschini *et al.*, 1997; Glasby, 1998; Glasby and Connell, 2001; Holloway and Connell, 2002). Features of mussel-beds can also differ among different types of artificial structures. For example, those on pontoons are generally thicker (have more layers of mussels) than those on other structures (J. People, personal observation, 2006) and may, therefore, contain a different or more diverse assemblage of associated animals. Hence, any comparisons of assemblages that live on different types of artificial structure should also include comparisons of those species inhabiting biogenic habitats that are themselves living on the structures.

This was done by comparing assemblages living in mussel-beds on pontoons, seawalls, pilings or natural reefs in four locations in Sydney Harbour. Considering only the number of types of animals present, there were no differences among structures or locations. Abundances of some types of animals differed among structures and/or locations, while others showed no patterns. For example, isopods were most abundant within mussel-beds on pilings than on pontoons, whereas amphipods showed the opposite pattern (Fig. 9.3a and b). Nemertean worms were most abundant on pontoons and seawalls, although their numbers varied according to location (Fig. 9.3c). Another group of worms (syllid polychaetes) showed no consistent pattern among structures or locations (Fig. 9.3d). These complex patterns are not easy to explain as many of these taxa are of similar size, need similar resources and have similar life histories.

Considering the group of species as an assemblage (i.e. taking into account the types and abundances of all animals in the samples), differences among structures and locations were more consistent. In each bay, assemblages differed among structures. For each type of structure, assemblages differed among bays. Therefore, what type of structure these animals are colonising is important, but equally important is what part of the harbour the structure is in. Assemblages in mussel beds on pontoons, however, differed most from those on all other structures in all places (they contained a different combination of varieties of animals

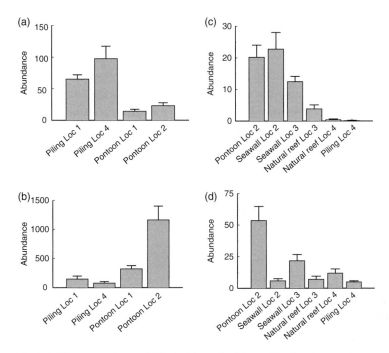

Fig. 9.3. Mean abundances (S.E.) of (a) isopods; (b) amphipods; (c) nemerteans and (d) syllid polychaetes from mussel-beds on different types of urban structures in different locations in Sydney Harbour. For all comparisons $n = 10$ except for natural reefs in Location 3 where $n = 9$.

and plants and many more individuals; People, 2006). This lends support to the concept that pontoons are unique habitats that differ considerably from other types of marine urban structures, both for the organisms that inhabit or attach to the structures' surfaces directly, but also for those that inhabit them indirectly (living on the species that themselves live on the structures).

Mussels are very strong competitors and, once they settle, often overgrow other organisms and tend to form monocultures, replacing natural, patchy, pre-existing biogenic habitats (Chapman et al., 2005). When mussels die or are removed from artificial structures by disturbances, such as wave action or harvesting, bare patches are created. Through time, these patches can be colonised by other sessile organisms which, in turn, provide a different type of biogenic habitat. Different biogenic habitats, such as algae, mussels, barnacles, are often inhabited by different assemblages of associated organisms (e.g. Thompson et al., 1996; Chapman et al., 2005). Therefore, in order to understand fully the effects of replacing natural shores by urban structures, it is necessary to measure the changes in biogenic habitat and any secondary effects of these on the species that live on and in them.

As part of a study of overgrowth by mussels, mussel beds on sections of seawalls were manually removed to allow recolonisation by natural patches of coralline algae. The assemblage of algae and small invertebrates that lived in the remaining patches of mussels was then compared with that developed in natural algal turf, which grew up from remnants in the space previously overgrown by the mussels. Very different assemblages developed in the two types of habitat (Chapman *et al.*, 2005). Many of the taxa were, however, common to mussels and *Corallina*, but most taxa, including polychaetes, amphipods and chitons, were more abundant in *Corallina*, even though the algae had been available for habitat for a shorter time than the mussels. Therefore, on seawalls in Sydney Harbour, overgrowth by mussels reduces the suite of species that live on the substratum below them and they do not provide similar biogenic habitat for species that live within them. Replacement of natural shores by artificial structures that are commonly invaded by mussels can therefore not only lead to changes in the type of biogenic habitat provided, but also in the assemblage that inhabits it. Therefore, effects of artificial structures may be complex, cryptic and easily overlooked.

Urban structures as habitat for fish

In addition to the benthos which lives directly on their surfaces, urban structures, such as marinas, piers, wharfs and seawalls, provide habitat for fish, throughout most of their lives (Bohnsack and Sutherland, 1985; Rilov and Benayahu, 2000), or only while they are juveniles (Hair *et al.*, 1994; Able *et al.*, 1999). The fish eat the organisms living on the surfaces of these structures (López-Jamar *et al.*, 1984) and/or use the complex habitat for shelter (Connell and Jones, 1991). Because of the apparent similarities between the assemblages of fish living on natural reefs and those living around marinas etc., it has been suggested that habitats formed by urban structures can potentially mitigate the loss of natural habitats for fish (Pollard, 1989; Pratt, 1994). This will, however, depend on whether they are able to support types and numbers of fish similar to those on natural rocky habitats.

It is evident from the research that has been done that artificial habitats of all types attract many species of fish, sometimes within hours of their deployment. An artificial reef off the coast of Florida was colonised by fish within several hours of deployment. After 11 days, more than 50 fish were observed on the reef (Cummings, 1994). Such rapid colonisation of artificial reefs has been well documented (e.g. Molles, 1978; Grant *et al.*, 1982). In most cases though, this rapid increase has been believed to be a result of the redistribution of fish from nearby natural habitats (Alevizon and Gorham, 1989).

Research generally shows that most species of fish common to nearby rocky reefs are found around urban structures (e.g. Carr and Hixon, 1997; Rooker *et al.*, 1997; Tupper and Hunte, 1998; Rilov and Benayahu, 2000; Fig. 9.3a). In Sydney Harbour, the fish exploiting urban developments include commercially import-ant species, such as yellowfin bream (*Acanthopagrus australis*), luderick (*Girella tricuspidata*), yellowtail (*Trachurus novaezelandiae*), sweep (*Scorpis lineolatus*) and leatherjackets (Monocanthidae). In addition, those species of fish that were most likely to be present prior to the building of marinas and other structures are also still found around such structures. Therefore, sting rays, small gobies and goat-fish (Mullidae) that live and feed on the sandy bottom are often present on the soft sediment under marinas in similar abundance to sandy habitats where no additional structure exists (Alevizon and Gorham, 1989).

This apparent increase in number of fish should not necessarily be considered a good thing, although anglers may think so. It is a change from natural condi-tions and therefore should rightly be considered an environmental impact. An increase in the abundances of fish can have impacts on surrounding habitats where they forage for food, similar to the impacts that artificial reefs may have on surrounding habitats (Davis and van Blaricom, 1992; Baine, 2001).

Fish display very predictable spatial distributions around urban structures. Larger mobile species, such as bream and yellowtail, move between the pilings and pontoons and in the open water immediately surrounding the structures (B. G. Clynick, unpublished data). Many smaller species, such as damselfishes, wrasses and hula fish (*Trachinops taeniatus*), are concentrated only around the pilings and pontoons themselves.

A study in Sydney Harbour examined the distribution of fish in marinas. Out of a total of 50 species sampled, 28 were only present directly adjacent to pilings or under pontoons and not in the open water between these structures. Interest-ingly, there appeared to be no difference between the types and numbers of fish associated with pilings and those found under pontoons, despite the different nature of these two types of structures – pilings are narrow vertical structures and pontoons large floating structures (Clynick, 2008; Fig. 9.4a) and they have different epibiota, as discussed earlier.

These spatial patterns may be determined by the way fishes respond to either the physical or biological structure of the habitat, i.e. the biota living on the structures. The abundance and diversity of fish associated with marinas in Sydney Harbour were strongly correlated with the amounts of foliose algae, mussels and solitary ascidians growing on the pilings. In general, marinas that had large amounts of mussels, solitary ascidians and algae also had a large diversity of fish. In contrast, marinas where such conspicuous epibiota were mainly absent had very small numbers and few types of fish (Clynick *et al.*, 2007).

Fig. 9.4. Marinas typically have many pontoons and pilings, which provide habitat for fish, increasing local densities (a). Colonisation by seaweeds, fish and invertebrates of small patch reefs made of different types of urban waste material (b) is adding to our knowledge of value of different urban structures as marine habitat.

These biota may provide fish with food, both directly and indirectly. In some instances, fish eat the larger organisms (e.g. ascidians; see Keough (1984)). In other cases, small epifauna living in the larger attached biota are a source of food (e.g. crustaceans and polychaetes living among mussels; see López-Jamar *et al.* (1984)). Habitat produced by sessile plants and animals may also provide shelter for small, cryptic fish, such as blennies and gobies that live within refuges created by the attached organisms (Behrents, 1987). Therefore, the composition and amount of the attached biota, which itself varies considerably among different types of structures (as described previously), may influence the numbers and types of fish associated with the different types of habitats (Coleman and Connell, 2001).

Correlative evidence, such as this, must, however, be supported by experiments designed to be able to identify the different factors to which fish respond. Therefore, a manipulative experiment was done at two marinas to test the model that the amount of conspicuous epibiota (e.g. mussels, ascidians and algae) on pilings directly influences the numbers and types of fish found around them. Removal of these encrusting organisms on pilings showed a marked decrease in numbers of all types of fish. At one marina in particular, fish numbers dropped from up to 100 fish per piling to almost zero (Clynick *et al.*, 2007).

In addition to common and commercially exploited species, urban structures may provide critical habitat for endangered species of fish, such as populations of seahorses. Many species of seahorses have recently been added to the World Conservation Union's (IUCN) 'Red List' of threatened animals (www.iucnredlist.org). Seahorses are generally found in shallow coastal habitats, such as seagrass beds, coral reefs and mangroves. In Australia, the demise of these fish has been exacerbated by the degradation and fragmentation of coastal habitats (Vincent, 1998) which is so common around urban cities.

Seahorses are, however, also often observed among the netting used in swimming enclosures in different areas in Sydney Harbour. These nets appear to provide a surface onto which seahorses grasp. They are also generally located in sheltered areas within the harbour, where it is safe for people to swim and where the nets will not be exposed to large waves that damage the netting. These areas are not unlike areas where seagrass beds can be found, although within the harbour, seagrass beds have been significantly diminished in recent years (Keough and Jenkins, 1995). These nets are, however, often removed during the winter months. This may have serious implications for the seahorses within the harbour, since they may not have alternative habitat during these months (see Clynick (2007) for more detail).

Although much of the research on artificial reefs has examined existing structures, such as oil platforms and pier-pilings, in many parts of the world, other kinds of reefs are specifically constructed from different types of materials, such as tyres, car bodies and shipwrecks, and deployed for the specific purpose of attracting fish (Bohnsack and Sutherland, 1985). Whether these habitats merely redistribute fish from surrounding areas, or do, in fact, increase overall size of fish populations, is still not clear (Grossman *et al.*, 1997) and is not a question that can be easily answered. The value of these structures as habitat can be measured, to a certain extent, by how closely they mimic natural reefs. As mentioned above, although some previous work has identified many of the same types of fish around artificial structures and natural reefs, the results are not very consistent. In some cases, artificial structures supported more species than nearby natural reefs (Rilov and Benayahu, 2000). In other studies, the opposite pattern has been found (Rooker *et al.*, 1997). At this point, more information on the relative value of artificial structures as habitat for fish and other species is needed, before it can be ascertained whether the loss of natural habitat can be compensated for by the provision of artificial structures. Again, this information will best come from experiments where different types of structure are provided and rates of colonisation by fish (and invertebrates) measured.

Urbanised estuaries are also usually littered with large amounts of material that has been dumped into the water over many years. Therefore, in harbours such as Sydney Harbour (New South Wales, Australia), car bodies, tyres, wood and scraps of metal scattered over the seafloor may create habitat, although this was not the aim when they were dumped. Despite the fact that this rubbish is unsightly and may cause pollution and/or physical damage to existing marine life, these hard surfaces also provide a refuge for many types of animals, including small species of fish and a range of invertebrates. Therefore, removing this dumped material may disturb assemblages and potentially remove useful habitat. Before appropriate managerial decisions can be made, it is important to determine what sort of animals and plants use different types of material as habitat and assess their vulnerability to removal.

To understand the role of dumped materials on fish populations, small replicated reefs, each approximately $1.5\,\text{m} \times 1.5\,\text{m} \times 0.8\,\text{m}$, were deployed in Sydney Harbour in a relatively undisturbed sandy area of the harbour, in approximately 6–8 m of water. These artificial 'reefs' were constructed out of pieces of metal, wood, tyres or sandstone blocks, with replicate sets of artificial reefs made of different types of material (Fig. 9.4b). Colonisation of the different reefs by seaweeds, invertebrates and small fish was measured to try to understand which animals and plants use different materials as habitat (Chapman and Clynick, 2006). These results should ultimately provide useful data for managing and restoring marine habitats within urbanised waterways.

Improving quality of urban structures for conservation

It is clear that many marine species can live in harbours where much of the natural habitat has been replaced by urban structures. In particular, intertidal and subtidal biota that traditionally live on hard surfaces can exploit a wide range of artificial material. Many have probably extended their range into parts of estuaries that originally had little or no rocky reef. Nevertheless, increases in urban structures can have subtle effects on marine biota, including inability of some native species to use these structures effectively. Some introduced species can also thrive on these structures, potentially pre-empting space that would otherwise be colonised by natives and thereby reducing diversity.

As previously discussed, many urban structures lack features associated with natural rocky shores, particularly those that add complexity and heterogeneity to the surface. For example, most structures do not have the pits, crevices, overhangs, rock pools or horizontal surfaces that are common on natural shores or reefs. Many will never have these features. As seawalls deteriorate and degrade, however, holes and cracks do appear, perhaps ameliorating the severity of initial conditions and providing microhabitats for many creatures. Because seawalls form important infrastructure in an urban environment, their degradation, while potentially beneficial to marine organisms, is detrimental to the purpose for which they were built, particularly when slumping of the wall may affect human safety. Seawalls undergo regular maintenance in order to maintain their primary function. This work may be minor, such as filling crevices between blocks or patching cracks, or major, such as rebuilding entire sections of walls. This inevitably means that these potential additional microhabitats, that might mimic important features of natural shores, are constantly being removed. In addition, depending on the extent of repair works, continual repairs to and rebuilding parts of a seawall may disturb the assemblages in the surrounding area.

While the necessity of the repairs cannot be denied, it is possible that they can be undertaken in such a way as to minimise disturbance to surrounding assemblages and to try to maintain or create some of the habitats that are missing from many seawalls. Where new seawalls are being built, or old ones repaired, there is scope to incorporate elements into the design that may mimic natural microhabitats found on rocky shores. This requires close co-operation between managers, engineers and ecologists to establish what would be most desirable from an ecological point of view, what is necessary for maintaining the viability of the seawall and what is technically possible.

A number of examples of such collaboration are leading to much greater understanding of the role of seawalls in the ecology of Sydney Harbour. For example, in one experiment, the seawall at Farm Cove, in Sydney Harbour, which has important heritage value, needed repair. The fill behind the wall was washing out through crevices that had developed between the large sandstone blocks. The need to stop this loss of material meant that these crevices, which may have been acting as refuges for some species, would no longer be available. With the co-operation of the managers responsible for maintaining the wall and the contractors doing the work, it was possible to incorporate new features into the repaired wall. These included small depressions and grooves at different densities and combinations to test the model that these features could serve as habitat for species to replace those lost during the repairs. In this case, the main concern of the managers was to maintain the heritage quality of the wall, while trying to improve its value as intertidal habitat. Other concerns might include maintaining access, structural integrity, especially in rough conditions, and safety. Studies to evaluate the benefits to marine species of such managerial modifications are currently being done.

Because of the variety of goals of management in different parts of the harbour and restrictions on what might be technically feasible, proposing changes to seawalls in order to maximise the diversity of habitats has to be adaptable to different situations. In addition, information is still needed on what changes might be most beneficial, or on the relative costs and benefits of different approaches. This knowledge will only come from field experiments, where managers of urban structures make their resources available, the people repairing or building new structures are prepared to incorporate different experimental designs (with replication, control sites, etc.) into their works, and ecologists are prepared to do the research to investigate this. Such efforts are progressing well in Sydney Harbour through collaboration between government, business and university researchers.

Acknowledgements

First and foremost, we would like to acknowledge all of our friends and colleagues who have contributed ideas and discussion to our thoughts on this subject, particularly Tony Underwood, Tim Glasby, Sean Connell and Fabio Bulleri. The University of Sydney and the Australian Research Council, through its Special Research Centres Scheme, have supported this research, as have North Sydney Council, Woollahra Council, the Sydney Ports Corporation, John Nixon Engineering and Commander J. Shevlin of HMAS *Penguin*. Tony Underwood, as usual, made helpful comments on an earlier draft. We would also like to thank Mark McDonnell and two anonymous referees for helpful comments to clarify and focus this chapter.

10

Comparative studies of terrestrial vertebrates in urban areas

CHARLES NILON

Introduction

Comparative studies of terrestrial vertebrates are one approach that can be used by researchers to build on the extensive work done by animal ecologists and applied ecologists in cities (Luniak, 1990; VanDruff *et al.*, 1994; Nilon and Pais, 1997). Much of this work pre-dates the renewed interest in cities by mainstream ecologists. The new emphasis on the ecology of cities provides new tools and approaches to conducting comparative studies that will be useful in answering questions about vertebrates in cities. In this chapter I will discuss why comparative studies of vertebrates are important to ecologists, managers and people who live in cities by reviewing the comparative studies that have been done on the vertebrate fauna of cities. I will describe some of the research on vertebrates that occurs within the framework of urban ecosystems research, and I will propose a comparative study that illustrates how contemporary approaches to urban ecology can be applied to a conservation issue.

Comparative studies ask and answer questions about the ecology of cities

The need for comparative studies comes from a need to answer questions about animals in cities. The questions are shaped by different groups (i.e. scientists, the public, resource managers, policy makers and conservationists)

Ecology of Cities and Towns: A Comparative Approach, ed. Mark J. McDonnell, Amy K. Hahs and Jürgen H. Breuste. Published by Cambridge University Press. © Cambridge University Press 2009.

that care about animals in cities. Traditional ecologists studying cities ask questions about ecosystem structure and function. Ecologists working on the Baltimore Ecosystem Study, funded by the US National Science Foundation, consider terrestrial vertebrates as part of the question, 'How does the spatial structure of ecological, physical, and socioeconomic factors in the metropolis affect ecosystem function?' (Pickett *et al.*, Chapter 3). This question is framed by the goals of understanding how urban ecosystems work and testing models about human ecosystems.

Residents of cities have their own understanding of important questions about vertebrates that is shaped by individual experience and by socially constructed views of nature and animals. Their questions might include, 'I've seen some dead birds on my street: does this mean we are at risk for West Nile virus?', 'Will cleaning up the vacant lots in our neighbourhood get rid of rats?', or, 'I really enjoy the birds in the patch of woods near my house. Will the new housing estate hurt them?'

Conservation and management questions are at the interface between questions raised by ecologists studying cities and urban residents. Management questions are shaped by the two sometimes conflicting goals for wildlife conservation in cities: to maintain regional biodiversity, and to provide opportunities for urban residents to have day-to-day contact with wildlife (Tylka *et al.*, 1987). These goals lead to multiple questions: 'Are these small forest patches sources or sinks for small mammals?', 'How is bird species richness influenced by garden management decisions and practices?', or 'How do government policies on brownfield development impact biodiversity at a local scale?' The rest of this chapter will consider how comparative studies can address management questions about vertebrates in cities.

Approaches used in comparative studies: developing a framework for comparisons among cities

Earlier comparative studies of vertebrates have focused on the distribution of species among cities. These studies have considered not only the distribution of cities but questions about kinds of cities where species occur and places within cities where species occur, an approach to comparison that requires an objective way of describing and grouping cities and areas within cities. Ecological, social and economic factors influence both the location of cities and how those cities grow and change over time. The same factors shape the physical structure and layout of cities and shape their physical environment and ecological characteristics (Bridgman *et al.*, 1995). Applied ecologists have used classifications based on ecological characteristics and on urban form to group cities for comparison.

Luniak *et al.* (1990) classified cities in central and eastern Europe based on their ecological setting: vegetation zone and presence/absence of sea coast or big rivers. Harris and Raynor (1986) classified British cities using a scheme developed by urban geographers to group cities with similar development histories (Moser and Scott, 1961). Sanders (1984) classified metropolitan areas in the United States using a system that combined potential natural vegetation (Kuchler, 1964) and period of maximum urban growth (Borchert, 1967).

Although most studies of vertebrates in cities have focused on remnant habitats, there is a growing recognition that a wide range of habitats exists in cities, and the need to identify these habitat types is an important step in comparative studies (McDonnell and Hahs, Chapter 5). Ecologists and managers need a way to define types of habitats or patch types within cities. In the United States this classification has often been based on land-use cover (Anderson *et al.*, 1976). Recent studies on the distribution of urban bird species illustrate how land use and land cover have been used as a surrogate for habitat or patch type (Hadidian *et al.*, 1997; Turner, 2003).

The recognition that land-use classifications may not accurately account for the heterogeneity of habitats in cities has led to efforts to classify cover types found in cities. Brady *et al.* (1979) developed a 'typology of the urban ecosystem' that defined different biotic zones in cities and linked land use and land cover. Matthews *et al.* (1988) used a protocol based on the US National Wetlands Inventory that combined 26 land-use categories and 31 land-cover categories to classify and compare seven cities in New York State.

Since the 1980s, biotope mapping approaches have been developed that use a hierarchical approach to habitat classification (Werner, 1999). These approaches have been developed to link habitat classification both to planning decisions (Freeman and Buck, 2003; Shaw *et al.*, 1998) and to broader ecological land-cover classifications (Löfvenhaft *et al.*, 2002a; Löfvenhaft, Chapter 24). Habitat classification using biotope mapping has been a key part of comparative studies of vertebrates in European cities.

Comparative studies: species composition

Three studies from Europe and North America serve as examples of comparative studies designed to answer questions about the distribution and abundance of species in cities. They are useful examples because they illustrate how the classification of cities, and of habitats within cities, has been used as a framework for comparison.

Ornithologists in Poland developed a survey of the avifauna of cities in central and eastern Europe (Luniak, 1990; Konstantinov *et al.*, 1996). Both studies used a standardised questionnaire sent to ornithologists in several cities. The ornithologists were asked to provide information on the breeding status, abundance and population trend for each city. They were also asked to provide a list of new species occurring in their city. The goal of the original study (Luniak, 1990) was to provide a standardised list of species for cities, and to determine new species occurring in cities since the 1950s. The study by Konstantinov *et al.* (1996) was designed to provide information on changes occurring in the avifauna of eastern European cities since 1984. An important part of the comparison was to understand bird species composition in the context of regional features: vegetation zone, presence of sea coast, and presence of big rivers, that might be influenced by urbanisation (Luniak, 1990).

Cringan (1987) compared Christmas bird count data from four cities in the Rocky Mountain region of the United States that was collected over a 30-year period to determine whether the similarity in species composition was increasing as a result of urbanisation. His study focused on cities within a geographical region where cities had different types of pre-development vegetation but were showing similar patterns of growth and development.

Since 1990, ornithologists have developed the Urban Ornithological Atlas project to compare bird species composition in 14 Italian cities (Dinetti, 1996). The project developed standard methods for habitat classification and for conducting bird counts. Participants in a project working group developed a standard classification for habitats in cities that helped to standardise counting methods. Dinnetti (1996) noted that the Atlas Project seeks to answer scientific questions about birds in cities as well as questions dealing with urban planning and conservation.

Comparative studies: populations

Comparative studies been used to answer questions about patterns of distribution and abundance that are relevant to managing populations. Conover (1995) surveyed state conservation agencies in the United States to determine cities with urban deer (*Odocoileus* spp.) populations. The survey asked biologists to identify when deer were first observed in a city and when complaints about deer abundance were first recorded. Conover (1995) received responses for 195 cities and attempted to develop general ideas about the occurrence of deer in cities that could be used to guide management-orientated research.

Luniak *et al.* (1990) studied the distribution of the blackbird (*Turdus merula*) in central and eastern Europe and used the results of the study to develop hypotheses about the kinds of species that become abundant in cities. Jerzak (2001) compared the distribution of the black-billed magpie (*Pica pica*) in 12 Polish cities to understand how species respond to urbanisation. Tree planting associated with urban redevelopment, ameliorated climate and anthropogenic food were factors that contributed to increased abundance of crows over a 12-year period.

A long-term study of red foxes (*Vulpes vulpes*) in British cities has focused on understanding the factors controlling fox occurrence and population size. The core of the study is the development of a fox population model using data from several cities (Harris and Raynor, 1986). Part of this study included developing a model to predict fox occurrence that relied on socio-economic data on 158 British cities (Harris and Smith, 1987). The model predicted both the cities in which foxes occurred and the areas within cities that are likely to contain foxes. The development of the model was also used to understand the socio-economic factors and planning conditions that were associated with foxes becoming established in British cities.

The previously described studies are relevant to the questions asked by ecologists, urban residents and managers because they developed ways of classifying types of cities and methods for classifying habitats within cities. They have documented patterns of species occurrence and abundance among cities and linked these patterns to ecological and social factors. This information has been useful in understanding similarities and differences among cities in patterns of vertebrate species composition and abundance. However, as descriptive studies they have not focused on mechanisms that provide answers to questions raised by ecologists, residents and managers.

How can the current focus on urban ecosystems contribute to comparative studies of urban fauna?

The recent focus on the ecology of cities promises an approach that seeks to identify the mechanisms that underlie patterns and processes (Pickett *et al.*, 2001, Chapter 3; Niemelä *et al.*, Chapter 2). One method used by ecologists in their new focus on cities is the patch dynamics approach used by researchers working on the Baltimore Ecosystem Study, a project funded by the US National Science Foundation (Pickett *et al.*, 2001, Chapter 3). This approach considers the ecological properties of a patch, in this case habitat features and species composition, as being determined by: the history of the patch (patch origin), the spatial setting in which the patch occurs and current influences on the patch. I will describe how patch dynamics and patch setting have been used as a framework to identify and understand potential mechanisms that determine vertebrate species composition and abundance in cities. It is important to understand that patch dynamics is proposed as an approach to studying vertebrates in cities rather than the only way to study vertebrates in cities. Of equal importance is the recognition that the patch approach, as it is used in Baltimore, recognises that patches should be defined by the species that are being studied rather than an a priori assumption of what is a patch and what is a matrix.

Patch origin

Zipperer *et al.* (1997) described three types of patches that occur in urban areas: remnant patches of natural or semi-natural vegetation, emergent patches resulting from changing land uses within the patch, and planted patches. Although remnant patches are important in conserving biodiversity, planted patches offer unique opportunity for comparative studies among cities because they reflect international approaches to design, species selection and approaches to management (Forbes *et al.*, 1997).

Neighbourhood parks in US cities are an example of planted patches with similar design and management. Because most cities in the United States follow a standard set of park planning guidelines, neighbourhood parks are similar in size (5 to 10 ha) and typically are designed to serve residents living within 1 km of the park (Ignatieva and Stewart, Chapter 23). Researchers in Baltimore and Phoenix have collaborated on a study of birds using small neighbourhood parks in the two cities (Paige Warren, personal communication). The studies use identical census techniques and compare small parks in very different cities to determine if there are similar species or groups of species in small parks, and to determine if small parks support different species from the neighbourhoods surrounding them. A key part of the study is the hypothesis that neighbourhood parks are similar in habitat structure and design and that these similarities would result in similar bird communities between the two cities. By focusing on planted patches they intend to focus on the role that park design, maintenance and management activities, and people's activities play in influencing the composition and abundance of bird species.

Patch setting

Ecologists use a number of metrics to describe the spatial setting of a patch (McDonnell and Hahs, Chapter 5; Yang and Zhou, Chapter 16). Landscape ecologists often consider the matrix of land uses surrounding the patch. Animal ecologists often look at metrics such as patch isolation or patch connectivity to describe the degree of isolation of the patch from similar habitats. Studies considering patch setting have been useful in studying factors that influence population growth and survival (Catterall, Chapter 8; Natuhara and Hashimoto, Chapter 12).

Williamson and DeGraaf's (1980) and Johnsen and VanDruff's (1987) studies of birds in urban neighbourhoods were some of the first to consider how socio-economic factors influence the landscape in which species occur. The recent research focus on humans as a component of urban ecosystems has resulted in more research on the ecology of vertebrates in patches in different social landscapes (McDonnell and Pickett, 1993b). Cities and subdivisions of cities can be classified using a number of indicators of human social, economic, and demographic characteristics (McDonnell and Hahs, Chapter 5; Yang and Jinxing, Chapter 16). These characteristics can be used to develop scales and indices that allow comparison of cities and their subdivisions. Because socio-economic and census data are available for a number of cities it is possible to make comparisons of the social landscape surrounding patches in a number of cities and to compare how this landscape defines mechanisms shaping species composition and abundance.

Nilon and Huckstep (1998) used census data to define the social landscape surrounding small woodlands in Chicago neighbourhoods. Small woodlands are an important component of natural and semi-natural greenspaces in cities in the Northern Hemisphere. The patches they studied were similar in plant species and in vegetation structure. Patches surrounded by low-income neighbourhoods with rental housing and black American residents had more rubbish and human-related disturbance and had lower numbers of native small mammal species and more exotic species.

The previously described study comparing bird communities in small neighbourhood parks in Baltimore and Phoenix considered the socio-economic setting of urban parks. Each park was classified by the socio-economic status of the adjacent neighbourhood. This initial comparison led to a number of additional questions that could form the core of other comparative studies. Researchers in Phoenix found that socio-economic status is correlated with several metrics for bird communities. Additional research might focus on how ownership and management of pets, bird feeding, and yard or garden management practices vary with socio-economic status and might be predictors of bird survival or other population characteristics.

A proposed comparative study using a patch dynamics approach

Comparative studies exist because there is a need to answer questions about the ecology of cities. I have described how comparative studies have been used to answer questions about the distribution of species among cities. I have also described how a focus on patch setting and patch type can be useful in understanding the ecology of vertebrates in cities. In this final section, I will describe how the approaches can be combined to answer questions about the mechanisms that shape species distribution and abundance, key factors in wildlife conservation programs.

Central cities of metropolitan areas in Europe, North America and Australia contain large parks and cemeteries built during the last half of the nineteenth century. These greenspaces, including large cemeteries in several US cities, were built following design principles based on European romantic landscapes and can be viewed as planted patches of similar origin (Darnall, 1983; Forbes *et al.*, 1997). These sites are valued as important cultural resources but their conservation value for vertebrate species is largely unknown. Large greenspaces also occur in specific spatial settings, often older residential neighbourhoods that were developed to provide housing for wealthy residents. This combination of patch origin and spatial setting allows comparison among a group of cities selected based on location, ecological characteristics and pattern of development.

A comparative study focused on large greenspaces could take advantage of patches of similar origin and management history but occurring in very different settings to answer questions about the conservation value of the sites:

(1)   Do large greenspaces built with similar designs support similar species or guilds?
(2)   Are there differences in the presence, abundance, and population characteristics of native and exotic species among large greenspaces?
(3)   Do species using habitats in large urban greenspaces within the selected cities differ in reproductive success and survival?

Engaging ecologists from cities in different settings to develop projects that address the mechanisms that form the basis of questions about species occurrence and survival is the key to a successful study. Comparisons offer a framework for study and a way for bringing together researchers and managers to address important questions. An excellent example of the benefits of comparative ecological studies in different cities is the GLOBENET initiative which examined carabid beetle assemblages in several cities around the world (Niemelä *et al.*, 2002, Chapter 2).

11

The ecology of roads in urban and urbanising landscapes

RODNEY VAN DER REE

Introduction

Roads are conspicuous and pervasive components of most landscapes throughout the world, occurring in both highly modified urban areas and relatively pristine areas of wilderness. Roads the world over are remarkably similar in both form and function and are designed to transport people and goods between places as quickly and efficiently as possible. Road networks are typically designed and classified according to a hierarchy that at one end allows for high mobility and limited local access (arterial roads, variably termed highway, freeway or motorway) to roads with low mobility but high local access (local roads) at the other extreme (Forman *et al.*, 2002).

Roads and traffic have ecological and biological effects on adjacent habitats and biota that can extend for hundreds or thousands of metres from the road itself (Trombulak and Frissell, 2000; Forman *et al.*, 2002). Estimates for the United States of America and the Netherlands indicate that about one-fifth of the surface area of both these countries is directly affected ecologically by roads and traffic (Reijnen *et al.*, 1995; Forman, 2000). Our understanding of these impacts has been well summarised previously (Forman *et al.*, 2002), and includes the loss and fragmentation of habitat; input of pollutants (e.g. noise, chemicals and dust) into adjacent air, soil, vegetation and water; direct mortality; and the creation of barriers to wildlife movement. Most research on the ecological effects of roads has been conducted in landscapes and systems that still have relatively

Ecology of Cities and Towns: A Comparative Approach, ed. Mark J. McDonnell, Amy K. Hahs and Jürgen H. Breuste. Published by Cambridge University Press. © Cambridge University Press 2009.

intact ecosystem processes, such as rural or wilderness areas (e.g. Fahrig *et al.*, 1995; Reijnen *et al.*, 1995; Miller *et al.*, 1996; Ortega and Capen, 1999; Wilkie *et al.*, 2000; Develey and Stouffer, 2001). These examples suggest that many of the ecological effects of roads and traffic on relatively intact systems are potentially large.

In contrast to these relatively natural landscapes are urban and suburban areas that are an extreme example of the consequences of anthropogenic change. The almost complete replacement of natural habitats with grossly modified land uses, the introduction of exotic plants and animals, and alteration to heat and energy fluxes are just a few of the extreme and essentially permanent changes caused by urbanisation. In urban areas, roads and traffic are one of a number of processes and altered states that may affect plants, animals and ecological processes. Therefore, given the mix of other disturbances in urban and suburban areas, to what extent are urban areas influenced by roads and traffic? What are the main effects of roads and traffic in urban areas and to what extent are they similar to those reported from more natural areas? Are the ecological effects of roads exacerbated or mitigated by urbanisation?

The inability to answer these questions highlights the lack of a synthesis of the ecological effects of roads in urban and suburban areas. The two aims of this chapter are to highlight some of the main effects of roads and traffic in urban and urbanising landscapes; and to outline research questions and a methodology to move towards a synthesis of the ecology of urban roads.

The classification of roads

The objective of road classification schemes is to allocate roads into discrete groups based on their intended function. Three broad criteria are primarily used to classify roads: (1) the size of the urban settlements connected by the road; (2) the volume of vehicular traffic carried and the typical distance travelled by people on the particular road; and (3) location of the road (urban or rural). A typical hierarchy ranges from local roads with low traffic volume, high levels of local access and typically short trip durations to arterial roads, which have very high traffic volume, extended trip duration and restricted access to local areas. Collector roads, which connect local roads to arterial roads, are intermediate in these parameters. However, there are no definitive or universal cut-off points that can be used to classify roads because traffic volume, length of trips and size of human settlements vary greatly among and within regions, and between developed and developing nations. Furthermore, some regions include extra divisions within these categories, such as major or minor collector roads, and high or low volume local roads. Nevertheless, the simple hierarchy of road type and function (local–connector–arterial) is a useful system that would allow for comparison between regions, provided additional detail about road width, number of lanes and traffic volume is given.

The majority of roads in most regions appear to be the local access roads, comprising about 70% of all roads in the USA (Forman *et al.*, 2002). Similarly, local access roads in the State of Victoria, Australia, accounted for 68% of all roads (of a total of 153 010 km of declared roads and about 40 000 km of roads in National Parks and wilderness areas), compared with 4% of highways and freeways (AustRoads, 2005). Traffic volume on local access roads is typically of the order of hundreds of vehicles per day, and in the USA, around 80% of all roads carry very low volumes of traffic (<400 vehicles per day; Forman *et al.*, 2002). The density of local roads in urbanised areas is likely to be much higher than at broader spatial scales, with 95% of roads in the metropolitan region of Melbourne classified as local roads. While local roads may be the more common landscape feature, they also carry less traffic. In the USA, the combined extent of major and minor arterial roads accounted for 11% of road length, but served 72% of all travel (Forman *et al.*, 2002). Traffic volume on these major arterials typically exceeds 10 000 vehicles per day, exceeding 50 000 per day on some roads. Collector roads carry between 2000 and 10 000 vehicles per day.

The balance between the proportion of roads that are paved or unpaved is likely to depend on the relative wealth of the country as well as the function of the road. For example, almost 60% of roads (of 6.3 million km of public road) in the USA are paved (Forman *et al.*, 2002), compared with <2% (of 145 100 km) of roads in the Democratic Republic of Congo (Wilkie *et al.*, 2000). Finally, arterial roads are more likely to be paved than not, while local roads, particularly in rural and urban–rural fringe areas, are more likely to remain unpaved (Forman *et al.*, 2002).

Road density, measured as the length of roads per unit area (km per km^2, or miles per mile^2) is a useful measure of the road network within an area. Road density varies greatly among regions and countries. National estimates of road density range from lows of 0.09 km/km^2 in Canada and 0.10 km/km^2 in Australia, through intermediate levels of 1.52 and 1.62 km/km^2 in the United Kingdom and France, to 3.07 km/km^2 in Japan (AustRoads, 2003). Within Australia, the Australian Capital Territory and State of Victoria have the highest density of roads (1.11 and 0.69 km/km^2, respectively), whereas Western Australia and Northern Territory have the lowest densities at 0.06 and 0.02 km/km^2, respectively. Within the State of Victoria, road density across metropolitan Melbourne (including rural and undeveloped land on the urban fringe) is 3.48 km/km^2 (R. van der Ree, unpublished data).

The ecological effects of roads and traffic

Roads as barriers to movement and a source of mortality

One of the most visible effects of traffic is wildlife mortality caused by collision with vehicles. Most assessments of road kill have occurred in natural or rural landscapes (e.g. Bellis and Graves, 1971; Mallick *et al.*, 1998; Bonnet *et al.*, 1999; Mumme *et al.*, 2000; Clevenger *et al.*, 2003), with large effects recorded for some species (e.g. badgers, *Meles meles*; van der Zee *et al.*, 1992) or groups of species, such as amphibians and reptiles (e.g. Rosen and Lowe, 1994; Fahrig *et al.*, 1995). The most important variable related to the decline in badger setts (an index of population size) in the Netherlands was road density, with approximately 10% of the total badger population (*c.* 150 out of *c.* 1400) reported as casualties of collision with vehicles in 1986 and 1987 (van der Zee *et al.*, 1992), equating to about half of the yearly potential growth of the population (Berendson, 1986, cited in van der Zee *et al.*, 1992).

While systematic counts of the number of road-killed wildlife in urban areas are rare, the rate or effect of mortality due to road kill may be gleaned from some autecological studies. For example, a study of the movement of common brushtail possums (*Trichosurus vulpecula*) in suburban areas of Launceston, Australia, found that of the 23 animals that were radiotracked for up to 444 days, nine were confirmed killed and two injured by collision with vehicles (Statham and Statham, 1997). It was also considered possible that some or all of the five individuals that could not be relocated at the end of the study had also been run over. Statham and Statham (1997) conclude their study by suggesting that urban possums may have a shorter life span than animals in more natural settings, primarily owing to increased mortality rates from collision with vehicles. However, it is unclear what the population level effects for common brushtail possums are likely to be as the species is relatively abundant in many urban areas of southeastern Australia (e.g. van der Ree and McCarthy, 2005).

The probability of collision with a vehicle appears to be specific to the species and to the age/sex-class. A 6-month study of the movement patterns of 17 blue-tongued lizards (*Tiliqua scincoides*) in Sydney, Australia, reported that mortality due to road kill was low, with resident animals appearing to avoid roads consistently (Koenig *et al.*, 2001). A subsequent analysis of a dataset of over 2000 'rescued' blue-tongued lizards collected by wildlife carers between 1994 and 1998 from across Sydney reported that collision with vehicles accounted for 12% of 757 known deaths (Koenig *et al.*, 2002). However, it is difficult to quantify the true threat from vehicles to wildlife in urban areas without an assessment of other causes of mortality. The major cause of mortality of blue-tongued lizards in Sydney was predation by cats and dogs, accounting for 52% of deaths (Koenig *et al.*, 2002). However, the actual rate of mortality due to collision with vehicles is likely to be significantly underestimated because animals that are found dead are unable to be 'rescued' and are therefore less likely to be reported (Koenig *et al.*, 2002).

Mortality due to collision with vehicles is likely to have greater impacts on population viability if particular groups of animals are more vulnerable, such as terrestrial vertebrates with low mobility or particular age/sex classes. The loss of reproductively active adult females may affect the viability of some species more than the loss of males (Bonnet *et al.*, 1999). Similarly, the continual loss of dispersing juveniles from a habitat surrounded by roads, and the prevention of new individuals from reaching a habitat, could also decrease the viability of local populations. The decline of many species in urban areas (van der Ree and McCarthy, 2005) suggests that the rate of loss does not need to be high for there to be demonstrable impact at the population level. Populations of many species of wildlife are likely to be smaller and more fragmented in urban areas, and thus any additional increase in the rate of mortality may threaten local viability. Therefore, while rates of road kill of some species may appear to be low compared with other sources of mortality in urban areas (e.g. blue-tongued lizards around Sydney; Koenig *et al.*, 2001; Koenig *et al.*, 2002), it is necessary to attempt to reduce sampling bias and fully quantify all causes of mortality in all age and sex classes.

Roads may act as complete barriers or a partial filter to the movement and dispersal of wildlife. This may occur because animals cannot safely cross the road or because they actively avoid the road or traffic. The barrier effect of roads is related to the combined effect of both traffic volume and road width. For example, woodchucks (*Marmota monax*) living near highway interchanges in Ottawa, Canada, were more likely to complete a successful road crossing at narrower roads with fewer vehicles (Woodward, 1990). In another example, the movement of bumblebees (*Bombus impatiens*, *Bombus affinis* and *Xylocopa* species) in metropolitan Boston, Massachusetts, was found to be restricted by roads and railroads, even though they were physically able to cross (Bhattacharya *et al.*, 2003).

A challenge in urban ecology is to separate out the negative effects of urbanisation and that of roads and traffic. A recent study of the composition of pond-breeding frog communities conducted along an urban–rural gradient in the city of Melbourne, Australia, found that species richness was negatively correlated with road density (Parris, 2006). This is probably due to a combination of effects including increased mortality and isolation due to roads and traffic, as well as factors associated with urbanisation, such as the drainage and alteration of ponds. However, traffic intensity was identified as the primary cause of decline in the density of local amphibian populations on the outskirts of Ottawa, Canada (Fahrig *et al.*, 1995). Fahrig *et al.* (1995) concluded their study by suggesting that road mortality, particularly in urban areas, may be a major cause in the decline of amphibian populations.

Roads, roadsides and unused road reserves as habitat

In some highly cleared landscapes, vegetation occurring along roads may represent a significant proportion of indigenous or natural habitat, particularly in many rural areas of southern Australia (Bennett and van der Ree, 2001). The value of this vegetation for the conservation of biodiversity is being increasingly recognised as studies demonstrate their habitat and connectivity functions for both rare and common species of plants and animals (Cale, 1990; Major *et al.*, 1999; Norton and Stafford Smith, 1999; van der Ree and Bennett, 2001, 2003). There appear to have been fewer studies that investigated the role of roadsides in urban areas, but the small numbers of studies show that they provide habitat for birds (Fernández-Juricic, 2000; Bolger *et al.*, 2001; White *et al.*, 2005), invertebrates (Munguira and Thomas, 1992), plants (Cilliers and Bredenkamp, 2000) and mammals (Woodward 1990; Bolger *et al.*, 2001).

The value or quality of the habitat for conservation appears to be variable, and dependent, at least in part, on several aspects of landscape and habitat. For example, the richness of bird species using wooded streets in Madrid, Spain, was found to be intermediate between urban parks and non-wooded streets (Fernández-Juricic, 2000). Furthermore, wooded streets that were connected at each end to urban parks supported a greater number of bird species than streets that were not directly connected to parks. There was also a negative relationship between traffic density and the density of ground species and tree-hole species (Fernández-Juricic, 2000). Similarly, streets containing mostly native species of plant in urban Melbourne supported a larger number of foraging guilds and fewer species of introduced bird than streets lacking vegetation or containing primarily exotic plantings (White *et al.*, 2005). Plant species diversity appears to be largely influenced by natural processes such as gradients in soil nutrients or moisture, as well as invasion by exotic species (Cilliers and Bredenkamp, 2000).

Habitat along roadsides can support very high densities of some species. For example, the highest density of woodchucks (*Marmota monax*) ever recorded in any habitat was at a single suburban interchange along a major four to six lane highway in Ottawa, Canada (Woodward, 1990). The maximum density recorded at the interchange (5.4 individuals per ha) exceeded that recorded from a vegetable garden in Ontario at 3.3 individuals per ha (Woodward, 1990). Although being lower, the densities at the urban and rural interchanges were still relatively high compared with studies of woodchucks in a range of other habitats (e.g. old fields, urban parks, hedgerows, roadside adjacent to agricultural land, agricultural land; various references in Woodward, 1990). Woodward (1990) hypothesised that the high densities within the interchanges were due to a combination of factors, including a lack of domestic and endemic predators, abundant growth of suitable food, successful reproduction and recruitment of young, adequate drainage of burrows by sloping earthworks, and ability of the species to cross two-lane roads regularly and successfully.

As well as providing habitat, roadside vegetation may also have aesthetic value and other roles in ecosystem function (Wolf, 2003). A recent study in the USA found that road users preferred vegetation along roadsides to screen out commercial land uses (Wolf, 2003). Vegetation may also assist in the collection of air-borne particulate matter, including dust and chemicals.

Roads as watercourses

Studies in forested landscapes have demonstrated that the frequency and size of flood events, the amount of debris (soil, sediment and wood) carried by normal and peak water flows, the chemical composition of water bodies and barriers to the movement of aquatic organisms are all affected by the presence of roads (see Jones *et al.* (2000), Trombulak and Frissell (2000) and Forman *et al.* (2002) for examples). Importantly, the effects of roads on biodiversity were often not immediately evident upon construction, and some were not observable until decades later (Findlay and Bourdages, 2000).

Roads and traffic in urban areas are likely to have generally similar impacts on wetlands and waterways to those reported in forested landscapes. A major difference in urbanised systems will be the large proportion of the landscape with impermeable surfaces. In effect, roads are an extension of waterways because they collect and divert rainfall into channels, drains and ultimately into rivers and streams. Thus, even minor rainfall results in the almost immediate influx of water and pollutants from the road surface into drains and water-courses. In natural systems, most rainfall would be filtered by the soil before entering watercourses. Thus, roads are likely to increase the amount of water and pollutants reaching waterways and decrease filtration time.

A relatively new housing development to the southeast of Melbourne, Australia has incorporated principles of water-sensitive urban design in the collection, treatment and disposal of stormwater (Lloyd *et al.*, 2001a). Among a number of measures being trialled is the replacement of impervious concrete guttering on the road edge with vegetated swales. These act as biofiltration systems to remove solids and chemicals as runoff water filters down through the soil into an underlying gravel-filled trench, which eventually drains into a piped collection system. The biofiltration system was designed to withstand a 1 in 5-year flood event, with a 1 in 100-year flood event catered for with an overland flow system (Lloyd *et al.*, 2001a). Preliminary results show reductions in total suspended solids (60%), total phosphorus (47%) and soluble phosphorus (66%), with mixed and complicated results for nitrogen (Lloyd *et al.*, 2002).

Roads as conduits for non-indigenous species

Alteration to plant community composition and invasion of roadside vegetation by non-indigenous species is a significant problem in some areas. For example, most of the plant communities found along road verges in the Potchefstroom Municipal Area in South Africa were previously undescribed and depended on adjacent land uses, type and intensity of management and disturbance, and the time since road construction (Cilliers and Bredenkamp, 2000). This diversity of new communities may be a reflection of high vehicle density in urban areas, because vehicles may act as vectors for weeds and pathogens, rapidly transferring propagules from place to place (Lonsdale and Lane, 1994).

Roads have also been implicated in the geographical range expansion of a number of species of animals. The cane toad (*Bufo marinus*) is one such species whose range expansion in northern Australia is probably related to the presence of roads (Seabrook and Dettmann, 1996). Introduced to Australia in 1935, cane toads have had deleterious impacts on native fauna, particularly predators who are poisoned by toxins contained in their skin and parotid glands. In the study, cane toads were found at higher densities along roads and vehicle tracks than in adjacent habitat, and they travelled longer distances along the road (Seabrook and Dettmann, 1996). These effects were strongest where the vegetation at ground level next to the road was most dense. Hence, the effect of roads on movement patterns of cane toads in urban and suburban areas may be reduced by clearing the ground-layer vegetation. However, the imposition of other potential barriers in urban areas (e.g. fences, buildings) may increase the importance of roads as conduits for movement. Outside of urban landscapes, features along roadsides (e.g. trees, drainage ditches, sandy verges) have been identified as potential movement corridors for small terrestrial mammals (Getz *et al.*, 1978), beetles (Vermeulen, 1994) and ants (De Mers, 1993; Stiles and Jones, 1998).

Future directions

The ecological impact of roads and traffic on flora, fauna and ecological processes has been described as a nascent field of research (Forman *et al.*, 2002).

Within road ecology, a synthesis of effects of roads and traffic in urban areas is particularly understudied, and we are a long way from the identification of general principles. A priority for future studies on the effects of roads and traffic should be to: (1) identify the main effects of roads and traffic in urban and suburban areas; and (2) design and test systems that eliminate or mitigate those main effects. There are a number of approaches that may prove useful in developing generalisations that are applicable in urban settings around the world. These approaches include the establishment of co-ordinated, integrated research programmes across roads, species and geographical locations, and the use of future road constructions as replicated experimental units in controlled experiments. Finally, to increase the scientific rigour and improve accessibility to results, the research must be published in international refereed journals.

Traditionally, most research on the ecology of roads has been relatively site- or species-specific and has rarely compared the effects of roads on a range of different taxa or habitats. A notable exception is the research programme being undertaken along the Trans-Canada Highway through Banff National Park, which has investigated the barrier effect of the highway and the effectiveness of wildlife crossing structures on birds, small mammals, ungulates and carnivores (Paquet, 1996; Clevenger, 1997; Clevenger and Waltho, 1999; Gloyne and Clevenger, 2001; Clevenger et al., 2003; St Clair, 2003; McDonald and St Clair, 2004). A potentially powerful approach to identifying the ecological effects of roads in urban areas is to develop collaborative research programmes that are integrated across different cities to answer the same questions. While this increases the logistical difficulties, this approach will ensure that the observed results are more reliable and generalisations will be more widely applicable. This does not preclude the use of results from species- or location-specific studies, as they may potentially be pooled and summarised later.

The rapidly urbanising landscapes common to many sprawling cities provides excellent opportunities for experimental research. New local, collector and arterial roads are frequently being constructed and smaller roads expanded to cope with increasing human populations and vehicle travel demands. While this occurs throughout the landscape, the greatest rate of change occurs in urban areas, particularly on the urban–rural fringe for new building work and housing. Thus, there is an opportunity to influence the design and construction techniques for new and expanded roads to minimise environmental impact and improve prospects for the conservation of biodiversity. In contrast, the relatively high cost of retrofitting existing roads with wildlife-friendly structures that increase permeability, or with features to reduce noise, light or chemical pollution will limit the conservation gains.

Another approach is to develop viability models for populations or meta-populations that attempt to approximate and predict the effects of different variables. Lopez (2004) modelled the effect of urban development and road mortality on the endangered key deer (*Odocoileus virginianus clavium*), endemic to the Florida Keys, USA. The risk of the metapopulation declining to certain levels was evaluated for a range of different scenarios, from which acceptable levels of development could be decided. The work by Lopez (2004) also highlights the importance of assessing impacts of roads at the regional scale (across two islands), rather than on an *ad hoc* or parcel by parcel approach that is unlikely to evaluate fully the potential cumulative effect of incremental road construction over time.

An important step in minimising the deleterious effects of roads and traffic is to test models experimentally based on field data. Gutzwiller and Barrow (2003) outline in detail an experimental protocol to test the hypotheses about the influence of roads on nighthawks (*Chordeiles acutipennis*) in the Chihuahuan Desert, USA. They suggest that when roads are being closed to traffic, appropriate and statistically rigorous comparisons be made with control sites that remain open to traffic. To improve precision and power to detect significant differences, studies should also include before and after measurements across a number of replicate sites. While closing roads in urban landscapes may be problematic, the principle of using management as an experiment is still valid. In urban areas, the treatment may be to reduce vehicle speed, close the road at certain times of day or year, reduce or increase rate of traffic flow, erect sound barriers, or replace concrete gutters with permeable vegetated swales.

The key areas of research that need to be addressed to provide innovative solutions centre on quantifying the main effects of roads in urban areas and testing mitigation techniques. Furthermore, research questions should focus on elucidating the mechanisms responsible for observed responses which will assist in the transfer of findings across different urban areas as well as into rural and natural landscapes. More specifically, the questions include the following:

(1) What are the main ecological effects of roads and traffic in urban areas? For example, is the mortality of wildlife a greater concern than the pollution of waterways or interruption to the acoustic communication of wildlife? And under what circumstances does the relative effect of each vary?

(2) What species, habitat and ecological process within urban and urbanising landscapes are most affected by roads and traffic?

(3) What are the characteristics of the species, habitat or process that make it most vulnerable to the effects of roads and traffic?

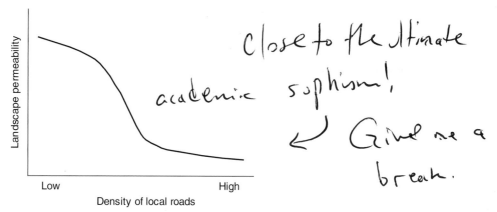

Close to the ultimate academic sophism! ← Give me a break.

Fig. 11.1. Hypothesised relationship between various measures of the road network and ecological effect.

(4) How does road density and traffic volume influence the severity of the effects of roads and traffic in urban areas?

(5) What are the relative effects of the road and traffic per se, compared with the associated development that occurs as an area is urbanised?

(6) What are the secondary effects of roads and traffic? If pollinators are unable to traverse roads, what are the consequences for viability of plant communities?

(7) To what extent are new roads and the use of motor vehicles as a primary means of transportation a cause or consequence of urban sprawl?

These questions generate predictions or hypotheses that can provide a foundation for the design and analysis of future research and experiments. For example, Fig. 11.1 attempts to relate the density of local roads to the landscape permeability. However, to understand fully the ecological effect of roads and traffic within urban areas, a third axis, measuring some aspect of the extent of urbanisation, such as human population density or extent of habitat loss or fragmentation, needs to be added to Fig. 11.1.

In this example, the *y*-axis is a measure of landscape permeability against road density (*x*-axis). The *y*-axis could be a measure of rate of road kill, population viability, extent of degradation to adjacent habitat or alteration to acoustic communication, while the *x*-axis could measure traffic volume, road width, traffic noise or extent of pollution.

Conclusion

Much of our current understanding of the ecological effects of roads and traffic on flora, fauna and ecological processes in urban landscapes is derived from studies in rural or wilderness areas. However, urban landscapes lie towards the other end of a continuum that describes human impacts on landscapes. Thus, it is unclear how far the general principles of road ecology from more natural systems can be applied to urban roads. Nevertheless, roads and traffic are likely to have ecological effects in urban, suburban and urbanising landscapes. To develop generalities and theories of road effects in urban areas, a number of key questions and approaches are proposed. The questions should focus on identifying the main effects of roads in urban areas, and on the effectiveness of mitigation approaches designed to ameliorate those negative effects.

12

Spatial pattern and process in urban animal communities

YOSIHIRO NATUHARA AND HIROSHI HASHIMOTO

Introduction

Urbanisation provides an environmental gradient from a highly developed core to a rural or natural area (Numata, 1976; McDonnell and Pickett, 1990). Urban–rural gradients provide a useful laboratory in which to examine environmental effects on communities. Analysing changes in a biological community along such a gradient provides a scientific basis for planning ecological cities, but also makes it easier to test hypotheses through management of urban landscapes.

Urban ecosystem studies in Japan started in 1971 as a part of a project on 'human survival and environment' (Numata, 1976). Numata defined an urban ecosystem as one consisting of man-modified and man-made ecosystems, and he proposed three approaches to urban ecosystems: (1) examining the flow of energy, matter, people and information; (2) studying the impact of an urban environment on terrestrial and aquatic ecosystems; and (3) studying reactions to the abiotic environment (in the Clementian sense). He and his colleagues reported a series of urban ecological studies of metropolitan Tokyo (see Numata, 1982).

Although urban ecological study in Japan covers many fields, such as pollution of air and water, urban climates and the water cycle, one important subject is the impact of urbanisation on flora, fauna and the biological community. Early studies focused on biological indicators of urbanisation; lichen (Taoda,

Ecology of Cities and Towns: A Comparative Approach, ed. Mark J. McDonnell, Amy K. Hahs and Jürgen H. Breuste. Published by Cambridge University Press. © Cambridge University Press 2009.

1973), alien plants (Hotta, 1977), soil arthropods (Aoki, 1979), and the retreat of wild animals (Chiba, 1973) were used as indicators. Through comprehensive study of urban ecology, Numata (1987) identified the importance of landscape ecology in urban ecosystem studies. He emphasised this approach as a holistic or integrated approach to the anthropocentric ecosystem.

The different academic streams of landscape ecology in Japan can be traced to three sources: geography, landscape architecture and ecology. Nishikawa (1951) introduced the works of Carl Troll to the Geographical Society in Japan, and Sugiura (1974) reviewed the theory and methodology of landscape ecology in Troll's context. Their geo-ecological approach was further developed by Yokoyama (1995). Takeuchi (1975, 1991) introduced a geo-ecological approach, derived from geography, to the field of landscape architecture in Japan and proposed 'regional ecology' that aims for the management and restoration of regional environments for human welfare. Ide and Kameyama (1993) also argued that landscape ecology research is conducted to inform management, conservation, restoration and the construction of new landscape features. This broad definition of landscape ecology encompasses the work of landscape architects and has stimulated the uptake of ecological studies in the Japan Institute of Landscape Architecture. As mentioned, Numata introduced landscape ecology to the Japan Ecological Society and organised the creation of the International Association of Landscape Ecology (IALE)-Japan Chapter in 1991. Nakagoshi has recently been vigorously pursuing this defined landscape ecology as a spatial approach to investigating ecological phenomena, such as circulation, productivity and biological communities (Nakagoshi, 1995). Most of the important studies on the landscape ecology of Japan have focused on rural landscapes (Kamada and Nakagoshi, 1996; Fukamachi et al., 2001).

Although the importance of the fusion between urban ecology and landscape ecology has been emphasised, only a few papers have been published in Japan. Some of these are on pattern analysis of urban landscapes (Yokohari and Fukuhara, 1988; Hasebe and Suzuki, 1997; Ochi et al., 2000), and others are on function of urban landscapes as habitat (Hamabata, 1980; Higuchi et al., 1982; Hashimoto et al., 1994; Hattori et al., 1994; Toyama and Nakagoshi, 1994; Imai and Natuhara, 1996; Natuhara and Imai, 1996; Yabe et al., 1998; Goto et al., 1999; Hashimoto et al., 2005).

In this study we identify the effects of habitat fragmentation on species in urban and suburban areas. In particular, by making use of comparative studies of different taxonomic groups, we test the hypotheses that: (1) habitat fragmentation in urban gradients generally increases species diversity; and (2) the effects of urbanisation depend on the life histories of the species. We also explore methods for conservation of species diversity in the urban area.

Study area

Osaka Prefecture occupies an area of $1864\,km^2$ in the western region of Japan and has a human population of 8 830 000. The annual mean temperature and precipitation are 16.2 °C and 1400 mm, respectively. The monthly mean temperature varies from 5.5 °C in January to 28.2 °C in August, and monthly mean precipitation varies from 34 mm in December to 206 mm in July. Elevations in Osaka vary from sea level at the Osaka Plains to 1125 m at Mt Kongo. The dominant potential natural vegetation types are evergreen broad-leaved forest, consisting of *Castanopsis cuspidata* var. *sieboldii* and *Quercus glauca* from plain to hilly areas, and deciduous forest of *Fagus crenata* in the upper mountain. Analyses of pollen in geographical strata reveal that lowland forests were cleared and converted to paddies 2000–3000 years ago.

Habitats along urban gradients

In Osaka Prefecture, as in other cities, built areas decrease from the centre of the urban core to the suburbs, while the area of cultivated field increases and then decreases with increasing forest area (Fig. 12.1). In urban areas, fragmented habitats appear as islands in a matrix of built, cultivated and natural areas. Many studies have used island-biogeography theory to analyse fragmented habitats in urban areas, reporting that important variables affecting the species were forest area, degree of isolation, age since isolation, and combinations of these factors (Willis, 1979; Higuchi *et al.*, 1982; Howe, 1984; Opdam *et al.*, 1984; Askins *et al.*, 1987; Soule *et al.*, 1988; Bolger *et al.*, 1991; Haila *et al.*, 1993; Ichinose and Katoh, 1994). The determinants of species diversity are often too complex to be modelled by area alone. The incorporation of other variables such as a measure of habitat heterogeneity or resource availability may be necessary (Boecklen and Gotelli, 1984). Another important finding was that bird species in isolated habitats tended to show high nestedness (Simberloff and Abele, 1976; Patterson and Atmar, 1986; Hashimoto *et al.*, 2005). Species are not distributed randomly among the isolated habitats; instead, their response to fragmentation is influenced by their population and life-history traits (With *et al.*, 1997; Natuhara and Imai, 1999).

At the same time, urbanisation creates land mosaics (Forman, 1995; Natuhara and Imai, 1996). A gradient can be seen in the land cover, and in the intermediate zone, mosaics of forest and open field are detected (Fig. 12.1). Formation of the mosaic landscape sometimes increases the biodiversity, although urbanisation is generally a major cause of the loss of biodiversity. We examine this mosaic model of habitat and its meaning in the urban area.

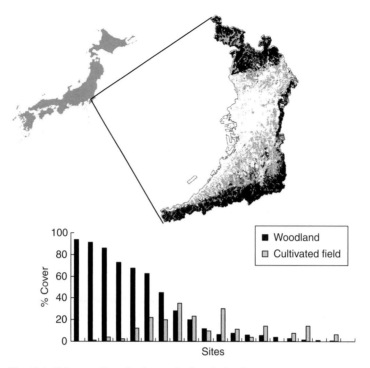

Fig. 12.1. Urban gradient in the study site, Osaka, Japan.

The effects of landscape mosaics on biodiversity are the result of various mechanisms, and are exerted at various spatial scales (Hansson, 1979; Helle and Muona, 1985; Yahner, 1988). Species richness may increase in a mosaic of habitats by the following mechanisms: the formation of a new habitat at a boundary between neighbouring elements, such as the vegetation of forest edges with shrub layer forming the mantle and the lianas forming the veil; and the mosaic effect per se, which is that a mosaic of forests and open lands can contain habitats for both forest species and open land species. Several butterflies use a set of resources in the habitat, e.g. food plants for larva and a nectar source for adults, and their habitat must be a mosaic of different vegetation. However, some species may disappear from the mosaic because of the fragmentation of habitat, and less mobile species cannot move beyond a barrier between patchy habitats.

Furthermore, the quality of urban and suburban habitats is changing in the study area; the traditional coppicing in the Satoyama landscape (Natuhara *et al.*, 1999; Fukamachi *et al.*, 2001), which is a mosaic of secondary forests, grasslands, farmlands and irrigation ponds, has been abandoned over the past 40 years. The lucidophyll (evergreen broad-leaved) forests in southwestern Japan have been converted to deciduous *Quercus* forest by human use over the past several thousand years. These forests have historically been fragmented by farmlands,

Table 12.1. *A comparison of species–area relationships in taxonomic groups in Osaka, Japan.*

Group	$S = cA^z$			$S = b \ln A + c$		
	c	z	r^2	c	b	r^2
Birds[a]	1.595	0.235	0.880	1.296	3.717	0.687
Butterflies[b]	6.580	0.293	0.762	4.088	4.594	0.699
Ants (Osaka)[c]	10.751	0.050	0.048	11.453	0.696	0.083
Ants (Kyoto)[d]	15.109	0.101	0.135	16.046	1.398	0.124
Trees[e]	37.8	0.301	0.671	43.4	11.295	0.780
Ferns[f]	9.387	0.408	0.636	13.5	5.347	0.668

Notes:

[a] Natuhara and Imai (1999);

[b] Imai and Natuhara (1996);

[c] Natuhara (1998);

[d] Yui *et al.* (2001);

[e] Murakami and Morimoto (2000);

[f] Murakami *et al.* (2003).

but more recently both the remaining forests and farmlands have been covered by buildings and asphalt during urbanization. The gradient of urban habitats includes the following components: reduction, isolation, mosaic formation and ecological succession of habitats.

Urban habitats as islands

We compared species–area curves among five taxonomic groups: birds, butterflies, ants, trees and ferns. Generally the relationships can be described either by a power function (Eq. (12.1)) or log function (Eq. (12.2)), although we were also able to fit the data to a logistic curve.

$$S = cA^z \tag{12.1}$$

$$S = b \ln A + c \tag{12.2}$$

where S is species richness, A is habitat area, and b, c and z are constants. Coefficient of determinants (r^2) was high for most groups in both power and log models, but ants had low coefficients of determination in both models (Table 12.1). In the power function analysis, the species richness in 1 ha areas was highest for trees, followed by ants, ferns and butterflies, with the lowest richness for birds, although statistically significant regression could not be

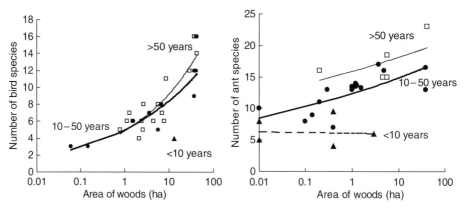

Figure 12.2. A comparison of species–area curves between birds and ants in Osaka, Japan. Symbols indicate years after plantation of forests: squares and thin lines, more than 50 years; circles and thick lines, 10–50 years; triangles and broken lines, less than 10 years.

estimated for ants. The slope was highest for ferns, then trees, butterflies, birds and lowest for ants. When the log function was used, the slope was highest in trees.

We assessed the affect of age since development of habitats on species richness by classifying them as younger than 10 years old, between 10 and 50 years old, and older (Fig. 12.2). Using an analysis of covariance we found that ant species richness varied with age group, but there were no significant differences in the species richness between age groups in birds and butterflies with the exception of the Nanko power station. The Nanko power station had extremely few bird species and many butterfly species. This habitat consisted of 3-, 7- and 10-year-old woods; most trees were evergreen, shorter than 2 m in the youngest stands and grew 10 m with high density (20 individuals per 100 m^2) in the older stands. In contrast, the species–area curve for ants varied among the three age groups.

We used linear regression to analyse the effect of distance to species source or continuous large forests on the species richness of birds, butterflies and ants in Osaka. The effect of distance was greatest in butterflies and least in ants, and there were no significant correlations in trees and ferns (Table 12.2). Differences in proportion of occurrence in urban areas and the distance effect are influenced by movement ability (i.e. dispersal for plants) and habitat size of the species. But these figures are biased, because species–distance relationships are not linear. There are 55 forest birds breeding in Osaka, but the intercept is 13.7. This means 75% of bird species do not breed in fragmented habitats even if the location is close to the continuous habitats. The intercept for butterflies is 43.7, which is about 56% of butterfly species recorded by transect counts in Osaka Prefecture. The intercept for ants is 17.7, which is 20% of 87 ant species recorded in Osaka Prefecture (Natuhara, 1998). But the distribution of ants is random among

Table 12.2. *The effect of distance (D) to species source or continuous large forest on the species richness of birds, butterflies and ants in Osaka, Japan.*

Group	b	c	r^2
Birds	−0.530	13.7	0.601
Butterflies	−2.356	43.8	0.730
Ants (Osaka)	−0.377	17.7	0.162
Trees	−	−	−
Ferns	−	−	−

Note:

$S = c + bD$. The Nanko power station was not included in this analysis. The values for trees and ferns were too small to include. S = species richness, D = distance, and c and b are constants.

fragmented habitats, and total number of species recorded in the fragmented habitats was 50 (or 57% of total species).

Possible causes of the lack of significant species–distance correlations in trees, ferns and ants in Kyoto are little or no recruitment of seeds from street trees and gardens in the urban matrix, and the long-distance dispersal ability of fern spores. In ants, passive dispersal with gardening materials causes long distance dispersal. Furthermore, possible metapopulation structure in urban habitats for these taxonomic groups may reduce the slope of the species–distance curve (Hanski and Gyllenberg, 1997). For most bird species, urban forests are too small to maintain a large enough population for long-term persistence. Thus, populations in urban forests are a sink supported by source populations in mountainous areas. On the other hand, many species of ants can maintain large populations in the urban forests, and a metapopulation is formed.

In our original analysis of the butterfly data, the distance relationship was not significant ($r^2 = 0.294$, $P = 0.0884$), but when the results from the Nanko power station site were removed from the data, a significant regression was estimated (Table 12.2). This site is located at a harbour far from the species source, but many butterflies were recorded here because Rutaceae trees, which are important food plants for butterflies, are more abundant than at other urban parks. Furthermore, some butterfly species migrate along the sea coast where the Nanko power station is located.

The species composition of birds in smaller habitats was a nested subset of the larger habitats (Table 12.3). The occurrence pattern varied according to species. Fifteen species could potentially breed in urban parks. *Streptopelia orientalis*, *Hypsipetes amaurotis*, *Zosterops japonica*, *Passer montanus* and *Sturnus cineraceus* were

Table 12.3. *Nestedness of occurrence in urban habitats for bird species in Osaka, Japan.*

	Area of woodlands (ha)			
	≥20.1	5.1–20	2.1–5	≤2
Number of sites	8	7	6	7
Average area (ha)	38.5	7.99	3.12	0.96
Species	Percentage of occurrence sites			
Japanese green woodpecker (*Picus awokera*)	13	0	0	0
Varied tit (*Parus varius*)	13	0	0	0
Common pheasant (*Phasianus colchicus*)	25	0	0	0
Short-tailed bush warbler (*Cettia squameiceps*)	25	0	0	0
Japanese grosbeak (*Eophona personata*)	25	0	0	0
Bush warbler (*Cettia diphone*)	63	0	0	0
Japanese pygmy woodpecker (*Dendrocopos kizuki*)	88	0	0	0
Siberian meadow bunting (*Emberiza cioides*)	50	14	0	0
Bamboo partridge (*Bambusicola thoracica*)	38	29	0	0
Long-tailed tit (*Aegithalos caudatus*)	75	29	0	0
Jungle crow (*Corvus macrorhynchos*)	88	14	33	0
Carrion crow (*Corvus corone*)	100	43	17	14
Bull-headed shrike (*Lanius bucephalus*)	63	43	33	14
Great tit (*Parus major*)	100	29	33	14
Oriental greenfinch (*Carduelis sinica*)	88	29	33	29
Japanese white-eye (*Zosterops japonica*)	100	57	67	71
Gray starling (*Sturnus cineraceus*)	88	100	83	71
Rufous turtle dove (*Streptopelia orientalis*)	100	100	100	100
Brown-eared bulbul (*Hypsipetes amaurotis*)	100	100	100	100
Tree sparrow (*Passer montanus*)	100	100	100	100

recorded at all forests, and the other ten species were primarily restricted to forests greater than 5 ha. In areas with lower amounts of forest, the numbers of carnivorous and insectivorous species decreased more rapidly than those of granivores and omnivores.

The distribution of species in urban habitats depends on their life history. The most important trait is the variety of microhabitat used by the species. Nakamura (1988) classified the habitats in the study area into open spaces in forests, open space edges, forest edges and forest interiors, and reported an occurrence pattern of species in those microhabitats. Species using the forest edge, *Parus major*, *Aegithalos caudatus* and *Emberiza cioides*, occurred in middle-sized urban forests in the present study (Table 12.3). *Cettia diphone*, which uses not only forest edges but also open space in forests, occurred only in large forests. Forest interior species did not occur in the urban forest.

The distribution of carnivorous birds and insectivorous birds was limited to large forests. This is understandable for carnivores because they need a large home range. Canaday (1997) discussed the causes of the negative relationship between the number of insectivorous species and the degree of human impact. His list of important factors includes: microclimatic changes that have altered the insect prey base, greater habitat sensitivity among insectivores resulting from their high degrees of ecological specialisation, changes in predation upon these birds, and interference competition from opportunistic, disturbance-adapted omnivores (Canaday, 1997). In California, out of 12 species of birds found in non-developed areas, half (six species) were insectivores, and no insectivores were found in developed areas (Blair, 1996). In Canada, Lancaster and Rees (1979) reported that 63% of species in forests were insectivores, in contrast to 1% of species in commercial industrial areas.

In Osaka, *Parus major* and *Carduelis sinica*, in particular, increased in occurrence as urban forest patches increased from 1 to 20 ha (Table 12.3). Habitats for these species at forest edges or scattered forest may emerge in this size of forest. Similarly, habitats in the forest interior and open spaces in forests for *C. diphone* and *Dendrocopos kizuki* may emerge in forests of more than 20 ha. The way that these species use habitats in urban parks has not been studied so far. Studies of microhabitat use by these species and comparison of microhabitat structures among urban parks are needed to confirm the habitat diversity hypothesis.

Generalist or forest edge species adapt their behaviour to urban landscapes. *Parus major* (which includes *P. minor*) is found in both forests and urban parks in Japan, but the population density is very low in downtown Tokyo and downtown Osaka. In our study of 85 parks in Osaka, *P. major* was present in only 12, with an additional three occurrences noted in areas outside the study sites (Hashimoto *et al.*, 2005). Although these three occurrences were not study sites, we counted them in the number of surrounding habitats. The average areas of parks where *P. major* were recorded and not recorded were 26.0 ± 42.1 ha (1 S.D.) and 2.1 ± 2.9 ha, respectively. The smallest park was 0.56 ha. Breeding behaviour was compared between two areas with different percentage of wood cover (Inoue *et al.*, in press). Interestingly, the home range areas of breeding pairs were larger in the area with the lower percentage of wood cover. Mean home range size was 4.70 ha at the site where the percentage of tree cover was 31.5%, and 0.76 ha at the other site where the percentage of tree cover was 76.6%. *Parus major* breeding in the former site probably required a larger home range to get food for their fledglings.

In comparison with birds and butterflies, ants, trees and ferns did not show nestedness, partly because they usually need smaller areas as habitats. Peintinger *et al.* (2003) also reported a random pattern in distributions of vascular plants, bryophytes, butterflies and grasshoppers; species richness increased with the area of habitat islands, but overlap among them was so low that even small habitat islands contributed to overall species richness.

From the above results, we conclude that the requirements of a species for space and mobility strongly affect its distribution in urban habitats. The hypothesis of random immigration and extinction in the equilibrium theory of island biogeography is not realistic (Patterson and Atmar, 1986). Occurrence of bird species is not random; instead, each species follows a specific pattern (Lancaster and Rees, 1979; Higuchi et al., 1982; Ambuel and Temple, 1983; Blake, 1991; Hansen and Urban, 1992; Canaday, 1997), the nested subset pattern, in which most species present in small habitats also occur in larger habitats. A species' abundance in its source habitat, its body size (Soule et al., 1988; Bolger et al., 1991) and its need for a forest interior (Blake, 1991) are important factors among life-history characteristics that influence the nested subset pattern.

The distribution of species in urban habitats affects strategies for conservation. Consider two hypothetical patterns of species in habitats: nested subset and heterogeneous. In the former case, habitats holding fewer species do not contribute to species diversity at a regional scale. In the latter case, few species occur in multiple habitats because of differences in their habitat requirements, and habitats holding fewer species contribute species diversity at a regional scale. By simulating random arrangement of samples, we found that several small habitats contain more species of ants than a single large habitat of the same size. We obtained the opposite results for birds and butterflies. However, this pattern of butterfly distribution is not universal. No nestedness was detected in butterflies inhabiting mountainous wetlands (Peintinger et al., 2003).

Faunal change along the urban gradient

The intensity of habitat fragmentation by urbanisation varies from the suburbs to the urban core, influencing the arrangement of habitat. Forests are fragmented by farmlands in rural areas, and both forests and farmlands change to buildings and asphalt in the urban core. Examination of faunal change along this environmental gradient from continuous large habitats to habitat mosaics is important for conservation planning. In the intermediate level of forest reduction (forest cover from 65% to 10%), increasing farmland area forms land mosaics (Fig. 12.1) and the number of fragmented forests increased in the $4\,\text{km}^2$ grids as forest cover increased from 10% to 35% of the grid. In this section we focus on the effects of the habitat mosaics in Osaka on bird and butterfly assemblages at the landscape scale.

For bird assemblages, we recorded the proportion of nine types of land use (forest, scattered forest, farmland, grassland, bare ground, residence, city centre,

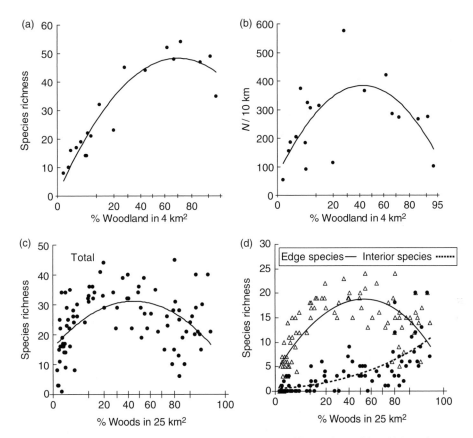

Figure 12.3. Relationships between percentage of forests in a grid and (a) species richness of butterflies, (b) population density of butterflies, (c) species richness of birds, and (d) species richness of forest interior birds and forest edge birds. In the plots for butterflies (a, b), $N/10$ km means number of individuals recorded along a 10-km transect route with width 10 m, giving an area of 0.1 km². But we indicate percentage forest within a 2×2 km² square that includes the transect route. In the case of birds (c, d), bird records in a 5×5 km² square were used instead of route transect records, giving $N/25$ km².

pond and river, and sea) and the presence or absence of each of 76 breeding birds in 5 km square quadrats on a map of Osaka Prefecture (Natuhara and Imai, 1996). For butterfly assemblages, 78 butterflies were recorded along 19 transect routes in various land covers (Natuhara, 2000).

The number of bird species is shown against percentage of forest in Fig. 12.3. The highest richness is detected at around the 50% level. The relationship varies among species groups with different habitat use. Species richness changed according to the proportion of forest in the 5 km square and showed a unimodal curve. However, the response was different in forest-interior species from forest-edge species; the former increased approximately linearly with increasing proportion of forest, whereas forest-edge species had highest species richness when 50% of the sample grids were covered by forest.

Butterflies showed a similar pattern to birds; the peak in population density occurred when about 50% of the area was covered by forest and the peak in species richness occurred for about 70% coverage (Fig. 12.3). Hogsden and Hutchinson (2004) also reported that butterfly assemblages had equal or higher numbers of individuals and species richness at moderately disturbed sites compared with the least disturbed site. Increased habitat heterogeneity, measured as the number of land-cover types within an area, is a strong predictor of butterfly richness and diversity. This pattern of butterfly assemblages along the human-disturbance gradient is a result of patchy fragments of suitable habitat, in even highly disturbed areas, in which butterflies can persist (Hiura, 1973, 1976; Hardy and Dennis, 1999; Kerr, 2001).

However, individual species responded differently (Table 12.4). Although most species showed a unimodal curve with a peak at intermediate levels of wooded area, some species appear only in large continuous forests. The relationship between percentage forest and abundance of butterfly species varies among species groups with different life history. There are several patterns of changes in abundance by food habit (e.g. tree, bamboo, herb, forest edge) of larvae (Table 12.4). Univoltine species of tree feeder are distributed only in sites with continuous forests. Vagrant species (Dennis and Hardy, 2001), r-strategist species (Kitahara and Fujii, 1994), and oligo- or polyphagous species (Koh and Sodhi, 2004) are reported to be relatively more abundant in urban sites than non-urban sites.

These changes in bird and butterfly diversity along the Osaka urban gradients were also detected by ordination (Natuhara and Imai, 1996; Natuhara, 2000). The proportions of forest and of farmland are two major environmental gradients, according to Principal Components Analysis of the nine types of land use. Ordination by Canonical Correspondence Analysis (CCA) showed that breeding bird distribution differentiated along the two major clines, forest and farmland (Natuhara and Imai, 1999). There were no discrete boundaries of the distribution of bird-species groups. We tentatively classified five groups of 25 km^2 grids and five groups of bird species in CCA.

Five grid groups were characterized by the bird species and land use as follows. The first grid group was characterized by a large woodland area (91.4%) and appearance of forest birds such as Hodgson's hawk-eagle (*Spizaetus nipalensis*) and white-backed woodpecker (*Dendrocopos leucotos*). These species are rare in Osaka Prefecture. The second group seem to have more fragmented woodland (forest area 69.5%) than the first group and was characterized by appearance of forest birds such as the copper pheasant (*Phasianus soemmerringii*) and Japanese lesser sparrowhawk (*Accipiter gularis*). Farmland area increased in the third group

Table 12.4. *The abundance of butterfly species as a function of percentage of woods and food type.*

Decrease1: species whose population density decreases with decreasing forest cover and which are not distributed in urban core (left side of each figure). Decrease2: similar to Decrease1 but distributed in urban core. Increase: number of species whose population density increases with decreasing forest cover. Unimodal1: species whose population density shows unimodal curve with the peak at higher percentage of forest cover. Unimodal2: similar to Unimodal1 but population peak appears at lower percentage of forest cover.

Butterfly abundance					
	←	Forest cover (%)			→
	Decrease1	Decrease2	Increase	Unimodal1	Unimodal2
Tree, U	4				
Tree, M	2	1	1	2	
Edge	4			5	
Bamboo	4			1	
Herb, U	4			1	
Herb, M	2	1		4	6

Note:

Tree, edge, bamboo and herb are food type, where 'edge' means that the food plants often appear in the forest edge. U: univoltine, M: multivoltine species

(farmland 19.2% and forest 17.0%). The third group did not have a distinctive avifauna and contained a variety of bird species from water birds to birds inhabiting scattered woodland. The fourth and fifth groups are characterized by water, built-up areas and no forest in both groups, and the fifth group was discriminated from the fourth by the presence of sea shore and decreasing area of scattered woodland. The fourth grid group was characterized by birds of paddy and marsh, such as the ruddy crake (*Porzana fusca*) and grey-headed lapwing (*Microsarcops cinereus*). The fifth group was characterized by birds of the river mouth, such as the European coot (*Fulica atra*) and snowy plover (*Charadrius alexandrinus*).

The average number of species per grid for the five groups was 34.5, 26.2, 36.3, 23.4 and 21.8, respectively. The fact that average species richness in a grid was highest in the third group suggested that diversity of land use could increase species richness. However, the first group, consisting of continuous woodland, contained as many species as the third group.

These effects of landscape mosaics (patchworks of forest and open land) may appear on various spatial scales, and butterfly assemblages can be studied on several spatial scales, such as the region, landscape and local habitat. On the landscape and smaller scales, the landscape mosaic enhanced the species richness of butterflies, but the diversity indices and specialist species (univoltine tree feeder) decreased in the mosaic landscape (Natuhara *et al.*, 1999).

At the same time, the abandonment of traditional coppicing in the Satoyama landscape, which is a mosaic of secondary forests and farmlands (Natuhara *et al.*, 1999; Fukamachi *et al.*, 2001), has changed the species composition of butterflies (Ishii *et al.* 1995). Lucidophyll (evergreen broad-leaved) forests have historically occurred in southwestern Japan, and a considerable proportion of them have been changed to deciduous *Quercus* forest by human use. An important process in forest succession in southwestern Japan is the recovery of the evergreen broad-leaved (lucidophyll) oak forest from the deciduous *Quercus* forest that used to be maintained by human interference, such as coppicing. We compared the proportion of butterflies having strong relations with the lucidophyll forest. The lucidophyll forest species were *Graphium sarpedon*, *Papilip helenus*, *Narathura japonica*, *Narathura bazalus*, *Ussuriana stygiana* and *Melanitis phedima*. The proportion of the lucidophyll forest butterflies was high not only in lucidophyll forest but also in urban areas. The high proportion of lucidophyll forest butterflies in urban areas is caused by the planting of *Cinnamomum camphora* in shrines and public parks, and as street trees. Thus, the gradient of habitats includes two components: the degree of habitat mosaics and the stage of ecological succession.

Mosaics at fine scales

Fine-scale heterogeneity also enhances the species diversity of birds (MacArthur and MacArthur, 1961). In our study, ant species diversity increased with increasing microhabitat diversity. Yui *et al.* (2001) reported that species richness of ants was positively correlated with the number of microhabitat types, such as stones and herbaceous patches. They explained the species richness of ants at two different scales by using a structural equation model (Fig. 12.4). The area and shape index of forest affected the habitat quality at larger scales, and management intensity and microhabitat diversity in the forest were important at smaller scales. The effect of habitat quality was stronger at smaller scales than at larger scales.

The mosaic at a fine scale is also important for butterflies. Chikamatsu *et al.* (2002) monitored the effect of gap clearance in the study area on butterfly assemblages. The average number of species and number of individuals were higher at the gaps (11.3 species, 40 individuals) than the interior of forest (3.2 species, 7 individuals). Among four gaps where the sky factor (proportion

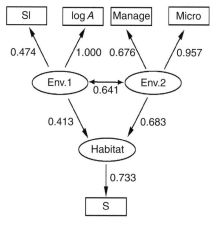

Fig. 12.4. Structural equation model for species richness of ants in urban habitats. Circles indicate latent variables: hypothetical variables that cannot be observed directly, but are derived from observed variables (boxes). Env.1: combination of area (log A) and shape index (SI) of woodlots. Env.2: combination of management (Manage) and microhabitat diversity (Micro) of woodlots. Together, Env1 and Env2 determine the species richness of ants (S). Numbers are standardised factor loadings that represent the strength of relatedness between variables (after Yui *et al.*, 2001).

of open area to all-sky area observed from the forest floor) was measured using hemispherical photographs, population density and species richness correlated with the sky factor. Pollard and Yates (1993) summarised the butterfly monitoring in Monks Wood (Cambridgeshire, UK) by saying that clearance at the edges of the ride is beneficial to butterflies. On the scale of individual movement, butterflies can sample a much more diverse array of habitat types in fine-grained landscapes (Debinski *et al.*, 2001).

Urban landscape planning and adaptive management

A goal of urban landscape ecology is to restore ecosystems in urban areas. Fauna in urban areas are influenced by the size and shape of the habitat, percentage of forest in the surrounding areas, and distance to the species source. Among these, as mentioned in the previous section, habitat size is the most important factor for most groups. An isolated forest does not perform well as a habitat for many birds. Askins *et al.* (1987) reported that there were no differences in population of edge species between larger forests (>187 ha) and smaller ones (i.e. forests from 186 to 20 ha). But there were significant differences in populations of forest interior species. In particular, insectivorous species are the most sensitive to the reduction of forest interior habitat in smaller patches which results from fragmentation. Edge species, on the other hand, are less sensitive and can inhabit forest of all sizes as long as there is an edge habitat. If a larger area of forest cannot be supported in cities, increasing the percentage of forest in urban regions by planting small groves can help the colonisation by forest edge species. It is important to realise that urban areas, which represent the fragmentation of potential habitats, can support a diversity of several groups such as butterflies, even species that avoid disturbance, if we create and maintain suitable environments (Hogsden and Hutchinson, 2004). For bird species in Osaka, planted forests (age >10 years) were not inferior to older forest with the same area (Natuhara and Imai, 1999). Vale and Vale (1976) reported that garden plantings seem most influential in determining the distribution and density of birds. Horticultural plantings are typically more luxuriant and provide more diverse habitats than the pre-suburban environments. This is also true for insects; distribution and abundance are more likely to be limited by the availability of suitable habitat than by their migration ability (Wood and Pullin, 2002). Several methods for increasing urban biodiversity were tested with replication (Gaston *et al.*, 2005), and some of the methods, such as bamboo sections as a nesting site for solitary bees and wasps, were found to be effective in increasing biodiversity.

From an ecological viewpoint, in urban areas it may be better to design habitats for individual species than for species richness or abundance as a whole, owing to their relatively small size. Hashimoto *et al.* (in press) focused on the great tit (*P. major*) for reasons mentioned in the previous section, and found that the best-fitting logistic regression model for describing the distribution of *P. major* in Osaka was

$$\text{logit } P = -18.144 + 3.799\, A250 + 0.688 N1 \tag{12.3}$$

where P is the probability of occurrence, $A250$ is the area of tree cover within a radius of 250 m (19.6 ha) and $N1$ is the number of other habitats (i.e. tree patches) within 1 km of the centre point, excluding the central 19.6 ha (Fig. 12.5). More tree cover is needed for great tits if the number of nearby habitats is small. By applying the model it was found that to achieve a probability of occurrence of 0.5 when the number of other habitats within a 1 km buffer was 0, 1, 2 and 3, tree areas of 6.0 ha (31%), 4.0 ha (20%), 2.6 ha (13%) and 1.8 ha (9%) are required.

From the model and its examination (Hashimoto *et al.*, 2005), a minimum of 1.8 ha tree cover in a radius of 250 m or 9% of the area, and at least three other habitats within 1 km, are factors necessary to provide habitat for *P. major* in urban areas. Thus, more than 10% of tree cover is a realistic target figure for an ecologically sustainable environment for urban areas. The tree cover of Osaka City in 1991 was only 4.1%, but its target figure for 2005 is 15% (Osaka City Greenery Promotion Division, 1995), which includes trees in large parks. A target

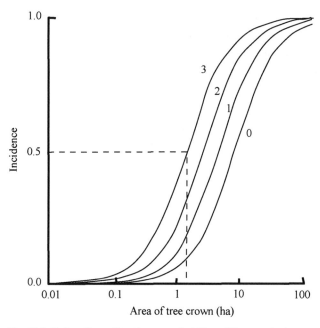

Fig. 12.5. Estimation of incidence probability of *Parus major* by area of tree crown and number of neighbouring habitats in Osaka, Japan. Each line represents the number of neighbouring habitats from 0 to 3 within 1 km. When there are three neighbouring habitats within 1 km, incidence probability is 0.5 with a tree crown area of 1.2 ha.

of 10% tree cover for areas outside large parks is required to maximise avian biodiversity. This target is rather high and difficult to achieve in the urban area of Osaka, but there will be chances to create habitat for *P. major* by using combinations of park networks, roadside trees and rooftop gardens.

Ecosystems are unpredictable and it may be useful to modify plans in response to the results of biodiversity monitoring. Adaptive management is a useful method for conservation of biodiversity in urban landscapes. In 2001, six artificial gaps (15 × 15 m) were created in an urban forest (98.5 ha) at the Expo'70 Commemorative Park in an urban area of Osaka. Thirty years have passed since the completion of land reclamation, and the broad-leaved evergreen trees that were planted are now established. Planners thought that the broad-leaved evergreen forest was the potential natural vegetation of the site. However, low penetration of solar radiation to the forest floor seemed to restrict the diversity of vegetation there (Nakamura *et al.*, 2005) and the effect of gap clearance on butterfly assemblages was monitored (Chikamatsu *et al.*, 2002). Butterflies were recorded in 15 × 15 m quadrats for 10 minutes at six gaps, six plots of interior forest adjacent to the gaps, a vegetable garden and an area of turf. Average number of species, *S*, and number of individuals, *N*, were, respectively,

13 and 55 at a vegetable garden, 11.3 and 40 at gaps, 3.2 and 7 at forest interiors, and 2 and 6 at the turf site. Five species, including *Papilio bianor*, were recorded only at the gaps, and the gaps changed the species composition of butterflies and increased the species diversity in the park as a whole. Future monitoring and a clearance programme are planned because population densities of some species of butterflies and birds change with years after coppicing (Warren, 1987; Fuller *et al.*, 1989).

Summary

Urban gradients provide a useful laboratory for landscape ecology. Along the gradient, the amount and arrangement of habitat for animals change. We compared the response of various taxonomic groups in the large city of Osaka, Japan, in order to examine relationships between the abundance and arrangement of the habitats, and life-history traits of the species. We have presented species-specific responses to habitat fragmentation. We compared changes in urban habitats in birds, butterflies, ants, trees and ferns. Species richness decreased more rapidly in birds than ants from the urban to rural ends of the urban gradient, and butterflies were intermediate. Birds were influenced by the habitat area and distance to species source. In contrast, ants were less influenced by habitat area, but were susceptible to the history of the isolated habitats. In ants, trees and ferns, some rare species occurred even in small habitats and the small habitats contributed to species diversity in the urban areas of Osaka. Simultaneously, variation of the life history affected the distribution of species. For example, *Parus major* was able to breed in urban areas by using scattered trees in an urban matrix; their home range enlarged in the urban area to secure sufficient food. One of the major goals of urban landscape ecology is to use scientific information to restore and preserve biodiversity in urban ecosystems.

Acknowledgements

We acknowledge the following people for their help: Yukihiro Morimoto, Hisayuki Maenaka, Akihiro Nakamura, Ayuko Yui, Minako Chikamatsu, Yasuko Mizutani, Kentaro Murakami, Chobei Imai and the Expo'70 Memorial Park Office. We would like to thank Michael McCarthy for his help in improving the manuscript.

13

Invertebrate biodiversity in urban landscapes: assessing remnant habitat and its restoration

DIETER F. HOCHULI, FIONA J. CHRISTIE AND BORIS LOMOV

Introduction

Remnants of natural ecosystems in urban environments are at the centre of an emerging discipline in ecology, reflecting population shifts towards towns and cities and the urgent need to understand the ecology of the environments in which most of the world's population live (McDonnell and Pickett, 1993b; Grimm *et al.*, 2000). Major themes focus on understanding the way in which these landscapes have responded to the effects of urbanisation and how these impacts can be ameliorated (Kendle and Forbes, 1997). The importance of urban ecosystems is further enhanced by their social implications; these systems are a first connection with nature for much of the world's population and as such are important tools for education and contributions to emotional well-being (Kaplan, 1995). There are dramatic shifts in biodiversity in urban habitats, driven by local extinctions and invasions by exotic species. Terrestrial arthropods, the drivers of many ecological processes in urban environments, are under-represented in the emerging field of urban ecology, despite their abundance, diversity and importance (Kremen *et al.*, 1993; Natuhara and Hashimoto, Chapter 12; McIntyre and Rango, Chapter 14).

The development of a conceptual framework of urban ecology is crucial to the development of this emerging field (Peters, 1991; Ford, 2000; Bastian, 2001; Niemelä *et al.*, Chapter 2; Pickett *et al.*, Chapter 3). The main emphasis of urban ecology, as with much of landscape ecology, is on the descriptive, with the search

Ecology of Cities and Towns: A Comparative Approach, ed. Mark J. McDonnell, Amy K. Hahs and Jürgen H. Breuste. Published by Cambridge University Press. © Cambridge University Press 2009.

for general principles and patterns hampered by the enormous variation in systems and methodological approaches adopted. In this chapter we describe the responses to urbanisation by terrestrial invertebrates and the consequences of shifts in species composition for ecological interactions in urban remnants. We also examine how these responses can be applied to the assessment of the ecological state of remnant vegetation and measures of the effectiveness of restoration efforts. Our aim is to develop a conceptual framework for evaluating the responses of terrestrial invertebrates to urbanisation, integrating survey-based approaches with experimental approaches, revealing the extent to which ecological interactions and ecosystem processes are affected by species shifts. Ultimately, we hope to identify the potential to use terrestrial invertebrates in urban environments to reveal disruptions to fundamental ecological processes and their restoration after replanting and management.

Searching for general principles in urban landscapes

Ecology's rich history of struggling to develop general principles (Peters, 1991; Beck, 1997; Ford, 2000) is reflected in the emerging disciplines of urban ecology and landscape ecology. Many of the specific criticisms of ecology target its seeming lack of progress, the absence of a general unifying theory, inadequate concepts founded without clear operational definitions and the general failure to test theories (Peters, 1991; Ford, 2000). The need to integrate descriptions of patterns in nature with explanations of the processes driving them has also been emphasised in many reviews of emerging themes in ecology (e.g. Lewin, 1983; Underwood, 1995a; Simberloff, 1998). In urban ecology, the search for general principles describing ecological patterns and processes is further complicated by the semantics and history underpinning this emerging discipline and the desire to apply it in multiple landscape contexts (Bastian, 2001). In short, landscape ecologists appear to be very good at describing patterns in specific contexts and not very good at identifying the processes causing them.

Few general themes have emerged in urban ecology, although ecosystems in urban areas are often perceived as being depauperate in biodiversity and irreparably modified owing to the apparent and pervasive anthropogenic impacts associated with cities and their growth (e.g. Davis, 1982; McDonnell et al., 1993; Grimm et al., 2000). Many urban remnants are actively managed for a range of often competing interests, including recreation, conservation and heritage values (Ehrenfeld, 1976; Grimm et al., 2000; Davies and Christie, 2001) despite being subjected to extreme anthropogenic pressures (McDonnell et al., 1993). Remnant habitat in urban environments tends to occur in small, disturbed fragments with diverse ecological and management histories. These remnants are located in numerous climatic zones (e.g. tropical, arid or temperate regions) and vegetation types (e.g. around Sydney, Australia, a city of 5 million people, urban habitats include areas of heath, woodlands, rainforest, wetlands and grasslands separated into over 20 different vegetation communities). The expectation that we should be able to develop general principles about the effects of urbanisation independently of issues such as scale, ecological history, biome and habitat is clearly a formidable challenge for ecologists and one that leads many to advocate the pursuit of general principles at finer scales (Lawton, 1999).

Nevertheless, urban ecologists are expected to develop the framework from which we can answer a range of questions. For an ecologist these would include:

- Are patterns of species loss from urban habitats predictable?
- What are the causal mechanisms underpinning change in urban habitats?
- Does species loss affect ecological functioning?
- Do patterns of species loss or change hold across cities?
- Can we repair damage to and/or recreate habitat in urban systems, such that they take on the ecological properties of suitable reference sites?

Urban contexts

As with most aspects of ecology, a lack of clear operational definitions hinders progress towards a conceptual framework. The development of a taxonomy of cities (McDonnell and Hahs, Chapter 5) is a major advance for urban ecology as is the formalising of approaches to studying the ecology 'of cities' and ecology 'in cities' (Niemelä et al., Chapter 2; Pickett et al., Chapter 3), themes developed throughout this volume.

The ecology of urban areas has previously been explored in a number of contexts, from the predominant descriptions of the fauna and flora in urban areas through to complex approaches integrating the effects of urbanisation at multiple scales. Our focus is on biodiversity in remnant habitats in cities and towns and how a range of approaches examining ecology of and in cities can be used to evaluate the ecological state of urban sites, generating hypotheses identifying how differences among and within these areas arose.

General responses to urbanisation

Mechanisms driving biotic responses

Of the pervasive modifications urbanisation imposes on the natural environment, the most apparent consequence is habitat fragmentation and loss

(Connor *et al.*, 2002). Recent reviews reveal numerous general principles outlining the effects of habitat loss and fragmentation, with small habitat fragments generally supporting fewer species than larger fragments, and with those species often represented by relatively low numbers of individuals (e.g. Lindenmayer and Franklin, 2002; Fahrig, 2003). Smaller fragments are also disproportionately affected by a range of edge effects (Turner, 1996; Ozanne *et al.*, 1997) which may aid colonisation by invasive species (Suarez *et al.*, 1998; Crawley *et al.*, 1999). Evidence for differential species losses from trophic levels (with higher trophic levels being more susceptible to local extinction) is equivocal at general levels although demonstrated in others (Crooks and Soule, 1999), with parasitoids known to be particularly susceptible to adverse effects of fragmentation (Kruess and Tscharntke, 2000).

These reviews also reveal that difficulties in separating the effects of habitat loss from those of habitat fragmentation per se pervade the literature (Fahrig, 2003). The emphasis of studies outlining responses to habitat fragmentation has been on mensurative approaches, mostly detailing shifts in species composition in habitat fragments with few studies outlining the ecological consequences of those changes. Furthermore, the importance of the landscape matrix surrounding fragments for biodiversity conservation has also been underestimated (Lindenmayer and Franklin, 2002).

Urbanisation may also affect invertebrate diversity through changes to habitat quality, independently of the effects of size, shape and isolation associated with habitat fragmentation (Natuhara and Hashimoto, Chapter 12; McIntyre and Rango, Chapter 14; Eisenbeis and Hänel, Chapter 15). Remnant habitat in urban areas may be subjected to nutrient inputs (King and Buckney, 2002), pollutant inputs (Gregg *et al.*, 2003), altered disturbance regimes (Zipperer *et al.*, 2000), and heat island effects (Landsberg, 1981). Current landscape contexts may also be inadequate predictors of biotic responses as the ecological history of urban remnants can have strong influences on current biotic composition (Cam *et al.*, 2000; Knick and Rotenberry, 2000).

Invertebrate responses to urbanisation

Although work on many terrestrial invertebrates in cities is still in its infancy, the growing literature examining their ecology ranges from relatively small-scale surveys examining their ecology 'in cities' (e.g. Nuckols and Connor, 1995) to ambitious global efforts describing the ecology 'of cities' (e.g. Niemelä *et al.*, 2002). Table 13.1 outlines the general patterns of terrestrial invertebrate responses to urbanisation, summarising results describing changes in species composition (Gibb and Hochuli, 2002), species richness (Niemelä *et al.*, 2000) and invasion assisted by urbanisation (Bolger *et al.*,

Table 13.1. *Responses of terrestrial invertebrates to urbanisation.*

Target group	Context/location	Collecting method(s)	Responses and key findings	Source
Hemiptera – Scale insects	Urban trees/urban forest remnants Maryland, United States	Branch clipping; Visual counts of adult females	Decreased plant water potential equates to high abundance and increased performance of insects; High mortality of scale from generalist predators in forests	Hanks and Denno (1993)
Hemiptera – Scale insects	Urban Oxford, United Kingdom	Visual observations	Impermeability of substrate surface under trees increases susceptibility to herbivory; Trees near roads/concrete support a higher abundance of scale insects	Speight et al. (1998)
Lepidoptera – Leaf mining	Urban and rural remnants San Francisco Bay, United States	Leaf analysis – for evidence of mining	Extent of urbanisation did not affect overall abundance or species richness; Species responses to urbanisation are highly variable	Rickman and Conner (2003)
Lepidoptera – Larvae	Urban–rural gradient São Paulo, Brazil	Hand collection; Dissection	Higher pupal success on sheltered sites in urban areas where larvae are using man-made structures for safe pupation; High mortality further from city where vegetation cover is high	Ruszczyk (1996)
Leaf-damaging insects – Inferred from leaf analysis	Urban and natural forests Virginia, United States	Leaf analysis	No difference in total herbivory; Higher chewing damage in natural forests compared with urban trees	Nuckols and Connor (1995)
Lepidoptera – Gall-forming larvae	Rural-urban gradient Pretoria, South Africa	Hand collection	Larval densities and species richness at city sites lower than urban reserves; Suburban sites transitional between rural and city for assemblage structure; Larval assemblage different in highly disturbed in city sites	McGeoch and Chown (1997)

Table 13.1. (cont.)

Target group	Context/location	Collecting method(s)	Responses and key findings	Source
Lepidoptera – Butterflies	Urban Manchester, United Kingdom	Visual counts – atlas data	Increased urban cover leads to decreased abundance and richness for most species because of reduction of host plants and nectar sources Overall impact of urban cover on species richness is weak	Hardy and Dennis (1999)
Lepidoptera – Butterflies	Urban–suburban gradient São Paulo, Brazil	Visual counts	Increased diversity with increased area, connectivity, permanent water, vegetation and flowers Decreased diversity with human impacts (e.g. pollution) Connectivity key to butterfly management in urban areas	Brown and Freitas (2002)
Lepidoptera – Butterflies	Urban gradient – forest/ reserve/office park/ Central Business District (CBD) California, United States	Visual observations	Greatest richness at moderately disturbed sites Greatest abundance at natural sites Multi-use areas will not conserve butterfly diversity	Blair and Launer (1997)
Arthropods – Ground-dwelling	Urban and natural forest Sydney, Australia	Pitfall trapping Water trapping	Small fragments support fundamentally different fauna Highlights possible consequences for ecosystem functioning	Gibb and Hochuli (1999, 2002)

Taxa	Location	Methods	Findings	Reference
Arthropods – Ground dwelling and arboreal	Urban and natural forests Sydney, Australia	Pitfall trapping Water trapping Leaf analysis	Arthropod assemblage in small remnants differs from large; Higher trophic levels most affected; Higher levels of herbivory in small remnants; Hypothesise that invertebrate herbivores may be released from pressures of predators and parasitoids leading to increased survival and herbivory	Hochuli et al. (2004)
Arthropods – Ground-dwelling	Urban–rural gradient (residential/industrial/agricultural/desert) Arizona, United States	Pitfall trapping	Arthropod composition different for different land types; Richness was not affected by gradient; Taxon-specific responses to habitat structure; Predators, herbivores and detritivores more abundant in agricultural sites, omnivores cosmopolitan. Hypothesise that ecosystem functioning is affected by species responses	McIntyre et al. (2001)
Arthropods	Native and exotic site (lawn and fallow) Botanic Gardens Pietermaritzburg, South Africa	Pitfall trapping Malaise trapping Sticky trapping Sweep netting Visual sampling	No difference in mean number of species in different sites; Differences in abundance and richness between trapping methods within site and 18% of species in common between sites; Conserving a diversity of habitat types (vegetatively and structurally) will conserve a greater diversity of arthropods	Clark and Samways (1997)

Table 13.1. (cont.)

Target group	Context/location	Collecting method(s)	Responses and key findings	Source
Arthropods – Non-ant Hymenoptera Hymenoptera – Argentine ant (non-native)	Urban fragments California, United States	Pitfall trapping Vacuum sampling	Diversity and abundance of arthropods are positively related to fragment area but negatively related to fragment age Abundance and diversity of ground spiders increase with fragmentation Predators (spiders and carabids) increase with fragment age Argentine ants are a significant conservation threat to arthropod fauna of the area Hypothesise that significant changes in arthropods may affect ecosystem functioning	Bolger et al. (2000)
Coleoptera – Carabid ground beetles	Derelict urban areas West Midlands, United Kingdom	Pitfall trapping	Increased species richness on early successional sites Urban derelict sites provide important habitat for carabid species	Small et al. (2003)
Coleoptera – Carabid ground beetles	Urban–suburban– rural Canada Finland Bulgaria Japan	Pitfall trapping	Weak response of carabids to urbanisation Suggest some support for decreased species richness Opportunists/generalists become dominant in urban areas Abundance and richness decreased from rural to urban	Niemelä et al. (2000) Ishitani et al. (2003)

Taxon	Habitat/location	Method	Findings	Reference
Odonata – Dragonfly	Plantation/parkland/residential/industrial Pietermaritzburg, South Africa	Visual counts	Species respond differently Vegetation physiognomy not botanical taxon determines the presence or absence of species Conservation should aim at maximising habitat structure	Samways and Steytler (1996)
Hymenoptera – Bees	Urban–rural gradient xeriscaped residential yards/mesiscaped residential yards/urban desert parks/natural desert parks Arizona, United States	Water trapping (yellow and blue water traps)	Increase in diversity in the order mesic–xeric–desert park–natural desert Type of habitat features (exotic/native trees/shrubs/cacti/man-made structures) influence bee numbers and diversity Bees generally responding negatively to urbanisation Preservation of native desert habitat both within and around urban area will help preserve native pollinators and the plants they pollinate	McIntyre and Hostetler (2001)

2000). Evidence for differential losses from different trophic levels and functional groups is equivocal (Niemelä *et al.*, 2000; McIntyre and Hostetler, 2001; Hochuli *et al.*, 2004) but reveals that, as for plants and vertebrates, certain components of assemblages will be more susceptible to urbanisation (Steffan-Dewenter and Tschartntke, 2002).

A common theme in the small body of work reviewing the effects of urbanisation on forest insects (Dreistadt, 1990), carabids (Niemelä *et al.*, 2000), arthropods (McIntyre, 2000), butterflies (New and Sands, 2002), lepidopterans broadly (Connor *et al.*, 2002) and ecological interactions among arthropods (Hochuli *et al.*, 2004) is that the major impediment to the establishment of general principles describing terrestrial invertebrates in urban environments is a gaping lack of knowledge. Table 13.1 also reveals considerable geographical, taxonomic and methodological biases in existing literature. The focus on ground-dwelling arthropods (particularly carabids and ants) reflects trends in insect ecology (Majer, 1997; New, 1998), as does the reliance on survey-based approaches. However, while there is clearly a need to broaden the collecting methods used and the groups examined, numerous testable hypotheses emerge from the existing small body of work. Chief among these is that the marked response of terrestrial invertebrates to urbanisation is likely to affect the functioning and integrity of urban ecosystems.

Disruptions to ecological interactions and ecosystem processes

A major consequence of focusing on survey-based methods to investigate the impacts of urbanisation is that we know little about what the consequences of these changes in species abundance and distribution mean. The differential loss of trophic groups from urban remnants has led to predictions of disruptions of ecological processes in smaller fragments, such as the release of herbivore populations from regulation by parasitism and predation (Kruess and Tscharntke, 1994; Marino and Landis, 1996). Other ecological processes may also be depressed in small fragments, including pollination and seed set resulting from loss of pollinating species or reduced pollinator efficiency (Cunningham, 2000; Kremen and Ricketts, 2000). Table 13.2 summarises a suite of ecological interactions driven by the activities of terrestrial arthropods and how these may be disrupted by species loss associated with urbanisation and habitat fragmentation. Work examining these specifically in urban contexts is sparse, although outlining disruptions to herbivory, predation and pollination in urban environments suggests that common themes are emerging.

Table 13.2. *Ecological interactions of terrestrial invertebrates affected by landscape disturbances and the ecological consequences of disrupting them.*

Biotic interaction	Major contributing taxa	Key disturbance	Consequences of disruption to interaction	Source(s)
Pollination	Coleoptera Hymenoptera Lepidoptera Diptera	Disruption by introduced pollinators	Low-quality pollination leading to low seed output; reduction of plant fitness	Paton (1993) Gross and Mackay (1998) Roubik (2000) Kremen and Ricketts (2000) Aizen and Feinsinger (1994) Cunningham (2000) Cox and Elmqvist (2000) Brown and Mitchell (2001)
		Habitat fragmentation, change of habitat complexity and microclimatic conditions	Depauperate pollinator community; decline in pollination levels and seed production; restricted pollen flow; inbreeding	
		Exotic plant invasion	Replacement of native floral host leading to pollinator extinction; reduction of seed set through foreign pollen transfer; increased competition for pollinators	
Herbivory	Coleoptera Lepidoptera Hemiptera Diptera Hymenoptera	Habitat fragmentation and/or degradation	Change of the host plant quality leading to herbivore outbreaks	Port and Thompson (1980) Zabel and Tscharntke (1998) O'Dwyer and Attiwill (1999) Sands et al. (1997)
		Altered fire regime	Change of floral composition leading to herbivore extinction	
		Exotic plant invasion	Herbivore cannot complete lifecycle on toxic host, local extinctions	

Table 13.2. (cont.)

Biotic interaction	Major contributing taxa	Key disturbance	Consequences of disruption to interaction	Source(s)
Predation and parasitism	Araneae Hymenoptera parasitic wasps Hemiptera Chilopoda	Habitat fragmentation and/or degradation	Reduction of prey abundance leading to predator/parasite decline; herbivore outbreaks due to release from predator control leading to severe plant damage and dieback	Kruess and Tscharntke (1994) Alaruikka et al. (2002) Zabel and Tscharntke (1998)
Decomposition	Collembola Acarina Isopoda Diplopoda Isoptera Coleoptera	Increased levels of CO_2 Habitat fragmentation and/or degradation	Changes in soil fauna and rates of decomposition Species loss, decrease in nutrient supply and retention leading to ecosystem instability	Jones et al. (1998) Souza and Brown (1994) Didham (1998)
Seed dispersal	Hymenoptera Formicidae	Habitat fragmentation and/or degradation Invasion of exotic seed-removing ant species	Decline in diversity of seed dispersers leading to decreased seed dispersal and survival Decline or displacement of native seed dispersers, decrease of seed dispersal, increased seed loss	Grimbacher and Hughes (2002) Majer (1980) Pudlo et al. (1980) Christian (2001) Carney et al. (2003)
Food source for vertebrates	Most taxa	Habitat fragmentation	Decline in insectivorous birds owing to food shortage	Zanette et al. (2000)

Herbivory

The state of vegetation of urban remnants has been the focus of many studies in urban ecology (e.g. Rudnicky and McDonnell, 1989; Cilliers and Bredenkamp, 2000; Florgård, 2000). Increased levels of insect herbivory have been implicated as a major cause of changes to plant 'quality' through localised dieback (Houston, 1985; Hochuli *et al.*, 2004), and regular outbreaks of insect pests in urban remnants (Reader and Hochuli, 2003) have raised serious concerns over the long-term viability of these habitats. The well-known effects of urbanisation on the landscape are also potential mechanisms driving changes to rates of defoliation by herbivorous insects; nutrient input (King and Buckney, 2002), heat island effects (Landsberg, 1981) and increases of CO_2 and O_3 (Gregg *et al.*, 2003) could all affect host plant quality.

Evidence for increased herbivory in urban remnants is equivocal (Hochuli *et al.*, 2004), although outbreaks of herbivorous insects along motorways in the United Kingdom have been associated with changes in the composition and status of foliage driven by anthropogenic pressures (Port and Thompson, 1980). Others have found little evidence for the contention that urban or ornamental plantings are more susceptible to insect attack, and receive more damage to foliage by insect herbivores than trees in natural forests (Nuckols and Connor, 1995). Patterns of herbivory are also likely to be affected by the loss of higher trophic levels regulating populations of insect herbivores (Marquis and Whelan, 1994). High levels of herbivory on dominant trees in urban remnants in Sydney (Burrows, 1999; Hochuli *et al.*, 2004; Christie and Hochuli, 2005) have been associated with the loss of higher trophic levels from those remnants (Gibb and Hochuli, 2002). Fine-scale studies, targeting the causal mechanisms by which levels of herbivory are affected, are required to support general arguments for the disruption of ecological processes in urban remnants (Debinski and Holt, 2000).

Predation and parasitism

Landscape-driven mechanisms affecting the success of predators and parasites are well known from agricultural systems (Wratten *et al.*, 2007), with these groups likely to be more susceptible to habitat fragmentation than herbivores and plants (Steffan-Dewenter and Tschartntke, 2002). Evidence for the effects of urbanisation on arthropod predators and parasites in urban contexts is primarily correlative (Ruszczyk, 1996; Miyashita *et al.*, 1998; Gibb and Hochuli, 2002) and the hypothesis that predators and parasites are lost from urban sites is not always supported (Bolger *et al.*, 2000). Gall-inhabiting lepidopterans using acacias in urban remnants in South Africa show low levels of gall occupancy, larval density and species richness at disturbed city sites (McGeoch and Chown,

1997). Although most causal mechanisms are inferred from patterns, recent manipulative experiments excluding predators and parasitoids from foraging groups of larval *Doratifera casta*, a common outbreaking species on dominant Eucalyptus trees in urban environments in Australia, showed dramatic consequences of predation and parasitism for larval survival (Reader and Hochuli, 2003). The clear link from disruption of predation and parasitism to insect–plant interactions in urban remnants indicates that future investigations into invertebrate biodiversity and ecological interactions in urban remnants need to integrate multiple approaches to both survey and experimental work to disentangle pattern and process.

Pollination

Pollination has been described as an 'endangered mutualism' (Kearns *et al.*, 1998; Kremen and Ricketts, 2000), owing to disruptions to pollination syndromes, declines in endemic pollinator assemblages, reductions in pollinator effectiveness (Cunningham, 2000), and invasions by ineffective pollinators (Roubik, 2000). Many taxa known to be pollinators respond negatively to urban environments (Hardy and Dennis, 1999; McIntyre and Hostetler, 2001; Gibb and Hochuli, 2002), and this coupled with the extent of invasion in many of these environments indicates that pollination is likely to be significantly affected by urbanisation. However, despite this conjecture, there is little evidence for depressed pollination in urban environments (Kremen and Ricketts, 2000), a reversal of the common but controversial practice of inferring pollinator declines from pollination deficits (Thomson, 2001).

Ecological restoration and urban ecology

The enormous effort put into repairing and restoring damaged systems globally is reflected in urban landscapes (Robinson and Handel, 2000; Davies and Christie, 2001; McDonald *et al.*, 2002). Urban restoration is often driven by widespread public interest and community involvement and has a primary focus on restoring vegetation to damaged areas (Davies and Christie, 2001). Many restoration efforts are poorly integrated and their effectiveness is rarely assessed, leading to growing concerns over the rationale underpinning these efforts (Allen *et al.*, 1997). An understanding of their effectiveness may be compromised by inappropriate, unrealistic or poorly defined goals and the use of inappropriate sampling designs to assess restoration success (Grayson *et al.*, 1999). The desire for restoration to ensure the return of ecological integrity (Grumbine, 1994) and ecological fidelity (Higgs, 1997) needs to be considered in ultimate assessments. This requires identification of suitable reference and control sites in replicated designs in restoration efforts. If urban remnants are inherently and irrevocably altered as a result of anthropogenic pressures, it is critical that the goals for choosing these sites accommodate these characteristics. These issues are critical when setting and assessing the goals for restoration in these remnants, as appropriate control and reference sites will need to incorporate any constraints imposed by the remnants in their landscape context.

Many restoration efforts also explicitly build the 'field of dreams hypothesis' (Palmer *et al.*, 1997) into their goals, actively pursuing the restoration of faunal assemblages and ecological interactions into their restored landscapes. Given the fine scales at which urban restoration efforts are often pursued, terrestrial invertebrates are an excellent candidate for assessing the success with which these goals are met (Kremen *et al.*, 1993). Assessment of restoration efforts using terrestrial invertebrates has focused on snapshot surveys creating inventories of fauna and flora in restored sites (e.g. Andersen, 1997; Majer and Nichols, 1998), sometimes characterising long-term trends in faunal responses (Nichols and Nichols, 2003). Although these are important components of any assessment, it is also critical that the functional attributes of faunal assemblages be considered and measured in restored areas so that the fundamental hypotheses underpinning restoration, that ecological characteristics of remnant reference areas are returning to once-damaged areas, can be tested.

A toolbox for entomologists in urban ecology

The reliance on survey-based methods to investigate the ecology of insects in urban habitats (Table 13.1) is unlikely to reveal the processes driving patterns in biodiversity observed in urban landscapes or the ecological significance of any of these patterns. An approach integrating traditional surveys with experimental approaches outlining the consequences of shifts in species composition is essential to developing a conceptual framework. In Fig. 13.1 we outline the three essential components of future investigations into the urban ecology of terrestrial invertebrates in work examining both impacts and the restoration of these systems.

The scheme builds on and enhances the surveys that make up the bulk of previous urban ecology, arguing that classification into broad functional groups based on ecological and trophic groups (pollinators, herbivores, predators, parasites) and within well-known taxonomic groups such as ants (Andersen, 1990, 1997), spiders (Churchill, 1997) and carabids (Niemelä *et al.*, 2000) is a critical step beyond conventional estimates of faunal structure. Central to this scheme is the notion that surveys should adopt multiple sampling methods to survey a range of taxonomic and ecological groups; the trapping and taxonomic biases

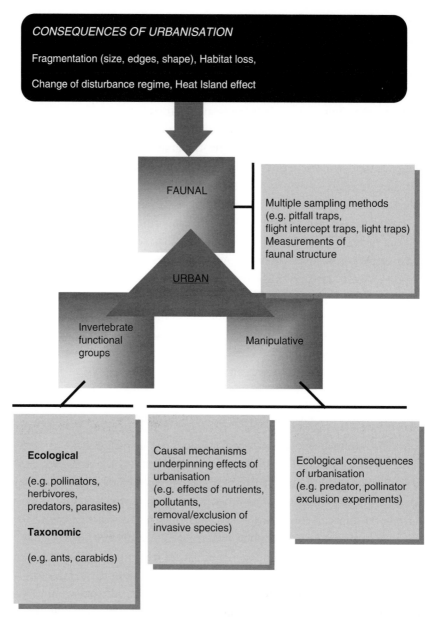

Fig. 13.1. Concept diagram outlining a synthesis for an urban ecology of terrestrial invertebrates.

prevalent in previous work (Table 13.1) impede the development of a true general synthesis and the generation of testable hypotheses about their functional role in urban remnants. This approach will not only identify the causal mechanisms underpinning responses to urbanisation (e.g. small-scale manipulations of the characteristics known to be modified by urbanisation) but also describe the extent to which ecological interactions have been disrupted (e.g. exclusions of predators, parasites and pollinators). Terrestrial invertebrates are amenable to an enormous range of experimental approaches that enable us not only to identify how urbanisation has affected biodiversity but why this has occurred and what it means to the ongoing functioning of these systems. Although the main stumbling blocks towards wider acceptance and use of terrestrial invertebrates for environmental assessment remain taxonomic impediments and broader community awareness, these are clearly outweighed by the enormous opportunities these components of biodiversity provide to urban ecologists (New, 1998).

The future for urban ecology – of and in cities?

Although scaling problems pervade most attempts to generalise in landscape ecology, clear operational definitions and testable hypotheses are paramount to the development of a conceptual synthesis for this emerging discipline. The cry that 'all cities are different and there is no point trying to generalise across them' owing to their intrinsic variation and inherent confounding simply requires the specificity provided by a clear classification of urban environments (McDonnell and Hahs, Chapter 5). The rapid development of tools to define patterns more precisely and carry out experiments to disentangle causal relationships will lead to meaningful meta-analyses synthesising the findings of the growing body of work in urban ecology. This description of the ecology of cities will create the opportunity to test clearly defined hypotheses in a number of urban contexts both of and in cities, as well as their satellites and budding suburbs.

However, we argue that this ecology of cities for terrestrial invertebrates will only be meaningfully synthesised when the breadth of their ecological roles is considered across the range of urban contexts. This will require substantial extensions of the techniques adopted by most insect ecologists and dramatic shifts in the descriptive approaches that characterise much previous work in these environments. Furthermore, we believe that urban ecology would benefit from a bottom-up approach to establishing general principles, generating the detail of its conceptual framework from the studies investigating the ecology both of and in cities. The desire to separate these components in any conceptual framework provides greater clarity when seeking general principles but has the unintended consequence of shrouding what is perhaps a more important direction for insect ecologists in urban environments: the integration of survey-based approaches with measures outlining how ecological interactions have been disrupted by urbanisation.

Conclusions

Terrestrial invertebrates are fundamental components of the biodiversity of urban ecosystems, playing roles in interactions crucial to maintaining the ecological integrity of these systems. Although only a small body of work examines their responses to urbanisation, their sensitivity to anthropogenic impacts coupled with the fine scales at which they operate makes them an ideal target group for work in remnant habitat in urban environments. The immediate benefits of increasing the emphasis on the use of invertebrates in urban ecology will be realised in its developing conceptual synthesis and through the emergence of general principles. In addition, the long-term benefit of creating a nexus between species diversity and ecological function will be a powerful tool with which the educational and scientific value of urban remnants can be promoted using landscapes surrounded by a majority of the world's population.

14

Arthropods in urban ecosystems: community patterns as functions of anthropogenic land use

NANCY E. MCINTYRE AND JESSAMY J. RANGO

Introduction

The prophetic words of geographer Chauncy Harris (1956), who believed that global urbanisation was a 'gigantic and pervasive revolution', hold even more true now than when he uttered them in 1956. Whereas less than a third of the world's population lived in urban areas in 1950, over half currently lives in urban areas (World Bank, 1984), nearly half of the Earth's terrestrial surface has been altered by human activities, and human-induced losses to biodiversity are occurring at unprecedented rates (Vitousek *et al.*, 1997b). Urbanisation is thus among the most influential factors shaping biological communities today, but the scope and magnitude of its consequences have only recently been glimpsed.

Urbanisation is the process whereby humans convert indigenous ecosystems to a type of ecosystem in its own right, the urban ecosystem. An urban ecosystem is not merely an area under human domination; rather, it is characterised as an area of high-density human habitation (see McIntyre *et al.*, 2000). The amount of energy consumed in an urban ecosystem is over 1000 times greater than that in other types of ecosystems (Odum, 1997). As such, cities and towns have an ecological 'footprint' (sensu Wackernagel and Yount, 1998) that extends far beyond recognisable urban boundaries (Luck *et al.*, 2001). An urban ecosystem is at least as heterogeneous as native ecosystems in terms of three-dimensional

Ecology of Cities and Towns: A Comparative Approach, ed. Mark J. McDonnell, Amy K. Hahs and Jürgen H. Breuste. Published by Cambridge University Press. © Cambridge University Press 2009.

structure, land-cover types, microclimate zones and resource availability. Within urban ecosystems, the presence of anthropogenic impervious surfaces and building materials may alter climatological and hydrological cycles (Arnold and Gibbons, 1996). All of these features create a system that has been traditionally viewed as antithetical to 'natural' systems and devoid of interesting ecological questions concerning biodiversity.

Recently, however, ecologists have begun to embrace urban ecosystems as locations in which to conduct research (Niemelä et al., Chapter 2; Pickett et al., Chapter 3). Urban ecosystems provide a novel opportunity in which to examine interactions between humans and wildlife, the effects of human activity on biogeochemical cycles, and the interplay of socio-economic and ecological patterns and processes. Arthropods are immediate candidates for model organisms in such studies for many reasons (see Niemelä et al., Chapter 2; Natuhara and Hashimoto, Chapter 12; Hochuli et al., Chapter 13; Eisenbeis and Hänel, Chapter 15). First, arthropods are abundant, constitute over 50% of the Earth's described biodiversity and are relatively easy to sample (Kim, 1993). Second, arthropods play a variety of important ecological roles (e.g. pollinators, decomposers) and are indicators of environmental integrity (Kim, 1993). Third, many arthropod groups have worldwide distributions; consequently, the same taxa can be compared in different cities around the globe. Fourth, arthropods are economically and socially important, considering the amount of money and effort that goes into combating termites, cockroaches, and other home and garden pests. Finally, arthropods are vectors for many infectious diseases, with urban human populations at especial risk because of the density-dependent nature of disease spread. These properties make the study of arthropods in urban ecosystems broadly applicable and representative of the biotic changes elicited by urbanisation.

In this chapter, we have three objectives: (1) to summarise the current state of understanding regarding the ecology of arthropods in cities and towns; (2) to encourage comparative studies that will be vital in advancing ecological understanding of urban areas; and (3) to discuss why interactions between ecological research and urban planning have been relatively limited yet are critical to successful conservation and management efforts. In addressing these objectives, we identify limitations to obtaining general principles in urban ecology that come from difficulties in conducting comparative studies among cities.

Current state of understanding of arthropod ecology in cities and towns

A review of the literature revealed that most work on arthropods in urban environments has dealt primarily with pest management or with arthropods as

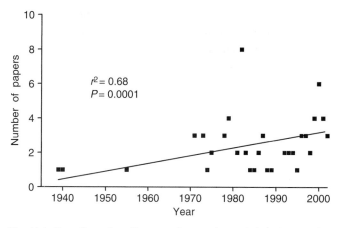

Fig. 14.1. Plot of number of papers about arthropods in urban environments by year, 1939–2002. Line is a significant linear regression line.

disease vectors; most of the remaining studies examined the effects of pollutants such as heavy metals on arthropod density and diversity (McIntyre, 2000). Many of these studies adopted a gradient approach, where the intensity of urbanisation is considered to vary with distance from the city centre (Matson, 1990; McDonnell *et al.*, 1997; Pickett *et al.*, 2001; also see Zipperer and Guntenspergen, Chapter 17; Carreiro *et al.*, Chapter 19; Pouyat *et al.*, Chapter 20). In this approach, urbanisation is considered to be a form of ecological disturbance.

To examine how interest in the ecology of arthropods in urban ecosystems has grown, we conducted a search of the Web of Science journal database (http://www.isiwebofknowledge.com) using the Boolean search statement 'urban* AND (arthropod OR insect)' as well as the bibliographies of the references thus obtained. Papers devoted simply to pesticide trials or to urban arthropods solely as disease vectors were excluded, leaving only those with an ecological focus. Our search revealed a significant recent increase in papers devoted to the study of arthropods in urban environments (Fig. 14.1). These papers have increased our knowledge about how arthropods respond to urbanisation, yet they also illustrate the depth of our ignorance. The vast majority of studies were relatively short in duration and conducted in temperate biomes of the Northern Hemisphere, primarily on Lepidoptera and Coleoptera (see also McIntyre, 2000). Few cross-city comparisons were identified, which will be addressed in a separate section below.

Most studies were conducted in only a single patch type, usually in remnants of native habitat and often applying principles from island biogeography to native habitat remnants in a 'sea' of urbanisation (see e.g. Gibb and Hochuli, 2002; Niemelä *et al.*, 2002; Hochuli *et al.*, Chapter 13); yet the urban ecosystem is a heterogeneous mosaic of many forms of land use, including residential, agricultural, industrial/commercial and other property forms. Relatively few studies have compared arthropod community structure among different forms of urban land use, yet urban areas in different biomes are similar because of the highly managed characteristics of human land use. Despite differences in cultures and climates, cities around the globe possess commonalities because they serve common needs, namely housing citizens (homes), providing goods and services (factories, stores), maintaining transportation corridors (roads, railways, airports), and supporting education and recreation (schools, churches, parks, playgrounds). Few studies have examined the effects of this heterogeneity on urban arthropods; some case studies that have addressed this oversight are presented below.

Case studies from Phoenix, Arizona (USA)

Phoenix, Arizona, is home to ~2.7 million people distributed over ~3900 km^2 (AZB, 1998). Although it comprises nearly three dozen contiguous yet independent municipalities (e.g. Tempe, Mesa, Scottsdale), only one of which is the city of Phoenix proper, the metropolitan area as a whole is referred to as 'Phoenix'. It is located within the Sonoran Desert, a hot desert biome (Fig. 14.2a, b). Although the Sonoran Desert experiences two rainy seasons per year (averaging 180mm/yr), water is a key limiting resource in Phoenix (Fig. 14.2c). With an annual population growth rate of 23%, Phoenix is one of the fastest-growing urban areas in the world (AZB, 1998). As such, it has become one of two focal locations in the United States for studies in urban ecology (the other being Baltimore, Maryland; see Pickett *et al.*, Chapter 3). Funded by the National Science Foundation, the Central Arizona–Phoenix Long-Term Ecological Research (CAP-LTER) project is a multi-year, interdisciplinary examination of the interplay between biophysical and socio-economic factors that generate the urban ecosystem in the Phoenix metropolitan area, and of the effects of such a process on the region's human and non-human inhabitants (see http://caplter.asu.edu for more information).

Like other cities, Phoenix possesses a diversity of land-use types, including residential, industrial and agricultural forms, as well as native habitat remnants preserved as parks. Long-term and ongoing monitoring studies are comparing arthropod diversity and abundance among different land-use types along an indirect gradient of urbanisation in the Phoenix metropolitan area (McIntyre *et al.*, 2001). Results after five years of monitoring indicate that community evenness is highly skewed in all months and in all forms of land use, with springtails (order Collembola), mites (Acari) and ants (Hymenoptera: Formicidae) being the most abundant urban taxa. The abundance of particular arthropods in

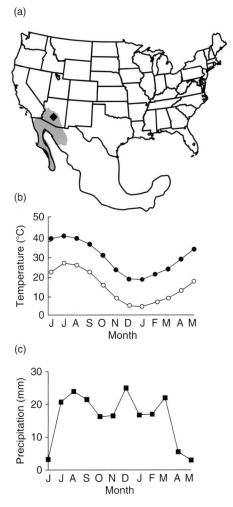

Fig. 14.2. (a) Location of Phoenix, Arizona (black diamond) within the Sonoran Desert of North America (grey shading). (b) Average daily maximum (solid symbols) and minimum (open symbols) air temperatures by month in Phoenix, Arizona. (c) Average daily precipitation by month in Phoenix, Arizona.

urban areas may exceed that in non-urban locations. Urban areas are dominated by a few synanthropic species that achieve high populations (McIntyre *et al.*, 2001; Shochat *et al.*, 2004), a pattern also seen with arthropods in other areas (Denys and Schmidt, 1998) as well as with birds (Emlen, 1974). Arthropod richness was higher in urban forms of land use than in native habitat, even when exotic taxa were excluded from the urban totals (McIntyre *et al.*, 2001; Shochat *et al.*, 2004). Ignoring urban forms of land use, when the arthropod community associated with a single species of shrub in patches of native desert in urban locations was compared with that in patches in non-urban sites, richness and abundance were consistently lower in the urban sites (Rango, 2002). In addition, arthropod community composition was extremely variable in both site types (Rango, 2002). Thus the overall urban context of even native habitat patches exerts a strong influence on coarse community-level traits (richness, abundance) but not necessarily on finer traits (composition).

One likely explanation for these patterns, at least in Phoenix, is that many forms of urban land use supplement the naturally limited availability of water in the desert. In particular, agricultural lands and residential yards (even xeris-caped yards and gardens – those using desert-adapted plants in landscaping) experience considerable anthropogenic subsidies of water (Martin, 2001), which may compensate for mortality incurred from pesticides applied by farmers and homeowners alike. Cities in more mesic biomes may not experience such an effect; it would be instructive to determine whether arthropod richness in temperate or tropical cities is higher than that in surrounding native habitats.

Although most of the above studies examined community-level responses to urbanisation, other studies have focused on particular taxa such as scorpions (McIntyre, 1999), native bees (McIntyre and Hostetler, 2001) and spiders (Shochat et al., 2004). From these and other studies, it is known that certain predatory taxa (e.g. certain scorpion species (Scorpiones), pseudoscorpions (Pseudoscorpiones) and large ground beetles (Coleoptera: Carabidae)) are consistently lost when native desert is converted to anthropogenic forms of land use (see also Klausnitzer and Richter, 1983; Blair and Launer, 1997). A similar response to urbanisation has also been noted for birds (Emlen, 1974; Parody et al., 2001) and lizards (Germaine and Wakeling, 2001). Some taxa (e.g. tarantulas (Araneae: Therapho-sidae)) are especially sensitive indicators that are lost from even remnant patches of desert when those patches are enclosed by urban development. Other taxa are indicative of urbanisation by their presence rather than their absence: roaches (Blattaria), spitting spiders (Araneae: Scytodidae), Argentine ants (Hymenoptera: Formicidae, *Iridomyrmex humilis*), European cabbage butterfly (Lepidoptera: Pier-idae, *Pieris rapae*), common fruit fly (Diptera: Drosophilidae, *Drosophila melanoga-ster*) and termites (Isoptera) are especially associated with humans (Kocher and Williams, 2000; McIntyre et al., 2001; Vega and Rust, 2001; Avondet et al., 2003). Most of these taxa are now found worldwide, leading to a global homogenisation of the urban arthropod fauna. An upside to this homogenisation is that the same taxa can be compared in different cities around the globe, similar to the work of Niemelä et al. (2002 and Chapter 2). They collected data on carabid beetle assemblages across urban–rural gradients in Bulgaria, Canada and Finland and discovered that the average size of the organisms decreased with increasing urbanisation (Niemelä et al., 2002). Effective maintenance of key ecosystem functions will hinge on conservation of taxonomic and genetic diversity of arthropods in the face of this homogenisation; certain urban areas are already experiencing declining plant recruitment and lower decomposition rates because of the loss of key taxa that are involved in ecosystem services (Carreiro et al., 1999; Liow et al., 2001). Conservation, in turn, hinges on effective co-operation between urban ecologists and land-use planners, but forming such coalitions is easier said than done (Sukopp et al., 1995).

Interactions between ecological research and urban planning

Arthropods and especially arthropod conservation are a hard sell to people (Kim, 1993). Most people actively try to eradicate arthropods when they encounter them, for arthropods are associated with unhygienic conditions, disease and low socio-economic status. We need to move beyond thinking of urban arthropods only in terms of pests, however. Entomophobia and ignorance about the many beneficial roles played by arthropods in ecosystems have erected a barrier to ecologically sound urban planning. Education and outreach are the ultimate solutions to this problem.

Another barrier to incorporating insights gained from ecological research into urban planning and conservation is that ecologists and planners seldom meet or discuss findings in a common forum. Even when these hurdles are overcome, there is then the obstacle of not using common terms in a similar fashion (see McIntyre et al., 2000; Theobald, 2000, 2004). In addition, although much of the urban ecology literature treats urbanisation as a disturbance (e.g. Blair and Launer, 1997; Niemelä et al., 2002; Zerbe et al., 2003), perhaps what is needed is recognition that urbanisation is in fact not a classical disturbance because there is no return possible to a pre-disturbance state: urbanisation perturbs the system to a new phase state, effectively resetting the parameters as to what is 'normal' and what is 'disturbed'. (This shift should not negate the usefulness of the gradient approach in urban ecological studies sensu Matson, 1990; McDonnell et al., 1997; Avondet et al., 2003.) Symposia designed to bring ecologists and planners together, along with precise use of defined terms, are necessary first steps in integrating ecological research into urban planning (Sukopp et al., 1995).

One of the issues ecologists and planners must grapple with is whether it will be preferable to support urban infill rather than spreading development. More specifically, should urbanisation be concentrated into smaller areas (meaning that there will be few or no remnant patches, parks, etc.), or should it be allowed to grow outwards (not necessarily the same thing as sprawl) to incorporate such remnants? The work that has been done on arthropods would argue for the former position, but compelling sociological arguments can be made for the latter. This is an issue that all cities face, and increasing urban growth will only make the matter more urgent.

The role of comparative studies in advancing ecological understanding of urban areas

Each urban ecosystem is unique in terms of history and culture, so comparisons among cities must be made with caution. Although the identities of the arthropod species may differ among cities, patterns of arthropod community simplification and homogenisation are hypothesised to be consistent and attributed to similarities in land use (which translate to similarities in vegetative/habitat composition and structure) among cities regardless of biome. Such similar response patterns may aid in urban planning for biodiversity conservation. For example, it is possible to compare patterns among similar land-use categories in different cities (Niemelä *et al.*, 2002; see also http://www.helsinki.fi/science/globenet/) or as functions of human population growth rates, resource-use statutes and so on.

One commonality of urban ecosystems that has made some cross-city comparisons easier is the presence of trees in residential yards or gardens, parks and forest remnants. (In many cities, these woodlots represent native habitat. In Phoenix and elsewhere, however, woodlots contrast sharply with the indigenous surrounding habitat. Differences in the environmental contexts of urban areas will assuredly complicate cross-city comparisons.) Like woodlots, turfgrass lawns are another feature common to urban areas around the world. These areas do not mimic indigenous grasslands, being wholly anthropogenic features that typically experience a very high degree of human maintenance. They often receive water and nutrient supplementation, are exposed to chemicals in the forms of pesticides and herbicides, and have a physiognomy that is maintained by mowing. Despite their artificial nature, lawns support a myriad of surface and fossorial arthropods that regulate soil fertility and nutrient cycling (particularly Collembola and Acari), but the different ways in which lawns are managed influence the ability of arthropods to carry out these functions. Like urban entomology in general, most research on arthropods in lawns has focused on pest management (Potter and Braman, 1991), although a smaller body of research has examined the effects of lawn management on beneficial arthropods such as spiders and beetles (e.g. Potter *et al.*, 1985; Arnold and Potter, 1987). The effects of chemical applications in lawns on arthropods are highly variable and depend on the type of chemical, its application rate and the arthropod group (Kunkel *et al.*, 1999). Nevertheless, the ubiquity and anthropogenic origins of lawns may aid cross-city comparisons of arthropod communities.

Much more information is needed from other urban locales to make better decisions about the placement and design of future urban development. Urban ecology offers a great many research opportunities for the future, for there is clearly a need for more studies on arthropods in urban areas around the globe. Many cities still lack fundamental information on their biodiversity, precluding cross-city comparisons. Comparative studies should be a high priority, which will be critical in identifying suites of indicator species that may serve as barometers of resource availability, contaminant levels and so forth. Research in Phoenix, Arizona, on arthropod community composition and dynamics revealed patterns of deterministic loss and replacement. If Phoenix is any gauge, then loss of large, predatory arthropods from the community is a signal of degradation; a mere change in species richness is not informative, for some forms of urban land use harbour as many species as native habitat, if not move.

Conclusions and synthesis

Urbanisation is not a fad. Despite acknowledgements that human sprawl has contributed to declines in standards of living for human and non-human organisms, the human population continues to grow (and indeed is encouraged to grow by political and religious leaders). Just as an oncologist might view a melanoma with fascination and clinically disguised revulsion, the emergence of a new and spreading entity on the face of the Earth has elicited similar responses among ecologists. The implications of the continued growth of both entities are ominous. As a consequence, the importance of research in urban ecology cannot be overstated, and numerous questions remain to be answered. Urban ecology, as a relatively young and growing field, holds many research opportunities.

Like most emerging disciplines, urban ecology has primarily been concerned with documenting patterns and dynamics in urban ecosystems. We now need to move beyond pattern description to obtaining an understanding of mechanistic relationships. Doing so will require an integration of urban ecology with planning and management, which in turn will require stronger efforts at communication by all parties.

Human needs are the same the world over, and native ecosystems are being altered in similar fashions to satisfy those needs. Urbanisation is thus effectively homogenising the world. It is also creating an arthropod assemblage that may be no less diverse but may differ in composition from the indigenous community. Effects of these changes are already being seen in terms of alterations in ecosystem functions such as pollination efficiency/fruit and seed set, lowered decomposition rates and simplified food-web structure (Carreiro et al., 1999; Lerberg *et al.*, 2000; Liow *et al.*, 2001). City dwellers of the future will have to learn to live with these changes, or take counteractive steps, but at least the choice is in our hands: do we settle for a depauperate environment, or do we acknowledge that the fates of arthropods are linked to our own?

Acknowledgements

We are grateful to Mark McDonnell, Amy Hahs and Jürgen Breuste (and the associated members of the Steering Committee) for organising the symposium on urban ecology at the Sixth World Congress of the International Association for Landscape Ecology (16 July 2003), followed by the International Workshop on Urban Ecology (19–22 July 2003); interactions with colleagues at both helped shape this manuscript. Much of our thinking about urban ecology has also been influenced by discussions with colleagues from Arizona State University, particularly Stan Faeth, Bill Fagan, Nancy Grimm, Diane Hope and Chuck Redman. Our research on urban arthropods at the CAP-LTER has been funded by the National Science Foundation (DEB-9714833 to N.B. Grimm and C.L. Redman). We thank Loren Byrne (Penn State University) for information and discussions on lawns. Loren Byrne and Mike Willig (Texas Tech University) suggested improvements on a draft of this chapter.

15

Light pollution and the impact of artificial night lighting on insects

GERHARD EISENBEIS AND ANDREAS HÄNEL

Introduction

The creation of urban environments has significant impacts on animals and insects throughout the world (Niemelä *et al.*, Chapter 2; Catterall, Chapter 8; Nilon, Chapter 10; van der Ree, Chapter 11; Natuhara and Hashimoto, Chapter 12; Hochuli *et al.*, Chapter 13; McIntyre and Rango, Chapter 14). During recent decades both landscape and urban ecologists have been confronted with a new phenomenon associated with cities and towns: 'light pollution'. Fast-growing outdoor lighting as a threat to astronomy was first described by Riegel (1973). Astronomers need dark sky conditions to discriminate the faint light of astronomical sources from the sky background, which is due to a natural glow (airglow, scattered star light, etc.) and artificial light scattered in the Earth's atmosphere. Since the invention of electric light and especially since World War II the outdoor lighting level has increased steeply and the natural darkness around human settlements has disappeared almost totally. Unwanted skylight produced by artificial night lighting is spreading from urban areas to less populated landscapes, generating a modern sky glow.

The primary cause of this new phenomenon is the excessive growth of artificial lighting in the environment. It is related primarily to general population growth, industrial development and increasing economic prosperity, but there has also been a technical shift to lamps with higher and higher luminous efficiency. For example, the light output efficacy of an old-fashioned incandescent lamp is

Ecology of Cities and Towns: A Comparative Approach, ed. Mark J. McDonnell, Amy K. Hahs and Jürgen H. Breuste. Published by Cambridge University Press. © Cambridge University Press 2009.

10–20 lumens/watt and for a modern low-pressure sodium vapour lamp it is nearly 200 lumens/watt. Still another significant contribution is the excessive and, at times, careless use of artificial outdoor lighting, as well as the use of poorly designed fixtures that allow a high proportion of upward flux of radiation. All these components contribute to an increase in sky brightness often visible as 'sky glow' or as a 'light dome' covering city centres and visible from afar.

This ubiquitous increase in night lighting in human settlements has resulted in a significant change in environmental conditions and should be regarded as a new challenge for ecologists involved in the conservation of biodiversity. Mizon (2002), Cinzano (2002) and Marisada and Schreuder (2004) have provided comprehensive reviews of the topic of light pollution. Several conference proceedings that are mainly focused on astronomical observations also discuss the negative influence of light pollution (Isobe and Hirayama, 1998; Cinzano, 2000; Cohen and Sullivan, 2001).

Although bright lights are associated with the world's thriving cities, there are some voices that are increasingly warning of the 'dark side of light' and its negative effects on plants, animals and humans. The harmful impacts of night light on natural habitats and ecosystems have only recently been studied. An advisory report on this subject has been published by the Health Council of the Netherlands (Sixma, 2000). There are many adverse effects of lighting known for animals, especially insects and animals (see de Molenaar et al., 1997, 2000; Schmiedel, 2001; Rich and Longcore, 2006). The main effects are the disturbance of biological rhythms, orientation and migration, and of basal activities such as the search for nutrition, mating behaviour and the success of reproduction. Artificial night light can affect plants in many ways including altering their direction of growth, their flowering times and the efficiency of photosynthetic processes (Briggs, 2006).

The aim of this chapter is to discuss the ecological impacts of light pollution in cities on insects. Insects are known for their great sensitivity to artificial light sources and in this context they can be regarded as a model group to demonstrate the negative effects of artificial lighting to nature. In addition, some thoughts on bad and good lighting design and placement are presented. Finally, our overall goal is to promote an environmentally friendly illumination system as an integral part of cities, towns and villages and the open landscape.

Light pollution from global to home level

The magnitude of artificial night lighting worldwide is best visualised by remote sensing techniques with the DMSP (Defence Meteorological Satellite Program) satellites applied by the NASA Goddard Space Flight Centre (data David

Fig. 15.1. Global map of artificial night lighting based on remote sensing techniques with the Defence Meteorological Satellite Program – DMSP of the NASA Goddard Space Flight Center (data from David Imhoff/Christopher Elvidge).

Imhoff/Christopher Elvidge). The hot spots of night lighting in a continental view from the west coast of the USA to the east coast of Australia can be seen in Fig. 15.1. It is evident that global city lights are concentrated into the Northern Hemisphere of the Earth. In the Southern Hemisphere only a few big conurban areas (i.e. aggregations of urban areas) are visible, e.g. the area around Johannesburg, whereas most of the land mass belongs to the huge sparsely populated areas of South America, Africa and Australia. Further bright sources of artificial illumination can be found along many coasts of the Mediterranean, such as the Cote d'Azur in France, Costa Brava in Spain and the coastal lines of Florida in the USA. Another striking example is the big river valleys with a high population density, e.g. the valley of the Nile which is visible as a winding light ribbon (Fig. 15.1). This kind of mapping gives a first impression of the distribution of artificial night lighting on Earth.

While these images show the direct light emitted from Earth into space, Cinzano et al. (2000a) have calculated the brightness of the sky background from calibrated satellite data. The upward emitted light is scattered in the atmosphere. Using model calculation methods developed mainly by Garstang (1991), Cinzano et al. (2001) derived a world atlas of light pollution. They also compared the lighting level between years beginning with 1971. One of the best documented examples is that of Italy (Cinzano et al. 2000b). Cinzano and his group compared the increased level of artificial sky brightness with the level of natural sky brightness. They also compared the lighting levels in 1971 and 1998. Based on

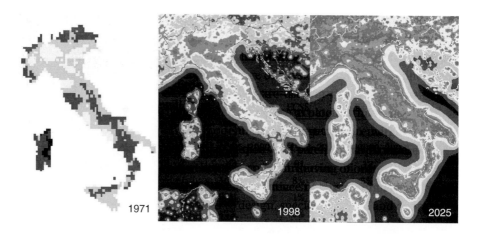

Map 1971		Map 1998		Map 2025	
<0.05	black	<0.11	black	<0.11	black
0.06–0.15	grey	0.11–0.33	blue	0.11–0.33	blue
0.16–0.35	blue	0.33–1.0	green	0.33–1.0	green
0.36–1.1	green	1–3	yellow	1–3	yellow
>1.1	yellow	3–9	orange	3–9	orange
		>9	red	9–27	red
				27–81	violet
				>81	white

Fig. 15.2. Maps showing artificial sky brightness in Italy according to Cinzano *et al.* (2000b). The artificial sky brightness is given as the increase above a reference natural sky brightness of $8.61 \times 10^{-7}\,V\,phot\,cm^{-2}\,s^{-1}\,sr^{-1}$ (photons in the visual spectral range), corresponding approximately to $252\,\mu cd\,m^{-2}$ or $21.6\,V\,mag\,arcsec^{-2}$ (astronomical visual magnitude). The higher the value, the greater the artificial brightness. See also colour plate.

known growth rates for lighting between these periods they made a prediction for the year 2025 (Fig. 15.2). In 1971 the maximum sky brightness is about 1.1 times the natural night brightness.

In 1998, the centres of conurbation of Milano and Roma were more than 9 times brighter than the natural night brightness, and for the year 2025 they predict that these areas will have more than 8 times the natural brightness. The same will occur in other parts of Europe, such as Belgium, the Netherlands,

Fig. 15.3. Artificial lighting panorama of Los Angeles, 19 February 2002, taken 9:00 p.m. from Mount Wilson with Nikon Coolpix 995, 100 ASA and 4 s at F3.

Great Britain and selected parts of Germany. Consequently it is possible that natural darkness will disappear in extended areas of Europe, and also in other developed areas of the world.

A current example of a city with high levels of lighting is illustrated by a night photograph of Los Angeles from the nearby Mount Wilson Observatory (Fig. 15.3). On a smaller scale such over-lighting is visible in modern cities but nowhere is such an extended illuminated area found as in Los Angeles. City lighting planners distinguish different sorts of lighting: (1) primary lighting (public must lighting) which includes lighting for streets and public places; (2) secondary lighting (commercial must lighting) which involves lighting for each kind of advertising, public buildings and monuments; and (3) tertiary lighting or non-obligatory 'event lighting'. Floodlighting with cut-off floodlights, e.g. of sports grounds used for normal activities, should be classified as secondary lighting. But if a mega soccer stadium is illuminated from the outside all night, or if floodlights are visible from many kilometres away, we clearly have a case of tertiary lighting. Citizens also contribute to light pollution by illuminating their gardens and houses for security or prestige reasons. White house fronts are true insect traps, and gardens are losing their function as refugia for nature. If a residential building is illuminated by 20 000 Christmas lights it must be regarded as a very bad case of tertiary lighting. There is an urgent need to educate city planners, architects and the public to prevent the excessive use of bad lighting which can have a variety of bad effects on insects, animals and plants. It is apparent from the photograph of Los Angeles that all sorts of lighting sources contribute to the observed high overall lighting level. In a standard city it must be assumed that the main sources of lighting are primary and secondary. Some cities, however, are introducing more tertiary lighting as a special local feature such as the city of Lyon (Cité lumière) in France and the city of Lüdenschein in Germany (Stadt des Lichtes). If this becomes common practice, then the light levels projected by Cinzano will become reality sooner than expected. Secondary and tertiary lighting are the main components of a new marketing strategy for cities which is known as 'city marketing with light'. It is obvious that light will be more and more used to promote the economic status of towns and cities. We regard this development for purely commercial and economic reasons as a great danger for the urban environment with potential unknown consequences. Some cities now plan to establish lighting master plans to improve their appearance and image. In principle, we can support the idea of developing lighting master plans, but these plans need to include physical, social, economic and ecological considerations in order to develop truly sustainable cities.

Strong growth of settlement areas, and consequently of artificial lighting, can be observed more and more in the rural landscapes throughout the world. Haas *et al.* (1997) estimate that the increase of developed land in Germany is about $1km^2$ each day. The total yearly loss of the open, undeveloped landscape in Germany is about the size of Bremen County, one of the smaller Federal States in Germany. The typical European landscape shifts to a fine-meshed mosaic of settled areas, small isles of forests and open rural space. Sprawling like an octopus, the illuminated areas penetrate deeply into formerly undeveloped and dark landscapes. As a consequence of this development, streetlights are increasing exponentially and the local sky domes and bright horizons are reducing the darkness. According to Kolligs (2000) the streetlight pool of the city of Kiel increased from 380 in 1949 to nearly 20 000 in 1998. Based on a population size of 240 000 in 1998 this equates to about 12 streetlights per person. Similar trends have been reported for Great Britain (Campaign to Protect Rural England, 2003). Another example of the loss of darkness comes from the Eifel region of Germany. In the 1950s the Hoher List Observatory at Bonn University was an excellent location for viewing the night sky, but today with the growth of nearby towns it is affected by light pollution.

Animal behaviour around street lamps and other light sources

Many animals appear to be attracted by night lights (Schmiedel, 2001; Rich and Longcore, 2006). This applies primarily to flying insects (Frank, 1988; Eisenbeis and Hassel, 2000; Kolligs, 2000), but also birds flying in swarms and those that migrate at night. Sometimes they are trapped by big light sources, particularly during periods of inclement weather. Approaching the lights of lighthouses, floodlit obstacles, ceilometers (light beams generally used at airports to determine the altitude of cloud cover), communication towers or lighted tall buildings, they become vulnerable to collisions with the structures themselves. If collision is avoided, birds are still at risk of death or injury. Once inside a beam of light, birds are reluctant to fly out of the lighted area into the dark, and often continue to flap around in the beam of light until they drop to the ground with exhaustion. Then there is a secondary threat of predation resulting from their aggregation at lighted structures. In early August 2003, Eisenbeis (unpublished) observed a floch of silver gulls flying around the lighted top of Sydney's AMP Tower (305 m in height). It is possible that the gulls were searching for food, but for whatever reason, they were attracted by the tower's light space. From other observations it is known that if the light is turned off such a swarm is dispersed very fast (Cochran and Graber, 1958).

Flight-to-light behaviour of insects around artificial light sources disturbs the ecology of insects in many ways and can lead to high mortality (Bauer, 1993; Eisenbeis, 2001a). On the other hand there are many external factors, especially clear or cloudy conditions, that can also affect insect night behaviour (Mikkola, 1972; Kurtze, 1974; Blomberg et al., 1978; Bowden, 1982; Eisenbeis, 2001a). Hsiao (1972) distinguished a 'near' from a 'far' phase for the approaching behaviour of insects to lamps. Bowden (1982) emphasises that most studies have focused on the 'near' phase within the zone of attraction, but 'far' effects derived from a changing background illumination, e.g. by moonlight, are very important in determining how many insects are brought within the influence of a light source at all.

In this section we discuss observations of insect behaviour near lamps which can be used to classify three different scenarios in which flight-to-light behaviour manifests itself (Eisenbeis, 2006). In the first scenario, insects are disturbed from their normal activity by contact with an artificial illumination source such as a street lamp. For example, the scenario may begin with a moth searching for flowers. When it comes into the 'zone of attraction' of a street lamp it can react in different ways. The insect may fly directly onto the hot glass cover of the lamp and die immediately. Far more frequently, the insect orbits the light endlessly until it is caught by predators or falls exhausted to the ground where it dies or is caught. Some insects are able to leave the nearest light space and fly back seeking the shelter of the darker zone. There they rest on the ground or in the vegetation. It is assumed that the trigger for this behaviour is a strong dazzling effect of the lamp. Some are able to recover and fly back to the lamp once more, and others proceed to be inactive, being exposed to an increased risk by predators. Many insects may fail to reach the light because they become dazzled and immobilized approaching the light. They may also rest on the ground or in the vegetation. Hartstack *et al.* (1968) have shown that more than 50% of moths approaching a light stopped their flight on the ground. We have termed all these variants of behaviour the 'fixation' or 'captivity' effect, which means that insects are not able to escape from the near zone of lighting. Schacht and Witt (1986) neglect the fact that insects are actively attracted by lights themselves, for they argue that the flight-to-light behaviour is only a blinding effect. The animals would try to flee, but were blinded by the light.

The second scenario describes the disturbance of long-distance flights of insects by lights encountered in their flight path. The scenario begins with three insects flying through a valley along a small stream. They use natural landmarks such as trees, stars, the moon or the profile of the horizon to orient themselves. The course of the flight is then intersected by both a street and a row of street lamps. The lights prevent the insects from following their original flyway. They fly directly to a lamp and are unable to leave the illuminated zone, suffering the same fate as described above for the first scenario. We have termed this the 'crash barrier' effect because of the interruption of the insects' long-distance flyway across the landscape.

The third scenario is called the 'vacuum cleaner' effect. During a summer season, insects are attracted to the lights in large numbers. They are 'sucked' out from their habitats as if by a vacuum, which may deplete local populations. Work by Kolligs (2000) and Scheibe (2003) suggests that outdoor lighting can significantly eliminate insects.

The magnitude of each of the effects on insect behaviour depends on background illumination. Moonlight always competes with artificial light sources (Bowden, 1982; Danthanarayana, 1986). Illumination from artificial lighting often creates higher illumination levels than natural night light sources such as the full moon. Kurtze (1974) measured near a parking lot at the city centre of Kiel, Germany, an illumination level of 0.5 lux, about double the value for the full moon (0.3 lux), and the overall illumination by the urban sky glow of Vienna with a cloudy sky was measured at 0.178 lux (Posch *et al.*, 2002). As yet no data are available about insect activity within settled areas that are constantly illuminated. More research is necessary to characterise such fundamental changes in the level of darkness.

Insects therefore perceive artificial lights at full moon only when they are close to the lights and consequently fewer insects are attracted to any given light. Under natural conditions, therefore, the zone of attraction changes during a lunar cycle. Additionally, changes may occur during a single night depending on weather, as the sky changes from clear to cloudy. Consequently the efficiency of catches around lamps depends on background illumination. On the other hand the low flight activity at artificial light sources during full moon does not necessarily mean that fewer insects fly on bright moonlit nights. For insects and many other animal groups it is known that the moonlight steers their rhythmic activity (Bowden, 1981, 1982). Numerous animals are particularly active at full moon or the days before or after. Others, in contrast, are active around the new moon (Endres and Schad, 1997). To investigate insects' true nocturnal activity, other catch methods in addition to light trapping have to be used.

The importance of lamp type

Several older studies reported that sodium street lamps are approached much less by insects than mercury lamps. The reason for is that the white shining mercury lamps emit radiation in both the ultraviolet and blue–green spectral ranges which are known to be very attractive to insects (Cleve, 1967; Mikkola, 1972). However, some of these examinations were not carried out under practical conditions, and the data sets often were too small to analyse statistically. Therefore, in 1997, a new project was established by the nature conservation group BUND (the German branch of Friends of the Earth) in co-operation with the University of Mainz and supervised by the local energy provider (Electric Power Plant of Rheinhessen, EWR; see Eisenbeis and Hassel, 2000). The aim of the project was to study insects' flight-to-light activity around street lights during a full summer season in the rural landscape of the Rheinhessen district in south-west Germany.

The area is nearly treeless and characterised by viticulture and cultivation of cereals and sugar beet. Three sites were studied: (1) a housing area of Sulzheim village (with some garden ponds); (2) a farmhouse site (far from any water bodies); and (3) a road site near Sulzheim village. Nineteen light traps (Fig. 15.4) were mounted just below street lamp fixtures (luminaires) to capture insects. They were prepared each day before dusk, and remained exposed during the night until morning. We used two slightly modified trap models, but at any particular site, only one kind of trap was used. Insects were trapped in receptacles containing soft tissues and small vials filled with chloroform. The trapping period was June until the end of September 1997. The types of luminaires and lamps in the study were standard types commonly used for outdoor lighting in Germany. The lamps were high pressure mercury vapour (80 watts) or high pressure sodium vapour (70 or 50 watts).

Additionally, we tested high pressure sodium–xenon vapour lamps (80 watts), and for special purposes some of the high pressure mercury vapour lamps were fitted with an ultraviolet-absorbing filter membrane covering the glass cover of

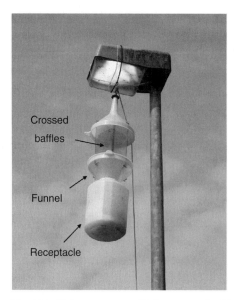

Fig. 15.4. Light trap exposed below a standard luminaire (street light).

luminaires. From beginning of June to the end of September we collected 536 light trap samples containing a total of 44 210 insects, which were categorised into 12 orders. The main flight activity was in July with a maximum night catch of nearly 1700 insects in a single trap, and some other catches were around 1000 insects per trap per night. Normal catch rates were under 400 insects per trap per night. The main result is shown in Fig. 15.5 which gives the average catches for lamps and control in a single night. Most important are the data for high pressure mercury and high pressure sodium which are used to obtain the catch ratio. When we include all insects of the three study sites, we obtained a catch ratio of 0.45 which indicates that 55% fewer insects have been caught around high pressure sodium lamps. If we include only moths then the catch ratio is 0.25, which represents a 75% reduction in flight activity.

These data indicate that insects react differently depending on the light source. These data are only representative for the specific street light system used in our study. Beside the quality of lamps some other accessory parameters such as construction of luminaries, permeability of glass covers, the height of light fixtures and the composition of the insect fauna in the adjacent habitats determine the rates and the catch ratio. Therefore the catch ratios given above should be regarded as an estimation of the potential reduction for the flight activity of insects around street lights.

The pattern of 12 insect orders (plus two groups of arachnids) found at the three study sites is shown in Fig. 15.6. The community at the road site near an

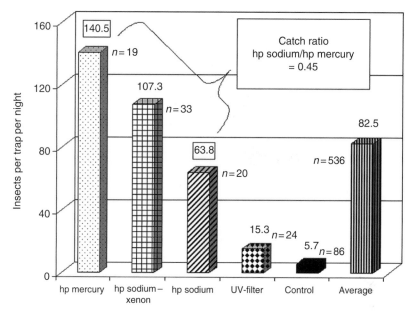

Fig. 15.5. Average insect catch rates for different lamp types in the rural landscape of Rheinhessen, southwest Germany, according to Eisenbeis and Hassel (2000).

open landscape with fields and vineyards was dominated by flies (Diptera, 67.6%), and the percentage of each of the other orders was under 10%. Insects caught at the housing area of Sulzheim village were dominated by beetles (Coleoptera, 30.7%) followed by moths (Lepidoptera, 15.9%), aphids (Aphidina, 14.3%), flies (Diptera, 9.8%), caddis flies (Trichoptera, 8.1%), bugs (Heteroptera, 8.0%) and hymenopterans (Hymenoptera, 5.9%). The proportion of each of the remaining orders remained less than 5%. At the farm site three orders dominated the insect community: beetles (Coleoptera, 38.9%), moths (Lepidoptera, 19.4%) and bugs (Heteroptera, 12.8%). Each of the others contributed less than 10%. The aquatic caddis flies (Trichoptera) were found in high proportions (5.0%, 8.1%) only at two sites, which were near small bodies of water such as ponds in gardens. The proportion of this order was small (0.7%) at the farmhouse site, where there were no aquatic habitats. These results indicate that each site has its specific insect community which reflects the type of vegetation and land use.

Further evaluation of the catches revealed that the ambient temperature and the moon phase are important key factors (Eisenbeis, 2001b). If the ambient temperature at 10 p.m. Central European daylight saving time was significantly lower than 17 °C then the flight activity dropped to zero. When temperatures were significantly higher than 19 °C at 10 p.m. Central European daylight saving time, the number of captured insects rose and peak activity occurred. Our data agree with previously published research in that the lowest flight activity around

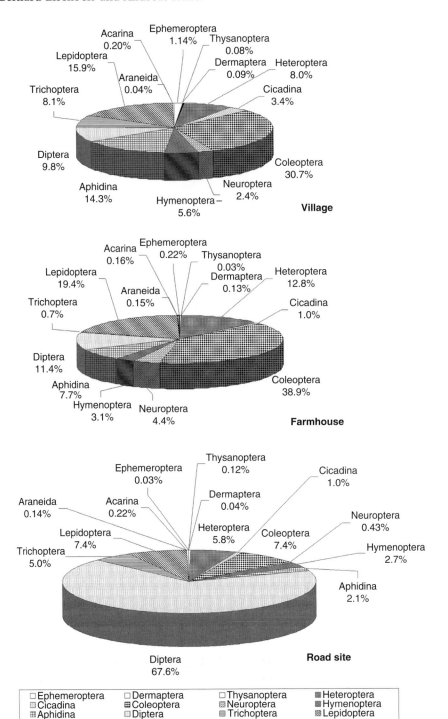

Fig. 15.6. Faunal diversity of insect groups at three sites with different levels of night lighting in Germany.

lamps occurred during the full moon, and the peak activity accumulated at and near the new moon. This can primarily be explained by the competition between moonlight (as a background light) and the artificial light source. Previous research also indicates that insects behave very differently depending on the moon phases, and both weather and cloudy conditions are important co-factors (Williams, 1936; Kurtze, 1974; Nowinszky *et al.*, 1979; Bowden, 1981; Danthanarayana, 1986; Kolligs, 2000).

One interesting observation often discussed is that insect flight activity is different if street lamps such as high pressure mercury or high pressure sodium are used competitively (simultaneously) or non-competitively (only one type of lamp is visible for insects). According to Scheibe (1999), increased flight activity to high pressure mercury would only occur under the condition of light competition, i.e. if high pressure mercury and high pressure sodium were switched on together. Therefore Eisenbeis and Hassel (2000) made a separate study in which the types of lamps were changed from day to day over a period of weeks. The site for this experiment was at the farmhouse in a true dark area without any other light sources. The high pressure sodium lamps attracted significantly fewer insects (1164 versus 2739; U-test, $p = 0.004$) than high pressure mercury lamps with a catch ratio of 0.48. In addition, the average catch rate per night was higher in traps under mercury bulbs (average of 114 insects per trap per night) as opposed to those under sodium bulbs which had an average of 55 insects per trap per night. Bauer (1993) conducted a similar experiment and found that each type of lamp had its own power of attraction, although he noted that the data could not be confirmed statistically because only a few night catches were taken. To summarise, it is evident that the flight-to-light behaviour of insects is influenced by the quality of light. High pressure mercury and high pressure sodium vapour lamps differ significantly. Comparing all known data about light trapping, it is evident that insects are significantly less attracted by high pressure sodium lamps. Comparing the results of six German studies, the insect attraction is reduced to about 57% (average catch ratio 0.43; Fig. 15.7) for this lamp type.

On the other hand there are some 'losers' among insects which prefer to fly to high pressure sodium vapour lamps. In a recent study, A. Schanowski (Institut für Landschaftökologie und Naturschutz−ILN, Buhl, unpublished) reported 53 specimens of glow worms caught at high pressure sodium lamps and only two specimens found around high pressure mercury vapour lamps. Other insect species show an indifferent behaviour, e.g. the bug *Pentatoma rufipes*, which was found in equal numbers around high pressure mercury and high pressure sodium lamps (Bauer, 1993). There are also some groups of aquatic insects, especially the Chironomids, that seem to prefer the yellow light (Scheibe, 2000,

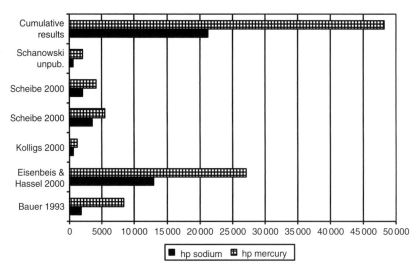

Fig. 15.7. Comparison of insect catch rates for high pressure (hp) sodium and hp mercury lamps based on six German studies (Scheibe (2000) includes two different datasets).

2003). Therefore Scheibe (2003) recommended not to use yellow lighting near water. In our opinion this recommendation is questionable. On the one hand, the bulk of insects in Scheibe's experimental series near a stream bank were attracted by a high pressure mercury lamp; on the other hand, Scheibe never tested the yellow low pressure sodium lights. The relatively high number of aquatic insects showing a preference for the high pressure sodium lamps is reflected by the comparatively high catch rates found in Scheibe's investigation. Also, the spectrum of insects trapped in Scheibe's investigation is comparatively small; for instance, there were no nocturnal Lepidoptera (moths) and hardly any Coleoptera, Heteroptera (bugs), Hymenoptera or Neuroptera. Normally these groups are also found near water and they should never be neglected in the context of the ecological consequences of artificial night lighting. In our opinion, Scheibe's unfounded statement contradicts all efforts to minimise the dying of insects around lamps used for outdoor lighting.

The decline of insects in cities

In January 2003, the *Wall Street Journal* published an interview with Gerhard Tarmann, a Lepidopterologist from the Tyrolean State Museum Ferdinandeum at Innsbruck/Austria. The topic was the decline of butterflies in the Alps during the past decades. Dr Tarmann is one of the founders of the Austrian

Action against the ecological consequences of artificial night lighting, which is called 'Die helle Not' (freely translated 'The lighting disaster') and which has engaged the people to preserve the formerly very rich insect and butterfly fauna in Austria by the conversion of public lamp systems to sodium lamps. In Tarmann's opinion, the biggest impact on the butterfly fauna in Innsbruck was the Winter Olympics in 1964. The spectacular hyper lighting of bridges and walkways was succeeded by devastation of city's butterflies. Within just three years the rich fauna disappeared to a minimum level. According to Tarmann, the same sequence has been observed in remote valleys of the Alps. There, the meadows contained a remarkably diverse fauna with hundreds of butterfly species, but after these valleys were opened for tourists and new lighting was installed for petrol stations, billboards, hotels and restaurants, etc., the rich fauna significantly declined within a few years of the installation of the lights.

Similar observations have been described in the older entomological literature. Malicky (1965) reported from his observations around newly built and strongly illuminated fuel stations that there was a high initial flight activity of insects during the first two years, which then quickly faded away. In our opinion such personal observations must be considered as a serious indicator of a significant change of a local insect population caused by the 'vacuum cleaner' effect mentioned above.

Entomologists from the second half of the twentieth century frequently reported extremely large light trap catches of many thousand insects in a night, but more recent catches have been much smaller. For example, Robinson and Robinson (1950) caught more than 50 000 moths in a single trap (equipped with a 125 watt mercury lamp) in the night of 20/21 August 1949. Worth and Muller (1979) caught 50 000 moths with a single 15 watt black light trap from 2 May to 12 September 1978 on an isolated farm site not close to competing lights. Eisenbeis and Hassel (2000) caught only 4338 moths with 192 light trap samples at 80 watt high pressure mercury lamps from 29 May to 29 September 1997, which corresponds to a rate of 22.6 moths per trap per night. Of course such simple enumeration (the sites, the lamps and the traps were different) does not allow for statistical evaluation, but these data strongly suggest a progressive decline in insect populations.

Eisenbeis (2001a) has calculated that about one-third of insects approaching a street lamp are caught by a light trap. Based on Bauer's observations (Bauer, 1993) he estimated a death rate in the same order of magnitude. Thus, if about 450 insects approached a high pressure mercury street light during a night, we would expect about 150 would perish. As yet there are no quantitative data on the number of animals that become inactive in the nearer surroundings of a streetlight and are ultimately lost by secondary predation. There are estimated to be 8.2 million street lights in Germany, and based on these early data on insect catches the loss of insects due to the lights throughout the country could be in the order of one trillion during a summer season.

Heath (1974) describes in his report 'A century of change in the Lepidoptera' some profound changes in Macrolepidoptera in Great Britain, which can mainly be attributed to changes in land use. Most changes involved extinction, declines or restriction of species to few local spots, but there were some examples of colonisation of new species and extension of existing ranges. Heath notes that the main causes for the change of insect habitats are: (1) clear-cutting of many acres of deciduous forests and their replacement with coniferous plantations; (2) conversion of heath lands and forests to agricultural use; (3) the agricultural revolution and changes in woodland management; (4) use of chemicals such as herbicides and insecticides in the environment; (5) urban sprawl; (6) construction of motorways; (7) human recreational pressure on the countryside; and (8) periods of climatic change. At the time the report was written, there was no discussion of light pollution as a serious new hazard for insects.

Taylor *et al.* (1978) reported on the Rothamsted Agricultural Research Centre's insect survey with relation to the urbanisation of land in Great Britain, which was based on a light-trapping network. The industrial region of middle England and the London area were clearly identified on faunal maps as islands of low diversity and density. The authors used light trapping as their basic method, but they offered no comments about the possible role of increasing artificial lighting for the decline in diversity.

Bauer (1993) investigated the insect activity of three housing areas normally illuminated by street lamps and a semi-natural habitat that was not regularly illuminated before the study. He used light traps exposed in the light space of street lamps in the suburban area of Konstanz, a mid-sized town in Southern Germany. In the illuminated areas, the catch rates (5, 29 and 47 insects per trap per night in the city centre and two housing areas) were between 4% and 30% of those in the semi-natural non-illuminated habitat (143 insects per trap per night), but altogether the results from the illuminated areas were heterogeneous. Moths were the dominant species and showed an average proportion of 14.9% for the illuminated sites and 34% at the non-illuminated site, but the differences among illuminated sites were high (2.7, 11.6 and 30.5%). For this reason, such data should only be regarded as a first quantitative monitoring of changes in the insect population.

Scheibe (1999) used suction trapping to study night-flying insects along a wooded stream bank in a low mountain range of the Taunus area in Germany far from any artificial lighting. During eight nights he caught 2600 insects per trap night with maximum catches of 11 600 and 5100 insects. These data for flight activity outnumber all other data recently reported from illuminated areas in Germany. The results must be regarded as further evidence that the dark zones in the landscape have a much richer insect fauna than do lighted zones.

In his Ph.D. thesis, Scheibe (2000) tried to determine the capacity of such a trap to catch insects flying within the zone of attraction of a single street lamp. He measured the number of all aquatic insects (mayflies, caddis flies, dipterans, etc.) emerging from a small stream in the low mountain range of the Taunus area, standardised as 'number of emerging insects' per 72 h per 1 m length of the stream bank. During the night following such a test of the emergence, he determined the number of aquatic insects flying to a street lamp positioned near the bank. He found that different taxa of aquatic insects reacted differently, but in many instances light catches significantly outnumbered the number of emerging insects. For example, the number of caddis flies caught in an August night by the lamp was approximately the same as the number of caddis flies emerging along 200 m of the bank. Therefore it can be concluded that the lamp has a long-distance effect for light-susceptible insect species and that far more insects are attracted than would potentially be found in the area immediately surrounding a lamp. By extrapolation, if there were a row of street lamps along a stream, a species could become extinct locally in a short time, which can be explained again by the 'vacuum cleaner' effect of street lamps.

Another example of attraction of large numbers of insects around lamps is reported from mayflies along riversides and bridges. The swarming of the species *Ephoron virgo* (or other species) is described as summer snow drifting (Kureck, 1996; Tobias, 1996) because the insects are attracted in such masses that the ground near lights is covered by a centimetre-thick layer of these insects. An estimated 1.5 million individuals have been recorded in one night on an illuminated road surface of a bridge. It is part of the fatal destiny of the animals that each female loses her egg cluster upon first contact with an object. Eggs that are not released into water must be regarded as a loss for the population, with potentially significant effects on the local population.

As discussed by Frank (1988), rare species are vulnerable to effects of artificial lighting. Kolligs (2000) reported capturing endangered 'Red List' species as single individuals in a large study of assimilation lighting at a greenhouse. Such species can be regarded as endangered by artificial lighting. K-selected species (i.e., slow maturation and long-lived species) with specialised habitat requirements and stable population sizes are most likely to be disrupted by artificial lighting (see also Eisenbeis, 2001a, b). Reichholf's (1989) research on moth populations revealed a steep urban gradient between the outskirts of a village with house gardens close to nature (650 species), intermediate housing density with parks (330 species) and city central housing area (120 species).

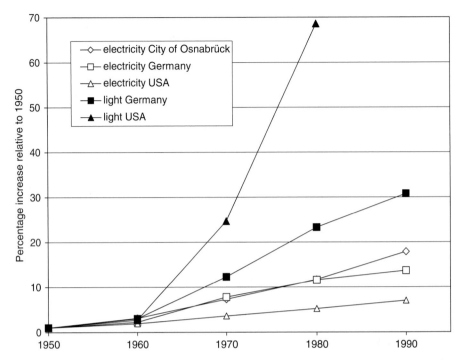

Fig. 15.8. The increase of electric power consumption and of light emission in the city of Osnabrück, Germany, and in the countries of Germany and the USA.

This growing body of evidence strongly suggests that the diversity of insects has declined dramatically in Germany and England during recent decades. Insect-friendly lighting systems may reduce the negative impacts, but if the absolute lighting levels continue to increase then our cities will develop to nearly insect-free (and perhaps bird-free) ghost towns far removed from the formerly rich animal life.

Street lighting in Germany

Riegel (1973) and Sullivan (1984) estimated the growth of emitted light from electric power consumption for road lighting in the USA. While the power consumption increased linearly, the emission of light increased exponentially at an annual rate of 23% between 1967 and 1970. This is due to the use of more efficient lamps, changing from incandescent to mercury high pressure and even sodium high pressure lamps. We have tried to estimate the light emission for Germany (Hänel, 2001). Therefore we compared the percentage increase of electric power consumption for the city of Osnabrück with Germany and the USA (Fig. 15.8).

Assuming also a gradual change to sodium high pressure lamps we estimate a growth rate for light emission of 7% annually between 1980 and 1990 and even less since then. These values provide an estimate of the increase of light. The amount of light emitted to the sky which ultimately increases the artificial sky brightness cannot be estimated because we lack data on the numbers and type of lamp housings. Nevertheless, these indirectly derived values can be compared with the measurements of sky brightness in Italy which increased by about 10% annually between 1960 and 1995 (Cinzano, 2000b). The growth of light pollution in Europe is less than in the USA, probably for a variety of reasons. In addition, in Europe road lighting is regulated by norms, which require only minimal luminance values at the road surface. By German environmental legislation light is classified as potentially hazardous. A technical regulation ('Licht-Richtlinie') sets limits on illuminance from non-public light sources at 1 Lux (in residential areas) and 5 Lux (in industrial areas) on private windows. For public illumination a limiting value of 3 Lux is often assumed.

Good lighting and steps for the protection of the dark sky

In Europe, light pollution regulations have been issued in the provinces of Catalonia and Tenerife in Spain, in Lombardy and others in Italy, and in the Czech Republic for the first time on a nationwide level. These regulations mainly forbid any use of upward light and demand a cautious use of light. In addition, some cities in the USA have developed regulations for the use of artificial light during the night. Table 15.1 provides a list of suggested measures that could reduce the harmful impacts of night lighting on insects.

There are typically economic reasons proposed as to why measures to reduce light pollution are not feasible. But there are examples such as the western Canary Islands (Tenerife and La Palma) where strict regulations allow only full cut-off luminaries (lights) in order to maintain a dark sky for their world-famous astronomical observatories. Despite these regulations, tourists continue to visit the islands and the economy flourishes (Benn and Ellison, 1998).

In addition to regulations, it is important to develop programmes that inform the public about the problem of light pollution. Some positive examples are brochures like 'Die helle Not' in Austria (Tiroler Landesumweltanwalt, 2003) or programmes such as 'Wieviele Sterne sehen wir noch?' [How many stars do we see?] in Austria (Posch *et al.*, 2002) or 'Night blight!' in England (Campaign to Protect Rural England, 2003). Because of the growing worldwide concern about

Table 15.1. *Suggested methods to reduce the harmful impacts of night lighting on insects.*

1. Lighting should be used only when necessary and then only as dim a light as possible.
2. Direct illumination of the sky should only be allowed if absolutely necessary; searchlights for commercial purposes must be forbidden.
3. Only full cut-off luminaries help to reduce the light glow domes over cities. Light emitted in horizontal planes contributes even more to these light domes than the direct upward light (Cinzano, 2000b). Even luminaries installed with small inclinations to illuminate the opposite road side should be avoided and when possible they should be installed horizontally.
4. There is some research (Schanowski and Späth, 1994) indicating that sodium low pressure lamps attract fewer insects. Therefore these lamps should be used when colour vision is not important and on streets in or close to rural landscapes. Colour perception with these lights is reduced because of the monochromatic sodium light (589 nm wavelength). But small amounts of broad-spectrum lights from house lighting or automobile headlights can render colour perception essentially normal (Luginbuhl, 2001).
5. Elsewhere sodium high pressure lamps should be used while mercury pressure lamps should not be used.
6. Road lighting should be dimmed or even switched off when road use is negligible (e.g. 11 p.m. to 5 a.m.).

light pollution, in 1988 the International Dark Sky Association was founded to educate people about the problem and to develop methodologies to mitigate the effects of high levels of night lighting.

As a result of the UN Conference on Environment and Development (Rio de Janeiro, 1992) a global programme for sustainable development was brought into being, the Agenda 21. In section II, the main topics are the management of the Earth's resources, the protection of major biomes and conservation of bio-diversity. It is recommended that all energy sources will need to be used in ways that respect the atmosphere, human health and the environment as a whole. As a consequence of Rio, a 'Local Agenda 21' was established in Germany. It is used as a guideline for cities and regions to realise the ideas and recommendations of the global Agenda 21 on a local level. But unfortunately there is no mention of the huge waste of light that dissipates energy and changes the night environment. In our opinion, over-lighting is recognised as a modern component of atmospheric pollution. Therefore we recommend that the environmentally friendly use of artificial lighting should be a fixed part of strategies to promote sustainable development at all municipal levels. It contributes both to saving energy and to conserving the diversity of organisms, especially of animals.

Summary

Artificial night lighting is increasingly affecting nature and ecosystems. Many groups of animals are affected directly or indirectly, especially birds and nocturnal insects. Our study in a rural landscape in Germany clearly demonstrates the importance of light quality for street lighting. Insect flight activity around high pressure sodium lights was less than half that around high pressure mercury lights. In the spirit of the theme of this book, there are numerous opportunities for comparative studies of the effects of light pollution in cities on insects and other organisms because they all have very similar lighting fixtures, design and placement.

16

A comparison of vegetation cover in Beijing and Shanghai: a remote sensing approach

JUN YANG AND ZHOU JINXING

Introduction

Comparative studies of cities are important for understanding the structure and dynamics of urban ecosystems (McDonnell and Hahs, Chapter 5). Comparative studies also contribute to the development of urban ecology. However, as McDonnell and Hahs point out, information on non-human components of urban environments is very limited. It is more problematic in cities where environment data are not available because of financial difficulties, lack of necessary investigation techniques and human resources. Even in cities where information is available, the usefulness of the data for comparative study can still be doubtful because the data are often not collected in a uniform way. The lack of information poses a challenge when conducting a comparative study of cities (McDonnell and Hahs, Chapter 5).

Non-human environmental data can be gathered through ground surveys. Methods such as biotope mapping (Sukopp and Weiler, 1988; Breuste, Chapter 21; Wittig, Chapter 30), urban–rural gradient analysis (McDonnell et al., 1997; Zipperer and Guntenspergen, Chapter 17; Carriero et al., Chapter 19; Pouyat et al., Chapter 20) and others (Rogers and Rowntree, 1988; Nowak et al., 1996) have been used successfully in many cities. However, these methods require extensive funding and labour support that are not always easy to get. There are also other restrictions that make ground surveys infeasible: for example, the cities under

Ecology of Cities and Towns: A Comparative Approach, ed. Mark J. McDonnell, Amy K. Hahs and Jürgen H. Breuste. Published by Cambridge University Press. © Cambridge University Press 2009.

study may be inaccessible for political and safety reasons. A comparative study of cities therefore needs a tool to provide reliable, uniform and cost-effective data.

Remote sensing is a useful tool in urban studies (Donnay *et al.*, 2001). It can provide spatially consistent data sets that cover almost any part of the Earth with both high spatial detail and high temporal frequency. The history of using remote sensing in urban studies is not short. Its earliest application was by Tournachon, who used a camera carried on a balloon to study parts of Paris in 1858 (Campbell, 1987). Since then, aerial photos taken from various platforms, mainly aeroplane, have been interpreted to describe the structure of the urban physical environment as well as to predict socio-economic variables (Estes, 1966; Lillesand and Kiefer, 1994). From the 1970s, with the launch of Landsat Multi-spectral Scanner (MSS) satellite and the subsequent series of Earth observation satellites, including Landsat Thematic Mapper (TM), SPOT, IKONOS and EO-1, satellite imagery has become a valuable data source for urban studies (Forster, 1983, 1985; Foresman *et al.*, 1997; Jensen and Cowen, 1999).

Vegetation, including all trees and herbaceous plants, is among one of many urban features studied by remote sensing. Vegetation is an important component of the urban ecosystem. Its most common use in cities is for aesthetic enhancement (Appleyard, 1980), but it can also reduce air pollution (Taha, 1997), alleviate urban heat islands and save energy (Akbari and Taha, 1992; Avissar, 1996). Urban vegetation can contribute to the psychological well-being of urban dwellers (Ulrich, 1986) and generate economic value (Kuchelmeister *et al.*, 1993). The amount and extent of vegetation cover are mainly determined by urban morphology, natural factors and human management system (Sanders, 1984). While the natural environment decides the major vegetation type, the urban morphology shaped by the history and the development of the city will decide the distribution and quantity of urban vegetation. Thus vegetation cover is thought to be an important index in comparative studies of cities (Emmanuel, 1997).

Information on vegetation cover in a city can be derived from aerial photos. Aerial photos with high resolution provide accurate and detailed information. However, it is very expensive to obtain aerial photos covering the entire city at regular intervals, and interpretation of hundreds of photos is a time-consuming job. Satellite imagery overcomes these difficulties with its frequent coverage of large areas. From the early Landsat MSS image, which has a ground resolution of 80 metres, to the latest IKONOS (1 metre resolution in panchromatic band) and QuickBird images (0.65 metre resolution in panchromatic band), satellite images can reveal more and more detail. By now, most studies done on urban vegetation cover use Landsat TM images (Wang and Zhang, 1999; Vogelmann *et al.*, 2001). Each Landsat TM image has a ground resolution of 30 metres and covers an area of about 30 000 km^2. Landsat TM satellites have been able to provide consecutive coverage of almost any city every 16 days since 1982.

Various techniques have been used to extract the vegetation cover information from Landsat TM images. Traditional hard classification methods such as supervised and unsupervised classification are easy to use but the accuracy of results is relatively low in urban areas. The spatial scale and the spectral variability of urban land cover are problematic for the traditional classification algorithms (Small, 2001). The vegetation–impervious–soil (V-I-S) model developed by Ridd (1995) assumes that land cover in urban areas is a linear combination of three components: vegetation, impervious surface, and soil. This model provides a way to decompose urban landscape and link the components to the spectral characteristics in remote sensing. However, it cannot account for various land-cover types in urban areas, so the accuracy of classification results is not always high (Madhavan *et al.*, 2001). Spectral mixture analysis (SMA) can be seen as an improved form of the V-I-S model. It assumes that the reflectance spectrum of an image pixel is the linear combination of the spectra of the different land-cover types on ground. By decomposing the spectrum, the area percentage of each land cover in a pixel can be obtained. SMA is useful to reduce the influence of spatial and spectral heterogeneity in urban areas and has been used in various urban land-use/land-cover studies (Small, 2001; Wu and Murray, 2003). The result of spectral mixture analysis depends on the selection of suitable endmembers. Selection of endmembers requires good knowledge of the possible land-cover types in the study area, and the procedure itself is complicated compared with hard classification methods (Lu and Weng, 2004). Other classification methods such as knowledge-based classification and the expert system approach use ancillary data like texture and contextual information as well as spectral information during classification or in post-classification sorting. The accuracy of classification can be generally improved by incorporating ancillary information (Moller-Jensen, 1990; Stefanov *et al.*, 2001). In this study, because the assumption made at the beginning is that data about certain cities are not easy to obtain, the traditional classification method is adopted. The objective is to use two cities in China as an example to show how the vegetation covers in different cities can be compared by analysing the Landsat Enhanced Thematic Mapper (ETM+) images with simple remote sensing techniques.

Methods

Study sites

Beijing and Shanghai were chosen for this study. They are two of the most important cities in China. Beijing, the capital city of China, is the political

Table 16.1. *Basic information about Beijing and Shanghai.*

	Beijing[a]	Shanghai[b]
Location (latitude and longitude of the centre)	39° N, 116° E	31° N, 121° E
Annual precipitation (mm)	630	1428
Average temperature (°C)	11.5	17.8
Total population (million)	13.8	13.3
Planned city area[c] (km^2)	750	667
Administration area[d] (km^2)	16 800	6340
Gross domestic production (US$ billion)	37.9	65.6

Notes:

[a] Data source: www.beijing.gov.cn

[b] Data source: www.sh.gov.cn

[c] Planned city area is that part of the administration area designated as central city on the master plans by the Beijing and Shanghai municipal governments.

[d] Administration area includes all planned city area, rural counties and outer suburbs administrated by the Beijing and Shanghai municipal governments.

and cultural centre. Shanghai is the largest coastal city and the financial centre in China. The basic information about each is shown in Table 16.1. Study areas are defined by the outermost ring road for both Beijing and Shanghai (Fig. 16.1). Areas are 614 km^2 and 667 km^2 for Beijing and Shanghai, respectively.

Image acquisition and processing

A Landsat ETM+ image taken on 24 May 2002 covering the Beijing area and a Landsat ETM+ image taken on 3 July 2001 covering the Shanghai area were acquired for this study. Both images have a cloud cover of less than 5%. They were chosen at leaf-on time of vegetation for both cities. All images are a geometrically and radiometrically rectified level-G product so no further correction was applied. We used 1:25 000 street maps of Beijing and Shanghai to delineate the urban parts of the two cities. These parts of the two cities were cut out from the image for study purposes.

Deriving vegetation cover through unsupervised classification

An unsupervised classification method was used to derive the vegetation cover from the satellite images. Such methods can automatically classify image pixels into clusters with similar spectral features. With visual interpretation, these clusters were put into meaningful land-cover classes (Schowengerdt, 1997). In this study, the ISODATA procedure embedded in the ERDAS IMAGINE 8.4

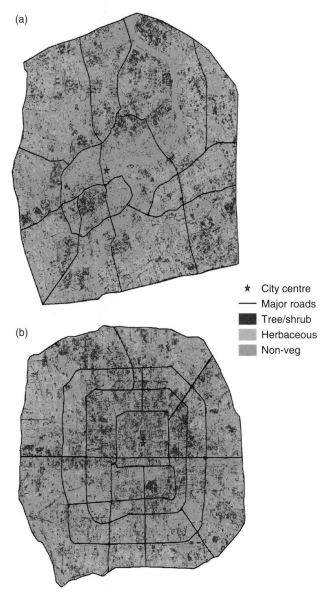

Fig. 16.1. Classification results show tree/shrub (dark green), herbaceous (bright green), and non-vegetation (violet) covers in Shanghai and Beijing. (a) Shanghai; (b) Beijing. See also colour plate.

software package (ERDAS Inc.) was used. The parameters were set up as 50 classes, 100 iterations and a convergence threshold at 0.95. After running the ISODATA procedure, the 50 clusters formed were merged into three classes – tree/shrub cover, herbaceous plant cover and non-vegetated cover – on the basis of class values and visual interpretation. Accuracy assessment was conducted by selecting 100 randomly distributed check points per class, and the source ETM+ images were used as the basis for assigning reference labels to each classified test pixel. It would be desirable to use an independent source of reference data of higher precision and known accuracy for validating the classification. However, as stated earlier, such data are not available. The overall accuracy and Kappa coefficient were generated. Overall accuracy is a measure of the number of sample pixels correctly classified, and the Kappa coefficient is a measure of how different the classification results are from those expected by chance alone (Congalton and Green, 1999).

Calculating landscape metrics

The raster images that resulted from the classification were converted to vector files. Patch Analyst 3.0, an extension developed by Rempel (2003) for ArcView 3.2 (ESRI), was used to calculate landscape metrics for the vegetation class in two cities. The landscape metrics calculated were: patch numbers, patch density, mean patch size, edge densities and percentage of total landscape area. Those landscape metrics were selected because they describe the degree of fragmentation of urban vegetation patches.

Results

Classification results

The classification results are shown in Fig. 16.1. The overall classification accuracy for Beijing was 84% and the Kappa coefficient was 0.75. For Shanghai, the overall classification accuracy was 81% and the Kappa coefficient was 0.71. Those numbers show that the classification results are at an acceptable level compared with other studies (Small, 2001; Lu and Weng, 2004).

Tree cover in Shanghai was mainly concentrated in few parts of the city. In Beijing, the tree cover was distributed more evenly all over the city. The large herbaceous plant patches at the lower right corner of Shanghai are mainly farmland. This can be judged from the flat, regularly divided and rectangular texture of the vegetation on the classified images.

Landscape metrics

Landscape metrics calculated for the vegetation patches are shown in Table 16.2. The table shows that Beijing has roughly same number of vegetation patches as in Shanghai. However, the number of tree patches in Beijing is more than that of Shanghai. The mean sizes of tree and herbaceous plant patches are small in both cities.

Table 16.2. *Comparison of landscape metrics of vegetation patches in Beijing and Shanghai.*

	Beijing		Shanghai	
	Tree (shrub)[a]	Herbaceous	Tree (shrub)	Herbaceous
Patch number	69 757	26 153	41 477	51 922
Patch density (number per 100 ha)	113.5	42.55	62.18	77.84
Mean patch size (ha)	0.17	0.19	0.19	0.20
Edge density (m/ha)	186.76	71.96	111.42	141.46
% total landscape area	19.13	7.89	10.22	14.07

Note:

[a] Tree cover includes the surface covered by shrubs.

Discussion

The extent of tree cover in Beijing is about 9% higher than that of Shanghai. If only the climate is considered, Shanghai is more suitable for tree growth. Shanghai is located in a subtropical monsoon zone, Beijing in a semi-arid continental monsoon zone. The contradiction may be explained by the different development history of these two cities. Beijing has been the capital city of China for about 800 years. Numerous royal gardens, officials' residences and temples have been extensively planted with trees and other vegetation (Dember, 1993; Liu *et al.*, 2004). While the city expanded around the old districts, these trees were kept for their historical and aesthetic value (Profous, 1992; Dember, 1993). And now, after winning the right to hold the 2008 Summer Olympic Games, the municipal government has initiated large-scale urban greening projects inside and outside the city. In 2000, the municipal government invested US$172 million in urban greenspace construction (Beijing Statistics Bureau, 2003).

Shanghai is located in the region that has the most productive farmland in China. The long history of extensive agricultural activities cleared the original vegetation cover. From 1950 to the end of the 1980s, Shanghai developed as an industrial centre. As in other industrial cities in China, the land in Shanghai was mainly used for building factories and housing for workers. Few greenspaces were built during that time (Le, 1994). From 1990 to the present, Shanghai has been transforming into the financial centre of China. The municipal government invests heavily in urban greening in the city. However, the high population density in the central city and the skyrocketing real estate values make it very difficult to add more new greenspace in the central city (Yan, 1998).

The distribution pattern of vegetation is more reasonable in Beijing than in Shanghai. From Fig. 16.1, it can be seen that the vegetation patches, mainly the tree patches in Beijing, are dispersed more evenly, whereas in Shanghai, the bulk of vegetation cover, mainly the herbaceous plants, consist of agricultural lands far from the city centre. Researchers have found that ecological benefits such as microclimate modification produced by urban vegetation are local phenomena, constrained inside the vegetation patch and its immediate adjacent area (Oke et al., 1989). Thus the urban vegetation in Beijing is more effective in providing city dwellers with ecological benefits. Also, for sports and leisure purposes, the citizens of Beijing have easier access to greenspace than people living in Shanghai.

In the future, the vegetation cover in Beijing will be potentially more stable than that in Shanghai. The tree patches interspersed in the city can be well protected through strict government regulation (Dember, 1993). The few patches of herbaceous plants near the boundary of the city may possibly be lost to development. However, these losses can be partially offset by the urban greening activity of the government. In Shanghai, the vegetation cover may further decrease in the future. The large farmland patches at the lower right corner of Shanghai are likely to be developed to incorporate the need for commercial and residential spaces. According to Liu et al. (2005), 75.3% of the newly expanded urban land in Chinese mega-cities, including Shanghai, came from cultivated land in 1990–2000, and we can reasonably expect this trend to continue into the future considering the rapid economic growth in China.

If we compare the tree cover patterns and population density in Beijing and Shanghai with those of several American cities, the Chinese cities are not performing badly at all (Fig. 16.2). Beijing is quite close to New York both in population density and extent of tree cover. The tree cover extent of Shanghai is close to that of Chicago, but Shanghai has a population density three times higher than that of Chicago. The overall trend of tree cover extent among all compared cities follows the conclusion by Nowak et al. (2001) that percentage of tree cover in urban areas tends to decrease as population density increases.

Conclusion

The study showed that Beijing has a higher extent of vegetation cover than Shanghai. Furthermore, Beijing is likely to keep relatively stable vegetation cover while Shanghai may face reductions in the future. There are some limitations in this study. For example, the classification method used here can only classify image pixels dominated by vegetation. In the city there are mixed pixels where vegetation exists but is not the dominant land-cover type. So the

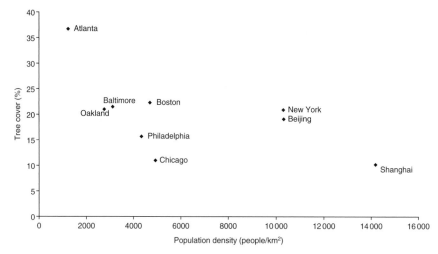

Fig. 16.2. Comparison of tree cover (%) and population density in Atlanta, Beijing, Shanghai, Chicago, New York, Philadelphia, Boston, Oakland and Baltimore. Except Beijing and Shanghai, the tree cover data for other cities are from Nowak *et al.* (2001) and the population density data are from Wikipedia (http://en.wikipedia.org). The population densities for Beijing and Shanghai were calculated for the studied area with the information obtained from the website of the Beijing Bureau of Statistics (http://www.bjstats.gov.cn) and Shanghai Bureau of Statistics (http://www.stats-sh.gov.cn).

classification results underestimate the vegetation cover in these two cities. Also, owing to the coarse resolution of the Landsat ETM+ image, more detailed information about the structure of the vegetation, such as the percentage of lawn, crop, pasture and vegetable garden, the species composition, or details of horizontal and vertical layers, cannot be derived from the image. In future studies, high-resolution satellite images, more advanced image interpretation methods and ancillary data could be used to overcome these limitations. Despite these limitations, the method used in this study can still be a quick, cost-effective and relatively accurate way to generate information for comparative studies of cities. At the same time that this study was conducted, two projects using similar methods to analyse large-scale urban vegetation cover were running. The Comprehensive Urban Ecosystem Studies (CUES), conducted by the United States Geological Survey (USGS) with the participation of American Forests, generated a national map containing tree cover information for all urban areas in the United States by using Landsat data taken in 2001 (Gary, 2005). The Dynamics of Global Urban Expansion project, run by the World Bank, generated urban land-cover information for 90 cities worldwide through analysing the Landsat images in 1990 and 2000 (Angel *et al.*, 2005). We can expect remote sensing to be more widely used in comparative studies of cities as the satellite data become more available and the cost of software and hardware becomes more affordable.

Acknowledgements

We want to thank Peng Gong (University of California, Berkeley), for providing the Landsat ETM+ image of Beijing. Also, without the generous support from Joe McBride (University of California, Berkeley), this study would not have been possible.

17

Vegetation composition and structure of forest patches along urban–rural gradients

WAYNE C. ZIPPERER AND GLENN R. GUNTENSPERGEN

Introduction

The urban landscape is highly altered by human activities and is a mosaic of different land covers and land uses. Imbedded in this are forest patches of different origins (Zipperer et al., 1997). How these patches influence and are influenced by the urban landscape is of ecological importance when managing the urban forest for ecosystem goods and services.

To evaluate how forests respond to altered environmental conditions of urban landscapes, McDonnell and Pickett (1990) proposed an urban-to-rural gradient approach. The approach builds on an established ecological methodology, gradient analysis, to evaluate species response to changes in environmental conditions (Whittaker, 1967; Pickett et al., Chapter 3). Two basic categories of gradient analyses exist – direct and indirect. Simplistically, direct gradient analysis is typically employed when a single factor is used or the underlying environmental factors are organised linearly, whereas indirect gradient analysis is used when the multiple interacting factors and the environmental factors are not organised linearly across a landscape or in a regular pattern (Ter Braak and Prentice, 1988). Other approaches exist for studying the response of ecosystems to altered environmental conditions in urban environments, such as biotope mapping (Breuste, Chapter 21) and patch dynamic approaches (Nilon, Chapter 10).

Ecology of Cities and Towns: A Comparative Approach, ed. Mark J. McDonnell, Amy K. Hahs and Jürgen H. Breuste. Published by Cambridge University Press. © Cambridge University Press 2009.

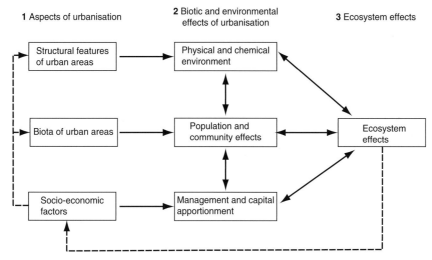

1 Aspects of urbanisation

2 Biotic and environmental effects of urbanisation

3 Ecosystem effects

Fig. 17.1. A composite model showing the effect of urbanisation on ecological components. The solid lines represent the original model proposed by McDonnell and Pickett (1990). The dash lines are feedback loops to link ecosystem effects (altered goods and services) back to socio-economic components.

Unlike many environmental gradients where environmental factors (e.g. in temperature, moisture, elevation) change linearly, urbanisation does not change linearly (high to low) across a metropolitan region (McDonnell et al., 1993). Consequently, urbanisation actually is best represented by indirect gradient analysis, where population, community and ecosystem responses are analysed and urban gradients are identified.

The urban–rural gradient is not a new idea and has been used by individuals prior to McDonnell and Pickett (1990) (see Airola and Buchholz, 1984; Dorney et al., 1984; Moran, 1984). But McDonnell and Pickett (1990) moved the science from merely describing species changes along an urban continuum to framing how ecosystems – their structure, function and change – are altered by urbanisation and the consequences to society (Niemelä et al., Chapter 2; Pickett et al., Chapter 3; Natuhara and Hashimoto, Chapter 12; Carreiro et al., Chapter 19; Pouyat et al., Chapter 20). To portray the effect of urbanisation on ecosystems, they proposed a composite model with three components: (1) aspects of urbanisation; (2) biotic and environmental effects of urbanisation; and (3) ecosystem effects (Fig. 17.1). The model emphasises the effect of the urban landscape on ecosystem structure and function without any ecological feedback on the social system (Zipperer et al., 1997). See Pickett et al. (Chapter 3) for more discussion of the feedbacks between ecological and social systems.

A second type of urban–rural gradient is proposed by Porter et al. (2001). Rather than evaluating a specific ecosystem in different urban contexts, they

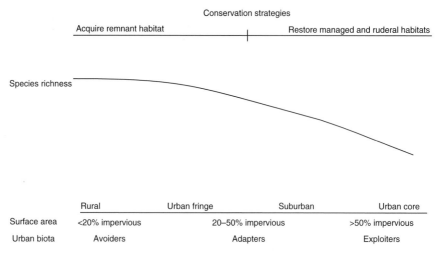

Fig. 17.2. A graphic representation of changes in impervious surface, species richness, species composition and conservation strategies along urban–rural gradients as proposed by McKinney (2002).

propose to compare different land-use cover types to a natural ecosystem. For example, Blair (1996) examined how bird diversity varied from a forested patch to various urban land-use types including residential, recreational and commercial (see also Catterall, Chapter 8). The analysis provides insights into species responses to different land-cover types. Yang and Zhou (Chapter 16) and McDonnell and Hahs (Chapter 5) discuss other remote sensing and GIS variables that can be effectively used to define urban–rural gradients.

McKinney (2002) reviewed the current literature on how urbanisation alters ecosystems and offered conservation strategies for managing ecosystems and educating the public about the importance of maintaining ecosystems in urban and urbanising landscapes. From the review, he identified several general patterns from rural to urban (Fig. 17.2): impervious surface increases, native species richness declines, species composition shifts from interior to ruderal species, and conservation strategies shift from acquiring remnant patches to restoring managed and ruderal habitats (McKinney, 2002). These observations often were derived from studies examining species responses to different land covers rather than a specific ecosystem in different urban contexts.

In this chapter, we will use McDonnell and Pickett's (1990) composite model of urban effects on ecosystems and McKinney's (2002) descriptive model of species and management responses to urbanisation to examine patterns of species composition and structure in remnant and reforested forest patches, and remnant forest productivity, along urban–rural gradients in Maryland, New Jersey, New York and Wisconsin (Levenson, 1981; Airola and Buchholz, 1984;

Table 17.1. *General descriptions of urban–rural gradients used to compare vegetation composition and structure.*

Milwaukee	24 remnant upland forest patches (Guntenspergen and Levenson, 1997). Patches were dominated by sugar maple (*Acer saccharum*) and occurred on soils with similar characteristics. All patches had mature forest edges and were devoid of recent disturbances such as grazing, cutting, fire and windthrow. Patches ranged from 0.59 to 21.0 ha.
Palisade	Only five forested patches along the Palisades escarpment in New Jersey (Airola and Buchholz, 1984). Patches were remnant forests. Three occurred within the Palisades Interstate Park and showed little signs of disturbance. The other two patches were on unprotected urban sites. Patch sizes ranged from 2.5 to 16 ha.
Baltimore	45 remnant upland forest patches (W. C. Zipperer, in preparation) along an urban–rural gradient in the Gwynns Falls watershed. Patches were >5 ha in size. All patches had mature forest edges and were devoid of recent disturbances such as grazing, cutting, fire and windthrow.
Syracuse	Both remnant (44) and reforested (52) upland forest patches (Zipperer, 2002). All sites had established canopies and did not show any signs of recent large-scale disturbances. Patch sizes ranged from 0.25 to 85 ha.

Kostel-Hughes, 1995; Guntenspergen and Levenson, 1997; Kostel-Hughes *et al.*, 1998a; Zipperer, 2002; Table 17.1). Although urbanisation is best represented by indirect gradient analysis, in this analysis we used the direct gradient as outlined by the researchers in each of the mentioned studies because indirect gradient information was not available for all of the studies.

Aspects of urbanisation

In their composite model, McDonnell and Pickett (1990) identified three elements – structural features, biota and socio-economic factors of urban areas (Fig. 17.1) – as the principal drivers influencing ecosystem structure and function. Here, we specifically examine how structural attributes define the urban landscape and their effect on forested ecosystems.

Structural features

European settlement of North America fragmented large tracts of forest into smaller forest remnants as forest lands were cleared for agriculture (e.g. Curtis and McIntosh, 1951), altering external allogenic and autogenic processes (Saunders *et al.*, 1991). As landscapes became more urbanised, landscape context changed, and allogenic and autogenic processes changed as anthropogenic disturbances (e.g. trampling and arson) supplanted natural processes and disturbances such as fire (Parker and Pickett, 1997). Further, with the shifts in landscape context, the functional aspect of the edge changed (see Cadenasso *et al.*, 1997). The conversion of non-urban land to urban land use has been extensively studied. For example, Godron and Forman (1983) examined landscape modifications by humans and identified several effects including linearisation of feature, reduction of patch size, increase in patch isolation and fragmentation, and a shift from interior to edge habitat. It is not the purpose of this section to review the literature on conversions to urban land use, but instead we use three studies – Zipperer *et al.* (1990), Medley *et al.* (1995) and Luck and Wu (2002) – to characterise general patterns of structural features observed along urban–rural gradients. Zipperer *et al.* (1990) conducted a spatio-temporal analysis of forest patches in five different landscape types – forest, forest+agriculture, forest+urban, agriculture, agricultural+urban, and urban. The dominant or co-dominant land use or cover defined a landscape. His analysis showed a similar pattern to that seen by Godron and Forman (1983), but it also showed that even though a landscape was urban (dominant land use), fragmentation and deforestation continued to reduce patch size and eliminate patches, increasing the isolation of the remaining forest patches.

Medley *et al.* (1995) quantified the New York urban–rural gradient by using a set of landscape parameters along a linear transect from highly urbanised New York City to rural Litchfield County, Connecticut. Social parameters included population density, traffic volume, road density and percentage of land use (residential, urban-mixed, forest, agriculture, wetland, abandoned land and water). Forest patch attributes included mean patch size, patch density, and percentage of total forest edge adjacent to urban-mix and residential land uses. Although the results were similar to the previous study, Medley *et al.* (1995) also revealed that disturbances associated with urbanisation show a complex spatial pattern not clearly related to a linear distance from urban to rural.

Looking more closely at patch dynamics and applying different patch metrics to an urban landscape, Luck and Wu (2002) conducted a detailed patch analysis in the urban and urbanising landscapes of the Phoenix Metropolitan area. They observed patterns for desert vegetation similar to those described by Godron and Forman (1983), Zipperer (1990) and Medley *et al.* (1995) – declines in size and total number of patches and increased isolation with an increase in urban land use. They also reported that urban landscapes can be quantified using known patch metrics, and land-use types did differ to some extent with regard to these metrics (Luck and Wu, 2002). Land-use types, however, did not show a distinct landscape signature but rather a 'landscape pattern profile'. Further, their analyses supported McDonnell and Pickett's (1990) hypothesis that a gradient analysis using patch metrics can help to quantify complex urban landscapes and subsequently relate attributes to ecosystem patterns and processes.

Biota of urban areas

Human activities lead to a high diversity of non-native species in urban landscapes (Kowarik, 1990; Porter *et al.*, 2001; Catterall, Chapter 8; Nilon, Chapter 10; van der Ree, Chapter 11; Natuhara and Hashimoto, Chapter 12; McIntyre and Rango, Chapter 14 and Meurk *et al.*, Chapter 18). Although most species introductions do not affect ecosystems, about 5% can become invasive and affect ecosystem structure and function (Reichard and White, 2001). Ecologists are just beginning to understand how these non-native species are altering urban forest patches. For example, exotic earthworms alter denitrification in urban forest soils (Steinberg *et al.*, 1997). Similarly, Ehrenfeld (2003) reports that non-native species increase biomass and net primary production, increase nitrogen (N) availability, alter nitrogen fixation rates and produce more litter than co-occurring native species. Non-native species also compete with native species for available growing space and nutrients. Understanding how non-native species alter community and ecosystem dynamics is a central theme for today's urban ecologists.

Socio-economic factors

In addition to these structural and biotic effects, urban woodlands also are strongly influenced by socio-economic factors and processes (Grove and Burch, 1997). Collectively, these factors and processes can be defined as sociogenic, and are often accounted for in ecological studies by land-use patterns. However, a land-use classification does not capture the wealth of social heterogeneity within a land use and how that heterogeneity influences the movement of energy, species and materials (Machlis *et al.*, 1997). Several studies indicate the importance of accounting for social heterogeneity with respect to species availability and performance (see Whitney and Adams, 1980; Richards *et al.*, 1984). To account for sociogenic processes, Grove and Burch (1997) recommend defining social areas as patches based on socio-economic attributes and capital, such as ethnicity, education, home ownership and income. These socio-economic patches are then overlaid on ecological patches (e.g. forest patches) to examine interactions and relationships between social and ecological patterns and processes. In addition, the patch approach enables hierarchical analyses to examine how the different social attributes influence ecological processes at different scales (Pickett *et al.*, 1997b).

Alberti *et al.* (2003) present a conceptual framework that differs from the patch approach of Pickett *et al.* (1997b). The framework accounts not only for the interactions between human and biophysical patterns and processes, but also the feedbacks from these interactions. Regardless of the approach, both Pickett *et al.* (1997b) and Alberti *et al.* (2003) recognise the importance of social context within an urban landscape and its influence on ecosystems. The urban–rural gradient can be used to assess how different social contexts influence ecosystem structure and function, and how different ecosystems can affect social contexts (Pickett *et al.*, Chapter 3).

Biotic and environmental effects

Physical and chemical

Environmentally, urban landscapes are highly altered when compared with natural systems. For example, a comparison of urban and rural forest soils shows that urban forest soils have a higher organic content (i.e. decomposed material) in the O_2 horizon, possibly the result of earthworm activity (Pouyat *et al.*, 1995a; Steinberg *et al.*, 1997), a lower litter depth (Kostel-Hughes *et al.*, 1998a) and, in some areas, greater bulk density from compaction. Internal functions of urban woodlands also differ from those in rural woodlands. Urban woodlands have higher rates of decomposition, nitrification and seed predation (Nilon, 1996; Pouyat *et al.*, 1996; Carreiro *et al.*, 1999; Zhu and Carreiro, 1999; Carreiro *et al.*, Chapter 19 and Pouyat *et al.*, Chapter 20), and possibly have lower soil moisture (White and McDonnell, 1988). Decomposition, nitrification and soil moisture influence the concentration and type of nutrients available for plant growth. Higher rates of seed predation may influence successional development of the site. And because of a concentration of human activities (e.g. hiking and biking), more soil erosion and reduced infiltration from compaction occur in urban woodlands than in rural woodlands. In addition to these direct effects, urbanisation affects the woodland indirectly by altering the disturbance regime; increasing ambient temperatures (urban heat island); increasing pollution deposition of heavy metals, nitrogen, calcium and manganese; modifying hydrology; and introducing non-native species (Pouyat and McDonnell, 1991; Lovett *et al.*, 2000; Reichard and White, 2001). A more detailed evaluation of environmental effects is presented by Carreiro *et al.* (Chapter 19) and Pouyat *et al.* (Chapter 20).

Population and community effects

Changes in the physical, biotic and structural attributes along urban–rural gradients affect species composition and structure in vegetation. McKinney (2002) describes a shift in composition from a dominance of interior species to a dominance of ruderal species as one moves from rural to urban sites. This pattern seems to hold true for both flora and faunal communities. For example, Porter *et al.* (2001) observed no changes in structural attributes of woody vegetation (>3 cm diameter at breast height, dbh) across six land-use types (forest preserve, recreational, golf course, residential, apartments and industrial), but did observe changes in species richness. The richness analyses did not show a decline in native species richness, but did show an increase in non-native species richness, principally from ornamental planting and gardens. The occurrence of native species across these land-cover types was attributed to planting of native species and to remnant individuals (e.g. McBride and Jacobs, 1976). Porter *et al.* (2001), however, did observe a greater faunal change across the land-cover types. The social context of each land-cover type significantly influenced flora and fauna (see also Meurk *et al.*, Chapter 18; Florgård, Chapter 22; Ignatieva and Stewart, Chapter 23). And, although this and similar studies (Blair, 1996) identify changes associated with urbanisation, these changes are based on changing land-use types. We will show that comparisons of forests along urban–rural gradients also show shifts in species composition and structure.

Remnant forests

To evaluate how species composition and structure varied across an urban–rural gradient, we separated forest structure into three categories of vertical structure: canopy, shrub/sapling and seedling. For upland remnant forests, non-native species richness for canopy, shrub/sapling, and seedling strata increased from rural to urban, regardless of patch origin (Tables 17.2, 17.3 and 17.4). However, two distinct patterns of native species richness were observed. Along the New Jersey Palisade gradient, native species richness declined in the canopy, shrub/sapling and seedling strata (Airola and Buchholz, 1984). By comparison, native species richness for each stratum was unchanged for the Milwaukee (Levenson, 1981; Ranney *et al.*, 1981; Guntenspergen and Levenson, 1997), Baltimore and Syracuse remnant forest patches (Zipperer, 2002; W. C. Zipperer,

Table 17.2. *Changes in native and non-native species richness in the canopy stratum for different urban–rural gradients.*

Gradient	Native species	Non-native species
Palisade	↓	↑
Milwaukee	↔	↑
Syracuse: Remnant	↔	↑
Syracuse: Reforested	↔	↑
Baltimore: Remnant	↔	↑

Notes:
↑: increased from rural to urban
↓: decreased from rural to urban
↔: no change

Table 17.3. *Changes in native and non-species richness in the sapling/shrub stratum for different urban–rural gradients.*

Gradient	Native species	Non-native species
Palisade	↓	↑
Milwaukee	↔	↑
Syracuse: Remnant	↔	↑
Syracuse: Reforested	↓	↑
Baltimore: Remnant	↔	↑

Notes:

↑: increased from rural to urban

↓: decreased from rural to urban

↔: no change

Table 17.4. *Changes in native and non-species richness in the seedling stratum for different urban–rural gradients.*

Gradient	Native species	Non-native species
Palisade	↓	↑
Milwaukee	↔	↑
Syracuse: Remnant	↔	↑
Syracuse: Reforested	↓	↑
Baltimore: Remnant	↔	↑

Notes:

↑: increased from rural to urban

↓: decreased from rural to urban

↔: no change

unpublished data). This difference may be related to sampling intensity and patch disturbance regime. Airola and Buchholz (1984) sampled only two forest patches in the urban landscape, so they did not have sufficient data to give an adequate representation of forest conditions. In addition, the Palisade gradient did not control for disturbance. In the urban forest patches, canopy cover was not continuous and tree density was much lower than in the undisturbed sites along the Palisade. For the Syracuse, Baltimore and Milwaukee gradients, canopy cover was maintained and disturbances were limited to small-scale events (Sharpe *et al.*, 1986; Zipperer, 2002).

Structurally, with the exception of Palisade, each gradient showed an increase in tree stem density. All the gradient studies showed an increase in shrub/sapling

Table 17.5. *Changes in structural characteristics for different urban–rural gradients.*

Gradient	Tree density	Shrub/sapling density	Seedling density
Palisade	↓	↑	↓
Milwaukee			↓
Syracuse: Remnant	↑	↑	↓
Syracuse: Reforested	↔	↑	↓
Baltimore: Remnant	↑	↑	↓

Notes:

↑: increased from rural to urban

↓: decreased from rural to urban

↔: no change

density, but also a decline in seedling density. In the New Jersey gradient, tree density declined. Unfortunately, long-term monitoring of species composition and structure of forest patches along an urban–rural gradient is lacking. However, a number of studies of temporal changes in structure and composition of forest patches in the urban landscape have been conducted (e.g. Rudnicky and McDonnell, 1989; Botkin, 1990). In each case, we do not see a loss of native species, but rather a shift in species importance and an increase in non-natives. In general, the structure shifted from long-lived, shade-tolerant species (*Acer saccharum*, *Quercus* spp. and *Fagus grandifolia*) to short-lived, shade-intolerant species (*Liriodendron tulipifera*, *Prunus serotina* and *A. rubrum*).

Reforested patches

Unlike the studies examining remnant forest patches along urban–rural gradients, analysis of reforested patches is limited (Zipperer, 2002), so the pattern that we observed, a decrease in native species richness but an increase in non-native species across all structural categories (Tables 17.2, 17.3 and 17.4), needs to be verified for other locations. Reforested patches in Syracuse, New York, were dominated by non-native species (Zipperer, 2002), and those species differ from the dominant species occurring in rural reforested patches. In the urban landscape, *Acer negundo, A. platanoides* and *Fagus pennsylvanica* are the dominant tree species. In the rural sites, *A. rubrum* and *Fraxinus americana* are the dominant species. Structurally, sites are similar in tree density, but differ with respect to shrub/sapling density and seedling density (Table 17.5). Rural sites had lower shrub/sapling densities but higher seedling densities. A number of factors could cause these differences including site disturbances, species availability and altered site conditions. Additional research, however, is needed to identify how these factors influence the observed species distribution and structural characteristics.

Ecosystem effects

The analysis of urbanisation on ecosystem function has focused principally on soil processes (see McDonnell *et al.*, 1997) rather than forest processes, such as productivity. Nevertheless, the soil studies have pointed out two factors that can significantly affect productivity: warmer soil temperatures and higher levels of available nitrogen. Analysis of phenological differences between urban and rural areas also indicates that the growing season was 7.6 days longer in urban than in rural broad-leaf deciduous areas in the eastern United States (White *et al.*, 2002). Coupling this observation with an increase in carbon dioxide in urban landscapes (Idso *et al.*, 2001), one would predict a higher rate of productivity in urban areas than rural areas. Using eastern cottonwood (*Populus deltoides*) clones planted along an urban–rural gradient in the New York metropolitan area, Gregg *et al.* (2003) showed higher productivity rates for the urban plantings. These higher rates, however, were not attributed to higher urban temperatures and CO_2 concentration but rather to higher levels of ozone in rural areas, which reduced productivity.

A comparison of leaf weight for the permanent plots established within the Gwynns Falls watershed in Maryland and a forested reference site in Oregon Ridge State Park located north of the watershed (part of the Baltimore Long-Term Ecological Research Project) showed that rural sites had a greater mass per leaf area suggesting thicker leaves (W. C. Zipperer, unpublished data). Carreiro *et al.* (1999) also observed the same pattern for oak forest patches along a New York urban–rural gradient. Ozone is known to affect leaf thickness (Berish *et al.*, 1998). The observed differences in leaf weight per area for both Maryland and New York gradients suggest that some environmental factor is influencing stand growth, possibly ozone as hypothesised by Gregg *et al.* (2003).

No differences in the mean annual growth increment of trees in remnant stands greater than five hectares in the Gwynns Falls watershed were observed between the upper section (rural) and the lower section (urban). No differences in tree growth were observed between rural and urban areas. Regardless of tree age, the middle or 'suburban' section had the lowest mean annual increment. These observations differ from what would be predicted from Gregg *et al.* (2003). The lower or urban section should have the highest productivity. The mean annual increment analysis did not involve saplings. A more detailed analysis of individuals from each stratum – tree, shrub/sapling, and seedling/herbaceous – is needed to understand the complexity of forest productivity along an urban–rural gradient.

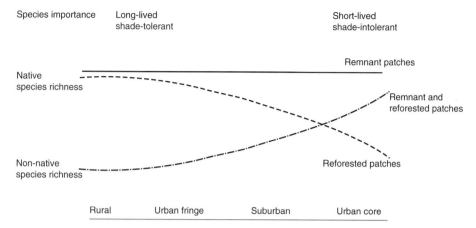

Fig. 17.3. A modification of McKinney's (2002) model for changes along urban–rural gradients to illustrate changes in species richness and importance observed for remnant and reforested patches.

Revised urban–rural model

By comparing only forest patches with similar disturbance regimes and origin along urban–rural gradients, we observed that native species richness remains relatively constant but non-native species richness increases. As the disturbance regime changes, native species richness declines (Airola and Buchholz, 1984; Zipperer, 2002). This decline, however, needs to be substantiated with additional studies. Regardless of the disturbance regime, non-native species increased in both remnant and reforested patches. Seedling density declined with an increase in urban land use. In reforested sites, native species richness also declined, and unlike their rural counterparts, urban reforested patches were often dominated by non-native species.

Even with similar disturbance regimes and compositions, upland remnant forest patches may be shifting in species importance as shade-tolerant species give way to shade-intolerant species. This pattern is suggested by McKinney (2002) as a shift from interior to ruderal species. Structurally, the forest is composed of a higher density of smaller diameter trees. More studies are needed to understand how the environment of an urban landscape affects tree growth and patch productivity.

We propose the following modifications to McKinney's (2002) model (Fig. 17.3). First, no single model can capture the variation observed in urban landscapes because of differences in site legacies and disturbance regimes. Second, for woody plant species, species richness needs to be separated into native and non-native categories to capture changes along the gradient. Finally, the use of species importance, rather than interior and ruderal categories, may capture potential changes in stand structure.

These modifications do not suggest that McKinney's (2002) model is wrong or incomplete; to the contrary, we are adding another dimension to our understanding of how the urban landscape affects flora and fauna. Actually, how one views the urban landscape depends on perspective. Looking across similar land-cover types in different urban contexts will yield different patterns than examining how different land covers differ in urban landscapes. Because of the social, physical and ecological complexities in urban landscapes, we need to initiate detailed studies that examine these differences to better understand urban effects on ecosystem patterns and processes.

18

Environmental, social and spatial determinants of urban arboreal character in Auckland, New Zealand

COLIN D. MEURK, NADYA ZVYAGNA, RHYS O. GARDNER, GUY
FORRESTER, MIKE WILCOX, GRAEME HALL, HEATHER NORTH,
STELLA BELLISS, KATHRYN WHALEY, BILL SYKES,
JERRY COOPER AND KATHRYN O'HALLORAN

Introduction

To date, nearly all vegetation studies in New Zealand have been carried out in pristine to semi-natural systems. Thus, urban ecology in New Zealand is in its infancy as compared with the centuries of observation, documentation and mapping of vegetation, biotopes and natural history in urban areas of Europe (Gilbert, 1989; Breuste *et al.*, 1998; Sukopp, 2002; Breuste, Chapter 21; Florgård, Chapter 22; Wittig, Chapter 30) and 30-plus years of study in North America (Zipperer and Guntenspergen, Chapter 17). The relatively few studies of urban vegetation in the New World have typically focused on remnant natural systems enveloped by residential and commercial dwellings (Airola and Buchholz, 1984; Rudnicky and McDonnell, 1989; Kuschel, 1990; Molloy, 1995; McDonnell *et al.*, 1997). Accordingly, there is a distinction to be made between the ecology of remnant primary ecosystems (those that retain at least some thread of biological and pedological continuity with the primeval system) and the ecology of synthetic or spontaneous recombinant systems on anthropogenic substrates (i.e. most vegetation in cities and towns). In New Zealand, we know quite a lot about natural forest, wetland and grassland vegetation, whether in National Parks or as remnants in cities (Wardle, 1991); but little about recombinant communities of cultural landscapes (that is, human-inhabited landscapes in the sense of

Ecology of Cities and Towns: A Comparative Approach, ed. Mark J. McDonnell, Amy K. Hahs and Jürgen H. Breuste. Published by Cambridge University Press. © Cambridge University Press 2009.

Nassauer (1997)). They have been traditionally shunned in New Zealand because they almost totally comprise exotic, planted and/or weedy species. This is in sharp contrast to the United Kingdom where Thompson *et al.* (2003) report that 90% of the most frequent plants in garden quadrats are natives. Nevertheless, there is growing evidence that New Zealand's indigenous flora and fauna is colonising the cities (Stewart *et al.*, 2004; Crossland, 2005). Despite their modified state, it has been shown that New Zealand cities are biodiversity refugia and have restoration potential (Given and Meurk, 2000), but this biodiversity is under great threat because it occurs primarily in small and degraded remnants invaded by exotic species. Many of them are subject to land owners and city managers unaware that cryptic indigenous species occur on their land and that they might be of value. Traditionally and universally, most of New Zealand's conservation has been practised in mountainous, cold or wet areas. Lowland species and habitats are therefore not only the most fragmented and degraded, but also the least protected (Meurk and Buxton, 1990). In particular, lowland herbaceous floras are being squeezed out of existence by intensification of agriculture on the one hand, and the rampant growth of tall, dense exotic grasses in waste places or lightly managed land in the cultural landscape on the other. This unique low-land flora may survive in small patches of habitat – such as short tussock grasses in the 1–2 m wide tension zone between the shade of an exotic conifer shelter belt, the tree root zone which sucks the water out of the surface soil layers, and the mown road verge which all diminish exotic grass competition and thereby favour a few native species (Meurk and Greenep, 2003).

Meurk and Swaffield (2000) have also suggested that visibility of nature is an important element of conservation; thus it is important to raise the profile of nature where most people are likely to experience it – in cities. A recently developed science programme in New Zealand addresses low-impact urban design and development or application of soft-engineering principles to management of stormwater, waste, toxins and energy – to reduce impacts of urbanisation (Eason *et al.*, Chapter 27). We identify a parallel and urgent need to understand more about the natural environment and biodiversity of New Zealand's cities in order to address both the ecological and socio-cultural needs of biodiversity conservation. This is the study of the green fabric within the built infrastructure – its status and potential for enhancement as a living part of our urban environment that contributes to the legibility of our landscapes (in landscape architecture terms, the ability to read the history in the landscape) and consequently our quality and richness of life experience (Louv, 2005).

In the absence of baseline information on the ecology of cities in New Zealand, we initiated a programme to study residential vegetation, its biodiversity value and potential, biosecurity load, regenerative dynamics of indigenous species, coexistence of nature and culture, community knowledge and interest in biodiversity, and management attitudes and practices (Meurk and Hall, 2000; Stewart *et al.*, 2004; Meurk, 2005). The study of these habitats poses methodological problems, such as how to sample fine-grained mosaics or small disjunct vegetation patches. Unpredictable human disturbance drives successional pathways in cities and creates a bewildering array of ephemeral plant communities. And finally, scientists must contend with community suspicions, while peering at lawns or emerging unexpectedly from shrubberies, and avoid being distracted from the task at hand.

We focused this study on the most classic of urban environments in New Zealand cities – the front yard of the home garden. New Zealanders are inveterate gardeners (this and walking are the two top recreational pastimes), but there has been a preoccupation with using exotic species (at least since the 1930s, Strongman, 1998), many of which have escaped and become invasive weeds. With an indigenous vascular flora of about 2500 species, New Zealand has of the order of 30 000 exotic species (W. R. Sykes, personal communication), a tenth of which are naturalised; and the number is being added to at a rate of over four per year for Auckland alone (Esler, 1988b). Introduced plant species thrive in New Zealand's benign climate, especially when free of their natural biological controls and harsh homeland winters. The successful weeds also do well owing to their co-adaptations to other imported influences alien to New Zealand such as mammal grazing and continentally honed competition (Meurk and Swaffield, 2000). The propagule rain and seed bank of the cultural landscape is now overwhelmingly dominated by exotic species (Partridge, 1989). If New Zealand is to maintain its indigenous plant biodiversity it will be important in the future to redress this imbalance.

This chapter reports our work on the vegetation of Auckland, the largest city in New Zealand, with over a million people spread over a larger area than occupied by many other major cities of the world. Auckland can also rightly claim to be one of the weed capitals of the world. The large and growing number of exotic species in the region has been documented by Esler (1988a, b). We use front gardens, not only because these can be readily seen from the street, but also because in general in New Zealand, these are the showpieces of lawn, flowers, shrubberies and ornamental or amenity trees. Back yards were traditionally used for vegetable and herb gardens and small orchards. This pattern is undergoing a major shift with changing activity patterns and as house infilling and the availability of food at supermarket and fast food stores are reducing the amount of productive garden per residence. The surviving 'gardens' may be paved as car parks, grassed over, or left to become semi-wild with increasing localised opportunities for regeneration of both native and exotic 'weeds'.

Our aim is to report on the density, composition and proportions of native and exotic, mainly woody, plant species in residential front yards of Auckland, New Zealand. We assess the biosecurity risks due to exotic species and the consequences for the sustainability of urban wildlife. Finally, we present some preliminary information on the ecological and social causes of the patterns observed. This information is critical for developing intelligent management and restoration priorities in urban planning that will enhance biodiversity in Auckland and other New Zealand cities.

Methods

We sampled tree vegetation, weeds and regeneration in front gardens as seen from the roadside from a stratified random sample of residential Auckland properties, excluding the Central Business District (CBD), other major shopping and industrial centres, and waterways or bodies. For stratifying this large city we identified environmental and social gradients that are seen across most cities. The most direct is a rainfall gradient with higher rainfall in the western uplands. A greenness index, derived from multi-spectral satellite imagery (30 m combined to 250 m pixels), divided into five equal wavelength classes, was the basis of the stratification. Twenty compound pixels were chosen randomly from each of the five classes and then two to six random street numbers, spread between the two sides of a street at the centre of the pixel (Fig. 18.1).

A subsample of one of the properties from each side of the street was used for an 'intensive survey' in which the property was entered, a more detailed examination was made of the land cover, regeneration, weed infestation and soil acidity, and the property resident was interviewed. The remaining, approximately four street numbers, were subject to the 'extensive survey' – only what could be seen from the footpath; and only those tree or bush species that projected above the standard high fence line (*c.* 1.7 m) were surveyed. This approach was chosen so as to allow rapid inventory on a consistent basis. High fences were only encountered occasionally and the level of obscuration (of regeneration and weeds) was noted. Often the 'extensive survey' samples could only be conducted on the property if permission was given. This would contribute to some sampling bias.

For both extensive and intensive surveys the key variables that were measured or estimated included: area of front garden, topographic position, rainfall, the 'greenness' or leafiness of the street and property (independent of the satellite-based index), the proportion paved, 'tidiness' or neatness, the number and cover of trees in three height categories, the numbers (index) of regenerating

Fig. 18.1. Study area (*c.* 38 km across) in Auckland City, northern New Zealand with 100 sample blocks indicated within the pale blue to grey–green coloured areas representing the built-up residential/industrial city. Dark blue is sea/water, pink is grass/pasture, and red is forest. The base map is down-sampled to 250 m spatial resolution from a Landsat multispectral satellite image. A five-level greenness index was derived from these data and used to stratify the urban environment for (random) vegetation sampling as described in the text. Numbers are deprivation index (1–10 with 10 being greatest socio-economic deprivation) for each sample block. There are gradients of rainfall (positive) and air pollution (negative) from the central city to the west and southeast. See also colour plate.

Table 18.1. *Data classes collected from each front garden.*

Cover classes for trees, greenness (total tree cover), weeds and paving
0 = 0%   1 = > 0–1%
2 = >1–5%   3 = >5–25%
4 = >25–50%   5 = >50–75%
6 = >75–100%
Height classes
1 = 1.7 m (fence height) to 1st floor ceiling (*c.* 3 m)
2 = 1st floor ceiling to top of roof or 2nd floor ceiling (*c.* 6 m)
3 = top of single-storey pitched roof or 2nd floor ceiling to 20 m
4 = over 20 m
Regeneration categories
1 = 1 seedling seen (usually some could be seen from the footpath or *en route* to and from the front door while permission was being sought)
2 = 2–5 seedlings
3 = 6–10 seedlings
4 = >10 seedlings
'Tidiness/sterility/neatness' scale
1 = concreted over or largely sterile/hard surface
2 = manicured (no weeds in garden, grass cut, neat rows)
3 = average tidy (garden a bit weedy, edges not sharp, etc)
4 = untidy (tall grass or weeds in garden but some order)
5 = seriously overgrown and rubbish in garden

seedlings, and cover of weed species (Table 18.1). A number of the trees are also classed as 'weeds'. Plants were identified to species where possible, but genus level was accepted, especially for the extensive survey. 'Untidy' gardens usually had more native plants and regeneration than highly managed gardens (both ecological and social causes), so the term is not intended to be pejorative. Nevertheless, residents often thought we were judging their gardens for tidiness rather than biodiversity and might be accordingly quite apologetic – showing the power of neighbourhood peer pressure. Each property was considered the sample unit and, as in most cities in New Zealand or Australia, the front gardens were relatively similar in size (about 0.07 ha).

In the intensive survey the additional factors measured were soil pH (with a universal colour indicator-based field kit) separately under lawn and the garden proper. The property occupier was interviewed using a set of standard questions in order to ascertain: knowledge about natural history (native plants and wildlife), observations of wildlife, interest in such matters (desire to know more), and relevant property management behaviour (ownership of pets, frequency of garden watering, fertiliser input and use of chemicals).

Summary statistics were compiled for many of the variables, and multivariate statistics (DCA ordination and multiple regression) were used to determine the role of the physical environment and social factors as predictors of vegetation character, wildlife resource values and biosecurity risks. All regression and correlation analyses were carried out using the statistical package GenStat v6.2 (GenStat Committee, 2002).

Results

Plant biodiversity

From the entire survey of 441 Auckland front gardens a total of 4704 'trees' were recorded (1343 indigenous, 3361 exotic) representing an average of 464 'trees'/ha and a relatively high incidence of indigenous stems (28.6%). These contain over 90 different taxa of indigenous trees, shrubs, tall tussocks and lianes. The four most abundant taxa were: *Pittosporum* spp., *Coprosma* spp., *Cordyline* spp. and tree ferns (Table 18.2). Over 400 taxa of exotic trees/large shrubs or tussocks also were recorded. The more prominent genera with over 100 occurrences include: *Camellia*, *Cupressus*, *Rosa*, *Prunus*, *Acmena smithii* and *Betula* (Table 18.2).

Biosecurity

The national vascular flora contains *c.* 2500 indigenous species and a similar number of naturalised species, but there are about 30 000 aliens altogether and naturalised species are becoming more widespread. In our sample of front gardens in Auckland the most common 'weed' was *Pennisetum clandestinum* which occurred in over 38% of the properties (Table 18.3). This is a smothering grass when not controlled by repeated mowing or herbicide. Next was *Ligustrum sinense* (35%), *Ligustrum lucidum* (24%), and *Nephrolepis cordifolia* (23%). All other weed species occurred in less than 20% of the gardens.

There are several dozen weeds known to be common in Auckland that were rarely recorded in our study (e.g. *Ageratina adenophora* (mist flower) (1 record here), *Salix cinerea* (grey willow) (3), *Acer pseudoplatanus* (sycamore) (4), *Buddleja davidii* (buddleja) (3), *Galeobodolon luteum* (aluminium plant) (1), *Plectranthus* (5) and *Rhamnus alaternus* (buckthorn) (1), to name a few. These may have been overlooked from the footpath vantage point, and so our quoted values are minima for at least the herbaceous or less conspicuous species. These species may also be under better control in gardens than in wild or nature reserve sites.

Regeneration of indigenous trees and shrubs

Gardens can be havens for regeneration of native plants, especially when shaded by trees that suppress rank herbaceous growth and where there

Table 18.2. *The most abundant trees, large shrubs or tussocks, with total number of occurrences in 441 Auckland front gardens in parentheses.*

Indigenous taxa

pittosporums (347)	coprosmas (172)	*Cordyline* (163)
tree ferns (100)	*Metrosideros* (90)	*Myrsine* (78)
araliads (74)	podocarps (54)	myrtles (53)
NZ flax (46)	Malvaceae trees (34)	*Sophora* (29)
Corynocarpus (20)	*Alectryon* (18)	*Griselinia* (18)
hebes (14)	*Vitex* (12)	*Dodonaea* (10)
other conifers (13)	*Corokia* (6)	*Rhopalostylis* (5)
Geniostoma (4)	*Melicytus* (4)	tree daisies (4)
Aristotelia serrata (3)	*Lecupogoon fasciculatus* (3)	*Pisonia brunonis* (3)
Calystegia sepium (2)	plus 11 others	

Exotic taxa (species or genera with an asterisk exhibit weed characteristics)

Camellia (277)	*Cupressus* (158)	*Rosa* (135)
Prunus (127)*	*Acmena smithii* (115)*	*Betula* (105)
Magnolia (96)	*Ligustrum sinense* (87)*	Pacific *Cordyline* (85)
Ligustrum lucidum (73)*	*Tecomaria* (71)	*Citrus* (65)
Hibiscus (57)	*Euonymus* (57)*	*Callistemon* (56)
palms (48)*	*Toona* (46)	*Nandina* (45)
Oleander (44)	*Wisteria* (42)	*Acacia* s.l. (42)*
Acer (41)	*Jasminum* (39)*	*Rhododendron* (39)
Bougainvillea (37)	*Cotoneaster* (36)*	*Liquidambar* (31)
Feijoa (30)	*Cedrus* (30)	*Malus* (25)
Hedera (25)*	*Fatsia* (24)*	*Photinia* (24)
Fraxinus (23)*	*Quercus* (22)	*Cryptomeria japonica* (22)
Impatiens (21)	*Monstera* (21)	bamboos (20)*
Solanum mauritianum (19)*	*Populus* (19)	*Strelitzia* (17)
Eucalyptus (17)	*Tibouchina* (16)	*Cassia* s.l. (16)
Hydrangea (16)*	*Casuarina* (15)	*Lavandula* (14)
Schefflera actinophylla (14)	*Viburnum* (14)	*Rhus* (13)
Yucca (13)	*Juniperus* (13)	*Vitis* (13)
Abelia (13)	*Cestrum* (13)*	*Banksia* (12)
Fuchsia (12)	*Jacaranda* (12)	*Abutilon* (12)
Arecastrum (12)	*Albizia* (11)	*Clematis* (11)*
Escallonia (11)	*Polygala* (11)	*Melia* (10)
Robinia (10)*	*Eriobotrya* (10)	*Laburnum* (10)

is periodically bare soil or litter cover. The three most common native species found regenerating in Auckland front gardens were *Coprosma* spp. (2.1 per ha), *Pittosporum* spp. (1.2 per ha) and *Myrsine australis* (1 per ha) (Table 18.4). The regeneration of other species was less than 1 plant per hectare. These results,

Table 18.3. *The most abundant weeds found in Auckland front gardens listed with percentage frequency of gardens sampled in parentheses.*

Pennisetum clandestinum (>38%; ubiquitous, but not always recorded)	
Ligustrum sinense (35%)	*Ligustrum lucidum* (24%)
Nephrolepis cordifolia (23%)	*Hedera helix* (18%)
Asparagus spp. (18%)	*Acmena smithii* (16%)
Cotoneaster spp. (16%)	*Araujia sericifera* (15%)
Tradescantia fluminensis (14%)	*Jasminum polyanthum* (12%)
Ehrhata erecta (10%)	*Lotus pedunculatus* (10%)
Phoenix, Washingtonia, other palms (9%)	*Crocosmia* spp. (8%)
Erigeron karvinskianus (7.4%)	*Solanum mauritianum* (7.2%)
Cyperus spp. (7%)	*Hedychium garderianum* (5%)
Lonicera japonica (3%)	*Berberis* spp. (2.3%)
Rubus fruticosus (2%)	*Paraserianthes lophantha* (1.8%)
South American *Cortaderia* (1.4%)	*Iris* spp. (1.4%)
Selaginella kraussiana (0.9%)	

Table 18.4. *Seedling density (stems/ha) of the most common native woody plants regenerating in front gardens in Auckland, New Zealand.*

Coprosma spp. (2.1)	*Pittosporum* spp. (1.2)	*Myrsine australis* (1)
Podocarpus totara (0.3)	*Cordyline australis* (0.3)	*Pseudopanax* spp. (0.19)
Kunzea ericoides (0.13)	*Alectryon excelsus* (0.11)	*Hoheria populnea* (0.1)
Hebe spp. (0.07)	*Corynocarpus laevigatus* (0.06)	*Sophora* spp. (0.06)

apart from a greater appearance of warm temperate species, parallel preliminary findings in Christchurch (Stewart *et al.*, 2004).

Regeneration of native herbaceous plants

A number of native herbaceous species were noted commonly as spontaneous or planted specimens in yards, gardens, footpaths and walls. These were not recorded systematically but the most common species were: *Hydrocotyle moschata, Gamochaeta coarctata, Pteris* spp., *Oxalis exilis, Cyathea dealbata* (silver tree fern), *Dicksonia squarrosa* (wheki – a tree fern), New Zealand flax (some planted), *Dichondra repens, Pyrrosia eleagnifolia, Carex* spp., *Centella uniflora, Pteridium esculentum* (New Zealand bracken fern), *Astelia chathamica* (planted) and New Zealand *Cortaderia* spp. (planted). Some of these flat or turf-forming species (together with other genera such as *Leptinella, Pratia, Plantago* and *Mazus*) can form the basis of biodiverse lawns – an untapped potential for threatened New Zealand lowland herbaceous species (Ignatieva *et al.*, 2000).

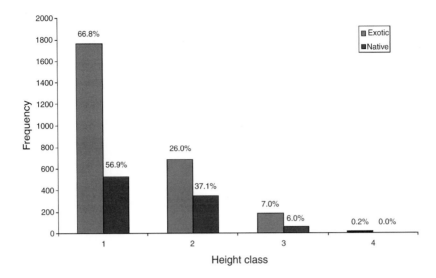

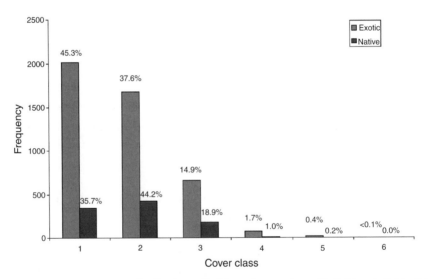

Fig. 18.2. Frequency distributions of height and cover classes (definitions in Table 18.1) for indigenous and exotic species in the Auckland front garden survey. Numbers over bars represent proportion of each class for native and exotic species separately. Exotic species are seen to be dominant in all categories.

Phenological and functional attributes of plants

The frequency distributions of cover and 'tree' height classes show that exotic species are dominant in all categories (Fig. 18.2). A breakdown of flower and fruit types reveals the roles that the larger native and exotic plants perform in the Auckland urban environment. Most tree flowers (69%) are insect-pollinated, but

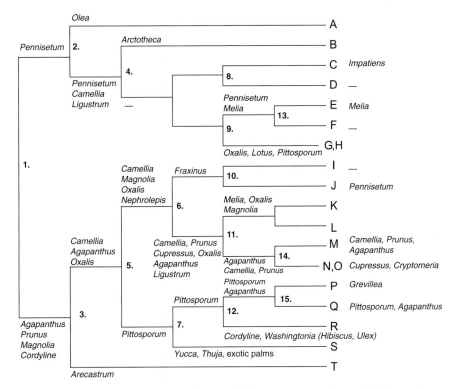

Fig. 18.3. Diagram of the results of a TwinSpan cluster analysis of 437 vegetation samples from front gardens in Auckland. Letters represent community types, numbers represent order of splits, and taxa represent indicator species for each split (full names are given in Table 18.5).

bird nectar flowers are more common among native trees and non-weed aliens such as proteas and myrtles (11.8% of natives and 6% of exotics when plants pollinated by birds or insects are included).

Native trees are the main source of small (<1 cm diameter) fleshy fruit (67% of natives and 37% of total). This is an important consideration for native birds and reptiles which are co-adapted to this food supply and preferentially use native species when there is a choice (Burrows, 1994a, b; Williams and Karl, 1996). On the other hand, non-weed aliens have mostly dry (>44% of total) or large fleshy fruits (19% of total; e.g. domestic fruit trees), whereas weeds produce small fleshy or dry fruit in equal proportions.

Garden plant associations

The results of a 20-group cluster analysis of 437 vegetation samples from front gardens in Auckland are presented in Fig. 18.3 and Table 18.5. The analysis included only the 426 species that occurred in more than two front yards.

Table 18.5. *Results of cluster analysis of the vegetation of 437 front gardens in Auckland, New Zealand.*

The analysis (Fig. 18.2) identified 20 different community types which are listed below as types A to T. The number (*n*) of sampled front gardens included in each cluster is given as well as those species that had >10% frequency (herbaceous species first) – with species overall <10%, but sometimes dominant, in parentheses. These are considered character species for each community type. Significantly discriminating species composition, and characteristics of the section or neighbourhood are depicted in abbreviated form under the Community Class letter if outside the norm: < or >, less or more than average of the factor; spp, species richness; I, indigenous spp; X, exotic spp; R, indigenous regeneration; character indicated as affluent or deprived, new or old (dwellings), hard (impervious) or soft (grassy) and maintenance style (neat/controlled or relatively wild/unordered).

Community class	*n*	Character species (>10% frequency)
A <spp <I <X <R affluent new soft	1	*Olea europaea*
B <spp <I <X <R deprived old soft wild	4	*Arctotheca calendula, Oxalis* pink, *Arujia sericifera*
C <spp <I <X <R hard	1	*Chlorophytum comosum, Ehrhata erecta, Impatiens walleriana*
D <I >X <R deprived old hard wild	4	*Ehrhata erecta, Citrus* spp., *Cupressus* spp., *Prunus* spp., *Weigela floribunda*
E <I >X <R affluent old soft	1	*Euonymus japonicus, Hibiscus* spp., *Melia azeradach, Photinia serrutina*
F >spp deprived old wild	67	*Ehrhata erecta, Euphorbia peplus, Nephrolepis cordifolia, Oxalis* pink, *Pennisetum clandestinum, Tradescantia fluminensis, Arujia sericifera, Callistemon* spp., *Camellia* spp., *Citrus* spp., *Cupressus* spp., *Euonymus japonicus, Impatiens sodenii, Impatiens walleriana, Leptospermum* cv (I), *Ligustrum lucida, Ligustrum sinense, Nerium oleander, Rosa* spp.
G >spp >R wild	31	*Galium aparine, Lotus pedunculatus, Oxalis* pink, *Pennisetum clandestinum, Arujia sericifera, Camellia* spp., *Cassia/Senna, Ligustrum lucida, Ligustrum sinensis, Pittosporum eugenioides* (I), *Pittosporum tenuifolium* (I)
H <I <X >R deprived old wild	1	*Cirsium vulgare, Crocosmia* x *crocosmiiflora, Oxalis* pink, *Soliva sessilis*
I <spp <I <R deprived wild	3	*Fraxinus* spp. (*Soliva sessilis, Betula* spp.)

Table 18.5. (*cont.*)

Community class	*n*	Character species (>10% frequency)
J >spp >I >R deprived old wild	2	*Crocosmia* x *crocosmiiflora*, *Mentha* spp., *Pennisetum clandestinum*, *Soliva sessilis*, *Zantedeschia aethiopica*, *Cordyline australis* (I), *Fraxinus* spp., *Magnolia* spp., *Metrosideros excelsa* (I)
K <spp <I old	1	*Cestrum* spp., *Melia azeradach*
L <spp <I >X affluent	5	*Oxalis* pink, *Magnolia* spp., *Melia azeradach*
M >spp >I >X >R wild	270	*Agapanthus orientalis*, *Asparagus asparagoides*, *Galium aparine*, *Nephrolepis cordifolia*, *Oxalis* pink, *Pennisetum clandestinum*, *Phormium tenax* (I), *Tradescantia fluminensis*, *Zantedeschia aethiopica*, *Acmena smithii*, *Arujia sericifera*, *Betula* spp., *Callistemon* spp., *Camellia* spp., *Citrus* spp., *Coprosma robusta* (I), *Cordyline australis* (I), *Cotoneaster franchetii*, *Cupressus* spp., *Cyathea dealbata* (I), *Fatsia japonica*, *Hedera helix*, *Hibiscus* spp., *Impatiens sodenii*, *Jasminum polyanthemum*, *Ligustrum sinensis*, *Ligustrum lucida*, *Liquidambar styracifolia*, *Magnolia* spp., *Metrosideros excelsa* (I), *Nerium oleander*, *Pittosporum eugenioides* (I), *Pittosporum tenuifolium* (I), *Prunus* spp., *Rosa* spp., *Solanum mauritianum*, *Wisteria sinensis*
N >R new	10	*Asparagus scandens*, *Callistemon* spp., *Cryptomeria japonica*, *Cupressus* spp.
O >I >X <R new soft wild	3	*Cryptomeria japonica*, *Cupressus* spp., *Leptospermum macrophylla*, *Plagianthus regius* (I), *Sophora* spp. (I), (*Acer japonica*)
P >I >X deprived new wild	3	*Acer japonica*, *Albizia julibrissins*, *Fraxinus* spp., *Grevillea robusta*, *Lagunaria pattersonii*, *Pittosporum eugenioides* (I), *Pittosporum tenuifolium* (I)
Q >I >R affluent hard wild	20	*Pittosporum eugenioides* (I), *Pittosporum tenuifolium* (I)
R <spp <X <R new soft neat	4	*Cordyline australis* (I), *Pittosporum eugenioides* (I), *Washingtonia filifera*
S <spp <I <X <R affluent new hard neat	2	*Yucca* spp. (exotic palm, *Griselinia lucida* (I), *Thuja* spp.)
T <spp <N <X <R affluent new hard neat	4	*Arecastrum romanzoffianum*, *Rosa* spp.

Fig. 18.4. (a) Dense, predominantly native bush front garden dominated by the podocarp *Dacrydium cupressinum* and various native hardwoods (Community Type M). (b) Species- and structure-poor front garden with small, scattered compact flowering or fruit trees and shrubs with lawn (Community Type F). (c) Structure-poor front garden with central *Prunus* and ordered herbaceous border and shrubbery, and some native species: *Phormium, Cordyline, Meryta, Griselinia* (Community Type F). (d) Front yard dominated by a few large trees and bushes – *Phoenix* and *Rhododendron*, with *Tecomaria* hedge and *Alectryon* street trees (low diversity variant of Community Type M).

Table 18.5 lists the character species, which are those that occurred in a greater than 10% frequency class in at least one of the 20 community types.

The vast majority of the sites (270) fall into one ubiquitous front garden woodland association (M, Table 18.5). It is characterised by 23 frequent trees or tall shrubs of which six are indigenous (including a tree fern) and eight are weedy, six vines of which four are weedy, and eight herbs of which one is native and four are serious environmental weeds. Total species richness and indigenous regeneration are consistently high. *Camellia* (46% of front gardens in this class), privets (*Ligustrum*), cupressoid trees, plums, roses, monkey apple (*Acmena*), birch, magnolias, citrus, hibiscus and bottle brush (*Callistemon*), and the other species listed in Table 18.5, are the common elements. Indigenous species are found in over 30% of these gardens (Fig. 18.4a, d). These are generally found in well-established, middle income neighbourhoods.

Gardens with similar species, but lower diversity (smaller area with less scope for large trees), are represented by community types D, F and G (cf. Figs. 18.4b, c, 18.5a). A variant is the garden with one or two massive trees (e.g. *Phoenix canariensis, Cupressus macrocarpa* or *Metrosideros excelsa*) that are out of scale with the surroundings and suppress other species (community types: J, O, P and some less

Fig. 18.5. (a) Impoverished lawn-scape garden with sparse *Citrus* and *Feijoa* shrubs and arum lily border (Community Type D). (b) New suburb with *Pittosporum* hedge, *Meryta*, *Griselinia* and short tussock sedges (Community Type Q). (c) Very new house and garden with exotic palm, *Yucca* and small sedge tussocks in early stages of growth (Community Type S, T). (d) Social housing gardens with almost no structure apart from a *Camellia* and *Hebe* shrubs in distance (Community Type B).

diverse M; Fig. 18.4d) each with their own dominant species. Some associations have a higher proportion of indigenous species suggesting a definite intent to plant native (e.g. community types G, J, M, O–R) or to let natural regeneration take its course (G, H, J, M, N, Q).

Front gardens with low richness include community types A–E, H, I, K, L, N and Q–T, typically comprising a few compact flowering or fruit trees, exotic palms, dwarf conifers, roses or flowering shrubs (Fig. 18.5a) that just reach the minimum height for inclusion (*Impatiens*, *Cestrum*) or that form a low hedge of *Tecomaria*, *Euonymus*, *Escallonia*, *Acmena* and native *Olearia paniculata*, *Griselinia*, *Pittosporum* or *Hebe* (cf. Fig. 18.5b). These are generally associated with proportionally extensive lawns (*Pennisetum*, *Cynodon*, *Digitaria*, *Arctotheca*, *Soliva*, *Gamochaeta*, *Lotus*, New Zealand *Oxalis*) and weeds found along broken paths, garden edges and woodland borders – such as *Euphorbia peplus*, *Polygonum capitatum*, *Erigeron karvinskianus*, *Crassula multiclava*, *Ehrhata*, thistles, pink flowered oxalis, *Picris*, New Zealand flax (*Phormium*), *Pelargonium*, *Mentha* and *Galium*.

In the most barren cases, the front yard is largely paved and impervious and only the forb weeds may be present in the cracks. These sparse conditions reflect either new (raw) suburbs (A, N, Q–T) with small yards (Fig. 18.5c), manicured or heavily paved and with low growing species (outside the range of this survey) or minimalist gardens, rental accommodation, quasi-commercial or poorer areas where landlords have imposed a low maintenance, 'scorched earth' regime of grass or paving (B–D, H, I, K) (Fig. 18.5d).

The recognisable vegetation forms or styles in Auckland front gardens can be summarised as follows: (1) middle to deprived, older suburbs with no trees and either grassy (B, H) or paved gardens (C); (2) old-money or older leafy suburbs with high diversity on larger sections often including a large proportion of mature indigenous species (M); (3) similar but lower income, with indigenous species but lower diversity (F, G); (4) new middle income or rental but leafy neighbourhoods with a few large trees and less-manicured smaller sections (J, O, P); (5) new or medium age wealthy to middle class suburbs with few sparse, compact, flowering or fruiting trees and 'neat' gardens dominated by lawn and low native species diversity (A, E, L, N, R); (6) similar but newer, small gardens with a greater proportion of pavement and a few architectural, exotic palms (the next generation of weeds), yuccas or bedding plants (S, T); (7) new middle class suburbs with simple *Pittosporum* hedges and low diversity drawn from a broad palette (Q); (8) similarly spartan to (5) but in poorer neighbourhoods with older sections, higher proportions of pavement and less tidy, with one or two dominating exotic trees, shrubs or vines (D, I, K); and (9) Japanese-style minimalist pebble gardens with simple form and low diversity of large plants (not covered in this study). Overall, it was found that, regardless of socio-economic status, gardens that are 'neat and tidy' (by the criteria of Table 18.1) have lower species richness (especially indigenous) and indigenous regeneration than those that are deemed 'untidy'.

Ordination of communities and species

The ordinations, based on species composition, revealed little discrimination between sites and clusters and hence these analyses have not been presented in detail. Measured variables accounted for more of the variance in Axes 2 (up to 24%) and 4 (43%) than for either Axis 1 or 3. Axis 4 was negatively correlated with both Axes 1 and 2. While having weak statistical power, Axis 4 distinguished associations with prevalent grass, forbs and scatterings of trees (A–H; positive), albeit rich in overall species in F, from those generally with dominant tree cover regardless of diversity (I–T; negative). In summary, Axis 4, the only one with a relatively clear pattern, represents a vegetation gradient from dense woodland to open parkland or shrubland. Woody species segregated positively were hedge plants (*Tecomaria, Acmena, Euonymus, Escallonia, Hydrangea, Thuja, Rubus fruticosus* agg., *Wisteria, Ligustrum* and native *Lophomyrtus, Griselinia, Pittosporum, Olearia paniculata, Calystegia sepium*) and large stand-alone trees (*Phoenix, Nerium, Pinus, Acacia, Quercus, Leucadendron*), with ample space for grasses and forbs (and lavender). This contrasted with the centrally ordinated, medium density, species-rich woodlands (both native and exotic).

The negatively ordinated species are *Laburnum, Alnus, Teucrium, Abelia, Jacaranda, Abutilon, Fagus, Robinia, Eucalyptus,* Australian *Leptospermum, Acer japonica, Arecastrum, Liquidambar* and the New Zealand *Plagianthus regius, Melicope ternatus, Macropiper excelsum, Cordyline banksii, Corynocarpus, Meryta, Nothofagus menziesii* and *Sophora tetraptera.* Although physiognomically similar to the 'positive' species, they represent a different mix of imposing trees and shrubs, or uncommon species entering the frame only where vegetation is dense or species-rich.

The open grass/forb associations are dominated by the grasses and weeds listed with lawns in the previous section. Other woodland edge species positively ordinated are *Hedychium, Astelia,* fennel, *Tradescantia fluminensis, Galeobdolen, Crocosmia* and *Monstera.* In the middle to negative end of Axis 4, in shaded garden woodlands, are herbs such as *Plectranthus ciliatus, Allium triquetrum, Chlorophytum comosum, Viola, Agapanthus, Acanthus, Selaginella, Petasites, Gladiolus, Iris, Zantedeschia, Asparagus* and *Impatiens.* Large tussocks that occupy unshaded simpler gardens are *Strelitzia, Cyperus* and *Cortaderia* with *Soliva* and *Lotus* specifically in the lawns.

Significant factors positively regressed on Axis 4 are shady aspect, street leafiness, weediness, wildness, air pollution and deprivation, whereas negative correlates are sunny aspect, section leafiness (both native and exotic), imperviousness, soil pH and section neatness.

Although most physical and social factors were significant in ordination axis regressions, the overall segregation of community types in ordination space was weak. We interpreted this to mean that management for fashion (style of garden), rather than the uncontrolled physical environment, is the main driver of urban woodland vegetation type in Auckland, although size of section (and socio-economic circumstances) constrains options for diverse vegetation on a grander scale. We found that nearly all the character species of all the associations are either prevalent or at least present in 'M'. The only associations that fall fractionally outside the ordination envelope of 'M' are B, D, F–H, L, N, O, T and these (12% of samples) are at the more exotic-tree end of Axis 2. Thus most associations are merely less diverse and idiosyncratic variants of M. They may be seen as personal and almost random selections from the palette of approximately 400 typical garden species available in Auckland plant nurseries. The total richness and composition is then a barely predictable function of section size (affluence), personal preferences (species) and fastidiousness (weediness, regeneration, species richness). The social behaviour relationships have only been touched on in this study. Also, greater discrimination in species composition may occur in the herbaceous tier. Selection of vivid colour is a strong indicator of garden style, but falls largely outside the scope of this survey.

The physical and social gradients are spatial in nature with rainfall and greenness increasing to the west and southeast (Fig. 18.1) and socio-economic layers strongly segregated by suburb.

Social factors

Based on the interviewed subsample of home occupants, we infer that knowledge of or interest in biodiversity varies according to: location, socio-economic indicators, ethnicity of residents, residence time and age of suburb. Some 56% of respondents recognised at least a few native plants in their section or neighbourhood and 60% recognised some native birds. Thirty-three percent were very interested to know more about the local natural history, 23% had some interest or did not know, and 44% had no interest. A factor that may have a direct impact on wildlife, and in some cases a bearing on community awareness of biodiversity issues, is the ownership of domestic pets. Over 50% of households own cats while 20% had dogs. This translates to at least 130 000 cats and 50 000 dogs in Greater Auckland. There is still much to be learned about the optimum balance of various domestic and feral predators in urban or cultural landscapes. It has been suggested that cats may be a net benefit to native wildlife because of their mesopredation of rats and mustellids, which are more voracious killers of birds (John Flux, personal communication). Whereas uncontrolled dogs are known to take a high toll on ground birds such as kiwi and weka in wilderness environments, in leafy urban environments they may deter possums and ferrets.

Surrogate measures of 'control' may be used to infer garden style patterns. For instance, about 60% of respondents water, 40% fertilise, 30% apply herbicide and 40% apply pesticide to their gardens more than once per year. Altogether, knowledge, social attitudes, values and behaviour (including pet ownership, conformity and chemical use) will influence urban vegetation; but the magnitude and details of this relationship remain elusive and complex.

Discussion and conclusions

There are floristic convergences with other urban woodland studies around the temperate world. Dorney *et al.* (1984) reported, for Shorewood, Wisconsin, boreal trees or shrubs (elm, ash, maple, apple, spruce, oak, cedar, birch, *Tilia*, *Prunus*, *Syringa*, barberry, *Cotoneaster*, privet and rose) which are all present but less common in Auckland. Their 96 stems/ha of trees and saplings, with an unstated, presumably high density of shrubs (totalling 42% cover of woody vegetation), equates with our 462 'trees'/ha. Smith *et al.* (2005) listed for Sheffield, England, gardens with hedges – *Ligustrum*, non-native conifers, *Fagus*, *Crataegus* and *Prunus laurocerasus*. In Hobart, Tasmania (Daniels and Kirkpatrick,

2006), the top species are also familiar: *Prunus*, *Rosa*, *Callistemon*, *Hebe*, *Hedera*, dwarf conifers, *Agapanthus*, *Cotoneaster*, *Malus* and *Betula*. Less showy gardens occurred in rented properties and new homes were more showy. On the other hand unemployment levels correlated with showy front gardens. Daniel and Kirkpatrick surmised that emphasis on individualism in western society pushes infinite variety, but people are also conforming to community pressure. Kirkpatrick *et al.* (2007) showed that the percentage frequency of trees in front gardens was best predicted by household income. Other variables were tertiary education, older age, renting, unemployment, local birth and suburb age. All garden components responded individualistically to these variables. Arboriphobia was detected in poorer suburbs marked by exotic shrub gardens of small, tidy, planted trees. The well off, non-tertiary educated preferred shrubs and trees to complex gardens. Our simple grass or paved yards would be called 'non-gardens' by Grove *et al.* (2006b) who found them in areas of high unemployment. The apparent contrast between Grove's research and that of Daniel and Kirkpatrick (2006) may mean that working class areas often had tidy, showy gardens indicating retention of pride and hope, whereas the most deprived areas with high unemployment had neglected gardens attributable to management by absentee landlords.

Thus the influence of the physical environment is indirect, parabolic (such as for house age) or inconsistent. In Hobart, garden size is not a good predictor of garden type, but in Sheffield, Smith *et al.* (2005) showed that (back) garden area was the overwhelming predictor of vegetation. Perhaps this is because of limited space (mean of $173\,\mathrm{m}^2$ compared with $230\,\mathrm{m}^2$ in our study). While the larger gardens of New Zealand and Australia may be above some threshold, urban infilling may soon change this.

Grove *et al.* (2006b) calculated that life style behaviour was a better predictor of urban vegetation than population or social stratification. The garden is one of the few places in which people of lower socio-economic circumstance can exercise control, and in general, those over 65 do not like native gardens. These various observations from temperate urban woodlands demonstrate the common themes of globalised species composition, the often overriding – albeit difficult to measure – complex influence of socio-economic factors and yet the universal retention of at least some indigenous elements. This component may be gaining momentum, as the influence of the educated baby boomers permeates (western) society.

Urban landscapes are highly altered mosaics of primary habitat (remnant forests), parkland, gardens and industry, linked by generally fragmented stream and transport corridors and modified catchment processes. Paradoxically, cities provide refugia and restoration potential for significant elements of regional biodiversity. They frequently straddle biome junctions, nationally serious animal pests may be absent, human and economic resources are abundant, and social impact of conservation successes is high (Given and Meurk, 2000; Meurk, 2005). However, the resource values of urban woodland (second in area only to lawns in New Zealand cities), and the threats to them, are poorly known in New Zealand. If regionally indigenous biodiversity is to survive it must contribute to local cultures and to do that it must be a part of people's everyday experience, aesthetically, and as an amenity and utility (Meurk and Swaffield, 2000). The positive reinforcement of biodiversity must therefore take place in populous cities and in the wider cultural landscapes, or it is likely to become irrelevant (Meurk and Hall, 2006). There is an ongoing debate among some sectors of the urban community in New Zealand about the merits of native versus exotic species. Many, especially older, urban dwellers prefer exotic species, perhaps because the historical dominance of exotic species in the colonial New Zealand landscape makes them familiar and accepted (Meurk and Swaffield, 2000).

The future of New Zealand's biodiversity will depend on adequate food (nectar and fruit) and secure shelter for breeding wildlife. This in turn entails pest and weed control and critical mass of indigenous plants for habitat and visibility. The high value of indigenous flowers, fruits and foliage to the endemic wildlife (Wilson, 2002) puts a premium on expanding the presence of native plant species across the lowlands. This will ensure ecological sustainability of indigenous biodiversity as viable populations of plants and animals, but also socio-cultural sustainability. This may be manifest as legible landscapes engendering a sense of place, and culturally viable imagery built from landscapes that prominently celebrate nationally and regionally unique vegetation.

One of the solutions to meeting community needs and familiarity with the exotic flora is to provide indigenous alternatives for desired growth forms, and knowledge about their propagation and values. For plants there is a great diversity of indigenous species now being used in gardens (Gabites and Lucas, 1998) and a target may be to increase the proportion of native trees and shrubs to 50% in the urban residential matrix, to have habitats and groves of podocarps in every neighbourhood, and in particular more producers of nectar and fleshy fruits (Meurk and Hall, 2006). As for pets, a case has been made for encouraging greater use or even breeding of indigenous birds and reptiles as semi-wild pets, replacing the contemporary preoccupation with cats and dogs (Craig *et al.*, 1995).

There are many biodiversity opportunities in garden habitats, both informal and formal (Baines, 2000; Thompson *et al.*, 2003; Meurk, 2005; see also Breuste, Chapter 21; Florgärd, Chapter 22; Ignatieva and Stewart, Chapter 23). Examples include lawns, herbaceous borders, rock gardens and other urban biotopes, with weedy native species that colonise footpaths, pavement cracks, dry stone walls, railway embankments and waste sites, alongside the usual exotic species (Ignatieva *et al.*, 2000; Breuste *et al.*, 1998) that are adapted to being human associates. The goal here is to increase the proportional propagule pressure and seed banks of indigenous species in urban environments. There are also many native riverbed, coastal and rock ledge species suitable for life in the suburbs (Meurk and Greenep, 2003) that can be introduced.

Results like these in Auckland provide city biodiversity planners and educators with new biological and spatial data to better target education and to design/manage sustainable wildlife habitat patches, corridors and matrices (residential gardens). This green framework or ecostructure should eventually become self-reinforcing for urban ecological integrity and sense of place.

Acknowledgements

Great thanks are owed to Mark McDonnell for his judicious and patient editing of the draft manuscript. I am indebted to my colleagues Maria Ignatieva, Glenn Stewart and Helen Greenep for ongoing discussion. The work was funded by a NZ Foundation for Research Science and Technology contract.

19

Carbon and nitrogen cycling in soils of remnant forests along urban–rural gradients: case studies in the New York metropolitan area and Louisville, Kentucky

MARGARET M. CARREIRO, RICHARD V. POUYAT,
CHRISTOPHER E. TRIPLER AND WEI-XING ZHU

Introduction

During the past 50 years urban and suburban areas in the United States have been expanding rapidly at the expense of agricultural land and natural ecosystems (Richards, 1990; Douglas, 1994). Between 1960 and 1990, 12.6 million ha of cropland, forest and pasture in the United States were converted to urban and suburban land (Frey, 1984; Dougherty, 1992). An additional 4.5 million ha of rural land were developed in the 5 years between 1992 and 1997 (USDA National Resources Inventory, 2000), indicating that the pace of land conversion in the United States has been accelerating. While cities and towns now cover 3.5% of the conterminous United States, their associated sprawl into adjacent counties designated as Metropolitan Areas has resulted in 24.5% of the area of the United States being categorised as urban land cover (Dwyer et al., 2000). These areas, including their natural components like forested land, are thus becoming increasingly exposed to the effects of diverse urban activities. The states that have experienced the greatest population growth per unit land area between 1990 and 1996 occur in the eastern third of the country, where human settlement is expanding mostly into forested land (Dwyer et al., 2000). These eastern rural

Ecology of Cities and Towns: A Comparative Approach, ed. Mark J. McDonnell, Amy K. Hahs and Jürgen H. Breuste. Published by Cambridge University Press. © Cambridge University Press 2009.

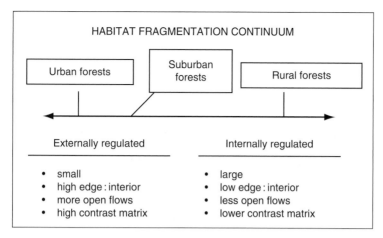

Fig. 19.1. Urban and suburban forest remnants are smaller than rural forest counterparts resulting in their having higher edge-to-interior ratios. For urban forests, proportionately greater edge length would therefore be in contact with the matrix, permitting more open and frequent exchanges of species, matter and energy between forest and matrix. Since urban matrix conditions differ markedly from most rural matrix types and forests in species composition, atmospheric chemistry and thermal regime, the intensity and type of flows is accentuated. Both higher edge-to-interior ratios and the high contrast matrix increase the potential for surrounding conditions to regulate ecological processes inside small, urban forests. Ecological processes, such as decomposition, primary production and population dynamics, in larger forests with less edge in contact with their surroundings are more likely to be regulated by internal factors.

forests have been increasing in area in the past 100 to 150 years because of secondary succession following farmland abandonment in the nineteenth and early twentieth centuries (Foster, 1993). Because of varied public and private land ownership patterns, forest fragments of different sizes have been and are being created in these urbanising landscapes (e.g. Medley *et al.*, 1995; Vogelmann, 1995; Heilman *et al.*, 2002). These forests are often privately owned and not intensely managed. Hence the suburban and urban conditions that surround them will play a large role in determining their long-term health, species composition and sustainability.

As forests become fragmented, their edge-to-interior ratios also increase, resulting in forests being exposed to greater inputs of energy, matter and species from their altered surroundings (Saunders *et al.*, 1991; Matlack, 1993a). External influences on these ecological systems then become at least as important as internal feedback regulation in defining the species composition and functioning of biological communities (Fig. 19.1). This may be especially true for forest remnants that become surrounded by cities, since, as opposed to agricultural lands, urban land-cover properties (e.g. impervious surfaces) and land-use activities (e.g. fossil fuel combustion) contrast greatly with those of forests. Compared with forests in rural areas, these urban forest remnants would be likely to be subjected to greater external inputs of thermal energy (urban heat island effect; Oke, 1995), greater atmospheric inputs of both injurious pollutants and fertilising nutrients (Turner *et al.*, 1990; Lovett *et al.*, 2000), increased colonisation by exotic species (Kowarik, 1990; Rebele, 1994; McKinney, 2002) and increased human visitation (recreational and residential activities along forest boundaries; Matlack, 1993b).

Therefore, populations, communities and ecosystem processes in these forests are likely to be disproportionately more affected by their external surroundings than rural forests. Despite their small size and fragmented nature, these forest remnants are functionally important since they provide human society with: (1) ecosystem services (air and water pollutant filtration, maintenance of the landscape's hydrological function, biological control of pest species, conservation of native species); (2) sites for educating the public about the natural world; (3) recreational and aesthetic opportunities; and (4) a cultural identity and connection with the original native landscape. Currently our scientific knowledge of how these forest remnants are faring as they become increasingly surrounded by dense human settlement is scant and scattered (Zipperer and Guntenspergen, Chapter 17). While species lists for urban woodlands and forests may be available in many cities, integrated information on forest functions, community trajectories and ecosystem processes is particularly lacking. Such process-level information would allow us to improve our understanding of the ecological roles that remnant forests perform in the greater landscape, and the time lags and resiliency thresholds for particular functions as land use changes around them. A deeper ecological understanding of the roles and responses of urban and suburban forest remnants could underpin the development of more pro-active management strategies as conditions surrounding these forest patches continue to change.

The urban–rural gradient approach and comparisons among cities

Several scientific approaches are currently used to determine urban effects on natural ecosystems (Pickett *et al.*, 1997b; Alberti, 1999; Grimm *et al.*, 2000, Pickett *et al.*, Chapter 3). Since many cities in the United States have grown in a concentric fashion, with a densely populated urban core and development that diminishes further from the city, McDonnell and Pickett (1990) conceived of applying the multi-variate, ecological gradient approach to compare responses of natural habitats to varying degrees of human settlement. This urban–rural gradient approach has been used in the New York metropolitan area (McDonnell *et al.*, 1997) and other locations (Guntenspergen and Levenson, 1997; Iakovoglou *et al.*, 2001; Niemelä *et al.*, 2002; Niemelä, Chapter 2) to understand how cities affect species and ecosystem processes in natural habitats, such as forests.

Although many cities share similar physical attributes (e.g. roads, buildings, parks), the magnitude and type of impacts that cities have on natural habitats may depend on their geographical location, size, age, growth rate, socio-political values and economic status. Therefore, comparisons among cities can allow us to correlate these urban characteristics with more proximate factors that affect natural communities within their boundaries, such as pollutant deposition loads, degree of temperature alteration, and extent and type of human visitation. Comparative studies can also allow us to determine which natural population, community and ecosystem level responses are shared across cities in different regions or biomes. The threshold values for such responses are related to the magnitude of particular sets of urban factors, which natural habitat types are more sensitive to urban impacts than others, and which responses may be idiosyncratic to specific cities (Lehvävirta and Kotze, Chapter 31).

Rationale for focus on soil carbon and nitrogen cycling in urban–rural gradient studies

The urban–rural gradient approach permits a variety of comparative ecological studies to be conducted in remnant natural habitats. In the New York metropolitan area and Louisville, Kentucky, we and our colleagues focused our experiments on carbon and nitrogen cycling in forest soils for reasons that were simultaneously pragmatic and reflective of the importance of these processes in sustaining forest productivity. Decomposition and soil nitrogen transformations are regulated by microbes and invertebrates, organisms characterised by rapid growth rates and short generation times. Therefore, in contrast with tree communities, their activity levels, population sizes and community composition are likely to respond more rapidly to variation in abiotic conditions along urban–rural gradients. In addition, many decades of exposure to urban and suburban land use may not only have changed decomposer species populations and communities, but may also have stimulated rapid evolutionary adaptation through natural selection. Decomposers are also sensitive to alterations in the quantity and chemical quality of inputs of plant organic matter from leaves, wood and roots, factors that urban conditions can potentially alter as well. Therefore, one of the advantages of studying decomposition and soil nitrogen cycling is that these processes integrate the effects of many factors that have a high likelihood of being influenced by urban land use and land cover. These include: (1) climate (urban heat island); (2) atmospheric inputs of matter,

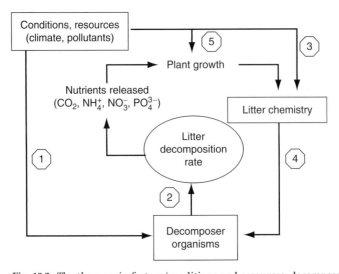

Fig. 19.2. The three main factors (conditions and resources, decomposer organisms, litter chemistry) that control the decomposition rate of organic plant litter (dead leaves, roots, wood). Cities and suburban environments can alter all three of these main factors and hence the rate at which litter decays. Pavement and buildings warm local surroundings through the heat island effect, and fossil fuel combustion and industrial processes produce air pollutants that settle onto soil. Heat and pollutants (such as heavy metals, nitrogen and sulphur) can affect the types, numbers and activity levels of decomposer organisms (arrow 1) that break down organic materials (arrow 2) into nutrients that plants use to grow. Urban conditions and pollutants, such as ozone, can also directly affect the chemistry of plant foliage and subsequent leaf litter (arrow 3). Decomposers respond to these chemical changes by either accelerating or decelerating litter breakdown (arrow 4). Urban environments can also change the way plants grow and incorporate nutrients into their cells (arrow 5) such that their foliage, wood or roots become chemically altered. Again, decomposers can react to such changes in chemical quality by becoming more or less abundant and thereby either speeding up or slowing down litter decay. These processes (1, 2, 3, 4 and 5) combined can alter the average depth of the forest floor organic layer.

both nutritive (e.g. forms of inorganic nitrogen, basic cations) and damaging (e.g. ozone, sulphur dioxide, heavy metals); (3) quantity and chemical composition of plant matter; and (4) decomposer community composition and activity levels (Fig. 19.2). Since these processes integrate abiotic and biotic factors that vary during the course of a short-term study and those that have accumulated in the past, studying soil processes increases the likelihood of detecting differences in ecosystem responses linked to land-use variation within a few years of initiating an experiment. In addition, soil carbon and nitrogen cycling are key ecosystem processes that can change forest productivity by altering the rate of inorganic nutrient supply within the forest. These processes also affect the flux of matter between the forest remnant and its surrounding matrix, exchanges of importance at landscape and global scales. These ecologically important as well as utilitarian reasons made soil organisms and the processes they regulate an important focus for initial urban–rural gradient studies in both New York and Louisville.

Description of the New York and Louisville urban–rural gradients

In the late 1980s a transect of forest sites, constituting the New York Urban–Rural gradient study (URGE; see also Pickett et al., Chapter 3), was established running 130 km northeast from the Bronx (a borough in New York City) to rural Litchfield County, Connecticut (Fig. 19.3a). New York City (40° 47′ N, 73° 58′ W), settled by Europeans in the early seventeenth century, attained a population of 8 million with a mean density of 10 300 people/km^2 in the year 2000. The New York City Metropolitan Statistical Area (MSA), with a population of approximately 20 million, is the largest among the 280 MSAs in the United States (US Bureau of the Census, 2000). Population density at the urban end of this gradient was 10 000 people/km^2 and declined to 10 people/km^2 at the rural end (Medley et al., 1995). The 40-km-long urban–rural transect of forests in Louisville, Kentucky, was established in 2001 and runs southward from Louisville in Jefferson County to rural Bullitt County (Fig. 19.3b). Louisville (38° 15′ N, 85° 46′ W) was first settled in the late eighteenth century and by 2000 had a population of 259 000 with a mean density of 1600 people/km^2. The Louisville MSA, with a population of 1 161 000, ranks 43rd in the nation (US Bureau of the Census, 2000). Population density within a 1.5-km radius of forest sites studied along this transect varies from 1665 people/km^2 at the urban end, through 183 people/km^2 in the suburban section, to 20 people/km^2 at the rural end.

The cities have similar climate and are located within the eastern deciduous forest biome where the oak–hickory forest type is common. The climate in the New York region consists of warm humid summers and cold winters with mean annual air temperature of 12.5 °C. Precipitation is evenly distributed throughout the year and averages 1080 mm annually (NOAA, 1985). Louisville's climate is of the mild mid-latitude type with a mean annual air temperature of 13 °C, and mean annual precipitation of 1143 mm, also distributed evenly throughout the year (Ulack et al., 1998).

To maximise the ability to detect land-use effects on soil communities and soil processes, forest plots along the urban–rural gradients in these two cities were chosen using the following standardised criteria: (1) canopy dominance by the same tree species (Quercus rubra–Q. velutina complex (red oak–black oak) in

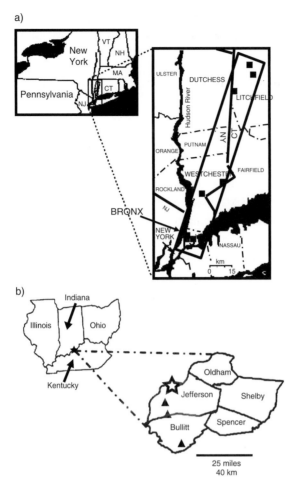

Fig. 19.3. (a) The New York urban–rural transect of sites in the Bronx (urban land use), Westchester County, New York (suburban) and Litchfield County, Connecticut (rural). Forest sites are denoted with solid black squares. This transect was 130 km long. (b) The 40-km-long Louisville, Kentucky, urban–rural transect of sites in Jefferson and Bullitt Counties. The Knob forest sites (solid black triangles) are Iroquois Park (urban), Jefferson County Memorial Forest (suburban) and the Bernheim Forest (rural). The star represents Louisville.

New York, and *Q. prinus* (chestnut oak) in Louisville); (2) location on the same or closely related soil series (in New York Charlton–Hollis soils, which are sandy loams, mixed, mesic Typic or Lithic Dystrochrepts; and Tilsit soils in Louisville, which consist of fine silt loams, mixed, semi-active, mesic Typic Fragiudults); (3) no canopy gaps; (4) no signs of recent natural or human disturbance such as fire, severe insect infestation or selective logging; and (5) similar within-stand land-use history. By holding these internal characteristics as constant as possible, we could increase confidence that any differences in forest properties measured along the urban–rural gradient would be due primarily to current and past cumulative effects of land use surrounding the stands.

Soil carbon and nitrogen transformations, in a nutshell

To maintain primary productivity, forest trees require inorganic nutrients, and in many temperate forests the nutrient that most limits tree growth is nitrogen (N) (Vitousek and Howarth, 1991). Nitrogen in inorganic forms (typically ammonium (NH_4^+) and nitrate (NO_3^-)) can be supplied to a forest either from external sources via atmospheric deposition, or from internal sources generated during decomposition of organic matter. Most studies of litter decomposition in North American forests have been conducted in large forests far from cities. Therefore, rates of nutrient return from internal reservoirs (e.g. dead plant matter) have received greatest attention, since the dependence of primary production on externally derived nutrients is often much smaller.

Litter decay studies follow not only rates of mass loss and the production of CO_2 (C mineralisation), but also the conversion of organic N in dead plant matter to inorganic ammonium (NH_4^+) and nitrate (NO_3^-) (N mineralisation). During decay (Fig. 19.2), fungi and bacteria enzymatically break down complex carbon compounds, take up a portion of these compounds into their cells for growth, and respire others for metabolic energy. Microbial respiration (and therefore CO_2 production), along with invertebrate fragmentation and grazing, results in mass loss of the litter during decay. To produce their own proteins and nucleic acids, microbes take up nitrogen not only from litter but also from precipitation and the soil. As a result, total N mass as well as N concentration often increases in litter during the early stages of decay (a phenomenon referred to as net N immobilisation). However, as the plant litter is transformed by microbial and invertebrate activity to organic humus, mineralisation of N from organic to inorganic forms exceeds N uptake by microbes. Consequently, there is a net release of N from the litter to the soil where it becomes available for plant uptake. In some forests NH_4^+ predominates in soil as the main inorganic N form. In others, NH_4^+ is converted to NO_3^- primarily by the action of specialised chemoautotrophic nitrifying bacteria (although heterotrophic nitrification pathways conducted by other microbes have also been discovered in some forests (Killham, 1990)). Production of NO_3^- via nitrification can be ecologically important at the landscape scale because NO_3^-, being more mobile than NH_4^+, is leached readily from the soil and exported to groundwater, streams and other receiving water bodies where it can contribute to eutrophication. Furthermore, under conditions of high soil moisture, NO_3^- can be converted by anaerobic denitrifying bacteria to N_2 gas or nitrous oxide (N_2O), a greenhouse gas. In this case, nitrogen leaves the forest via the atmosphere. Therefore, NO_3^- production at levels that exceed plant and microbial uptake (a condition called N saturation; Aber *et al.*, 1998) can make a forest more vulnerable to N loss and change the forest's role in the greater landscape to being a N source rather than a retentive N sink.

Findings from the New York urban–rural gradient experiments

Litter decomposition studies

Several studies were conducted from 1989 to 1997 to determine if atmospheric N deposition, decomposer communities, decomposition of leaf litter and soil N transformations differed in oak-dominated forests along the New York urban–rural gradient. One of the earliest objectives was to determine whether the rates at which leaf litter decomposed and N was released from decaying litter differed along the gradient. Our expectations of the outcomes were uncertain because we anticipated that stimulation of process rates from potentially warmer urban soil temperatures could be offset by higher concentrations of heavy metals often found in urban soils (Chaney *et al.*, 1984). Also, Findlay and Jones (1990) had found that ozone altered the chemistry of living leaves such that the subsequent decay rate of senesced leaves was depressed. So the potential degree of difference and even the direction in decomposition rates and litter N dynamics between urban and rural forests were not predictable at the outset.

For this initial decomposition study (Pouyat and Carreiro, 2003), senesced leaves from red oaks were collected from urban, suburban and rural stands, weighed into mesh bags and returned to decay in their stands of origin. However, to separate the potential effects of leaf litter quality on decay rate from those of site factors (such as climate, pollutant inputs, differences in activity or composition of decomposer organisms), a reciprocal litter exchange was also carried out such that litter collected in rural stands would decompose in both rural and urban stands, and likewise for litter collected in urban stands. Since litter of urban and rural origin would decay side by side, if their decay rates differed, then variation in within-species litter quality must be responsible. In turn, since litter of urban and rural origin decayed in both urban and rural forests, if the litters of similar origin decayed at different rates in the different locations, then variation in site factors must be the cause. Only urban and rural litters were exchanged in this way, not suburban litter, which was left to decay only in suburban stands. Comparison of litters that decayed in their sites of origin would reveal the net effects of potential litter quality and site factor interactions on litter decay rate.

At the end of a 22-month period, no statistically significant difference in mass loss rates for litter types decaying in their sites of origin was detected along this gradient, although the decay rate in the urban forests was faster than in their suburban and rural counterparts (32.5%, 37.1% and 41.1% mean mass remaining, respectively). However, the reciprocal transplants revealed that these results were obtained for different reasons in the urban versus the rural forests. Regardless of whether litter incubated in the urban or rural forests, oak litter collected from the urban stands decayed more slowly than oak litter collected from the rural stands (across-site mean mass remaining after 22 months was 41.8% for urban litter versus 29.8% for rural litter). This study indicated that soil decomposers found the quality of urban litter to be lower than the quality of rural litter. Also, regardless of stand origin, litter decayed more quickly in the urban forests than in the rural stands, indicating that urban site factors accelerated decay relative to rural forests (across-litter type mean mass remaining was 25.6% in urban forests compared with 46% in rural forests). This independently validated the findings of another decomposition study along this gradient that had used a single litter type (sugar maple) from a single location to assay variation in site conditions (Pouyat *et al.*, 1997). Since urban site conditions accelerated the litter decay rate but urban litter quality reduced it, decay rates of urban litter in urban forests were similar to those of better-quality rural litter decomposing in rural forests. Similar decay rates across the gradient for litters incubating in their sites of origin obscured the fact that controls associated with site conditions and within-species chemical quality of litter differed in a compensatory manner along this land-use gradient. These mechanistic insights would not have been possible if a litter transplant had not been incorporated into the experimental design for this decomposition study.

Seeking explanations: differences in litter quality

Other experiments occurring simultaneously with the above study revealed some of the reasons for these shifts in controlling variables along the New York City urban–rural gradient. Chemical analyses of senesced oak leaves collected from the same urban, suburban and rural forests in the subsequent year showed that urban oak litter contained less labile material, more lignin and higher lignin:N ratios than rural leaf litter (Carreiro *et al.*, 1999). All of these chemical characteristics are known to correlate with slower rates of litter decay (Melillo *et al.*, 1982). Indeed, when these leaves were incubated under similar moisture and temperature conditions in the lab, urban litter decayed most slowly (25% more slowly than rural leaves) and sustained less fungal and bacterial growth (50% less than rural leaves) than rural or suburban oak litters (Carreiro *et al.*, 1999). The results of this laboratory experiment independently corroborated the findings of the field litter transplant study regarding differences in urban and rural oak litter quality. The reasons for this variation in litter quality are unclear, but ozone damage to the living leaves before senescence is a possibility. Differences in the chemical quality of senesced leaves along the urban–rural gradient were consistent with those of other studies that investigated acute ozone effects on leaf litter quality and subsequent litter decomposition rate (Findlay and Jones, 1990; Findlay *et al.*, 1996).

Seeking explanations: differences in abiotic conditions and decomposer communities

Knowledge of litter quality variation along the gradient could not, of course, address the question of how urban site conditions promoted decay rates of litter. Pouyat and McDonnell (1991) found that heavy metal concentrations (e.g. lead, copper, nickel) were two to four times greater in mineral soil of urban than of rural forest stands along the urban–rural gradient. While this indicated a greater atmospheric deposition history for heavy metals near the city, the mean concentrations found were not considered high enough to depress soil organisms and microbial processes greatly. Average precipitation did not vary substantially along this gradient, although there is generally greater year-to-year variability in the city than in outlying rural areas (NOAA, 1985). Pouyat (1992) found, as expected, that soil temperature in the urban forest stands averaged 2 to 3 °C warmer than their rural counterparts. However, using a simple exponential model and assuming a Q10 of 2, the mean temperature increase of 2.5 °C above the 12.5 °C annual mean for the region would result in a litter mass remaining of 37% in the urban stands rather than the 25.6% that was obtained (the across-litter type means were used in this calculation). Therefore, the temperature differential across the gradient could not account for the entire difference in litter decay rate.

The discovery that there were two major differences in decomposer community composition along the gradient provided a likely explanation for the large variation in litter decay rates and litter N immobilisation patterns (more below) in response to site factors found in the litter transplant study (Pouyat *et al.*, 1994). First, growth in fungal biomass over a 9-month period on oak leaf litter in the urban stands was half that in the rural stands, with suburban stands intermediate. However, negative urban impacts on fungal biomass could not explain the faster decay rate of litters placed in the urban forests, since less fungal growth should result in slower decay. Likewise, microinvertebrate abundance, especially of those functional groups (mites, collembola, nematodes) that feed on fungi, was also greater in forests at the rural end of the gradient, and so could not account for faster urban litter decay either. However, densities of large earthworms in urban and suburban forests were found to be as much as 10 times those in rural stands (Steinberg *et al.*, 1997). Most of these earthworms consisted of two epigeic species of *Amynthas*, originally from Asia. The distribution of exotic worms across the gradient is strongly correlated with the decay rates observed. Through their fragmentation and feeding activities, worms accelerate leaf litter decay and create mull soil conditions characterised by thin leaf litter layers and mixed A soil horizons (i.e. upper mineral soil horizons have been bioturbated). Therefore, in addition to warmer soil temperatures, it is very likely that the presence of these worms can account for a large proportion of the rapid litter decay rates observed in these urban and suburban forest stands.

Ecological implications of faster litter decay in urban forests and verification from other studies

The slightly faster, although statistically non-significant, decay rates of *in situ* bagged oak litter at the urban end of the gradient were found to scale up to variation in stand-level thickness of the mixed-deciduous litter layer along this gradient of forest sites. While forest litter production was similar across the gradient, the mass per square metre of the leaf litter layer in the urban forests was only 33% that in the rural forests (Kostel-Hughes *et al.*, 1998b). Since tree litter inputs were similar across the gradient, this indicates that the ratio of decomposition to primary production is greater at the urban end of the gradient. Litter depth has important implications for plant regeneration (Facelli and Pickett, 1991; Kostel-Hughes, 1995) and abundance of litter macrofungi in these forests.

These gradient trends were also corroborated by findings from other studies using different techniques. Groffman *et al.* (1995) conducted a study in forests along this gradient to assess the amount of carbon in four soil pools operationally defined by laboratory incubation methods into categories with different turnover times. They found that pools of: (1) readily mineralisable C (turnover within days to weeks); (2) microbial biomass C (turnover within days to weeks); and (3) potentially mineralisable C (turnover of weeks to months) were higher in the rural stands. However, pools of passive C with turnover times of years to centuries were 33% higher in the urban stands. These results were consistent with expectations that earthworm activity accelerates the loss of labile C fractions in soils and yet sequesters some C in soil aggregates, protecting it from rapid microbial breakdown for long time periods. Higher recalcitrant C pools in urban stands could also be the consequence of proportionately greater inputs of recalcitrant litter compounds. Substantially lower microbial biomass in the urban soils compared with the rural soils was also found by Groffman *et al.* (1995) and Zhu and Carreiro (2004b).

Because different methods were used and studies conducted in different years, collectively these studies independently verified that, relative to the rural forests, urban sites contained: (1) less microbial biomass (particularly fungal biomass); (2) less labile material in oak leaf litter; (3) more recalcitrant material such as lignin in oak leaf litter; (4) less easily mineralisable soil carbon; and (5) a larger passive soil carbon pool. For these urban stands in New York City, it appears then that altered chemical quality of plant detrital inputs and the presence of exotic earthworms may be increasing the forest soil's potential to sequester passive recalcitrant carbon relative to similar reference forests in rural areas. Also, despite the fact that litters decaying in their sites of origin lost mass at statistically indistinguishable rates across the gradient, because the controls on decomposition differed across the gradient, year-to-year variation in factors such as precipitation and pollution inputs would be expected to have differential impacts on this ecosystem process in urban and rural forests. For example, warm, sunny drought years could lower earthworm populations and increase ozone levels closer to the city. In such years one could anticipate that leaf litter decay rates would be relatively more reduced in urban than in rural forests.

Nitrogen cycling in forests along the New York urban–rural gradient

Internal nitrogen sources: release from decomposing litter

Since nitrogen is often the nutrient that most limits primary productivity in terrestrial systems, it is important to determine whether urban conditions can alter the rate at which organic N in plant litter is transformed by microbes and invertebrates to inorganic N available for plant uptake. Breakdown and transformation of organic C and N during microbial processing in the soil are intricately linked, and therefore can affect each other in numerous ways. Rates of organic C mineralisation by bacteria and fungi during litter decay can be either accelerated or depressed by N availability (Carreiro *et al.*, 2000), and the rate at which organic N becomes mineralised to inorganic forms depends in part on the quality of C compounds available to microbes and invertebrates. Therefore, the effects of litter quality and site factors on net N retention and loss in decaying leaf litter were also examined in the litter transplant study described above (Pouyat and Carreiro, 2003).

This study showed that relative to the urban forests, the litter layer in these rural forests was a stronger N-immobilising environment, and hence a longer-term reservoir of N in forms not available for plant uptake. Interaction effects between site factors and litter quality were also discerned in that rural litter lost N far more rapidly than urban litter when incubated in the urban stands, but not when both litter types were incubated in the rural stands. After 22 months of decay, the across-litter-type, mean N immobilised in the rural forests was 15% more than they originally contained, while the across-litter-type, mean N in the urban forests was 30% less than they originally contained. The effect of litter origin (and hence litter quality) was only observed in the urban forests. Urban litter contained 92%, while rural litter contained only 51% of its original N content after 22 months of decay in the urban forests. In contrast, urban and rural litters decomposing in the rural plots did not differ greatly in their N content and retained 18% and 12% more N, respectively, than they had to start with.

Again, the different compositions of the decomposer communities along this urban–rural gradient provides a plausible explanation for these contrasting patterns of N retention and release in the litter layer of urban versus rural forests. Leaf litter with high fungal biomass, as occurred in the rural forests, would be expected to retain N for a longer period of time than that with a smaller fungal component (Swift *et al.*, 1979). Because leaf litter initially has a higher C:N ratio than fungal cytoplasm, fungi augment N supplied from litter by translocating more of it from lower soil horizons into the leaf layer via filamentous hyphae that grow into and tap both substrates simultaneously. In addition, fungi and bacteria can incorporate N from precipitation and throughfall into their biomass, which then becomes an integral part of the decaying litter mass. Therefore, it is not surprising that the rural forests with their greater fungal biomass than urban forests should immobilise N in the litter layer for a longer period. In addition, Pouyat *et al.* (1994) and Zhu and Carreiro (2004b) noted that fungal and total microbial biomass, respectively, grew exponentially from winter to spring, particularly in the rural stands. Microbial biomass can therefore conserve forest N capital during this vulnerable period of low plant uptake. It appears that these rural forests with their greater microbial biomass pool than urban counterparts may be able to retain N more effectively. In contrast, the urban forests contained high densities of exotic earthworms that consume litter and mix litter fragments and partially digested detritus into the upper mineral soil horizons. The net effects of their activities would be to accelerate C and N loss from litter through digestion of the material and by creating a disturbed forest floor environment (mull soils) that could reduce the hyphal growth of longer-lived macrofungi (McLean and Carreiro, unpublished data) that would immobilize N for longer periods than most bacteria and microfungi.

Nitrogen transformations in the humus and upper mineral soil horizon

Most soil nitrogen consists of organic rather than inorganic compounds; a portion of these organic compounds is soluble and may be leached from the system, taken up by microbes and plant roots, or microbially transformed into soluble inorganic compounds (Paul and Clark, 1996). Over a 16-month period, Zhu and Carreiro (2004a, b) examined the temporal dynamics of both soluble organic N (ESON or extractable soil organic nitrogen) and soluble inorganic N (ESIN) compounds in surface soils containing the humus horizon (Oa, Oe) and the upper mineral soil horizon of nine oak forests along the New York gradient. Not only did urban soil produce 35% more soluble N annually than soils in rural forests, but a greater fraction of that N was in inorganic form. ESIN comprised 70% of total soluble N produced annually in the urban forests, but only 54% of the total soluble N pool in the rural forests. Also, as found earlier by Pouyat (1992), not only were N-mineralisation rates in the upper mineral horizon (upper 7.5 cm) of the urban forests higher, but the fraction of NH_4^+ transformed to NO_3^- was far greater in these urban and suburban forests (48% and 44%, respectively) than in the rural forests (2.8%) (Zhu and Carreiro, 2004a). These field results were consistent with those from N-mineralisation experiments conducted with laboratory-incubated soil (Pouyat *et al.*, 1997; Zhu and Carreiro, 1999). Through the use of the acetylene block technique Zhu and Carreiro (1999) also verified that chemoautotrophic nitrifying bacteria, not heterotrophic microbes, controlled the nitrification process in these acidic soils, and that low nitrification rates in the rural soils were not explained by removing limitations in NH_4^+, phosphorus or low soil pH, at least over short (14-day) incubation periods.

Again, it is likely that earthworm activity would explain the higher nitrification rates in the urban and suburban forests, since they are known in other systems to increase N availability, N transformations and frequently nitrification (Scheu and Parkinson, 1994; Blair *et al.*, 1995). This was experimentally demonstrated in the New York area forests by Steinberg *et al.* (1997) who found that adding the exotic Amynthas earthworms to soils collected from both urban and rural forests stimulated both N-mineralisation and nitrification rates over those of controls without worms. Not only might soil mixing and excretion by worms promote N mineralisation, but earthworm casts may well provide a microsite where nitrifying bacteria find conditions and resources more conducive to their activity (circumneutral pH, greater soil moisture, more organic matter, more NH_4^+) than the non-cast soil (Carreiro and Zhu, unpublished data). This was shown by comparing nitrification rates in earthworm casts collected from one urban and one suburban forest with rates in the mineral non-cast soil collected immediately beneath the cast layer (Carreiro and Zhu, unpublished data). After a 14-day laboratory incubation, nitrate production in the worm casts was 10 times as great as that in the non-cast soil.

Atmospheric nitrogen deposition: an external source to forests

While internal N cycling during decomposition provides a forest with most of its annual N capital for supporting plant growth, a certain amount of the total forest budget originates from outside the forest and enters in precipitation in both wet (as rain, snow, cloud fog) and dry (as particulates and N-containing gases) forms. Therefore, owing to greater fossil fuel emission in urban-industrial areas, the amount of N entering forest remnants from atmospheric sources would be expected to increase with proximity to cities. For several decades there have been many studies of atmospheric and precipitation chemistry in urban areas (Gatz, 1991). However, until recently we knew little about the magnitude of atmospheric N deposition to urban forest remnants. To address this knowledge gap, Lovett *et al.* (2000) quantified atmospheric N inputs over two growing seasons in oak forest stands along the New York urban–rural gradient. They measured N in both throughfall (precipitation falling onto the forest floor after passing through the forest canopy) and precipitation (rainfall collected in open areas near the forest stands). Throughfall N contains not only the amount of N entering the system in rainfall, but also any additional amount captured as dry dust particles by foliage between rain events. However, canopy processing in forests not receiving high N deposition can actually reduce the amount of N in throughfall relative to the amount in rain. If N in throughfall exceeds that in rainfall, then the difference serves as a conservative estimate of the amount that the canopy foliage captured in particulate form between rain events. Lovett *et al.* (2000) found that N entering urban forests in throughfall was 50 to 100% greater than the N flux into rural and suburban forests. Additionally, they found that the difference was due mostly to N entering in particulate form rather than rainfall. Particulate N deposition in forests was at least 17 times greater at the urban end of the gradient (15.5 mmol N per m^2 in urban stands versus 0.9 mmol N per m^2 in rural stands), with nearly 70% of this inorganic N in NO_3^- rather than NH_4^+ form. These inputs did not decline linearly with distance from the city, but instead fell off rapidly somewhere between New York City and the suburban stands 45 km to the north. This steep drop-off threshold can be explained by the reaction of acidic anions with alkaline dust particles (Ca^{2+} and Mg^{2+}) thought to originate mostly from construction and demolition activity within the city. Since the particles were large ($>2 \mu m$), most sedimented in the city itself and were not blown further away. If these N deposition trends are also found in other cities, then urban forests would receive a large N subsidy in dry particulate deposition during the growing season relative to suburban and rural forests nearby.

Conclusions for the New York urban–rural gradient studies

While abiotic factors of air pollution, atmospheric deposition of nutrients and heavy metals, and warmer temperatures undoubtedly play roles in modifying C and N cycling in forest soils along the New York urban–rural gradient, perhaps the factor that has had the most noticeable impact is biotic – namely, the invasion of these urban and suburban forests by exotic earthworms. These worms have accelerated C and N cycling rates and indirectly changed the direction and products of a major biogeochemical cycle – the N cycle. By stimulating nitrification, these worms have also potentially altered the role that these forests play in the greater landscape. As one moves closer to New York City from the north, the likelihood that forests will shift from being sinks to sources of nitrogen increases greatly. The production of NO_3^- is pivotal, therefore, not only to the internal dynamics of the forest community itself, but also to the forest's role with its local surroundings and the atmosphere. Counterintuitively, while the worms are accelerating soil C and N cycling rates, they may also be increasing the rate at which a portion of that carbon is being sequestered into a long turnover C pool. Sequestration rates of passive C would be accelerated if ozone or other factors consistently alter leaf chemistry to increase the relative size of recalcitrant C inputs to the soil. Interactions between worm activity and greater N deposition to urban forests would also stimulate nitrification rates, since chemoautotrophic nitrifying bacteria, primed by worm activity, could convert both detrital and atmospherically deposited NH_4^+ into NO_3^-.

Increased soil N availability through locally greater worm activity and atmospheric N deposition has several important positive and negative implications for urban forest communities in the New York vicinity. Greater N supply could differentially stimulate primary production of species able to take advantage of its increased availability and therefore alter plant community composition (Tamm, 1991). The plants thus favoured may not only be native species. High rates of N-mineralisation and nitrification have been strongly correlated with a greater degree of invasion by non-native plant species in hardwood forests in the New York City area (Howard *et al.*, 2004). Since propagule supply of non-natives is typically high in urban and suburban landscapes (Kostel-Hughes *et al.*, 1998a; McKinney, 2002), increased soil fertility may make forest remnants particularly vulnerable to fast-growing non-native plants. Increased soil N is also often associated with higher N concentration in foliage (Magill *et al.*, 1997). While this can translate into higher primary productivity rates, it can also increase a plant's vulnerability to attach by insects and fungal pathogens (Huber and Watson, 1974; Mattson, 1980; McClure, 1991). Increased N deposition can also either accelerate or reduce C mineralisation rates during litter decomposition, depending on the litter's relative lignin and cellulose content (Carreiro *et al.*, 2000). Should N availability exceed plant and microbial sink strength for many years (N saturation), then a syndrome of clustered responses can ensue (Aber *et al.*, 1998), resulting in accelerated tree mortality and N export from the forest to surrounding habitats. However, if there is consistently greater Ca^{2+} and Mg^{2+} deposition in cities, then one negative aspect of high NO_3^- inputs and high nitrification rates in urban forests could be mitigated – namely leaching loss of basic cations from soils (Likens *et al.*, 1996).

Other cities, other patterns?

Urban–rural gradient experiments investigating the effects of land use on soil C and N cycling in temperate forests have also been initiated in other metropolitan areas in the United States (Carreiro, 2003; Pavao-Zuckerman, 2003). Such studies permit comparisons among different cities to ascertain whether forest responses found in any one city are also applicable to others (Lehvävirta and Kotze, Chapter 31).

The results obtained from the New York urban–rural gradient serve as a benchmark for these studies because of their extent, detail and duration. The New York gradient also provides data on forest responses to the high human density and intense commercial activity of the largest metropolitan area in the United States. Comparisons of the same response variables in forest remnants in smaller cities would help us discover whether: (1) certain responses and effects are idiosyncratic or common; (2) the magnitude of some responses varies linearly or non-linearly with city size and other urban attributes; and (3) thresholds related to population density, size and other urban characteristics exist (see also McCarthy, Chapter 7; Lehvävirta and Kotze, Chapter 31).

Findings from the Louisville urban–rural gradient study

Louisville, Kentucky, with a population of 700 000 is a continental city an order of magnitude smaller than New York City, but located at a similar latitude and within the same eastern deciduous forest biome. The Louisville area possesses many forest fragments with the same canopy and sub-canopy tree species as found in forests in the New York urban–rural gradient. Therefore, establishing a gradient of sites here permits an initial examination of the effects of city size on forest communities with similar plant species composition. Since the Louisville gradient studies were started in 2001, not all are complete and only interim results are reported here.

Litter decomposition study

A litter transplant study, similar in design to that in New York, was initiated to ascertain the potential effects of site factors and litter quality on the decay rate of chestnut oak (*Q. prinus*) leaf litter. Leaf litter bags were set out in urban, suburban and rural plots in their sites of origin, and urban and rural litter exchanges were also made. Despite the fact that the lignin:N ratios for urban and suburban litter were about 15% greater than rural litter, differences in mass loss rate after 21 months of field incubation have been small along the gradient of forests. No detectable differences in litter quality or site factor effects have been observed. With respect to N dynamics in the decomposing litter, all nine forest stands along this gradient have shown strong immobilisation patterns with the amount of N remaining in the *in situ* litters after 18 months of decay ranging from 188% to 160% of original N mass in the suburban and urban stands, respectively.

Soil N mineralisation study

Nitrogen-mineralisation studies were conducted from July 2001 to December 2002 in the Louisville area forests using cores of the upper 10 cm soil horizon. Unlike the urban–rural pattern observed in New York, N-mineralisation rates from December 2001 to December 2002 were greatest in the rural plots, followed by the urban and then suburban plots. On a dry mass soil basis, the upper 10 cm horizon of the rural stands mineralised 26% and 69% more N than the urban and suburban stands, respectively. Also unlike the New York City gradient, urban forest plots in Louisville contained more soil organic matter than the rural plots. When these N-mineralisation rates were normalised on a soil organic matter (SOM) basis, the discrepancy in N-mineralisation rates between the urban and rural forests increased further, with rates in rural stands becoming 47% higher than rates in urban stands. This indicates that quality of soil organic matter is more recalcitrant in the urban stands, a result similar to that found in the New York City gradient. The urban forests mineralised 2.2, suburban 1.96, and rural 3.23 mg N per kg SOM per day over that 1-year period. Compared with forests along the New York gradient, annual N-mineralisation on an SOM basis in the Louisville urban and suburban plots was 50% and 56% that of their New York forest counterparts. However, the rural plots in Louisville mineralised 130% more N than the rural forests in the New York gradient. The nitrification pattern across the sites in Louisville differed greatly from that in New York as well. In the urban and suburban stands in New York as much as 70% of mineralised NH_4^+ was transformed to NO_3^-, with net nitrification being negligible in the rural forests. However, in Louisville nitrification in the rural stands was 10 times that in the urban plots, and negligible in the suburban forests. On average 65% of the total N mineralised was converted to nitrate in rural stands in Louisville. These results cannot be fully explained at this time. However, potential explanations may include the fact that exotic earthworms are not as obviously abundant in the urban, suburban or rural forests in Louisville as they were in New York. This comparison suggests that the exotic earthworms may have been primarily responsible for the steep differences in N-mineralisation and nitrification patterns observed along the New York urban–rural gradient.

Atmospheric N deposition

From May to October 2002 rainfall (bulk precipitation) was collected weekly from a total of three stations in open areas near the urban, suburban and rural forest sites. Throughfall was also collected simultaneously from beneath the canopies of 27 Q. *prinus* trees, nine trees each in the urban, suburban and rural forests. As opposed to the soil N-mineralisation results, urban–rural gradient trends in atmospheric N and nutrient deposition were similar in forests in both the Louisville and New York areas. The amount of total inorganic N (combined N from NH_4^+ and NO_3^-) entering the urban forests in throughfall was 31% and 53% greater than that entering suburban and rural forests, respectively. The particulate component in throughfall was responsible for most of the difference along this gradient (7.01, 4.66 and 1.43 mmol N per m^2, for urban, suburban and rural, respectively) rather than the amount entering via bulk precipitation. The proportion that entered as NO_3^- instead of NH_4^+ increased monotonically (65–72%) from urban to rural ends of the gradient, as was found in the New York City study. This indicates that NO_x in fossil fuel emissions is the likely major source of N entering these forests from the atmosphere. Bulk deposition fluxes of Ca^{2+} and Mg^{2+} to the urban stands in Louisville were also two to three times those to rural forests. Since greater inputs of these basic cations were also found in New York, urban forests may generally receive greater inputs of these nutrients than rural forests nearby.

In summary, the trends in deposition fluxes of N, Ca^{2+} and Mg^{2+} to forests in the Louisville area are very similar to those in New York City, which were also collected over the growing season and over a similar number of weeks. In addition the absolute amounts of N, Ca^{2+} and Mg^{2+} entering the urban forests in both cities were very similar. Louisville had approximately half the N inputs of New York City, but slightly greater inputs of Ca^{2+} and Mg^{2+}, despite the fact that the Louisville Metropolitan Area (1 million inhabitants) has a population just 5% of that of New York, and a mean population density 7.5% of that of New York City. City size and density alone, therefore, are unlikely to explain most of the variation in atmospheric deposition trends. This is not surprising since other geographical, socio-political and economic factors can influence air quality in a particular city. For example, the Louisville area has a number of large, coal-burning power plants nearby along the Ohio River, and depending on dominant wind directions these can contribute to atmospheric deposition in the local area. The fact that N deposition to the rural plots in the Louisville gradient was greater than the amount entering the rural plots in the New York City gradient is perhaps indicative of greater contribution of emissions from these large point sources to the region surrounding Louisville. In addition, automobile traffic may also be greater per capita in Louisville than in New York City, since the fraction of New Yorkers who own or drive cars within their city limits is likely to be less than in Louisville. Local and state air quality regulations on emissions from both stationary and mobile sources (automobiles) may differ between the two cities as well.

Concluding remarks

Detailed study of urbanisation's effects on soil processes within forest remnants is still in its early stages, and studies in more cities are needed to determine the range of possible responses. Nonetheless, the notion that soil processes in urban forests are uniformly depressed by pollutant accumulation, low biotic activity and soil compaction have not been born out by the examples in New York and Louisville. In fact, rates of carbon and nitrogen cycling in these urban plots are comparable to, or, in the case of New York, greater than those measured for other temperate forests in the United States (Pastor *et al.*, 1984; Zak and Grigal, 1991). Whether urbanisation may alter the decomposition to primary production ratio in some forest remnants would be an important focus for future studies. Such a shift could have important implications for the long-term composition of plant and microbial communities in these forests and for the role these forest patches may play in the greater landscape as net sinks or sources of C, N and other nutrients.

These two case studies suggest that the direction of some abiotic driving variables across the land-use gradient, such as atmospheric deposition and temperature, may be similar among different cities. For example, greater atmospheric N, Ca and Mg deposition into forests at the urban end of the gradient may be a common urban phenomenon. However, the magnitude of the variables and their rates of change across the gradient may vary among different cities. If the differences in abiotic conditions and resource inputs are found to be steep across urbanisation gradients, then these systems would constitute useful 'natural experiments' for understanding integrated forest responses to variation in these variables. Conversely, the expectation that forests in different cities will respond similarly to these abiotic drivers is not likely to be supported. Since forest remnants in different cities vary in terms of climate, age, historical usage, soils and species (including exotics), forest responses to variation in urban-derived abiotic drivers would depend on the degree of control that those factors have over a particular process under a specific set of ecological conditions. Measurement and documentation of the key abiotic drivers likely to vary along urban–rural gradients (temperature, atmospheric deposition of nutrients, CO_2 and O_3 concentrations and fluxes) would therefore augment our mechanistic understanding of the C and N cycling responses of urban forest remnants, and improve our predictions of the behaviour of forests that may become surrounded by cities and suburbs in the near future.

Acknowledgements

Funding support for these studies was provided by the National Science Foundation (DEB 0196319 to M.M.C.), the University of Louisville Research Foundation, and the USDA Forest Service (Northern Global Change Program to R.V.P.).

20

Investigative approaches to urban biogeochemical cycles: New York metropolitan area and Baltimore as case studies

RICHARD V. POUYAT, MARGARET M. CARREIRO, PETER M. GROFFMAN AND MITCHELL A. PAVAO-ZUCKERMAN

Introduction

By 2007 more than half of the world's population is expected to reside in cities (United Nations, 2004). As urban populations and the number of cities expand, natural and agricultural lands are transformed into highly altered landscapes. These changes in demography and land use have contributed to the alteration of biogeochemical cycles at local, regional and global scales (Vitousek *et al.*, 1997a; Pouyat *et al.*, 2003). Yet we lack sufficient data with which to assess the underlying mechanisms of land-use change (Groffman *et al.*, 2004), largely because of the difficulty encountered when applying established biogeochemical research methods such as large-scale field manipulations to urban and suburban ecosystems (Pouyat *et al.*, 1995a). Moreover, current conceptual and quantitative biogeochemical models incorporate human effects only indirectly (Groffman and Likens, 1994).

As a result, most urban ecosystem studies have relied on a comparative approach or 'natural experiments' to investigate urban effects on biogeochemical cycles in ecological remnants characteristic of a particular area or region (Pickett *et al.*, 2001). This approach takes advantage of remnant systems as 'whole ecosystem' manipulations by which the effects of multiple urban stress and disturbance factors are assessed with established statistical methods and modelling approaches (Pouyat *et al.*, 1995a; Breitburg *et al.*, 1998; Carreiro and Tripler, 2005; Carreiro *et al.*,

Ecology of Cities and Towns: A Comparative Approach, ed. Mark J. McDonnell, Amy K. Hahs and Jürgen H. Breuste. Published by Cambridge University Press. © Cambridge University Press 2009.

Chapter 19). Examples include comparisons of remnant forest patches with different land-use histories within an urban area (Hobbs, 1988b; Zipperer, 2002) and between remnants in urban, suburban and rural areas (McDonnell *et al.*, 1997; Pavao-Zuckerman and Coleman, 2005; Carreiro *et al.*, Chapter 19).

Apart from the comparative approach, patch dynamic and watershed approaches have been promoted to study the interaction of the human and ecological domains of the entire urban landscape (Pickett *et al.*, 1997b; Grimm *et al.*, 2000; Grimm and Redman, 2004). Urban landscapes are diverse spatial mosaics representing a variety of ecological conditions that are useful in comparing the effects of urban land-use change on ecological structure and function. Natural sources of spatial heterogeneity in ecosystems still underlie and constrain the effects of land-use and land-cover change. These factors include the geophysical setting, physical environment, biological agents, and processes of disturbance and stress (Pickett and Rogers, 1997). Humans introduce an additional source of heterogeneity by altering landforms and drainage patterns, constructing structures, introducing non-native species, and modifying natural disturbance regimes (Turner *et al.*, 1990; Pouyat *et al.*, 2007a). Additional patchiness also results from variations in human behaviour and social structures that function at different scales (Grove *et al.*, 2006). By comparing human and natural sources of heterogeneity within the spatial context of watersheds, the processes and patterns of human and ecological systems can be linked (Pickett *et al.*, 2001, Chapter 3).

In this chapter we investigate urban biogeochemical cycles from studies conducted in the New York City and Baltimore, Maryland, metropolitan areas. Since the United States is an industrialised country, our approach may not be applicable in cities within developing nations, where urban populations are expanding at a tremendous rate and development patterns differ from those of cities in developed countries (Zipperer and Pickett, 2001). We focus on carbon (C) and nitrogen (N) cycling, both of which have environmental importance from a local to global scale (Vitousek *et al.*, 1997a; Schlesinger and Andrews, 2000). The biogeochemistry of these elements might be a useful indicator of the long-term accrued effects of urban stress and disturbance on ecosystem structure and function (Pouyat *et al.*, 1995a). Here we evaluate: (1) the effects of urban land-use change on native ecosystems; and (2) the relative strengths and limitations of three approaches used to investigate urban land-use effects on C and N cycling: the urban gradient, patch dynamic and watershed approaches.

Urban land-use change

When land is converted from forest, grassland and farmland to urban land use, novel management and disturbance regimes are introduced by humans (Pouyat *et al.*, 2003). Most large-scale disturbances, such as site grading and vegetation removal, occur in the construction phase of urban development, whereas finer-scale disturbances, such as demolition of old buildings and conversion of vacant lots into community gardens, generally occur later. Horticultural management introduces even finer-scale disturbances and includes the establishment and maintenance of lawns, shade trees and planting beds on parcels of land that typically are smaller than the parcels that were managed in the previous forest or agricultural landscape. Horticultural management generally does not result in continuous physical disturbance of soil or plant communities, so it has less impact on biogeochemical cycles than management of agricultural systems, which disturbs plant and soil systems annually or continuously throughout the year (Pouyat *et al.*, 2003).

Urban environmental factors that could affect biogeochemical cycles are overlaid on these novel patterns of disturbance and management. These factors include the urban heat island effect; increased atmospheric concentrations of carbon dioxide (CO_2), and oxides of nitrogen and sulphur; atmospheric N deposition; heavy metal and organic chemical contaminants; and the introduction of invasive plant and animal species (Carreiro *et al.*, Chapter 19). In some metropolitan areas, the net effects of these multiple factors may be analogous to predictions of global environmental change, e.g. increased temperatures and rising atmospheric concentrations of CO_2 (Pickett *et al.*, 2001; Carreiro and Tripler, 2005). In fact, some of these environmental factors seem to affect biogeochemical cycles in remnant forest ecosystems within metropolitan areas (Grodzinski *et al.*, 1984; McDonnell *et al.*, 1997). The results of these and other studies are reviewed by Carreiro *et al.* (Chapter 19).

The net result of human disturbance, landscape management and environmental changes associated with urbanisation is a mosaic of land patches with varying environmental conditions (Pouyat *et al.*, 2003). In this heterogeneous landscape, distinctly different patch types lie near each other, e.g. a forest patch adjacent to a residential area. As landscapes become more densely developed, the structure and function of the managed patches should become more distinctive and correspond more closely to the management preferences of the individual land owner, e.g. whether a parcel is landscaped primarily with native or exotic plants (Zipperer *et al.*, 1997). Typically, the development pattern of a metropolitan area results in a configuration where patch size tends to decrease from rural outlying areas towards the urban core while the diversity tends to be greatest at the urban fringe (sensu Burghardt, 1994) (Fig. 20.1). Management of these parcels depends on ownership (public or private) and/or on the socio-economic status of the owner (e.g. Hope *et al.*, 2003; Law *et al.*, 2004). By contrast, remnant patches such as a forest or wetland patch typically are not managed and will have

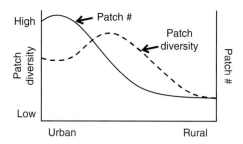

Fig. 20.1. Conceptual relationship of patch diversity and density going from a highly urbanised to rural landscape. Patch density peaks near the urban core while patch diversity peaks at the urban fringe (sensu Burghardt, 1994). Figure used by permission, after J. Russell-Anelli.

characteristics of the native ecosystem, but with significant changes resulting from the effects of the urban environment (Pouyat *et al.*, 1995a; Guntenspergen *et al.*, Chapter 29). In urban landscapes, the immediate surroundings of individual patches are likely to exert a strong influence on biogeochemical cycling, which is due to higher edge-to-interior ratios and thus more open flows of energy, matter and organisms between the patch and adjacent urban matrix (Carreiro *et al.*, Chapter 19).

Based on these observations, it is important to consider and map the arrangement of patches and their relationships with each other in urban landscapes (Forman, 1995). Individual patches can be studied as black boxes with fluxes and cycles of resources that interact with neighbouring patches (Zonneveld, 1989; Grimm *et al.*, 2003). For example, patches within a watershed might function as sources or sinks of nutrients and contaminants and also regulate matter and water flows. Thus, in modelling watersheds hydrologists calculate the inputs of water, nutrients and contaminants to streamflow depending on the cumulative biotic and abiotic attributes of individual patches and their spatial location within a watershed (Black, 1991). In the case of remnant patches such as a forest or wetland, the environmental context of individual patches, whether it be an urban, suburban or rural matrix, can be related to C and N cycling within the patch (Pouyat *et al.*, 1995a).

Urban–rural gradient approach

The gradient approach has been used to investigate effects of urban environmental changes on C and N dynamics in remnant forest patches (McDonnell *et al.*, 1997; Carreiro *et al.*, Chapter 19). The approach is particularly effective as urban environments consist of many factors and effects that otherwise would be difficult to manipulate (Pouyat *et al.*, 1995a). The use of the environmental gradient paradigm to investigate responses of forest ecosystems to urban land-use change was first proposed by McDonnell and Pickett (1990), although the approach had been used earlier by Santas (1986) to study soil organisms. McDonnell and Pickett recognised that complex environmental gradients also may occur when human population densities, human-built structures and human-generated processes vary spatially on a landscape. The environmental gradient paradigm was introduced by Whittaker (1967) as a method for examining and explaining species composition of forest communities along an elevation gradient. Whittaker's assumption was that environmental variation is ordered in space and that the spatial pattern of the environment constrains the structural and functional components of ecosystems (McDonnell and Pickett, 1990). McDonnell and Pickett suggested the term urban–rural land-use gradient to describe environmental gradients in metropolitan areas caused largely by variations in land use (Pickett *et al.*, Chapter 3).

Applying the gradient approach to metropolitan areas

Gradient analysis techniques can either be direct when the underlying environmental factor is ordered linearly in space or indirect when a gradient of underlying factors is organised non-continuously across the landscape (McDonnell *et al.*, 1993). These techniques may require multi-variate statistical approaches when the gradient consists of several environmental factors, some of which may co-vary and interact. For a discussion of the theory of gradient analysis, see Ter Braak and Prentice (1988), and as it is applied to urban–rural gradients, McDonnell *et al.* (1993). Indirect techniques entail measuring ecological system parameters and then ordinating these values to represent the underlying environmental gradient (Whittaker, 1967; Ter Braak and Prentice, 1988). The ordinated response variables, or surrogate variables, are then compared with actual site factors or environmental measurements such as soil type and the availability of soil moisture. These site factors and environmental measurements can then be related to other ecosystem attributes. For example, Brush *et al.* (1980) conducted a gradient analysis of woody vegetation data for the State of Maryland, USA. The authors found a spatial correlation between forest associations (surrogate variables) and soil type (site factors). They concluded that patterns of soil type (soil texture, slope position) were related to water availability, which was ultimately controlling the distribution of woody species in the state.

McDonnell *et al.* (1993) suggested that urban–rural gradients are complex and non-linear, and thus best described by indirect gradient analysis (Pickett *et al.*, Chapter 3). Although measures or indices of urban land cover and land use are easily obtained, often there are few data that describe the spatial variation in environmental factors such as soils that underlie cities and suburbs. As a result, it is difficult to determine how environmental variation interacts with and relates to attributes of the urban ecosystem and diverse human activities. In other words, we do not fully understand how urban environmental factors vary spatially or what causes the spatial pattern – a relationship that is assumed when performing a gradient analysis. Moreover, even if relationships are found, we may not be able to describe the mechanistic links behind a particular response. For example, in describing forest associations in Maryland, Brush *et al.* (1980) understood the relationship between plant species and soil texture, and between soil texture and soil moisture. This was possible because the interrelationship between soil texture and moisture had been well studied, and such soil patterns had been well described at the scale of landscapes and physiographic regions. In urban ecosystems, we lack the knowledge base for making such connections, so before attempts are made to correlate an ecosystem response to a suspected urban environmental gradient, we need to quantify the relationships between human activities, urban features in the landscape and pre-existing (underlying) spatial patterns for environmental variables known to drive the responses of interest.

Landscapes are commonly classified by geographers as urban, suburban or rural/wildland on the basis of socio-economic data and political entities. However, the ecological implications of these classifications remain unclear (McDonnell and Pickett, 1990; Medley *et al.*, 1995; Yang and Zhou, Chapter 16). The following example illustrates this point. Pouyat *et al.* (1995b) measured several soil variables (heavy metals, basic cations, content of soil organic matter, electrical conductivity) in oak forest stands along an urban–rural land-use gradient in the New York metropolitan area. Soil data were submitted to indirect gradient analysis (Principal Component Analysis) in which the scores for the first two principal components of each forest patch were plotted (Fig. 20.2). Using the results of this analysis, we assigned each forest patch to a land-use type (U = urban, SU = suburban and R = rural in Fig. 20.2) based on the criteria of a regional planning agency (Yaro and Hiss, 1996), which used political boundaries (counties) and population density to distinguish urban from suburban and suburban from rural land-use types. Inspection of the groupings with respect to the PC1 axis shows that the suburban and rural forest patches are overlapped, while one of the patches in the urban group is more closely aligned to the suburban patches (Fig. 20.2).

In this example, the qualitative assignment of patches to a land-use type based on planning criteria did not correspond directly to the ordination of plots based on soil criteria, suggesting the need for a more quantitative ecological definition of land use. Indeed, in a review of research using urban–rural land-use gradients,

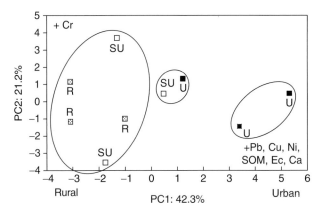

Fig. 20.2. Scatter plot of the first two principal component scores of soil chemical properties measured along an urban–rural land-use gradient in New York metropolitan area. Percentage of variation explained by each component is given on each axis. Each square represents a forest patch ($n = 9$ plots). Land use (U = urban, SU = suburban and R = rural) based on urban planning designations is next to each patch. Solid lines show cluster analysis of quantified geographical features (modified from Pouyat *et al.*, 1995b).

Theobald (2004) identified a lack of quantifiable metrics in the description of human-modified systems in the studies reviewed. For the New York urban–rural land-use gradient, Medley *et al.* (1995) used quantitative metrics such as patch size, traffic volume and population density. In the previous example, the landscape context of each forest patch along the gradient was then quantified by Pouyat *et al.* (1995b) using the Medley measures. Using results of this analysis and for illustrative purposes here, we regrouped the patches (Fig. 20.2, solid lines) and found more clearly defined groupings that corresponded to the ordination of patches better than those defined qualitatively by planners.

Nonetheless, even if a quantitatively defined urban–rural land-use gradient is available, the spatial extent and variation of underlying environmental factors may be poorly understood. To illustrate this point, we again used soil data from the New York urban–rural land-use gradient study. However, this time we used a direct gradient approach to compare relationships between different quantitative measures of urban land use and soil response variables. We first used distance to the urban core (a variable that is easily measured) to serve as a surrogate (and continuous) variable for the extent of urban development and as a predictor of soil characteristics of the urban, suburban and rural forest plots. There was a significant relationship between soil lead (Pb) content and distance from the urban core (Central Park in Manhattan) ($r = 0.677$, $P = 0.05$ using Pearson Correlation). The relationship was even stronger when soil Pb levels were related to traffic volume within an area of $1 km^2$ around each stand ($r = 0.953$, $P = 0.001$ using Pearson Correlation). That soil Pb content was correlated more highly with traffic volume than with distance to the urban core suggests that Pb emissions from automobiles may be more responsible than other Pb sources for the variation in soil Pb contamination along this urban–rural gradient. Moreover, traffic volume may not necessarily be strongly related to distance to the urban core. The use of more quantitative measures of urban development revealed a functional relationship among a site environmental variable (soil Pb content), an urban environmental factor (Pb deposition) and its probable source (automobile exhaust).

This example suggests that when possible, urban gradients should be defined quantitatively using both geographical features, e.g. road density or traffic volume, and environmental factors, e.g. heavy metal deposition. The latter can be substituted with site variables that are related to a particular environmental factor, e.g. content of soil heavy metals, as a temporal integrator and index of atmospheric heavy metal deposition (Table 20.1). Further, using distance to the urban core as a surrogate measure for urban land use may not always be appropriate to describe an underlying environmental gradient (McDonnell and Hahs, Chapter 5). Once these relationships are better understood, additional ecological meaning and explanatory power can be derived from statistical relationships between urban land use and the ecosystem response that is measured. A similar conclusion was reached by plant ecologists, who now recommend submitting environmental variables prior to vegetation variables to plant community ordination analyses (Fralish, 2002).

Another challenge in quantifying urban–rural land-use gradients and the underlying environmental factors associated with such gradients is separating the effect of non-urban and urban environmental factors. For example, soil characteristics of oak/tulip-poplar forests in the Baltimore metropolitan area were measured along an urban–rural land-use gradient (Szlavecz *et al.*, 2006). After correlations among the soil variables were explored using Principal Component Analysis, the plots were labelled according to their land-use context (Fig. 20.3). However, whereas canopy cover was similar among plots, soil type varied because of the variability in surface geology of the region. Thus land-use type is confounded with variation in soil type, so it is unclear whether differences in soil characteristics (and C and N processes) measured along the urban–rural land-use gradient were due to urban environmental factors or natural soil-forming factors (Fig. 20.3).

To increase our ability to separate urban from non-urban effects, Pouyat (1991) suggested using the Factor Approach, a conceptual model first proposed by Jenny (1941) to describe the formation of soil at landscape scales. This approach

Table 20.1. *Potential quantifiable metrics that can be used to define urban–rural land-use gradients.*

Urban features	Environmental factors	Site environment variables	Ecosystem variables (C and N)
Distance	**Atmosphere**	**Soil chemical**	**Primary productivity**
Human population	• Wet/dry deposition	• Heavy metals and other contaminants	**Decomposition**
	• Ozone	• Acidity/alkalinity	**N mineralisation**
• Density	• Carbon dioxide	• Hydrophobicity	**Nitrification**
• Per capita use		• Calcium	**Denitrification**
		• Phosphorus	**Soil respiration**
Human structure	**Climate**	• C:N ratios	**Food web structure**
			Species diversity
• Road density	• Precipitation		**C pools**
• Impervious (%)	• Air temperature UVB radiation	**Soil physical**	**N pools**
• Urban land (%)			**N retention**
• Housing density		• Temperature	
• Density of birdfeeders	**Biological**	• Moisture	
	Non-native	• Infiltration	
	species propagules	• Bulk density	
Human function			
		Biological	
• Traffic volume			
• Energy use		• Seed bank	
• Water use		• Number of species	
• Pollution emissions		• Number of invasive species	
Habitat measures			
• Fragmentation			
• Connectivity			
• Patch size distribution			
• Vegetation structure			
• Disturbance frequency			

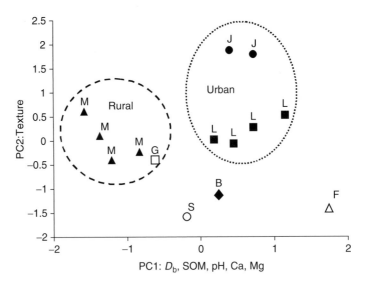

Fig. 20.3. Scatter plots of the first two principal component scores of soil chemical and physical properties measured along an urban–rural land-use gradient in Baltimore metropolitan area. Each symbol represents a forest patch ($n = 3$ plots). Soil type is designated with a capital letter adjacent to each symbol. Forest patches are grouped by either an urban or a rural context (hatched lines). D_b = soil bulk density; SOM = soil organic matter concentration.

posits that soil and ecosystem development is determined by a combination of state factors that include climate (*cl*), organisms (*o*), parent material (*pm*), relief (*r*) and time (*t*), where the characteristics of any given soil (or ecosystem), *S*, are the function $S = f(cl, o, pm, r, t)$. Amundson and Jenny (1991) and Pouyat (1991) proposed that human effects can be incorporated into the factor approach by including a sixth or anthropogenic factor *a*, such that $S = f(a, cl, o, pm, r, t)$. To investigate the relative importance of individual factors, Jenny (1961), Vitousek *et al.* (1983) and Van Cleve *et al.* (1991) identified 'sequences' of soil bodies or ecosystems on landscapes in which a single factor varies while the other factors are held constant, e.g. a chronosequence where age, *t*, is the varying factor. Likewise, Pouyat (1991) and Pouyat and Effland (1999) proposed that urban–rural land-use gradients can create situations in which the anthropogenic factor *a* (in this case, an urban factor) varies for relatively short distances (km) so that it is possible to hold the remaining factors as constant as possible, i.e. an 'anthroposequence', where $S = f(a)_{cl,o,pm,r,t}$. With the Factor Approach, the null hypothesis that there is no detectable difference in the response variable along the urban–rural gradient is essentially predetermined (Pouyat *et al.*, 1995b). Further, a study design that emulates an anthroposequence should a priori account for the potential of confounding urban (*a*) and non-urban (*cl, o, pm, r, t*) factor effects.

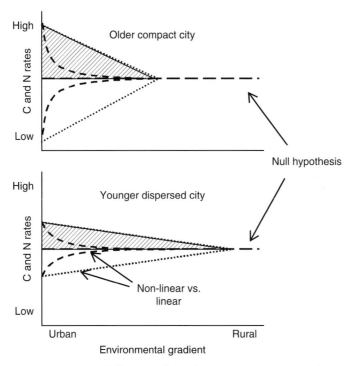

Fig. 20.4. Conceptual diagrams of C and N rate responses to an urban–rural environmental gradient for an old, compact city (top) and young, dispersed city (bottom). Hatched lines under response curves represent stimulation of C and N rates. Null hypothesis is represented by horizontal dashed line, i.e. no change in rates.

Other considerations related to the urban gradient approach

When using the gradient approach to study urban environmental effects on remnant patches, it is important to consider the physical, biological and socio-economic characteristics of the metropolitan area under investigation (Niemelä *et al.*, Chapter 2, Pickett *et al.*, Chapter 3). Consider a suite of potential response curves of C and N measurements in forest patches situated along an urban–rural land-use gradient (Fig 20.4). As stated earlier, the underlying environmental gradient consists of many factors that can affect C and N cycling. These factors are themselves related to the development pattern of the city and its surrounding area, for example population density (effects also separately dependent on aerial extent of the city and total population), dominant commercial activities and age of the city (see McDonnell and Hahs, Chapter 5). In older more compact and industrialised cities, the differences in atmospheric pollution between urban and rural ends of the gradient should be steeper and less linear (with a more abrupt threshold effect evident) than in newer less industrialised cities that have a dispersed development pattern (Fig. 20.4).

Table 20.2. *Comparison of trends in soil characteristics and C and N process rates along urban–rural land-use gradients in three cities that range in population from over 61 607 (Asheville, NC) to 7 420 166 (New York City, NY) inhabitants.*

Population	New York City 7 420 166		Baltimore 645 593		Asheville 61 607	
Soil variable	Rural	Urban	Rural	Urban	Rural	Urban
pH	4.7	4.5	4.6	5.2	4.9	4.9
SOM (g kg^{-1})	75	108	110	90	97	79
Annual temperature (°C)	8.5	12.5	12.8	14.5	11.9	13.0
N-mineralisation (mg N kg^{-1} SDW d^{-1})	4.02	10.3	2.2	8.0	0.11	0.26
Leaf decay (mg d^{-1})	0.0068	0.0113	n.a.	n.a.	0.0012	0.0009

Note:
Modified from Pavao-Zuckerman and Coleman, 2005.

In some cases, both the direction and the magnitude of a variable or biogeo-chemical process can differ along urban–rural land-use gradients in different cities (see litter decay rate, soil pH and organic matter content in Table 20.2 and Carreiro *et al.*, Chapter 19). These results suggest that the net effect of urban environmental factors can stimulate or suppress C and N process rates (Fig. 20.4). In the former case, factors such as N deposition, CO_2 enrichment and temperature increases can increase C and N processing when these factors limit biological activity, which is true for most terrestrial ecosystems. In the latter case, environmental factors such as heavy metals and ozone might constrain biological processes gradually as contamination increases or rapidly after reaching a certain threshold (Fig. 20.4). In either case, the age, dominant commerce and industry, and developmental pattern of the metropolitan area affects the amount of contamination or inputs of C and N and, therefore, the response of C and N processing along an urban environmental gradient (Carreiro *et al.*, Chapter 19).

Another consideration in using the gradient paradigm is the difficulty encountered in determining the underlying mechanisms when a property is correlated with a particular environmental gradient (Vitousek and Matson, 1991). Because many factors underlie an existing environmental gradient, the gradient paradigm can only suggest possible explanations, and the patterns within a particular system may not be valid for other systems (Duarte, 1991). Obviously, the inability of the gradient approach to attribute cause to a gradient correlate is a disadvantage, although one can identify the relative importance of environmental factors and the measured range in which those factors occur in the field. Once identified, the effect of individual factors can be verified and the mechanism of the response can be tested in field and laboratory experiments.

Assessing relationships between environmental factors and ecosystem responses along urban gradients is clearly a complex task. However, not only are these relationships difficult to uncover but they can also lead to erroneous conclusions if field observations are not combined with experimental approaches. Again, we use the New York urban gradient study as an example. In measuring the decay of red oak leaf litter in laboratory incubations, Carreiro *et al.* (1999) found that litter collected in urban forest remnants decayed more slowly than suburban litter, which, in turn, decayed more slowly than rural litter. The authors attributed the differences in decay to intraspecific differences in leaf-litter quality; the urban litter had the poorest quality. Later, oak litter incubating in forest remnants of origin showed that decay rates did not differ statistically across the gradient even though urban litter quality was demonstrably lower in the laboratory assays (Pouyat and Carreiro, 2003). A simple manipulation – exchanging bags of rural and urban litter – showed that warmer temperatures and the presence of invasive earthworm species in the urban plots were likely to compensate for lower quality of urban litter (Pouyat and Carreiro, 2003). The use of field and laboratory studies in combination provided greater explanatory power than otherwise would have been possible.

Finally, the previous example suggests the importance of invasive species in the processing of C and N in ecosystems. Indeed, urban land-use change can modify native habitats and thus elevate indigenous species extinction rates while increasing invasions of non-native species (McKinney, 2002). As a result, the combination of these effects has created a pattern in which native species richness decreases from outlying rural areas to urban centres while invasive species richness increases (Blair, 2001). Since invasive species can play a disproportionate role in controlling C and N cycles in terrestrial ecosystems (see Ehrenfeld, 2003; Bohlen *et al.*, 2004), the relationship between invasive species abundances and habitat change along urban–rural land-use gradients has important implications for the biogeochemical cycling of C and N.

Patch dynamic and watershed approaches

In non-urban ecosystems, spatial heterogeneity can help or hinder the flow of materials and energy across boundaries, affecting biogeochemical cycles within particular patches and across the entire landscape (Gosz, 1991). Patch dynamics treats spatial heterogeneity at any scale as a mosaic whose elements and overall configuration can shift through time. This concept is an important organising principle in ecology and has contributed to the elucidation of the role of spatial control in ecological systems (Wu and Loucks, 1995; Cadenasso *et al.*, 2006). For example, patch dynamics has been cited in explanations for long-term variations in nutrient cycling in forested ecosystems (Likens and Bormann, 1995), and, more recently, in the biogeochemical cycling of nutrients and contaminants in urban landscapes (Pickett *et al.*, 1997b; Grimm *et al.*, 2000; Pickett *et al.*, Chapter 3).

How patches function and interrelate are important questions in urban ecology (Grimm and Redman, 2004). Urban landscapes are more complex than natural landscapes and the importance of human activities makes it difficult to predict their interactive effects on ecosystem processes and structure. If we are to understand biogeochemical cycles in urban ecosystems we must integrate human behaviour and socio-economic factors with ecological factors. Although social heterogeneity is not addressed in this chapter, Pickett *et al.* (1997b; 2001) discussed this topic in detail. They concluded that in urban landscapes, the heterogeneity of both social and natural components can be organised hierarchically around drainage patterns. Thus, the watershed approach is an important tool in assessing the interaction of these components.

Baltimore LTER: using landscape heterogeneity as an asset

Environmental patchiness can be studied at various spatial scales (Wu and Loucks, 1995). In the Baltimore Long-Term Ecological Research (LTER) site, a hierarchical study design is being used to test the hypothesis that ecological and socio-economic heterogeneity operating at different scales affects biogeochemical cycles in urban ecosystems (Pickett *et al.*, Chapter 3). In this study, patches were delineated by their land use and cover and were organised using a nested hierarchy of increasingly larger hydrologic units and watersheds (Pickett *et al.*, 1997b, 2001). Each watershed and their arrangement of different patches were used as whole-ecosystem studies to compare within-patch C and N pools and fluxes among different patch and watershed units at different scales (Table 20.3).

To establish a hierarchical study design, a network of watershed monitoring stations was located within the 17 150-ha Gwynns Falls watershed. The network traversed a gradient in land use from the highly urban core of Baltimore City, through older high-density residential areas, to medium-density single attached houses in the middle reaches, and finally to the rapidly urbanising headwaters of Baltimore County (Doheny, 1999). As part of the network, longitudinal main channel sites were established that represented different land-use boundary zones along the Gwynns Falls. The smallest watersheds selected for monitoring in the network (<100 ha) were predominately of a single land-use type, e.g. high- or low-density residential, forest, or agriculture. Thus, differences in socio-economic factors, land use and cover among the smaller watersheds in

Table 20.3. *Nested hierarchical study design of the Baltimore LTER. Patches are delineated and classified by their land use, cover, built structures, and land management activities and organised using a nested hierarchy of increasingly larger hydrologic units and watersheds.*

Hydrologic hierarchy	Size in area (ha)	Classification system	Minimum patch size	Patch comparisons
Regional watershed	>50 000	Anderson II	15 ha	Land use/cover
Watershed	17 125	Anderson III, HERCULES[a]	4 ha	Land use/cover Vegetation, built structures and surfaces
Sub watershed	100–2500	Anderson III, HERCULES	0.5–4 ha	Land use/cover Vegetation, built structures and surfaces
Small watershed	<100	HERCULES, Ecotope Level I[b]	0.5 ha 25–100 m^2	Vegetation, built structures and surfaces Landscape features, cover/management
Neighbourhood catchment	<10	Ecotope Level I	25–100 m^2	Landscape features, cover/management
Stream reach/ hillslope, city block	<1	Ecotope Level II[b]	8 m^2	Land management, cover

Notes:

[a] Cadenasso *et al.* (2006).

[b] Ellis *et al.* (2006).

the hierarchy were used to set up comparisons much like the gradient analysis of remnant forest patches described earlier. These comparisons or 'natural experiments' substitute for the large-scale manipulations that have been used on small watersheds at other LTER sites (Bormann and Likens, 1979; Hornbeck and Swank, 1992). As a result, the monitoring of small watersheds has allowed comparisons with other LTER sites and more detailed analysis of input–output mass balance than those of larger watersheds of mixed uses (Groffman *et al.*, 2004).

Unlike the more homogeneous small watersheds, larger watersheds (>100 ha) in the hierarchy have mixed uses, so it is more difficult to connect outflows and nutrient loads to a particular land-use or patch type. For these watersheds, patch structure and function has been investigated using the variable source area approach to model watershed hydrology and nutrient dynamics (Band *et al.*, 2000; 2001). The net effect of patches of varying composition, management regimes and site histories can be estimated with variable source area approaches by modelling how the attributes of different patches cycle or contribute water, nutrients and contaminants depending on their location in the watershed (Black, 1991). Moreover, sensitivity analyses can be conducted in different modelling runs to determine how varying patch compositions and configurations affect quantitative and qualitative inputs to streams.

In addition to modelling, a network of 'intensive' and 'extensive' plots was established in representative patch types to capture the range of spatial and temporal conditions within each watershed in the hierarchy. The goals were to measure ecosystem response variables over time and conduct whole-ecosystem analyses in a representative patch type. The intensive plot measurements are important for calibrating models, developing mass-balance budgets and measuring ecosystem responses to stochastic events and climate fluctuations (Groffman *et al.*, 2006). Intensive plots require a high commitment of resources and time for sampling, so only a limited number have been established. By contrast, larger numbers of extensive plots are sampled intermittently to assess spatial variation in several ecosystem response variables in the metropolitan region, e.g. plant productivity (Nowak *et al.*, 2003) and soil chemistry (Pouyat *et al.*, 2007b).

Developing functional characterisations of patch structure that are ecologically based is important for identifying representative plots in different patch types and for aggregating C and N mass-balance measurements for a specified watershed or other ecologically bounded area. Until now, the location of extensive plots has been stratified according to Anderson land-use categories (Anderson *et al.*, 1976). However, new land-cover classification systems with higher categorical resolution are being developed to improve the stratification of plots primarily for highly heterogonous urban mosaics (Ellis *et al.*, 2006; Cadenasso *et al.*, 2007; Table 20.3).

Patch comparisons

The nested hierarchical design has allowed comparisons of C and N cycling processes of different patch types at different spatial and temporal scales. Measurements of trace-gas fluxes and nitrogen-cycling variables on our intensive plots revealed temporal variation in natural processes as well as spatial variation caused by land-use change. For example, *in situ* measurements of net N mineralisation and nitrification on our intensive forest plots showed that the magnitude and annual variation of natural fluxes are much higher than many anthropogenic fluxes. Net nitrification (a natural source of nitrate) ranged from approximately 5 to 15 kg N ha^{-1} yr^{-1}, equal in magnitude to atmospheric deposition and fertilisation fluxes in our watersheds (Table 20.4). Comparison of

Table 20.4. *Nitrogen budget input–output analysis (kg/ha per year) for a suburban and a forested watershed (<100 ha) in the Baltimore LTER study.*

	Suburban	Forest
Inputs		
Atmosphere	11.2	11.2
Fertiliser	14.4	0
Total	25.6	11.2
Outputs		
Stream flow	6.5	0.52
Retention		
Mass	19.1	10.7
Percentage	75	95

Note:

Adapted from Groffman *et al.* (2004).

grass and forest intensive plots has shown that grass areas have surprisingly high N retention and moderate leaching losses, which are likely to be due to an active carbon cycle (indexed by high total soil respiration) maintained by the young, actively growing grass (Pouyat *et al.*, 2007a).

Unlike the intensive plots, results from the extensive plots provide one-time measures of soil characteristics, C and N cycling, and vegetation structure. However, using a hierarchical classification system to stratify plots made it possible to compare among and within patch classes at different scales. For example, a network of 200 extensive plots was stratified by the relatively coarse scale Anderson Level II land-use and cover classes within Baltimore City (Anderson *et al.*, 1976; Table 20.3). The plots were sampled for vegetation structure and soil over 2 years (Nowak *et al.*, 2003; Pouyat *et al.*, 2007b). There was a wide range in soil characteristics among all plots, although a subset of the variables measured (P, K, bulk density and pH) showed a discernible and coherent pattern with Anderson land-use classes. Differences were greatest between land-use types characterised by intensive land management (lawns) and the absence of management (forests). In particular, concentrations of P and K, which are in most lawn fertilisers, differentiated the most between forest and grass cover (Pouyat *et al.*, 2007b).

In separate studies, N-transformation rates were measured on a subset of the extensive plots. For illustrative purposes, we compare potential nitrification rates among Anderson land-use classes (P. Groffman, C. Williams, R. Pouyat and I. Yesilonis, unpublished data) with results from remnant forest patches along an urban gradient in the Baltimore metropolitan area (Szlavecz *et al.*, 2006).

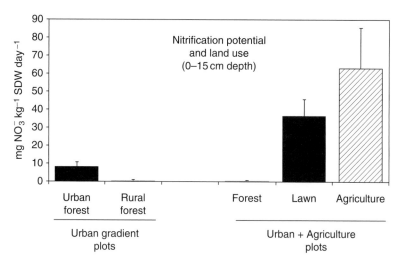

Fig. 20.5. Mean ($\pm$ standard error) of potential net nitrification rates (mg NO_3^- kg^{-1} day^{-1}) of mineral soil samples of forest, lawn and agricultural plots in the Baltimore LTER study. Bars on left represent comparison of urban ($n = 9$) and rural ($n = 9$) forest patches. Bars on right represent comparison of forest, lawn and agriculture land-use types ($n = 14$, 10 and 10, respectively). SDW = soil dry weight. Data from P. Groffman, C. Williams, R. Pouyat and I. Yesilonis (unpublished) and Szlavecz *et al.* (2006).

Differences were much higher among land-use types than between urban and rural forest patches (Fig. 20.5). These results suggest that soil management associated with different land uses has a much greater effect on C and N cycling than abiotic environmental variables that are altered in the Baltimore metropolitan area, such as the heat island effect and deposition of atmospheric pollutants.

Because of the wide distribution of a relatively large number of plots, it was possible to reclassify the extensive plots using criteria other than Anderson land-use classes. For the soil results cited, plots were reclassified by surface geology and parent material since they should have an important influence on initial soil element contents. The reclassification revealed that a subset of the variables measured, primarily Al, Mg, V, Mn, Fe, Ni and soil texture, were strongly related to the presence of a specific rock type in the region (Pouyat *et al.*, 2007b). These results suggest that natural soil-forming factors, parent material in this case, were more important than Anderson land-use classes in determining the spatial pattern of these elements in the Baltimore City landscape. However, at this coarse scale, the variation of some factors, e.g. Pb, was not explained by land use or surface geology, suggesting that spatial variation of certain characteristics is controlled by other factors operating at finer scales.

In using the extensive network of plots, it was possible to separate natural from urban influences on spatial variation of factors that determine rates of

Table 20.5. *Carbon storage and sequestration (±SE) in aboveground biomass of Baltimore City.*

Land use	Storage (t C)	(t C ha^{-1})	Sequestration (t C yr^{-1})
Forest	124 576 (25 250)	73 (15)	3009 (489)
Medium density residential	139 129 (27 272)	33 (7)	4195 (653)
High density residential	119 321 (31 811)	20 (5)	3423 (670)
Urban open	89 992 (29 734)	60 (20)	2052 (670)
Commercial/industrial	63 665 (34 625)	13 (7)	1862 (1204)
Institutional	29 223 (25 168)	16 (14)	814 (655)
Transportation	4792 (3931)	8 (7)	170 (121)
Barren	83 (82)	1 (0.4)	5 (5)
Total city	570 781	224	15 529

Source: Calculated using the UFORE model (Nowak and Crane, 2000). Data used to run UFORE model from Nowak *et al.* (2003).

C and N cycling processes and other soil characteristics, at least at the scale of the classification categories used. The designation of patches into specific classes within a hierarchical system also allowed like classes to be aggregated into a watershed or other bounded area, whether ecologically or politically defined. For example, vegetation data collected in the extensive plots were used to estimate the amount of C stored (± standard error) in aboveground biomass for Baltimore City using the UFORE model (Nowak and Crane, 2000). UFORE calculates the amount of C stored at the plot scale and then aggregates to the city or regional scale using a hierarchical classification system (Table 20.5). In a similar fashion, belowground storage of soil organic C was estimated using the extensive plot data (Pouyat *et al.*, 2006).

We also can delineate patches with higher categorical resolution and make comparisons at the finer scale of a neighbourhood or small watershed (<100 ha). At this scale, measurements can be related to patches with specific site histories and activities of individual land managers (Pouyat *et al.*, 2007a). In turn these can be compared with ecosystem-level measurements such as small watershed hydrological outflows like those mentioned previously, or above-canopy CO_2 fluxes from a tower. In two suburban neighbourhoods in the Baltimore metropolitan area, patches have been delineated using high-resolution ecotope mapping (Ellis *et al.*, 2000; Ellis, 2004). Preliminary results suggest that socio-economic factors, lot size, and age of the housing development are important explanatory variables for soil variables at this scale (Law *et al.*, 2004; Fig. 20.6).

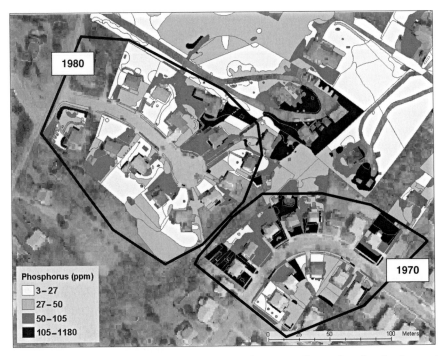

Fig. 20.6. Map of phosphorus (P) concentration ranges for two housing developments in the Cub Hill neighbourhood of Baltimore County. Developments differ by age (1980 upper left and 1970 lower right). Concentrations of P in lawns were significantly higher ($P < 0.01$) in the 1970 ($n = 11$) than the 1980 ($n = 13$) subdivision (J. Russell-Anelli, I. Yesilonis and R. Pouyat, unpublished data).

Whole-ecosystem comparisons

Our long-term watershed monitoring has enabled us to compare outflows of small watersheds dominated by different land uses. Results show that N exports are higher from urban watersheds than from forest watersheds, but lower from agriculture watersheds (Groffman *et al.*, 2004). That these exports were not markedly variable was surprising given the high spatial heterogeneity of these watersheds. Also, our low-density residential watershed (Baismans Run, >100 ha) is served by septic systems and has relatively high nitrate concentrations. This was unexpected given that nearly 75% of its area is forested and our 'reference' forested watershed (Pond Branch) is nested within it and had the lowest concentrations of our monitored watersheds (Fig. 20.7). These results suggest that septic systems can add high concentrations of nitrate directly to groundwater (Gold *et al.*, 1990). The nitrate in our other residential watersheds is likely to have originated from contamination from sanitary sewer systems because the households in these watersheds always have been connected to the sanitary sewer system.

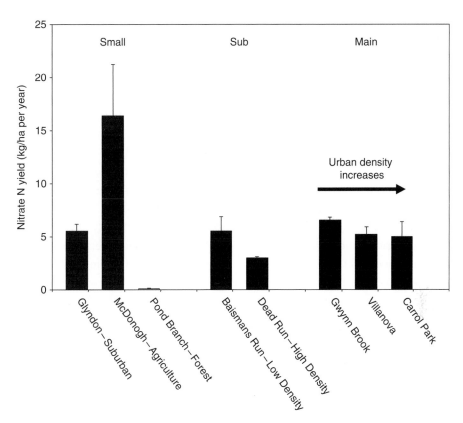

Fig. 20.7. Mean (± standard error) nitrate N yields (kg per ha per year) for three water years of small, sub, and main channel catchments of the Gwynns Falls watershed. Small catchments are dominated by suburban (Glyndon), agriculture (McDonogh) and forested (Pond Branch) land uses. Sub and main channel catchments have mixed land uses. Modified from Groffman *et al.* (2004).

The watershed mass-balance approach also allowed us to calculate the retention of N in individual watersheds. For example, N budget input–output analysis showed that retention of N in a suburban watershed (<100 ha) was surprisingly high compared with our reference forested watershed (Table 20.4). These analyses have raised questions about unique sources and sinks for N in urban and suburban watersheds, including residential lawns, leaky sewers, riparian zones, stream features such as organic debris dams, and stormwater detention basins (Groffman and Crawford, 2003; Groffman *et al.*, 2004), which we are addressing in ongoing research.

Concluding remarks

To date, our use of the gradient, patch dynamic and watershed approaches in studies of C and N cycling in urban ecosystems has produced useful and informative results, but additional research is needed before we can integrate these cycles with the behaviour of humans and the built environment. Moreover, there are only a few comprehensive, whole-ecosystem analyses of urban ecosystems worldwide from which comparisons can be made (Grimm *et al.*, 2000; Heinz Centre, 2002). As a result, we do not know whether we can generalise from these few comprehensive studies, especially with respect to the array of urban-development patterns, cultural differences and economies of cities around the world (McDonnell and Hahs, Chapter 5). The number of urban study sites worldwide needs to be greatly expanded to include the entire range of cities and human settlements, regardless of the approach taken, although we suggest combining all three approaches where possible.

A good example of a cross-system comparison is GLOBENET (Global Network for Monitoring Landscape Change), which compares carabid beetle populations along urban–rural land-use gradients throughout the world (Niemelä *et al.*, 2002; Chapter 2). Comparisons of urban–rural gradients among a suite of metropolitan areas allows for region-by-region assessments of changes in the composition of native species, the importance of specific urban environmental factors, and the net effect (native versus urban ecosystem) of these changes. These comparisons can be enhanced by adopting standardised methods (e.g. Robertson *et al.*, 1999; Niemelä *et al.*, 2002), quantifying the environmental gradient of each metropolitan area (e.g. Table 20.1) and 'normalising' the response data to calculate the environmental effect of urban land-use change for a particular gradient analysis (sensu Seastedt, 1984; Tian, 1998).

Similar to comparisons of urban–rural land-use gradient studies, comparisons of budgets of C and N of small watersheds across different cities have been useful. Of particular interest is the retention of N, which has generated a series of studies of unique urban N sources (leaky sewers, lawns, septic systems, degraded riparian zones) and sinks (in-stream processes, lawns, stormwater detention basins). We suggest a long-term iterative process using monitoring, modelling and experimental approaches to increase our understanding of complex urban watershed ecosystems (Carpenter, 1998; McCarthy, Chapter 7). In so doing, we will continue to monitor our streams, develop models and take advantage of natural climatic variation and human actions, e.g. a major upgrade of the sanitary sewer system in Baltimore.

By combining gradient and patch dynamic approaches with the existing watershed approach to ecosystem analysis, we have been able to take advantage of the inherent heterogeneity of urban landscapes to answer questions related to the effects of land-use change on biogeochemical cycles. The combined use of these approaches also has enabled us to conduct natural experiments that can substitute for large-scale manipulations such as the deforestation manipulations accomplished at the Hubbard Brook LTER. These approaches allow integration with the human socio-economic domain. With increasing populations of people living in urban areas worldwide, and with more cities continuing to expand in number and size, the importance of studies aimed at understanding the global and local ecological aspects of urban ecosystems will continue to increase.

Part III   INTEGRATING SCIENCE WITH
MANAGEMENT AND PLANNING

21

Structural analysis of urban landscapes for landscape management in German cities

JÜRGEN H. BREUSTE

Urban landscape: general characteristics and tendencies

Urbanisation is one of the most important processes changing the landscapes of our planet. Worldwide, urbanised landscapes are growing rapidly. Even in Europe where this process is not very fast, urban landscapes today cover a great deal of former agricultural and forest landscapes in the surroundings of cities and towns, creating a patchwork of large, often connected areas. Between areas with a strong urban influence, cultivated landscapes under modern agricultural use are often found. The interface of these two landscape types is an area of conflict between continued agricultural use and development pressure to expand the urban landscape. Therefore, urban landscapes cannot be reduced to the limits and administrative borders of existing towns and cities, but include a zone approximately 10 kilometres wide surrounding cities or towns – the suburban zone (Breuste, 1996). Figure 21.1 shows the distribution of urban landscapes in Germany where the daily total growth rate of urban land-use forms (settlements and traffic areas) is very high – 70.4 ha per day.

Urban landscapes consist of a mixture of land-use forms which can be divided into built areas, such as residential estates or industrial areas, and cultivated areas, such as the remains of former agricultural and forest landscapes. It is not easy to compare patterns and processes between different urban landscapes because they differ in the density of built-up areas, the composition of the land-use mixture

Ecology of Cities and Towns: A Comparative Approach, ed. Mark J. McDonnell, Amy K. Hahs and Jürgen H. Breuste. Published by Cambridge University Press. © Cambridge University Press 2009.

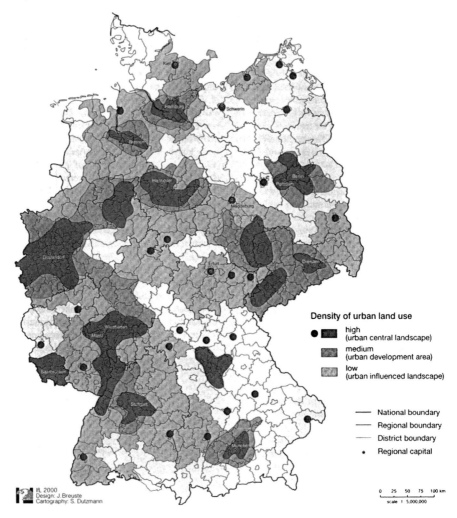

Density of urban land use

● ▨ high
(urban central landscape)

▨ medium
(urban development area)

▨ low
(urban influenced landscape)

—— National boundary
—— Regional boundary
—— District boundary
● Regional capital

IfL 2000
Design: J. Breuste
Cartography: S. Dutzmann

0 25 50 75 100 km
scale 1 : 5,000,000

Fig. 21.1. Map of urban landscapes in Germany (Breuste *et al.*, 2002).

and the nature of the pre-existing landscape (Breuste, 1995). The various forms of land use are located where the development conditions are optimal under specific time and financial constraints. In this regard, an urban landscape is an economically optimised landscape in that it is created to work effectively and properly in its parts – the different land-use forms – but not as a whole landscape (Sieverts, 1998a, b). This means that urban landscapes present various problems, including insufficient living conditions for many people, denaturalisation, pollution of water and air, and the decrease of indigenous plants and animals and their replacement by invasive organisms from other regions of the world.

The transformation of landscapes is not new and is not necessarily a 'dangerous' process. Transformations have taken place throughout history, but currently they are more rapid than in earlier decades and more concentrated and visible within urban landscapes (Sieverts, 1988b). To manage urban landscapes and the transition from agriculture and forestry to urban use, we need to understand the drivers of urban growth, the consequences of landscape change, and the best way to approach these transformations (Niemelä *et al.*, Chapter 2; Chapman and Underwood, Chapter 4).

One force driving urban growth in developed countries in Europe is the concentration of economic power and efficiency of organisation (e.g. education and communication). Although this process is not new, the largely unlimited and widespread use of automobiles has accentuated the process, with land occupation occurring faster and over larger spatial scales than 50 years ago (Mäding, 1997; Hesse and Schmitz, 1998). This increased mobility allows people to live in residential areas 10–20 kilometres away from their workplace, to take advantage of environments near forests, lakes and rivers that are more natural than would have been possible in the central city. So the city grows, and indigenous vegetation, often the only remains in a highly cultivated landscape, comes under increased development pressure for building and recreation purposes (Löfvenhaft, Chapter 24; Mörtberg, Chapter 25). To increase our understanding of how urban development is changing the ecological conditions of the landscape, research is needed to investigate both the patterns and processes that characterise urban landscapes. Of particular research interest, as previously described by Breuste (1996), are investigations of:

- land use as an indicator of urbanisation;
- structural characteristics of land use within urban landscapes;
- influence of different biomes, natural landscapes, etc., on urban development;
- urbanisation as a landscape-changing process;
- speed of urbanisation;
- duration and intensity of changes.

This chapter will address some of these questions, particularly land use as an indicator of urbanisation, and will outline an improved method for investigating the structure and function of landscape elements in urban areas. To place these questions into context, it is important to understand why there is a demand for urban landscape management, and therefore to understand the type and scale of information required to direct management decisions (see also Snep *et al.*, Chapter 26).

History and current demands of urban landscape management

The landscape is a mosaic of structures covering the Earth's surface. The patterns within landscapes are the result of numerous interacting factors, and areas are in a constant state of change (Neef, 1967). Dominant factors of influence can be determined, pattern can be recognised, comparisons of landscapes can be made and landscapes can be managed as parts or as a whole. After dominant characteristics have been determined (e.g. agrarian landscapes, high mountain landscapes, post-mining landscapes) they can form the framework for investigations, evaluations or planning. This viewpoint was recently transferred to urban landscapes following a rising demand for improved environmental conditions in cities, reduced human impacts and the protection of existing intact natural structures (nature protection), and after recognising the need for complex environmental or landscape management.

In the 1970s, there was rising social awareness of the value of nature in the city and the realisation that extensive losses had already taken place. Spatial planning authorities in Central Europe (and elsewhere) came under pressure from public and political opinion and were required to achieve clear improvements in the environmental management of cities and to act as moderators in the reconciliation of the different interest groups. Politicians and planners were requested to react. A methodological framework was needed for the protection of nature in cities. In Bavaria, they adapted the 'Kartierung schutzwürdiger Biotope in Bayern' (mapping of habitats in need of protection in Bavaria; Kaule, 1975) to create this framework. Planning departments began to conduct comprehensive surveys of the urban landscape and surrounding countryside. These surveys involve broad-scale spatial analyses of landscape components, particularly by remote sensing and GIS, in conjunction with detailed investigations of the condition and interrelationships of the individual elements of the urban ecosystem (e.g. plant communities, climate conditions, soils). Similar frameworks were implemented in nearly all other federal states of the Federal Republic of Germany in the following 10 years (1975–1985), and habitat mapping became the most important means for fulfilling the requirements outlined by the new Federal Nature Protection Law in Germany (Fig. 21.2). The central goals of the law were the protection of species and scenic (landscape) values as well as landscape functions. This often reduced the protection to very specific elements of the urban landscapes, such as wetlands or flood plain forests (Breuste, 2001).

By focusing nature protection on a small subset of the entire urban landscape, there was a tendency for selectively mapping 'habitats valuable for protection' (Brunner et al., 1979; Müller and Waldert, 1981), rather than obtaining a complete overview of the landscape. Over time, the understanding of nature protection was extended to include goals such as recreation, environmental education, production of fruits, vegetables and ornamental plants, ecological processes and landscape functions, and scientific research (Sukopp and Weiler, 1986). Nature protection in cities and towns had to change from primarily protecting

The 11 nature protection areas (local names)

1 Hohenweidener Holz
2 Beesener Holz / Teiche
   nördl. u. südl. von Planena
3 Reidebachniederung von
   Reideburg bis zur Mündung
4 Rabeninsel
5 Forstwerder
6 Götschemündung / Saalealtarm
   am Tafelwerder
7 Osendorfer See
8 Tagebaurestgewässer südl. Dieselstr.
9 Steinbrüche und Porphyrkuppen Siedlung Neuaufbau Dölau
10 Ehemalige Kiesgrube Kröllwitz
11 Fuchsberg Kröllwitz

Fig. 21.2. Protected areas of the territory of the city of Halle, Germany, showing wetlands, floodplain forests and other forests (Stadt Halle, 1994).

threatened plants and animals to a broader remit that could incorporate additional aspects of the urban landscape. The current aim of urban nature protection is to maintain organisms and biocoenoses (i.e. ecosystems) because this is where urban dwellers can come into direct contact with natural environmental elements (Sukopp *et al.*, 1980; Sukopp and Weiler, 1986; Sukopp and Trepl, 1990). Floristic and vegetation-science-based surveys of the urban landscape began with the initial goal of using easily recognised homogeneous areas as the basic landscape components for investigation (Kunick, 1978; Sukopp *et al.*, 1979b).

In 1986, habitat mapping on the basis of land use became the standard method for mapping the habitat of urban landscapes; this programme was revised in 1993 (Arbeitsgruppe Methodik der Biotopkartierung im besiedelten Bereich [Working Group for Biotope Mapping in Developed Areas], 1986, 1993).

Between 1978 and 1986 urban habitat mapping using land use as the basic component had become the most widely accepted approach underpinning urban nature conservation in Europe (Breuste, 2001).

With the increase of urban ecological research, information was emerging on the ecological conditions within the urban ecosystem. Much of the early research was based on the premise that land use is the most important process influencing plants, animals and their communities.

Sukopp et al. (1980) describe the specific ecological conditions of urban landscapes as depending primarily on the forms of land use, which in turn influence the pattern and distribution of organisms. They believe that to protect nature in the city, it is important to analyse systematically the most important types of land use and characterise their species content and ecological characteristics. Those land-use forms that support low species diversity and require management actions for the re-establishment of nature can then be clearly identified (Sukopp et al., 1980).

Following from this idea, land use became the key tool for undertaking applied urban ecological research and urban nature conservation. An entire field of pure and applied research was developed that involved urban habitat mapping, and the research relied heavily on the concepts of 'land-use types' or 'urban structural types' to create a hierarchical classification system. This enabled structural units in urban landscapes to be used as reference content in urban ecology in the 1970s and 1980s. Classification systems were developed and recommended for a broad, comparative use in urban and non-urban nature protection (Arbeitsgruppe Methodik der Biotopkartierung im besiedelten Bereich, 1986, 1993). Land-use types were initially used as ecological units without detailed investigations into the way that human usage affected natural ecosystems and without including available scientific information from landscape research.

Several European countries, and Germany in particular, have taken a leading role in ecological investigation, and application of its results in spatial planning (Löfvenhaft, Chapter 24; Mörtberg, Chapter 25). Pioneering urban ecological research conducted by the Sukopp-School in (West) Berlin in the 1970s rapidly developed and expanded to other German cities over the following 10 years. Accompanying this development was an increasing need to develop spatial models that were suitable for the application of the scientific results, and at the same time would contribute to the practice of environmental management. These spatial models had to balance differences in the environmental conditions (soil, water regime, climate, vegetation, etc.) and their relationships with existing processes in the area. The models also had to be compatible with the spatial planning of the cities which is based primarily on land-use structures (e.g. commercial, residential and open space development).

In spatial models, efficiency of data collection must be balanced against the need for a dataset covering all components of the urban landscape. Owing to the enormous temporal and financial expense of collecting detailed information in larger cities, the determination of 'ecological landscape types' can be helpful in urban environmental management. Ecological landscape types are defined by specific combinations of the soil, vegetation and climatic conditions (etc.) within a defined area. As these types have well-defined physical characteristics, it is possible to deduct general functional aspects of the landscape conditions on this level. However, to begin to define ecological landscape types, it was necessary to develop an adaptable assessment method based on specific criteria, which must be assessed along with models of the urban landscape from the viewpoint of spatial planning.

To summarise, for spatial models to provide useful information for landscape management, they must have the following characteristics:

- completeness of the spatial overview;
- fast and cost-effective collection of the data;
- illustration of interrelations of several environmental elements;
- ability to complement other spatial planning instruments;
- link into the hierarchy system of spatial planning;
- compatibility with land-use structures;
- development and use of assessment methods.

The following conditions help these models achieve the above requirements:

- environmental data collected on the same scale as land use;
- development of landscape types as typical structure and process combinations;
- ability to define spatial units in different hierarchical levels;
- ability of the model to evaluate data in its spatial relation;
- development of assessment systems, using limits of the regeneration ability of the ecological systems or/and the conditions of a healthy environment;
- flexible, simple and transferable models;
- spatial models consisting of analysis, spatial structure, assessment system and recommendations for management.

Given the demand for the management of urban landscapes, these areas could no longer be seen as extraordinary edge features of agrarian-forestry cultural landscapes, but had to be accepted as special, dynamically growing cultural landscapes, which must be treated as landscapes in their own right. This shifted urban landscapes from an 'extraordinary position' in the 1970s into a central position of interest to landscape planning. A complex, independent discipline – urban ecology – was developed to investigate the ecological conditions of urban landscapes and their application in planning (Breuste, 2001; Niemelä *et al.*, Chapter 2; Pickett *et al.*, Chapter 3; Snep *et al.*, Chapter 26).

Methods for investigating urban landscape structure

Good management of urban systems requires an understanding of the nature of the different landscape components, how their features influence the processes within the area, and how the components interact to modify the influences or even create new ones. This section will outline two of the current approaches to investigating the urban landscape, and a third method for describing landscape components which incorporates pattern and process.

Land use: basic information on how humans influence ecosystems

Landscape components are currently described using the terms 'land cover' or 'land use'. These terms are often used interchangeably, but this is incorrect as they represent fundamentally different aspects of the landscape. Land cover describes the physical attributes of the space (i.e. the existing material elements), whereas land use describes how this space is being used by humans (i.e. what it is currently used for). Given the fundamental difference between these two terms, it is important to define clearly which term is being used, and the reason for using it (see also Yang and Zhou, Chapter 16). Clear definitions are particularly important for comparative work in order to reduce communication problems, especially in the face of a wide variety of additional terms (land-structure, actual use, spatial use, etc.). For the purpose of this chapter, land use will be the main term used to define landscape components, as this term encapsulates more of the social processes occurring in urban landscapes, and therefore can provide greater insight into the social drivers that determine landscape structure and pattern.

'The utilisation of technical (e.g., agriculture, forestry, settlement) and natural conditions of the environment by humans at the level of the individual, group or society determines how space/land is ultimately used.' Utilisation or land use is not a condition, but a process. The available space can be subject to several requirements at the same time – multi-functional (targeting) utilisation. Because land use relates to procedures, there is also a temporal dimension composed of retrospective land use (history) and projected land use in planning (e.g. masterplan). The complex term land use covers very different things such as using open spaces or building use. However, there are general patterns of use that make it possible to classify general land-use types. Land use varies over time

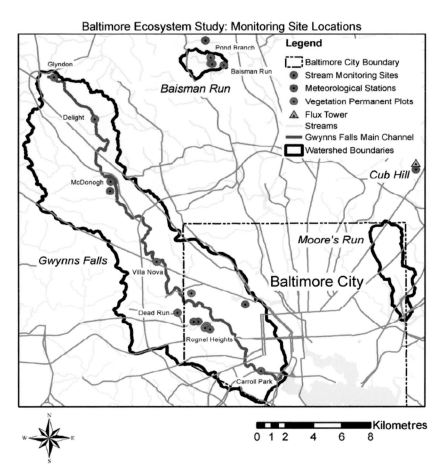

Plate 3.5. Sampling sites for the Baltimore Ecosystem Study, based on major watersheds. Watersheds are used as integrators, and reflect different degrees of urbanisation. The Baisman Run watershed contains Pond Branch, which serves as a forested reference for the project. Different kinds of sampling plots or facilities are identified across the urban landscape.

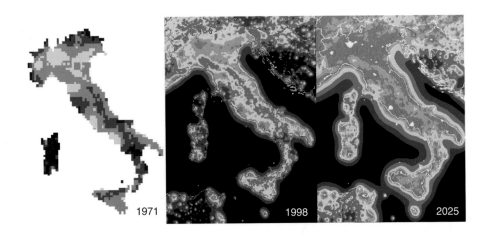

Map 1971		Map 1998		Map 2025	
<0.05	black	<0.11	black	<0.11	black
0.06–0.15	grey	0.11–0.33	blue	0.11–0.33	blue
0.16–0.35	blue	0.33–1.0	green	0.33–1.0	green
0.36–1.1	green	1–3	yellow	1–3	yellow
>1.1	yellow	3–9	orange	3–9	orange
		>9	red	9–27	red
				27–81	violet
				>81	white

Plate 15.2. Maps showing artificial sky brightness in Italy according to Cinzano *et al.* (2000b). The artificial sky brightness is given as the increase above a reference natural sky brightness of 8.61×10^{-7} V phot cm^{-2} s^{-1} sr^{-1} (photons in the visual spectral range), corresponding approximately to 252 μcd m^{-2} or 21.6 V mag arcsec^{-2} (astronomical visual magnitude). The higher the value, the greater the artificial brightness.

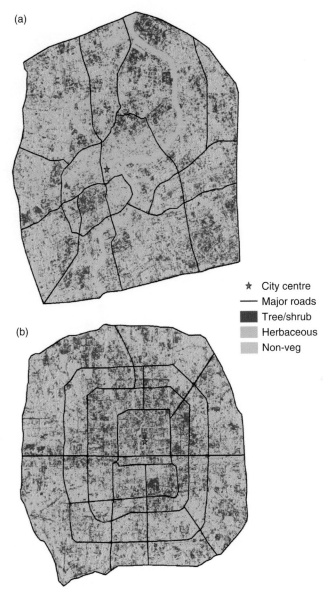

(a)

★ City centre
— Major roads
■ Tree/shrub
▨ Herbaceous
▨ Non-veg

(b)

Plate 16.1. Classification results show tree/shrub (dark green), herbaceous (bright green), and non-vegetation (violet) covers in Shanghai and Beijing. (a) Shanghai; (b) Beijing.

Plate 18.1. Study area (*c.* 38 km across) in Auckland City, northern New Zealand with 100 sample blocks indicated within the pale blue to grey–green coloured areas representing the built-up residential/industrial city. Dark blue is sea/water, pink is grass/pasture, and red is forest. The base map is down-sampled to 250 m spatial resolution from a Landsat multispectral satellite image. A five-level greenness index was derived from these data and used to stratify the urban environment for (random) vegetation sampling as described in the text. Numbers are deprivation index (1–10 with 10 being greatest socio-economic deprivation) for each sample block. There are gradients of rainfall (positive) and air pollution (negative) from the central city to the west and southeast.

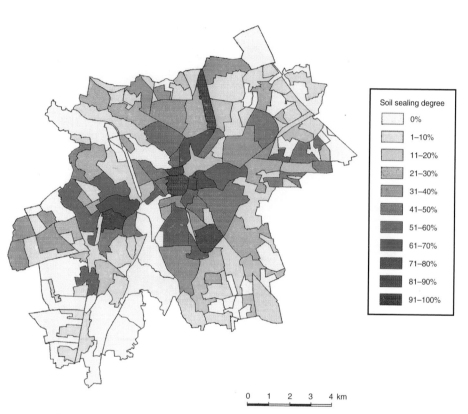

Plate 21.4. Soil sealing map of Leipzig, Germany (in 10% classes) (Kabisch *et al.*, 1997).

Plate 21.7. Urban structure units occurring in Leipzig, Germany. After Breuste and Böhm (1997).

Residential land and land of mixed use

City centre
Detached kerb-close apartment buildings with built-up courtyard (1870–WW I)
Terraced kerb-close apartment buildings with built-up courtyard (1870–WW I)
Detached kerb-close apartment buildings with open courtyard (1900–WW II)
Terraced kerb-close apartment buildings with open courtyard (1900–WW II)
Free standing blocks of flats in rows (since WW I)
Large new prefabricated housing estates (since 1960)
Detached and semi-detached houses
Villas
Former village centres

Industrial areas

New, medium density industrial and commercial areas
Old, high density industrial and commercial areas

Special estates

Large public facilities
Shopping centres
Public utilities and waste management plants

Infrastructural facilities

Infrastructural facilities

Recreational areas

Parks and green spaces
Allotments
Cemeteries
Sports fields, playgrounds

Agricultural areas

Agricultural areas

Woodlands

Woodlands

Rivers and standing water

Standing water
Rivers

Waste ground and changing areas

Waste ground and changing areas

Quarries, pits, mines and related facilities

Quarries, pits, mines and related facilities

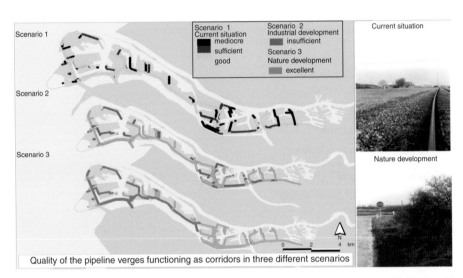

Plate 26.3. Connectivity function of pipeline verges for the brown argus (*Aricia agestis*) in three spatial scenarios. Scenario 1 describes the current situation, whereas scenario 2 shows a more industrial use and scenario 3 the possibility to implement nature development. The LARCH analysis shows that scenario 2 will decrease the connectivity between butterfly populations, especially in the eastern part, while in scenario 3 the connectivity will increase in the western part of the Port of Rotterdam.

and space. Thus, the term encompasses both the temporal and spatial components of the change process (Richter and Kugler, 1972; Haase and Richter, 1980a; Richter, 1989). The utilisation process is also highly complex. To be modelled, it must be reduced to selected parameters. The basic positions, procedures and goals of this reduction must be explained in each case, as otherwise the term land use can be misinterpreted.

The development of ecological research in urban areas was also connected with the expansion of geographical landscape research, landscape ecology and ecological landscape planning in urban areas. The early research in the 1970s was largely in the field of geographical landscape research, although it was influenced by biology, in particular vegetation science. In the 1980s the need to incorporate explicit locations for results from different research disciplines became a priority in an effort to gain a clearer understanding of the spatial distribution of ecological conditions within an urban area. Geographical landscape research tried to address this challenge by drawing upon theories from geography and landscape ecology which had already been well established from studies outside urban areas (Neef et al., 1961; Neef, 1963). This focus gave rise to a wave of landscape-ecological work conducted in cities (Haase and Richter, 1980b; Hülbusch, 1982; Richter, 1984; Kaerkes, 1985; Breuste, 1985, 1986; Kaerkes, 1987; Schönfelder, 1988; Breuste, 1989), particularly through habitat mapping. Identification of land-use structures provides an initial way to differentiate components within the urban cultural landscape.

If one peruses the geographical research on land use, it becomes clear that it represents primarily a linkage of geography, biological sciences, and spatial and regional planning. It strengthened investigations into the process of land-use change and its relationship to natural components of the landscape. In the process, it became apparent that the social function of areas was not of the greatest importance for determining spatial landscape pattern, and 'the process of landscape influence and change' or 'the degree of transformation of the natural balance of matter and energy of a landscape' (Schrader, 1985) became the centre of interest. Urban structure units of homogeneous physiognomical form were developed for urban landscapes using land-use types, spatial ecological units, and urban landscape units (e.g. Breuste, 1985; Duhme and Lecke, 1986; Breuste, 1986, 1989; Leykauf et al., 1989; Duhme and Pauleit, 1992b). Researchers interested in a larger scale than that used for habitat mapping (e.g. wetlands, urban structure units) created the science of landscape ecology to address issues that require a broader level of investigation and reflection.

In the 1980s, mesoscales were primarily used to provide an overview of the whole city or urban landscape. An example is the investigation of general urban

Fig. 21.3. Soil sealing of a public open space in Leipzig, Germany (Kabisch *et al.*, 1997).

climate and the urban heat island (Oke, 1982). With the development of urban bio- and ecological climatology, it became necessary to investigate the specific characteristics of smaller areas. This led to a shift to microscale research (climate topes, the smallest climate units). The same process is reflected in other branches of urban landscape ecological research (Breuste, 2001).

Soil sealing: main indicator of processes and functions in urban landscape

Soil sealing is a form of land cover that becomes more prominent as increasing urban influence creates more impermeable surfaces in the landscape. It involves removal of the vegetation cover of soils and replacement with less permeable materials (bitumen, concrete, stone pavements, etc.) to create building grounds or pavements, plazas, streets and roads (Figure 21.3; Breuste *et al.*, 1996). In replacing the natural soil–air interface with an artificial surface, the ability for soils to exchange nutrients and energy with the surrounding elements is reduced, thus altering the ecological conditions of the site. In this way soil sealing can be seen as a complex indicator for changes in the flow of water, nutrients and other materials as well as changes to the general ecological conditions without the need for additional measurements. This does not replace measurements of ecological process but provides an initial indication for an

Table 21.1. *Effects of soil sealing on the environment.*

Soil and water regime (by 'loss' of the vegetation cover and physical change of the soil surface and the upper soil layer)

- partial or complete removal of the upper soil layer;
- decreased infiltration of precipitation water into the soil and thus reduced groundwater renewal;
- increased evaporation;
- more increased and accelerated rates of storm water runoff;
- more frequent high levels in drains and streams with heavy rain and thaw.

Urban climate (by 'loss' of the vegetation cover and thermal and energetic effects due to human modifications (creation of new technical surfaces))

- increased thermal capacity and thermal conductivity of the sealing materials;
- increased air temperatures;
- increased particulates, and thus more frequent precipitation events;
- lower volume and shorter periods of snow cover;
- reduced humidity in temperate regions (not always true for arid regions).

Vegetation and fauna (by destruction of the vegetation cover and change of the local ecological conditions, intensive use by trampling and driving on)

- reduced, usually minimal colonisation opportunities for plants;
- lower oxygen and water supply for soil fauna, and decreased exchange of matter and gases between the soil and the near-surface air layer;
- depletion of the native flora;
- loss of levels of the food pyramid;
- loss of habitat;
- increasing isolation of populations.

Source: Breuste *et al.* (1996).

expected system characteristic. The changes to the ecological conditions can be grouped into three major categories: changes to the physical soil structure and the water regime, changes to the microclimate conditions (temperature, humidity, periodicity of snow cover) and changes to the surfaces available for use by plants and animals (Table 21.1).

Soil sealing is usually used as a general indicator of anthropogenic denaturalisation. There are also attempts to connect the term with clearly understandable, ecologically relevant functions. Some authors understand soil sealing as the complete covering of surfaces by impermeable substances, which halt all exchange processes between soil and near-surface air layer (Böcker, 1985). Another definition states that soil sealing can be applied to any surface that exceeds certain values of runoff and evapotranspiration rates (Pietsch and Kamith, 1991).

Both definitions attempt to describe and scientifically support a term which is already firmly embodied in ecology, planning and politics.

In Europe, soil sealing data were collected using empirical landscape-ecological mapping (e.g. habitat mapping) and initially only used to describe the areas without vegetation cover. These predominantly 'vegetation-hostile' surfaces combined into the category 'soil sealing'. Investigations showed that these surfaces can have a profound impact on the urban ecological system, depending on their material and form of construction. While these impacts are generally well acknowledged, there is a need to differentiate further between types of soil sealing, as the current use of the term is too broad. A similar problem exists for the biological aspects of land cover, which often use the broad term 'vegetation cover', without any further qualifications as its composition and structure.

The term soil sealing persists because it can be useful to differentiate generally between 'favourable surfaces' (Schulz, 1982) or 'vegetation-capable' (Reidl, 1992) surfaces, and 'non-favourable surfaces' (Schulz, 1982) or 'vegetation-hostile' surfaces. The greater the extent of vegetation-hostile surfaces in a given area, the further the area is from its natural state. Therefore the proportion of sealed surfaces within a spatial unit plays an important role in urban ecological management as a method for evaluating the level of 'denaturalisation'. Sealed surfaces are metahemerobic (i.e. extremely disturbed) areas (Bornkamm, 1980). Their prevalence in urban landscape components leads to these components being defined as meta- or polyhemerobic structures in their own right. See Blume (1992) for a compete explanation of this soil classification system.

Thus soil sealing is useful as both a general indicator for denaturalisation in cities (loss of vegetation, changes to soil structure), and for anthropogenic changes of natural processes (climate, water regime, species diversity, etc.). For example, Figure 21.4 shows the distribution of soil sealing within census districts for Leipzig, Germany. The areas with the greatest proportion of soil sealing are also the areas with the densest housing development and the oldest areas of the city.

However, while the term soil sealing is useful for examining human influence at a broad spatial scale, it is also subject to problems of interpretation:

- the term covers very different kinds of anthropogenic changes, ranging from buildings to layers of stone arranged as pavement, and even layers of water-bound gravel and sand within trails and sports grounds;
- the term does not extend to compacted soils which are constantly driven on or trampled;
- soil sealing does not always indicate the magnitude of changes to soil structure and the water regime; and

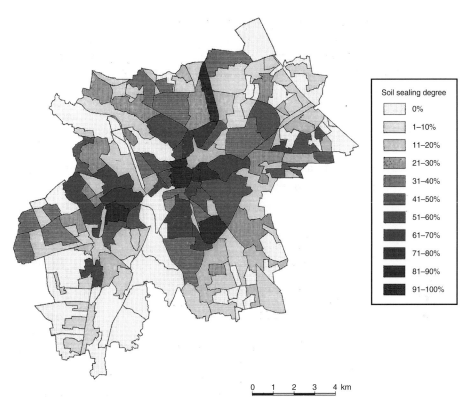

Soil sealing degree

☐ 0%

▨ 1–10%

▨ 11–20%

▨ 21–30%

▨ 31–40%

▨ 41–50%

▨ 51–60%

▨ 61–70%

▨ 71–80%

▨ 81–90%

▨ 91–100%

0   1   2   3   4 km

Fig. 21.4. Soil sealing map of Leipzig, Germany (in 10% classes) (Kabisch *et al.*, 1997). See also colour plate.

- sealed soils are not completely hostile to plant and animal life – incompletely sealed surfaces such as a pavement of stone layers can carry a nearly closed herb coverage within one or two years after the end of intensive use, irrespective of changes to the sealing surface.

Soil sealing alone is also insufficient to explain the intensity of human influence on the area. If additional anthropogenic influences are of interest, alternative indicators must be used, depending on the type of influence. These additional indicators would be required to address questions related to:

- displacement of vegetation cover due to continuous trampling and driving (monitoring and evaluation of the real use of the surfaces);
- influence of the surface structure on the infiltration of precipitation into the groundwater table (monitoring and evaluation of the different infiltration rates for different soil sealing textures and soil conditions) (Fig. 21.5);

Fig. 21.5. Examples of pavement types found in cities. The number and size of
the spaces between pavement blocks alter water infiltration (Breuste *et al.*, 1996).

- influence of surface structure on rainwater runoff (monitoring of the
  runoff promoted by different surface textures, soil conditions and angle
  of inclination of surfaces);
- influence of surface structure on evapotranspiration (evaluation of
  evaporation promoted by surface characteristics such as thermal
  conductivity, thermal capacity, the degree of energy accumulation and
  transformation into heat); and
- influence of the surface structure on the temperature characteristics of
  locations (analysis and evaluation of thermal factors such as radiation
  benefit, material characteristics and anthropogenic thermic supply).

Clearly, additional characteristics of sealed soils may be required depending
on the target of the investigation. A strongly infiltration-promoting surface
(pavement of smaller stones) is not always accompanied by an equivalent change

in surface temperature. We need to move away from using the proportion of soil sealing as a comprehensive term, and to begin to acknowledge the complex range of characteristics that soil sealings possess. The level at which the different surface types can be grouped will depend on the question being asked. For these questions addressing the process-level characteristics of sealed surfaces, there are still neither reliable data, nor appropriate equipment to collect and analyse data properly (Pietsch and Kamith, 1991). Until these limitations are addressed, we cannot fully answer these questions.

Apart from the general loss of vegetation in cities, the most noticeable effects of soil sealing are the changes to the urban water regime. High stormwater runoff and low groundwater tables are increasingly common in cities. This justifies the need to expand our knowledge of the extent of soil sealing (e.g. by aerial photographs and satellite images), and begin to address the factors that drive the current patterns of soil sealing (e.g. adjusting economic instruments), in order to reduce its impacts. A general goal of ecologically sustainable urban development must be to substantially increase the infiltration opportunities for precipitation in cities and thus reduce the stormwater runoff. This goal requires a stronger understanding of the infiltration capacity of different types of soil sealing. Investigations show that typical classifications, using physiognomic characteristics such as gaps between individual paving elements (e.g. stones), do not fully reflect the hydrogical functions. Vegetation density of the gaps, collected fine-material enrichment (indicator of 'aging'), intensity, duration and frequency of the precipitation events are also highly influential. The description and typical characteristics of different soil sealing types could be summarised in 'soil sealing catalogues' which would contain statements about infiltration capacity, runoff and evaporation rates under different precipitation conditions, and allow assessments of soil sealing to improve urban environmental management (Breuste et al., 1996; Münchow and Schramm, 1997; Breuste et al., 2002).

Reducing the impact of sealed surfaces by increasing their water permeability and providing additional infiltration opportunities are goals requiring a complex approach to management. To achieve these goals, there is a need to improve the monitoring methodology (remote sensing, GIS) and to develop techniques that can be used to quantify and analyse these options at different spatial scales (experimental determination of sealing characteristics for different functions).

Urban structural units as reference units and tools of landscape management

The two previous methods (land use, and soil sealing as an example of land cover) outlined for use in classifying the components of urban landscapes have been widely used as a basis for modelling patterns within urban areas. But while both of these methods are useful for describing patterns, they are less useful for examining processes because of their general definitions and broad applications. One method available when information is required at a finer spatial scale is the use of 'urban structural units'.

Urban structure types delineate areas of homogeneous physiognomic development, predominantly identified by clearly distinguishable characteristics in built-up structures and open spaces (vegetation and soil sealing). They are, to a large extent, homogeneous in type, density and portions of the built-up areas of various forms and of different components of open spaces (soil sealing areas, vegetation types and urban forest). Urban structure types offer an opportunity to combine the structural information available from the soil sealing classification system with the utilisation processes associated with the land-use classification system. They therefore allow modelling of processes within the urban system at a finer level of detail than the other methods, whilst maintaining the advantages of comprehensive and cost-efficient data collection.

Substantial ecological characteristics of a space can be described by its land-use form and structural characteristics. Spaces with uniform structural equipment and the same land-use form exhibit comparable habitat or landscape household functions (e.g. water cycle functions, climatic functions, biotope functions). Urban structural units thus summarise spaces with similar complex environmental conditions. Therefore they can be used as the basis for collecting information on the ecological or landscape characteristics of urban areas, as each unit has a predictable type of habitat and vegetation structure, climatic conditions, soil structure, intensity of soil sealing and rate of groundwater recharge.

The main types of urban structural units found in urban areas are residential estates and areas of mixed use, industry and commercial areas, areas of specific use, traffic areas, leisure and recreation areas, agricultural areas, forest areas, water bodies, derelict lands and landfills, quarries and disposal sites (Fig. 21.6, 21.7; Wickop, 1997). These structural units can be further divided on the basis of more specific forms of development (see Table 21.2).

Characteristics used to define the urban structure types are frequently connected with the utilisation process such as: utilisation and maintenance intensity, degree of soil sealing, age of land-use form and spatial position (isolation, neighbourhood of other uses) (Landesanstalt für Ökologie, Landschaftsentwicklung und Forstplanung Nordrhein-Westfalen [State Institute for Ecology, Landscape and Forestry Development Planning, North Rhine–Westphalia], 1989). As previously demonstrated, the utilisation form (economic function of the land) alone is not an effective indicator for ecological characterisation. Their further 'explanation' by additional characteristics is recommended (Arbeitsgruppe Methodik der Biotopkartierung im besiedelten Bereich, 1993).

Table 21.2. *Examples of sub-types of residential estates in Leipzig, Germany.*

- City centre
- Detached kerb-close apartment buildings with built-up courtyards (1870–World War I)
- Terraced kerb-close apartment buildings with built-up courtyards (1870–World War I)
- Detached kerb-close apartment buildings with open courtyards (1900–World War II)
- Terraced kerb-close apartment buildings with open courtyards (1900–World War II)
- Free-standing blocks of flats in rows (since World War I)
- Large new prefabricated housing estates (since 1960)
- Detached and semi-detached houses
- Villas
- Former village centres

Fig. 21.6. Example of detached kerb-close apartment buildings with open courtyards (1870 to World War I) (photograph J. H. Breuste).

Function-orientated land-use types (maps, listings, etc.) nevertheless lend themselves to planning applications because they are easily integrated into management recommendations. Indicator characteristics can be used to further differentiate the ecological conditions within urban structure types. Soil sealing as an indicator of human influence is currently far more advanced than vegetation structure as an indicator. We can see this from the small number of different urban structural units used to cover a wide range of vegetation types (see Figure 21.7). So far, data for the characteristics of vegetation used in ecological urban spatial patterns, in particular habitat mapping, are often non-uniform and ambiguous. The term 'vegetation structure' (or green areas) is frequently regarded as an indicator of utilisation and maintenance intensity in urban areas and also for areas just outside the city, with a cover of predominantly vegetation. There are many competing definitions for the term vegetation structure (e.g. Kunick, 1974; Bornkamm, 1980; Schacht, 1981; Auhagen and Sukopp, 1983; Kowarik, 1983; Wittig and Schreiber, 1983; Trepl, 1984; Schmidt, 1985; Breuste, 1986; Arbeitsgruppe Methodik Biotopkartierung im besiedelten Bereich, 1986, 1993). Some examples of current definitions are shown in Table 21.3.

Because of the defining characteristics of utilisation type and building structure, there are direct relations between the scientific framework of the urban structure types and the instruments of urban planning (master plan, zoning plan and site/property planning). Scientific findings can be readily converted

Fig. 21.7. Urban structure units occurring in Leipzig, Germany. After Breuste and Böhm (1997). See also colour plate.

Residential land and land of mixed use

City centre

Detached kerb-close apartment buildings with built-up courtyard (1870–WW I)

Terraced kerb-close apartment buildings with built-up courtyard (1870–WW I)

Detached kerb-close apartment buildings with open courtyard (1900–WW II)

Terraced kerb-close apartment buildings with open courtyard (1900–WW II)

Free standing blocks of flats in rows (since WW I)

Large new prefabricated housing estates (since 1960)

Detached and semi-detached houses

Villas

Former village centres

Industrial areas

New, medium density industrial and commercial areas

Old, high density industrial and commercial areas

Special estates

Large public facilities

Shopping centres

Public utilities and waste management plants

Infrastructural facilities

Infrastructural facilities

Recreational areas

Parks and green spaces

Allotments

Cemeteries

Sports fields, playgrounds

Agricultural areas

Agricultural areas

Woodlands

Woodlands

Rivers and standing water

Standing water

Rivers

Waste ground and changing areas

Waste ground and changing areas

Quarries, pits, mines and related facilities

Quarries, pits, mines and related facilities

Fig. 21.7. (cont.)

Table 21.3. *Examples of types of vegetation structures used by working group on habitat mapping within urban areas.*

Vegetation structure type	Description
Decorative green	Flower beds, small lawn patches, bushes, hedges, etc. (well cared for)
Accompanied green	Green strips along traffic lines or as addition to fill up the space between apartment blocks
Gardens/parks	Urban open spaces, well maintained
Allotments	Privately used garden plots (allotments) territorially organised in groups of 100 or more as closed-up area
Urban lawns	Large open lawns regularly mown for recreational uses
Urban forests	Forests as remnants of former semi-natural landscape in the urban areas, used for recreation

Source: Arbeitsgruppe Methodik der Biotopkartierung im besiedelten Bereich (1993).

into administrative, political and legislation documents which become the basis for actions. Urban structure types therefore form an interface between science and planning. Many different urban structure units are currently used in the environmental documentation and monitoring of cities, in the environmental management of identified problem areas, and for urban ecological analysis and comparison within and between cities. They provide a crucial means for understanding the environmental development of cities, and their utility has been demonstrated in the cities of Munich (Blum, 1991; Duhme and Pauleit, 1992a, 1994), Berlin (Stadt Berlin, 1996), Leipzig (Kabisch *et al.*, 1997) and Halle (Frühauf *et al.*, 1993). All of these cities have successfully used urban structure types for their environmental planning. Their monitoring has been aided by the development of new technologies, such as aerial photographs and satellite images, and the advent of computer programmes that can combine existing maps and data (Breuste *et al.*, 2002).

The need for comparative ecology

There is a strong need for the comparison of urban ecological studies worldwide (McDonnell and Hahs, Chapter 5), to separate local and individual results from broadly applicable general trends. On the other hand regional and local studies can only be evaluated if the spatial circumstances (natural and anthropogenic) are clearly defined. A formalised clear description of the spatial conditions of an investigation will allow comparisons between research conditions and the associated findings. Also, the characteristics of the selected spaces can be compared between cities (for instance, residential estates in different countries) and even the spaces themselves. New and interesting information on urban ecosystems can be expected from undertaking comparisons between different urban ecosystems (and their elements) and between different research results in various locations.

Comparison of general human influence on urban ecosystem on large spatial scale: land use as comparative factor

The main factor of human influence on urban ecosystem is land use (see above). It makes sense to start comparisons by definition and typification of this factor. The aim is to create categories which reflect different levels of human influence on urban ecosystems at a large spatial scale (urban ecosystems, cities, ecology of cities, etc.). Following this, comparisons between different urban ecosystems, such as Beijing and Berlin, are possible by describing their land-use structure and ecologically relevant characteristics. The comparison can be made on small scale or at a structural level (overview). The object can be the identification, qualification and quantification of areas representing different degrees of human influence. Different land-use categories can be grouped to represent each of the categories high, medium or low human influence on ecosystem. This is an easy initial form of assessment, which offers a lot of possible interpretations and answers to questions. The following are examples of questions that can be addressed at the level of the entire urban ecosystem.

(1) Comparison of human pressure on the ecosystem: How much space (square kilometres, percentage of the space, etc.) of the urban ecosystem is under high, medium or low human influence? This allows an initial quantification of human input on the urban ecosystem as a whole.

(2) Comparison of the spatial structure of the ecosystem: How can the urban patterns in general be described? Where in the urban ecosystem are these areas located? What is the spatial structure of the landscape? This allows for the comparison of structural information between cities. The description can be made by maps, by distance zone around the city centre (Central Business District, CBD) or even by mathematical methods (landscape metrics, etc.).

(3) Comparison of the speed of changes: How fast are the changing processes between these main categories? Next to space, time is the most important factor for urban ecological changes. The timescale of ecological changes can be shown and compared.

(4) Comparison of the quality of changes: Is the quantitative spatial growth connected with qualitative changes? Urban growth is commonly

measured as the expansion of urban land use. This information is not qualitative, whereas the altered configuration of land use provides a more detailed and informative measure.

Comparison of the intensity of human influence on urban ecosystems using selected indicators: for example, soil sealing indicating hydrological processes

More and more urban ecological studies are directed towards understanding human influences on natural processes in order to improve their management or even to begin to manage them. These human influences must be investigated on the small scale by measuring the matter content (air, water, soil, vegetation, etc.) and/or the fluxes of matter and energy. Most of these fluxes are influenced and regulated by the urban surfaces ('land cover'). To compare investigations, the description of the physical consistency of these surfaces as a transformer of energy and matter is necessary. One rapid way to overcome this hurdle to information is to identify and assess the transformation properties of sealed soils (by different pavements). This can be done on all levels of investigation, by summarising information at a broad scale, by collecting structural information on a medium scale (ecological pattern) and by collecting detailed information on pavement types at a small scale, e.g. hydrological assessments.

Sealed soils are a useful approach to urban ecological comparisons. They are typical for all cities, cover large areas in all cities worldwide and are an indicator for general 'degradation/denaturalisation' of the urban ecosystem as well as a specific steering factor of the water cycle, micro-climate, habitat conditions, etc. This offers a lot of possible interpretations and answers to questions such as the following.

(1)   Quantitative approach on large scale: What area of a city is occupied by sealed soils? This allows a comparison between cities by using one main indicator which is widely applied worldwide. A quantity in square kilometres or in percentage of the total urban space can be given.

(2)   Growth rate of human pressure on urban ecosystem: How fast are these areas growing? Sealed soils as a general category can be easily identified by interpretation of satellite images or aerial photographs. A general overview of the whole urban area is possible for different time sequences, which provides an excellent opportunity to examine changes over time.

(3)   Increasing pressure of human influence on urban ecosystem: Which areas are changed into sealed soils? The location of newly sealed soils shows which ecological units are most susceptible to land-use conversion pressure. It shows which habitats (part of the urban and

peri-urban ecosystems) come under stronger urban influence and which are spatially reduced.

(4)   Soil sealing as internal factor of urban pattern: What is the degree of soil sealing in different land-use types? Soil sealing can be a factor of ecological differentiation between land-use types. It can show the extent of change to specific land-use types and which of these land-use types are really comparable in degree of soil sealing (e.g. residential areas, commercial areas).

(5)   Association of soil sealing: With what other ecologically relevant factors is soil sealing connected? Understanding how soil sealing is connected with other human factors (e.g. economy, income groups of population, age of built-up structures) can be an important point of comparison between cities. This comparison can highlight the interactions between socio-economic and ecological factors.

Determination and comparison of urban pattern qualified by process indication: urban structural units (USU)

A relevant and accurate way to compare ecological conditions of cities is to define urban structural units (USU) in each investigated city. It allows a direct connection between data on land use and land cover, indicating natural processes. This process is well established in medium-scale research in addition to small-scale investigations. It allows the assessment of not only a general degree of human impact on the urban ecosystem but also a detailed spatial view, which includes the assessment of relevant human-influenced natural processes (such as climate, hydrological and ecological processes). In particular, the definition of additional characteristics of land cover (soil surfaces) as sealed soil types, building types and types of vegetation can give a clear view on the main ecological factors of an area as representative of a spatial type. This can be used for a sharp and clear comparison of many other characteristics and even allow an assessment of the structure and components of the urban ecosystem. This offers a lot of possible interpretations and begins to address such questions as the following.

(1)   Structural approach: How differentiated are the land-use classes in an ecological sense? Which ecological types of urban structural units are useful to define? The identification, mapping or use of urban structural units in GIS allows the characterisation and assessment of its (internal) characteristics in different directions. This can even be used for a detailed and complete overview of the urban ecosystem.

(2)   Stability approach (internal changes): Which USU have characteristics that are generally stable over many years and which are rapidly

changing their characteristics? The urban transformation is not only connected by external growth but also by strong internal changes of urban ecological characteristics. These changes can be quantified in terms of changes to the characteristics of the urban structural units. It can be shown which of them are stable over many years. This provides important information on ecological conditions and allows the ecological stability of cities to be evaluated.

(3) Growth approach (external growth): Which USU are the most important in the urban growth process and which ecological consequences are connected with them? When it can be identified which urban structural units are consistently constructed on large newly created areas in the urban fringe zones of cities, a qualitative assessment of the growth process and its elements is possible. This allows an increased understanding of the urban growth process.

(4) Comparison of detailed small-scale investigations: Which are the ecological circumstances characterising detailed local investigations (often by measurements) of climatic, hydrological and ecological factors that will allow us to compare the results between cities? A very important question is the comparison of detailed studies, for example on urban climate, distribution of plants and animals, or pollution of water, soil or air. Previous studies in different cities have not sufficiently described the conditions under which they were undertaken. Even where the description is more detailed, a comparison with other studies is not possible because of the singularities of the locations. The use of urban structural units would aid in urban ecological investigations and their comparison between cities.

Conclusion

The landscape-ecological modelling of urban landscapes has grown substantially over the past 35 years, yet there is still room for improvement (McCarthy, Chapter 7; Snep *et al.*, Chapter 26). While the monitoring methods are now largely automated (e.g. remote sensing techniques), there is still the need for substantial research focusing on modelling process rather than structure. This research is not necessarily to the detriment of structural models, as these two types of research are intricately related. Progress in the ability to model processes will also help to refine the structural models of urban landscapes. Categories of land use in urban landscapes continue to be an important criterion for the demarcation and characterisation of ecologically homogeneous areas.

The contribution that land use makes in terms of acting as a major influence on ecological systems in urban areas and as an indicator of associated processes is confirmed in a broad sense. But there is still only limited research into the utility of this system as an indication of process. It is important to use and further develop the existing methods of landscape research and to adapt them to urban conditions. The existing and widespread application of land-use-based modelling is only partly effective, and should be extended by the addition of further characteristics. Depending on the questions being addressed, a further differentiation of the existing land-use-based urban ecological structures may be recommended, using the methods for creating urban structural units.

It is also important to remember that the urban landscape is not strictly separated from other cultural and natural landscapes. Thus models need to include and further examine natural characteristics that can be used to refine the methods for quantifying landscape pattern. There are currently methodological deficiencies in using general landscape-ecological methodology and with the current system of selecting, differentiating and evaluating the ecological characteristics of the urban landscape. These deficiencies have far-reaching consequences beyond those associated with the practical planning process, so it is important to obtain accurate and scientific results. Nature protection and ecologically orientated urban development will benefit from the further development of comprehensible landscape-ecological methods of analysis and evaluation of the urban landscape structure.

22

Preservation of original natural vegetation in urban areas: an overview

CLAS FLORGÅRD

Preservation of original natural vegetation in urban areas

Over the past decades models for sustainable development of towns and cities have been created and discussed (see Naess, 2001; Itoh, 2003). A component of such an 'ecological approach' is to preserve patches of the original vegetation as parts of the green structure in areas designated for future development, and to preserve remnant natural vegetation in already built-up areas. There are many examples from around the world where the original natural vegetation within cities has been preserved (e.g. Greller, 1975; Schmid, 1975; Florgård, 1978; Dyring, 1984; Olsen *et al.*, 1987). This concept involves the preservation of the original natural vegetation in areas where buildings, roads and other structures are to be built, and the preservation of remnants of such vegetation in already built-up areas. Typically, the vegetation will be close to houses, roads and other developed areas. The vegetation can be natural or semi-natural which has developed with little or no human intervention over time. It also comprises stable post-agricultural plant communities such as meadows and pastureland. Thus, vegetation types such as natural and semi-natural forests and woodlands, bushland, meadows, pasture land, heaths, mires and wetlands can be preserved in towns and cities.

The concept of preserving a functioning biotope or ecosystem is of crucial importance in preserving the original vegetation. Preserved solitary trees are usually not included in the biotope concept, but can be studied as remnants of

Ecology of Cities and Towns: A Comparative Approach, ed. Mark J. McDonnell, Amy K. Hahs and Jürgen H. Breuste. Published by Cambridge University Press. © Cambridge University Press 2009.

the original vegetation (Oguz, 2004). However, solitary trees, preserved together with natural or semi-natural ground cover vegetation so that a part of the biotope remains, can be important in maintaining biodiversity in cities and towns. The preservation of recent spontaneously established vegetation, such as ruderals, is not a key component of preserving remnant vegetation, but planting and sowing of trees, bushes, herbs and grass can complement existing remnants of natural vegetation.

The utilisation of natural vegetation within cities usually means that the vegetation should remain in a state as similar to the original one as possible. However, in certain cases vegetation changes can be tolerated (Airola and Buchholz, 1984). This is the case if the changes coincide with the goal set for the green area. For example, if the aim is to develop an exciting playing area, it might be possible to accept vegetation changes as long as they do not damage too much of the usefulness for play. In cases where vegetation changes are accepted, the ground and the vegetation can be looked upon as resources to be used in the best way. This allows for methods such as the establishment of vegetation using translocation of ground together with ground cover vegetation from one site to another. On the other hand, if the main purpose is to preserve biodiversity as such, it is probable that very little change in vegetation can be accepted. In most cases, preservation will mean that the vegetation will be protected against major impacts and subsequent vegetation changes. Care and maintenance are important to achieve the objectives set for an area, and are critical to the preservation of the vegetation (McDonnell, 1988). Usually, the need for maintenance (e.g. weeding and pruning) is much less for natural vegetation than for planted areas, but it still needs to be carried out. Stenhouse (2001) has pointed out the important role that non-governmental organisations can play, but also that there is need for professional support.

Research directed towards preserved and remnant natural vegetation in urban areas has been carried out at least since the late 1960s and early 1970s, and natural vegetation has also been viewed as a resource in development planning during this period (Bucht, 1973; Jaatinen, 1974; Greller, 1975; Kirkpatrick, 1975). The perspective has been broad. A main focus has been human-caused impact on preserved vegetation, and the subsequent vegetation changes. Importance, function, concepts and definitions have been taken into consideration, as well as planning, design, construction and uses. Care and maintenance have also been studied, including methods for the rehabilitation of damaged natural vegetation (Florgård, 2007a). The establishment of new habitats using translocation of ground and ground cover vegetation between sites has been studied in connection to infrastructure construction. The research has so far been geographically divided into two groupings, one with Australia and the

United States as a core, and the other in the Nordic countries Norway, Sweden and Finland. These two groupings have, surprisingly, not known of each other's existence until the present decade (Florgård, 2007b). The first international research meeting within this field of research was held in Uppsala, Sweden, in 2002 (Florgård, 2002). This symposium was followed by a symposium at the IALE World Congress in Darwin, Australia, and a workshop held in Melbourne in July 2003, both of which were focused on the comparative ecology of cities and towns. These latter two meetings were the impetus for this book.

The aim of this chapter is to present an overview of knowledge on preserved and remnant original vegetation in urban areas. Therefore it includes a presentation of a variety of topics including the benefits of the vegetation as part of the urban green infrastructure, the impact on the vegetation and subsequent vegetation changes, the planning and design for preservation, and the management.

Terminology and concepts

There are two main concepts used today in regards to vegetation in urban environments. One is 'urban remnant vegetation' and combinations connected to that, used mainly by American and Australian researchers, and the other is variations of 'preservation of natural vegetation in cities/urban areas', used mainly by Nordic researchers. This latter concept is a translation of the word 'naturmark', used in Norwegian and Swedish (Florgård, 2007b). As a part of the larger grouping of researchers, the American–Australian concept might today be more accepted than the latter. On the other hand, the latter concept is more useful in the planning and design process. Before vegetation was fragmented by development and agriculture, there were no remnants. The natural vegetation covered all of the land. Parts of the vegetation can be used as parts of the future green infrastructure in the cities. As such the concept 'preservation of natural vegetation in cities/urban areas' is a more active one, and is useful in the action-orientated planning and design process. If the word 'preservation' is excluded from the concept, it will become less active.

The use of the concept 'indigenous vegetation' in the title of the symposium in Sweden 2002 was an attempt to use an existing expression with a new and precise definition. The concept of 'indigenous plants' has been used for centuries (see Brookes, 1763 and Loudon, 1830). However, the combination 'indigenous vegetation' has been little used, and has, as far as can be found, not been clearly defined. The advantage of this concept is that it can be defined in such a way as to encompass most of the variables of this field of research, and that it is short and easy to use. However, there are also difficulties in establishing such a new concept.

In the title of this chapter I have used the concept 'preservation of original natural vegetation in cities'. But this has the disadvantage that it is long, and will probably almost always be shortened when it is used within a paper. 'Remnant' is easy to use and easy to understand, but not usable in the planning and design process. 'Preserved' does not cover all these patches which are just left over in the development process. But the expression 'preservation of vegetation' can be used when occasionally remnant vegetation is discussed, as well as when a more active approach including preservation of undeveloped areas is needed. As an active approach it also allows for the important interaction between researchers and practitioners.

Benefits of preservation

The presence of a green structure within residential areas, industrial parks and infrastructure areas provides many biological, economic and social advantages. Green areas have been found to improve the urban quality in many ways (Breuste *et al.*, 1998). Preservation of natural vegetation in urban areas has many additional advantages (Schmid, 1975; Rosengren, 1979; Simons, 1979; Florgård, 1981; Dyring, 1984; Hitchmough, 1993; Hörnsten, 2000).

Preservation of remnants of original natural vegetation in cities is a part of an ecological approach to planning and design. One recently discussed advantage is that preserved original vegetation can become an important source for biodiversity (McDonnell, 1988). Agenda 21, the document resulting from the UN environmental conference in Rio in 1992 (United Nations, 1993), states that biodiversity is a part of the natural resources. Often urban areas are looked upon as poor areas from the biodiversity point of view. But, as has been found in many urban ecology studies, this occurs primarily in heavily built-up areas. In moderately built-up areas, the number of animal as well as plant species can be very high (Davis and Glick, 1978; Burgess and Sharpe, 1981; Gilbert, 1989; Klausnitzer, 1993; Parsons *et al.*, 2003), and in some cases the number of native plants can be higher within the city than in the hinterland (Given and Meurk, 2000; Sukopp, 2003). Many suburban areas can support the presence of urban as well as rural species.

Preserved vegetation will support wildlife (Mörtberg, 1996; Löfvenhaft, 2002; Catterall, Chapter 8; Nilon, Chapter 10; McIntyre and Rango, Chapter 14; Mörtberg, Chapter 25). Detached houses built in areas where some original trees are retained are found to be the type of urban development with the most varied bird species composition (Geis, 1974; Hedblom, 2007). However, most studies of wildlife in cities do not discriminate remnant vegetation from planted vegetation, even if the presence of remnant vegetation is a part of the study (Hohtola,

1978; Vizyova, 1986). Sometimes the preserved habitats can become areas for colonisation by rare native species (Kirkpatrick, 1986), even though rare native habitats in cities are threatened (Vähä-Piikkiö et al., 2004).

Another important advantage of preserving natural vegetation in parks and residential areas is that the vegetation will already be mature when the houses are ready for occupation. This is a great advantage especially in areas with low plant growth potential, such as arid areas or areas with cool or cold climate (e.g. mountainous areas or far northern or southern areas).

Preservation of remnants of original natural vegetation in cities is also a part of a new planning and design philosophy centred on searching for a local identity of place. Preservation of natural plant communities within the city can be an important tool in breaking down the homogeneity of landscape design language in the urban environment. Areas with preserved natural vegetation are visually different from 'traditional' gardens and parks, and can thus be a comple-ment to designed areas, providing visual diversity and a sense of place. It is often difficult to develop a natural-looking vegetation using planting and/or sowing. It is usually expensive, and it usually takes a long time before the vegetation is mature. In many cases it is not possible to develop vegetation which is visually equal to the desired natural vegetation.

Natural vegetation has been found to provide exciting playgrounds for chil-dren. In accordance with Florgård (1978), children will use designed playing areas more frequently than more natural areas if they have access to both types. However, the natural areas seem to be of great importance because they are used for special purposes. Florgård et al. (1984), Kylin (2003) and Hedblom (2007) found that natural-looking areas were very much used by children for the construction of hiding places as dens. Natural areas were also much used for fantasy play. These studies imply that access to natural vegetation develops another type of play than that of designed playgrounds, and that play in natural and semi-natural areas is complementary to play in designed areas. One could speculate about the importance of this. In Sweden, Norway and Finland, most children have access to large or small areas of preserved natural vegetation close to their homes, and thus become familiar with nature at a very young age (Fig. 22.1). This may have some impact on their attitude toward nature and the environment as adults, and may also have a connection to the strong environmental movement in the Nordic countries (Friberg, 1979). In any case, there are observations that children who did not have access to nature in the form of natural vegetation when they were very small have found nature frightening (Florgård, 1978). It has been shown that the third generation of city dwellers easily become alienated from nature (Heberlein and Ericsson, 2005; Louv, 2005). People who experience the natural environment in their daily lives have been found to appreciate these

Fig. 22.1. A site of natural revegetation in Stockholm, Sweden, which is much used by children and adults. (Photo by C. Florgård).

environments greatly (Saastamoinen and Sievänen, 1981; Lindhagen, 1996; Louv, 2005). Connected to their function as playgrounds is the function as areas for learning. Preserved natural vegetation and ground can be used as teaching areas, both in schools and in nursery schools (Titman, 1994).

An important reason for preserving natural vegetation in towns and cities is economic. Construction of outdoor environments can be costly. On the other hand, if preserved vegetation is used instead, costs will be very low. Costs are incurred for surveying and mapping, for protection measures such as information and fencing during construction and so on, but these costs are much lower than those for developed areas (Florgård, 1980). However, from an economic point of view, the most important phase is not planning, design and construction, but later use. Costs for care and maintenance of built outdoor environments usually exceed construction costs within 20 years. The maintenance costs of preserved vegetation (thinning, tidying up) are much less than those of lawns and planted areas.

Another economic aspect is the value of the existing natural vegetation for property prices in the neighbourhood. Tyrväinen (1997) and Morancho (2003) found that proximity of wooded recreation areas and watercourses had a positive influence on apartment prices, as did views onto forests (Tyrväinen and Miettinen, 2000). According to Tyrväinen and Väänänen (1998), up to half of the inhabitants were willing to pay to prevent the conversion of forested parks in the neighbourhood to other land use.

But the most important benefit of preservation of original natural vegetation is usually thought of as being the amenity of these areas, and the use of the areas for recreation (Gustavsson, 1986; Benson and Howell, 1990; Hitchmough, 1993; Plant, 1996). This includes increased visual diversity in the urban environment, as well as historical ties to the past (Schmid, 1975). Tyrväinen and Väänänen (1998) found that up to 80% of the population in a Finnish city visited an urban forest at least once a week. As mentioned above, these vegetation types are usually difficult to develop using traditional methods. If the preserved areas are carefully chosen in the planning and design process, they can provide visually attractive complements to designed areas. Many of the preserved areas in Australian cities are considered to be of unique quality in the urban environment, and many of the local governments have created specific staff positions for bushland conservation and management (Stenhouse, 2004b).

Indigenous vegetation as a part of the urban green infrastructure

The concept 'green infrastructure' within cities includes all green and blue (i.e. water) areas (Halvorsen Thoren and Nyhuus, 1993). Thus, such areas as parks, gardens, green areas connected to traffic systems, self-colonised vegetation areas and water bodies are critical components of 'green infrastructure', independent of administrative borders or whether they are public or private property.

Natural vegetation can be preserved in all these areas within the green infrastructure (McDonnell, 1988), but preservation is usually difficult to carry out in the very centre of a city, even though some examples exist. Areas just outside city centres are usually so heavily built up that there is very little green space left for preservation, even if it is possible to achieve remnants of natural vegetation in the parks (Given and Meurk, 2000). In these areas which surround the city centre, natural vegetation is seldom found on private property. In the Nordic countries, one often can find a type of green area called the 'City Forest', which means a forest preserved quite close to the city centre as a natural area of public access. Such a 'City Forest' can be found in a number of Swedish, Norwegian and Finnish cities. In suburban areas, however, natural vegetation can be preserved on private property as well as in public areas managed by local and state governments. In both cases, the reasons for preservation can be environmental as well as economic and social. In the Nordic countries, woodland cemeteries have become common sources of local natural vegetation (Westerdahl, 1996). The Skogskyrkogården (Woodland Cemetery) in Stockholm was the first cemetery to be included on the UNESCO World Heritage List because of its outstanding natural vegetation (Constant, 1994).

At the urban fringe, nature can be seen as a resource for further development as well as a resource for recreation and as habitat for maintaining biodiversity in towns and cities. Local and regional authorities have to make decisions concerning whether areas should be regarded as future development areas, or areas to be preserved for recreational and ecological purposes. To accomplish this, some sort of nature survey has to be carried out. The aim of such a survey should be to point out areas of natural vegetation of particular interest for the public, or for the preservation of biodiversity. These areas must, in some way, be protected and the vegetation within them preserved. Vulnerable vegetation will be affected to a great extent, even if the area has been designated a recreational reserve (Kirkpatrick, 1975). But even if an area should only contain vegetation without special qualities and be targeted as a development area, this does not exclude the vegetation in it from being of interest for preservation. In many cases, vegetation which is of little interest for nature conservation can be of great value when it is preserved in residential areas just because it is natural and preserved close to where people live (Jaatinen, 1974; Rydberg, 1998).

Impact on preserved and remnant vegetation in cities, and the following vegetation changes

When a rural area is transformed into an urban area, habitat conditions will be changed, with possible negative impacts on preserved vegetation (Davis and Glick, 1978; Burgess and Sharpe, 1981; Gilbert, 1989). The impacts can involve changes in climate, radiation, hydrological conditions, soil conditions, pollution situation, fragmentation of biotopes, and mechanical impacts such as littering, trampling, cutting and driving vehicles (Schmid, 1975; Ingelög et al., 1977; Florgård, 1978; Wuorenrinne, 1978; Bagnall, 1979; Pärnänen, 1979; Dyring, 1982; Clements, 1983; Dyring, 1984; Rudnicky and McDonnell, 1989; Saunders et al., 1991; McDonnell et al., 1997; Breuste et al., 1998; Malmivaara et al., 2002; Sukopp, 2004; Lehvävirta, 2005).

Natural patches of vegetation in urban environments are studied either by urban–rural gradients (McDonnell and Pickett, 1990; Medley et al., 1995; McDonnell et al., 1997; McKinney, 2002; Zipperer and Guntenspergen, Chapter 17; Carreiro et al., Chapter 19), or by comparing the conditions at a site before and after development. However, Florgård et al. (1977, 1984; also presented in Florgård, 1981, 1991 and 2000) studied a rural area in Stockholm before developmental impact and changes started, while development was in progress, and the impact and changes during later use. Factors studied were the planning process, impact due to construction and the ensuing changes in climate, hydrology and pollution, impact due to later use by the residents, and vegetation changes.

This study implies that habitat changes – climate, hydrology and pollution effects – were measurable in this suburban area, but not of the magnitude to explain the vegetation changes. Direct impact from constructors during development and from the residents during later use were found to be the most important factors. Numata (1977) suggested that an increasing concentration of SO_2 resulted in the extinction of needle-leafed trees such as *Pinus densiflora* and *P. thunbergii* in Tokyo. Such an effect was not found for *Pinus sylvestris* in Stockholm, which can be explained by relatively low SO_2 concentrations in the city (Florgård, 1991). Morgan (1998) has demonstrated that non-native plants have invaded natural grassland vegetation along roadsides in southeastern Australia, and that this colonisation was connected to an increasing amount of phosphorus in the soil. Rudnicky and McDonnell (1989) found that over a 50-year period natural disturbances in the form of hurricanes, as well as human-induced disturbances such as arson, trampling and vandalism, contributed to changes in tree canopy composition in a remnant oak–hemlock forest in New York City.

Changes in soil conditions have been studied as comparisons between soils in urban and rural forest stands in the eastern United States and to some extent in Finland. These studies mainly imply that soils and soil organisms are affected by anthropogenic impacts (Baxter *et al.*, 1999). Heavy metal concentrations may lead to a decrease in fungal densities and invertebrate populations (Pouyat *et al.*, 1994), but the fungal biomass can, in spite of this, be unaffected (Markkola *et al.*, 1995). However, activity of earthworms has been found to be higher in urban stands (Steinberg *et al.*, 1997), and has converted urban soils from mor to mull humus (Pouyat, 1992). Phosphorous availability and, to a lesser degree, nitrogen availability are lower in urban forest stands (Baxter *et al.*, 2002). Litter in urban forest stands is found to be of less depth, mass and density than that in rural stands (Kostel-Hughes *et al.*, 1998a,b). Decomposer activity can be affected by urban pollution (Carreiro *et al.*, 1999), but higher temperature and higher earthworm activity compensate for what otherwise should be slower litter decomposition (McDonnell *et al.*, 1997; Pouyat and Carreiro, 2003). Kostel-Hughes *et al.* (1998a, b) found a higher content of emergents and non-native species in the urban soil seed bank as compared with rural forests. The studies imply that urban effects on soils, and subsequently the vegetation, can be positive as well as negative. The negative effects appear to outweigh the positive, but not to an extent where changes in soil conditions become too limiting for successful plant growth and survival.

Regarding fragmentation and isolation, Janzen (1983) has pointed out that patches of pristine forests are heavily influenced by the surrounding landscape, which is the case when the surroundings are urban space with weeds, ruderals and planted exotic vegetation. Plant species richness (Honnay *et al.*, 1999), as well as bird and amphibian species richness (Vizvoya, 1986), are found to be more resistant to impacts in larger patches of remnant forest, whereas impacts on mammals and reptiles are more dependent on the degree of isolation (Vizvoya, 1986). Guntenspergen and Levenson (1997) found that changes in understorey vegetation can be due to urbanisation as well as natural disturbances. Connections between urban remnants and the surrounding landscape are broken if motorways are built (Pirnat, 2000). Löfvenhaft (2004) found that there can be a time-lag of several decades between changes in land use and the resultant changes in the prevalence of amphibian species, and Lehvävirta et al. (2006) did not find any overall negative effect on carabid beetle populations from trampling in an urban woodland. On the other hand, studies by Florgård (2000) in Stockholm imply that the response of the ground cover vegetation in boreal forests to trampling is very fast for vulnerable plant communities, and quite slow for more tolerant communities. But when you look at the response of the vegetation in more detail there can be different outcomes. One such difference is the observation that in pine and spruce forest remnants in Stockholm, the species turnover after 25 years of trampling is very small and in several areas non-existent. Instead of species turnover, heavy trampling results in the loss of vegetation, creating bare soil. In studies in other countries it has been shown that species turnover occurs which can be a threat to the preserved plant communities. The difference between the Swedish and other studies is not limited to studies of urban vegetation carried out in Australia and the United States. The same difference can be found towards Norwegian and Finnish projects.

There are numerous studies of the effects of trampling in forests and recreation areas (LaPage, 1967; Kellomäki, 1973; Kardell, 1974; Kellomäki and Saastamoinen, 1975; Kellomäki, 1977), but relatively few have been conducted in urban areas (Dyring, 1982; Malmivaara et al., 2002; Lehvävirta and Rita, 2002; Lehvävirta et al., 2004; Arnberger, 2006; Lehvävirta and Kotze, Chapter 31). Vulnerability of ground cover vegetation has been found to depend on many factors such as soil depth, soil characteristics such as texture, structure and fertility, ground water level, mobility of water, climate, vegetation community, slope angle and of course trampling intensity. Trampling intensity can be as much as three times higher at inner-urban areas than peri-urban areas (Arnberger, 2006), but small preserved natural areas very close to residential areas are even more trampled (Florgård and Forsberg, 2006).

In general, trees have not been found to be measurably affected by limited trampling except on special sites (Florgård, 1985), but trampling can occasionally result in decreased tree growth (Nylund et al., 1979), and reduction of the area of the tree canopy (Dyring, 1982). Levenson (1981) and Hoehne (1981) found that species richness of the tree canopy and woody plants was due to the patch area, while species richness of the ground layer was due to the intensity of trampling and other impacts. Species richness of the tree canopy initially increased with increasing patch size up to 2.3 ha. Over that patch size it decreased. Ground-layer species richness initially increased with increasing impact, then decreased. All these changes resulted in disturbance to the original vegetation. A study by Bhuju and Ohsawa (1998) in Japan showed that trampling resulted in soil compaction, which in turn resulted in decreased root and stem growth, followed by decreasing plant cover on the trampled areas.

A special and very serious type of impact occurs during the construction process (Gottberg, 1972; Florgård, 1978). These damages are, to a great extent, due to the design of the construction site. Close to where construction is carried out, observed damage includes: cutting tree roots while excavating, raising soil level which destroys the ground vegetation and also negatively affects tree roots, tree felling due to increased wind velocity, and increasing exposure to sunlight to trees that were originally sheltered and shaded. But some damage is due to the construction work itself. Areas to be preserved can, for example, be damaged by direct impacts by vehicles, by use as storing areas during construction, and by use for construction site huts. This damage can occur both close to the site and at a considerable distance (Florgård et al., 1979; Rosengren, 1979). Impacts during construction affect trees as well as ground-layer vegetation. However, an important conclusion of these studies is that trees are mainly affected during construction, whereas ground-layer vegetation is mainly affected by trampling and other impacts during later use. In pine and spruce forests of Myrtillus type, trampling was not found to result in invasion of species from the surrounding area during the first 25 years. Instead, the result of heavy trampling was the occurrence of bare soil devoid of ground-layer vegetation (Florgård, 2000). This is in accordance with the observation of only weak concordance between the soil seed bank and the actual vegetation in natural vegetation in Australian urban bushland (King and Buckney, 2001). There could be numerous seeds of non-natural plant species which were not represented in the vegetation. But plant species turnover has been observed in Australian suburbs over an 88-year period (Rose and Fairweather, 1997).

In Nordic vegetation there are also important differences in the resistance of different tree species to impact during construction (Florgård, 2000). For example, the most common tree species in Finland, Norway and Sweden, the Norwegian spruce (*Picea abies*), is found to be vulnerable to many types of impact. It is vulnerable to increased wind velocity due to clearcutting close to the tree and is thus easily felled; it is vulnerable to increased insolation if sheltering trees are cut; to root damage if vehicles are driven on the root system; to build-up of soil over the root system; to excavation close to the stem with damage to the roots; and to mechanical damage to the bark. On the other hand, the second most common tree, the Scots pine (*Pinus sylvestris*), is found to be resistant to most impacts. It is fairly tolerant to increased wind velocity even if it has formerly been sheltered by other trees; it is very tolerant to increased insolation even if sheltering trees around are felled; the main root system is rather deep and therefore not very vulnerable to vehicle driving or build-up of soil; and the stem and thick branches and roots contain a substance that protects against fungal infections and makes the pine tolerant to excavation and to damages to the stem. Observations at construction sites (Florgård, 1978) implies that of deciduous species, the pedunculate oak (*Quercus robur*) is even more tolerant to most types of impact than the Scots pine, whereas silver birch (*Betula pendula*) is quite vulnerable, but not as vulnerable as the spruce.

Strategies, planning and design for preservation

Until the nineteenth century, natural areas were seldom looked upon as a resource within cities (Hummel, 1983). Nature was not protected as such, but could remain as spaces left over in planning, such as areas for military defence, riparian zones used for flood control or areas too steep to be developed (Schmid, 1975; Florgård, 1981; Gilbert, 1989; Plant, 1996). In many cities such remnants are the only areas where vegetation from the time prior to development can be found. Unfortunately, most of the natural resources are destroyed during urbanisation (Sharpe *et al.*, 1986). But in the twentieth century, interest in preservation has increased in countries all over the world. In some countries it was part of a national romantic trend, influencing architecture and town and city planning (Simons, 1979; Ignatieva and Stewart, Chapter 23). In Sweden, for example, the chairman of the Swedish National Association for Nature Protection and Professor of Botany in Uppsala, Rutger Sernander, initiated a cooperative programme with the staff of the Stockholm City Park Administration. Together they developed a concept for Stockholm where vegetation was used in its natural state to form parts of future parks and green areas (Sernander, 1926). Since then natural vegetation has been used systematically in the planning of the green infrastructure in many Swedish cities and towns, and has become an integrated part of the planning and design approach throughout the country. In Norway, Sweden, Finland and Australia, governmental and other central recommendations for nature preservation in cities have been presented (Natur mellan hus, 1975; Luonto ja kaupinkien asuntoalueet, 1984; Naturmark i bebyggelsesplanen, 1986; Government of Western Australia, 1995).

However, Norwegian studies indicate that areas with preserved natural vegetation in cities were among the area categories most heavily destroyed when infill was built between 1960 and 1990 (Nyhuus and Halvorsen Thorén, 1996). This suggests that when infill buildings are planned in urban areas the remnant natural vegetation is more threatened than gardens and parks. Infill is a great threat to all green areas, but more to natural vegetation than other types of green areas.

Numerous philosophies for preserving natural vegetation in cities have been presented (Palm, 1973; Landskap, 1979; McDonnell, 1988; Rieley and Page, 1995; McKinney, 2002; Breuste, 2004) as well as development strategies and preservation plans (Greller, 1975; Kellomäki and Loikkanen, 1982; Mansikka, 1984; Plant, 1996; Vähä-Piikkiö et al., 2004) and ecological mapping methodologies (Freeman and Buck, 2003). The implementation of these strategies is of crucial importance for preservation, because natural biotopes in cities have been found to be severely threatened, and the official statistics of their availability misleading (Kucharik and Kakareka, 1998). Ønvik Pedersen et al. (2004) have pointed out the use of Geographical Information Systems (GIS) as important tools for conservation of biodiversity in cities. Hercock (1997) has presented a method for the involvement of non-professionals in the planning and design process.

If the goal is to preserve original natural vegetation as such in cities and towns, a crucial problem is that once the native vegetation is lost, it cannot be restored by just planting replacement species. Therefore, the damage is irreversible if it is greater than the resilience capacity of the vegetation. This, in turn, raises huge information and persuasion problems. Everyone involved in the development process, including decision-makers as well as planners, designers, labour management staff and construction workers, must be informed about the goal for the protected areas (Florgård et al., 1977). If not, any mistake can lead to irreparable damage.

The most important phases in the development process are found to be the decision-making, planning and design stages (Florgård, 2000) because it is in these phases that the most resilient vegetation types can be chosen to be preserved as future green areas. Suitable construction methods can be selected, and residential areas and roads can be located in a pattern developed to minimise future impacts on the natural vegetation (Fig. 22.2). Vegetative as well as zoological biodiversity should be increased by preserving or recreating natural islands of complete habitat profiles (Beissinger and Osborne, 1984).

As mentioned above, it has been found to be important to carry out a nature survey before the planning and design stages begin (Dyring, 1984). This survey should include vegetation, soil, hydrology, local climate and other factors of importance to the planning and design process (Perelman, 1979). Aspects that

Fig. 22.2. During construction (a) and after construction (b) of the IBM building in Stockholm, showing the preservation of natural vegetation. (Photos by C. Florgård).

should be considered are the vulnerability or resistance of the vegetation to disturbance, the resilience capacity of the vegetation, and its suitability for use as components of the urban structure. These factors and aspects should be based on an analysis of the probable main impact of the development. A final assessment should point out areas of interest for preservation, and possible counter-measures to minimise future impacts. A simple survey integrated in the process at the right time – which almost always means early in the process – is found to be much more efficient than a highly developed survey apart from the planning and design process, or late in the process (Florgård, 1981).

If the vegetation in an area is mosaic, with some parts deemed to be vulnerable and others considered resistant, it is not only the type and extent of the impact that has to be considered; the location of the area relative to areas that are yet to be developed must also be known. If the area is large and can be preserved as a whole, impacts might be small enough for some parts of the area to remain more or less undisturbed. Ecotones such as forest fringes have been found to be of special importance for preserving biodiversity (Ehnberg, 1991). In these cases, the biodiversity aspect should be taken into consideration when creating development plans. On the other hand, if the area is to be heavily built-up with only small parts of the original vegetation preserved, it is most likely that these parts would be severely damaged by trampling and other impacts (Niemelä and Halme, 1998). In this case, the planners and designers have to consider whether the vulnerable parts of the vegetation should be removed and these areas built upon, and more impact-tolerant areas be preserved instead. The structure of the development plan has to be adapted to the site (Naturmark i bebyggelsesplanen, 1986).

Some impacts are dependent on the type and location of the development and cannot be completely eliminated by mitigation measures in planning and design, while other types of impact can be reduced or prevented. Urban climate changes (Oke, 1989; Upmanis *et al.*, 2000) are due to both regional and local factors. The amount of fragmentation of a development site can also be influenced by planning (Kellomäki and Wuorenrinne, 1979; Saunders *et al.*, 1991; Niemelä and Halme, 1998; McWilliam and Brown, 2001; Stenhouse, 2004a), which is important for the species richness in remnant patches. Impacts such as changes in the hydrological situation, changes in pollution situation and increasing trampling are very much due to planning and design. Thus, they can be controlled by the implementation of ecologically sound planning and design schemes which can minimise impacts on the vegetation targeted for preservation. For example, storm water can be captured at roofs and asphalt areas, and infiltrated in green areas, thus compensating for loss in natural infiltration (Florgård and Palm, 1980), and an area can be planned in such a way that trampling in vulnerable areas is reduced.

Regarding impact during construction, much of it can be prevented by developing appropriate countermeasures. Dorney *et al.* (1984) emphasise the importance of the developer for the conservation of trees. The most important factor is the creation of a work environment where everyone understands and shares the goals of preserving vegetation (Florgård, 1981). All persons at a construction site have to be informed about why some areas are protected and why they are not allowed to be used during construction. This includes workers as well as labour management staff, designers and decision-makers. The second most important counter-measure is to erect fences around areas to be protected. These fences are temporarily erected during construction, and removed when construction is finished (Luniak, 1980). With the creation of a shared understanding of the conservation goals of the site and the erection of fences, it has been possible to preserve indigenous vegetation adjacent to both sides of highrise buildings even though the fences were put up only 2 metres from the façade on one side, and 4–15 metres on the other (Florgård *et al.*, 1979). Therefore, the construction site itself must be designed. For example, areas for storage and for construction site huts must be limited and their placement carefully planned (LaDell, 1986).

It is important to bear in mind that it is the values connected to the vegetation that should be preserved (Florgård, 2000; Breuste, 2004). A study by Hoehne (1981) revealed the fact that there were two objectives when preserving natural and semi-natural areas in towns and cities: preservation and recreation. In addition to these objectives, other objectives such as environmental improvement can be added. In some cases, the objective can be only to preserve the original vegetation. This is the case when biodiversity is the main value, and any change in vegetation composition would have negative consequences. However, in other cases preservation does not necessarily mean that all parts of the original vegetation must be preserved. The preservation should be looked upon more as preservation of certain values connected to the vegetation, rather than just the plant community itself (Florgård, 1981; Falck, 1996; Guntenspergen et al., Chapter 29). For example, if the value according to the nature survey and assessment is 'shelter belt', it might be possible to preserve the tree and bush layer, even if the ground cover vegetation is destroyed. And if the main purpose is to create a play area, its value may not be reduced even if trampling and playing results in some damage to the vegetation. In some cases, it will also be possible to change a part of the vegetation deliberately to fulfil the objectives for the area. Of course this has to be done in a sensitive and creative manner so that other values connected to the vegetation will not be lost.

Management of preserved vegetation

Preserving natural and semi-natural vegetation, instead of planting and sowing to establish vegetation, has economical benefits. One of the most important facts is that the care and maintenance costs are usually low and management activities relatively simple, which means they can easily be carried out by the management authorities (Geelmuyden, 1985). However, low cost does not mean that there is no need for maintenance (Stenhouse, 2001; McDonnell, 1988). Again, the need for maintenance depends on: (1) the goal for the vegetation in a specific area; (2) impacts on the area; and (3) the sensitivity of the vegetation to disturbance (Falck and Rydberg, 1996; Rydberg, 1998; Rydberg and Falck, 2000). Long-term changes must also be considered when planning the creation of a preserved patch of natural and semi-natural vegetation (Löfvenhaft, 2004, Chapter 24). Numerous goals and management approaches have been developed, as well as plans and guidelines for the care and maintenance of natural areas in Australia, Norway, Sweden and other countries around the world (Olsen et al., 1987; Mather and Laurence, 1993; Government of Western Australia, 1995; Vårdprogram för naturmarken i Hagaparken, 1995; Urban Bushland Council, 1999). Studies to date indicate that picking up litter and keeping the area tidy are as important in areas with preserved vegetation as in more traditionally developed areas such as squares and playgrounds (Heino, 1974). If not kept tidy, the areas will deteriorate. However, the definition of the term 'tidy' may be problematic. For adults, 'tidy' often means garden-like conditions with a few bushes and small trees under a higher tree canopy. This means that bushes, small trees, fallen dead trees, fallen branches and so on are often removed by the management organisation. This results in a lack of material to inspire children's play. It also means that the image of the area will be more cultivated, and according to Kylin (2003) less useful and less inspiring for children. In other words, it is not easy to find a way of tidying up which meets both the 'demand for order' by the adults and the 'demand for disorder' by the children. Care can also lead to a decreasing amount of biologically important organic matter, and decreasing biodiversity. Maintenance itself can become an impact (McDonnell, 1988) so it is critical that the goal of preserving the vegetation is clear and understood by everyone working at the site (Falck, 1996).

Pre-commercial thinning has been used to manage the vegetation to suit the demands of different groups of residents, and the value of the vegetation can be gradually increased step by step (Rydberg and Falck, 1998). But again, it is important to set specific goals and management plans for these activities. Thinning and replacement of native species by ornamental vegetation without a specific goal can negatively affect the recreational value of the vegetation as well as its importance for the bird population (Beissinger and Osborne, 1984). The traditional methods of commercial forestry are not appropriate (Hörnsten and Dahlin, 2000). Gundersen et al. (2005) states that a conservative felling policy in urban forests makes it likely that the proportion of old stands will increase.

Regeneration must also be considered. Lehvävirta (1999) found that there was regeneration by tree saplings even in fairly trampled urban woodlands, and that barriers such as rocks, tree stems, fallen trees and so on could be used to limit wear at small spots, and thus improve regeneration.

An ecological problem involving long-term care and maintenance is that impact on the vegetation and biodiversity does not only occur when an area is urbanised. Vegetation in a rural area could also be under stress, and some parts of this stress will disappear when the area is transformed from rural to urban. One could say that the process of removing original, natural impact factors in itself constitutes an impact. For example, in Sweden there has been a debate about the trampling tolerance of preserved vegetation, and whether certain vegetation types should be preserved because of their presumed vulnerability to trampling. One of the discussed vegetation types is the herb-rich pastureland on dry soil, a vegetation type providing not just great beauty, but also high biodiversity. As pastureland it has been grazed and trampled by cattle. However, it has been found that when it is preserved in urban areas, trampling by people has been less severe than that of cattle (Florgård, 2007c). Wear-and-tear by children, including cutting branches and ripping leaves to build dens and so on, has also been found to be a minor impact compared with the cattle grazing. Preserved pastureland, which was predicted to become worn down by the local occupants, has instead been found to be overgrown by bushes and trees. In this case, the impact of people has been less than that of the cattle, and maintenance should aim at keeping the pastureland open. Because this new impact differs from the original, vegetation changes in the ground cover will occur anyway. Whether or not changes in the preserved vegetation are acceptable should be considered in the planning and design process.

Once the goals of preserving the vegetation of a site have been established, the physical, ecological and social assets of the site need to be clearly identified along with the appropriate measures to maintain them through the construction phase and into the future.

If the resource is defined as biodiversity, then it will probably be best preserved if the vegetation is protected against most types of habitat changes. If the resource, on the other hand, is defined as 'beautiful vegetation' or 'soil with high biological potential' it may be possible to supplement or improve the quality of the site using resources from other areas. This approach allows translocation of vegetation. Translocation can be carried out in many ways and for many purposes (Buckley, 1989). For example, if a pipeline has to be built in an area where the image of nature is important, turf with ground cover vegetation can be removed before construction, and replaced when construction is finished. Parts of quarries or roadsides can be restored with turf from a part of the site where quarrying or road work is going on. Deposits can be covered with turf taken from the area where the deposit is enlarged. The transplantation will put the vegetation under stress. This will start a succession which must be accepted. However, in most cases the vegetation changes will not be severe, and the treated area will in a short period of time come to resemble the surrounding natural vegetation. In addition to the turf transplanting method, relocation of the topsoil as such can also be a method for developing a succession towards a natural-looking vegetation. The direction and the speed of the succession depend on the vegetation and soil used, and the habitat on the new site.

Summary

Preservation of original natural vegetation within cities means the use of the vegetation in areas where buildings and infrastructure are to be built. It also includes preservation of remnants of vegetation in already built-up areas. The approach encompasses vegetation types such as natural and semi-natural forests and woodlands, bushland, meadows, pastureland, heaths, mires and wetlands. Preservation of natural vegetation has many biological, economic and social advantages. It can provide high biodiversity, low costs for development of green areas, and exciting natural areas for children's play. One of the most important reasons for preservation is amenity. Vegetation types of this kind are unique and virtually impossible to recreate using traditional methods of planting and sowing. If the preserved biotopes are carefully chosen during the planning and design process, they can provide attractive complements to designed areas. However, remnants of natural vegetation are stressed by changes in climate, radiation, hydrological conditions, soil conditions, pollution, fragmentation of biotopes (habitats), and mechanical impacts such as littering, trampling, cutting trees and driving of vehicles. In most cases, preservation will mean that the vegetation will be protected against major impact and major vegetation changes, but the vegetation can, in certain cases, be altered if it is in accordance with the goal for the preservation objectives. Strategies for decision-making, planning, design and management are of crucial importance for the preservation of natural and semi-natural vegetation in towns and cities.

Acknowledgements

Thanks to Mark McDonnell for improving and final editing of the manuscript.

23

Homogeneity of urban biotopes and similarity of landscape design language in former colonial cities

MARIA E. IGNATIEVA AND GLENN H. STEWART

Introduction

When the Anglo settlers set out to establish colonies in the United States, Canada, Australia and New Zealand they were attempting to create a 'new England', a purified British society transplanted to another land. These countries have a lot in common in history, demography and interconnections: they are Anglo 'colonies of settlement' (unlike 'colonies of Empire') where Europeans dispossessed and almost exterminated the earlier inhabitants (Diamond, 1997; Dunlap, 1999). In the case of the United States and Canada there were also other significant European settlement influences such as French, German, Dutch and Spanish. In the nineteenth century the settlers made themselves at home in these new lands by making it like home. They used European plants and animals and tools of industrial civilisation to transform the countryside with a speed and thoroughness never seen before and on a scale that has never been repeated. The destruction of native ecosystems was a central process, eclipsed only by the subsequent enthusiasm for importing mammals and birds for sentiment and sport. Both had dire biological and social consequences.

Changing the land was not an event but a process characterised by a set of actions that created a suite of landscapes. The transformation was most complete around settler homes. European grasses spread to picket fences, roses and lilacs bloomed in North American yards, primroses and other English flowers by Australian and New Zealand homes. In parks from New York to Sydney people

Ecology of Cities and Towns: A Comparative Approach, ed. Mark J. McDonnell, Amy K. Hahs and Jürgen H. Breuste. Published by Cambridge University Press. © Cambridge University Press 2009.

walked on European grass growing in imitation English meadows, and the commonest birds they saw were starlings, pigeons and English sparrows. In rural areas, European crops filled the fields and European weeds the roadside ditches, but some native species persisted (Cronon, 2003). New habitats were created and the wild changed as plants and feral animals spread before the settlers.

After a lengthy period of redoing their new lands, governments by the late eighteenth century began to establish more systematic efforts in the service of 'empire'. They established experimental gardens in the tropics and at home for botanical studies and as a source of novelties for the gardens. They tested new species and shifted promising ones to their new lands. With the increased speed and volume of shipping by the mid nineteenth century commercial gardeners were stocking British greenhouses with tropical plants and sending British flowers to homesick colonials in the antipodes.

By the late nineteenth century settlers had formed societies to 'improve' their countries by stocking them with 'useful and beautiful' plants and animals. These societies concentrated on species from 'home' but in some instances also imported plants and animals from around the world. In New Zealand for example, more than a hundred species of birds and over 30 species of mammals, including deer, possums and wallabies, were introduced (Veblen and Stewart, 1982). Within a generation this fad had passed, but seldom have so few done so much over so large an area with so little effort or understanding. In the end of the nineteenth and the beginning of the twentieth centuries many former colonial cities experienced the 'beautification' movement based on a contemporary understanding of European forms and the monumental idioms of city planning, architecture and planting design.

In the twentieth century there arose a new appreciation of nature and along with it, the conservation movement – the beginning of searching for each country's particular ecological identity (Worster, 1977). Settlers began to examine seriously what effects the land had on them and to incorporate the land into their culture. Conspicuous or emblematic plants and animals became national symbols – the kiwi in New Zealand and the kangaroo in Australia are classic examples. Landscape paintings, nature literature, outdoor recreation and nature education became an integral part of urban middle-class leisure. Governments took new steps to protect nature, setting aside rural or wilderness areas for recreation and protection. This culminated in the strong environmental movements of the 1960s and 1970s when ecological knowledge became a cornerstone of the conservation movement.

The unique ecological identity of the former colonies therefore reflects similarities and differences in the cultural, historical and ecological aspects of the landscape. This is particularly obvious in urban environments. There has been a strong European influence in the way that cities were planned and the way in which they developed. The objective of this chapter is to explore some important principles of urban planning structure (grid system, downtown and suburban sprawl) and different landscape architecture styles (Capability Brown, Picturesque, Gardenesque and 'Wild' Garden), and to look at the peculiarities of using the same plant materials in parks and gardens. These principles are the main reasons behind the phenomena of homogenisation of urban environments and the creation of similar urban habitats in former colonial cities (creation of lawns, hedges, flower beds, walls, pavement cracks, etc.). These similarities of urban habitats can be an excellent starting point in initiations of comparative analysis in different cities and towns. This chapter also explores some practical planting design solutions ('freedom lawns', 'go wild', 'plant signatures' and indigenous gardens) that break the homogeneity of urban environments and help to create identity of cities. We use as examples cities in the northeastern United States, Australia (mostly Melbourne, Sydney and Adelaide) and New Zealand. We use the word 'homogeneity' in its broader meaning as consisting of similar design and plant materials that are similar to each other.

Starting points

Native landscapes of the northeastern United States prior to European colonisation were primarily forested landscapes (mostly deciduous forests). Native Americans cultivated many plants, including beans and squash, and they cleared some forests for agriculture (Cronon, 2003). In appearance and plant composition (and even fauna) European and northeastern landscapes had much in common. Both landscapes were influenced, and in many cases shaped, by the most recent glaciations and both were clothed with deciduous forests. The landscapes were much 'wilder looking' to Europeans because back at home there were few native forests remaining. On the other hand in the northeastern United States, Europeans could see not only a forested landscape with familiar trees but also familiar mammals such as deer, bear, wolf and fox.

Compared with this, native Australian and New Zealand landscapes looked completely different to the colonists. In New Zealand they were confronted with an essentially forested landscape (apart from the eastern side of the South Island) with an unfamiliar complement of plants and animals. The dramatic and breathtaking landscape ranged from boiling mud pools, volcanoes and geysers in the north to soaring mountains, primeval forests and glaciers in the south. Apart from two species of native bats there were no terrestrial land mammals and a highly endemic avifauna, many of which were flightless. In an attempt to make their new country 'more like home' the colonists voraciously cleared the forests and converted the land to pasture. That, and the introduction of familiar mammals, dramatically changed the landscape. In Australia, settlers found a hot, dry and unforgiving land (Flannery, 1999) – tropical forests in the north, eucalyptus forests for miles and miles, and endless deserts in the middle, full of strange and wonderful but utterly unfamiliar animals. As in New Zealand, cities and towns sprang up, mainly near the coast, and forests were rapidly converted to pasture.

European settlers applied to these completely different native landscapes on the other side of the globe the exact same principles of urban design and land-use practice, landscape and planting that they had practised in Europe.

The European influence

Urban planning principles

All human landscapes reflect cultural peculiarities in some way. When Europeans arrived in the New World countries they brought their own architectural styles for buildings and patterns to follow in urban planning. Even though American, Australian and New Zealand cities were established at different times, they all exhibit some similarity in the history of their development. All new towns and cities had mainly European design patterns with some peculiarities related to differences in climate, topography, politics and their economic situation.

The grid system

Initially, all colonial settlements explored a regular grid planning structure. The grid system is a logical way to survey land in straight lines, whether for a township or an urban lot. The grid system gave the city functional efficiency and was ideal for the equal distribution of land or easy parcelling and selling of real estate. Historically the urban grid served two main purposes. The first was to facilitate orderly settlement and colonisation in a broad sense. The second was its use as an instrument of modernisation and as a contrast to what was not as orderly. One of the first large US cities planned using a grid system was Philadelphia. The grid system was the most efficient way of using space for development where topography was non-limiting and was supposed to encourage economic development (Homberger, 1994). Syracuse, New York, founded around the 1840s, also demonstrated a classical grid structure intersected by the Erie Canal (Fig. 23.1a).

In New Zealand and Australia many towns were designed in Great Britain using the regular grid system as a model. For example, in the Edward Jollie plan of Christchurch a classical rectangular grid can be easily recognised (Fig. 23.1b). An early plan of Melbourne also shows a rectangular grid of streets one mile by half a mile (Fig. 23.1c). Adelaide was started as a simple grid that covered one square mile and was surrounded by parkland.

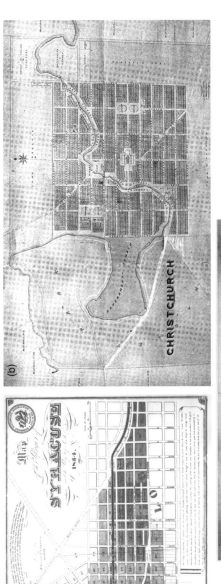

Fig. 23.1. Examples of cities with classical grid patterns: (a) plan of Syracuse, NY in 1834, (b) plan of Christchurch, NZ by Edward Jollie in 1850 and (c) view of Melbourne, AUS in 1880.

Downtown

The next influential chapter in the development of urban planning of colonial cities was a crystallisation of commercial urban cores in the end of the nineteenth and the first part of the twentieth centuries. Development of downtowns was driven by growing demand for limited amounts of good commercial real estate and by opportunities provided by modern technology. Earlier towns were transformed into intense and more exclusive settlements with single-purpose areas established, such as financial, shopping and administrative districts (Kostof, 1992). Densely urbanised areas with skyscrapers expressed the new assertiveness of technology and the modern urban spirit. The panorama of New York's Manhattan district started to be a world-famous symbol of American cities (Fig. 23.2a). This symbol 'served American national pride', it was also a symbol of 'power, energy, daring, and sophistication' (Meinig, 1979). This American pattern was later mirrored in Australian cities (Melbourne downtown, Fig. 23.2b), New Zealand (Wellington downtown, Fig. 23.2c) and even in Europe (La Defence in Paris and London's Canary Wharf; Kostof, 1992).

Fig. 23.2. Panorama views of three former colonial cities illustrating their roles as symbols of urban prosperity, technology and power: (a) New York's Manhattan district as world-famous symbol of American cities, (b) downtown Melbourne, AUS and (c) downtown Wellington, NZ.

Fig. 23.2. (cont.)

Suburbia

The third most influential urban planning element that has driven the development of all former colonial cities has been suburbia. The modern suburb is the result of an era of industrialisation and fast transportation. By the end of the nineteenth century a new pattern of residential settlement for commuters developed in Europe and the United States. Development of suburbs always reflected differences in local culture, banking systems, transportation, building technique and administrative authority. There are two major types of suburbia: a diffuse patchwork of detached houses, or high-density apartment blocks with open areas (Kostof, 1992). For example, English Georgian suburbs developed a pattern with rows of identical very closely attached houses. High density apartment blocks were a very common type of suburbia in Western and Eastern Europe. Rows of identical attached single-family terraced houses with tiny gardens have also been very influential in US seaboard cities (e.g. Philadelphia, New York, Baltimore, Boston, San Francisco). There are only a few surviving examples of this type of suburb in the USA.

By the beginning of the twentieth century, suburbia characterised by detached houses started to become most influential in the USA and later in Australian and New Zealand cities. The reason for the popularity of this type of suburbia in the USA was the right of landowners to develop their properties as they wanted. In the period after World War II, the USA experienced an unprecedented migration to the suburbs. Between 1946 and 1956 about 97% of all new single-family dwellings were detached and surrounded on every side by their own plots (Jackson, 1985). Typical lot sizes were relatively uniform around the country (averaging 0.1–0.2 acre or 810 to 405 square metres). These suburbs, which began as early as the 1930s in the United States, became completely automobile dependent, a condition exaggerated by Eisenhower's Interstate Defence Highway Act of 1956.

Another very important feature of American post-war suburbs was an architectural similarity. It was a result of reducing the design fees by simplifying the production methods and design solutions. After World War II, because of these mass-production techniques, government-financed high wages and low interest rates, it was easier to buy a new house in suburbia than to reinvest in central city properties (Jackson, 1985).

Suburbia effectively grew in all Australian and New Zealand cities in the post-war years. There are some differences of course in the design solution of the individual plots and residential architecture, but ideologically suburbia's structure was very similar in these countries to that in the United States (Fig. 23.3a, b and c). One of the reasons for sharing the US experience of suburbia in Australia, New Zealand and Canada is a strong frontier tradition of small populations, and a British cultural dislike of cities (Jackson, 1985).

(a)

(b)

Fig. 23.3. Examples of suburban development showing similarity in the ideological structure of suburban life: (a) Syracuse, New York in 2003, (b) Melbourne, Australia in 2003 and (c) Christchurch, New Zealand in 1998.

Fig. 23.3. (cont.)

Urban renewal

Urban renewal in the United States, Australia and New Zealand was equivalent to post-war reconstruction in Europe. It took place mainly in downtown areas in the 1950s and 1960s. Many places were completely cleared of structures and then re-developed. It was viewed as a way to install modern components in American downtowns (Kostof, 1992). The same tendencies can be seen in many Australian and New Zealand cities. Large buildings, tall monolithic structures (new skyscrapers), parking garages and huge parking lots, and new apartment houses transformed the traditional downtown colonial grid. However, it is important to note that many cities have historic buildings and districts that were preserved.

As a result of similar historical development of urban planning in cities in the USA, Australia and New Zealand, there are striking similarities in urban planning structures, such as the original simplified grid pattern, modern downtown, suburban sprawl and extensive transportation systems. The similarity in urban planning structure is one of the main reasons for the creation of similar urban habitats such as paved areas, roads, building walls, garden and park lawns, street planting and parking lots.

Landscape architecture styles

Landscape design styles were another very important part of European 'borrowed' baggage that arrived in the New World colonies. At the end of the eighteenth century and the beginning of the nineteenth century the most influential was 'Capability' Brown who was followed by the Picturesque style. Lancelot 'Capability' Brown (1716–83) edited nature and created an aesthetically 'perfect' landscape. The topography was shaped in the form of a series of gentle convex and concave curves. Trees were planted in groves, groups or belts. An emerald-green flowing lawn was one of the essential composition elements. He used only native deciduous trees (e.g. *Quercus robur*, *Tilia cordata*, *Fagus sylvatica*, *Ulmus laevis*, *Acer platanoides*, *Acer pseudoplatanus*, *Fraxinus excelsior*) and a few evergreen tree species. Brown's gardens were simply a productive working landscape arranged to be beautiful (Rogers, 2001).

In the last decade of the nineteenth century the principle of deriving landscapes from pictures was to be called 'Picturesque'. Advocates desired to add 'the bold roughness of nature' and suggested appreciation of wild nature as seen through the filter of art. William Gilpin, one of the main ideologists of the Picturesque style, promoted 'bold nature' by encouraging conversion of lawns to rugged oak woodlands, complete with wheel tracks, scattered stones and brush-wood. Instead of making landscapes smooth, Gilpin suggested making them rough, and therefore picturesque (Rogers, 2001). The Picturesque style was the most influential as a theoretical source, especially in new colonies. One of the most famous admirers of both Capability Brown and Picturesque was Frederick Law Olmstead, the designer of Central Park in New York City, who created park landscapes that were both pastoral and picturesque. Olmstead strongly believed that the pastoral and picturesque scenery of parks would be instructive to immigrants of the new democratic societies, through a process of scenic enjoyment of predominantly agrarian values (Rogers, 2001). Open spacious lawns with gentle rises and scattered clumps of trees, curvilinear lines of pathways, ponds and lakes all aiming to create scenic views appeared in public parks and gardens. Cities in the United States, New Zealand and Australia were influenced by Capability Brown and Picturesque ideology (Fig. 23.4a and b). Frederick Law Olmsted and the social reformer Charles Loring Brace helped in creating a new vision of suburbia in the USA and other colonial countries.

Suburban yards in former colonial countries also followed this romantic approach with their gently curving paths, irregular groupings of trees and shrubs, and often-rustic pavilions. Many authors see the presence of green lawns in suburban gardens as nostalgia for English motherland gardens. The appearance of sheep, cows, deer and other 'plastic' kitsch culture attributed to the middle-class front lawns in the USA, Australia and New Zealand is also a kind of intuitively nostalgic note on the pastoral English landscape. Especially in the USA the well-manicured yard became a symbol of wealth and social standing.

The Industrial Revolution in Europe in the nineteenth century opened a new era of stylistic diversity. Gardenesque style was opposite to Picturesque and

Fig. 23.4. Examples of Capability Brown and Picturesque ideology of gentle curves and open lawns with scattered clumps of trees: (a) Central Park (New York City) and (b) one of Sydney's (Australia) public parks.

introduced eclecticism of design styles and exoticism – use of new plant species that had just been discovered in different parts of the world. John Claudius Loudon introduced the principle of incorporating exotic species and a display of all plants in a way that would highlight individual species (Rogers, 2001). The Gardenesque approach in landscape design was a very powerful tool of the Victorian ethic of 'improvement'. Victorian gardens actually perpetuated the picturesque approach but used and displayed new exotic plants. The lawn was used as a special display where each plant can 'arrive at perfection' and the quality of plants can be seen especially clearly (Elliott, 1986). Around the 1840s new exotic plants started to be used in the system of 'change-bedding' – very elaborate floral displays planted mainly for temporary seasonal decorative effect. The introduction of the lawn mower in 1830 provided the opportunity to have a manicured lawn-display not only in large private or public parks but also in small gardens.

Capability Brown, Picturesque and Gardenesque styles were actively used in colonial countries. It resulted in the creation of similar types of habitats in public and private parks and gardens: lawns – the leading type – flowerbeds, tree and shrub groups, and groves.

The Edwardian period saw two very influential figures in landscape design. William Robinson introduced the 'Wild Garden' concept, where the garden should highlight natural development and express plant colour, form and growth habit (Zuylen, 1994). He advised the planting of alpine species in small rock gardens, the use of naturalised shrubs and ground covers in woodland parts, and native and exotic bulbs in grass and woodlands. Robinson created gardens where natural processes could be seen and appreciated. Gertrude Jekyll tried to combine the naturalistic approach within the more formal framework in her famous colourful herbaceous borders (Bisgrove, 1992).

Robinson's naturalistic gardens were incorporated in many private and public gardens in England and former colonial cities by using daffodils and bluebells in meadows and woodlands, on riverbanks and in private yards. Diverse or very simplified versions of Jekyll's herbaceous borders can be found in United States, New Zealand and Australian cities (Fig. 23.5).

Planting design

Classic romantic English parks were based on native broad-leaved trees (e.g. *Quercus robur, Tilia cordata, Fagus sylvatica, Ulmus laevis, Acer platanoides, Acer pseudoplatanus, Fraxinus excelsior*). There were only a few exotics used for solo planting such as *Cedrus libani, Salix babylonica* and *Populus nigra* 'Italica'.

In colonial parks deciduous trees were also essential plant material. For example, in Christchurch parks created in the middle to the end of the

Fig. 23.5. Simplified versions of Jekyll's herbaceous borders in one of the private gardens in Christchurch, New Zealand.

nineteenth century and the beginning of the twentieth century European deciduous trees were dominant. The image of 'the most English city outside England' was created because of wide use of European plants that were essential for Picturesque parks and gardens. In Australia there was a tremendous effort to establish deciduous trees all over the country to provide connections with home and to relieve the monotony of the naturally dull native Melaleuca, Callitris and Eucalyptus species with fresh green in spring and colour in autumn (Bligh, 1980).

In the USA, European deciduous trees were also used, but native deciduous trees such as *Acer saccharum*, *Quercus rubra*, *Ulmus americana* and *Fraxinus americana* were often planted. Native deciduous American trees were very 'lucky' because of their close resemblance and genetic relationships to European relatives in texture, and in colour, in other words to the general European image.

Gardenesque style introduced to European and colonial parks and gardens a whole range of tropical and subtropical plants from around the world. For carpet beds Central and South American plants such as *Tagetes erecta*, *Tagetes patula*, *Begonia semperflorens* or *Ageratum houstonianum* were among the favourites. The 'discovery' of the Chinese flora resulted in the appearance in gardens of *Chrysanthemum maximum*, *Dianthus chinensis* and *Callistephus sinensis*.

Chinese and American rhododendrons and azaleas were an excellent 'discovery' for William Robinson's wild garden. Many public parks or private gardens

Fig. 23.6. Influence of Robinson's 'Wild Garden' in Christchurch, NZ Hagley Park (note daffodils).

tried to organise small naturalised groups of blooming rhododendrons that would look very 'natural' and beautiful. Robinson's practice of introducing native and exotic bulbs in woodland and grassland resulted in the appearance in new colonies of the same species in public and private gardens. For example, in Christchurch's Hagley Park in New Zealand, the display of daffodils and bluebells (Fig. 23.6) is one of the major city attractions in the spring. According to our recent survey of three neighbourhoods in Syracuse, New York, in private gardens, daffodils and tulips are still the most popular spring decorative culti-vated plants. Gertrude Jekyll used classical perennial border plants such as *Delphinium*, *Lavandula*, *Rosa*, *Dianthus*, *Campanula* and *Alcea rosea*, and they can be found in practically every private colonial temperate garden.

Urban habitats today

The use of similar urban design structures, landscape architecture styles, plant material and construction materials has resulted in the creation of cities and towns around the world that have the same general appearance. For example, brick, sandstone, limestone, marble, concrete and granite are used for foundations, columns and steps, while asphalt is commonly used for roads and car parks. The use of gravel and mortar-joined material in cities and towns has resulted in the creation of specific urban biotopes (habitats) such as lawns, hedges, woodlands, flowerbeds, herbaceous borders, roadside and railway verges, walls and paving cracks (Breuste, Chapter 21). There are also remnants of natural vegetation that can be viewed as another type of urban habitat (Florgård, Chapter 22). Here we discuss several of these urban biotopes.

Lawns

Lawns are one of the most frequent and widespread urban biotopes (Muller, 1990). Lawns are found in parks, private gardens, playing fields, golf courses, along streets and roads, in plazas and schoolyards. In European parks, for example, lawns normally occupy between 75% and 95% of the park area (Gilbert, 1989). Lawns are nearly universal in front and back yards in suburban USA, Australia and New Zealand. For example, lawns average 52–80% of residential greenspace among ten older to newer neighbourhoods studied in Syracuse, New York (Richards et al., 1984). In Christchurch, New Zealand, lawns typically cover at least 50–60% of private gardens, and as much as 75% of public parks.

The first lawns were probably well maintained fields in Europe used for grazing cattle and sheep, but were also used as a setting for ornamental trees and shrubs. The origin of the lawn as a landscape feature is most likely due to the fact it occurs in natural European landscape as floodplain meadow vegetation. Lawns probably first appeared in the thirteenth century (Muller, 1990; Goryshina and Ignatieva, 2000) but the precise time of their appearance is unknown. In Medieval gardens a turf 'cut from good (meadow) grass' was used quite widely (Thacker, 1979).

Lawn was part of the English colonists' 'luggage' that they brought to new land, 'something domestic, or at least domesticated' (Teyssot, 1999). Lawn in former colonial private gardens and public parks symbolically represented the pastoral nostalgia of the English landscape. Domestic green 'carpet' was also a continuation of the interior of a house, explaining perfectly why lawn is supposed to be neat and tidy in all domestic gardens. In public spaces lawn always symbolised civic identity and democratic stability (O'Malley, 1999). One of the latest and very common theories to explain this 'passion' and love for lawns is the evolution of humans in the grassy, tree-scattered savannas of Africa (Bormann et al., 2001).

Lawn as a type of meadow plant community was completely alien to native landscapes of the northeastern United States, Australia and New Zealand. In the northeastern United States there is relatively little native (or long-evolved) meadow community associated with upland areas of the naturally forested region, so any meadow or lawn community had to be composed primarily of introduced species, especially from regions where there is a much longer history of livestock husbandry than in the northeastern USA (where it is less than 400 years). In Australia and New Zealand there are quite a few grasses in native biomes, but all of them are endemic to these countries and had a very 'foreign' appearance compared with green European meadow grasses.

Nowadays lawn can be seen not only as a symbol of the British Empire but also as a symbol of Western Civilisation. Because of the dominant economical and political role of the USA, its inhabitants have successfully transported this 'lawn aesthetic' around the globe. In the USA itself, lawns cover 27.6 million acres, an area about the size of the state of Pennsylvania. Lawn maintenance is about a $30 billion industry (Bormann *et al.*, 2001). Lawn is the major source of pollution in American suburbia as a result of mowing and herbicide application.

Comparison of available data on temperate lawns (in Europe (Gilbert, 1989; Muller, 1990; Wiltshire, 1994), Christchurch, New Zealand (Ignatieva *et al.*, 2000) and Syracuse, New York (M. E. Ignatieva, 2003 field data)) shows that in 'colonial lawns' exotic species completely dominate – *Lolium perenne*, *Poa pratensis* and *Festuca rubra* are the most frequent grasses. Among perennials other Eurasian herbaceous species can be found in almost any urban lawn – *Trifolium repens*, *Plantago lanceolata* and *Prunella vulgaris*.

European lawns are dominated by European or Eurasian species. There are some native plant species in Christchurch (16) and Syracuse (6) lawns but they are uncommon with normally only two or three at any particular site. As for the overall number of species, lawns can vary from five to six species in intensively managed lawns (using herbicides, fertilisers, regularly watering and mowing) to 10–25 in 'common' casually maintained residential lawns with a high diversity of low-growing herbaceous species. Lawns show not only homogeneity in cultural appearance ('green' as viewed from a distance), but also in structure (one layer cutting regularly) and in composition (domination of certain 'noble' grasses) in sown mixtures.

Hedges

Hedges are special habitats created by planting trees or shrubs in a line or in small dense groups a short distance from each other. There are both short and tall hedges, formal (cut) and informal types. Hedges can be found in urban private gardens and in public parks, along streets and roads. There are quite a number of tree and shrub species available for hedges, but there is a group of common species that have been used for centuries. In Europe the most common and 'oldest' species used for hedges are *Buxus sempervirens*, *Taxus baccata*, *Cupressus sempervirens*, *Cupressus macrocarpa*, *Chamaecyperus lawsoniana*, *Fagus sylvatica*, *Carpinus betulus* and *Quercus ilex*. In New Zealand traditional European, Asian and some

American species are very common in urban landscapes including *Photinia glabra*, *Camellia japonica*, *Cupressus macrocarpa*, *Chamaecyperus lawsoniana*, *Fagus sylvatica* and *Pinus radiata*. Recently some of the evergreen native species have also become popular such as *Olearia paniculata*, *Corokia cotoneaster* and *Pittosporum tenuifolium*. In the northeastern United States *Taxus cuspidata* and *Berberis thunbergii* from Asia, *Ligustrum* species from Europe and native *Thuja occidentalis* are among the most common species used for hedges. In Australia exotic plants are the most popular – *Ligustrum* species, *Berberis thunbergii*, *Plumbago* species and *Buxus sempervirens*.

Branches and trunks of trees or shrubs planted close to each other provide an excellent environment for the development of climbing species such as *Convolvulus arvensis*, *Calystegia sepium*, *Galium aparine* and *Hedera helix*. These plants can be observed in most hedges of European cities and in the colonies. The area at the base of the hedge under the canopy is usually bare ground or consists of a layer of mulch that is commonly colonised by weedy plants of Eurasian origin. Such plants as *Elytrigia repens*, *Euphorbia peplus*, *Chenopodium album*, *Coronopus didymus* and *Taraxacum officinale* commonly grow in these habitats.

Flowerbeds

The flowerbed is typically dominated by exotic herbaceous plants and occasionally sub-shrubs with decorative flowers or foliage. The species makeup of flowerbeds has always reflected the fashion of planting design. Nowadays the most popular summer bedding plants in public and private gardens are predominantly annuals derived from South Africa, Mexico and the Mediterranean. Floristic composition in former colonial cities is almost identical to the flowerbeds of European cities – *Tagetes*, *Pelargonium*, *Petunia*, *Narcissus*, *Tulipa*, *Cineraria* and *Rosa*. Flower borders in private gardens typically use a wider range of decorative plants. Among perennial exotic plants traditional English cottage plants are still popular and include roses, delphiniums, hollyhocks, peonies, lupins and lilies.

The most common spontaneous weeds of colonial flower borders are *Euphorbia peplus*, *Sonchus oleraceus*, *Oxalis* spp., *Senecio vulgaris* and *Poa annua*. A very important feature of this habitat is regular disturbance by cultivation, weeding, irrigation and fertiliser applications.

Pavement cracks and walls

Pavement cracks in all colonial cities have similar environmental parameters. First of all, plants that appear in cracks experience many stresses such as pollution from cars, extremes of temperature, compaction and trampling, and in some cases salt from de-icing (Woodell, 1979). The mechanical damage to plants and the compaction of soil lead to poor moisture retention and lack of aeration making pavement cracks a difficult environment for plants to survive. Because of the use of similar construction materials for buildings and roads and similar technology, the gaps between paving stones accumulate a similar soft soil-like substratum. Plants that occupy such habitats commonly do so in cities around the world. There are a lot of annual plants among 'pavement' plants. The four most common cosmopolitan species include *Poa annua*, *Plantago major*, *Polygonum aviculare* and *Taraxacum officinale*.

Brick, sandstone and limestone, concrete and granite are the most frequent materials for walls in most cities. The physical characteristics of mortar-joined materials for brick and stonewalls are very similar too. Similarity of environmental conditions such as moisture, light and temperature create conditions for growing similar plants. The Eurasian plant *Cymballaria muralis* is the most common urban wall plant around the globe. Some ferns are also very common among wall plants. For example, *Dryopteris filix-mas* has been found growing on many European and New Zealand urban walls.

Searching for ecological identity in colonial cities

Alternative or 'freedom lawns' in the Unites States of America

Many factors, including homogeneity of landscape, lack of natural biodiversity, air and soil pollution, and the use of fossil fuels associated with the creation and upkeep of lawns, the most common urban habitat, have resulted in a new interest in developing alternative solutions to traditional 'velvet' carpet lawns in America (Bormann *et al.*, 2001).

The first and the oldest initiatives of an alternative to traditional lawns started around the turn of the twentieth century in the Midwest of the USA where the native 'prairie' grassland community was maintained and extended by wildfire. Jens Jensen (1860–1951), one of America's great landscape designers, created the 'Prairie Style' in landscape architecture. Instead of cultivating traditional exotic vegetation in tightly ordered patterns, he started to use native prairie plants in designed parks. 'Prairie school' architects used the Illinois tall-grass prairie and oak savannah as sources of inspiration. Jensen also encouraged the restoration of native landscapes along roadsides. At the same time Illinois landscape horticulturists pioneered the idea of using native plants and their natural plant associations, and the reintroduction of native plants in small yards as an alternative to traditional private gardening (Egan, 1990). Nowadays the Midwest is leading the USA in a number of projects in gardening with prairie plants in urban and suburban communities (Wasowski and Wasowski, 2002).

With growing environmental awareness and ecological education over the past two decades, many Americans have begun to question the environmental and economic costs, and aesthetic quality, of the traditional lawn. New terms such as 'alternative lawns' and 'freedom lawns' have started to be used in popular gardening and scientific literature. Publications such as Michael Pollan's *Second Nature* (Pollan, 1991), *Redesigning the American Lawn* (Bormann *et al.*, 2001) and *The Lawn: A History of American Obsession* (Jenkins, 1994) recount many stories of how ordinary Americans over the country have rethought their front and backyard designs and transferred their conventional lawns into prairie gardens, natural or wildlife gardens in the Midwest and northeastern USA or 'xeriscape' in dry areas throughout the country.

There are numerous publications available in the US landscape design and horticultural literature dedicated to landscaping with native plants (Diekelmann and Schuster, 1982; Stein, 1997; Knopf *et al.*, 2002). Brooklyn Botanic Garden is the leading institution on this topic (Sawyers *et al.*, 1990; Marinelli, 1994). Over recent decades the number of nurseries specialising in propagating native plants has grown dramatically. Today Americans can easily order cans of wildflowers.

There are also disadvantages of using 'alternative lawns', such as the fire hazard and insect problems, and also the occurrence of deer ticks which carry Lyme disease in some areas of the United States. The potential health risks are a concern to homeowners and have been widely discussed in local newspapers. Nevertheless, in most cases there are ways to eliminate such disadvantages using appropriate ecological design.

Unfortunately the average numbers of non-traditional native gardens in urban areas are still very low. For most people 'messy', unkept-looking 'freedom lawns' are associated with neglected landscapes. This is just the beginning of a change in traditional lawn psychology of conservative Americans towards sustainability and native biodiversity in urban landscapes.

'Go wild' in Europe

In the United Kingdom a new environmental movement towards increasing native biodiversity through designing with native plants is having real visible results. A dramatic decline of native habitats in the country forced a search for alternative ways to enhance native biodiversity. Today 20% (1 million acres) of urban areas in Great Britain are private gardens and they have the greatest potential for serving as new nature preserves. There is a large campaign in the country to increase native biodiversity by minimising traditional lawn areas and planting native plants that attract butterflies, insects and birds. In 2003, an exhibit called 'Go Wild', in Kew Botanic Gardens, illustrated ways of increasing urban biodiversity (butterflies, insects and birds) (Fig. 23.7). Among

Fig. 23.7. 'Go Wild' exhibit where lawn was not mown and looks like a meadow. Royal Botanic Gardens, Kew, UK, in May 2003.

Wow!

other European countries, the Netherlands and Germany have also been successful in designing with native plants in urban areas.

Towards a new individual ecological identity: plant signatures in New Zealand and Australia

Southern Hemisphere cities found their own way of breaking homogenous urban patterns and searching for a new way of creating an ecological as well as cultural identity. For Australia and New Zealand the concept of 'wild lawn' is not appropriate, because there is no native meadow vegetation (similar to traditional European) in the natural landscape. New Zealand and Australia have natural tussock vegetation dominated by grasses but this type of plant community looks very different from European floodplain meadows or American prairies. European patterns in architecture, planning structure and landscape design have dominated Australian and New Zealand landscapes for over 150 years. Native vegetation has only survived in the form of remnant patches throughout urban landscapes.

In the 1970s the environmental movement in Australia and New Zealand resulted in a blooming interest in native vegetation, and design with native plants in combination with interest in aboriginal art and culture. Restoration of native plant communities along rivers and coastlines, and woodlands has changed the appearance of many Australian and New Zealand urban settlements. There is also a strong movement towards creating indigenous or native gardens in Australia and New Zealand (Gabites and Lucas, 1998; Snape, 2002; Wrigley, 2003).

In 1993, Nick Robinson introduced the new concept of the 'plant signature' (Robinson, 1993). Plant signatures express the essence of a place through plant composition. The novelty of plant signatures is in the use of native plants and their combination to express the character of a particular place, offering distinctive and memorable designs. Plant signatures are about using plant combinations not only for environmental improvement, for these plants are adapted much better to existing environmental conditions, but as a way of adding distinctive identity to a neighbourhood through the design of streetscapes, street intersections, public parks, private gardens and public plazas.

In Australia and New Zealand plant signatures are often combined with sculptural or architectural works expressing aboriginal culture. For example, in New Zealand, tussock grasses are combined with stone sculptures or gravel stones having direct references to Maori culture. Nowadays plant signatures are used as a special tool for expressing national identity. For example, groups of native plants have appeared next to the Australian Parliament in Canberra and the Art Gallery of New South Wales in Sydney and next to significant buildings in all cities throughout the country. In Wellington the 'Bush City' next to the Museum of New Zealand (Te Papa) celebrates and symbolises natural New Zealand vegetation (Hicks, 1998).

Today, many native plants have become very symbolic in urban landscapes. In New Zealand, for example, one of the most common native plant combinations is cabbage tree (*Cordyline*) with flax (*Phormium*) and tussock grasses. Plant signatures are much more visible in the urban landscapes of New Zealand and Australia than in North America. But the plant signature concept could also be applied in American cities. For example, in Syracuse (New York) for plant signatures we recommended the use of a combination of plants from diverse and colourful native edges and pioneer successional herbaceous plant communities to replace part of extended lawns. This would make the urban landscape more environmentally friendly and provide new design dimensions (Carter and Ignatieva, 2002).

Conclusions

Former colonial cities have remarkable similarities in their urban biotopes and landscape designs. Given their similar settlement histories this is perhaps not surprising. The similar grid system, principles of development of downtown and suburbia, the most influential landscape architecture directions (Capability Brown, Picturesque and Gardenesque), use of urban construction materials and technique, and similarity in using introduced plant species (European deciduous trees for example) have produced an array of urban habitats that are replicated around the globe. From urban lawns to hedges and vegetation in pavement cracks and walls, the compositional and structural similarity in urban biotopes is remarkable. But now, this spreading social and ecological homogeneity in urban environments is recognised as dangerous and ending in loss of native biodiversity and general local identity. New concepts in planting design such as indigenous or native gardens, 'plant signatures', 'Go Wild' and 'alternative' or 'freedom lawns' in the United States, the United Kingdom, Australia and New Zealand offer new hope in searching for ecological and cultural identity in the cities.

24

Tools to assess human impact on biotope resilience and biodiversity in urban planning: examples from Stockholm, Sweden

KATARINA LÖFVENHAFT

Introduction

In Sweden, the political ambition is to integrate the convention on biological diversity (UNCED, 1992) into physical planning and monitoring of urban areas. These ambitions are, however, hampered by a lack of significant information on the ecological landscape context. The responsibility for implementation lies with the local municipalities, through physical planning of land and water uses, and development. According to the Planning and Building Act every municipality shall have a comprehensive up-to-date plan for its geographical area and the local government should develop the plan in co-operation with inhabitants and other interested stakeholders. The expectations on planning as an arena for discussions and implementation of environmental issues and sustainable development have increased in international and Swedish national politics. In this context it is important for the different players to bring forth the best possible grounds for making decisions on future planning and building.

To increase the comprehensive understanding of urban ecosystems, new theoretical frameworks are needed (Pickett *et al.*, 2001 and Chapter 3). The study I describe in this chapter stresses the importance of including spatio-temporal aspects in this work. It focuses on how urban monitoring procedures can be designed on the local level to provide complementary spatial and temporal

Ecology of Cities and Towns: A Comparative Approach, ed. Mark J. McDonnell, Amy K. Hahs and Jürgen H. Breuste. Published by Cambridge University Press. © Cambridge University Press 2009.

information on biodiversity that supports assessments in physical planning. By addressing questions considering biotope (i.e. habitat) fragmentation, this enables comparisons to be made at the scale of the entire municipality. This chapter will illuminate some aspects essential for including ecological information in the planning process, i.e. how to develop data needed for this purpose, and how to process the data to provide visualisations that can be used in planning work and in the planning process.

The first step in this process, in view of the absence of existing appropriate data, was the creation of a biotope database (Löfvenhaft et al., 2002a) and a record of species changes over time (Löfvenhaft et al., 2002b). The next step was to combine these datasets to analyse changes in biodiversity in the biotopes over time (Löfvenhaft et al., 2004). The framework is customised for physical planning, and is based on patterns of ecologically defined biotopes (Forman, 1995; UNEP, 1995) and land-cover types (Marzluff and Hamel, 2001), taking into account ecological and historical aspects of the landscape. Physical planning in Stockholm, Sweden, is used as the starting point.

To meet the need for geo-referenced and context sensitive ecological data in urban Stockholm, neither existing data nor previous methods for biotope mapping were sufficient. The Stockholm approach differs from others (e.g. Nyhuus and Halvorsen Thorén, 1996; Zerbe et al., 2003) in several ways. Physical planning is used as the starting point, ecologically defined biotope cover is used instead of land use as the classification tool, and spatio-temporal analyses are used as a way to obtain new knowledge and useful planning tools. Urban studies found in the literature often consider selected sites and do not relate the study of change to a wider context (e.g. Freeman, 1999; Cilliers and Bredenkamp, 2000; Florgård, 2000). This study considers a trans-disciplinary approach to provide a comprehensible reference for the landscape with enhanced interpretation possibilities for physical planning.

Objectives

The main goal of this project is to aid in maintenance of biodiversity in urban areas, by developing tools for visualising spatial and temporal aspects of the biodiversity concept, applicable to physical planning. Specific objectives are: (1) to illuminate aspects of integrating ecological–geographical information into physical planning from a user perspective; (2) to identify methods that consider area-specific ecological data, and that can be formed into complementary tools supporting contemporary planning work, by being readily used by urban planners, politicians and the public; (3) to consider longer timescales (decades to centuries) than is normal in physical planning (1–5 years) for assessing ecological effects of land-cover changes in urban areas; and (4) to test the methods developed, within the framework of real planning situations at the Stockholm City Planning Administration, using an integrated framework and a probability-orientated approach.

The probability-orientated approach was used to increase certainty when assessing effects – positive as well as negative – on biodiversity of land-cover changes. This is to widen the more commonly used problem- or risk-orientated approach, which by definition rather refers to negative effects (Suter, 2001). This definition also goes beyond the statistical probability concept.

The study was initiated in the City of Stockholm in 1990. Parts of the work have been conducted within the framework of real planning situations at the Stockholm City Planning Administration. Because the spirit of this work lies within the applied foci of land-use and land-cover changes, interdisciplinary research is necessary. We selected information from three research disciplines, with partly different views on how to apply the biodiversity concept: physical and ecological geography, conservation biology and systems ecology. The implications of integrating ecological information with urban planning have been discussed in detail by Healey (1997) and Shannon (2002). The objectives of our study were formulated from an applied perspective, emanating from experience of physical planning and management in Stockholm.

Background

Urban planning and monitoring

In Sweden, maintenance of biodiversity is part of the national environmental objectives. One reason for recognising active planning of biodiversity issues in urban areas as an urgent task is that, by 2030, more than 60% of the world population is expected to live in an urban setting (UN, 1997). Cities are open systems, with a great impact on, as well as dependency on, their rural and natural hinterlands (e.g. Folke *et al.*, 1997). One other reason is that parks and natural areas are important for people's well-being and health (e.g. Grahn, 1994; Elmqvist *et al.*, 2004). According to a recent study in the municipality of Stockholm, 75% of the citizens visit green open spaces every week in summer time, and 48% in winter time (Stadsbyggnadskontoret, 2002). Large natural and semi-natural areas, such as Djurgården, top the list of favourite places mentioned.

It is essential for successful policy integration to develop ways to handle uncertainties and risks in regards to maintaining biodiversity (Shannon, 2002). The Swedish government stresses the need for an increased focus on ecological resilience, i.e. the ability of ecosystems to buffer land-use changes. To maintain the resilience of ecosystems it is essential to know about land-cover changes.

Some of the obstacles to increasing the awareness of ecological values and risks on a landscape level in physical planning include the following.

- Spatial and temporal data are often weak or lacking, making it difficult to visualise ecological values and risks on a landscape level, and assess effects of land-cover changes in planning work. Existing species and biotope data have been collected for different purposes, with different scales and methods, leading to confusion about terminology and utility.
- In physical planning a developed plan should express all relevant interests in one representation, where biodiversity is one interest amongst others. However, in a geographical perspective there is no such thing as a single representation of biodiversity that incorporates every possible viewpoint of the concept.
- Physical planning is concerned with area-specific qualities, functions and problems. Because geo-referenced and context sensitive ecological knowledge is difficult to achieve and will be forever limited and incomplete, it must be adaptive. Approaches have been developed to deal with these issues, such as adaptive management by experiment and monitoring (e.g. Walters and Holling, 1990). To apply an adaptive approach within traditional organisations is, however, a challenge (Löfvenhaft, 2002).
- Improved interaction between research and land-use planning, as well as between research disciplines, is needed (e.g. Hobbs, 1997; Niemelä, 1999b; Theobald et al., 2000; Antrop, 2001; Fry, 2001; Robertson and Hull, 2001).
- Since urban planners often have to deal with rapid and sometimes large-scale structural changes, ecological information must be designed for such planning. In the United States, where systems for environmental monitoring and ecological risk assessments have been put in place, differences in approaches and procedures have resulted in a mismatch between monitoring and assessment (Suter, 2001).

The problems outlined above indicate that in order to strengthen the capacity of ecosystems to buffer land-use changes and sustain biodiversity through urban planning, knowledge from different disciplines must be combined and adapted for this purpose. This constitutes an important basis for the present study.

Theoretical background

When applied, landscape-ecological concepts are put into different historical and practical contexts – into old cultural landscapes of Europe where the concerns for biodiversity are closely related to the cultural history, as well as into relicts of natural landscapes in America and Australia (Brandt, 1998;

Florgård, Chapter 22). This must be considered while trying to apply research results to the urban situation in Sweden. Also, the different degree of fragmentation between Sweden and more densely populated countries in Europe, such as the Netherlands, must be recognised (Snep *et al.*, Chapter 26). The connectivity concept of corridors seems to be the most commonly applied. However, the role of corridors as an effective tool in the conservation of biodiversity is vigorously debated (e.g. Gustavsson and Hansson, 1997; Hobbs and Wilson, 1998; Bennett, 1999; Hilty *et al.*, 2006). Corridors must be part of a broader integrated approach considering all aspects of the connectivity concept including pattern, function and change.

Many landscape studies have found that fragments of habitats, such as forests, are not pieces of the original habitat. Indeed, in such cases their biotas may be drastically altered (e.g. Andrén, 1994; Skånes, 1996; Harrison and Bruna, 1999; Käyhkö and Skånes, 2006). Such fragmentation effects can be assumed to be crucial also in urban landscapes. A considerable decline in the floral diversity is, for example, documented in a geographically isolated woodland park in urban Boston (Drayton and Primack, 1996). Findlay and Bourdages (2000) discovered that populations of wetland species susceptible to land-use changes (e.g. road traffic) decline gradually, with complete loss occurring some decades later. Put together, this indicates the need to consider area-specific as well as retrospective conditions, i.e. to build up landscape complexes for urban landscape planning through analyses of both past and present biotope patterns.

To predict the implication of landscape changes on ecosystems, knowledge of the ecosystems' resilience and certain ecological thresholds are needed. Regarding resilience, many definitions can be found in the literature (e.g. Holling, 1996; Carpenter *et al.*, 2001). So far, most studies have used the concept as a theoretical construct, and not for empirical studies (Carpenter *et al.*, 2001). The resilience of ecological processes depends on the distribution of functional groups (Tilman, 2001) within and across scales (Peterson *et al.*, 1998). The habitat requirements of these species, and the ability of ecosystems to buffer land-use changes are, in turn, largely dependent on the biotope configuration in the landscape. Hence, spatial and temporal data on both species and biotopes are required, data which rarely exist for most systems of interest (Findlay and Bourdages, 2000; Pickett *et al.*, 2001). This study explores some components that may be operational for assessing effects on biotope resilience of land-cover changes in physical planning, focusing on biotope continuity and direction of change.

Stockholm as study area

The study area includes the City of Stockholm and parts of the surrounding region covering an area of 260 km^2 (Fig. 24.1). With approximately

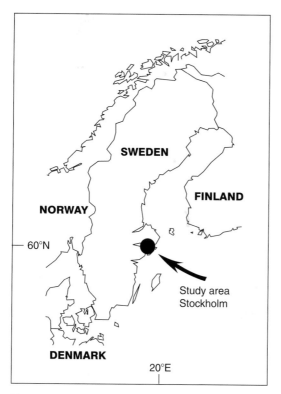

Fig. 24.1. The study area – Stockholm, Sweden – covers approximately 260 km^2.

1.6 million inhabitants, the Stockholm region is located on the coast of the Baltic Sea and includes the inlet to and parts of Lake Mälaren. Stockholm lies within the boreonemoral vegetation zone and mixed coniferous and decid- uous forests dominate. The vegetation types reflect the topography and the sedimentary deposits, as well as the favourable climatic conditions and previ- ous land use.

Archaeological findings are common in the region. In some areas, parts of the old rural landscape prior to mechanisation in the 1950s can be recognised. Small remnants of grasslands influenced by hay mowing occur as well. Grasslands and woodland successions with old broad-leaved deciduous trees, especially peduncu- late oak (*Quercus robur*) and linden (*Tilia cordata*) often dominate the historical spots and the historical parks of Stockholm. The seventeenth- and eighteenth- century royal parks of Ulriksdal, Haga-Brunnsviken and Djurgården which in part make up the National City Park are good examples of Stockholm's historic landscapes. The grasslands and woodlands originate from previous land-use practices with grazing and hay mowing and are characteristic of the old agricultural landscape of the Stockholm region and southern Sweden. They are crucial components for biodiversity, and today are threatened by modern forestry and urban development.

Stockholm, the capital of Sweden, was founded in the thirteenth century. Farming activities existed within the urban sprawl until the 1970s. From the mid twentieth century the city expanded along the transport routes, giving Stockholm its typical star-shaped structure of preserved forest and agricultural landscapes between radial urban settlements. So far, the topography has been an important factor for the city's expansion and the shaping of the city. The planning strategy for future expansion is to build the city inwards: that is, to re-use already exploited land and save valuable green open spaces.

The long-term history has governed characteristic biotope (i.e. habitat) configurations such as old-growth coniferous and deciduous forests with numerous, often small-sized, wetlands, old broad-leaved deciduous trees and natural shore lines with wet forests. These biotope components are also interwoven in historical as well as recently created parks. Their existence explains to a large degree the high species diversity found in natural and semi-natural areas of Stockholm. In this project, the Djurgården area has been especially studied. It constitutes part of the National City Park in Stockholm and represents a historical and cultural landscape of national interest.

Material and methods

The present framework used to provide spatial and temporal data which support physical planning includes deliberate choices considering: (1) what sources, scales and approach for data collection are to be used; (2) what components should be considered to make context-sensitive analyses possible; and (3) how to use available information to obtain complementary tools for the planning work. We chose to combine interpretations of aerial photographs and GIS with field surveys and logistic regression analysis of species presence/absence data and applied these methodologies to urban Stockholm in the context of physical planning. To receive feedback on the applicability of obtained information, results were used in the comprehensive physical planning of Stockholm.

Three datasets (comprehensive reference data) were explored in order to describe, and explain causes behind, the present conditions: (1) target biotopes; (2) roads with heavy traffic; and (3) focal species, broadly defined (Fleishman et al., 2000). We developed a biotope database from 1998 (Löfvenhaft, 2002; Löfvenhaft et al., 2002a), and used the most recent data on traffic intensity of the municipality (road patterns), and species data on amphibians (using logistic regression) collected in 1992, 1993 and 1996 (Löfvenhaft et al., 2002b). Past patterns were determined using aerial photographs from 1945 and 1950, scale 1:10 000, traffic information from 1950, and documentation regarding lost and destroyed breeding sites for amphibians for the period 1940–90. For data developed to supplement the spatio-temporal analyses, see Löfvenhaft *et al.* (2004).

The data give snapshots of two important phases of the city development in Stockholm:

- 1945–50 describes the conditions before large-scale structural changes that took place, predominantly, in the 1960–70s.
- 1996–98, like the whole of the 1990s, is characterised by relatively slow city development. This snapshot describes the conditions after large-scale structural changes during the 1960–70s, and the increasing density impact occurring in the mid 1970s and 1980s, but excludes the present (2000s) period of city expansion.

The biotope database targets crucial components for the biodiversity in Stockholm, such as: soil moisture, woodland successions, wetland networks, and the distribution of developed land and impermeable surfaces. It includes biotope qualities considering the habitat requirements of selected focal species groups: amphibians and existing data on invertebrates in the Red List connected to continuity in deciduous tree cover. Since these species groups depend on the access to certain biotope configurations during decades and even centuries, studies on them can show further information about the state of nature (Blaustein *et al.*, 1994; Diamond, 1996; Gärdenfors, 2000).

The GIS software PC Arc/Info and ArcView were chosen for all spatial analyses and the presentation of digital data. To check for specific ecological values and functions and depict the distribution of biotopes in space and time, all biotopes were reclassified (weighted) with respect to the continuity of deciduous tree cover (Löfvenhaft *et al.*, 2002a) and wetland networks (Löfvenhaft *et al.*, 2004). For statistical analyses of species' presence or absence, and changes in amphibian distribution, stepwise logistic regression was chosen (Sjögren-Gulve and Ray, 1996; Löfvenhaft *et al.*, 2002b).

Results

This chapter summarises results and outcomes from the Stockholm study in order to provide a platform for the discussion on the potential use of spatial and temporal data and how to provide them. It also provides a glimpse of what is going on right now in physical planning of Stockholm, with examples based on new background information for planning obtained by applying results from this study.

By using geographical methods and ecologically defined biotope cover for the biotope classification (Löfvenhaft *et al.*, 2002a), we found that:

- Crucial biotope configurations exist within green open spaces, as well as built-up areas, indicating that changes in ecological conditions can be planned for and assessed only if a new perspective on built-up areas is applied.
- The biotope database is sufficiently flexible as background information for physical planning, allowing an adaptation to the conditions in each individual area and landscape context, and to the level of detail suited to the planning situation. This is due partly to colour infrared aerial photographs allowing modifications and reinterpretations according to new planning specifications.

By examining the issue of biotope fragmentation from a conservation-biological perspective, we found, with statistical significance (Löfvenhaft *et al.*, 2002b), that:

- The regional distribution of three (out of five existing) amphibian species had decreased during 1992–1996 because of geographical isolation, by geographical distance and/or presence of road traffic.
- Roads with heavy traffic strongly increased the probability of local extinction of the common frog (*Rana temporaria*) and decreased the probability of colonisation of the crested newt (*Triturus cristatus*).
- High nitrate, ammonium or phosphate levels in the water had significantly negative effects on species occurrence in general but did not overshadow the effects of geographical isolation.

Because amphibians are sensitive indicators of environmental qualities and changes, we suggest that the results are indicative of what is happening to the wetland ecosystems in general in Stockholm. Information obtained clearly helped in environmental assessments regarding wetland biodiversity in comprehensive planning work in Stockholm. However, when the statistics were applied, some difficulties emerged owing to the limited geographical representation of results.

By combining the above perspectives and complementing them with temporal data on biotope and road patterns, we provided further information on the capacity of ecosystems to buffer land-use changes observed over the past 50 years (Löfvenhaft *et al.*, 2004). We found that:

- Temporal distributions of amphibians are related to changes in biotope patterns, suggesting that short-term environmental assessments are likely to underestimate real effects of biotope loss and deterioration.

- Use of so-called comprehensive reference data as complementary tools provides better insight into the ability of ecosystems to buffer land-cover changes.
- The biotope proportions of the areas that have experienced regional loss of focal biotopes and species (here wetland networks and amphibians), can be used as reference tools to visualise the direction of change in given areas (increased or decreased biodiversity).
- There is a time-lag of several decades between changes in urban land and road traffic and the resulting changes in biodiversity. This time-lag is not appreciated in present day short-term planning.

The spatial and temporal data increased the insight into the relative importance of subsequent biotope loss and changes in stress levels within different areas. The need for developing complementary assessment and monitoring procedures is therefore stressed.

When applied in physical planning work, the concept of a landscape ecological zone was developed: core areas with surrounding connectivity and/or buffer zones, which are holding and/or supporting unique and characteristic features of the urban region (Löfvenhaft et al., 2002a). In the developed background information for planning, the landscape ecological zones are expressed in terms of action (Stadsbyggnadskontoret, 1997; Löfvenhaft and Wikberger, 2004). They are presented on a scale adapted to comprehensive planning work that can be related to the instruments for action taking in subsequent planning.

Figure 24.2 gives one example that depicts three major landscape ecological zones of Stockholm (marked dark grey on the sketch), and highlights their dependency on the hinterlands (light grey). Also, the dependency of the 'inner networks' (i.e. remaining green open space within the cross-hatched inner city) on the landscape ecological zones becomes clearer. Figure 24.3 shows how the landscape zone of Djurgården – part of the National City Park in Stockholm – has changed during the past 50 years from being one coherent area many years ago to becoming the highly fragmented landscape it is today. Also, Fig. 24.3 illustrates how these conditions most probably will change in 50 years' time if (1) we choose to introduce protection and care of valuable biotopes in certain populated areas within and adjacent to the park; and (2) if we do not. Seen in a time span of approximately 50 years it could lead to the complete isolation of the Park's larger natural areas, and to great biotope losses, i.e. to rapid and severe deterioration. About 30% of the Park's oak woodlands lies outside the conservation areas suggested in the City Plan. Today these biotopes have no legal protection.

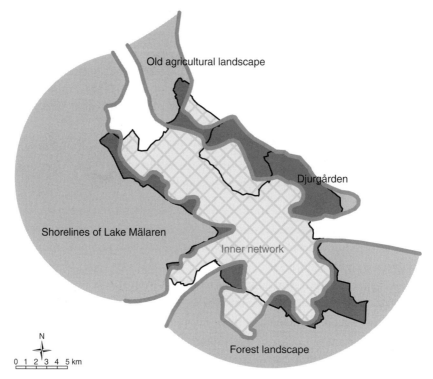

Fig. 24.2. Principal sketch of the landscape ecological zones identified for the comprehensive planning of Stockholm municipality (Löfvenhaft and Wikberger, 2004). From the point of view of biodiversity, it is especially important to develop further the guidelines for planning in this fringe area, marked dark grey on this sketch.

Discussion

This discussion focuses on two questions: (1) how effective is the implementation of spatial and temporal data on biodiversity in improving environmental assessments in physical planning; and (2) what implications might integration of such information have for urban planning and monitoring? Our experiences in Stockholm show that no single theory or method currently used may be sufficient to fulfil the needs for extended spatial and temporal perspectives in physical planning. In Stockholm, several methods – geographical and ecological – had to be combined. Moreover, the methods had to be adapted to the urban situation and the specific planning context. To succeed, an integrated framework with close cooperation between users and researchers was a prerequisite.

Implementation of spatial and temporal data

Naturally, continuous development in the urban environment must be allowed. By stating this, the goal of maintaining biodiversity becomes a

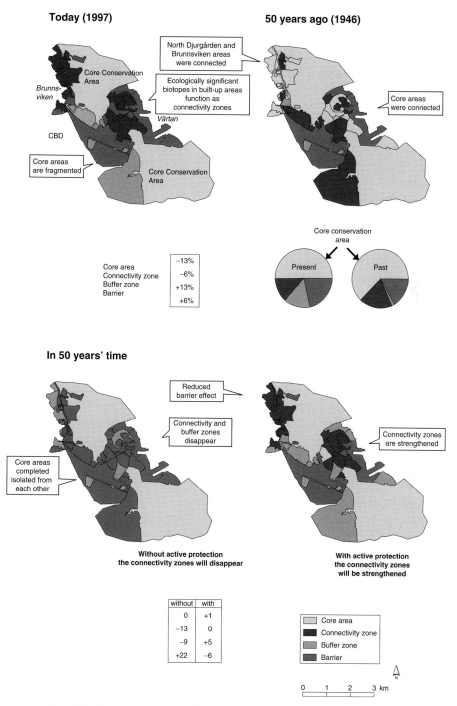

Fig. 24.3. Discussion platform for future planning. Djurgården, part of the National City Park in Stockholm: today (1997) and 50 years ago, and in 50 years' time, with and without protection. Introducing active planning and management of ecologically valuable biotopes in the connectivity and buffer zones will increase the possibilities for maintaining the core area's biodiversity (Löfvenhaft, 2002).

challenge of national as well as international concern. The methods used in this study provide spatial and temporal information sufficient for supporting landscape ecological considerations in comprehensive planning of Stockholm, and have improved the knowledge base of the municipality.

At the expense of statistical analysis, we have chosen a cartographic approach, which is more appropriate for the present purpose: to accomplish integration. The results are, however, consistent with the findings in the previous logistic regression analysis of the amphibians in Stockholm that indicated a relaxing system under change, with extant amphibian populations confined to clustered suitable localities surrounded by a hostile environment (Löfvenhaft *et al.*, 2002b). The calculated comprehensive reference data used as tools of comparison for assessing biotope resilience (Löfvenhaft *et al.*, 2004) have similarities with the ecological thresholds found in previous model studies (e.g. Andrén, 1994).

To be truly interdisciplinary, socio-economical parameters should be included (e.g. Pickett *et al.*, 2001 and Chapter 3), but this has been beyond the scope of this study. This study highlighted problems involved in collecting and processing long-term spatial and temporal data. We have, so far, used data from only two reference points in time – with a time span of about 50 years – and have related the findings only to changes in biotope cover and road traffic (Löfvenhaft *et al.*, 2004). The analysis includes only one organism group, amphibians. Hence, the approach has weaknesses and needs further development and refinement.

As in all landscape studies, biotope classification is subjective and the results must be interpreted. The principal ways of collecting land-cover data are aerial photography, satellite imagery and field survey. In this study aerial photography was chosen and it proved to be the least time-consuming method (Löfvenhaft *et al.*, 2002a). It gives an overview as well as detailed information, and makes it possible to consider developmental trends, at least over the past 50 years. Because of the stereographic view of the landscape, qualitative ecological features and properties, such as soil type and moisture gradients, can be assessed. Interpretation accuracy is about the same as is documented for field survey, 74–83% (Wyatt *et al.*, 1994).

The biotope database and map is both illustrative and useful on its own, and is widely used in today's planning and environmental management. For insight into the dynamics between different biotopes in the landscape it must, however, be analysed together with other information. The idea of the classification system is to assist in such analyses, where biotope data can be aggregated into larger units to reveal new patterns and structural connections seen from different perspectives.

In this way we try to show how a wider landscape perspective and longer timescales can bring new information to the planning work. Propositions for new development projects can be put into greater context. Despite knowledge gaps, the use of spatial and temporal data on species and biotopes improved our knowledge with clear indications on the direction of change, towards or away from the objective of sustaining biodiversity. Such information is a prerequisite to identify the areas where action needs to be taken.

To find ways to deal with uncertainty and knowledge gaps is one great challenge for successful integration of biodiversity issues in urban planning. The given examples from Stockholm (Figs. 24.2 and 24.3) are based on geo-referenced biotope data and scenarios defined within the framework of a real planning situation. The biotope data give meaning to the coarse measures of landscape changes, and they can be expressed as amount of significant biotopes that may increase or decrease. One advantage of the framework presented here is that the data can be extended, stepwise, and developed for additional areas, with new information and new time layers.

Illustrations such as Figs. 24.2 and 24.3 are used as a platform in the current discussion about the future of Stockholm. They raise questions in need of answers if maintenance of biodiversity is to be integrated into the city planning. In Stockholm, this means that partly new approaches and working methods need to be developed – not least for the engagement and knowledge of the citizens. Again, I would like to point out that one can never give complete information. However, if you are to pose questions concerning biotope resilience and buffering capacity in the decision-making process, simplifying and classifying is necessary and this study has attempted to demonstrate how this can be accomplished.

The question is how much can we nibble at Stockholm's large green areas, such as Djurgården, without risking the same thing happening there which we unfortunately have witnessed in so many places during the past decade. Our spatio-temporal study shows that environmental qualities of both the site (wetland) and the surrounding landscape (i.e. biotope configuration and road traffic patterns) are critical issues for maintaining wetland biodiversity in urban Stockholm. The results indicate that the wetland ecosystems in Stockholm are changing, including areas rich in biotopes. Similar to the results found by Findlay and Bourdages (2000), in which there was a time-lag of several decades between changes in urban land and road traffic, the response changes in biodiversity were apparent in my study (Löfvenhaft et al., 2004). What appears to be fine today, may be balancing on a threshold. This highlights the importance of considering past effects and future consequences, in terms of 50–100 years, when suggesting new developments and planning strategies.

Our study highlights the need for a procedure to determine what active responses are required in a given landscape and specific planning context. The principles for providing comprehensive reference data – through deliberate choices and analyses of temporal biotope patterns and species records – can be applied to other systems, areas and regions. The components to be studied will, however, differ from one place to another, because of environmental differences and degrees of fragmentation. To summarise, comprehensive and retrospective landscape studies are essential to the understanding and control of land-cover changes.

Implications for urban planning

Use of spatial and temporal data demands new planning practices. Background information for Stockholm has even been used in legal processes (Schantz, 2002). The use of the material by citizens and non-governmental organisations indicates a great concern for landscape values, which may contradict the common perception that citizens are most engaged in small concrete projects. It highlights the importance of making landscape ecological information accessible to the public.

However, available landscape information does not guarantee successful implementation of ecologically sound planning. To accomplish the planning examples given in this study, important prerequisites were: (1) the increased demands on a landscape perspective generated by the law on National City Parks; (2) the integrated organisation that allowed close co-operation between physical planners and ecologists; (3) co-operation between experts and researchers; and (4) communication with interest groups such as non-governmental organisations. In line with Shannon (2002), we stress that the degree of uncertainty over environmental conditions and change needs to form one part of the template for the method of organising the work and designing the participatory process.

Conclusion

Although the political ambition in Sweden is to integrate maintenance of biodiversity as well as human well-being into urban planning and monitoring, this is hampered by a lack of significant landscape data. The main goal of this study was to visualise spatio-temporal properties of the biodiversity concept for use in contemporary physical planning in Stockholm through: (1) applying a user perspective; (2) identifying methods forming complementary planning tools considering the landscape context; and (3) mapping and analysing comprehensive biotope patterns.

The lack of standardised methods for biotope mapping in urban areas clearly complicates comparisons between cities. The results from this study indicate, however, that the approach may be useful for providing important information and comparative tools suitable for physical planning in a given municipality.

These are complementary tools to: (1) extend the assessment scale back in time and to a landscape level; (2) aid assessments of how alternative planning strategies and plans will affect the city's biodiversity; and (3) improve background information for land-use decisions.

Increased knowledge of biodiversity patterns over time is a key link to support urban planning. Land-cover changes in the transition zone between urban land and remaining natural and semi-natural areas can be monitored and assessed only if a modified perspective on built-up areas is applied, as defined in this study. If the natural and semi-natural biotopes within built-up areas are not monitored, the potential to maintain the resilience of ecosystems diminishes.

Crucial biotope configurations and land-cover changes were both positive and negative with regards to preserving biodiversity. To assure the quality of subsequent planning, it is important to translate the ecological information into guiding principles, as well as legally binding land-use and management provisions, that are adapted to the different conditions of quality, risk and uncertainty in given areas. The biotope level (i.e. habitat) is suitable for such land-use planning in urban areas, if the components are chosen and processed within an integrated framework addressing the user perspective.

When developing programmes and plans for wetland biodiversity in urban areas, a time-span of several decades must be included in the analyses in order to understand what is happening within the ecosystems of today. If emphasis is put on comprehensive planning, development of complementary assessment and monitoring procedures on local and regional levels is one way to obtain the spatial and temporal information needed.

Finally, this study has provided important data on the comprehensive biotope patterns in Stockholm and demonstrated the potential of using matched species data with a time-span to obtain new spatio-temporal information on biodiversity and tools for applying it in physical planning work. Although the findings presented here do not provide a complete template applicable to all urban landscapes, they show how different approaches and perspectives within different disciplines may be combined and put to use in urban landscape planning.

Acknowledgements

Karin Holmgren and Helle Skånes have made valuable comments on the manuscript. Caroline Hainer contributed to the English translation. Gunilla Lundstedt and Tina Ekström drew some of the figures. Figures are reprinted with permission from the Stockholm City Planning Administration (Fig. 24.2), and the Swedish Environmental Protection Agency (Fig. 24.3). Without the active co-operation of the Stockholm City Planning Administration, this research would not have been possible. Financial support was provided by the City of Stockholm and the Swedish Environmental Protection Agency, but also by generous grants from the Office of Regional Planning and Urban Transportation (Miljövårdsfonden), the Ahlmann and Carl Mannerfelt research foundations, and from MISTRA–Foundation for Strategic Environmental Research, within the Swedish research program RESE–Remote Sensing for the Environment. My participation in the Australian Research Centre for Urban Ecology workshop held in Melbourne and the completion of this book chapter was facilitated by the Swedish Research Council for Environment, Agricultural Sciences and Spatial Planning (Formas).

25

Landscape ecological analysis and assessment in an urbanising environment

ULLA MÖRTBERG

Introduction

Urbanisation is a dominant source of land-use change worldwide, and causes profound alterations of natural habitat as cities and towns expand. To achieve sustainable land-use development in urbanising regions, the impacts on biodiversity of urbanisation, infrastructure and other development must be considered on landscape and regional scales. This requires that important decisions are made on a strategic level in the planning process, with a systematic evaluation of environmental impacts and alternatives. However, there is a lack of knowledge of the effects of urbanisation on the natural and semi-natural habitats that support biodiversity in urbanising regions (McDonnell *et al.*, 1997; Miller and Hobbs, 2002), and remnants of natural habitats have often been considered as reserve land for future exploitation. More recently, though, the value of natural vegetation in urban and urbanising areas has been recognised, since human settlements often are located in highly productive ecosystems, in proximity to rivers and coasts, reliable water sources, well-drained sites and high-fertility soils, which are ecosystems that also support high levels of biodiversity (Falkenmark and Chapman, 1989; Cincotta *et al.*, 2000; Given and Meurk, 2000; Ricketts and Imhoff, 2003).

Ecology of Cities and Towns: A Comparative Approach, ed. Mark J. McDonnell, Amy K. Hahs and Jürgen H. Breuste. Published by Cambridge University Press. © Cambridge University Press 2009.

A number of political decisions have been made in Sweden and throughout Europe that emphasise nature conservation and biodiversity as important issues for sustainable development. According to the Swedish government's environmental objectives, biodiversity is to be preserved in urban areas. The Convention on Biodiversity created at the 1992 Rio Earth Summit states that biodiversity should be taken into account in environmental impact assessments, with a view to avoiding or minimising negative effects (Official Journal of the European Communities, OJEC, 1993). The recent enactment of a new EU Directive, concerning the assessment of the effects of certain plans and programmes on the environment (OJEC, 2001), makes stricter demands on the integration of environmental concerns into planning and decision-making. In response to the directives, environmental issues need to be considered in initial decisions on urban expansion and major infrastructure investments, a strategic stage in the planning process. For this type of decision, a strategic environmental assessment needs to be prepared so that new plans for urban development can be presented in various scenarios of environmental effects. Based on these development scenarios, environmental effects can be identified and described (Balfors and Schmidtbauer, 2002). Because of the high level of abstraction of policies, plans and programmes, the prediction of impacts is a major methodological problem in strategic environmental assessment (Hildén *et al.*, 1998). According to Geneletti (2002), environmental impact statements often fail to provide quantitative predictions concerning nature conservation and biodiversity. These difficulties and the implementation of the Directive necessitate adequate tools and methods, which provide a systematic evaluation of environmental impacts of a proposed decision and of its alternatives.

Urban land-use changes alter the structure and nature of the physical landscape and will affect the fauna and flora inhabiting the area. Effects of development and other human activities involving the loss and fragmentation of natural habitats are major causes of biodiversity decline (Fahrig, 1997; Niemelä, Chapter 2; Chapman and Underwood, Chapter 4; Nilon, Chapter 10; Snepp *et al.*, Chapter 26). To protect biodiversity, considerations are needed at genetic, species and ecosystem levels. Further, the quality, quantity and spatial cohesion of natural habitats are essential. This means that a site-based conservation approach will not be sufficient to protect biodiversity. Instead, it will be necessary to consider persistence requirements of species and communities across the entire landscape (Saunders *et al.*, 1995). The application of landscape ecological knowledge and concepts in sustainable landscape planning is a growing issue (van der Zee and Zonneveld, 2001; Botequilha Leitão and Ahern, 2002). An example of integration of biodiversity issues and landscape ecological knowledge in planning is the Ecological Main Structure of the Netherlands (Ministerie LNV,

1990), which comprises a network of interconnected areas in the Netherlands where nature is of highest priority. It was introduced by the Government in 1990 in the Nature Policy Plan, aiming to prevent extinction of species and promote biodiversity. An example of integration of landscape ecological knowledge in impact assessment is Fernandes (2000), who used habitat networks of a prioritised species to evaluate the potential ecological effects of a highway project.

Several projects have been carried out in Germany and the Netherlands in order to integrate urban and recreational land uses with nature conservation (Knol and Verweij, 1999; Harms *et al.*, 2000). Suitable and accessible habitat can be planned in habitat networks. These networks often consist of core areas sufficient for species persistence in the landscape, which are linked together through corridors to allow dispersal (Bennett, 1999; Opdam *et al.*, 2002). Still, according to these authors, there is a gap between knowledge development and knowledge application in landscape ecology, and a lack of tools for integration in multi-disciplinary landscape studies, which impedes biodiversity conservation. Further, to use the landscape ecological concepts in urbanising environments, more information is needed on the wide-reaching effects of urbanisation (Miller and Hobbs, 2002).

Effects of urbanisation

The urbanisation process causes loss and fragmentation of natural habitats, puts a high pressure on the remaining areas of nature in urban regions, and at the same time creates new habitats. In this way, a complex land-use pattern often emerges. The ecological consequences of these changes can be complex and involve numerous confounding factors (Gilbert, 1989; McDonnell and Pickett, 1990; McDonnell *et al.*, 1993, 1997; Pickett *et al.*, 2001). Urbanisation adds new green infrastructure such as non-native trees, lush ornamental vegetation and lawns (Ignatieva and Stewart, Chapter 23) as well as grey infrastructure such as buildings, obstacles in the air, and hardened surfaces with and without traffic. From a wildlife perspective, exploited areas form barriers to movement for many species, particularly roads with a high traffic intensity, and contribute to the fragmentation problems (Trocmé *et al.*, 2002; van der Ree, Chapter 11). Other examples of urban effects are: a warmer climate, availability of anthropogenic food, impoverished vegetation cover and fauna, artificial lighting, noise, and pollution and nutrient loads to air and water (Luniak *et al.*, 1990; Botkin and Beveridge, 1997; Eisenbeis and Hänel, Chapter 15; Carreiro *et al.*, Chapter 19; Pouyat *et al.*, Chapter 20). Further, ecological processes such as fires and floods are altered, controlled and suppressed (Landres *et al.*, 1999), and a biotic homogenisation occurs (Lockwood and McKinney, 2001) ruled by human preferences of vegetation and hydrology (e.g. draining of wetlands, irrigation of arid land).

Human settlements may also act as a source of exotic and domesticated species, and of generalist predators, which compete with or prey upon native plants and animals (Haskell et al., 2001).

The remaining fragments of natural and semi-natural habitat are affected and altered by various disturbances in urban landscapes. Habitat types are commonly described by characteristics of vegetation and soil types, and, from a wildlife perspective, measures of habitat quality such as vegetation and age structure, occurrence of wetlands and decaying wood. For human-dominated landscapes, information on important characteristics is lacking (e.g. Dow, 2000). The origin and history of sites also are important factors shaping these characteristics, since there are significant differences between natural remnants and indigenous vegetation, parks with a long history of management, or sites with uncertain or no land use or management, and successional development on formerly open land (Florgård, 2004; Chapter 22). Further, human activities need to be taken into account. For example, park management often leads to a typical vegetation structure, with a half-open cover of large trees, mown lawns, exotic plants and a sparse or absent bush layer (Ignatieva et al., 2000; Meurk et al., Chapter 18; Ignatieva and Stewart, Chapter 23). Moreover, this type of park management is sometimes applied to native vegetation close to residential areas. Other types of human activities affecting habitat quality include recreation, children playing, rubbish dumping, collection of firewood and informal settlement. All these factors may occur around any human settlement, but in urban regions they can be concentrated and play a major role, not only as edge effects, but also as disturbance regimes and/or new forms of land use. These activities form complex and interacting patterns that can be quantified and modelled.

For the quantification of varying levels of urbanisation, and associated changes in ecosystem structure and function, the urban gradient approach has been proposed (McDonnell and Pickett, 1990; McDonnell et al., 1993, 1997; Pickett et al., Chapter 3), which can be combined with landscape ecology (Wu and David, 2002). Urban gradients can be measured as the distance to a city centre, the density of the human population, or the gradient of fragmenta-tion (McDonnell and Hahs, Chapter 5; Yang and Jinxing, Chapter 16). The latter can include measures such as size, shape and inter-patch distance of habitat fragments, density of road network, percentage of urban residential land and a vast number of landscape metrics (McDonnell et al., 1997; Alberti et al., 2001; Luck and Wu, 2002). When urban disturbances are quantified (Fig. 25.1), sample sites can be defined in a multi-dimensional space for use in multi-variate modelling. This will need careful consideration, though, for different reasons. One issue of concern is scale, since different processes are relevant on different scales, and there can be multiple interactions (Hostetler, 2001; Wu and David, 2002).

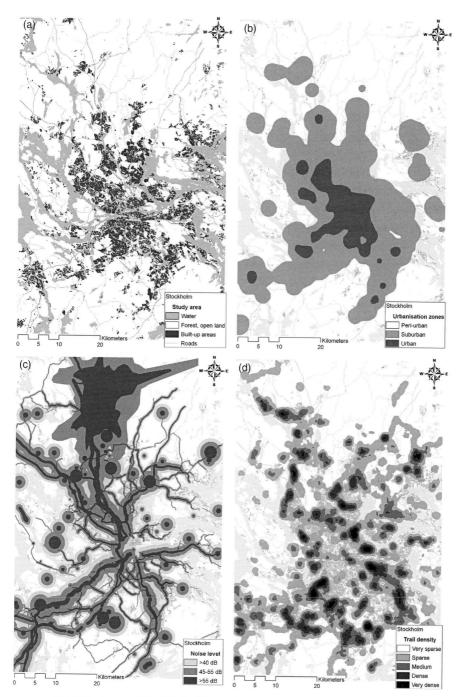

Fig. 25.1. A map of Stockholm illustrating three methods of measuring urbanisation. (a) study area; (b) density of the human population (urban zone: >5000 people/ha; suburban zone: 500–5000 people/ha; peri-urban zone: <500 people/ha); (c) traffic noise (dB); and (d) recreation pressure measured as density of trails.

Another problem that needs attention is redundancy among variables, and spatial autocorrelation (Borcard and Legendre, 2002; Overmars *et al.*, 2003; Mörtberg and Karlström, 2005). Further, as a result of urbanisation and infrastructure development, apparently small impacts on individual sites that seem insignificant can result in considerable cumulative effects on habitat loss and fragmentation when added up across an entire region.

Birds and urbanisation

The created, complex environmental gradient, from undisturbed nat-ural areas to highly modified urban landscapes, has been proposed as a base for exploring relationships between environmental heterogeneity and the diversity and abundance of species (McDonnell and Pickett, 1990; McDonnell *et al.*, 1993; Pickett *et al.*, Chapter 3). Birds in urban landscapes have been studied by, for instance, Catterall *et al.* (1991, Chapter 8), Jokimäki (1996), Blair (1996), Bolger *et al.* (1997), Hadidian *et al.* (1997), Sauvajot *et al.* (1998), Mörtberg (1996, 1998, 2001, 2004), Mörtberg and Wallentinus (2000), Marzluff (2001), Melles *et al.* (2003) and Crooks *et al.* (2004), and reviewed in Fernández-Juricic and Jokimäki (2001). Several studies of urban bird communities have reported that species richness generally decreases with urbanisation, while the total avian density increases (Emlen, 1974; Beissinger and Osborne, 1982; Jokimäki, 1996; Mörtberg, 1996, 2004). Abundance of dominant species, in particular non-migratory generalist species, usually increases with urbanisation, especially for those that benefit from anthropogenic food sources all year round (see also Catterall, Chapter 8). The abundance of migratory birds usually decreases with urbanisation, probably because of a decline of insect habitat. Ground nesters also decrease, the most likely reason being high predation rates by generalist predators (Jokimäki, 1996; Mörtberg, 1996; Haskell *et al.*, 2001; Mörtberg, 2004).

The size of forest fragments has been shown to be a strong, positive predictor of the total number of breeding bird species detected per fragment (Mörtberg, 1996; Crooks *et al.*, 2004) (Fig. 25.2 and 25.3). Figure 25.3 illustrates a comparison of species richness between urban and non-urban forest patches in relation to patch size (Mörtberg, 2004). For the comparison, two earlier studies were used, one of urban and suburban patches (Mörtberg, 1996) and one of rural forest fragments in the form of real islands in Lake Mälaren, west of the city (Ahlén and Nilsson, 1982). The composition of forest types was similar in the sites of the two studies, comprising coniferous, mixed and deciduous forest in a pattern following the undulating topography, but the urban forest patches were mainly surrounded by an urban matrix instead of water. Here, the urban disturbances varied considerably, and low species richness compared with forest area seemed

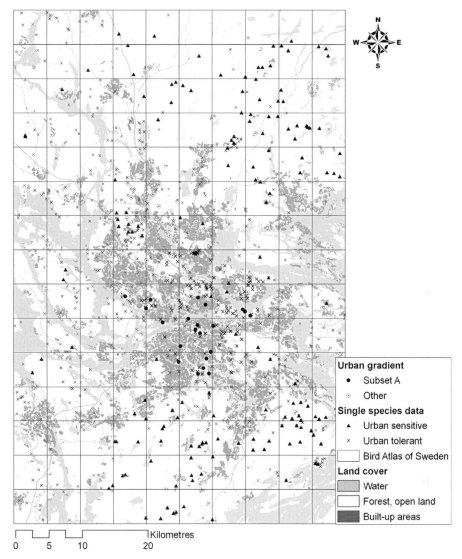

Fig. 25.2. The city of Stockholm showing the sample sites along the urban–suburban gradient, including Subset A (see Figure 25.4), observations of urban-sensitive forest birds, and observations of the urban-tolerant lesser spotted woodpecker (*Dendrocopos minor*). Data on *D. minor* come from the Bird Online Database maintained by the Swedish Environmental Protection Agency, and the location of sample squares is from the Bird Atlas of Sweden (Svensson *et al.*, 1999).

to be related to both vegetation structure and high disturbance from traffic noise. By contrast, when the number of individuals in each sample was taken into account (Connor and McCoy, 1979) species richness showed no correlation with forest area (Mörtberg, 1998) (Fig. 25.4). Instead, multi-layered deciduous

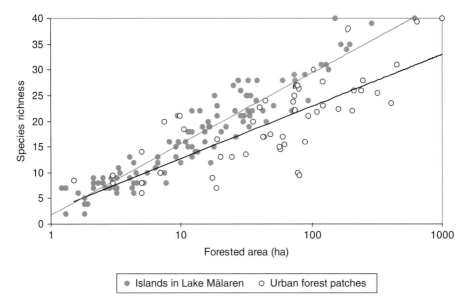

Fig. 25.3. Species richness of breeding forest birds in relation to forest area of urban forest patches in and around Stockholm (Mörtberg, 1996) compared with forested islands in Lake Mälaren, west of Stockholm (Ahlén and Nilsson, 1982). Trend lines are included for the forest patches on the islands in Lake Mälaren (thin line) and the urban forest patches (wide line). Similar methods for breeding bird census were used in the two investigations.

forest habitats with a large amount of dead wood, associated with natural shoreline, were preferred (Fig. 25.5). This example shows the importance of local habitat characteristics, as found by many previous studies (e.g. Beissinger and Osborne, 1982; Blair, 1996; Clergeau *et al.*, 1998).

As the relative species richness did not increase with sample size in Fig. 25.4, one plausible explanation is that the bird community in a small habitat fragment contains fewer individuals and can be considered as a random sample from a larger one. This would mean that the probability of occurrence of a species could be determined by its regional abundance (Connor and McCoy, 1979). However, analyses along an urban–rural gradient did not support this explanation, as several species that were found in larger forest areas were absent in urban fragments. Further investigations on single species, such as sedentary forest tits (Mörtberg, 2001), suggested that both habitat and landscape variables need to be considered (see also Melles *et al.*, 2003; Catterall, Chapter 8). Likewise, two of the most urban-sensitive bird species, the capercaillie (*Tetrao urogallus*) and the hazel grouse (*Bonasa bonasia*), were only present in larger forest areas outside the city (Fig. 25.2). Both these species could be significantly predicted by a combination of fine- and coarse-scale variables describing suitable habitat and

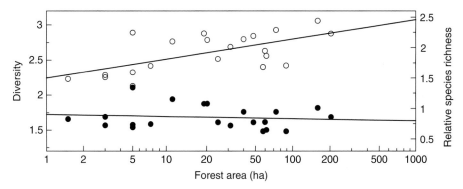

Fig. 25.4. Diversity index (Shannon) and relative species richness (Connor and McCoy, 1979) in relation to forest patch size, using only a subset of data shown in Fig. 24.2. Open circles are density and closed circles are relative species richness (Mörtberg, 1998).

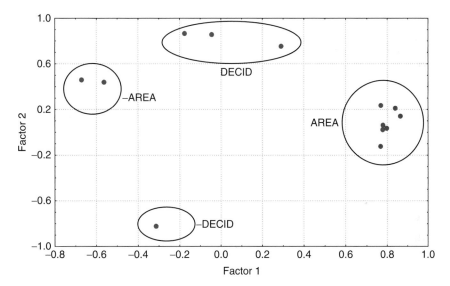

Fig. 25.5. PCA ordination diagram of variables related to patch area (AREA) and to multi-layered deciduous forest habitats (DECID). The area-related factor AREA was positively associated with the variables forest core area, spruce forest, moist forest and small wetlands, and negatively with variables such as distance to nearest neighbouring forest and edge density. Factor DECID was positively associated with proportion of deciduous forest, amount of dead and decaying wood, and natural shoreline, and negatively associated with disturbance from human visitors (Mörtberg, 1998).

accessibility (Mörtberg and Karlström, 2005). Additional explanation of the species distribution was gained by adding disturbance variables, as both species seemed to respond to variables describing traffic noise, and to some extent recreation pressure (Fig. 25.1). Further investigations on cause–effect relations are needed before any conclusions are drawn. For example, various studies have

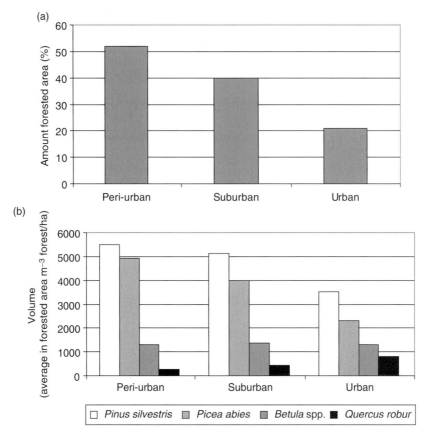

Fig. 25.6. Differences in the proportion of area in forest cover and composition along the urban gradient (see Fig. 25.1a for location of zones). The proportion of coniferous and deciduous tree species in the peri-urban zone reflects the situation in much of the boreal and hemi-boreal forest, while in the urban zone the proportion of deciduous trees is much higher, especially that of oak. Data from estimation of forest variables using satellite imagery (see Holmgren *et al.*, 2000).

documented reduced densities of birds breeding near heavily travelled roads, regardless of size of habitat fragment (e.g. Reijnen *et al.*, 1997; van der Ree, Chapter 11). Studies have also shown the effects of recreation pressure on birds (Jokimäki, 1996; Sauvajot *et al.*, 1998).

The effects of urbanisation were not the same for all vegetation types. Deciduous trees are predominantly planted and favoured in cities and towns (Gilbert, 1989; Jokimäki, 1996; Mörtberg and Wallentinus, 2000; Fig. 25.6). This can be detrimental when exotic species are used, but seems to have some interesting effects when native species are favoured. Since deciduous trees are sparse in boreal and hemi-boreal landscapes, landscapes shaped by industrial forestry, there are several Red List species tied to deciduous, broad-leaved deciduous or mixed forest in Sweden (e.g. Gärdenfors, 2000). In Stockholm, some Red List forest birds breed in relative abundance because of the occurrence of native deciduous trees in the urban area (Mörtberg and Wallentinus, 2000). Both the presence of old hardwood deciduous trees with nest-holes, and dense successions of deciduous trees on formerly open land, often along natural shorelines, supported these species and others such as the lesser spotted woodpecker (*Dendrocopos minor*, Fig. 25.2). Thus, it seems that physical conditions and a long history of human preferences together with unintentional land-use changes have created opportunities for native vegetation and native avian species.

A basic requirement for the prediction and assessment of impacts of human settlements on biodiversity is some type of indicator that is sensitive to the effects of the development processes, at different scales (Noss, 1990; Larsson, 2001). To use the overall findings of the responses of bird fauna to urbanisation for evaluation of planning scenarios, analyses were needed of how to represent a high diversity of forest bird species. One way of quantifying whether sites with high species richness also host rare species is to test for 'nestedness' (Fleishman *et al.*, 2000). This test reveals whether biological communities show a random or a non-random distribution pattern. A nested subset structure of occurrences means that the taxa present in species-poor assemblages are also found in increasingly species-rich assemblages, with the implication that more species-rich assemblages also contain more rare species. The overall forest bird fauna as a group, with birds more or less tied to each of coniferous, mixed and deciduous forest, was tested for nestedness within the study area (Mörtberg, in preparation), using data from the Bird Atlas of Sweden (Svensson *et al.*, 1999) (Fig. 25.2). In this urbanising landscape, with a mosaic of forest, open land, water and urban structures, forest birds revealed a high degree of nestedness, which means that sites with a high species richness also contained more rare species within the dataset. Single species that showed a high correlation with species richness were capercaillie, hazel grouse and willow tit (*Parus montanus*). Where these species were found, there was also relatively high species richness. By contrast, certain forest birds that are more closely associated with deciduous forest, like the lesser spotted woodpecker, did not. This could be interpreted as a need for a different set of indicators for species associated with this type of habitat, since deciduous forest did not decline at the same rate with urbanisation as other forest types in this region (Fig. 25.6).

Landscape ecological assessment

To integrate biodiversity considerations in regional planning in an urbanising environment, a landscape ecological assessment (LEA) was applied.

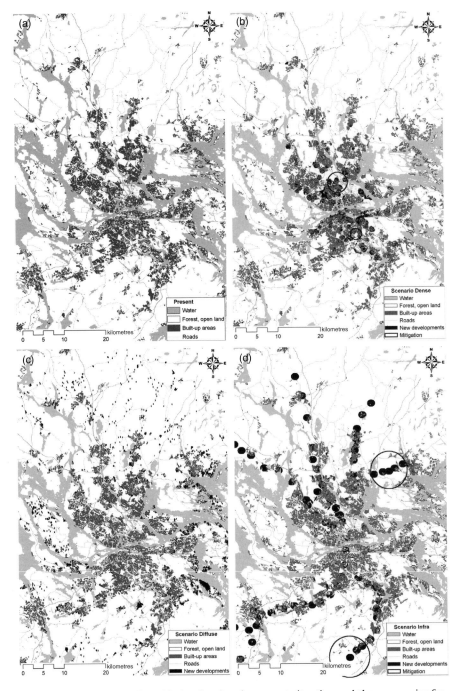

Fig. 25.7. Maps of Stockholm showing the present situation and three scenarios for future development in the region created by the Office of Regional Planning and Urban Transportation (1995). These assume the creation of additional housing for 250 000 more households in year 2030. Scenario Dense: almost all new development

The aim was to develop methods for the prediction and assessment of impacts on biodiversity components at the landscape scale. A case study was conducted in the Stockholm region, Sweden's capital and largest city, and the study area embraced the city, suburbs and peri-urban areas (Fig. 25.2; Mörtberg et al., 2007). The city has mainly grown along radial transportation lines, leaving large areas of natural and semi-natural vegetation in between. In the urban zone, forest fragments are embedded in an urban matrix, in the suburban zone residential areas dominate, and within the peri-urban zone large, quite undisturbed natural areas are found, with relatively few buildings and roads. Here, rural activities such as forestry, agriculture and hunting take place, but most people work in the city. When service and infrastructure start to develop within these areas, the gradual urbanisation process could accelerate, with associated disturbances, shrinkage and isolation of wildlife habitat and lowering of habitat quality.

Development in the region has been estimated to reach 250 000 additional households by the year 2030, and three alternative scenarios for this development (Fig. 25.7) have been created by the Office of Regional Planning and Urban Transportation (1995). In Scenario Dense, almost all the new development was concentrated within the inner suburbs. In Scenario Diffuse, the development was allowed to spread throughout the whole region, without planning efforts. Scenario Infra placed all development around stations of the long-reaching transport lines. To evaluate these alternative scenarios, conservation targets were defined on regional and landscape levels. Two different biodiversity targets for forest habitats were tested. These were relevant for different stages of urbanisation, but still significant for the city as a whole. The first target was to preserve the large forest tracts in the peri-urban zone, with characteristic combinations of habitat types and bird fauna. The second target was to maintain a connected network of forest remnants in the suburbs, to sustain non-urban, sedentary (i.e. non-migratory) forest birds. In the selection of indicators, both the problem – the effects of the proposed plans and alternatives – and the biodiversity targets had to be considered. For the large forest tracts we focused on two resource-demanding forest birds, the capercaillie and the hazel grouse, of which the latter also is dispersal-limited. For the suburban forest network, we focused on non-urban, sedentary forest tits, here represented by the willow tit.

Caption for Fig. 25.7. (cont.)
concentrated within the inner suburbs. Scenario Diffuse: development allowed to spread throughout the whole region, without planning efforts. Scenario Infra: all development around stations of the long-reaching transportation lines. The circles represent examples of detected conflict areas, where mitigation measures would be effective (Mörtberg and Balfors, 2007).

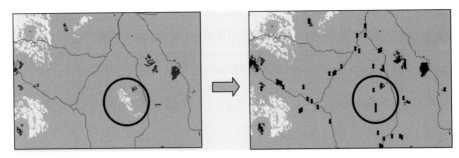

Fig. 25.8. A detailed illustration of the change from current conditions to Scenario Diffuse (Mörtberg and Balfors, 2007). A predicted effect of this scenario is the loss of available habitat for the capercaillie (*Tetrao urogallus*), one of the focal species, which may lead to extinction of local populations. White in the figure is predicted suitable habitat for the capercaillie, light grey is built-up areas and black is new development of residential areas in Scenario Diffuse.

From statistical analyses of empirical data (Mörtberg, 2001; Mörtberg and Karlström, 2005), GIS-based habitat models were used to predict focal species occurrences throughout the study area. In the next step, predictive habitat models, created for the present situation, were applied to each scenario to evaluate development impacts on the focal species. The results indicated that Scenario Diffuse led to adverse effects on biodiversity values of regional concern, including local extinctions and habitat loss in core areas of the focal species connected with the large forest tracts (Figs. 25.8 and 25.9). Scenario Infra would also lead to adverse effects, including substantial habitat loss and isolation. Scenario Dense mainly would lead to effects on the cohesion of the forest habitat network in the suburbs. However, both Scenario Infra and Scenario Dense could be substantially improved through mitigating alterations. Thus, if these scenarios were to be altered in a way that left certain train stations unexploited (Fig. 25.7), most of the predicted adverse effects on the investigated biodiversity conservation targets could be avoided.

In the evaluation, essential biodiversity values were addressed on a landscape scale. Still, an obvious problem with the use of species as indicators, even if carefully chosen, is that unforeseen needs of other species or groups may be left without consideration. For instance, most bird species may not be representative of dispersal-limited species (such as amphibians and several other non-flying species) or of species that need a long historical continuity of vegetation (such as many beetles confined to old trees). Another example of differences in response to urbanisation is the pattern mentioned above, that deciduous forest habitats are favoured in urban areas, while other nature types are more sensitive to the urbanisation process (e.g. Mörtberg and Wallentinus, 2000). These questions need to be addressed in further research, where several indicators will be tested

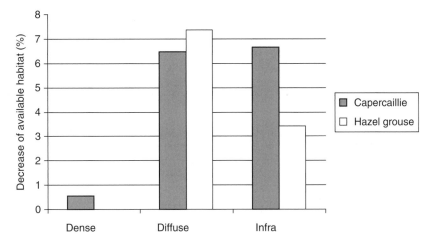

Fig. 25.9. Decrease of available (suitable and accessible) habitat for two urban-sensitive species, capercaillie (*Tetrao urogallus*) and hazel grouse (*Bonasa bonasia*), with the urbanisation scenarios Dense, Diffuse and Infra (modified from Mörtberg *et al.*, 2007).

systematically. A constructive and repeatable way of selecting indicators is to group species into functional groups, according to their properties, such as resource requirements and dispersal capacity, and their sensitivity to disturbances or threatening processes (Lambeck, 1997; Vos *et al.*, 2001; Coppolillo *et al.*, 2004) (Fig. 25.10). The functional properties of species groups will determine whether they will be affected by development. This approach can be done for a set of prioritised habitat types or combinations of these, and at different scales, corresponding to the biodiversity targets that were formulated in the beginning of the LEA process. In this way, a suite of functional groups of species will be selected, with the hypothesis that the requirements for persistence of the focal species collectively represent a variety of landscape characteristics and will encompass an essential part of biodiversity in a landscape (Lambeck, 1997).

The assessment of development impacts needs to be based on systematic, quantitative and spatially explicit predictions of effects on prioritised biodiversity components. One method is to use prediction tools in the form of GIS-based habitat models, which in the case study presented here were built on statistical analyses of empirical data. Another type of predictive, GIS-based habitat model is built solely on expert opinion (e.g. Yamada *et al.*, 2003). Our predictive habitat models were based on established relations between the occurrence of a species or guild and environmental variables, describing the species' suitable habitat, and applied over large areas (Natuhara and Imai, 1999; Guisan and Zimmermann, 2000; Scott *et al.*, 2002; Gontier *et al.*, 2006; Mörtberg *et al.*, 2007; Natuhara and Hashimoto, Chapter 12). Environmental variables included habitat variables on both local and landscape scales, and disturbance variables. Thus, sample sites

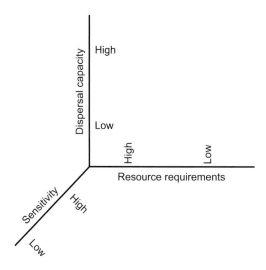

Fig. 25.10. A graph representing important properties of species that influence the risk of extinction and colonisation ability. Further dimensions can be added, such as sensitivity to disturbances like noise and recreation. In the diagram, vulnerable species will be located towards the origin. It should be noted, that to some extent, species' sensitivity to disturbances may change, as some native taxa are involved in a continuous process of adaption to urbanisation (e.g. Luniak *et al.*, 1990). Modified from Vos *et al.* (2001).

and study areas were defined in a multi-dimensional space, and for comparison, they were related to the size and characters of the relevant urbanisation centre. By doing so, knowledge about species distributions was expressed spatially in a format suitable for scenario testing and applicable to the planning process. In the field of scenario creation and testing, other planning support tools are available and could be used. For example, cellular automata and multi-agent systems can simulate activities of individual households and units of the built environment (Torrens, 2003), the sum of which causes drastic land-use changes. These kinds of tools for dynamic modelling also may be applied on biological units. Further, when analysing relations between urbanisation and wildlife, loss and fragmentation of natural habitats can be seen as proximate causes, but in order to incorporate the causal drivers behind the changes, the integration of social and economical factors will be necessary (Homewood *et al.*, 2001; Pickett *et al.*, 2001, Chapter 3).

The prediction of environmental impacts is an essential part of a strategic environmental assessment, which in Europe is required throughout the planning process. The assessment must consider the potential impacts of planning options, select alternatives that minimise environmental risk and plan measures for the mitigation of potential adverse impacts (Balfors *et al.*, 2005).

The LEA method will enable planners to consider biodiversity by defining specific landscape targets, and to take into consideration given sets of taxa related to these landscape targets, through a relatively transparent and repeatable framework and process (see also Florgård, Chapter 22). The spatial predictions of the impacts on habitats of focal species make it possible to quantify, integrate and visualise the effects of urbanisation scenarios on aspects of biodiversity across a broad area rather than just at the site-based level. The ecological and environmental advantages of a certain policy, plan or project could be visualised and when the final decision is made, this option could be selected. Through the LEA approach, effective mitigation and restoration measures also can be developed. By linking targets for landscape types with explicitly urban processes the LEA method is a useful tool in planning and impact assessments, and thus has the potential to improve the quality of strategic environmental assessments and ultimately contribute to sustainable planning and decision-making.

26

Applying landscape ecological principles to a fascinating landscape: the city

ROBBERT SNEP, WIM TIMMERMANS AND ROBERT KWAK

Introduction

This chapter describes the urban ecological research carried out by Alterra, a research institute at the Wageningen University and Research Centre (WUR) in the Netherlands. Our research group applies landscape ecology and spatial planning concepts to the study of urban environments, on the basis of a practical, learning-by-doing, approach. This specific approach of urban ecology, known as 'urban landscape ecology', is especially useful in an overpopulated country such as the Netherlands.

The chapter starts with a brief introduction on the concept of urban landscape ecology, followed by a description of four case studies, in which urban ecology and landscape ecology, spatial planning and architecture principles are combined into new concepts about preserving urban biodiversity and planning urban green space for 'People' (employees and residents), 'Planet' and 'Profit' (companies and developers). The chapter closes with an overview of our current research, which focuses on the contribution of business parks to regional ecological networks.

Introduction to urban landscape ecology

Cities have a size, structure and internal heterogeneity that distinguish them from other landscapes. The configuration and mutual relations of the

Ecology of Cities and Towns: A Comparative Approach, ed. Mark J. McDonnell, Amy K. Hahs and Jürgen H. Breuste. Published by Cambridge University Press. © Cambridge University Press 2009.

landscape elements of cities and towns differ significantly from those of other surrounding areas. Furthermore, the urban landscape has its own collection of underlying patterns and processes, which provide the conditions for a self-supporting ecosystem, the urban ecosystem, within which ecological, physical and socioeconomic components of metropolitan areas interact (Pickett *et al.*, 2001).

As described by Luck and Wu (2002), the relationship between the spatial patterns of urbanisation and ecological processes has been a topic for scientific research for over 50 years (mainly, however, with a focus on biotope mapping), but only became 'popular' and broadened to include all relevant aspects of urban ecology during the past 5 years. Current studies indicate that the spatial factor, and thereby the landscape ecological approach, has an important role in maintaining biodiversity. One outcome of the development of landscape ecology as a subfield of ecology has been that researchers have become more aware of the spatial configuration of habitats, barriers and gaps between habitats as important explanatory factors for the presence or absence of local biodiversity. This trend of applying spatial approaches within urban ecology can be seen as an integration of concepts, methods and ideas from both urban ecology and landscape ecology, and provides opportunities for a new integrated field of research: 'urban landscape ecology'. Within this research field three main objectives can be discerned:

(1) Evaluate the importance of urban ecosystems, and their networks, for ecology as a discipline;
(2) Determine how urban landscapes and urban green networks contribute to the conservation of biodiversity;
(3) Determine how urban landscapes and urban green networks contribute to human perceptions of biodiversity.

In relation to the first objective, the highly dynamic characteristics of urban ecosystems serve to intensify interactions between humans and wildlife in general. An urban plant or animal species needs to find a niche in a world dominated by humans and cars, and where landscape fragmentation, disturbance, pollution and other aspects of human activity are much more abundant and intense than in other ecosystems. Throughout the world, wild species have successfully adapted to life in urban ecosystems, providing some insights as to how other species might adapt to the future urbanisation of landscapes (e.g. Rapoport, 1993; Goode, 1998). Figure 26.1 shows how urban animal species might consider our direct living environment, a residential area, somewhat differently from the way we would look at it.

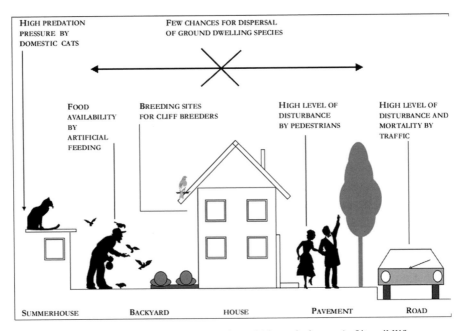

Fig. 26.1. The urban landscape experienced 'through the eyes' of its wildlife.

The second objective concerns the contribution of urban nature to the conservation of biodiversity. These days in Europe the value of urban ecosystems is much better understood and appreciated. Cities not only provide habitats for specific urban species, but also for increasing numbers of (common) species, which adapt to the urban environment, leading to an increased level of urban biodiversity (Morneau et al., 1999).

Despite the higher level of urban biodiversity, fragmentation and habitat isolation still appear to form a barrier for dispersal and (gene) exchange between the urban populations of some species, thereby posing a threat to their long-term occurrence (e.g. Hitchings and Beebee, 1997). A focus on the spatial configuration and connectivity of green areas within and around cities and towns can play an important role in helping maintain the presence of these species within cities (Mörtberg and Wallentinus, 2000; Rudd et al., 2002).

Finally, in relation to the last objective, the existing structure and composition of the urban green environment contributes significantly to human perceptions of biodiversity. As McIntyre et al. (2000) suggest, scientific research on the urban environment can only really be undertaken by a combination of natural and social sciences. By linking the conservation of urban biodiversity with human perceptions of urban greenspaces, opportunities arise to improve the quality of life for both humans and wildlife (Harrison et al., 1987; Burgess et al., 1988).

Research questions for urban landscape ecology

These points and our research experience in the Netherlands lead us to the formulation of the following main research questions for the scientific field of 'urban landscape ecology':

(1) Which factors are important to local population dynamics, such as the recruitment and mortality of urban wildlife?
(2) What is the influence of urban green structures on the long-term survival of species in cities (metapopulation level)?
(3) What is known about human perceptions of urban biodiversity (social relevance)?

The urban ecological research that the Alterra research institute has conducted in Dutch cities and towns since the millennium has shown the relevance of these questions. We expect these questions to be equally relevant for ecological researchers who work in other urbanised areas, and for researchers who combine more fundamental studies with a 'learning-by-doing' approach.

In the following sections the background of Alterra's research is outlined in more detail, followed by a description of five research projects that illustrate our way of conducting research. This is followed by a discussion on the contribution of Alterra's research in answering the research questions formulated above.

Dutch research in urban landscape ecology

Alterra has a long history in landscape ecology. For more than 20 years, the Landscape Centre has been carrying out pioneering research into the presence of plants and animals in fragmented landscapes (e.g. Opdam, 1991). During the past few years, landscape ecologists in this department have worked together with researchers in other disciplines (landscape architecture, planning, social administration and town planning) as a team to develop new concepts for balancing the needs of humans and animals in cities and towns. Our team, which studies urban–rural relations, focuses mainly on linking ecological principles to social needs in (sub)urban environments. During a comprehensive series of fundamental and applied research projects the team has developed a unique approach to the study of urban landscape ecology in the Netherlands (see e.g. Timmermans, 2001).

Our group has successfully applied two models, originally developed for rural areas, to the urban environment. Those models, called LARCH and SmallSteps, were developed by the Landscape Centre to study individuals and populations in fragmented landscapes. LARCH is a spatial expert system that calculates the configuration and volume of population networks for a wide range of species on the basis of habitat maps and population dynamic norms (Vos et al., 2001). These calculations can form the basis for evaluating the sustainability of the networks. To do so, the expert system determines the capacity of, and the distances between, all habitat patches and the existence of possible key patches with a potentially sustaining role. The model is especially suitable for comparing the ecological potential of all sorts of different planning scenarios that can be entered into the model. LARCH runs in a geographical information system (GIS) environment with norms and guidelines linked to the map material through a database. During the past few years LARCH has been used in several research projects on urban landscape ecology (e.g. Timmermans and Snep, 2001).

SmallSteps does not work at a population level like LARCH, but focuses on the individuals of a species. Hans Baveco (http://webdocs.alterra.wur.nl/internet/land schap/EMM/smallsteps/index.html) describes SmallSteps as a simulation model in which movements of fauna are simulated by means of the correlated random walk principle. This simulation is done in a heterogeneous landscape made up of polygons and linear landscape elements. These elements are represented by data in a vector format (GIS). The purpose of this model is to investigate whether, and how, individual butterflies or small mammals, for instance, move around the city. This then provides insights into whether habitats are isolated or linked, which elements in the city contribute to the ecological structure and what major opportunities and bottlenecks exist. To date, SmallSteps has been applied successfully within the urban context of the Rotterdam Borough of Hoogvliet (Snep et al., 2006).

Both expert systems are used in a GIS environment and are therefore largely dependent on digital information on the location of habitats, buildings, roads and so on. The coverage and amount of detail contained in map material collected by municipalities in the Netherlands are usually insufficient for this application. The possibility of using remote sensing techniques to develop reliable habitat maps from digital aerial photographs has recently been explored and seems to be an effective way of obtaining adequate map material (Snep et al., 2005). With the application of computer models such as LARCH and SmallSteps, and the use of detailed and up-to-date maps derived from satellite or aerial photos, a start has been made on 'reading' the urban ecosystem and understanding its complex patterns and processes.

Linking disciplines

Urban ecosystems can only be meaningfully understood if we see urban ecology in the context of the urban landscape, one that is designed, constructed and used by humans. Up until now this chapter has only described those human activities that influence the occurrence of plants and animals. But humans are more than just designers and users of urban landscapes; we also have clear wants and needs with regard to nature and greenspace (Chiesura, 2004). Nature is attractive in certain instances (e.g. butterflies in the garden) whereas other forms of nature are clearly unwanted (e.g. mosquitoes in the garden). The specific wants and needs of citizens are probably best expressed in public green spaces (see for example Van den Berg, 2003). Such areas must provide an attractive environment, yet dense urban woods, which are unsafe at night, are generally not wanted. In short, many competing social factors influence the design, layout and management of urban greenspaces. Therefore, urban ecological research requires a multi-disciplinary approach that also includes researchers from other disciplines, such as landscape architects and planners. The following cases describe the successful application of such a multi-disciplinary approach within a number of research projects.

Project 1 – how peri-urban areas can strengthen animal populations within cities: a modelling approach

We explored the extent to which source areas located in peri-urban zones can provide a response to a decreasing quality and size of green habitats within cities and thereby enhance populations of inner-city fauna (Fig. 26.2; for details, see Snep et al., 2006). The objectives of the study were to get a better understanding of: (1) the interactions between animal populations in urban and peri-urban areas; (2) the role of urban green structures within this relationship; and (3) the extent to which peri-urban areas can contribute to urban animal populations. We illustrated the idea of peri-urban support by using a simulation model for individual animal movements, applied through a specific case study using model species of butterflies as an example. The results show a relationship between the mobility of the model species and the accessibility of inner-city areas. The impact of peri-urban populations on populations of inner-city habitats differed for different source scenarios. It was calculated that the peri-urban individuals could enlarge the inner-city butterfly population by 7 to 36% in the case of 'moderate dispersers' and by 19 to 56% for 'good dispersers'. The results also showed that well-connected habitat patches within existing urban green structures were more likely to be visited by peri-urban individuals than isolated habitat patches. We concluded that peri-urban nature areas, if large enough, can have a potentially positive influence on the presence of fauna in inner-city neighbourhoods. In addition, the results suggest that the connectivity between inner-city and peri-urban habitat patches enhances the contribution of peri-urban migrants to inner-city populations. By providing a range of different habitats and linking the peri-urban areas to the inner city, moderately mobile

Fig. 26.2. Wishful thinking? Peri-urban nature development provides a source population and the opportunity for mobile species, like butterflies, to colonise the inner city – thereby increasing the density of urban butterfly species.

habitat specialists could compete better against the small but highly successful group of habitat generalists that are increasingly prevalent in urban environments all over the world (Snep *et al.*, 2006).

Project 2 – combining industrial activities and wildlife conservation:
contradictio in terminus *or unexplored opportunity?*

The next description of one of our research projects, conducted in 2001, is an early example of how biodiversity conservation can be successfully included in the design and management of areas planned for economic activities. We have since developed this topic in a longer-term and more intensive study, focusing on the biodiversity value of business parks, and a description of this work can be found in the last section of this chapter.

In the Netherlands, and other countries, specific areas are zoned for specific uses, and it is often assumed that these uses cannot be combined with other functions. 'Industry' is one such use that is rarely linked to a function like 'nature'. And yet, there can be all sorts of spontaneous nature values in industrial estates. The Port of Rotterdam, the world's largest harbour, more than 35 kilometres in length, contains many such examples and provides opportunities for nature to co-exist alongside industry. Alterra used the LARCH spatial expert system to study the nature values of wasteland and pipeline verges under various design and management scenarios (Timmermans and Snep, 2001). This spatial analysis showed that wasteland can be particularly good for hedgerow birds if they continue to be left undisturbed. This 'lack of management' means that vegetation succession will have a chance to create a natural shrubland vegetation which has a good carrying capacity for hedgerow birds. It was also found that pipeline verges play an important role as an ecological corridor for butterflies through the harbour area (Fig. 26.3). The nature value of industrial estates can be improved significantly if the design and management of existing greenspaces is more explicitly geared towards nature.

Project 3 – multi-functional wildlife overpasses: combining ecology, infrastructure and living

In a third project, described in more detail by Timmermans and Snep (2003), Alterra studied the ecological preconditions that a multi-functional wildlife overpass must meet. Wildlife overpasses (or viaducts) are overpasses that are surfaced with bushland vegetation, instead of asphalt. They act as 'natural' corridors and partially overcome the barrier effect of roads and highways for migrating ground-dwelling fauna. In the Netherlands, existing wildlife overpasses are currently all situated in, or near, natural parks (e.g. the Veluwe forest) and successfully provide Dutch wildlife, such as deer, wild boar, badgers and foxes, with an easy way to migrate from one part of the park to another.

The concept of a multi-functional wildlife overpass is an extension of this concept but includes more than just ecological functions. This makes it more reasonably priced (as the other functions will offset the total costs) and increases its relevance and applicability within more urbanised areas. The concept is intended as a bridging structure over a motorway that incorporates buildings (office space) as well as wildlife habitat (ecological corridor). It would consist of a building of one or more floors with a roof designed to function as an ecological corridor. The challenge here is to make the design sufficiently sophisticated that all the functions (infrastructure, building and ecology) can co-exist without compromising each other. From an ecological perspective it is important to create an attractive environment for all sorts of fauna, keeping disruptive elements such as light, sound and human presence to a minimum. This concept, called the 'officeduct', is currently being worked out in more detail for a specific case.

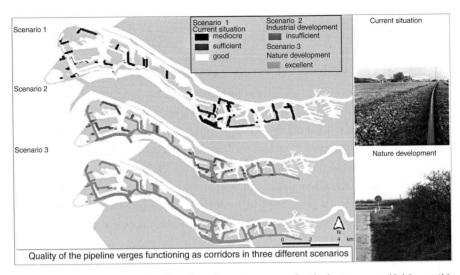

Quality of the pipeline verges functioning as corridors in three different scenarios

Fig. 26.3. Connectivity function of pipeline verges for the brown argus (*Aricia agestis*) in three spatial scenarios. Scenario 1 describes the current situation, whereas scenario 2 shows a more industrial use and scenario 3 the possibility to implement nature development. The LARCH analysis shows that scenario 2 will decrease the connectivity between butterfly populations, especially in the eastern part, while in scenario 3 the connectivity will increase in the western part of the Port of Rotterdam. See also colour plate.

Project 4 – new housing developments strengthening EU Bird Directive Area

Recently, more stringent European Union legislation for flora and fauna has placed tighter requirements on the protection of plant and animal species in development activities, such as building new residential areas and industrial estates. These new laws are often considered to be obstructive and restrictive. However, by taking the existing nature values into account in an early stage, problems can be prevented during construction, and in some instances, nature can profit from this approach. The planned new housing development of 'De Waalsprong' in the city of Nijmegen is situated next to an EU Bird Directive Area in the Dutch river region. The building site itself has limited nature value, but the design and the layout of the new area have been partially geared to the ecological functioning of the region as a whole, increasing the nature value of the adjacent Bird Directive Area. A broad ecological zone has been incorporated into the design of the new housing development, including an extensive system of water bodies (lakes and streams). Thus the birds, other animals and plants of the river system will be provided with a substantial area of new suitable habitat. In this way the ecology of the region as a whole will benefit from this urban development.

Discussion: Alterra's contribution to urban landscape ecology

As yet, the scientific field of urban landscape ecology is still largely unexplored and the main research questions, formulated earlier in this text, still await sufficient future research to be answered satisfactorily. As an institute with a tradition of landscape ecology research and located in one of the most densely populated and man-made countries of the world, Alterra is well positioned to conduct applied research on urban landscape ecology. The research projects described above show that we have started to explore some of the underlying patterns and processes of the urban ecosystem, especially with regard to the spatial aspects of urban animal populations. These all go some way to addressing the key research questions facing urban landscape ecology, which we posed earlier in this chapter.

> *Research question 1: what factors, such as recruitment and mortality,*
> *are important to the local population dynamics of urban wildlife?*

Several of our research projects have illustrated the effects of local habitat management on the local abundance of urban animal species. It is already known that the management of urban green areas is an important factor in the suitability of urban habitat for both animal and plant species. But while most of the existing studies focus on public green areas (e.g. urban parks), Alterra's studies, like the business park research (see section on 'Further research', below) and the multi-functional wildlife overpass (Project 3, above), show that architecture can also contribute to the conservation of endangered species. These habitat opportunities are often neglected by urban ecologists, who unfortunately are rarely involved in the design of buildings and other man-made structures.

Besides widening the focus of urban ecologists to other opportunities for developing urban habitats, some of the projects described above also show that, with intelligent configuration of urban and rural habitats, it is possible to achieve a more effective use of those habitats by animal species. Simulation studies (Project 1) illustrate that incorporating the ecology of plants and animals into the planning of urban and rural greenspaces can strengthen populations, for example of urban butterfly species. When important parts of the habitat required by a species (in this particular case vegetation that provides host plants) are missing from the urban environment, a sophisticated design and management of peri-urban source locations can be used to fill the gap. By doing so, the reproductive circle can be completed and local population dynamics will be positively influenced.

> *Research question 2: what is the influence of the urban green structure*
> *on the long-term survival of species in cities (metapopulation level)?*

The role of urban green networks in the metapopulation dynamics of urban species is an important research theme in all the Alterra research projects described in this chapter. They have investigated not only the role of traditional urban ecological structures, such as road verges (Project 1), but also pipeline verges (Project 2), buildings (Project 3), business parks (see Further research) and large urban parks (Project 4) in supporting exchange within animal metapopulations. The research results show that the concept of an urban ecological corridor can be stretched much further than the traditional strip of land, often located adjacent to the main road structures, that is designated as an 'ecological corridor' and managed as 'natural' urban greenspace. Most animals are able to make use of alternative corridors that can be located outside the public urban greenspace, that often do not have 'nature' as their dominant function and that sometimes are even not perceived as part of the ecological structure by town planners. These pioneering animals show that applying the concept of multi-functional land use for ecological purposes (e.g. the city's ecological structure) could be potentially even more successful if architects, planners, developers and landscape architects are willing to include habitat requirements within their plans.

Parts of cities and towns can play a potentially important role as habitats or ecological corridors for urban animal species, and this illustrates that the exchange of animals between local urban populations can be greatly enhanced. Yet it is difficult to comment on the sustainability of these urban ecological networks and the viability of urban populations, as there have been too few studies on the long-term effects of city dynamics on metapopulations of plants and animals.

Research question 3: what is known about human perceptions of
urban biodiversity (social relevance)?

Alterra explores the field of urban landscape ecology, and applies this new knowledge directly into plans, concepts and advice for urban planners and developers. Human perceptions about these development plans act as an important filter. If the role of human perception is not incorporated into the research methodology it will be much more difficult to implement the results and recommendations. In Project 1, the study on the contribution of peri-urban nature to inner-city animal populations, the human perception of urban nature played an important role in the design of the research. Inner-city areas contain few greenspaces, despite the well-known fact that people appreciate a green living environment. By planting host vegetation for butterflies, which is often not so attractive to humans, butterflies can be guided via urban green corridors to backyard gardens where they can exploit the inner-city flowers (sources of nectar) and humans can enjoy their presence. Similar beneficial combinations are applied to the multi-functional concept of business parks, where biodiversity conservation is included in the parks' design and management (see Further research) and to the design of the new housing development where a large urban park functions as both a recreation area and an ecological corridor for endangered animal species (Project 4). These projects illustrate how biodiversity conservation of urban animal species can be combined with positively increasing people's perceptions and experiences of nature in their immediate living environment.

Alterra's principles of research

A number of basic principles were taken into account and guided all the projects described above: (1) the importance of fitting a mono-functional view (wildlife ecology) within a multi-functional approach; (2) not to lose sight of reality but also not to let the current views on urban nature influence thinking too much; (3) the fact that unexpected combinations of functions often create opportunities for nature; and (4) the opportunities that nature provides in a specific situation should be approached by considering ecological conditions rather than zoning designation, function or current use.

Even though our research projects may be labelled 'successful' as concepts or plans, they also show that there is still much (empirical) research on nature in cities and towns that needs to be conducted, and that researchers in urban ecology face many challenges in developing better insights into the underlying patterns and processes of urban landscape ecology.

Further research – concepts for business parks that contribute to ecological networks

In 2004 we started a new, long-term and extensive research project in which we are applying the knowledge and experience that we have developed in urban ecological research to new multi-functional land-use concepts, particularly appropriate for urbanised countries like the Netherlands. This study focuses on the potential role that business and office parks, industrial and distribution areas can play as urban-edge habitats in regional ecological networks.

Although multi-functionality has in itself become a target within land-use planning, business areas, office parks and industrial sites are surprisingly still planned, built and managed with a mono-functional pattern of land use. Traditionally there is a separation of functions within these areas, and economic activities are seldom combined with other functions. Because of the current pressure for space in the Netherlands this tradition is being challenged. New ways are being explored to use the available space more efficiently by combining different functions. Within this context a new research project focuses on the opportunities to integrate conservation of biodiversity with business parks, as part of a new multifunctional concept (Ph.D. study; R. Snep, in preparation).

Several studies illustrate the opportunities that the design and use of business parks potentially provide for the conservation of biodiversity, but urban planners and developers in the Netherlands have not yet taken on board the concepts of multi-functionality, through which biodiversity conservation can be integrated into the design and management of business parks. The opportunity that such development sites offer for biodiversity conservation has, up to now, largely been ignored because the mutual benefits, for all stakeholders, have not yet been fully appreciated. The current state of scientific research does not provide enough detail about the ecological and socio-economic aspects of such multi-functionality. This project seeks to address this shortcoming. First, it aims to develop options for the design and management of multi-functional business parks that enhance such opportunities. Second, it will seek to develop an assessment framework which can explore both the socio-economic and ecological implications of those options. Finally, it will analyse the potential that multi-functional business parks, incorporating elements to promote biodiversity, can make to local and regional ecological networks. To achieve these objectives, a series of studies has been set up.

One of these studies, currently under way, will determine the existing local habitat value of business parks by analysing and comparing a set of urban bird inventories in Dutch cities and business parks to quantify relationships between land use at business parks and the abundance of urban bird species. This study focuses on those bird communities that potentially could best make use of business parks if their habitat value were improved. Coastal birds (e.g. terns, oystercatchers) are one example. They could take advantage of gravel roofs at business parks along the Dutch coast, in cities such as Amsterdam, Rotterdam, The Hague and Groningen. At present many of the traditional nesting places (beaches) are disturbed by human activities, and the dunes have recently also been invaded by foxes. Coastal birds therefore need to search for safe alternative nesting sites as, in some regions, their population is controlled by a lack of suitable nesting sites. Gravel roofs could provide a solution. Few of the flat roofs of business park buildings in the Dutch coastal zone are currently covered with gravel, yet many of these roofs have already been colonised by several EU Bird Directive species, including the common tern (*Sterna hirunda*), the lesser black-backed gull (*Larus fuscus*) and the oystercatcher (*Haematopus ostralegus*). This indicates that more gravel roofs could enlarge the populations of endangered coastal birds. The survey of urban bird data will seek to identify and quantify the key factors for successful nesting of such species at business parks.

In a follow-up study the identified key factors will be used to develop new concepts for business parks. These design and management measurements, to optimise the habitat value of business parks, will be put into future development scenarios which in turn will be used for ecological network analysis (by using the LARCH expert system) to determine the potential contribution that business parks can make to regional ecological networks.

Results from these two studies will subsequently be used for a multi-criteria analysis of several different business park concepts whose design and management will incorporate biodiversity conservation. By doing so, the advantages of such measurements will be determined for 'Planet', for 'Profit' and for 'People'.

27

A trans-disciplinary research approach providing a platform for improved urban design, quality of life and biodiverse urban ecosystems

CHARLES T. EASON, JENNIFER E. DIXON AND MARJORIE R. VAN ROON

Introduction

In this chapter, we report on the development of a trans-disciplinary research programme now under way in New Zealand which is designed to bring low impact urban design and development (LIUDD) practices into the mainstream. The development of LIUDD in New Zealand has drawn on earlier initiatives such as Low Impact Development (LID; Shaver, 2000), an alternative approach to stormwater management in North America. LID has much in common with Water Sensitive Urban Design (WSUD) in Australia (Lloyd *et al.*, 2001b) which deliberately embraces LID as well as other elements. A strong driver has been the need to enhance sustainability of the built environment through an integrated approach to urban design and development (van Roon, 2005). LIUDD aims to avoid a wide range of adverse physiochemical, biodiversity, social, economic and amenity effects that arise from conventional urban development and, at the same time, aims to protect aquatic and terrestrial ecological integrity (van Roon and Knight, 2004; van Roon and van Roon, 2005). With appropriate planning, funding and management, it is possible to have different patterns of development and intensities of development, whilst still meeting environmental standards and economic aspirations.

Ecology of Cities and Towns: A Comparative Approach, ed. Mark J. McDonnell, Amy K. Hahs and Jürgen H. Breuste. Published by Cambridge University Press. © Cambridge University Press 2009.

The chapter first provides some commentary on urban development practices in Auckland and New Zealand which provides a rationale for the development of the research approach. Second, key environmental, economic and social benefits of implementing LIUDD are identified through stakeholder interviews and literature reviews. Finally, the research programme and its four themes are outlined.

Opportunities for the implementation of LIUDD

Metropolitan Auckland is New Zealand's largest urban conurbation, consisting of four cities, Auckland, Waitakere, North Shore and Manukau. The region contains 1.2 million people, representing 31% of the country's population. Currently, Auckland grows by 49 people and 21 houses per day (Auckland Regional Council, 2003a). The accelerating rate of urbanisation in Auckland is increasing the rate of urban ecosystem deterioration.

Rapid urban growth puts pressure on the capacities of natural resources and physical infrastructure (Ministry for the Environment, 2000). Both greenfield development and urban retrofitting lead to increasing demands on conventional infrastructure (e.g. stormwater piping). The costs of maintaining existing and new stormwater and sewerage systems using conventional design and engineering approaches are escalating. The Auckland region will be spending NZ$5 billion over the next 10 years to replace aging pipes and meet the demands of new development (Manukau City Council website, 2003). This investment in infrastructure will not, by itself, reduce adverse environmental impacts on the receiving estuaries and rivers since current development practices and infrastructure lead to continued and cumulative adverse effects from stormwater runoff in urban areas. Contaminants and sediment reduce water quality, damaging streams and estuaries, and reduce aquatic biodiversity (van Roon and Moore, 2004). While extensive piped systems remove discharges from the site, urban stormwater discharges (flow peaks and contaminants) are unpleasant and are degrading coastal and inland waterways (Curry, 1981; Williamson, 1991; Wilcock, 1994; Snelder and Trueman, 1995). After decades of debate over 'cause and effect' relationships, stormwater impacts remain an unresolved priority concern (Parliamentary Commissioner for the Environment, 1998; Ministry for the Environment, 2002b).

Millions of dollars have been spent on research and monitoring the fate and effects of contaminants (e.g. heavy metals, solids, trace organics) and sediments (Hicks, 1993, 1994), and the adverse effects of excessive urban runoff both in New Zealand and overseas (Kingett Mitchell and Associates, 1992; McKergow, 1994; Colandini et al., 1995; Boxall and Maltby, 1995; Snelder and Trueman, 1995; Macaskill et al., 1996; Mikkelsen et al., 1996; Huser and Wilson, 1996, 1997; Boxall and Maltby, 1997; Robien et al., 1997). Current approaches in environmental research focus on the entry, distribution and 'end of pipe' monitoring of biological effects (Eason and O'Halloran, 2002), but have failed to put sufficient emphasis on removing the cause of these adverse effects.

Conventional approaches to residential land development in New Zealand substantially contribute to the problems (De Kimpe and Morel, 2000). In particular: (1) new building developments alter the land surface, increasing impervious surfaces and compacting hard ground to the extent that there is a near-total loss of permeability after development (Basher, 2000; Auckland Regional Council, 2000; Zanders et al., 2002); (2) topsoil is commonly compacted or destroyed, washed away in storms, discarded into landfills or sold, reducing groundwater recharge possibilities and increasing the need for irrigation of gardens and green spaces and the cost of planting and restoration strategies (Zanders et al., 2002); (3) during infill housing, retrofitting and new development, impervious surfaces proliferate across whole districts, resulting in increased stormwater runoff and catchment-scale impacts (McConchie, 1992; Schueler, 1994; Arnold and Gibbons, 1996; Schreier and Brown, 2002); (4) isolation of gardens from surface water flows by raised kerbs increases the unsustainable practice of watering gardens with potable water supplies; (5) new subdivisions often result in removal of native vegetation and an increase in weed spread to nearby remnants of indigenous vegetation through the proliferation of alien plant species in residential gardens and street plantings.

New research findings into loss of habitat and biodiversity conclude that 'houses are becoming worse than people'. New Zealand, with Brazil and China, is cited as a hot spot where the number of households is rising at nearly twice the rate of the population (Keilman, 2003; Lui et al., 2003). This situation, and the resulting urban sprawl, is acute in Auckland. The Auckland Regional Growth Strategy (Auckland Regional Growth Forum, 1999) anticipates that 70% of all new growth over the next 50 years will take place within metropolitan Auckland, making application of LIUDD in a brownfield situation a critical component for achieving urban sustainability.

As a consequence of conventional urban development, Auckland is arguably the weediest city in the world (Esler, 1988b). While Auckland occupies only 2% of the New Zealand's land area, it is home to thousands of introduced plant species (Auckland Regional Council, 2002). Colonial-style gardening approaches of planting predominantly alien plant species have led to a current naturalisation rate for alien plants of 10 species per year in Auckland (see also Ignatieva and Stewart, Chapter 23). More than 70% of environmental weeds were introduced to New Zealand as garden plants and have subsequently naturalised and become invasive (Owen, 1998). There are an estimated 17 000 introduced plant species held domestically in New Zealand, with approximately 2000 capable of naturalising (Buddenhagen *et al.*, 1998). The intensity of the environmental weed problem is explained almost entirely by factors associated with human settlement: subdivision age, housing density, proximity to reserves and species planted in gardens. Alien plants and weeds provide very poor habitat for native fauna. Abundance and diversity of birds, mammals and invertebrates is in general substantially lower for alien plants and weeds (Clout and Gaze, 1984; Kennedy and Southwood, 1984; Adair and Groves, 1998). Millions of dollars are spent on controlling plants that have become weeds, rather than preventing the establishment and spread of weeds. There is an opportunity for new developments to become low impact urban developments in terms of impacts of pest plants on indigenous biodiversity (Florgård, Chapter 22). Retaining and planting native plants will not only help to maintain the integrity of ecosystems close to the development by reducing weed impacts, but will also increase indigenous plant and animal biodiversity within the development itself (Nilon, Chapter 10; van der Ree, Chapter 11). Native plants and the wildlife they will attract will have flow-on effects in terms of aesthetic appeal and provision of ecological services, such as decomposition and nutrient cycling.

Development of the research approach

In constructing our research approach and methodology we reviewed international and New Zealand literature and practices, focusing on environmental, social and economic implications. We conducted a literature review of the costs and benefits of LIUDD approaches from a 'triple bottom line' perspective. We examined the literature on comparative assessments of sediment, pollution and flow discharges from LIUDD versus conventional building sites, and LIUDD versus conventional urban catchments. We have included in the review publications on the costs and benefits of the pollution-control infrastructure associated with LIUDD and conventional developments where possible.

In addition, we conducted preliminary interviews with five key stakeholder groups involved in urban development, including consumers, community, developers, and regional and city councils, to identify impediments to LIUDD and opportunities for change. We explored through interviews the reasons for the poor uptake of LIUDD practices by key stakeholder groups.

Findings

LIUDD is based on both ecological (McHarg, 1969; Arendt *et al.*, 1994; Hough, 1995; Steiner, 2000) and energy-efficient, compact approaches to urban design (Newman and Kenworthy, 1999). It comprises design and development practices that use natural systems and new low-impact technologies to avoid, minimise and mitigate environmental damage, energy requirements and waste. Key elements include working with nature, moulding land use to landform, avoiding or minimising impervious surfaces, using vegetation to assist in trapping pollutants and sediment, limiting earthworks, incorporating design features that reduce impacts, and enhancing biodiversity. In addition, LIUDD must also be cost-effective by reducing the need for construction and regular renewal of physical assets, such as piping (Christchurch City Council, 1999, 2000). Internationally, 'low impact' initiatives are still comparatively new, with demonstration developments and elements of LIUDD in many cities (van Roon and Knight, 2003, 2004).

New York's water supply (CH2MHILL, 2002) is an example at the catchment scale of huge cost-savings achieved by working with natural systems once community support was elicited (Daley, 1997). In contrast, New Zealand has few examples of LIUDD. Urban design and management professionals have in general responded appropriately to information on soil type (Basher, 2000), soil permeability and erosion sensitivity. By contrast the uptake of LIUDD is disappointing in view of the considerable technical knowledge and expertise in the design and application of LIUDD derived from overseas and New Zealand experience. Some Auckland councils, and other city councils in New Zealand, have recognised the opportunities for environmental protection and infrastructure cost-savings by producing a variety of comprehensive low-impact strategies and guidelines to encourage the use of swales, 'rain-gardens', 'roof-gardens', decreased imperviousness and other technology and strategies at the development site and catchment scale (North Shore City Council, 2001, 2002; Auckland City Council, 2003; Auckland Regional Council, 2003a,b). Structure plans prepared by Auckland councils for greenfield sites show significant shifts toward LIUDD principles (e.g. for Long Bay; North Shore City Council, 2002). However, developments depend on political willingness to implement relevant council plans and policies over a long time period. The Christchurch City Waterways and Wetlands Natural Asset Management Strategy 1999 (Christchurch City Council, 1999, 2000) is an early example of an innovative approach yet is still not fully integrated with other council plans and strategies. Benefits from LIUDD are readily identified at a site level, although not all can be easily quantified.

Environmental benefits

Compared with conventional development, LIUDD practices reduce sediment and pollutant loads, reduce stormwater flows, and have less impervious surface area and more vegetated areas. In turn, these lead to off-site benefits in waterways (improved fish habitat), in estuaries (improved habitat derived from reduced contaminant and sediment accumulation), and for terrestrial local biodiversity (native vegetation corridors). Typically reported benefits of LIUDD practices are as follows:

- Schueler (1994) reports reductions of 83% for sediments and approximately 70% for pollutants when 'low impact' approaches were used in North America.
- Monitoring data reported in Schueler (1994) indicate that 'low impact' stormwater practices (ponds, wetlands, filters or infiltration practices) can reduce phosphorus loads by as much as 40–60%.
- Vegetated swales, an element of LIUDD, have been shown in a study in Austin, Texas, to be effective sedimentation and filtration systems for reducing concentrations and loads of contaminants in runoff from roads (Barrett *et al.*, 1998). The reduction in pollutant mass transported to receiving waters was above 85% for suspended solids; 69–93% for turbidity, zinc and iron; and 36–61% for organic carbon, nitrate, phosphorus and lead.
- In studies in Auckland and Hamilton, New Zealand, Pandey *et al.* (2003) have shown that stormwater treatment walls remove over 90% of heavy metals and polycyclic aromatic hydrocarbons (PAHs) from stormwater generated from roads.
- Models of the hydrological benefits from low impact design predict that they will decrease peak flows for a 2-year storm by 7–14% compared with standard subdivision practice, and total storm runoff volume by 10–13% (Auckland Regional Council, 2000). Actual reductions should be greater. The model does not incorporate native vegetation in the low impact design. Auckland Regional Council considers revegetation using native species as the only effective way to reduce total runoff to predevelopment levels (Auckland Regional Council, 1996).

There is an opportunity for new urban developments to become low impact in terms of effects on indigenous biodiversity. Retaining and planting native plants will increase indigenous plant and animal biodiversity within the development and urban landscape. Native plantings within the matrix of individual residences will be important for creating 'islands' of suitable resources for wildlife. Native plants and the wildlife they will attract have additional benefits in terms of aesthetic appeal and provision of ecological services, such as decomposition and nutrient cycling. Landscape design within new developments, including plant selection and spatial distribution and the provision of structural elements, such as woody debris or rock features, will be critical to determining whether suitable food and shelter resources are available for native wildlife. There is also an opportunity for urban ecologists to determine whether there are measurable benefits of LIUDD in terms of biodiversity and potentially demonstrate an improvement in the functioning of 'urban ecosystems' in terms of processes such as nutrient cycling.

Economic benefits

Our reviews suggest that:

- LIUDD has reduced energy requirement to <25% of conventional housing at a number of sites (BRESCO, 2000). Bedzed is a development of 100 dwellings in South London combining reduced energy requirements with reduced potable water demand (by 40%) through recycling of rain and wastewater (Shirley-Smith, 2002).
- A 237-unit residential 'low impact' development in the City of Port Phillip, Melbourne, demonstrates reduced need for costly and scarce potable water supplies by recycling treated greywater and rainwater for garden irrigation and toilet flushing (City of Port Phillip, 2003). Similarly, at the 60L Green Office Building in Carlton, Melbourne, potable water savings of 90% and energy savings of 70% have been achieved through recycling and efficient design (The Green Building Partnership, website, 2004).
- LIUDD reduces infrastructure costs through the use of new design approaches and natural methods of stormwater avoidance and treatment. Auckland Regional Council (2000) estimates that at-source stormwater management will deliver savings of approximately 10% of current stormwater infrastructure and maintenance costs – that is, a saving of $5 million per year by 2008 – with increased savings in the longer term.
- LIUDD incorporates vegetated waterways rather than pipes. The Christchurch Waterways and Wetlands Natural Asset Management Strategy (Christchurch City Council, 1999, 2000) identified that restoration with natural drainage systems costs NZ$30–1000 per metre compared with pipe replacement at NZ$500–1300 per metre, with the latter requiring higher maintenance costs and replacement after 150 years as well.
- LIUDD is likely to be, on average, cost-neutral to developers. In recent modelling of the development of three sites (Auckland Regional Council, 2000), the financial performance of the low impact design was variable, being better, the same and poorer than that for standard subdivision at the site.
- Coffman (2000) reports a 25% reduction in both site development and maintenance costs for the 'Somerset' 'low impact' style subdivision in

Maryland, USA. The developer saved US$4500 per lot, or a total of US $900 000, by eliminating the need for kerbs, ponds and drainage structures.

- There is evidence that suggests that communities value the benefits accruing from LIUDD. In a community benefit survey (URS, 2001), Waitakere City residents indicated that they were willing to pay a combined total of $44.6 million per year in order to reduce the current levels of pollution in stormwater by 50% over the next 10 years.

Social benefits

LIUDD has the capacity to improve amenity values on- and off-site. LIUDD practices provide small, but significant, benefits to homeowners and the local community:

- Streams are retained in natural states. Walking for fitness and enjoyment is the single most popular recreational activity in the Auckland region. Many people like to take frequent walks in their local area, and there is increasing demand for scenic interest – and therefore natural habitat – to be retained in new subdivisions (Auckland Regional Council, 1996). Stream corridors can accommodate cycleways, increasing transport sustainability.
- Native vegetation is retained where possible. Residential streets may be narrowed and curved but street corridors can remain wide to accommodate 'rain gardens', large trees and swales. The existence of native vegetation on the properties is a frequent selling point.
- Ecological restoration in terms of urban form that is less colonial in style with restoration of native vegetation and traditional food sources will benefit Maori (indigenous people of New Zealand) and contribute to social and cultural restoration (Matunga, 2000).
- In comparison with conventional subdivision practices, subsoils are less compacted, and less topsoil is removed or stockpiled with a LIUDD approach. Soil layers are not mixed and returned on-site as heterogeneous composites devoid of natural structure and microfauna (Simcock, 2004). This means that soils are in much better condition, street trees establish and flourish, and lawns are lush and not flooded after rain because of poor drainage in the compacted subsoils.

Preliminary interviews

Interviews revealed that our five main stakeholder groups have specific needs (Table 27.1) that influence positively or negatively their willingness and ability to exploit LIUDD. Collectively these conflicting needs are often

Table 27.1. *Main issues for major stakeholders (identified in a preliminary survey by the University of Auckland and Landcare Research in Auckland and Christchurch, 2002–2003) relevant to Low Impact Urban Design and Development (LIUDD).*

Stakeholder group	Issue of concern
Community	• resistance to 'user pays' and price increases
	• disassociation between 'user pays' (water + waste) and local environmental quality
	• lack of understanding of city or regional council LIUDD goals
Maori[a]	• maintaining low-cost housing imperative whilst meeting Maori values
	• restoration and retro-fitting native vegetation
	• European identity predominates
Developers and professionals[b]	• lack of profit margins
	• council disincentives rather than incentives
	• LIUDD subsidises city council infrastructure costs
	• short payback requirement
	• time commitment to absorb LIUDD manuals
	• need to maximise land cover to maximise profit
	• lack of consumer demand
	• lack of demonstration projects to emulate
	• professional risk to engineers who use non-conventional (piping) approaches
Councils (local authorities)	• lack of data to define financial contribution/ incentives in district plans
	• maintenance cost
	• biophysical data on land resilience, planting and biodiversity for district plan
	• concern about disconnection between regional strategies and district plans that incorporate LIUDD & current engineering codes
	• need robust information to use in new guidelines for developers and regional plans
	• lack of understanding by community of goals
Consumer	• house prices
	• running costs
	• unaware of choice

Notes:
[a] Based on discussion with Ngarimu Blair, Ngati Whatua o Orakei (and from Matunga, 2000).
[b] professionals = engineers, planners, architects.

perceived as competing or insurmountable impediments to change. Disagreement and litigation between some stakeholder groups can be a costly deterrent. Poor uptake of LIUDD results from many of the reasons summarised in Table 27.1. Among the specific interests of each group were price concerns, willingness to change, and both planning and institutional barriers. Some council policies were identified as restricting change, as were some conservative development practices. This was compounded by a lack of local technical and economic data to influence plans and codes of practice. Also, while members of the wider community were dissatisfied with urban pollution, they were not really aware of LIUDD or the need to conserve resources and their impacts on local or regional environments.

New housing development provides different opportunities and challenges for different stakeholders (Dixon *et al.*, 2001; Standards New Zealand, 2001; Ministry for the Environment, 2002a). For developers, profit margins are tight, often at 5% or less (P. Rhodes, personal communication). Our survey identified house price and household running costs as key issues for buyers; thus, changes to development practices to reduce environmental impacts must be cost-neutral or better.

Councils want to reduce adverse environmental impacts but are constrained by the limited information available to underpin defensible rules to control development. City and district councils are concerned about rising infrastructure costs, which are exacerbated by design approaches that are costly to maintain. On one hand, urban communities expect traditional forms of infrastructure, such as kerbs, channels and extensive pavements, which reinforce current investment patterns by councils. On the other hand, these communities are demanding increasingly higher levels of environmental quality, such as clean streams and beaches (North Shore City Council, 1999; Auckland City Council, 2000), as well as increased numbers of native birds, and fish in streams (Heremaia, 2000).

Trans-disciplinary programme design

Our 6-year programme has several features that we consider constitute a trans-disciplinary approach to our research. First, it draws on a range of disciplines beyond those traditionally involved in this field to examine how the uptake of LIUDD can be increased. Second, it is collaborative in that we work alongside partners in the public and private sectors over a period of some years. In turn, this collaboration assists in disseminating knowledge of the programme and its findings. Third, the programme is strongly orientated, through participatory research and the use of demonstration projects, towards the transfer of research findings to practitioners and consumers, thus encouraging the uptake of new practices. Finally, the researchers have a strong commitment to the integration of data across objectives and disciplines so that results will be presented in forms that are easily accessible for residents as well as practitioners. For example, a national task force of leading planning practitioners has been established to work with the research team to assist in changing practices at local levels, such as modifying and aligning various types of council plans and development practices.

The research activities focus on metropolitan Auckland with sites in Taupo and Christchurch. There are also close links to Australian and North American case studies. The context for our work ranges from development sites to catchments and includes both greenfield and brownfield applications. We have established six case study sites in urban and rural locations with varying spatial scales that we are drawing on to develop and apply concepts, techniques and processes. The large research team drawn from several institutions encompasses researchers with expertise in environmental sciences, engineering, social sciences, economics and planning. Regular meetings and work programmes encourage trans-disciplinary collaborations. We are also interacting with a significant number of stakeholders in councils, private sector, Iwi (tribal) and other organisations through our various activities. This collaboration assists the education of researchers as well as stakeholders. The programme has four themes:

- Getting buy-in: the human and social dimension – identifying ways of overcoming social and institutional barriers to LIUDD;
- Innovative science and design – integrating natural features and treatment processes in urban development and catchment management to reduce stormwater impacts and enhance biodiversity;
- Economic tools for LIUDD – comparing cost–benefits of different approaches to underpin rational choices;
- Changing plans and practices: making it happen – developing a policy framework with a range of planning instruments that can aid in the uptake of LIUDD by councils and developers.

These four research themes will continue during the life of this progra-mme from 2003 to 2009 with considerable interaction between the themes (Figure 27.1).

Discussion

In achieving better uptake of LIUDD, there is a need to better understand the values and perceptions of stakeholders, including consumers. To this end, we are adopting a collaborative learning approach and working with stakeholders on a range of specific topics, such as rain tanks, to determine how uptake of specific components of LIUDD can be improved. We see 'buy-in' as a critical element for success of the programme. The communication of research results to stakeholders is also a critical element of the research process. The production of an online user's guide should assist dissemination of findings to a wide range of stakeholders.

Second, data on the on- and off-site environmental performance of LIUDD practices are not comprehensively available in a form that is credible for

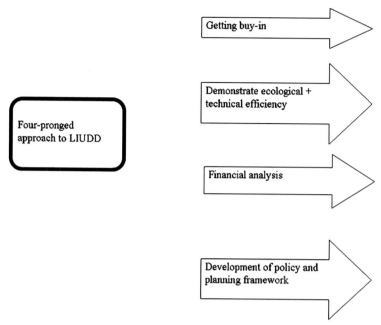

Fig. 27.1. Research approach used by the Centre for Urban Ecosystem Sustainability to encourage change in urban design and development.

practitioners or suitable for cost–benefit analysis. We are conducting comparative assessments of sediment, pollution and flow discharges from LIUDD versus conventional building sites, and LIUDD versus conventional urban catchments. We propose to establish how specific LIUDD practices (including re-engineered soil, vegetated swales, riparian strips, rain gardens and catchment revegetation) can reduce runoff, and improve water quality and urban biodiversity. Results from this theme will lead to defensible rules for housing developments and codes of practice for LIUDD.

The third theme focuses on developing economic tools for LIUDD. Currently, there is insufficient information to reliably translate estimates of improved hydrological performance, reduced contaminant loads and improved urban biodiversity into economic benefit. Economic signals sent by current pricing mechanisms (such as the price of water) or through council rates on house owners and businesses do not encourage improvements in urban development practices. The costs of managing or mitigating the impacts of housing developments are hidden. We will value the costs and benefits of LIUDD approaches from the perspective of the developer, house buyer, local council and community. Our valuation will include an estimate of the comparative savings through the pollution-control infrastructure and maintenance, reduced potable water consumption, reduced road area, and reduced stormwater associated with catchments with LIUDD, as opposed to catchments with conventional developments.

Finally, the uptake of LIUDD is directly influenced by a raft of instruments, such as statutory and non-statutory plans, strategic plans and codes of practice administered by regional and city/district councils. Despite some very supportive codes (such as Auckland Regional Council, 2000, 2003b) planning and regulatory processes are impeded by variable technical and economic information. Currently, planning instruments (such as district plans) vary widely, and there is poor integration among different types of instruments (such as district plans and codes of practice) that impedes the implementation of LIUDD as mainstream practice (Beca Planning, 2001). There are also few incentives to encourage developers to change traditional development practices and take on board innovations. We are developing a policy framework within which sits a range of planning tools that stakeholders can use and modify, depending on their particular needs.

Increasingly, however, as we work with our national task force, we are appreciating the need to address issues of organisational change as a first priority and to examine how best to manage the change process. Change in respect of accepted organisational practices is a precursor to achieving fundamental shifts in the way that local implementation occurs through a series of connected activities such as investment in infrastructure, the alignment of strategic and development plans within councils and the shaping of future urban form.

LIUDD is a critical means for making growth more sustainable, given the population increase predicted for the Auckland region over the next 50 years. Auckland is now identified as the priority focus in the Government's Sustainable Development for New Zealand Programme of Action (Department of Prime Minister and Cabinet, 2003). However, implementation is dependent on the willingness of stakeholder groups to embrace principles of LIUDD (van Roon and van Roon, 2005). For example, there will need to be substantial shifts in investment in infrastructure not only by individual households but also by local and regional government as major funders.

While the programme is well under way, it will be some time before we can determine comprehensively the impact of our research. However, we can already cite examples, such as our work with Taupo District Council on the Taupo West Structure Plan, where our interventions have influenced council practices and processes through the adoption of new concepts and tools. We are confident that the research design and methodology underpinning the programme is robust enough to assist the development of more sustainable practices and outcomes in the urban environment.

Summary

We have outlined a platform for a trans-disciplinary urban research approach underpinned by a literature review on Low Impact Urban Design and Development (LIUDD) and presented preliminary results from working with five key stakeholder groups: consumers, Iwi, community, developers, and regional and city councils in New Zealand. Conventional development practices in Auckland lead to adverse effects from stormwater runoff in urban areas and contribute to escalating costs of infrastructure. LIUDD comprises design and development practices that use natural systems and new low impact technologies to avoid, minimise and mitigate environmental damage, energy requirements and waste. Some Auckland councils, and other city councils in New Zealand, have recognised the opportunities for environmental protection and infrastructural cost-savings by producing a variety of low impact strategies and guidelines. Barriers to these are consumer and practitioner behaviour, deficient pricing of resources such as water, conflicts between stakeholder groups, and variable quality of planning instruments.

Significant practical work and research is required to overcome obstacles to broadscale uptake of LIUDD. With this in mind we have implemented a research programme that provides information on: (1) the performance of LIUDD at the development site and catchment scale; (2) the economics of conventional versus LIUDD; and (3) the range of policy and planning instruments available to local government as means of implementing LIUDD principles and methods that will, in turn, encourage the development community to embed LIUDD practices. The final part of our four-pronged programme, through a participatory research approach, will facilitate uptake of LIUDD by the range of stakeholders, professionals and consumers. Extensive opportunities exist for urban ecologists to compare urban biodiversity within and between different levels of spatial scale, such as sites, neighbourhoods and catchments, undergoing varying forms and intensities of development.

Acknowledgements

The authors would like to thank Margaret Stanley for provision of information on weeds in New Zealand cities, Ann Austin for her comments on the manuscript and the New Zealand Foundation of Research Science and Technology for its support.

28

Pattern:process metaphors for metropolitan landscapes

LAURA R. MUSACCHIO

Introduction

A broad-based consensus exists among the experts in the ecological, design and planning disciplines that the conservation and restoration of riparian landscapes and watersheds is one of the most important strategies for maintaining regional biodiversity, watershed health and landscape character (e.g. visual quality and sense of place) in the United States (e.g. Naiman et al., 1993; Smith and Hellmund, 1993; Beatley 1994; Forman, 1995; Naiman and Décamps, 1997; Noss et al., 1997; Beatley, 2000; Poiani et al., 2000). Yet this conservation and restoration still represents a unique situation because of the limited scientific research into urban ecosystems and the unique land-use and land-cover issues of metropolitan regions (Guntenspergen et al., Chapter 29). For example, riparian landscapes are part of floodplain systems, which have unique human-induced landscape transformation characteristics that involve regulation, infrastructure demands, stakeholders' environmental values, land-use patterns and recreational activities.

The metropolitan region is a perfect opportunity for linking conservation science to the design and planning of urban riparian landscapes and watersheds. Yet, experts in these disciplines have not reached consensus about the best approach for balancing concerns for regional biodiversity, water quality and quantity, landscape character and recreational use. At times, these disciplines have conflicting perspectives about which of these goals is most important in the

Ecology of Cities and Towns: A Comparative Approach, ed. Mark J. McDonnell, Amy K. Hahs and Jürgen H. Breuste. Published by Cambridge University Press. © Cambridge University Press 2009.

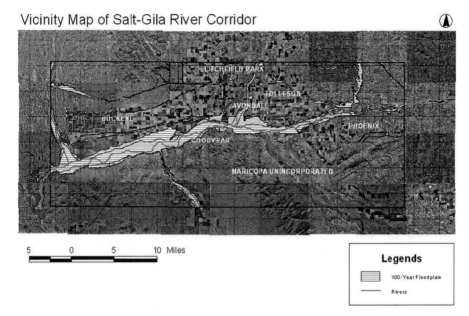

Fig. 28.1. Floodplain of the Salt–Gila River corridors in the Phoenix metropolitan region.

urban environment. Many scholars attribute this problem to a lack of a holistic vocabulary that aids translation of disciplinary theories and concepts (McIntyre *et al.*, 2000; Musacchio and Wu, 2004; Pickett *et al.*, 2004, Chapter 3). Given this circumstance, new integrative concepts are needed for urban riparian landscape conservation and restoration that aid communication and knowledge creation between conservation scientists, designers and planners, whether in academia or practice.

As a first step in this process, this chapter explores the challenge of how to develop integrative metaphors for urban riparian landscape conservation and restoration at the watershed level. In particular, I discuss the importance of the pattern:process metaphor as a means to promote cross-disciplinary communication and knowledge generation. Four aspects of this challenge are explored in this chapter: (1) the use of integrative metaphors in science, design and planning; (2) an introduction to the pattern:process metaphor; (3) the five recurring metaphors for streams, rivers and watersheds; and (4) pattern:process metaphors for riparian areas in the Phoenix metropolitan region (Figure 28.1).

Using integrative metaphors for cross-disciplinary communication and knowledge generation

Recent environmental legislation and policies, such as the National Environmental Protection Act (1969), Endangered Species Act (1973), Clean

Water Act (1970s), federal wetlands regulations (1970s–2000s) and ecosystem management (1990s–2000s), provide incentives for integrating conservation science (e.g. conservation biology, landscape ecology, restoration ecology and urban ecology) into urban land-use issues in the United States. Conservation scientists are playing a more important role in urban ecosystems, such as in endangered species issues, bioreserve design and habitat conservation plans. But landscape architects and environmental planners have a long history in similar areas, such as urban open space designs, greenway plans, wetland mitigation plans and habitat restoration plans. The result is knowledge growing in parallel in these disciplines with limited exchanges, especially between conservation biologists, landscape architects and urban planners.

An integrative metaphor is a promising concept for communication between the scholars and practitioners in conservation science, landscape architecture and urban planning. Prominent scholars have used the concept of integrative metaphor in three contexts: (1) as a means to understand complex ecological concepts (Pickett and Cadenasso, 2002); (2) as a means to communicate across disciplines (Pickett *et al.*, 2004); and (3) as a basis for design and planning concepts (Lyle, 1985, 1994; Spirn, 1998). These scholars strive to communicate one of the fundamental concerns in conservation science, design and planning: understanding the complexity of human-induced landscape transformations in metropolitan landscapes. The challenge of communication is how to translate concepts between disciplines without losing the integrity of ideas. Therefore, 'lost in translation' is perhaps one of the most challenging issues to address in the process of communicating and exchanging ideas and ultimately applying knowledge across disciplines.

A number of scholars have attempted to overcome the issue of 'lost in translation' by developing integrative metaphors to link science, design and planning. Examples include Lyle (1985, 1994), Steiner (2002), Capra (1996, 2002), Nabhan (1997, 2004), Pickett *et al.* (2004), and Musacchio and Wu (2002). John Lyle (1985, 1994), a landscape architect, draws on the principles of systems ecology to help explain why human-induced landscape transformations have particular properties, such as scale, hierarchy and self-organisation. His integrative metaphors, such as the title of his book *Regenerative Design for Sustainable Development* (1994), emphasise how the systemic properties of designed landscapes, which are particular types of human-induced landscape transformation, can be used to create more sustainable communities and watersheds (Lyle, 1985, 1994). He addresses this challenge by using a holistic approach that integrates ideas from the arts and sciences (Lyle, 1985, 1994). His approach is important for several reasons. He addressed the ecology and complexity of sustainable urban landscapes several decades before ecologists were concerned about these issues. In addition, these concepts are a connection to the field of study known as complex systems.

Frederick Steiner (2002), who is a landscape architect and environmental planner, also uses integrative metaphors to understand the systemic properties of designed landscapes. In his recent book, *Human Ecology*, Steiner reviews eight integrative metaphors for understanding the complexity and resiliency of designed landscapes (Steiner, 2002). These integrative metaphors are influenced by ideas in science, which he uses to explain the complexity of human ecology (Steiner, 2002). He builds on Ian McHarg's thoughts about human ecology and echoes the work of one of the most influential scientists, Fritjof Capra.

The writings of Capra (1996, 2002) introduced powerful integrative metaphors about changing ecological systems from his knowledge of the theories of physics, chaos and complexity. His undeniable strength is his communication skill because his integrative metaphors about living systems, such as the titles of his two books *The Web of Life* (1996) and *The Hidden Connections* (2002), resonate with many people. He has a particular concern about the negative effects and impacts of human-induced landscape transformations on the Earth (Capra, 1996, 2002). His writings have been very influential in the sciences, encouraging scientists to initiate new collaborations with social scientists, designers and planners and to take on the challenge of sustainable development.

Another example is Gary Nabhan (1997, 2004), who uses integrative metaphors about nature, culture and narratives. *Cultures of Habitat* (1997) are metaphors about the intertwining of cultural experiences, such as oral stories, in the natural cycles of other living organisms and the environment. His metaphors emphasise the coupling of human existence and local knowledge and nature and how this bond leads to more sustainable use of landscapes over many generations (Nabhan, 1997, 2004). In short, his metaphors encourage people to take the long view about their connection to past and future generations and reflect on their interactions with the natural world. He emphasises that indigenous cultures offer models of sustainable land-use and landscape change, which are important lessons for the twenty-first century (Nabhan, 1997, 2004).

Pickett *et al.* (2004) put forth the importance of 'resilient cities' as metaphors, which were inspired by 'cities of resilience' metaphors proposed by Musacchio and Wu (2002). All of these metaphors are important because they suggest a link between environmental performance and urban ecosystem patterns (Musacchio and Wu, 2002; Pickett *et al.*, 2004). Moreover, they suggest that a symbiotic relationship should occur between the disciplines of ecology, design and planning. These metaphors are reasons why human-induced landscape transformations should have a tighter evolutionary coupling with the natural world in metropolitan landscapes.

The use of integrative metaphors by Lyle, Steiner, Capra, Nabhan, Pickett *et al.*, and Musacchio and Wu are important precursors for the next level of integrative metaphors that are needed at the interface of conservation science, design and planning. Despite the valuable contributions of these scientists, planners and designers, better integrative metaphors are needed to describe human-induced landscape transformations in cities. Understanding the complex interactions among human decisions and land-use and land-cover changes is the key. For example, Nassauer (1995) emphasises that the culture–landscape relationship is a dynamic feedback system. But it is difficult to define what this means in growing metropolitan regions because of the complex relationship between rapid changes in culture and landscape structure and function. For example, one of the most visible manifestations of this complex relationship is the decoupling of riparian landscapes from their hydrological and ecological context, which cause changes in the hydrological cycle of watersheds and human experiences with water. Recoupling and protecting these riparian and wetland landscapes in their watershed contexts are important goals of pattern:process metaphors.

A first step – pattern:process metaphor

A pattern:process metaphor is a type of integrative metaphor that describes human-induced landscape transformations in metropolitan landscapes. First, the phrase pattern:process evokes ideas about the systemic relationship between structural and functional processes in landscapes. This concept is at the heart of the complex interactions between human decisions and land-use and land-cover changes. The words in the metaphor are carefully selected to communicate a particular landscape state and specific spatial and temporal properties that can be related to scientifically measurable variables and observable land-use and land-cover patterns. In this section, the usefulness of pattern:process metaphors for understanding these complex interactions is discussed.

First, a pattern:process metaphor can be used in a variety of contexts and circumstances to further understanding about changing cultures, habitats and landscapes. For example, because of their training, conservation scientists gravitate toward explanations that increase knowledge about ecological processes. Yet in human-dominated landscapes the influence of cultural processes is an important missing component in most ecological explanations of changing ecosystem patterns and processes (Nassauer, 1995). For example, human perception, behaviour and experience are some of the most potent functional processes not directly acknowledged in most ecological theories and explanations (Nassauer, 1995). But there are exceptions to this rule. For example, Kellert and Wilson's book *The Biophilia Hypothesis* (1993) seeks to explain human preferences for particular landscapes based on their evolutionary origins in the savannas of Africa. It is an important example of a pattern:process metaphor because functional processes are related to ecological and cultural properties of landscapes. Moreover, since it addresses the ecological and cultural basis for visual perception, this concept has enhanced cross-disciplinary communication between science and design. More pattern:process metaphors are needed that build on this foundation.

Second, a pattern:process metaphor addresses the broad challenge of translating disciplinary theories and concepts for practitioners and the public. For example, sustainability science is the hottest buzzword since ecosystem management, yet no one has figured out how to translate it into something meaningful for building more sustainable cities. Pattern:process metaphors are one potential solution that can connect sustainability science to sustainable design. For example, they can be used to educate practitioners and people about the preferred spatial concepts and relationships between habitat quality for different organisms and the desired level of landscape naturalness for human acceptance.

Third, a pattern:process metaphor can be used to describe and explain the unique dynamics of the land-use and land-cover change issues in metropolitan regions. It can be used to develop explanatory and predictive models for human-induced landscape transformations and as a practical tool for translating and communicating scientific concepts into observable phenomena, the cornerstone of human perception and experience. Moreover, pattern:process metaphors can be used to describe particular spatial patterns and processes, which can be used as the basis for spatial concepts for design and planning.

The current ecological and cultural metaphors for defining urban riparian landscapes

Certain ecological and cultural metaphors define the unique qualities of riparian landscapes. This section reviews five recurring metaphors that are important for understanding the dynamics of human-induced landscape transformation in streams, rivers and watersheds. They represent the intellectual evolution of ideas about riparian landscapes in general and in desert environments.

Riparian landscape as the ecological system

Ecological definitions of riparian landscapes are usually described as the riparian zone, area, ecotone, interface or corridor (Malanson, 1993; Naiman and

Décamps, 1997). Stream corridor, river corridor and floodplain are also used on a consistent basis to describe this landscape. Riparian zone or area is perhaps the most common term used to describe the ecology of riparian landscapes in the scientific literature.

Most definitions of a riparian area include a specific reference to location, hydrology, vegetation, soil conditions and gradients (National Research Council, 2002). One of the most recent definitions, which was developed by a team of scientific experts, emphasised the transitional biophysical, ecological and biotic characteristics of riparian areas (National Research Council, 2002). The Arizona Riparian Council (1994) describes riparian with an emphasis on the relationship of vegetation, habitats or ecosystems to perennial or ephemeral water sources. In contrast, Graf (2001), who is a geographer, emphasises that the biological and physical components of a riparian zone are important for understanding landscape patterns and change.

The spatial configuration of a riparian area influences flows of nutrients, energy and species (Malanson, 1993; Forman, 1995; National Research Council, 2002). The co-occurrence and concentration of these flows into linear corridors and networks make riparian areas some of the most biologically diverse and productive landscapes (Malanson, 1993). Yet the spatial extent of a riparian area is not precise because delineation is complicated by many interacting factors such as plant community dynamics and geographical location (Naiman and Décamps, 1997). In arid environments, the spatial extent and zone of influence of a riparian area is much easier to detect visually because of the abrupt transition of vegetation and moisture that occurs at the ecotone with the surrounding xeric uplands (Briggs, 1996).

The focus on the riparian area as a landscape is relatively recent and is typically used in landscape ecology and stream ecology. Interest has spread throughout ecology in recent years because of the increasing importance of understanding how ecological patterns and processes operate at the landscape scale. A number of explanatory concepts have been proposed to describe the spatial extent of a riparian area and these concepts emphasise the importance of using a geographic area to understand the patterns of flows of energy, materials and organisms in river systems. The 'river continuum concept', as proposed by Vannote et al. (1980), is an explanatory model for how the spatial patterns of energy, nutrients and organisms vary along a river corridor from its headwaters to its outlet. Forman (1995) described how the 'river continuum' creates a distinctive mosaic in the landscape. More recently, the 'river continuum concept' has been extended by Benda et al. (2004) in their 'network dynamics hypothesis' that relates watershed shape to the geographical distribution of stream habitat in a watershed network.

Moving along an urban–rural gradient, habitat loss and fragmentation increasingly affect the riparian landscapes in metropolitan regions. Several scientists have created spatial frameworks for habitat modification and naturalness that explain how these patterns relate to conservation strategies. McKinney (2002) proposed a model for how species richness, categories of urban biota, amount of impervious surfaces and conservation strategies change for an urban–rural gradient. From the urban fringe to city centre, these trends are observed: impervious pavement increases, species richness decreases and urban biotas become more disturbed (McKinney, 2002). He identified an important threshold for managing landscape change in suburban watersheds: when the amount of impervious pavement increases to 20–50%, conservation strategies change from acquiring remnant habitats to restoring habitats (McKinney, 2002). In another example, McIntyre and Hobbs (1999) conceptualised how landscape change creates four types of landscape states based on the degree of habitat destruction. Under the McIntyre and Hobbs' classification, most urbanising watersheds would demonstrate increasing spatial patterns of fragmentation, decreasing connectivity of habitats and increasing numbers of remnant habitat patches (McIntyre and Hobbs, 1999).

Riparian landscape as the engineered system

This metaphor of a riparian landscape emphasises the transformation of a natural system to an engineered system for human uses, including navigation, irrigation, water storage, commerce, electric power and flood protection. A riparian landscape as an engineered system is designed and maintained as an equilibrium system (Graf, 2001), which is different from the behaviour of unmodified riparian and floodplain systems.

Engineering works create a new spatial order that alters the natural co-occurrence and concentration of spatial patterns and ecological processes in riparian landscapes and watersheds. Graf (2001) characterises an engineered river system by the degree of human modification of a river's physical landscape. In order to classify changes in the naturalness of the geomorphology of rivers, Graf developed a scale with five classifications that is particularly helpful for understanding the rivers as engineered systems in arid environments. According to Graf's classification, an engineered river in a city would fit into three possible categories of modification depending on the extent of change (Graf, 2001).

In order to understand the riparian landscape as an engineered system, it is helpful to draw on an example from ecology that seeks to explain how human-induced landscape change reduces the natural resiliency of ecosystems. Gunderson and Holling (2002) proposed that two types of resilience exist in the environment: 'engineering resilience' and 'ecosystem resilience'. They argue that 'engineering resilience' does not represent a sustainable relationship between nature and people, while 'ecosystem resilience' does because it strives to maintain function when disturbances occur (Gunderson and Holling, 2002). The implications for the riparian landscape as an engineered system are clear: since the purpose of an engineered system is control of riparian structure and function, certain short-term benefits for humans are achieved through stability, but long-term sustainability is compromised because, over time, instability in the system is increased.

In urban watersheds, no better example can be found than the mass conversion of floodplains to urban land uses for residences and industry, which are 'protected' by an elaborate system of concrete channels and dams. The reality is that the removal of engineered structures is not likely because this measure would be considered a radical approach challenging the current paradigm of flood control and management. Therefore, the most realistic situation is to retrofit existing engineered systems that have land available for riparian restorations. In the case of new engineering systems, they should use ecologically based design principles that are grounded in ecological theory, such as resilience and persistence.

In Arizona, the power of this human-induced landscape change is evident with less than 10% of riparian landscapes remaining in their original form (Arizona Riparian Council, 2004). Engineered systems in Arizona's urbanising watersheds have modified the long-term sustainability of riparian areas in a number of ways: (1) the alteration of the hydrologic cycle by reducing infiltration capacity and increasing stormwater runoff; (2) the interbasin transfer of water from surrounding watersheds to cities; (3) the removal and fragmentation of the riparian vegetation and habitat systems; (4) the modification of the longitudinal profiles and cross sections of rivers and streams; (5) the decoupling of a river or stream bed from its water table and floodplain; and (6) the loss of alluvial fan and wash networks.

Riparian landscape as the picturesque

The naturalness of a riparian landscape has long been an important metaphor for scenic beauty in the United States. The most admired riparian landscapes have traditionally been those with the most exaggerated aesthetic and geomorphological structure. For instance, Hudson River (New York) has been admired for its primeval qualities and spawned the Hudson River School of landscape painting. These picturesque qualities influenced artists to travel in the western United States where they captured the awesome beauty on their canvases and swayed the lawmakers and public to protect these landscapes in national parks like the Grand Canyon and Yellowstone.

The challenge of the picturesque as a benchmark for resource protection and policy is that it has become associated with particular assumptions about which type of landscape is ecologically healthy and worth protecting (Nassauer, 1997). Some riparian landscapes in the Sonoran Desert have picturesque qualities that are icons of the Old West and wilderness of the United States, especially those in the foothills and mountains that have steep canyons, perennial water and gallery forests (large groupings of tall cottonwoods), such as Oak Creek Canyon near Sedona and Flagstaff, Arizona. These picturesque qualities are related to the hypothesis of Burmil *et al.* (1999) that two factors are most likely to affect perceived scenic beauty in arid environments: the presence of water and associated riparian vegetation. Zube (1982) found that these two factors of perceived scenic beauty are also recorded in settlers' historic accounts in Arizona. The verdant green of riparian vegetation also reminded travellers of humid climates in the eastern United States (Zube, 1982). In contemporary times, these same qualities are synonymous with places known for high biodiversity, endangered species and environmental sensitivity.

The picturesque as a socially defined metaphor for a healthy riparian landscape represents a quandary for scientists, policy makers, planners and designers who want to protect and restore riparian landscapes in the Sonoran Desert. Most riparian landscapes in this region do not have these picturesque qualities because they lack perennial water, high bluffs or large trees. Abused riparian landscapes have other issues with muddy banks, soil erosion and lack of vegetation, which is typical of overgrazing situations in rural areas, or they have been modified into engineered systems with single concrete-lined channels that have little vegetation or shade and have artificial flow velocities and volumes. Graf (2001) emphasises that cultural biases about the visual appearance of desert streams and rivers can lead to restoration policies in which desert streams and rivers are more likely to be managed and/or restored for unsustainable ecological states.

One explanation for the cultural biases is that a single channel has a higher level of visual legibility, coherence and order than a braided or compound channel of a desert stream and wash. The single channel and canopy trees communicate a certain type of naturalness and stability that is associated with the picturesque and savanna landscapes that are highly preferred by people. In contrast, a braided stream or wash has few canopy trees, low spiny shrubs, visually impenetrable underbrush and less open water, which is less favoured by people. Moreover, the multiple channels and lack of water do not communicate the magnitude of the potential flooding risk and other dangers found in arid environments. Because most people in the area come from humid climates, they do not realise that a dry desert wash is actually a dry stream bed and is prone to infrequent but devastating flash floods. Therefore, they do not fully perceive a risk when they drive through a desert wash because it can appear to be just a dip in the road with no water at the low point.

Riparian landscapes as the greenway

Another common metaphor of a riparian landscape emphasises its spatial extent as a network of linear corridors of habitat and water. This shape inspired an approach to resource protection known as greenways in design and planning, which Fábos (2004) defines as corridors with ecological, historical, cultural or recreational significance. Other related words include parkways, conservation corridors and ecological networks. Since Frederick Law Olmsted's development of the Emerald Necklace in Boston in the late nineteenth century, the use of greenways in the United States has been a common approach applied to open-space design, but the greenways as a movement did not take hold until the 1980s (Fábos, 2004).

Much of the greenways movement is built on the foundation of aesthetic principles of the picturesque, which is rooted in Olmsted's work in the humid, temperate climate of the Boston metropolitan area. Even the word greenway conjures up images of a single-channel, meandering stream with flowing water and lush vegetation. In deserts, this image is perhaps the most vivid because of the strong contrast between riparian vegetation and the surrounding desert. But these types are indicative of a river with perennial flow that is undammed and protected from intense grazing and recreation. This type of landscape is typical of a major desert river or stream, which is very rare in the Sonoran Desert and in the western United States. Some sections of the San Pedro River in the United States and Mexico come closest to this ideal Sonoran riparian landscape.

In reality, many desert rivers and streams are intermittent naturally or owing to diversion. For example, prior to World War II, the Phoenix metropolitan region had miles of riparian landscape along tree-lined channels that met the picturesque ideal, but these canals were geomorphically modified when all the riparian vegetation was removed and the banks of the canals were lined with concrete. The Salt River, which is one of the major rivers in Phoenix, now has concrete banks with scattered low vegetation in a gravel river bed. In addition, the Salt River's desert washes do not fit the picturesque convention of a stream because they are dry gravel and rock streambeds with a canopy of small trees, low shrubs and perennials.

The application of the greenways as a picturesque concept to Phoenix metropolitan region epitomises the concerns that Graf (2001) raised about the challenge of balancing social and ecological concerns in restoration projects, as described in the previous section. Yet the integration of social issues is an important part of managing the human dimension of greenway planning, so they have a place in urban riparian landscape conservation and restoration. For example, Gobster and Westphal (2004) identified six interdependent dimensions of the human perception of greenway recreational use that are important to consider in socially desired goals of greenway design. The reconciliation of these issues with the level of naturalness needed for high-quality habitats remains a challenge and can be a source of tension among ecologists, designers and planners.

The riparian landscape as a changing system

This metaphor is the underlying theory behind the recent scientific advances in fluvial geomorphology and stream ecology (Naiman and Décamps, 1997; Graf, 2001). Naiman and Décamps (1997) describe natural streams as changing systems. Since unmodified streams and rivers are non-equilibrium systems, resilience is an inherent characteristic of the tight coupling in landscape structure and function. Tabacchi et al. (1990) found that water discharges create two zones of change and floristic connectance. Yet in metropolitan areas, this pattern of floristic connectance would probably be different for riparian vegetation because of what McDonnell and Pickett (1990) call 'urban–rural gradients'. Theoretically, as riparian zones become more urbanised along the gradient, it is more likely that a new spatial order of built structures will replace the existing natural landscape.

The loss of resilience is an issue that affects not only riparian zones but also watersheds because of the transformative effects of urbanisation. For example, Snyder et al. (2003) discovered that riparian habitat becomes more fragmented in urban areas where watersheds with as low as 7% urban land use affected biotic integrity. They found correlations among urban land in relation to altered flow patterns, channel size and water quality (Snyder et al., 2003). The level of imperviousness in a watershed also affects species richness because of habitat loss and fragmentation. McKinney (2002) hypothesises that a threshold exists at or above 20% imperviousness in surburbia where forest interior species sensitive to the loss of core habitat are replaced by edge species that are more tolerant of human presence and habitat modification.

In the Phoenix metropolitan region, the loss of resilience and its implications for the region's identity are evident in the shifting public and governmental values for riparian landscapes. During most of the twentieth century, management actions emphasised the decoupling of water flow within the Salt and Gila watersheds because there was a desire to tame major floods and to provide a predictable flow of water for agriculture. The Theodore Roosevelt dam, which was established in 1911 on the Salt River, marked the introduction of the engineering paradigm in the region.

The environmental movement of the 1960s and 1970s increasingly caused the public to accept the idea of the Salt and Gila Rivers as changing systems. Rather than convert rivers to concrete channels, the public increasingly believed that rivers were intrinsic to the region's sense of place and should support multiple uses including recreation and habitat. The paradigm for floodplain management shifted away from exclusively the engineering paradigm to one addressing the ecological context of floodplain management. At this time, the first regional restoration plans for the Salt River occurred, but what was a unified vision soon disintegrated into a number of municipally based plans. More recently, the Flood Control District of Maricopa County has helped to create river corridor master plans for the Gila and Agua Fria Rivers that take into consideration engineering, ecosystem restoration and community goals that cross municipal boundaries.

Pattern:process metaphors for riparian areas

Most of the recurring metaphors reviewed in this section have certain limitations for explaining the dynamic relationship among culture, habitat and riparian landscape in the Sonoran Desert. Yet the riparian landscape as a changing system stands out because it has the potential to include a broad range of metaphors. It embraces the paradigms of general systems theory and complexity science, which have been used to explain the interactions in ecological and cultural systems. In the next section, this metaphor will be used as the foundation for conceptualising pattern:process metaphors that explain the interrelationship between the Phoenix metropolitan region's urban culture and landscape systems. In particular, the pattern:process metaphors can be used to develop explanatory and predictive models for how human decision-making has affected land-use and land-cover dynamics in relation to naturalness and habitat quality in the region's urban watersheds and riparian landscapes. Two types of pattern:process metaphors for changing urban riparian landscapes in Phoenix metropolitan region are discussed below.

Metaphors for changing urban watersheds

The pattern:process metaphors of resilience and persistence are key for understanding Phoenix's watersheds as changing systems. These metaphors have universal appeal to communicate across disciplines. Resilience and persistence are ecological concepts having certain spatial and temporal properties that can be linked to scientifically measurable variables and to observable land-use and land-cover patterns. As metaphors, they can be understood by designers and planners and relate to desirable qualities of sustainable communities in a watershed context.

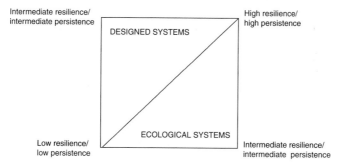

Fig. 28.2. The dual identity of urban riparian landscapes as designed and ecological systems.

In addition, resilience and persistence relate to human perception and experience, which can be associated with the naturalness of vegetation, presence of water and habitat quality.

In this chapter, the metaphors of resilience and persistence are linked to human-induced landscape transformation by conceptualising metropolitan landscapes as a gradient between designed and ecological systems. These two systems represent the duality of landscapes in metropolitan regions as they occur across the metropolitan region and its watersheds. A designed system is defined as any human intervention or modification, such as public infrastructure, parks, streets, neighbourhoods and other built projects that transform the spatial and functional order of land uses and land covers in a watershed's landscapes; often through manipulation of land form, vegetation, water and built structures. Human interventions can include the intentional manipulation of ecosystems for habitat management, such as burning to control and stimulate particular plant species. Designed systems of built forms are most prevalent in the urban core of a city and gradually shift in type, intensity and scale in the suburbs and finally to the urban fringe and ex-urban areas. An ecological system is defined as an ecosystem that has been slightly or moderately affected by indirect or direct human actions, but still has most of its landscape structure (e.g. vegetation and landform) and function (e.g. hydrological cycle) intact. These landscapes would be found in rural and ex-urban locations of the region's watersheds and extend into the urban fabric as riparian corridors and washes as well as remnant habitat islands.

These two systems have different characteristics of resilience and persistence – combinations of low, intermediate and high – depending on how their landscape's structure and function has shifted through human-induced land-use and land-cover changes (Fig. 28.2). In Fig. 28.2, the interface between the designed and ecological systems is of great interest because it represents hybrid systems and includes a broad range of partly modified landscapes. The common characteristic for all hybrid systems is that people have changed the structure (e.g. vegetation and landform) and function (e.g. water flow and habitat connectivity) of the riparian landscapes to benefit human uses. These systems have different characteristics of resilience and persistence depending on the type of human intervention – some have low persistence and resilience and others have high persistence and resilience.

Examples of hybrid systems with theoretically higher persistence and resilience would be those designed with ecological principles (known as ecological design and planning, or conservation design and planning) and improved watershed structure and function, such as greenways, stormwater wetlands, green roofs, brownfield redevelopments and wildlife corridors. Theoretically, they would have higher persistence and resilience because they potentially provide a broader range of ecological and cultural functions in a metropolitan region than conventionally designed systems. In addition, these examples are important strategies for protection of regional biodiversity, landscape character and recreational opportunities.

Metaphors for urban river identity

Pattern:process metaphors can be further differentiated into more specific ones that relate urban riparian structure and function to landscape character, including observable patterns of healthy and degraded riparian areas. My approach builds on previous research about rivers and sense of place. In particular, Pedroli and co-workers' (2002) proposed 'river identity' fits my approach because it addresses a river's ecological, spatial and visual characteristics in temporal and spatial terms. I hypothesise that six pattern:process metaphors help to explain and describe the spatial and temporal dimensions of urban riparian landscapes in the Phoenix metropolitan region (Table 28.1).

The first group of metaphors – sustenance, connectivity and health – represents the spatial order of an urban riparian landscape's structure and function. Sustenance emphasises the idea that riparian areas have long symbolised the importance of water for survival. This metaphor relates to habitat issues in riparian ecology and human preference for lush, green landscapes. Connectivity stresses the degree of continuity of an urban riparian landscape's ecological, physical and visual characteristics. Health represents the level of abuse and negative environmental impacts in a riparian landscape. For each of these three metaphors, the spatial order of the riparian landscape is divided into three major elements: water, vegetation and geomorphology. For these landscape elements, there are lists of characteristics that are associated with healthy or degraded landscape conditions, which also can be related to the levels of

Table 28.1. *Six pattern:process metaphors (see bold row and column headings) that help to explain the 'river identity' of urban rivers and streams in the Phoenix metropolitan region. Metaphors are inspired by Pedroli and co-workers' (2002) 'river identity' as a concept to address a river's ecological, spatial and visual characteristics.*

	Legacies (past landscape)	Indicators (existing landscape)	Precursors (emergent future landscape)
Sustenance			
Water	Evidence of floods and running water in the landscape	Perennial water Vigorous, green vegetation Sound of running water	Verdant vegetation Moist microclimate
Vegetation	Old trees and branches from floods Rich organic layer	Vigorous, green vegetation, especially cottonwood, willow and mesquite Lack of invasive species, such as tamarisk Moist microclimate near river Shade	Understorey of young willow, cottonwood and mesquite Rich ground layer (leaves, twigs and branches)
Geomorphology	Rich organic layer Intact floodplain and channel forms	Lack of soil erosion on channel banks Lack of headcutting Single or multiple channels	Fresh deposits of silt, sand and gravel
Connectivity			
Water	Evidence of continuous riparian landscape and channel	Single or multiple channels with perennial water and vegetation	Single or multiple channels with perennial water and vegetation
Vegetation	Lack of fragmentation of riparian landscape Lack of roads and trails Rich organic layer	Distinct boundary between riparian vegetation and surrounding vegetation Continuous green ribbon of riparian vegetation Complexity of vegetation strata and species diversity	Continuous green ribbon of young riparian vegetation Evidence of a seed bank Rich ground layer (leaves, twigs and branches) Understorey of young willow, cottonwood and mesquite

Table 28.1. (cont.)

	Legacies (past landscape)	Indicators (existing landscape)	Precursors (emergent future landscape)
Geomorphology	Continuous floodplain and channel(s)	Lack of soil erosion on channel banks	Fresh deposits of silt, sand, and gravel
	Lack of encroachment from agriculture and development	Lack of headcutting	
		Single or multiple channels	
		Shade	
Health			
Water	Evidence of vegetation removal, grazing or trampling	Concrete streambed and banks	Lack of green vegetation
		Lack of contact with the water table	Overpumping of water
		Discoloration of water from turbidity	
		Odours from the water	
Vegetation	Lack of old trees and branches from past floods	Lack of canopy vegetation	Lack of regeneration of native plant communities
	Fragmentation	Lack of cottonwoods, willows and mesquite	Lack of a rich ground layer
		Presence of invasive exotics, such as tamarisks	Lack of young trees
		Lack of shade	Soil compaction
		Lack of floods	Lack of seed bank
		Concrete channel	Early signs of headcutting
Geomorphology	Signs of mining (pits)	Dams	Soil compaction
	Encroachment from agriculture and urban development	Mining	
		Heavy dissection by roads and trails	
		Extensive erosion on stream channels	
		Denuded areas	

resilience and persistence. The different landscape characteristics can be used as targets for preservation, conservation and restoration activities.

The second group of metaphors represents the temporal order of an urban riparian landscape's structure and function: (1) legacies (past landscape); (2) indicators (existing landscape); and (3) precursors (the emergent future landscape). These metaphors emphasise the temporal continuity or discontinuity of the spatial patterns in the landscape structure and function of riparian areas. Each metaphor represents a bridge between the science of ecological monitoring and the observable patterns of landscape health. Legacies, representing the past landscape, are well known in ecology as a means to describe past land-use and land-cover changes. It is a concept that is a potential bridge to design and planning because landscape history is an important component of understanding a place's identity. Indicators, representing the current landscape, are used in contemporary ecological monitoring and have been successfully translated to environmental education. Precursors, representing the future, are patterns of potential future landscapes that provide clues about future trajectories of change in landscapes. These patterns may be related to natural and/or human processes that occur at different spatial and temporal scales (e.g. months, years and decades). These patterns relate to the list of characteristics that are associated with healthier or more degraded landscape conditions in Table 28.1.

Conclusion

The riparian landscapes along the Salt and Gila Rivers in the Phoenix metropolitan region are valued for their regional biodiversity, landscape character and recreational opportunities. The protection and restoration of such landscapes is perhaps one of the most important challenges for interdisciplinary approaches in the ecological sciences, landscape architecture, urban design and planning; yet there is a lack of foundation for theory, principles and guidelines for land-use management and policy. Integrative metaphors are an important communication device across disciplines and this chapter reviews examples from well-known scientists, designers and planners. Yet, as a concept, the integrative metaphor is general, so I introduced the concept of the pattern:process metaphor as a means to precisely describe the essential relationship for understanding changing landscape structure and function, ecologically and culturally. Five recurring metaphors for defining urban riparian landscape are reviewed: ecological system, engineered system, picturesque, greenway and changing system. The riparian landscape as a changing system is used as the foundation of the framework for pattern:process metaphors that is introduced in this chapter. The framework has two levels: (1) metaphors for changing urban watersheds; and (2) metaphors for urban river identity.

These pattern:process metaphors are directly linked to the spatial form and temporal dynamics in the riparian landscape. They are one step towards better theories, principles, guidelines and vocabularies to communicate about how human decisions affect landscape transformations.

Acknowledgements

This material is based upon work supported by the National Science Foundation under Grant No. DEB-0423704, Central Arizona–Phoenix Long-Term Ecological Research (CAP LTER). Any opinions, findings and conclusions or recommendation expressed in this material are those of the author(s) and do not necessarily reflect the views of the National Science Foundation (NSF).

29

Valuing urban wetlands: modification, preservation and restoration

GLENN R. GUNTENSPERGEN, ANDREW H. BALDWIN, DIANNA M. HOGAN, HILARY A. NECKLES AND MARTHA G. NIELSEN

Introduction

The increasingly rapid rates of land-cover and land-use change driven by the growth of suburban and urban areas threatens the sustainability of the world's natural resources. And nowhere has this phenomenon been more evident than in the world's coastal regions (Chapman and Underwood, Chapter 4). Urbanisation of the world's coastal area is accelerating (Tibbetts, 2002). Two-fifths of the world's major cities inhabited by 1–10 million people are located in coastal regions. One hundred per cent of cities with populations over one million in South America are coastal and 75% of those in Asia and Africa are as well (Berry, 1990). In the United States, coastal areas represent 53% of the population but only 17% of the land area (Pew Oceans Commission, 2003).

The rapid development and population growth associated with coastal areas is leading to the destruction and degradation of important habitats including wetlands, estuaries and coral reefs. It has been estimated that when 10% of the area of a watershed is covered in roads and other impervious surfaces, then rivers and streams and downstream coastal waters become degraded (Pew Oceans Commission, 2003).

The impacts of urbanisation on aquatic systems and especially streams are well documented. Urbanisation and associated stormwater runoff threaten receiving water systems (Watson et al., 1981; Schueler, 1987; Mensing et al., 1998; Magee et al., 1999; Reinelt et al., 1999; Shaffer et al., 1999; Groffman et al.,

Ecology of Cities and Towns: A Comparative Approach, ed. Mark J. McDonnell, Amy K. Hahs and Jürgen H. Breuste. Published by Cambridge University Press. © Cambridge University Press 2009.

2003). Urban stormwater runoff carries pollutants such as rubbish, sediments, hydrocarbons (oil and grease), metals, bacteria, pesticides and excess nutrients (Schueler, 1987; Paul and Meyer, 2001). Transport of sediment and nutrients is also facilitated in urbanising watersheds as a result of the increase in impervious surface cover and alterations to the hydrologic cycle (Schueler, 1994).

Wetlands are located at the interface between terrestrial and aquatic ecosystems and are also susceptible to the effects of watershed urbanisation. Ehrenfeld (2000) argued that the effects of urbanisation make wetlands function differently in urban settings than in non-urban lands. Wetlands are intimately tied to the hydrogeomorphic processes occurring in their watersheds, which if altered can threaten their sustainability. Changes in surface water runoff that affect peak flows, flow volumes and water quality can all affect wetland resilience (Guntenspergen and Dunn, 1998).

Despite the proximity of many large urban areas to coastal habitats, there are few studies that have assessed the impact of urbanisation on wetlands (except see reviews in Kentula and Magee, 1999; Santelman and Larson, 2004). All too often, urban settlement and development have led to the loss and degradation of wetlands (Schmid, 1994; Guntenspergen and Dunn, 1998; Ehrenfeld, 2000; Faulkner, 2004). Urbanisation may have accounted for as much as 58% of the total wetland loss in some watersheds in the United States. In Portland, Oregon, USA, Kentula *et al.* (2004) documented a loss of 40% of small palustrine wetlands between 1982 and 1992.

Because wetlands are strongly influenced by the character of their surrounding watershed, they are particularly susceptible to the changes associated with urbanisation. Land-cover change has led to altered hydrology and a diminution of the socially valued functions that wetlands provide (Ehrenfeld and Schneider, 1993; Holland *et al.*, 1995; Ehrenfeld, 2004). Both on-site and watershed stressors and hydrologic modification can have a significant impact on wetland condition. Kentula *et al.* (2004) rated 89% of the small palustrine wetlands they studied in the Portland metropolitan area as fair or poor and only 11% as in good condition.

Despite these losses, wetlands remain important parts of the urban landscape. Wetlands provide valuable ecological and societal services. Costanza *et al.* (1997) recently evaluated the economic value of the world's ecosystems. Wetlands and estuaries contributed US$4.9 trillion of the estimated US$33 trillion in annual ecosystem services and so managers increasingly value protection, restoration and creation to maintain these services (Streever, 1998; Baldwin, 2004; Ehrenfeld, 2004). The conservation and restoration of wetland habitat in urban settings is a challenge, but even in urbanised landscapes where substantial areas of wetland have been lost, restoration and creation of even small sites have a significant impact (Callaway and Zedler, 2004).

Our goal in writing this chapter is to use three case studies from the United States to illustrate the impacts of urbanisation and settlement on wetland processes, the complexities of wetland restoration, and the use of decision support models as an advanced identification tool to determine the impacts of residential development on wetland function. We use examples from our research in the Washington DC metropolitan area to illustrate the impact of urbanisation on riparian wetland function and the complexities of restoring tidal freshwater wetlands. Finally we illustrate the use of a GIS tool that can be used to assess the consequences of development in a rapidly changing rural watershed on Mt Desert Island, Maine, USA.

Tidal freshwater wetlands

Because wetlands are strongly influenced by the character of their surrounding watershed, they should not be viewed in isolation. This is especially true in highly urbanised watersheds, where wetlands may exist as small fragments in the landscape that receive large stormwater runoff volumes, toxins, excess nutrients and physical disturbance associated with human activities. Therefore, if wetland restoration efforts in urban areas are to be successful, the influence of the urban environment must be taken into account (Baldwin, 2004), or alternatively, the ecological condition of non-wetland areas within the watershed must be restored in concert with wetland restoration efforts.

The Anacostia River watershed (Fig. 29.1), located in the Washington DC metropolitan region on the eastern coast of the United States, is a prime example of an urban area with many ongoing restoration or environmental improvement activities. Because all of these efforts affect the quality of remnant wetlands and success of wetland restoration efforts in the watershed, we first present an overview of the broad range of restoration efforts within the Anacostia River watershed. Then we describe the ecological condition of a remaining fragment of tidal freshwater marsh, Dueling Creek, and compare this with a non-urban wetland to illustrate some of the effects of the urban environment on natural wetlands. Next we go on to describe three tidal freshwater marsh restoration projects: Kenilworth Marsh, Kingman Marsh and the River Fringe Marshes. Finally, we synthesise the major themes emerging from these studies and point to future directions for restoration and research.

Overview of restoration activities in the Anacostia River watershed

Like many urban rivers, the Anacostia River has been heavily affected by human activities. Intensive urbanisation in the Anacostia watershed has created extensive impervious surface coverage, causing rapid runoff of surface water

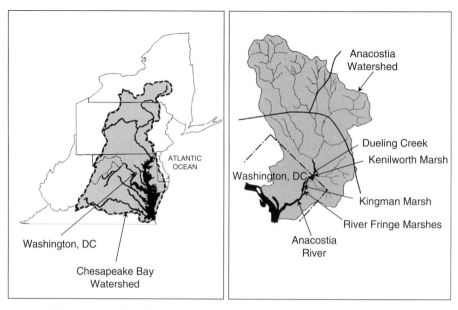

Fig. 29.1. Location of case study sites. The right panel is an enlargement of the Maryland and Washington DC area from the left panel.

that results in flashy stream hydroperiods and brings with it sediment, nutrients and other pollutants. Additionally, because of an antiquated sewage system design that combines runoff with sewage, wastewater volumes following many rainfall events exceed the capacity of wastewater treatment plants, necessitating the discharge of untreated sewage directly into the river. Furthermore, implementation of Charles L'Enfant's plan for Washington DC in 1901 and other development destroyed more than 3900 ha of swamps and marshes that were present in 1790, including about 1000 ha of tidal freshwater marsh along the Anacostia River (Schmid, 1994; US Environmental Protection Agency (EPA), 1997). By 1990 only a few hectares of fragmented tidal freshwater wetlands remained along the Anacostia River.

Increasing public awareness about the degraded condition of the watershed stimulated efforts to restore or improve the ecological condition of the Anacostia river. Beginning at least 20 years ago, federal, state and local governmental agencies and conservation groups started working together to rehabilitate the watershed (Metropolitan Washington Council of Governments, 2004). In 1987 the Anacostia Watershed Restoration Committee (AWRC) was formed, which has continued to co-ordinate the implementation of restoration projects throughout the watershed. Restoration goals developed by the AWRC include reducing pollutant loads, protecting and restoring streams, increasing ranges of resident and anadromous fish, protecting and expanding forest cover, restoring wetlands,

Fig. 29.2. Wetland vegetation at the Dueling Creek marsh, the largest remaining fragment of natural tidal freshwater marsh in the Anacostia River watershed.

and educating and involving citizens and businesses in the watershed. Since 1987 over $100 million have been spent on various restoration activities in the watershed, including reducing stormwater flows, stream restoration, wetland restoration, land purchases for conservation, and stream riparian buffer reforestation (Metropolitan Washington Council of Governments, 2004).

Dueling Creek: a natural marsh altered by watershed urbanisation

Dueling Creek Marsh is a remnant 0.41 ha urban wetland located in the tidal freshwater region of the Anacostia River (Fig. 29.2). It was once adjacent to the main channel of the Anacostia River until the river was redirected in the late 1930s by the US Army Corps of Engineers. This marsh represents the best remaining 'natural' urban wetland in the Anacostia, and has been used as a reference site for nearby tidal wetland restorations (Baldwin and DeRico, 1999; Neff, 2002).

While the Dueling Creek marsh is a natural wetland, it also appears to be affected by human activities in the surrounding watershed. Soil concentrations of chromium, copper, nickel, lead and zinc were higher in Dueling Creek Marsh than in a non-urban tidal freshwater marsh on the Patuxent River, located in a Maryland watershed east of the Anacostia watershed (Neff, 2002). This may be due to runoff from impervious surfaces in the watershed. Additionally, marsh soil at Dueling had lower organic matter content than the Patuxent River marshes or other natural tidal freshwater marshes (Mitsch and Gosselink, 2000), suggesting that mineral sediment inputs or decomposition rates are higher at Dueling Creek. In terms of vegetation, Dueling Creek has some dominant species that are similar to those of natural marshes such as *Peltandra virginica, Polygonum arifolium* and *Impatiens capensis* (Odum *et al.*, 1984; Neff, 2002). However, the invasive *Phalaris arundinacea* and non-native *Lythrum salicaria* are also abundant at Dueling Creek, while these species are rare or absent in many non-urban tidal freshwater marshes (Baldwin *et al.*, 2001; Baldwin and Pendleton, 2003). Together, these findings suggest that the urban environment influences hydrology, soil and plant communities, resulting in wetlands different from those in non-urban areas.

Kenilworth Marsh: the first major effort to restore tidal freshwater marshes

Kenilworth Marsh is located within Anacostia Park, a unit managed by the United States National Park Service in northeast Washington, DC. A tidal freshwater marsh existed historically at this location, but the site was dredged in the 1940s to create a recreational lake (Syphax and Hammerschlag, 1995). In 1992–93, the US Army Corps of Engineers restored wetlands at the site by increasing sediment elevation using river sediment dredged from the adjacent Anacostia River and planting more than 340 000 plants comprising 16 species of wetland vegetation (Bowers, 1995; Syphax and Hammerschlag, 1995). To our knowledge, Kenilworth was the first tidal freshwater marsh system to be restored anywhere. Some of the initial plantings did not survive or were out-competed by volunteer species, which began colonising the exposed sediment even before planting was complete. Owing to sedimentation from the watershed, the Anacostia river channel required dredging, and marsh restoration was seen as a beneficial use of dredge material. About 115 000 m^3 of sediments were dredged from the river and pumped into three areas, referred to as Mass Fill 1, Mass Fill 2 and Mass Fill 3, which differ slightly in elevation and together cover about 13 ha. By 1995, the vegetation in Mass Fill 1 had 62 plant species, Mass Fill 2 had 64 species and Mass Fill 3 had 71 species (Stauss, 1995).

As part of the restoration effort, the National Park Service and the US Geological Service monitored vegetation in transects during the growing season from 1994 to 1997. Monitoring indicated that plant coverage was similar across the 5-year period, reaching 90–100% during each growing season, while species density (number of species per 5 m^2 plot) increased from about five species in 1994 to about seven species in 1997 (R. S. Hammerschlag, US Geological Survey, unpublished data). Monitoring also indicated an abundance of *Lythrum salicaria*, *Phragmites australis* and *Typha* spp., species that are capable of colonising unvegetated or disturbed wetland sites rapidly and forming extensive monocultures. Monitoring of Kenilworth Marsh vegetation was continued beginning in 2000 as part of the monitoring effort for the Kingman Marsh restoration, described in the next section.

Kingman Marsh: applying the lessons learned from Kenilworth and learning new lessons

The restoration of Kenilworth Marsh was generally viewed as a success by the agencies that participated in the restoration process. One of the aspects of the marsh that was not seen as ideal, however, was the abundance of non-native plants such as *Lythrum salicaria* and invasive perennials such as *Phragmites* and *Typha* mentioned previously. These species tended to occur at higher elevations within the marsh. At another restoration site, Kingman Lake, the US Army Corps of Engineers restored marshes in early 2000 by adding sediment hydraulically dredged from the adjacent Anacostia River channel and planting 750 000 plants of seven wetland species, creating about 13 ha of vegetated wetland at a cost of US$5.2 million (Anacostia Watershed Restoration Committee, 2002). The design called for sediment elevations below those at Kenilworth Marsh in an effort to reduce colonisation by the invasive species and create a plant community more like that of a natural marsh.

Dense and diverse vegetation developed in the wetland during the 2000 growing season (Fig. 29.3), with high survival of planted species and colonisation by at least 150 other plant species. However, in August 2000, water tubes that were used to contain sediment while it dewatered and consolidated were removed, which restored tidal hydrology and possibly created more frequently flooded conditions. Elevation may also have declined after tube removal because of additional subsidence and erosion, further increasing water depth in the wetland. Additionally, temporary fencing was installed during planting to reduce grazing by a population of non-migratory Canada geese during 2000 but was removed by early 2001 because the vegetation seemed well established. This was premature, however, because the geese then selectively grazed almost all of the plantings of *Pontederia cordata* and *Sagittaria latifolia*. Other plantings fared better, notably *Peltandra virginica, Juncus effusus* and *Schoenoplectus tabernaemontani*. Greater herbivory and more flooding apparently combined to result in a plant community of lower vegetation cover and diversity in 2001 and 2002 (Hammerschlag *et al.*, 2003). By September 2002, total plant cover at Kingman Marsh was only 20–30%, compared with over 80% at Kenilworth, about 100% at Dueling Creek and over 100% at the non-urban Patuxent site. Despite the effort

Fig. 29.3. (a) The Kingman Marsh site before restoration in 1999. (b) The site during 2000, the first growing season following restoration. Note fence posts supporting fencing for excluding Canada geese. After fencing was removed in 2001, geese severely damaged the wetland vegetation.

to reduce elevations, *Lythrum salicaria* was an early coloniser, in some cases already established before planting began. Fencing to exclude geese was eventually installed again, but colonisation rates have not returned to those observed when the water tubes were in place, even where geese are excluded. Efforts are ongoing at the Kingman site to improve vegetation coverage by planting species less palatable to geese, such as *Peltandra*, and installing fencing. However, it is

Fig. 29.4. River fringe marshes along the Anacostia River, visible on the right of the photograph. Note plastic sheet piling protecting marshes from erosion. Not visible are fences to prevent Canada geese from grazing planted wetland vegetation.

clear that the potential effect of geese on plantings was underestimated in the Kingman Marsh restoration project.

The River fringe restoration: armoured wetlands

The most recent wetland restoration effort along the tidal Anacostia is that of wetlands fringing the banks of the river (Fig. 29.4). In 2003, the US Army Corps of Engineers again used dredged river sediment to raise elevations and planted vegetation to create wetlands, this time at two locations along the Anacostia River near the Kingman Marsh site. Because the river channel edges were expected to experience higher hydrologic energy than the Kingman and Kenilworth sites, plastic sheet piling was installed to contain sediments and left in place, unlike the temporary water tubes or hay bales used at the other sites. Additionally, to prevent decimation of plantings by Canada geese, fencing was installed around and throughout the wetland plantings, and string with survey flagging tape strung across the fences to dissuade geese from landing in the wetlands. These efforts appear to have been initially successful, as vegetation growth during 2004 has been vigorous. However, the sheet piling restricts tidal flushing (there are a few areas cut into the sheet piling to allow some water exchange between the river and the wetlands), and the fencing and string will not last indefinitely. This raises the question: if we are to restore wetlands in urban areas, must they be armoured to survive?

Synthesis of major themes

The ongoing restoration activities in the Anacostia watershed highlight the challenges of improving the ecological condition of urban environments. While it is possible to improve water quality and physical habitat in streams and rivers, it is more difficult to establish organisms typical of non-urban areas. This seems particularly true for restored wetland vegetation, which may require many years before resembling that of non-urban areas. It is also possible that vegetation may never resemble that of non-urban wetlands because of constraints imposed by the urban environment on vegetation establishment and growth (Baldwin, 2004). Perhaps a more realistic standard for evaluating restoration success is that of remnant natural urban wetlands such as the Dueling Creek Marsh. Successful restoration may thus necessitate accepting non-native species and altered soil and hydrologic conditions as part of the biodiversity and complexity of urban wetlands.

Urban forested wetlands

The Washington DC metropolitan area has experienced rapid urbanisation since World War II, especially in outlying suburban regions such as Fairfax County, Virginia, USA, incorporating 102 316 ha just west of Washington DC (Netherton *et al.*, 1978; Hooten, 1990; Masek *et al.*, 2000) (Fig. 29.5). Fairfax County began a rapid transformation in the 1940s, quickly altering the county from a primarily forested and agriculturally dominated region with a population of 40 929 persons to an urban and suburban community with a current population of greater than one million. Rapid continued growth is expected, such that Fairfax County's population is predicted to increase by approximately 15% by 2025.

The study of Fairfax County urban wetlands focused on the effects of increasing watershed urbanisation on riparian wetland surface soil and plant tissue nutrient (nitrogen and phosphorus) concentrations and soil P sorption capacities. Increased impervious cover necessitates stormwater management in response to flooding risks, redirecting watershed hydrologic flow in artificial channels (including road culverts and kerb and gutter systems), often directing urban runoff away from natural riparian wetlands and discharging directly into streams or stormwater facilities in the management of the new landscape permeability (Schueler, 1987; Paul and Meyer, 2001; Groffman *et al.*, 2003).

Therefore, urbanisation transforms the physical landscape, not only resulting in increased pollutants in urban runoff but also altering the watershed hydrologic regime. Although riparian wetlands occupy a landscape position between terrestrial and aquatic ecosystems, potentially making them well situated to

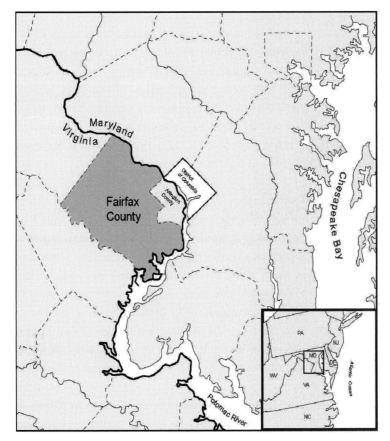

Fig. 29.5. The location of heavily urbanised Fairfax County, Virginia, just west of Washington DC.

intercept excess nutrient loads originating in urbanising environments, hydro-logic changes associated with urbanisation may compromise the ability of these systems to provide important wetland ecosystem services such as nutrient (i.e. N and P) removal and retention, wetland functions that result in the societal value of improved water quality (Johnston, 1991; Walbridge, 1993; Walbridge and Struthers, 1993; Reddy *et al.*, 1999; Reinelt *et al.*, 1999; Casey and Klaine, 2001; Groffman *et al.*, 2003; Zedler, 2003). Because of changed watershed hydro-logic pathways, wetlands in the most urbanised watersheds may no longer have the opportunity to improve the water quality of urban runoff before it enters an area's streams.

Fairfax County urban wetland study sites

Twelve forested riparian wetland study sites with watershed urbani-sation ranging from 1 to 29% were analysed. Watershed urbanisation was characterised by calculating the percentage of impervious cover in the watershed. Impervious cover was defined as any material that impedes water filtration into the soil, including building footprints and paved surfaces (e.g. roads, sidewalks, driveways) (Schueler, 1994). Impervious cover data were obtained from a land-use database derived from 1997 aerial photography, provided by Fairfax County Department of Public Works and Environmental Services. Based on percentage watershed impervious cover, wetland urbanisation was categorised as low (1.0–6.1%), moderate (8.6–13.3%) or high (25.1–29.1%), and was representative of the range of available sites in Fairfax County.

Wetland response

The effects of urbanisation on surface soil and plant tissue P accumulation and soil P saturation were found to be non-linear, increasing with moderate degrees of urbanisation, but decreasing in highly urbanised watersheds where hydrologic flows are likely to be directed away from wetlands by stormwater management infrastructure (Hogan, 2005). A second-order polynomial was statistically shown to describe this relationship best, accounting for the combined effect of two processes. The first part of the equation describes a linear increase in nutrient load, reflected in increased nutrient accumulation in wetland soils and plant tissues as a function of increasing watershed impervious surface cover (Schueler, 1994; Caraco *et al.*, 1998; Fig. 29.6a). As watershed urbanisation increased, the primary effects of urbanisation appeared to shift from increased wetland nutrient loads to watershed hydrologic modification, redirecting nutrient-rich urban runoff away from the more urbanised wetlands. This resulted in a negative effect on wetland nutrient accumulation, with no effect noted at sites with low impervious cover because of the absence of watershed stormwater management infrastructure and an increasing negative effect as impervious cover increased (Fig. 29.6b). The combined effect of these two processes resulted in an inverted parabola with lower nutrient accumulation at low and high watershed impervious cover, and maximum nutrient accumulation in the mid-range sites (Fig. 29.6c; Hogan, 2005).

In contrast to P, total Kjeldahl N accumulation in surface soil and plant tissue did not consistently vary significantly as a function of watershed urbanisation (Hogan, 2005). This may be due in part to the different mechanisms important for wetland N removal as compared with P removal, primarily denitrification, in which incoming nitrate may be converted to gaseous N and exported to the atmosphere.

The capacity of wetland soils to retain P can become saturated over time (Richardson, 1985), and concomitant with increases in P accumulation, an increased degree of saturation of wetland soil P sorption potential was noted

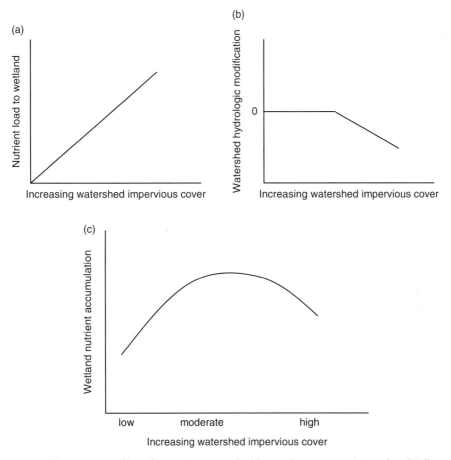

Fig. 29.6. The effect of increasing watershed impervious cover on (a) nutrient loading, (b) watershed hydrology and (c) wetland nutrient accumulation.

in the moderately urbanised watersheds (Hogan, 2005). The risk of wetland P release and export increases with the degree of soil P saturation and when soils do become P saturated, release of P to downstream aquatic environments can occur (Beauchemin and Simard, 1999; del Campillo *et al.*, 1999; Kleinman *et al.*, 1999; Pote *et al.*, 1999). These wetland soils were not currently found to be saturated to the point of spontaneous P release (Hogan, 2005). However, the more urbanised wetlands actually show a decrease in soil P saturation, suggesting either that more P from urban runoff directly enters streams or stormwater retention facilities, bypassing wetlands, and/or that desorption of P from the exchange sites may have already occurred.

Although the wetlands in this study were not intended to receive urban runoff as part of the stormwater management programme in Fairfax County, diversion of this runoff does not effectively sustain them by sparing them excess nutrient, sediment or toxin influx, but instead may negatively affect the ability of the wetland to provide ecosystem services in highly urbanised water-sheds. Most significantly, the natural ability of riparian wetlands to improve water quality is lost, as nutrient-rich urban runoff is instead directed towards streams or stormwater management facilities as evidenced by the lower soil P accumulation and saturation noted in the more urbanised wetlands in Fairfax County. This may result in an increase in excess nutrients entering Fairfax County streams directly, bypassing riparian wetlands and contributing to the impairment of the area's stream ecosystem health and associated eutrophication problems downstream in the Chesapeake Bay. Hydrologic regime is an important determinant of wetland function, and landscape-scale hydrologic modifications (i.e. stormwater management) in urbanising areas can degrade riparian wetland structure and function; the sustainability of wetlands in Fairfax County depends on future wetland nutrient influx and watershed hydrologic practices.

Tidal Creek estuaries

Increased nutrient loading to coastal waters from coastal watersheds has resulted in the degradation of many coastal aquatic systems (Goldberg, 1995; Valiela *et al.*, 1997; Roman *et al.*, 2000; Bertness *et al.*, 2002). In the northeastern United States, many coastal estuaries are becoming increasingly eutrophic in response to urbanisation in the surrounding watershed. In these systems, nitro-gen limits the production of phytoplankton and macroalgae (Valiela *et al.*, 1997). Howarth *et al.* (2002) predicted that at current rates of development, nitrogen inputs to US coastal waters in the next 25 years may increase by 30%.

Although estuarine ecosystems can tolerate some degree of enrichment with-out serious ecological ramifications, excessive nutrient inputs lead to dense algal growth, increased community metabolism, decreased dissolved oxygen concen-trations, shifts in dominant primary producers including losses of submerged vascular plant beds, and declines in habitat value for fin- and shellfish (Nielson and Cronin, 1981; Orth and Moore, 1983; Valiela *et al.*, 1992; Nixon, 1995). Shifts in autotrophic dominance from submerged vascular plants to phytoplankton, epiphytes and macroalgae have variously been recorded with estuarine nutrient enrichment (e.g. Harlin and Thorne-Miller, 1981; Sand-Jensen and Borum, 1991; Neckles *et al.*, 1993; Short *et al.*, 1995; Taylor *et al.*, 1995).

Managers urgently need the ability to predict ecosystem changes in the coastal systems that may result from changing land-use patterns. This requires identifying responses to nutrient enrichment, defining the critical nutrient thresholds causing shifts in estuarine ecosystem structure and function, and linking nutrient loads to watershed land use. Quantitative relationships linking land use, nitrogen loads and loss of submerged vascular plants have been defined for estuaries in southern New England, most notably for Waquoit Bay, Massachusetts (Valiela *et al.*, 1992; Short and Burdick, 1996). Valiela *et al.* (2000) subsequently used a modelling approach to assess the effect of varying management options for reducing nitrogen loading rates and to identify management options for coastal estuarine restoration. Serveiss *et al.* (2004) used an ecological risk assessment approach to discern the link between human activities, stressors and ecological impacts for a coastal estuary in Massachusetts. They developed models to help understand the impact of nitrogen export from the surrounding watershed on estuarine integrity and how management responses could mitigate or restore these degraded habitats.

We used a combination of these approaches to assess the vulnerability of a small coastal estuary on Mt Desert Island, Maine, USA, to increased settlement in the surrounding watershed. We first identified current land-cover patterns in the watershed, quantified nutrient loads from this watershed to the estuary, identified thresholds of nitrogen loading causing changes in ecosystem structure and function, and then linked land use, nitrogen loading and estuarine response within a decision support system model (DSS) to assess the impact of land-use change within the watershed on estuarine integrity.

Northeast Creek watershed and estuary

Northeast Creek is a small estuary on Mt Desert Island, Maine (a 280 km² island on the northern Atlantic Coast of the United States) that drains a 24 km² watershed. This system is dominated by a submerged vascular plant, *Ruppia maritima*, has an average depth of 0.75 m and a tidal amplitude of 3–20 cm. Although the combined population of the island is small (8770 people; US Bureau of the Census, 2001), certain watersheds have seen accelerated rates of population growth, and some estuaries on the island are already experiencing signs of degradation (Doering *et al.*, 1995; Kinney and Roman, 1998; Farris and Oviatt, 1999).

The Northeast Creek estuary, like many rural portions of the northeastern United States, has experienced increasing rates of residential development resulting in changes from natural habitat to residential land cover. In the Northeast Creek estuary watershed, wooded residential lots are replacing areas of continuous forested cover. The number of new houses in the watershed has increased 164% (from 158 to 417) during the period from 1981 to 2002 (Nielsen, 2002a, 2002b). Most of these dwellings are on septic systems and the lots have landscaped surfaces that enhance the export of nutrients to nearby streams. Nielsen (2002a) identified surface water discharge to the Northeast Creek estuary as the primary mode of nutrient delivery from the surrounding watershed.

Land cover and nutrient loadings

The land use in these watersheds was originally delineated in 1995 (National Park Service, unpublished data) based on colour infrared aerial photography at a scale of 1:15 830. This study delineated 20 vegetation-based land-cover types, which were generalised into six land-use categories for the current project. These land-use types for the current project are: wetlands, urban/suburban, forest, open water, agriculture and quarry/open rock/gravel pits. The primary residential land-use type in the watershed is urban/suburban. This type is characterised by areas with housing densities greater than 2.5 houses per hectare of land. Areas where house lot sizes are 2.5 ha or larger may have areas classified as urban/suburban if the actual houses are located fairly close together (fitting the criteria of more than 2.5 houses per hectare of land) and include contiguous lawn/paved area/landscaped area. No industrial or heavily urbanised areas exist in the watershed. Dwellings are present in some forested and agricultural areas but at densities less than 2.5 houses per hectare.

The 1995 land-use distribution was updated to reflect as well as possible the land use at the time the nutrient export data collection ended (2000). A 1998 digital orthophoto quadrangle of the area was examined for new roads, new houses and newly cleared land for rural housing developments. These new suburban land-use areas were field-checked in late 2000 and early 2001 to create the final land-use theme. The watershed is largely forested (68%) and has a small proportion of urban/residential land cover (8%). However, there has been a dramatic increase (77%) in new houses built within the watershed since 1996 (Nielsen 2002a). Nielsen *et al.* (2002a) calculated nutrient export loadings from 13 watersheds on Mt Desert Island. Total nitrogen loadings ranged from 0.42 to 2.50 kg ha^{-1} yr^{-1} across these 13 watersheds. We developed multiple regression models to examine the relationship between nutrient loading and land cover and physical variables. The proportion of unpaved roads (which can be used as an index of development) explained over 50% of the total variability in annual total nitrogen loadings. Spring total nitrogen loading was best explained by a combination of urban/residential land use and unpaved roads (Guntenspergen *et al.*, unpublished data).

Nutrient export coefficients

Instead of physically based models to predict nutrient loadings from watersheds, we used a model that simulates the export of nutrients from watersheds based on land cover. There is extensive literature that has provided empirical relationships between land cover and nutrient export from watersheds (Reckhow *et al.*, 1980; Beaulac and Reckhow, 1982; Frink, 1991). This literature has led to the derivation of nutrient export coefficients associated with specific land-cover types that when multiplied by the area of a specific land cover estimate the nutrient export from a watershed associated with that land-cover type. Summing the contributions from the land-cover types in a watershed provides an estimate of the nutrient export from a watershed.

Equations relating land use to total nutrient yield within basins were based on published literature values and 1999 nutrient load measurements from five subcatchments in the watershed. Nutrient export coefficients were derived using a minimum least squares approach to parameter estimation. Optimal values for nutrient export $kg\,ha^{-1}\,yr^{-1}$ from specific land-cover types were determined by minimising the sum of squared residuals between predicted and measured nutrient yields for the five basins on Mt Desert Island. Initial values for agriculture, forest and urban/suburban export coefficients during model optimisation were set as the means of published values that shared similar land-use, land-cover and climate characteristics, and parameter estimates were constrained to be less than the upper limits of these published ranges.

Export coefficients for agriculture, forest, urban/suburban, and wetlands land-use types were derived to be 4.7, 1.5, 6.9 and $-0.1\,kg\,ha^{-1}\,yr^{-1}$, respectively and these values fell within the range of values reported in the literature for these land-cover types. Coefficients for quarry/open rock/gravel pits and open water land-use types were assumed to be zero. The coefficient for wetlands area was constrained to be negative (i.e. less than -0.1), based on literature studies that suggest accounting for wetlands nutrient attenuation is essential for accurately predicting total export to coastal watersheds in southeastern Massachusetts.

Ecosystem response to nutrient loadings

Ecosystem response to nutrient loading was determined by experimentally manipulating the dissolved nitrogen loading to portions of the estuary that were mechanically isolated (Neckles *et al.*, 2002). This was done by adding slow-release fertiliser to estuarine water that was enclosed by mesocosms. These experiments ran for 10 weeks during the summer growing season in each of two successive years. The growth response of the major autotrophic groups – vascular plant Ruppia (*Ruppia maritima*), phytoplankton and epiphytes – to different nitrogen loadings were monitored during the experiment. Significant declines in Ruppia biomass and cover, and increases in phytoplankton and epiphytic abundance with enrichment, were then used to identify the thresholds of nitrogen loading causing changes in estuarine condition (Neckles *et al.*, 2002).

Decision support system tool

The Northeast Creek watershed has experienced rapid rates of development since 1995 and the potential for further growth and development exists. In order to protect the adjacent coastal estuary, managers and regulators need to

Table 29.1. *Total nitrogen export from the Northeast Creek, Mt Desert Island watershed associated with urban/suburban land development within the watershed.*

Development within the watershed	Total nitrogen export from watershed (kg ha^{-1} yr^{-1})
Current land use	1.86
25% developed watershed	2.56
50% developed watershed	3.25
75% developed watershed	3.97
100% developed watershed	4.68
No conservation status lands	5.70

be able to predict the threshold at which land-cover change results in excessive nutrient loading and subsequent degradation of the estuary.

One approach to effective planning has been the development and use of decision support systems (DSS). A DSS is an interactive, computer-based system designed to help managers deal with complex problems. The power of a DSS is in its ability to conduct simulations and examine the consequences of future management actions using the best available data and knowledge. A DSS has four major characteristics: (1) it incorporates both data and models; (2) it is designed to assist managers in their decision process; (3) it supports rather than replaces managerial judgement; and (4) its objective is to improve the effectiveness of decisions, not the efficiency with which decisions are being made (Keen and Morton, 1978). We used the Environmental System Research Institute's (ESRI) ArcView 3.3 software as the platform to link land cover/land use, nutrient loadings and results from the *in situ* field studies to predict how changes in land use would affect nutrient loadings from the watershed and estuarine response (Rohweder *et al.*, 2004).

We found that simulated conversion of even modest amounts of land cover to residential development in the Northeast Creek watershed resulted in increased loadings of total nitrogen that threatened the integrity of the estuary (Table 29.1). Nearly 20% of the watershed's land is protected with conservation easements (development restrictions) or owned by the US National Park Service and will not be capable of being developed. If not for this protected conservation status, a threshold of development less than 60% in accordance with current zoning standards would result in degradation of the estuary. The protection of this estuary will require the efforts of local land managers and regulators to consider sustainable management alternatives to development. Our decision support system provides an additional tool that simulates the effects of land-cover change in coastal watersheds and that all stakeholders can use to develop alternatives in the management of coastal estuaries.

Part IV   COMMENTS AND SYNTHESIS

30

What is the main object of urban ecology? Determining demarcation using the example of research into urban flora

RÜDIGER WITTIG

Introduction

The term 'urban ecology' can be used on two different levels (Sukopp, 1998): on the one hand it is used to describe 'urban design programmes at the political and planning level' (see Deelstra, 1998), while on the level of natural sciences it refers to 'that area of biology which is concerned with urban areas'.

Since Haeckel first introduced the term 'ecology' in 1870 (Haeckel, 1870), its meaning has changed from a purely biological science to a 'transdisciplinary' science covering not only biology but also including other areas of natural sciences and increasingly even areas of non-natural sciences. This is particularly true of the branch of ecology termed 'urban ecology'. Wittig and Sukopp (1998) define urban ecology both in a narrow sense and in a broader sense. In a narrow sense urban ecology is the branch of ecology which deals with urban biocenoses, biotopes and ecosystems, their organisms and location conditions as well as with the structure, function and history of urban ecosystems. In a broader sense urban ecology is a field of work integrated into various areas of science and planning with the aim of improving living conditions while ensuring a long-term and environmentally friendly urban development.

Irrespective of whether the term urban ecology is defined in a narrow or a broader sense, the question arises as to the spatial demarcation of the area which

Ecology of Cities and Towns: A Comparative Approach, ed. Mark J. McDonnell, Amy K. Hahs and Jürgen H. Breuste. Published by Cambridge University Press. © Cambridge University Press 2009.

is to be the subject of urban ecological research, i.e. the actual object of investigation. This chapter propounds a number of ideas on this subject (see also Niemelä et al., Chapter 2; Pickett et al., Chapter 3) and subsequently demonstrates that the demarcation of the area under investigation is not simply a question of a scientific theoretical nature but that it can have a decisive effect on the plausibility of the results of the investigation.

Criteria for the demarcation of a research area

Every science is based on an interplay between observations and exact measurements on the one hand and a logical chain of reasoning on the other. The name of a science (or a branch of that science) and the main object of research ought therefore to have a logical connection. It is logical, for example, that mountain ecology deals with the subject of mountains and not with the low plains which might happen to be situated at the foot of those mountains. Of course low plains are strongly affected by the neighbouring mountains (water draining from the mountains in the form of streams and rivers; deposition of sediments rinsed out of the mountains by these waters; cold air flowing down the mountainside; organisms which come down from the highlands to the lower plains in winter, etc.). Conversely, the mountains are influenced by the plains extending in front of them (water evaporating on the plain rains down on the mountains; dust whirled up on the plain is deposited on the mountain slopes; ozone building up on the plain damages the mountain forests, etc.).

The most striking example is that of a city situated on an island in the middle of a lake (Fig. 30.1a). No ecologist of inland waters (limnologist) will claim this city as their research area although the lake might have a significant influence on the city and the city might be highly dependent on the lake for the provision of its fresh water, fresh air and nutrition (fish). A lot of interesting questions arising out of the close proximity of a city and a lake could be investigated and solved jointly by a team of limnologists and urban ecologists working together. However, a city will never become an object of limnology. This statement should be true vice versa for an urban ecologist: research carried out in a lake should never be called urban ecology (Fig. 30.1b). According to the same rules of logic, the ecology of a desert, a steppe or a mountain situated within the political borders or geographically close to a city and influenced greatly by that city still remains desert ecology, steppe ecology or mountain ecology. This book contains several examples of fruitful co-operation between urban ecology and other ecological subdisciplines (see Chapman et al., Chapter 9; Carriero et al., Chapter 19; Pouyat et al., Chapter 20; Guntenspergen et al., Chapter 29).

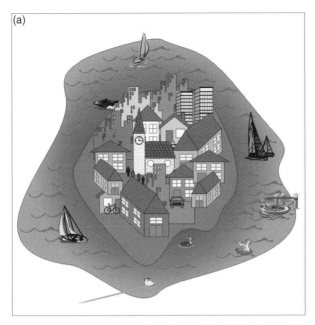

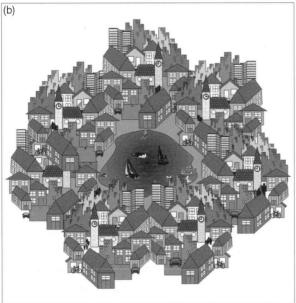

Fig. 30.1. The question of the determination of the research area of the ecological subdisciplines. (a) The ecology of a city situated in a lake is highly influenced by the surrounding lake. Does this city represent the object of limnology? Never! (b) The ecology of a lake in a city is highly influenced by the surrounding city. Does this lake represent the object of urban ecology? The reader is asked to use the laws of logic and give the answer.

Thus the question arises as to which biotopes or combination of biotopes constitute the object of urban ecology. As the examples given above (mountain ecology, ecology of inland waters, etc.) demonstrate, the main research object of urban ecology can only be an urban area and not any area subject to urban influence. So what characterises an urban area? An urban area is an area in which there is a condensed occurrence of human activity, production and use. These features can be found in the following areas:

- densely built-up housing areas;
- industrial estates;
- areas of intense trade and commerce;
- areas of high traffic (railway stations, airports, highways, harbours and inner-city roads);
- refuse pits and waste-heaps;
- recreation areas (urban parks, adventure parks, sport centres, etc.).

In comparison to the typification given by Brady *et al.* (1979) these urban biotopes comprise the following categories: cliff, derelict grasslands, derelict savannah, urban savannah, abiotic complex, rail- and highway, dump. Not included are the categories remnant natural islands and remnant agricultural islands. Among the land-cover classification system of Shaw *et al.* (1998) the classes residential, commercial/industrial/institutional can be regarded as totally, and the types graded vacant land and recreational as partly, belonging to the main object of urban ecology.

In the same way as it is of interest for a philologist of the English language to draw parallels with a Romance language, for example French (which would not make him/her a philologist of Romance languages), in order to gain a better understanding of the English language, comparisons between urban and non-urban biotopes are methods of research within the confines of urban ecology which produce promising results. Research along an urban–rural gradient has proved to be particularly useful in many respects (e.g. McDonnell and Pickett, 1990; Pouyat and McDonnell, 1991; McDonnell *et al.*, 1997; Zipperer and Guten-spergen, Chapter 17; Carriero *et al.*, Chapter 19; Pouyat *et al.*, Chapter 20). In the frame of the abovementioned studies tailored for use in an urban area and its hinterland, this is a well-known method of ecological research (e.g. Ter Braak and Prentice, 1988; Whittaker, 1967) and can naturally be applied for research work in all branches of ecology. However, it cannot be concluded from a correct application of this method that the rural side of the transect also falls into the field of work of urban ecology. An observation of the transect from the other (rural) side is also justifiable, in which case the whole urban area would become a component of 'rural ecology'.

Table 30.1. *Differences between the flora of a large German city (Frankfurt) and a small one (Oberursel) and the urban flora of these cities.*

	Frankfurt[a]	Oberursel[b]
Species number of the vascular flora of the city (species occurring spontaneously within the political border of the city)	1051[c]	552[d]
Species number of vascular water plants and indicators of humidity	215	116
Relative proportion of water plants and indicators of humidity among the urban flora	20.5%	21.0%
Number of vascular plant species of the urban flora	780	386
Number of water plants and indicators of humidity belonging to the urban flora	83	49
Relative proportion of water plants and indicators of humidity belonging to the urban flora	10.5%	12.7%

Notes:
[a] 650 000 inhabitants, 248 km^2.
[b] 43 000 inhabitants, 45 km^2.
[c] Unpublished data of the working group 'Biotopkartierung' of the Research Institute and Museum Senckenberg/Frankurt am Main.
[d] Unpublished data of the author and of the working group 'Taunus'.

The example of research on urban flora

Comparative research on the ecology of urban floras is not only an apt title for a book, but also presents us with the answer to a number of interesting and important questions, for example:

- What enables a species to survive under urban conditions?
- Do urban conditions serve as an evolutionary factor?
- Which species are particularly endangered by urban conditions?

Lists of their flora are available for many European cities (reviews given by Pyšek, 1989; Klotz, 1990; Pyšek, 1993; Wittig, 2002). However, these lists usually include the flora found growing in the political area of a city, irrespective of whether these biotopes are urban biotopes or natural or rural biotopes which happen to fall within the boundaries of a city. In the absence of a differentiated list of urban flora, these 'flora of cities' are often used as a basis for the evaluation of urban ecological statements. As the following example shows (see Table 30.1), this can lead to completely absurd results.

Biotope mapping carried out in Frankfurt (Germany) since 1985 (see Kramer, 1990) has meanwhile identified 1145 plant species. A critical examination, i.e. the removal of ephemeral species and species only representing garden relics but not spontaneously self-reproducing, causes the number of plant species to decrease to 1051. The ecological table drawn up by Ellenberg *et al.* (1992) identifies 215 (20.5%) of these species as indicators of humidity or moisture or as water plants. This proportion of 20.5% established for the city of Frankfurt is almost identical to the proportion of those plants for the whole of Germany (21.0%). In the small rural town of Oberursel, where the total number of spontaneous species is of the order of 552, the proportion of indicator plants of humidity or of open waters also amounts to 21.0%.

It is a well-known fact that Central European cities are not only heat islands (e.g. Sukopp and Wurzel, 2003), but, as a result of reduced relative air humidity (Landsberg, 1981), accelerated runoff (e.g. Benetin *et al.*, 1988) and reduced renewing of ground water (Berlekamp, 1987; Wessolek and Facklam, 1997), also dry islands in comparison with their surroundings. Therefore results that show the proportion of moisture- or water-indicating species occurring in cities as being equal to the proportion observed for the whole of Germany are misleading. In the same way, results are misleading which show no differences between a large city such as Frankfurt and a small rural town (Oberursel).

The results described here have nothing to do with the ecological characteristics of urban areas and have no correlation with the size of the two towns. The explanation goes back to the fact that a large river, the River Main, and a number of smaller tributaries and streams flow through Frankfurt, their banks providing habitats for reed vegetation. There are also a number of stagnant waters situated in Frankfurt which allow the existence of water plants. However, the small rural town Oberursel boasts only a few small streams which are partly canalised and partly overshadowed to such an extent by trees and forest debris that the growth of water and reed plants is rendered impossible. With the exception of a park pond which houses only a few species and a few fish ponds which are completely free of vegetation, there are no lakes here at all. But if we restrict our investigation to the core object of urban ecology, i.e. to the biotope complexes specified earlier, we arrive at a completely different set of results: of the 780 species of urban flora which exist in Frankfurt only 82 (10.5%) are indicators of humidity or water and among the 386 species of urban flora identified in the small rural town of Oberursel, 49 (12.7%) species belong to this ecological group (see Table 30.1).

If we focus our investigation on the strictly urban habitats, we arrive at a result which is in keeping with ecological reality: the list of the two urban flora contains considerably fewer indicators of humidity and water than the list of the entire flora of Germany, and the relative proportion of such indicators among the urban flora of a smaller town (Oberursel) is higher than among that of the large city of Frankfurt.

Conclusion and further remarks

It is not only a question of the logic of nomenclature that not all areas influenced by cities and not even all areas situated within the political border of a city can be regarded as characteristic objects of urban ecological research. As shown in Table 30.1, the selection of the object also decides whether the results are sound or misleading. Also, the identification of urbanophilous, urbano-neutral and urbanophobous species (Wittig *et al.*, 1985), which has been proved as a fruitful tool for the ecological characterisation of urban areas (Klotz and Kühn, 2002), is only possible if we differentiate clearly between urban and non-urban (rural and natural) areas. The paper of Crucitti *et al.* (1998) shows that from a zoological point of view, it also makes sense to focus on real urban habitats.

31

How to conduct comparative urban ecological research

SUSANNA LEHVÄVIRTA AND D. JOHAN KOTZE

Introduction

The human population is growing rapidly (Hopfenberg and Pimentel, 2001), in particular in Africa, the Middle East and Asia since 1950, and is becoming more urbanised (McDonnell *et al.*, 1997; Cohen, 2003). This influx of people from the rural landscape into cities creates major environmental concerns. Many cities are overpopulated and becoming more so, putting enormous pressures on urban green spaces. Furthermore, many cities are expanding in size, infringing on more natural suburban and rural environments.

What makes cities different from other environments? Obviously, and most importantly, cities and their suburbs are places where humans live. Ecologists agree that the main difference between urban and rural areas is the intensity of the impact of humans on nature (McDonnell *et al.*, 1997; Niemelä, 1999b). Humans have modified and constructed their environment to such an extent that most of the city surface is covered by artificial substrates (see also Breuste, Chapter 21). Not only buildings and roads, but also the soil beneath lawns is likely to be of foreign origin. As a result of human activities, a considerable amount of waste, exhausts, and sometimes toxic substances, are released into the environment (see also Carreiro, Chapter 19). Furthermore, urban environments are characterised by the presence of exotic species, and species that have been modified by selective breeding, i.e. domestic animals (see also Catterall, Chapter 8; Nilon, Chapter 10; Natuhara and Hashimoto, Chapter 12).

Ecology of Cities and Towns: A Comparative Approach, ed. Mark J. McDonnell, Amy K. Hahs and Jürgen H. Breuste. Published by Cambridge University Press. © Cambridge University Press 2009.

The consequences of these abiotic and biotic factors on the urban environment can be substantial. Buildings and roads fragment the landscape, causing habitat loss and creating a patchwork of indigenous and exotic vegetation plots of different sizes and levels of isolation (Trepl, 1995; Niemelä, 1999b). Light, chemical and noise pollution, and the risk of being trampled upon by feet or tyres, make life very risky for both indigenous and exotic organisms (see Eisenbeis and Hänel, Chapter 15). On top of this, the indigenous wildlife is quite possibly at risk of predation by domestic pets (Keitt et al., 2002; Lepczyk et al., 2003; Nilon, Chapter 10). Alternatively, these environmental characteristics may be favourable for some species, providing suitable growing space for those that can withstand these special habitat conditions.

There are three key arguments for doing research in urban ecosystems. First, urban environments, with intense human pressures, provide a great opportunity to study the causal effects of different anthropogenic activities on ecosystems. These causes can be studied singly or, importantly, simultaneously. This would increase our understanding of environmental changes, which is necessary in order to live sustainably in cities and on the planet. Second, urban environments provide a challenge for existing ecological theories. For example, understanding the effects of fragmentation on the biota has benefited greatly from two ecological theories, island biogeography theory and metapopulation dynamics (Haila, 1999). Of obvious importance in urban areas is whether the types of fragmentation brought about by humans are different from naturally occurring fragmentation and, critically, how these abovementioned theories translate to urban areas. Third, as a consequence of increased knowledge, we will be better able to establish and maintain natural-like green areas within cities.

In this chapter, we discuss the usefulness of urban theory and comparative research. We examine methods necessary for successful performance of comparative research. In particular, we will evaluate the need for clear concept definition, hypothesis generation and explicit testing, along with the need for quantification. We also suggest some parameters that should be given for explicit quantification and comparative purposes. Finally, we give an example of a study that was specifically designed for the purpose of international comparative research in urban ecology. We concentrate on ecological aspects, but acknowledge that the consideration of socio-economic aspects is often necessary, along with ecological research, to allow for the efficient application of ecological knowledge in urban planning (Pickett et al., 1997a; Niemelä, 1999a; Pickett et al., Chapter 3). Although our focus is on quantitative research, we acknowledge that the choice between qualitative and quantitative is determined by the research question. Our attitude here can be summarised in the words of Peters (1991): '... if we want to get someplace, then we must know where we are and where we want to go. For similar reasons, science progresses more easily when present limits and future goals are known.'

Is (urban) ecological theory needed?

The scientific perspective

The concept of theory and its role in ecology has been in dispute (Pickett *et al.*, 1994b). Also, a number of scientists are concerned with the apparent lack of progress in ecological theory, and question the ways in which ecological research is done (Peters, 1991; Weiner, 1995; Murray, 2001). Arguments have been raised that ecology should only focus on generating testable predictions (Peters, 1991); that ecology does not yet have universal laws and predictive theories because ecologists (and biologists in general) test their hypotheses only by verification (Pickett *et al.*, 1994b; Murray, 2001); that ecology is a science of case studies and cannot have general laws (Shrader-Frechette and McCoy, 1993); or that ecology already has a set of basic principles that are sufficient to describe, classify, explain and predict the dynamics of populations of living organisms (Berryman, 2003). Reasons given for this controversy are methodological, or linked to the character of nature. Methodological issues include the way in which biologists do science (see Peters, 1991; Pickett *et al.*, 1994b; Williams, 1997; Murray, 2001), while nature in turn is considered complex, dynamic, hierarchical, shaped by history, and generally considered not at equilibrium, and many phenomena have multiple, interacting causes.

For many of the reasons stated above, Vepsäläinen and Spence (2000) argued that broad, simple generalisations would rarely approach truth in ecology and evolutionary biology, and that general explanatory frameworks should be developed. This means that generalisations need to be scrutinised by defining their particular domains, and then by explicitly testing hypotheses derived from predictions within these domains (see Sismondo, 2000). This is a hierarchical approach in which specific hypotheses are tested within general explanatory frameworks, which in turn are used to evaluate and construct broader and higher-level, sometimes abstract, generalisations (i.e. theories; see Ford, 2000).

Our opinion is that ecological theory is necessary as a composition of knowledge that adds to our understanding of how ecological systems work, and it is indispensable as a guide and tool in our research attempts. We use the word 'theory' to mean a body of knowledge that can be used to construct potentially falsifiable predictions (i.e. hypotheses). Theories do not need to be established and/or extensive. They can also present new ideas (concepts by intuition; Ford, 2000), producing only a narrow chain of logical deductions. We believe that apart from generating testable hypotheses, theories should also explain commonalities between different examples and differences between them (Ford, 2000). In other words, theories should answer 'why' questions (Murray, 2001), not only pattern questions like how much, when and where (Peters, 1991).

The urban perspective

A debated topic in urban ecology is whether urban ecological systems need a specific theoretical framework (Trepl, 1995; Niemelä, 1999b). Niemelä (1999b) suggested that such is not needed because urban ecosystems function, in principle, in a similar way to any other ecosystem. For example, decomposition, predation and pollination take place in urban green areas, and species still interact with one another, in the same ways in which they do in natural systems. However, Niemelä (1999b) agreed with Pickett *et al.* (1997b) who suggested a conceptual framework, in which humans are considered as important ecological agents in the functioning of urban ecosystems, i.e. the human ecosystem model (see also Pickett *et al.*, Chapter 3).

Theories or frameworks that have been suggested as being useful in the urban environment include the theory of island biogeography (MacArthur and Wilson, 1967; Haila, 1999; Hubbell, 2001), metapopulation dynamics (Hanski and Gilpin, 1997; Hanski, 1998), the intermediate disturbance hypothesis (Connell, 1978; Wootton, 1998) and succession models (Trepl, 1995; Niemelä, 1999b). Island biogeography and metapopulation theory, for example, might be useful because habitat loss and fragmentation are among the main features of urban green environments (Trepl, 1995; Niemelä, 1999b), and these theories deal with the effects of patch size, isolation and connectivity on the biota (see Haila, 1999). The critical issue here is whether these theoretical constructs can be usefully translated into the urban context (see Ford (2000) for translating ideas, 'concepts by imagination', from one field of science to another).

In fact, working in the urban setting provides a great opportunity to evaluate the above theories – or any other essentially pristine-habitat theories – under new circumstances. We need to find novel and imaginative ways to test these theories in cities. If these theories pass the test in urban environments, they will gain power as their generality is extended. Alternatively, excessive human pressures may alter ecosystem structure and function to such an extent that these theories may become irrelevant to the urban environment, either because they simply do not work there, or because human impacts strongly confound the potentially observable patterns caused by the effects so that the underlying patterns are obscured and remain hidden from the researcher. When this is the case, alternative theories need to be used or constructed, and the domain of the existing theories needs to be redefined (see above).

The human component is, therefore, essential in understanding patterns and processes in urban nature (Pickett *et al.*, 1997b; Chapter 3). The challenge that urban ecologists face is to identify and assess the plethora of human effects in urban environments, and to relate their findings to urban planning and management. Examples of approaches in which humans are included in urban ecological studies are: (1) the 'human ecosystem model' that consists of social and ecological components (sensu Pickett *et al.*, 1997b; Niemelä, 1999b; Niemelä *et al.*, Chapter 2; Pickett *et al.*, Chapter 3); and (2) gradient analysis (urban–rural gradients, cf. McDonnell *et al.*, 1997; Niemelä *et al.*, 2002; Pickett *et al.*, Chapter 3).

The applicability perspective

Theory building, i.e. the search for general principles and domain specification, would be useful because it would allow the development of recommendations and guidelines for the planning and management of green areas, and the city as a whole. This will allow for the alleviation of anthropogenic pressures on urban environments (McDonnell, 1997; Pickett *et al.*, 1997b; Niemelä, 1999a; Niemelä *et al.*, Chapter 2). However, the translation from scientific theory to application in planning or management of the city is not automatically available. Niemelä (1999b) pointed out, for example, that the island biogeography theory did not offer immediate, straightforward applications, because of the controversy over whether it would be better to have several small areas or a single large one in order to maintain viable populations (see also Wu and Vankat, 1995; Duhme and Pauleit, 2000).

Or, take the intermediate disturbance hypothesis (IDH) as another example. According to this non-equilibrium hypothesis, species diversity is highest at intermediate levels of disturbance, both in terms of the time interval between disturbance events and the size of the disturbance event (Connell, 1978). Wootton (1998) restricted the domain of the IDH by showing that basal species in a food web tended to follow the IDH, while competitors at top trophic levels did not. So, if ecologists want to test the IDH in the urban setting, the following questions are crucial in their investigation: (1) can human disturbance be quantified? (2) If so, can an intermediate level of disturbance be identified between maximum and minimum levels? (3) Do the organisms studied fall within the domain of the IDH? And (4) if the answer is 'yes' to the previous questions, none of which are easy, then how would we apply the results to urban management and planning? And what kind of species diversity are we interested in? Or, is species diversity as such at all informative in the urban context?

For the sake of applicability it may occasionally be necessary to disregard the scientific theories and use practical questions as a starting point. The questions being asked from this perspective may be quite different from the sometimes abstract scientific theories. For example, what is the minimum size of a remnant patch to preserve viable populations of a species in an urban area? (Of course, theory is still needed to estimate what the size of a viable population is, for example using life history theory.) Or what kind of management is needed in order to promote a preferred characteristic, or to counteract unwanted effects on green areas? Thus we suggest that useful working hypotheses in urban studies do not necessarily have to be derived from ecological theories. The hypotheses can equally be logical descendants of any theoretical constructs, or models (sensu Peters, 1991; see also McCarthy, Chapter 7) originating from practical needs, i.e. city planning or management.

Finally, once the information has been produced, it has to be presented to decision-makers in such a way that it can be implemented in urban planning and development.

A call for international comparative research

What is comparative?

Comparative here means to work on the same scientific issues in different locations, under different environmental conditions, across the globe. Comparisons can be made at any spatial scale, for instance between cities and countries, as long as the comparisons are made at the same scale. Comparisons can be qualitative or quantitative. A typical example of qualitative, usually quite loose comparisons, is the way in which scientists discuss and evaluate their results in the light of other research performed in the same field, for example in scientific papers. Meta-analysis may aid in evaluating the strength and similarity of biological effects published, or in identifying the presence of selective reporting (Palmer, 2000). Tighter comparisons that are planned a priori and taken into account in the study design can be either qualitative or quantitative, depending on the research question, approach and level of comparison. Here we concentrate on the most stringent form of comparison, which is quantitative and planned a priori.

Comparisons can also be made at any hierarchical level (theory–hypothesis–data), again as long as they are made within the same hierarchical level. To compare at the theoretical level is to compare at the highest hierarchical level. For example, we can evaluate whether similar processes or cause-and-effect relationships exist in different locations. To make this comparison efficient, testable hypotheses should be derived from the theory. The theory under investigation will gain generality the more times the hypotheses are supported, and should be rejected or be modified as hypotheses get rejected. For this level, the hypotheses do not need to be similar for different locations, as long as they are descendants of the same theory. This comparison cannot be very accurate, but is likely to be qualitative and general. At the hypothesis level, similar research hypotheses are deduced from the theory and tested in different localities. However, the empirical predictions can differ, as well as the procedures for generating the data. Lastly, the comparison can be taken to the data level. In this case the research hypothesis is tested with an a priori planned data generation procedure in different locations. This method allows the most stringent comparison, possibly within one statistical analysis, as similar data are generated in different places. Obviously, the two latter levels of comparison include the theoretical level as well – if the data patterns are taken as corroboration or rejection of a specific theory, the same corroboration/rejection holds for all the sites under study. Thus the essential difference is in the stringency of comparison, increasing from the theoretical to the data level.

Why do comparative research?

International comparative work would be beneficial to urban ecology as a scientific discipline and to urban residents. The scientific benefits are obvious. The development of ecological theory occurs ideally through recurrent re-evaluation of a body of knowledge (Underwood, 1991; Ford, 2000). The generality of a theory is evaluated, and its domain defined through replication of studies in similar and different locations and ecosystems (see MacArthur, 1972; Underwood, 1997; Palmer, 2000). If theories 'borrowed' from other fields in ecology are capable of explaining patterns in urban environments, their general applicability will increase and they will, in the words of Ford (2000), 'have a right to exist'. If theories created specifically for urban areas (for example the human ecosystem model) pass the test in different cities, they gain in generality. These theories are, of course, not necessarily true, but they are currently the best explanations of the observed phenomena (e.g. Underwood, 1991).

The practice of ecology is by and large a social endeavour. Ecologists are quite likely to be among the key people to provide answers to environmental problems (Peters, 1991), making what we do important for numerous aspects of social welfare (Underwood, 1997). Identification of phenomena that most cities share (generalisations) will help to predict the response of remnant ecosystems or the city environment to urban development and forthcoming changes over time. Domain definition of theories is necessary to find out how the models or theories have to be fine-tuned (modified) at different locations for application. All of this is essential in maintaining environmental quality.

To conclude, we argue that there are convincing reasons for promoting international comparative research. If good, solid generalisations and local modifications to theories can be made, it will (a) help direct new research and (b) help focus on the potentially important aspects in the planning processes of cities and the management of green areas, to mitigate the unwanted effects on the city biota.

How to conduct comparative research

Much of what is being said below applies to any good quality research; however, we raise specific points that are central from an international comparative perspective.

Concept definition and operationalisation

Peters (1991) argued that progress in ecology is being held back by complex and inadequately defined terms. Clear concept definition is essential in any scientific work and especially to make comparisons; it is a prerequisite that concepts be explicitly and understandably defined throughout the research process, from the theoretical level through hypotheses to the empirical level.

For example, McIntyre et al. (2000) discussed the problems of defining 'urban'. They emphasised the importance of providing a benchmark for 'urban' to be able to compare studies performed in urban areas. They listed variables that might be used for defining 'urban', but recognised that some of them might not always be available to researchers, planners and managers. They also noted that, to some extent, the relevant definition of 'urban' depends on the study question. We feel that 'urban' may be used as a general concept that should be quantified to give an idea of the general characteristics of the study area. At minimum, this involves stating the human population density with corresponding area (McDonnell et al., 1997), but adding other attributes such as land-use and land-cover types, housing density or traffic frequency (McIntyre et al., 2000; Breuste, Chapter 21; Löfvenhaft, Chapter 24) may be necessary, or at least informative, for the study in question. We argue that even more important than defining 'urban' as an environment where the study is to be conducted, is to define explicitly all the concepts used to construct the focal theory or model and the research hypotheses derived from it.

To give another example, the concept of 'anthropogenic disturbance' is common in urban ecology. Urban environments are seen as 'more disturbed' than more natural suburban and rural environments, and this 'fact' is often invoked in explaining differences in the responses of the biota to urbanisation. In urban areas, disturbance is often thought of as an accumulation of all the human effects – pollution, fragmentation, trampling, soil sealing, etc. Disturbance is, however, rarely explicitly operationalised, in no small part owing to the complexity of the term (Attiwill, 1994). Open-ended and relative concepts, such as disturbance, may hinder progress if scientists get attached to them

(Peters, 1991), as not all ecologists define a particular concept in the same way (Ford, 2000). Developing specific hypotheses on the effects of a particular type of disturbance on the focal study object renders the whole concept of disturbance unnecessary: we can and should speak about things by their real names!

Concepts may not be fully defined at the beginning of a new research project; rather they represent novel, sometimes vague ideas (Peters, 1991; Pickett *et al.*, 1994b). However, when research progresses, we should consider our concepts critically. If the operationalisation of a concept is sound (i.e. the variables to be measured can be easily selected and logically deduced) then the concept can be used as a latent variable (Shipley, 2000) or verbal expression. However, if a concept lends itself to multiple meanings, allowing a number of variables to be measured, the study should be focused on a selection of the variables that have direct (hypothetical) links, causal or predictive, with the focal study object. For example, human disturbance in urban areas can be operationalised by quantifying trampling intensity (see the example below), by the number of residents in a specified radius around the study area or by the quantities of chemicals such as heavy metals in the soil, among other things. In this case the original concept can merely set the framework for the study, or may be abandoned as useless.

Theories, models and operationalisation

It is too common in science that the background theory and its link to the hypotheses and measurements are not explicitly stated in research papers. This hampers comparisons at the highest hierarchical level – the theoretical. If the link to the theoretical construct remains weak or implicit, it is not possible to compare the validity of a theory in different places (see for example Haila (1988) for different types of links between theory and data).

For comparative studies, as any study, we need to recognise the components of the focal systems and the critical processes linking the components in space and time (Shipley 2000). This may start as a vague idea that develops into a verbal or graphical conceptual model (Fig. 31.1). Because concepts may be imprecise and may have multiple meanings (Pickett *et al.*, 1994b; Ford, 2000), it is important to develop this further into a more precise qualitative, and if possible quantitative, model that shows the actual variables to be measured and the hypothesised mechanisms. Any model showing all the latent (or more conceptual) and measurement variables (and their errors), and the anticipated links between them, would be an efficient tool for a study, because the central processes and their operationalisation are described explicitly (see McCarthy, Chapter 7). A good way of picturing the hypothesised structure of a system (causal or correlational) is to draw causal graphs (see Shipley (2000) and Fig. 31.2).

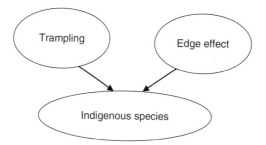

Fig. 31.1. A basic conceptual model of the anticipated effects of trampling and habitat edges on the indigenous biota in urban environments, as described in Grandchamp *et al.* (2000) and Lehvävirta *et al.* (2006).

An effective way to make comparisons is to use the same model with similar measurements from one study site, city and country to the next. In order to do this, sites, cities or countries need to have the focal characteristics in common so that similar measurements are possible. For example, if we want to investigate the effects of human trampling on forest vegetation and invertebrates in urban forests, the cities to be included need to have forests and people visiting them (to quantify trampling), and indicator vegetation and invertebrate taxa have to be identified. However, the effects of trampling on vegetation and invertebrates may be relevant for other kinds of biotopes (habitats) as well. For example, we might be interested in the effects of trampling on arid bushland vegetation and invertebrates. Now the original model should be used, with modifications in the operationalisation, i.e. variables to be measured, and possibly in the anticipated directions and magnitude of the effects (because, for example, the species composition and perhaps also the modes of trampling differ). The characteristics of the focal species will govern their response to different levels of trampling. Pioneer and generalist species may respond positively to moderate levels of trampling, while sensitive and specialist species may be negatively affected by even low levels of trampling. It is important that the focal species in both studies give information on the validity of the theoretical model in a similar way to allow for comparison. As more cities and circumstances (i.e. vegetation types and invertebrate taxa used) are included in a particular investigation, generality is increased (i.e. the domain is broadened) but often at the expense of accuracy (see Sismondo, 2000; Vepsäläinen and Spence, 2000).

Quantification is essential

To be able to compare within or between studies (i.e. sites, cities, countries) it is necessary to quantify the variables used and the results obtained. Furthermore, in order to provide applicable results, scientists have to be able to

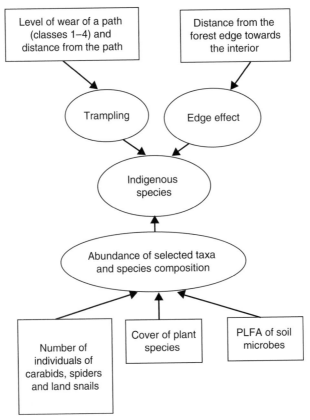

Fig. 31.2. An extended conceptual model or causal graph for the edge/trampling project, showing the factors (or more conceptual, i.e. latent, variables), enclosed in the ellipses, plus the measurement variables, enclosed in the squares.

give quantitative answers to questions like how much, how large, how far, and how big an impact. It is not enough just to describe what and where, or to describe the causal effects or correlations that exist (Peters, 1991 versus Shipley, 2000).

For example, McIntyre et al. (2000) were unhappy about the lack of quantification in a number of studies using the urban–rural gradient approach. The problem is that the gradients represent a complex combination of attributes (Medley et al., 1995; McDonnell et al., 1997; Pickett et al., Chapter 3; McDonnell and Hahs, Chapter 5) resulting in a large number of possible quantifications as discussed above. However, if these gradients are used unquantified, comparisons are impossible: without quantification we compare an unknown part of a gradient from one city with an unknown part of a gradient from another city. Furthermore, unquantified gradients remain black boxes that do not lend themselves to hypothesis generation or testing of causal mechanisms. Nevertheless, we acknowledge the usefulness of the multi-variate urban–rural gradient approach as a heuristic tool to explore patterns, and to generate hypotheses about processes and the magnitude of effects. To improve the gradient approach, McIntyre et al. (2000) suggested an a priori choice of ecological variables to construct 'a gradient of urbanisation dispersed across an urban area', with quantitative criteria. We agree completely, but note that constructing such a design does not produce a gradient as visualised by most people (i.e. city core – suburbs – rural surroundings); the design simply fulfils certain criteria where particular variables vary within selected limits. The use of the actual quantified variables, such as nitrogen deposition or population density, renders the concept of 'gradient' unnecessary (see Carreiro et al., Chapter 19, and Pouyat et al., Chapter 20, for alternative views).

Variables and patterns can be quantified by reporting their means, modes, medians, variances, ranges and quartiles, for example. If the study question included causal effects, the effect sizes have to be given with confidence limits. Parameters that are useful for comparative purposes include, for example, regression and correlation coefficients, R^2 statistics, differences between means in an ANOVA, partial correlation coefficients in path analyses, and the variance (for example standard errors or standard deviations) of the given parameter. The values have to be given in an understandable format, so that the reader does not have to know the techniques used by the authors. For example, if the variables have been transformed, the effect sizes should be back-transformed accordingly.

To understand the mechanisms, it is important to compare both numbers per se (numbers of individuals, objects, volumes, etc.) and the trends (patterns, effect sizes, etc.) between sites, cities and countries. If either of the perspectives is forgotten, the conclusions may be biased. If, for example, we find a negative effect, say 'trampling decreases forest vegetation cover', then looking only at the trends may obscure the fact that with similar trampling pressures the actual coverage may vary from place to place (cf. Peters, 1991). Or, looking only at the coverages may not make sense when different species or biomes are compared.

An example: the effects of habitat edges and trampling intensity on urban biota

In this section we discuss an ongoing research project that was designed particularly with international collaboration and comparison in mind. The study question has its origin both in the scientific debate and practical needs for knowledge in urban environments, and consequently, has both scientific and applied ambitions.

The theoretical framework

Previous studies (Heliölä et al., 2001; Lehvävirta et al., 2006), personal observations (S. Lehvävirta, D.J. Kotze), and discussions with colleagues suggested two potential key explanations for changes in the biota in urban woodland patches, namely the edge effect and human trampling. Much work has concentrated on the effects of human trampling on vegetation (Liddle, 1997), while we only found a few papers concerning the effect of trampling on other organisms (Duffey, 1975; Grandchamp et al., 2000). On the other hand, there is a wealth of information available on edge effects (e.g. Murcia, 1995; Harper and Macdonald, 2001; Heliölä et al., 2001). To our knowledge, no study exists where both of these two key factors had been investigated simultaneously. Thus, the question of the relative importance of these factors in modifying human-dominated urban ecosystems was scientifically interesting. Furthermore, the study has links to succession theory (trampling as part of ecosystem dynamics), the intermediate disturbance hypothesis (trampling seen as disturbance), the concept of fragmentation (edge effects) and the human ecosystem model (human behaviour).

Applicability

Both edge effects and trampling are factors that can be controlled and managed in urban planning and management of green areas. In order to maintain indigenous biota within and close to the urban setting, we need to know how these factors affect the ecosystems, and control them. Knowing the magnitude and spatial extent (how strongly and how far towards the interior of a patch) of the edge effect, and of trampling, will help planners and decision-makers to choose the minimum area of a patch, and human population density in relation to the amount of recreational land in a city (of course, other factors like the effect of patch size and population dynamics of the focal species should also be considered). Furthermore, means to restrict the areal extent of trampling can be applied if this turns out to be the main factor changing ecosystem remnants.

The study question

This was (following the above line of thinking) broadly defined as: what is the relative importance of the edge effect as compared to the effect of trampling on the indigenous biota of urban ecosystems?

International comparative aim

Edge and trampling effects are widely recognised in many human-dominated ecosystems. Scientifically, it is therefore interesting to define where these effects apply, i.e. their domains. This would be essential for those who want to apply the results of research in local planning and management of green areas – what kind of ecosystems do the results concern? If broad generalisations can be made, the knowledge can also be widely applied.

Concept definition and operationalisation

In this study there are three main concepts to consider: the edge effect, trampling and the indigenous biota. The edge effect is a complex term that can include anything from physical (wind, radiation, temperature, etc.) to biotic factors (invasion, dispersal, predation, penetration of pathogens, etc.). At the first phase of the study it is used as a black box term with no hypothesis on the actual mechanism causing patterns in the biota. We first wanted to test whether patterns existed in relation to the edge in general, and the mechanisms were to be studied later, if patterns get corroborated. Thus, we operationalised the edge effect simply as distance from the patch edge towards the interior.

Trampling is also ambiguous. In practice, trampling can include all kinds of physical pressure, including different human and non-human activities, for example cycling, or pet and wild animal walking. Furthermore, the effects of trampling may be direct (wear and tear or death of an organism) or indirect (altered physical environment through soil compaction). It is also debatable how the level (i.e. amount) of trampling should be measured. We took visible paths across the forest floor as indicative of trampling, and classified the levels of wear of the paths into four classes from light to extreme wear. The method of visual evaluation is based on our previous studies, first used and described by Lehvävirta (1999) and later assessed by Heiman *et al.* (2003). This method does not allow us to distinguish between different kinds of activities as a source of wear and tear. The method is easy, quick and cheap to apply anywhere, and reliable, which are prerequisites for international comparative work.

Indigenous biota here means species native to the area. Of course the species pool has to be locally defined, and history plays a role in the definition of what is native (how and when a species has invaded the area, and how established it is). We chose to measure certain unquestionably indigenous taxa of medium-fertility remnant forest patches. Some of the taxa were thought to represent key components of the ecosystem (i.e. soil microbes and vegetation), and some were thought to represent good indicator taxa (i.e. carabids, spiders and land snails). The actual measurements were vegetation cover in quadrats, number of tree stems in quadrats, phospholipid fatty acid (PLFA) spectrum of microbes in soil samples, number of individuals of carabids and spiders in pitfall traps, and number of land snails in litter samples.

The hypothetical model, empirical predictions and design

We stress the importance of making a priori predictions, and formulated our research hypothesis as a simple causal graph showing the key concepts and their relations (Fig. 31.1). A graph can also include information about the operationalisation (Fig. 31.2).

Our predictions are species or species-group specific (see Didham *et al.*, 1998; Haila, 2002) and incorporate the habitat requirements of the taxon in relation to its response to edge effects and trampling. For example, we hypothesised that with increasing distance from the forest patch edge towards the interior, forest specialist species will increase in number or cover, while edge and open-habitat species will decrease in cover or number. Similarly, sensitive species should be the ones with the most immediate and dramatic decrease in cover or number with increased levels of trampling and decreasing distance to the paths (see design below). For those species that could be classified a priori according to their ecological characteristics, a real hypothesis test can be performed. For species whose ecology is not well known, the study remains more explorative, as no direction of the pattern or effect can be specified a priori.

The design

The sampling was designed to be simple and cost-effective (Fig. 31.3). Ideally, each of 10 woodland patches (i.e. 10 replicates per condition, see below) was sampled at four distances from the woodland edge (approximately 0, 15, 30 and 60 m), and at three locations in relation to paths with four different levels of wear (at each distance from the edge). The locations in relation to paths were on the path, right next to it, or away from it (in the seemingly untrampled spots). In practice, however, very few urban woodlands satisfied all the 48 conditions (four edge distances × four trampling intensities × three locations) necessitating the inclusion of more patches to ensure adequate replication.

Vegetation, trees, land snails and soil microbes were sampled on the trampled path, next to the path, and away from the path. Samples were at least 10 m apart to ensure some level of independence, and samples 'away from the path' were at least 2 m from any path. Carabid beetles and spiders were sampled next to and away from the path, because the pitfall traps would not endure constant trampling on the paths.

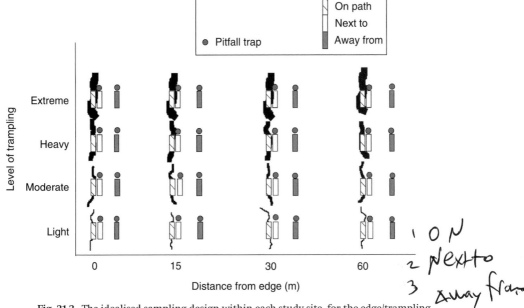

Level of trampling (y-axis)

Extreme

Heavy

Moderate

Light

0   15   30   60

Distance from edge (m)

Legend:
- ● Pitfall trap
- On path
- Next to
- Away from

Handwritten annotations:
1 ON
2 Next to
3 Away from

Fig. 31.3. The idealised sampling design within each study site, for the edge/trampling project. In Finland and Canada the study is focused on urban woodland patches. Soil microbes, vegetation and snails were sampled on the path, next to the path and away from the path. Spiders and carabid beetles were sampled next to the path and away from the path. Dark lines of varying size indicate paths. See text for details.

Handwritten: Good / Good!

Levels of comparison and quantification

Currently, this project is being run in two cities in Finland (Lahti and Helsinki) and in one city in Canada (Edmonton). The data collected from Lahti and Helsinki should be fairly similar, and for this reason comparisons will be made at the lowest level – the data level. The data collected from these two cities will be assessed within the same statistical analyses (Generalised Linear Models).

Comparisons between Edmonton and the two cities of Finland will be at the hypothesis level. The data collected will be different (i.e. different organisms with different habitat associations and in different site types), but the predictions will be the same for organisms sharing similar characteristics. For example, we expect to sample open habitat species more frequently at the edges as compared with the interiors in both countries. The cities will be compared by the direction and magnitude of the effects of trampling and distance from the edge (i.e. slopes for distances from the forest edge and the paths, and differences in relation to the level of wear). We also need to look at the actual numbers or coverages of organisms. This will allow us to evaluate which of the two factors, edge and/or trampling, is most important in shaping a species' response in Edmonton as compared with Lahti and Helsinki.

The statistics and parameters to be reported include the mean with standard errors and the range of both the independent and the response variables, plus the effect sizes of the Generalised Linear Models with p values. A number of graphs explicitly showing the response of the biota to both edge effects and trampling will also be produced.

Finally, we believe that this project is a good example of the implementation of a scientifically sound, collaborative research strategy that may ultimately aid in the refinement and development of urban ecological theory and in the management and planning of urban green space. The factors investigated (i.e. trampling intensity and edge effects) have been clearly defined and operationalised, and can therefore be measured in different cities, and the patterns obtained can be compared quantitatively.

Concluding remarks

The work ecologists do is important both from the scientific point of view, and in terms of human welfare. Researchers working in urban ecology have many challenging opportunities. For example, by generating novel hypotheses, existing ecological theories can be evaluated and modified to suit urban environments. Alternatively, the most creative individuals and groups may develop completely new explanatory models and frameworks. As urban ecology matures, the underlying causes of the observed patterns will be identified and developed into theories (see Williams, 1997), either as specifically urban or more general ecological theories.

This chapter has briefly summarised some views on how science might proceed in an urban ecological, comparative context. We relied greatly on the hypothetico-deductive method as described by Peters (1991), Williams (1997), Underwood (1997) and Ford (2000), for example, but we also stress the importance of explorative and descriptive approaches during some phases of a research project (cf. Haila, 1988; Pickett et al., 1994b).

Hypothesis testing or data exploration?

Enough urban ecological knowledge exists to start focusing studies more on testing causal effects and estimating the magnitudes of effects, rather than on exploration of data and hypothesis generation. We argue that the most efficient way to study urban ecosystems is to investigate a small set of factors at a time, and to control for other factors, preferably in the field or laboratory, or statistically if this is not possible (Shipley, 2000). Scientists should not hesitate to make clear predictions and test their validity, as this is an effective way for theory development (Romesburg, 1981; Underwood, 1990; Peters, 1991). It is also simpler, from both philosophical and practical points of view, to test simple, directional predictions (obtained from the dissection of complex causal models). Clearly, for comparisons between cities and countries, explicit quantitative theories and models are necessary.

An explorative approach may be needed at the very beginning of a new research project. For example, in our edge/trampling project for species whose ecological characteristics are not yet known well enough we cannot make predictions about the direction and magnitude of the effects of edges and trampling on them (see Haila, 1988). Also, an explorative phase is needed if the researcher is, after having conducted the study, faced with an unexpected result (Lehvävirta, 2005). Multi-variate explorative techniques (e.g. the urban–rural gradient; McDonnell et al., 1997) can help in hypothesis generation, keeping in mind that the complexity of multi-variate results lends itself to ad hoc explanations that may not be behind the observed patterns, or may be unique for the location under investigation (see Zipperer and Gutenspergen, Chapter 17; Carreiro et al., Chapter 19; Pouyat et al., Chapter 20).

Patterns or mechanisms?

It is important to establish that a pattern really exists, and is not just a product of beliefs, value-laden observations, or the difficulty of observing the focal object with similar precision in different places (MacArthur, 1972; Underwood, 1991; Palmer, 2000). Patterns can be explored or tested at large or small scales. The method of gradient analysis could be used to study whether patterns are real and recurring (see Zipperer and Gutenspergen, Chapter 17; Carreiro et al., Chapter 19; Pouyat et al., Chapter 20). An example of a large-scale gradient is that from the highly urbanised city centre to the rural surroundings (McDonnell et al., 1997; Niemelä et al., 2002), while a smaller gradient could be established from the woodland edge to its interior.

Whilst many patterns are described in ecology, their existence is often not tested, nor are the underlying mechanisms or causes of many of these patterns known. We suggest that it is time to move on from pattern exploration to test the existence of patterns, and more importantly, to test causalities. The reason for this is that similar patterns across cities do not necessarily mean that they are produced by similar causal mechanisms. Thus the ultimate aim for international comparative research should be to reveal the causal mechanisms, to allow for wider generalisations and consequently wider applicability.

To conclude, the key words for successful comparative, international research are concept definition; explicit expression of theories, research hypotheses and empirical predictions; simple cost-effective designs that can be widely put into practice; and quantitative results.

Acknowledgements

We thank the organisers and participants of the Urban Ecology Symposium of the IALE conference in Darwin, Australia (July 2003) and the Melbourne Urban Ecology Workshop, Australia (July 2003) for providing a very stimulating atmosphere during which a lot of interaction took place, and possible future collaboration was established. Katja Matveinen, Salla Heiman, Stephen Venn and Jari Niemelä provided very helpful comments on an earlier version of the manuscript.

32

Ecological scientific knowledge in urban and land-use planning

KRISTINA L. NILSSON AND CLAS FLORGÅRD

Introduction

As has been argued by Grimm *et al.* (2000), the study of urban ecology can be divided into ecology in cities and ecology of cities. The former is studied by natural scientists and the latter by natural as well as social scientists. Many of the natural scientists have found that their scientific results and collected knowledge are only used to a small extent as underlying data in urban and land-use planning and design processes. The question is why?

For the integration of scientific results into the planning and design process, we have to know how those processes work. Over the past few centuries, planning processes have changed as society has developed. At the same time, the conceptualisation of planning processes has progressed. Here we are going to describe seven main modes of planning processes. The modes are: survey-analysis, rational, incrementalistic, mixed-scanning, stakeholder-driven, communicative, and strategic planning processes. On the one hand, we can see these different modes of planning as showing how planning has developed and changed over recent decades, and on the other hand, we can see the modes still working in parallel in different situations.

In what follows, partners involved in planning processes are separated into actors and stakeholders. By 'stakeholders' we mean those partners who have interests in the planning subject but are not necessarily as active in the process as the 'actors'.

Ecology of Cities and Towns: A Comparative Approach, ed. Mark J. McDonnell, Amy K. Hahs and Jürgen H. Breuste. Published by Cambridge University Press. © Cambridge University Press 2009.

Seven modes of planning

We can identify seven main modes of planning processes that have been used during the past century. The mode of survey-analysis planning was described by Patrick Geddes in the late 1800s. He argued for a process where the planning team first had to carry out a survey of the natural conditions of the territory to be developed. The result of this survey provided the main underlying data to carry out a plan. The process was looked upon as two-stepped, going from the survey to the final plan. Geddes' idea of planning (1997) was normative, relying on 'rational rationalities' – that is, a search for optimal conditions as a base for decisions. It was an important step forward in that he emphasised the importance of knowledge about the natural conditions. However, for many decades it led to non-productive discussion between researchers and practitioners. In the past, as now, there was a discrepancy between researchers' and practitioners' views of how planning is managed. The researchers saw the practitioners work as not properly grounded, and the practitioners saw the planning theory launched by the researchers as nothing but theory, and of little use in practice.

The second mode of planning process is known as rational planning. This is a more active approach than the survey-analysis mode. In rational planning, goals for planning are set up, and alternative plans are developed and discussed. The alternatives are rationally evaluated, and the most appropriate is chosen. Several aspects are discussed, such as natural and cultural conditions at the site, function, social goals, technical issues and aesthetics. Such an objective-instrumental rationality is based on the idea that the most effective, logical and optimal instruments are used to achieve requirements. First, an actor becomes aware of a problem, when she or he posits a goal and weighs alternative means in a careful way. Second, the actor chooses among the alternatives according to the estimation of their respective merit, made with reference to the state of affairs the actor prefers (Etzioni, 1973). The action is based on economic, scientific and technical expert knowledge in achieving an optimal solution in a step-by-step linear process. We can see a technical and instrumental rationality in contemporary planning decisions even if there has long been criticism of the mode of planning. Part of this criticism sees rational planning as theory which is far from practice, since a planning process always consists of uncertainties. However, some processes seem to be limited and simplified in a rationalistic way.

The third mode is the incrementalistic planning approach. From this viewpoint, the decision-making is distributed between several actors, and every actor is working from their own interest. It is primarily political aspects that settle which alternatives are going to be assessed (Lindblom, 1973). Disjointed incrementalism seeks to adapt decision-making strategies to the limited cognitive capacities of decision-makers and to reduce the scope and cost of information collection and computation. Lindblom explains the planning process as 'muddling through' and summarises numbers of steps in the decision process in the following way. Rather than attempting a comprehensive survey and evaluation of all alternatives, the decision-maker focuses only on those policies that differ from existing policies. Only a relatively small number of policy alternatives are considered. For each policy alternative, a restricted number of 'important' consequences are evaluated. The problem confronting the decision-maker is continually redefined, owing to the numerous adjustments in the 'end-means' and 'means-ends' (see Lindblom, 1965). These adjustments make the problem more manageable (Lindblom, 1965). The incremental planning approach has also been criticised as a normative model.

To overcome this criticism there is the concept of mixed-scanning as a fourth mode. Etzioni (1973) presents this approach as being more responsive to societal decision-making, which he argues requires two sets of mechanisms. The first is the set of high-order, fundamental policy-making processes, which establish basic directions. The second is the incremental processes by which these fundamental policy decisions are parameterised and implemented. Etzioni argues that mixed-scanning provides both a realistic description of the strategy used by actors in a large variety of fields, and the strategy for effective actors to follow. He also states that the structures within which interactions among actors take place become more significant the more we recognise that the basis of decisions neither is, nor can be, a fully ordered set of values and an exhaustive examination of reality. In part, the strategy followed is determined neither by values nor by information but by the positions of and power relations among the decision-makers (Etzioni, 1973).

In the late 1970s the criticism of rational planning led to stakeholder-driven planning processes (Faludi, 1987). This fifth mode was the first one that can be said to rely on research to any great extent. The approach involves the stakeholders taking positions and deciding whether to be an actor or not. That means that the planning and design process can be initiated by any stakeholder, not just officials and planners, can be driven by this stakeholder or others, and can be obstructed by any stakeholder. Although most planning processes in Sweden are still initiated by the local planning administration, stakeholders can be officials, authorities, NGOs, companies, lay people – and scientists. The formal process given by law and other regulations is a framework within which anything can happen. Survey-analysis, rationality and strategy can be parts of the process, but the process can go on even without these approaches. At last the view of planning was founded on research, as a theory close to practice.

The sixth mode of planning process, and one of the most discussed in contemporary planning theory, is the idea of communicative planning processes. This view is influenced by the views of the sociologist Habermas, who described processes based on a discussion of free and equal inhabitants. Habermas draws on the conditions for a conversation between equals to derive principles for evaluating public debate, which can be brought into play in the process of public dialogue (Healey, 1997). Deliberative democracy, which utilises both consensus decision-making and representative democracy, makes no substantial distinction between good or bad, all views and arguments being welcome in the discussions. Deliberative democracy is based on dialogue, not only in the sense of being able to take part in discussions, but also in the sense of being justified through discussion. The choice of different processes or decisions must be through debate about their relative benefits, whether it be through discussion, negotiation or voting. These decision-making processes allow the evaluation of earlier known alternatives, while also generating new alternatives (Elster, 1998).

The idea of communicative planning is an answer to the view of a deliberative democracy and a reaction to the objective-orientated technical rationalistic planning traditions. Processes of spatial planning have always been dependent on dialogues and communication between all actors involved. Even in traditional rational planning, leading politicians and different types of planning experts have communicated planning issues. The communicative rationality is based on communicative ethics, where the best argument will win. This means that people in an open and transparent discussion can reach consensus about what is regulating community decisions. There must be a dialogue between equals to be able to assess planning alternatives in the form of a common planning process (Nylund, 1995). In planning practice, this means involving a manifold of actors – private, public and political – in the process. In a communicative process, all interests should be protected in the way everyone is expected to contribute honest and integrated arguments to the discussion. There are also requirements that individuals are only influenced by good arguments and that difference in power, status or prestige has little effect on decisions.

A communicative process should be designed to include all actors, stakeholders or representatives of stakeholder groups. In these arenas the participants exchange ideas, sort out what is to be judged and see what is important, and assess proposals for changes. All parties are expected to be aware of and accept contradictory standpoints and to identify eventual conflicts between parties. Also anticipated is a state of understanding, integrity and truth between the parties, which will give legitimacy to the decision-making. It is expected that solutions to eventual conflicts arising can be reached in consensus through forms of deliberative dialogues. As a result of the process the partners should be satisfied with step-by-step progress.

Several advocates for communicative methods also acclaim the learning processes between participating parties in communicative methods (Sjöström, 1985;

Forester, 1989; Healey, 1997; Molander, 1996; Wirén, 1998). In joint talks where views and opinions are discussed and tested, everyone learns from each other's knowledge. In the methods of communicative planning, the stakeholders are assumed to be involved from the start of the planning process and to be active during the entire process. Through this, participants in policy development processes learn about each other and about the problems they each face, and they develop shared meanings and understandings through which policy co-ordination in a shared-power world can take place.

An awareness of the power relations between the actors in planning processes motivates the idea of strategic planning, the seventh mode of planning processes presented here. From this point of view the planning process is seen as cyclic or spiral: first setting the goal and carrying out a preliminary limited survey; then development of alternatives, after discussion, revision of goals and deepening of survey; new sketches, new revision; and after a number of cycles, a final solution and decision. In a strategic planning perspective one is aware of the qualitative uncertainties and the plurality of values in the management of the planning process. There are efforts made to produce strategies that allow flexibility for new circumstances and/or new information. Instead of a linear order, as in rational planning, one can illustrate a cyclic order with several punctuated steps. Planners include several alternatives in their agenda in an effort to find measures of less complexity, where the uncertainties are easily understandable (Friend and Hickling, 1997; Healey *et al.*, 1997; Khakee, 2000; Vigar *et al.*, 2000). This approach is still normative, but can be seen as an approach to what the practitioners view as a real planning process.

The strategic planning process aims to find pragmatic, suitable strategies to manage a vision from idea to a concrete goal. However, strategic planning can be used for different purposes. It can be used to put a democratic planning process into practical operation using strategies to handle a high number of stakehold-ers and actors; or it can be used by powerful actors to achieve their own interests, using strategies to avoid undesired hindrances. Hull (1996) argues that strategic plan-making first and foremost provides a process to assess all the planning issues. She sees it as a legitimised documentary tool to co-ordinate and organise the disparate intentions of private sector development within wider community goals in the least conflictual way.

Perspectives on nature

The modes of planning presented above explain different ways in which actors can be involved in the process. However, another important part of how the processes are carried out is how different perspectives of the planning subject are managed. Perspectivism is described as the way we always observe and understand something from a perspective. It is characterised by the idea that knowledge is never separate from concrete situations or individuals; that is, perspectivism is always contextual. Rorty (in Danermark *et al.*, 1997) states that there are no fundaments on which we can base our arguments. To be able to discuss how our knowledge corresponds with the objective reality we need a joint language, which Rorty posits does not exist. He implies instead that knowledge must be seen in relation to its usability, related to a meaning, not to its degree of truth.

Even natural scientific knowledge that traditionally has been seen as 'real truth' is now identified in relation to different scientific perspectives. One example of this is different groups of scientists' contradictory view of the reasons for higher global temperatures. One larger group sees it as climate change caused by air pollution. Another much smaller group sees it as natural variation in solar warming. This means that even some natural scientific results will be seen as value-based knowledge and as such be managed as other value-based planning data.

In the communicative and strategic planning processes, the actors' and stakeholders' perspectives and values will be visible. In processes managing the natural environment and resources, the different perspectives of biocentrism and anthropocentrism will be of special importance. From the anthropocentric perspective, human beings carry an intrinsic value. The non-anthropocentrism perspective sees that even things other than human beings carry a moralistic value (Ariansen, 1993). The bio- or ecocentric perspective has its starting point in ecology.

Ecocentric, 'deep green' environmental fundamentalism holds that nature has an intrinsic value independent of human beings. From this perspective, biological diversity must have equal opportunities for surviving. Dryzek (1997) calls this green radicalism, which is both radical and imaginative. The green political parties and associations mainly advocate this perspective. Anthropocentrism can have a number of different philosophical or religious motivations. Human beings can have a unique position arising from one or other specific human characteristic such as the ability to talk, think, carry out working projects, make conscious plans for your life and so on. These characteristics are seen as specific to human beings, providing then with a moral status from the so-called 'criteria of distinctions'. Environmental philosophy provides some anthropocentric ideal modes around the extent of humans' attitudes and views on nature: conquest of the environment, repairing of the environment, resource administration, protection of the environment (Ariansen, 1993).

The ecocentric perspective with an ecological view of the world suggests that science will find a limit to what the environment can take, and man must keep to this to ensure the survival of the planet and biodiversity. There is a belief in strong sustainability based on the economy: material capital can be exchanged for natural capital. A balance can be produced based on physical principles. Natural capital must not be reduced. In contrast, according to the technocentric perspective, technology can reduce the load on the environment. Supporters of this view are looking for a balance between environmental considerations, technical aspects and other policy matters, particularly with respect to economic growth.

Scientists in planning processes

When discussing the possibilities of integrating results from natural science into planning, it is important to keep in mind that planning is an active practice. It is based on diverse scientific knowledge of natural, social, human, technical and design sciences as well as reflective experiential knowledge (Schön, 1983; Molander, 1996). The groups compiled for planning processes often consist of professional officers representing scientific knowledge. The planning activity is to weigh segments based on the different types of scientific knowledge to provide a solution that is possible to implement in practice. This is an activity reliant on technology, practical and tacit knowledge – a combination of episteme, techne and phronesis (Aristoteles in Ramirez, 1995; Flyvbjerg, 1998). This will be done inside a framework of planning legislation. How these segments are related to each other, and which basic underlying data will dominate, relies on values. In this respect, the planning activity, like politics, is very complex (Nilsson, 2003).

Planning is not science. Planning is action, and as such, basically a social process with a scientific, technological and juridical framework. It is carried out by professionals. Planning is mainly studied by social scientific theories. When scientists are actively involved in planning and design processes promoting segmented knowledge, they leave their positions as scientists and become stakeholders. In these situations they are competing with other stakeholders representing other knowledge and values. This is a core problem for scientists going into the planning and design process. The scientists are usually not aware of rules, legislation and decision-making systems. They are playing with and against professions with deeper insight into how to contribute information and manage the process.

In earlier rational planning processes, decisions were based on expert knowledge to find an 'optimal' solution. But rational planning has been heavily criticised for not being related to an open and democratic society where all stakeholders and their values are handled in the planning process. As an example, anthropocentric views will be set against ecocentric views, and, as we know, most planning legislation is based on an anthropocentric perspective.

In the mode of planning processes where stakeholders are involved in representing different interests and values, there will be competition to determine which interest and value will be dominant. In a power perspective (Flyvbjerg, 1998; Faubion, 2002), we can see that the interests with strongest support in society also will have strong support in planning processes. In other words, economic interests often are dominant over the ecological and biological interests (Nilsson, 2003).

An important fact is that in a specific situation a stakeholder will emphasise information that supports his/her/the organisation's interests, and will depreciate information that would support another position. As long as this is done without misleading information, this is a part of the play in a form of negotiative planning (Cars, 1992). It also means that the most important thing for taking scientific results into account is that these results are known by the stakeholder. Therefore, the first thing scientists have to do is to make their information known to crucial actors and stakeholders to consider.

However, it is not enough that the scientific information is known. It must also be available for all stakeholders and actors. This means that it must be easy to understand, and usually comprehensive. Generally, information in scientific papers is neither easy for planners to understand, nor comprehensive. Usually it has to be transformed into a format that practitioners can use. Another way to go, seldom used, is that researchers complement their competence to make it possible also to work as practitioners. A not so unusual option for practitioners is to continue their education concerning scientific theories and methods, so that they can inform themselves about such results.

33

Envisioning further steps in comparative urban ecology

ORIE LOUCKS

Introduction

The Melbourne Workshop on comparative ecology of cities and towns has challenged all participants in both expected and unexpected ways. The scope and diversity of research presented has been reassuring, even if complex. Two prominent directions are evident in the concepts and language used, one focused on understanding the parts, and the other on holistic comparative study. Beyond examining this dichotomy, my objective in this chapter is to highlight the important building blocks presented here and note some of the gaps evident in the vision for urban ecology. Finally, I offer some thoughts on the prospects for a comparative ecology of cities and towns that should emerge over the next decade.

One overarching view during the workshop has been the advancement of knowledge through comparative analysis of the ecology of cities and towns. This is a huge subject intellectually as well as technically, but one we seem to agree on, at least in principle. However, the number of papers dealing comprehensively and holistically with physical and ecological functioning of cities is modest, hardly enough to serve as a basis for comparative studies (although that was not an immediate objective of the workshop). Perhaps this is as it should be, given the variety of specific local questions we need also to ask about cities. However, would we come back 10 years from now with equally few comprehensive and holistic papers? I doubt it, and so we should look now to steps we can take to frame the scope of studies we expect in the future.

Ecology of Cities and Towns: A Comparative Approach, ed. Mark J. McDonnell, Amy K. Hahs and Jürgen H. Breuste. Published by Cambridge University Press. © Cambridge University Press 2009.

A second overarching view focuses on the components of cities and how we are to understand all the contributions from diverse scientific and professional fields that make up the framework for urban ecology. The workshop organisers suggested clearly that participants should just do what they do best: ecology, in a comparative mode if possible. Many participants, however, engaged us with language and concepts from quite diverse disciplines, ranging from the central role of hydrology in the Baltimore urban study (Pickett *et al*, Chapter 3), to the chemistry of runoff water in Baltimore and, finally, to water and biological responses to land-use change evident in the transport corridor studies of Stockholm (Löfvenhaft, Chapter 24). Even the field of air pollutant deposition and its effects on soil animals was shown as a component of the New York City and Louisville gradient studies (Carreiro *et al.*, Chapter 19; Pouyat *et al.*, Chapter 20). Each of these parts of urban ecology is important, but because each, for now, has been localised as only part of an overall picture for a site, we have had to stop short of learning through the comparative method. In this chapter, I would like to articulate a broad vision of comparative ecology for cities and towns, and bridge between the two views noted above, by drawing in part on well-defined and familiar work, and partly on conceptually broad but relatively unfamiliar work.

Structure and function in the comparative ecology of cities and towns

Our first challenge, then, is to consider whether urban ecology, as we are seeking to understand it through comparative studies, should be focused on nature in cities and factors influencing it (classical ecological structure), or on the interactions between activities of the human population, species of plants and animals that show effects, and the modified physical environment of urban areas (comprehensive function and integration). Pickett *et al.* (Chapter 3) use the term 'biogeophysical system' to be comprehensive about ecological processes in the city. Perhaps this term, more than ecology, facilitates engagement by scholars from the many disciplines evident in comparative urban studies. Bringing these fields together, as illustrated by the modelling work of McCarthy (Chapter 7), is a vision that workshop participants seemed to hope for, even as most reported research from their own more limited part of the full functioning of urban ecosystems.

To provide a framework for a critique and synthesis of the workshop then, I tried to think through what comprehensive aspects of structure and function would be most important for us to hear. I thought we should expect to hear coverage of broad themes that would frame comprehensively the essential components of comparative urban studies. Five such themes are summarised in

Table 33.1. *Themes for a comparative urban ecology.*

1. Size and scope of a city's ecological footprint: sources of used resources, waste and discharge.
2. Water: shortages, quality, floods and sea-level rise.
3. Temporal and spatial patch dynamics of people, institutions and biological complexity.
4. Accommodating the social and cultural needs and values of a city's people.
5. Planning and design to rationalise footprint, people, water and biology.

Table 33.1. During the workshop, I kept asking myself whether the subject presentations, in Melbourne and at the earlier meetings in Darwin, addressed the structure and function themes I expected to see in comparative studies.

Happily, the presentations, now captured in the chapters of this book, came through as adding systematically to our knowledge, both of the parts and of the whole, and all have contributed in one way or another to the themes in Table 33.1. There are gaps in the workshop proceedings, however, and while many may be due to the chance of who happened to be present, we can learn from all of them. Much as the material presented has been excellent, a critique, to be helpful, needs to ask whether the missing pieces could have been important.

Scope of the city's ecological footprint

One gap arises from the near-total absence from the workshop of reference to the 'ecological footprint' of cities, Fig. 33.1 (Wackernagel and Rees, 1996). Footprint investigations often have to focus on the links between cities and their surrounding support region, rather than on ecological functioning within the city, but close examination shows that footprints also tell us much about the metabolism of cities.

Consider, for example, the footprint associated with use and cycling of water in cities, from the conservation of water in source areas, beyond the city, to the disposal or reuse of wastewater (Postel, 1999) downstream from a city. A visit to any urban wastewater treatment plant, such as the one for Tel Aviv (a city in a desert; Fig. 33.2), reminds us of the hydrologic components of an ecological footprint, especially in a water-constrained environment. The planning and design of the regional system of water use and reuse, rural and urban together, shows this city's dependence on limited land upstream, as well as rural agriculture's dependence on urban wastewater supplies.

Another example can be seen in the release and transport of air pollutants in many urban and urban-to-rural environments. The emissions and their deposition tell us much about the ecological footprint of cities, as the city is usually

Fig. 33.1. The Ecological Footprint is a measure of the 'load' imposed by a given city or country on natural resources. It represents the land area necessary to sustain current levels of resource consumption and waste discharge by that population (after Wackernagel and Rees, 1996).

the source of pollutants, and rural areas are the sink. Adaptations made to automobile engines, and to stationary fossil-fuel burning facilities, have been designed to improve air renewal in the Los Angeles basin and have had moderate success. However, issues of cost and enforcement preclude the use of similar measures in urban areas such as Mexico City, Sao Paulo and Athens (see Fig. 33.3). The burden of urban pollutants is important, first and foremost for the health of the human population, but equally for the plants, birds and insect populations in the cities. These are all examples of how footprint analysis can lead to improved comparative study of cities and understanding of the interactions between cities and their resource support regions from around the globe.

Fig. 33.2. The wastewater stream from Tel Aviv, Israel, a water-limited site where the city depends on a limited share of available water supply, and the surrounding agricultural areas depend, in part, on treated waste water from the city.

The dynamics and functioning of water in cities

Because water functions so pervasively as the life-blood of ecosystems, terrestrial as well as aquatic, the details of human alterations of hydrologic cycling in cities can be seen as a guide to comparative ecology of cities. At a first order, cities such as Phoenix and Tel Aviv were at one time well-adapted to their limited water supplies. Other cities in the United States, southern Europe and Australia may have once believed they had plentiful water supplies for human use and nature's needs, but in recent years they have had to modify their urban infrastructure and water-use practices (hydrologic functioning) to adapt to new constraints on water supply. At the same time, many of these cities have found that expansion of urban land use (and the pavement and roof surfaces) has increased flood frequency in spite of expensive flood-prevention works. Sophisticated solutions, based on enhancement of ecological functioning, have great potential to solve flood and water supply problems, but urban institutions, with prior policies and priorities in place, would all have to make adjustments for such ecological solutions to work.

Water quality for full functioning of both human and natural systems also presents a challenge to comparative ecology of cities and towns. The broad picture includes increasingly serious disease risks in public water supplies, which are accommodated in developed countries by increasingly expensive

Fig. 33.3. Summertime air pollution over southern Greece and the Mediterranean Sea dimming the setting sun as seen from the Sanctuary of Poseidon, at Sounion, southeast of Athens.

systems for drinking water treatment. In arid regions, high salinity and low volume of return water following irrigation and local urban use are problems for the functioning of stream ecosystems. In many developing countries, however, degraded water quality leaves human populations and aquatic food resources at great risk from disease. These problems illustrate how a comparative ecology of cities may have to view humans as agents that are destructive of nature, while unmanaged nature's disease agents can be seen as destructive of the human community. Understanding the ecological balance among these forces, along with the role of economic development as the means for shaping and managing the balance of risks and benefits, is coming to be seen also as a part of comparative urban ecosystem ecology, a component that was hardly mentioned during the workshop.

The prospect of significant sea-level rise may be the ultimate water-related challenge for low-lying coastal cities. The city of Venice was noted during the meeting as the first city to begin an engineered adaptation to higher sea levels (only seasonally for now). However, the structures being built will lead to many other ecological responses within the urban-dominated lagoon complex. A comparative ecology of low-lying urban systems would greatly improve our global capacity to predict emerging ecological and human risks from these coastal engineering works.

An example of studies designed to predict coastal landscape change by modeling the effects of gradual sea level rise is available from the studies of Park *et al.* (1989). Their modelling of the effect of sea-level rise on low-lying Key Largo between 1987 and 2100 indicates that a median sea-level rise of 1 m would flood nearly all of the upland areas. Similar outcomes are projected for many low-lying Pacific Island communities and nations, and, importantly, for large coastal cities in the tropics where economic development may not be sufficient to pay for the engineering works that might protect the city from high flooding.

Dynamics of people, institutions and biological complexity in cities

For the third theme (Table 33.1), I looked for presentations on the internal patch dynamics (spatial demographics) of people in the cities, their institutions, and the biological complexity that people admire in cities. It should be axiomatic that comparative ecology of cities includes the temporal and spatial shifting of the human population over time, with its changing needs for services. Although transients in occupancy by humans have huge effects on surrounding resources, we heard only a few references to human demographics during the workshop, and these were mostly in relation to trends in the proper-ties of the urban watershed or in the growth of transportation systems and associated land-use change.

The dynamics across space and over time that characterise the biological complexity of cities were presented with sophistication and thoroughness in many papers, both at the Darwin symposium and at the Melbourne workshop. Perhaps the indigenous biological complexity is seen as a core subject for the ecology of cities, understood in terms of responses by the diverse native or introduced species sharing the environments of cities and towns with humans. But is this vision of ecology sufficient for a comparative ecology? Only a modest number of papers dealt analytically with causal agents that drive changes in biota of cities (such as habitat loss, nutrient enrichment and air pollutants). However, these alterations (or their absence) are central to understanding the responses of aquatic species and fauna such as birds, butterflies and urban soil organisms.

Probably more interesting in principle, but not covered in any detail, is what I have referred to in other papers (Loucks, 2001) as a metabolism of institutions that oversee and try to manage the landscapes of urban areas. The drinking water supply agency for New York City (Daily and Ellison, 2002), or the storm-water Management Commissions in Christchurch (Eason *et al.*, Chapter 27) probably exert a greater influence than any one physical factor on aquatic ecosystem functioning in these cities. Urban institutions can be a force for conservation, as in the watershed protection programs for the New York water supply (Daily and Ellison, 2002), or for impoverishment, when both groundwater and surface water flows are depleted as in Phoenix and Denver (Baron, 2002). Comparative ecology should include an assessment of ecological benefits (and risk of damages) stemming from the programmes and policies of resource-controlling agencies responsible for serving the area-wide 'public interest' of cities and towns.

Social and cultural needs and values of urban populations

Comparative ecology of cities also requires that we consider the social and cultural differences between cities, as these factors greatly influence the use or conservation of resources. Cultural traditions can be seen as both an historical and a modern expression of needs or expectations of the city and its people. The central challenge of such studies was presented by Ignatieva and Stewart (Chapter 23), contrasting patterns in use of urban landscaping, window-planters and other cultural–ecological resources in Moscow, Syracuse, USA, and Christchurch, New Zealand. The traditions in these cities have induced a unique urban ecology, but the reverse is true where a native ecology induces cultural traditions.

Another example of cultural expectations in urban ecology is illustrated by the 'dragonfly pond' created a few years ago in Yokohama, Japan (Loucks, 1994). The site had been a stormwater collection area surrounded by pavement and a roadside rock cut. However, given the importance of the dragonfly in art, litera-ture and spiritual traditions of the Japanese people, conversion of this small waste space into a living wetland and cultural symbol, with over 20 species of dragon-flies, was probably to be expected. Restoration of so many species, ecologically, was a great scientific challenge, but the reverence created for the site, through its richness and biological complexity, more than matched the scientific interest.

One should ask, also comparatively, what other cultures around the world would attach significance to such an unusual ecological system? Which cultures

Fig. 33.4. Far-sighted planning and good design often resolve conflicts between the needs of a human population and modified nature in urban areas, as illustrated here by a city with strong planning and design traditions, Toronto, Canada.

appreciate this kind of improvement in the quality of life for at least some of the local human population? Other cultures use their resources in ways that are important and unique to their society. Comparative ecology of cities will consider such knowledge and ensure a place for it, as we have sought to do in this book.

Designs for rationalising conflicts among priorities

Ultimately, a comparative ecology of cities will first document and understand the baseline resource states of these systems, and then plan for the protection of unique relationships among people, land, water, air and biological diversity in the city. All of these come together under the concept of urban planning and design for sustainable development, often with the idea of a sustainable ecological footprint (see Wackernagel and Rees, 1996). These steps for projecting future conditions, and planning and designing for desired outcomes, by themselves do not achieve resolution of conflicting priorities, but the process of planning and design helps. Issues of conflicting preferences for resource use are often rooted in differences between subsets of human needs desired by some, and the ecological goods and services sought for the essential human needs of others. Through strict planning, however, desired outcomes can be achieved, as has been illustrated by cities such as Toronto (Fig. 33.4) and the new urban areas of Shanghai.

Finally, it is knowledge of how the functioning of land, water, air and biological processes comes together to provide essential services to people that ensures long-term sustainability of these ecosystems. A comprehensive comparative ecology of cities and towns is needed to ensure that we develop that knowledge. The Melbourne workshop and this book have been a successful first step toward organising such knowledge.

34

Towards a comparative ecology of cities and towns

KIRSTEN PARRIS

Introduction

Much urban ecology to date has focused on the ecology of individual cities and towns, with limited comparison or synthesis of results. However, comparative studies between cities and between taxonomic groups are needed to improve our understanding of the structure and function of urban ecosystems, and to identify general principles such as patterns of biodiversity loss or changes to soil processes following urbanisation. The Melbourne Urban Ecology Workshop on the comparative ecology of cities and towns brought together researchers representing a diversity of continents, disciplinary backgrounds and approaches, with the aim of developing a conceptual and practical framework for comparative urban ecology. This broad mix of cultures and perspectives made for a very stimulating workshop, but on occasion it also led to some confusion and disagreement. I have based my summary on four themes that emerged from the workshop; definitions, diversity, tools and approaches, and identifying the common elements of cities and towns. I have also included an example of a comparative, urban ecological study using tools and approaches presented during the workshop in conjunction with established ecological theory.

Definitions

What is urban ecology and how do we do it? How should we define urban, suburban, peri-urban, rural? What is an urban ecosystem? Much time has

Ecology of Cities and Towns: A Comparative Approach, ed. Mark J. McDonnell, Amy K. Hahs and Jürgen H. Breuste. Published by Cambridge University Press. © Cambridge University Press 2009.

been spent and a number of papers written on questions such as these in recent years (e.g., McIntyre *et al.*, 2000; Collins *et al.*, 2000; Pickett *et al.*, 2001), and they were points of discussion and contention during the workshop. Urban ecology is regarded by some researchers as the ecology of the urban 'core' only – areas devoid of original vegetation and dominated by concrete, asphalt and buildings (e.g. Wittig, Chapter 30). In contrast, other researchers include all aspects of cities and towns (streets, industrial areas, private gardens, parks and remnant woodlands) and all species and habitats affected by the urban ecosystem (e.g. a city's water catchments, estuaries polluted by storm water and effluent) within the scope of urban ecology (e.g. Carreiro *et al.*, Chapter 19; Pouyat *et al.*, Chapter 20). Another dichotomy has been established between ecology in cities and ecology of cities, with the former focusing on the effects of urbanisation on species, habitats, climate, ecological patterns and processes within a city, and the latter focusing on entire cities, or cities as ecosystems (Grimm *et al.*, 2000; Pickett *et al.*, 2001). The two approaches differ largely in scale, although it has been argued that ecology of cities will best serve the integration of the biophysical and social sciences in urban ecology (Pickett *et al.*, 2001).

Urban, suburban and related categories can be defined in many ways – by the size or density of the human population, the proportion of impermeable surface in the landscape, time since urbanisation, or distance to the centre of the city (see review by McIntyre *et al.*, 2000). Pursuit of universally accepted definitions to be used in all urban ecological studies is unnecessary and maybe even pointless, as definitions will change with the questions being asked and the scale of a study. However, as advocated by McIntyre *et al.* (2000), it is important that the definitions used are both clear and quantitative to allow replication of the methods of a study and comparison between studies. It may be that the most effective comparative studies will be those designed as comparative from the outset, so the methods and definitions used are consistent across the different study sites or cities. *Post-hoc* comparisons or meta-analyses of different urban ecological studies are less likely to be successful.

Diversity

As mentioned in the introduction, the participants in the workshop represented a broad diversity of urban ecologists. This diversity could be classified in many ways, such as by geographical origin, interests, experience or disciplinary background (e.g. ecology, urban planning, conservation biology, forestry, soil science, ecotoxicology). However, I think that the most important difference between participants was that of motivation. Our reasons for studying urban ecology ranged from an interest in the structure of urban landscapes or assemblages of non-native plants that establish on vacant blocks (spontaneous vegetation; Wittig, 1998), through to the desire to conserve indigenous species and communities that are threatened by urbanisation. These different motivations were difficult to reconcile at times, particularly during discussions aimed at identifying important questions and emphases for future research. I believe that diversity provides interest, strength and a foundation for advances in the discipline, as long as it does not lead to division. Cities and towns are complex systems imposed upon complex natural or agricultural landscapes, and we would not expect a single approach to suit all questions and aspects of urban ecology.

Tools and approaches

The spoken and poster papers at the workshop presented a range of tools for and approaches to urban ecology, many of which draw on theory developed within other areas of ecology and environmental science. These include urban–rural gradients (McDonnell and Pickett, 1990), based on the gradient paradigm of Whittaker (1967); biotope mapping, based on the European concept of the biotope (Udvardy, 1959); analysis of urban landscape patterns (landscape ecology); analysis of ecological footprints (sustainability theory; Wackernagel and Yount, 1998); habitat modelling (niche theory; Hutchinson, 1957); and mathematical modelling of biotic processes such as dispersal, local extinction and colonisation (metapopulation and metacommunity theory; Levins, 1969; Gilpin and Hanski, 1991). There was some discussion about which tools we should be using, and whether some were outdated and/or less appropriate for comparative urban ecology than others. I think that the question is not whether we should still be using urban–rural gradients, but which tool or approach is most suitable for the question at hand.

Common elements of cities and towns

All cities differ in some way, such as the size of their human population, or their history, culture or biodiversity. European cities tend to be compact, while those in the United States and Australia tend to sprawl over a large geographical area. Cities in developing countries may have a substantial proportion of their human population housed in makeshift dwellings without running water or sanitation, and constructed without planning controls. Other cities are carefully planned to maintain areas of open space and natural vegetation. People have built cities across a wide latitudinal gradient from the tropics to sub-polar regions, in a corresponding diversity of climates and ecosystems. However, preoccupation with differences can lead to paralysis. Despite their differences, cities share many common features or elements such as houses, lawns, roads, industrial areas, native plants and animals, waterways, weeds, nutrients, pollution and a variegated, patchy landscape. These features are largely independent of the original ecosystem or the climate in which a city is built, and can be used as a basis for comparison (e.g. Grimm *et al.*, 2000; Niemelä *et al.*, 2002).

Even though different cities are constructed on or amongst the habitat of different suites of plant and animal species, these species can be placed into functional or taxonomic groups with broad representation such as predators, herbivores, nitrogen fixers, pollinators, amphibians, bats, trees, grasses and bryophytes. The geology and original hydrology may differ between cities, but all cities have soil and streams that are subject to similar processes such as compaction, nutrient deposition and pollution. General principles of urban ecology will emerge through broadly applicable comparative studies, and these must account for the differences between cities in a meaningful and relevant way to allow a focus on the similarities of interest. A classification of cities on one or two appropriate variables can also be used to identify hypotheses and useful comparative questions for further investigation.

Example: the response of garden gnomes to habitat loss and fragmentation in urban environments

Introduction

Originating in Scandinavia (Nuygen and Poortvliet, 1977), garden gnomes are now a common element of many cities throughout the world. The group has undergone a remarkable adaptive radiation in the past 1600 years, and currently consists of approximately 120 recognised species. However, all garden gnomes still use human-constructed gardens for at least part of their life cycle (the ancestral condition). In many countries, the increasing density of human dwellings in cities and towns and changing fashions in garden design are leading to the loss and fragmentation of habitat for garden gnomes. Networks of large gardens with lawns, herbaceous borders, established trees and dense shrubbery are being fragmented by medium- to high-density developments with small courtyard gardens or balconies that typically support only a lemon tree in a half-barrel and some potted herbs. Furthermore, the large gardens that do persist are undergoing dramatic structural changes with the expansion of paved areas, removal of trees, and a proliferation of water features and Balinese-style summer houses.

We must consider both the differences and similarities between garden gnomes in different cities when designing a comparative study of their response to habitat loss and fragmentation in urban environments. I have chosen to

Fig. 34.1. Some species of garden gnomes known from urban habitats: (a) the family gnome *Gnomus gregarius*, (b) the fishing gnome *G. piscatorius*, (c) the sleeping gnome *G. somnolus*, (d) the minstrel gnome *G. musicalus*, (e) the gardening gnome *G. hortulanus*, f) the football gnome *G. sporticus*. Part (c) reproduced with permission from Lori and John Ford of 'Gnomes, Pixies and More' (http://www.gnomespixiesandmore.com).

classify garden gnomes along two axes or gradients: social organisation (solitary species to those that live in extended family groups) and activity level (sleeping to playing football and fishing). Based on this classification, I hypothesise:

(1)   That social species will be affected by habitat loss and fragmentation more than solitary species, because they require a larger area of suitable garden habitat (social species are less likely to occur in small habitat patches).

(2)   That sedentary species will be affected more than active species with greater capabilities for dispersal between habitat patches (sedentary species are less likely to occur in isolated habitat patches).

Thus, I predict that social, sedentary species such as the family gnome *Gnomus gregarius* from Central and South America (Fig. 34.1a) will suffer local extinction in small and/or isolated patches of garden habitat, while solitary, active species such as the fishing gnome *G. piscatorius* from Britain and western Europe (Fig. 34.1b) will persist in fragmented urban landscapes. Solitary, sedentary species (such as the sleeping gnome *G. somnolus*, ubiquitous; Fig. 34.1c) should continue to inhabit small garden patches if they are not isolated from other suitable patches. Social, active species such as the minstrel gnome *G. musicalus* (Fig. 34.1d) will persist in large patches, both connected and isolated. I am publishing these predictions prior to data collection, so their accuracy can be assessed with the results of the study (after Mac Nally and Bennett, 1997; Mac Nally *et al.*, 2000).

Methods

In collaboration with five colleagues, I have chosen 20 cities where large gardens are being subdivided for medium- and high-density housing developments: Canberra, Melbourne, Auckland, Jakarta, Bangkok, Shanghai, Cairo, Johannesburg, Madrid, Lyon, Warsaw, Bristol, Edinburgh, Reykjavik, Boston, Seattle, Atlanta, Mexico City, Sao Paulo and Bogota. In each city, we will survey garden gnomes in 25 patches of garden habitat. The patches will range in size from 25 to 5000 m², and be situated along an urban–rural gradient defined by the proportion of impermeable surface in a 500-m radius around their perimeter (a measure of isolation). Each patch will be surveyed three times by a team of four people using diurnal searches, giving a total of 1500 gnome searches across 500 patches. Repeat surveys are needed to account for the variation in activity, and thus detectability, of some species.

Each species of garden gnome detected during the study will be classified on two variables describing their social organisation and activity level: average size of social group and average distance moved each day. Data on the daily movements and dispersal distances of most species of garden gnomes are readily available, because of the gnomes' habit of sending postcards from their destinations, while information on the size of social groups will be gathered during the survey. Species with an average social group of ≤ 2 individuals will be classified as solitary, and those that live in groups ≥ 10 as social. Species that move an average of ≤ 20 m per day will be classified as sedentary, and those that move ≥ 200 m per day as mobile. If hypothesis 1 were correct, we would expect patch size to have a greater effect on the probability of occurrence of social species than solitary species. If hypothesis 2 were correct, we would expect patch isolation to have a greater effect on the probability of occurrence of sedentary species than mobile species. Evidence in support of the two hypotheses will be assessed using four logistic regression models (Hosmer and Lemeshow, 1989) which will estimate the probability of occurrence of solitary and social species as a function of patch size, and sedentary and mobile species as a function of patch isolation (the proportion of impermeable surface in a 500-m radius around the patch).

Towards a comparative ecology of cities and towns

We have the knowledge, the conceptual and theoretical frameworks, the tools and the enthusiasm to undertake comparative studies that will help to identify and consolidate general principles of urban ecology. As we found during the workshop, the different interests, perspectives and motivations of urban ecologists make it unlikely that we will all agree on which comparative questions to address first. One way forward may be to form smaller research groups focused on different aspects of urban ecology, such as landscape ecology, population ecology, sociology and conservation biology. Each group could then identify a series of important questions to address in the first instance. I envisage that these groups would consist both of participants of the Melbourne Urban Ecology Workshop and of interested people who did not attend.

Summary

In summary, I have identified eight steps to successful comparative research in urban ecology:

(1) Stop arguing about definitions of urban or urban ecology.
(2) Accept diversity in the field of urban ecology, including diversity of interests, motivations, and disciplinary backgrounds.
(3) Form partnerships or research groups based on a common interest, motivation, or scale of investigation to focus on different aspects of urban ecology.
(4) Choose questions that compare the common elements of cities such as street trees, landscape structure, energy consumption, soil nutrient cycling, aquatic invertebrates or parasitic birds, while accounting for relevant differences between cities that are not the focus of the study.
(5) Identify an appropriate conceptual or theoretical framework derived from ecology, social science and/or the physical sciences.
(6) Choose local, national and/or international collaborators – these may be within or outside your own traditional discipline.
(7) Define terms and choose methods that are appropriate to the questions being asked – these may include tools and approaches that have or have not previously been used in urban ecological studies.
(8) Enjoy the intellectual challenge and stimulation of collaborative, comparative research!

35

A comparative ecology of cities and towns: synthesis of opportunities and limitations

AMY K. HAHS, MARK J. MCDONNELL AND JÜRGEN H. BREUSTE

Introduction

Over the past 20 years the study of urban ecology has made great progress. Our understanding of urban ecosystems and their influence on ecological patterns and processes is advancing to where we can begin to formulate some generalities. Many of these advances in understanding have been due to comparative studies at a local scale, such as those using a gradient approach within a metropolitan area. However, very few of the studies to date have taken a regional or global comparative approach, and therefore, many remain as little more than case studies. Comparative research between urban areas will allow us to test the applicability of these findings and generalities in cities with different social, historical and environmental contexts. They can also identify new research questions and help focus research on important components of urban ecosystems that require further attention (McDonnell and Hahs, Chapter 5; Lehvävirta and Kotze, Chapter 31). The aim of this book, and the workshops leading up to it, was to begin a dialogue on the value (i.e. opportunities and challenges) of comparative studies in advancing our knowledge of ecology in cities and towns, and how we might begin to foster a larger number of regional and global comparative studies. Therefore, this book should be seen as an exploration of the work that has been done so far, and a discussion about how we might move our science forward. From its conception, this book was designed to

Ecology of Cities and Towns: A Comparative Approach, ed. Mark J. McDonnell, Amy K. Hahs and Jürgen H. Breuste. Published by Cambridge University Press. © Cambridge University Press 2009.

explore how urban ecological research has been undertaken to date, what has been learnt, and where there are gaps in our knowledge. From this common understanding, we can then identify areas where we can perform comparative research both within and between cities to gain a more comprehensive understanding of the ecology of cities and towns. This will then enable us to identify strategies for developing more sustainable human settlements in the future.

As stated in the introductory chapter (McDonnell *et al.*, Chapter 1), we had three major goals in compiling this book: (1) to evaluate the current state of understanding regarding the ecology of cities and towns around the world, and the methodologies used to obtain this information; (2) to provide examples of how ecological information has been effectively integrated into urban management and planning schemes; and (3) to explore the opportunities and challenges of developing a regional and global comparative approach to the ecological study of cities and towns. In this chapter we will attempt to synthesise the major points that have been brought up in these three areas within the contributed chapters, and outline some directions for future opportunities for urban ecological research and the integration of scientific understanding into landscape and urban design.

Current approaches to studying the ecology of cities and towns

As identified in many chapters, urbanisation is occurring at a rapid rate across the globe. Understanding its impact on the ecology of these areas will help to identify measures that can be taken to minimise the detrimental effects on ecological patterns and processes. Urbanisation also presents an opportunity to test how well general ecological theories hold up in systems that have been highly modified by human actions (McDonnell and Pickett, 1990; Pickett *et al.*, Chapter 3).

This book has presented examples of many different studies which have been undertaken in urban ecosystems. These examples show the range and diversity of methodologies being employed and the variety of ecosystems and ecosystem components being investigated. This section will look at the major points regarding methods and tools currently being used in urban ecological studies.

Conceptual frameworks, models and theories

A variety of conceptual frameworks and other conceptual tools have been identified and described throughout the book. Pickett *et al.* (Chapter 3) began the discussion with a review of the role of frameworks, models and theories within scientific research. The role of models was further expanded upon by McCarthy (Chapter 7). The major frameworks and approaches that have been used repeatedly throughout this book include: urban–rural (urbanisation) gradients (Niemelä *et al.*, Chapter 2; Pickett *et al.*, Chapter 3; Carreiro *et al.*, Chapter 19; Pouyat *et al.*,

Chapter 20); patch dynamics (Pickett *et al.*, Chapter 3; Nilon, Chapter 10; Pouyat *et al.*, Chapter 20); the human ecosystem framework (Niemelä *et al.*, Chapter 2; Pickett *et al.*, Chapter 3; Cilliers *et al.*, Chapter 6; Lehvävirta and Kotze, Chapter 31); conceptual frameworks proposed by Grimm *et al.* (2000) (Cilliers *et al.*, Chapter 6), McKinney (2002) (Zipperer and Guntenspergen, Chapter 17) and Alberti *et al.* (2003) (Chapter 17); the watershed approach (Pouyat *et al.*, Chapter 20); landscape ecology and habitat fragmentation (Chapman *et al.*, Chapter 9; Natuhara and Hashimoto, Chapter 12); the ecology 'in' and 'of' cities (Niemelä *et al.*, Chapter 2; Nilon, Chapter 10; Hochuli *et al.*, Chapter 13; Parris, Chapter 34); island biogeography (Lehvävirta and Kotze, Chapter 31); metapopulation dynamics (Chapter 31); intermediate disturbance hypothesis (Chapter 31); succession (Chapter 31) and the pattern:process metaphor (Musacchio, Chapter 28). Of these conceptual tools, two have made a major contribution to the field of urban ecology, as evidenced by their recurrence throughout this book. Therefore, we will briefly examine the benefits and limitations of the ecology 'in' versus ecology 'of' cities approaches and the human ecosystem framework, particularly with respect to the points raised by various authors throughout this book.

Ecology 'in' versus ecology 'of' cities

Since the initial publication of the paper by Grimm *et al.* (2000) which proposed that there is a distinction between ecology 'in' cities and the ecology 'of' cities, there has been much discussion about the role of these two approaches in advancing our understanding of urban ecology. However, the majority of research published continues to fall under the umbrella of ecology 'in' cities, with very few studies successfully implementing an ecology 'of' cities approach. Several authors in this volume have suggested reasons why there has been little uptake of this research approach, even though the concept itself has been widely accepted (McDonnell *et al.*, Chapter 1; Niemelä *et al.*, Chapter 2; McDonnell and Hahs, Chapter 5; Nilon, Chapter 10; Hochuli *et al.*, Chapter 13; Parris, Chapter 34). One of the main reasons for a lack of uptake has been that our current under-standing of the ecological components of cities does not match the complexity and detail of understanding that we currently have for the socio-economic components of urban systems. However, while ecology 'of' cities has not been widely adopted as a primary scientific approach, several authors have stated that they believe that our increasing understanding of ecology 'in' cities will help to build our understanding of the ecology 'of' cities.

Human ecosystem framework

The human ecosystem model (Pickett *et al.*, 2001) has also received considerable attention within the published literature, as well as within individual chapters of this book (Niemelä *et al.*, Chapter 2; Pickett *et al.*, Chapter 3; Lehvävirta and Kotze, Chapter 31). However, while the ideas have been widely accepted within the discipline of urban ecology, their uptake in specific research projects has been limited. Niemelä *et al.* (Chapter 2) examined the applicability of this approach to the city of Helsinki, Finland. They found that while some components are useful, there were others that needed to be altered to make them relevant in a new setting.

Research methods

A variety of methods have been employed by the studies presented in this book to investigate the influence of urbanisation on the ecology of cities and towns. Most of these methods have been developed and are used regularly within the wider fields of ecology and landscape design and management. This reflects the move from viewing ecology as a study of pristine ecosystems (McDonnell *et al.*, 1993) to a field that studies all ecosystems, regardless of the degree of human influence and modification. These methods include the use of quantitative models (McCarthy, Chapter 7), intensive and extensive field surveys (Meurk *et al.*, Chapter 18; Pouyat *et al.*, Chapter 20), nested hierarchical sampling designs (Pouyat *et al.*, Chapter 20), urbanisation gradients (Niemelä *et al.*, Chapter 2; Carreiro *et al.*, Chapter 19; Pouyat *et al.*, Chapter 20; Florgård, Chapter 22; Lehvävirta and Kotze, Chapter 31), progressive research which builds upon the findings of previous studies (Catterall, Chapter 8), experiments in the field and lab (Chapman and Underwood, Chapter 4; Catterall, Chapter 8; van der Ree, Chapter 11; Carreiro *et al.*, Chapter 19; Florgård, Chapter 22), multi-variate classification and ordination (Catterall, Chapter 8), meta-analysis (Hochuli *et al.*, Chapter 13), and GIS (Florgård, Chapter 22; Ignatieva and Stewart, Chapter 23; Löfvenhaft, Chapter 24; Mörtberg, Chapter 25; Snep *et al.*, Chapter 26; Guntenspergen *et al.*, Chapter 29). We will briefly look at two of these methodological tools in more detail as they have been used extensively in previous studies and are important to the development of a regional and global comparative approach to the study of the ecology of cities and towns.

Urbanisation (urban–rural) gradients

The urban–rural gradient has been widely implemented as a research approach since the concept was first presented by McDonnell and Pickett (1990). Recently, the utility of the approach has been more widely recognised and the concept of the 'urban–rural gradient' has been expanded and replaced by the idea of 'urbanisation gradients'. As described by McDonnell and Hahs (Chapter 5), the study of urbanisation gradients provides many opportunities for local and regional comparisons within a single city or town, as well as comparisons between gradients created by different cities and towns. Several chapters in this book employed the gradient approach in their studies (Pickett *et al.*, Chapter 3; McDonnell and Hahs, Chapter 5; Carreiro *et al.*, Chapter 19; Pouyat *et al.*, Chapter 20), and several additional chapters contributed discussion points around their use (e.g. Niemelä *et al.*, Chapter 2). Some of the issues that were raised are that (1) the relationship between the gradient and the response variable is correlative, rather than causative, in nature (Catterall, Chapter 8; Pouyat *et al.*, Chapter 20); (2) some of the measures applied to describe the gradient have been too simplistic, thereby limiting the opportunities to develop and test hypotheses about causal mechanisms (Catterall, Chapter 8; Lehvävirta and Kotze, Chapter 31); (3) the gradient may be correlated with underlying environmental gradients (Chapter 8); and (4) variability in the non-urban end of the gradient may reduce its ability to act as a reference system (Chapter 8).

Owing to the widespread uptake of the urbanisation gradient approach in ecology, it is worth discussing these issues in more detail, as they represent areas where the implementation of the approach can be refined and improved. The first two points are related but it is worth discussing each on its own merit. The correlative nature of the findings from urbanisation gradient studies is an important point, especially as the implications for applying the findings without verifying the causative mechanisms could lead to unsatisfactory outcomes (Chapter 8). This highlights the importance of recognising that the urbanisation gradient approach is most suitable during the initial exploratory phase of research, when there is little known about the system. As in other gradient studies in ecology, the information revealed by urbanisation gradient studies can provide a solid foundation that can inform future correlative or experimental studies.

If the initial gradient has been defined too simplistically, there will be less information about which variables associated with urbanisation are worth focusing on. This can lead to difficulties in moving away from correlative relationships to more causative understandings. For example, if the initial gradient study defined the gradient as distance from the Central Business District (CBD), it will be more difficult to focus in on a particular component of the gradient as it could be related to any number of aspects of urbanisation. In contrast, if the initial gradient study had defined the gradient using the density of the human population and the density of roads, and had found a stronger correlation with the density of roads, it would then become possible to focus in on the aspects of the road network that are likely to be influencing the observed patterns. Therefore, for the same amount of effort in the initial study, you end up with a stronger indication of the direction future research should take. This links in with the points raised by McDonnell and Hahs (Chapter 5), who propose that the measures used to define the gradient can generally be categorised as either broad measures of urbanisation or as specific measures of urbanisation, both of which have their benefits and down sides.

The third issue around the urbanisation gradient approach relates to the possibility of the gradient being superimposed upon an underlying environmental gradient, especially in cities located on the coast or at the mouth of a river (Catterall, Chapter 8). This is again an important point, as drawing a conclusion about the patterns being related to urbanisation may lead to unsatisfactory outcomes when attempting to mitigate the effects of the urbanisation gradient. One potential way of addressing this is to include the potential underlying gradient as a predictive variable in the analysis of the data, and then evaluate the evidence for the ecological response being related to the environmental gradient against the evidence that it is related to the urbanisation gradient.

The fourth issue identified is that the sites at the rural end of the gradient may show too much variability to act as a reliable reference system (Catterall, Chapter 8). This point could possibly be addressed by including alternative explanatory variables in the analysis of the gradient, as suggested for the previous issues. It may also be a variable that is worth explicitly testing, as several authors have proposed that one of the ecological effects of urbanisation is the homogenisation of the biota (McKinney, 2004, 2006; Schwartz et al., 2006).

Geographic information systems

Geographic information systems (GIS) are a powerful tool for conserving biodiversity in urban environments (Florgård, Chapter 22). They have been used in visualising the spatial and temporal aspects of biodiversity in relation to planning applications; in developing predictive tools such as expert-based models (Mörtberg, Chapter 25; Snep et al., Chapter 26), scenario creation and testing (Mörtberg, Chapter 25) and decision support models to assess the consequences of specific development proposals (Guntenspergen et al., Chapter 29); and as a research tool for combining field survey data with additional data sources (Löfvenhaft, Chapter 24) that can act as input for spatially explicit analyses. The flexibility of GIS and the growing availability of digital spatial data present many opportunities to expand the research approaches being undertaken within this field and many others. Indeed, GIS is a key tool for addressing many of the issues identified in the discussion of urbanisation gradients, as it aids the characterisation of landscapes and the quantification of urbanisation within the study area, and between individual study sites. This characterisation and quantification is essential to developing a comparative approach between cities and towns. It can also act as a long-term data repository, as the data collected for previous studies remain available in an easily accessible form, which can be easily integrated into subsequent studies.

The potential obstacles to a more widespread use of GIS technology include a lack of basic spatial databases particularly in developing regions (Pickett *et al.*, Chapter 3; Cilliers *et al.*, Chapter 6); the efficiency and cost of using existing datasets combined with the general absence of specifically tailored spatial datasets; the costs involved in purchasing and licensing the major GIS software products and the acquisition of some spatial datasets; and the need for a minimum level of technical expertise – whether it is obtained through training existing personnel, hiring new staff, or collaborating with other research groups which have that expertise. Most of these obstacles are likely to be reduced as the use of GIS becomes more widespread and the accompanying investment in spatial data is increased, but other obstacles are better addressed by building a GIS component into funding applications and research proposals, particularly in the short term.

An additional benefit of an increased uptake of GIS is the potential to undertake local, regional and global comparative work more easily, as study sites would already be mapped, and common datasets could be applied across several studies to produce a common measure for meta-analyses, or even for studies that are explicitly comparative in their design. Spatial datasets are also easily shared between researchers, and well-constructed datasets can be submitted as data papers to journals such as *Ecological Archives*, thereby aiding in greater data exchange between researchers around the world.

Selection and measurement of dependent and independent variables

When conducting comparative research at the local, regional or global scale, the selection of measures used to characterise both the independent (predictor) and dependent (response) variables in a study, and the methods used to define those measures, become critical considerations (McDonnell and Hahs, Chapter 5; Catterall, Chapter 8; Nilon, Chapter 10; Hochuli *et al.*, Chapter 13; Pouyat *et al.*, Chapter 20; Parris, Chapter 34). Several chapters in this book identified the need to characterise cities objectively (Chapter 5; Nilon, Chapter 10; Hochuli *et al.*, Chapter 13; Parris, Chapter 34), and others provided examples of the measures which are currently in common use, including: biotopes (Nilon, Chapter 10; Löfvenhaft, Chapter 24); ecological landscape units (Breuste, Chapter 21); land cover (Catterall, Chapter 8) and vegetation cover (Yang and Zhou, Chapter 16); as well as a number of physical and demographic measures (McDonnell and Hahs, Chapter 5).

The previous measures can be used as either independent (predictor) variables or dependent (response) variables. The selection of measures used to characterise more ecological response variables was also discussed throughout the book. Some of the measures used to examine ecological responses included carbon and nitrogen cycling (Carreiro *et al.*, Chapter 19), trophic structures and functional groups (Catterall, Chapter 8; Hochuli *et al.*, Chapter 13), urbanophilous, urbanoneutral and urbanophobic species (Lehvävirta and Kotze, Chapter 31), and basic community measures such as species richness or abundance (Catterall, Chapter 8). The selection of measures and techniques used to quantify them requires similar attention if we are to move towards a more regionally and globally comparative ecology. Moving away from defining biotic assemblages in terms of broad community metrics (e.g. species richness, abundance, diversity) and towards using more functional definitions has been advocated by several authors, as the outcomes between studies have been more consistent (Marzluff, 2001; Catterall, Chapter 8), and it will make it easier to move towards a more mechanistic understanding of urban ecology (Shochat *et al.*, 2006).

In selecting the measures used for their study, several authors discussed issues that were considered during the selection process. For example, Löfven-haft (Chapter 24) discussed the difficulty of applying biotopes due to the lack of standardised methods to obtain them, Breuste (Chapter 21) highlighted the difficulties of using broad and undefined terms such as vegetation structure and soil sealing, and Catterall (Chapter 8) noted that land-use planning zones are not globally consistent, and other measures may be of limited use as their functionality may vary between regions. The lack of standardised terminology will be discussed further when we present some ideas on ways to move forward.

In selecting measures, the criteria that were considered to be important included the need for measures to be ecologically meaningful, to be measured at the correct scale, and ideally to have the ability to capture changes in the magnitude and scale of environmental variation between studies (Catterall, Chapter 8). It is also important that the measures be reliable, uniform and cost-effective (Yang and Zhou, Chapter 16) and that we develop an understanding of how the measures perform in terms of scale, redundancy and autocorrelation (Mörtberg, Chapter 25).

Another important consideration that was repeatedly identified was the need to include more specific measures in the group of predictor variables, such as the environmental context (e.g. desert or temperate biomes) (McIntyre and Rango, Chapter 14), geographical and environmental factors (Pouyat *et al.*, Chapter 20), and more direct measures of urbanisation (e.g. pollution, nutrient levels) (Catterall, Chapter 8).

As articulated by Parris (Chapter 34), until we have a greater understanding of the potential information that can be gained by using specific measures within a study, it will remain very important to define the terminology and methodology used in a study, including a definition of what is meant by the term 'urban' (McIntyre *et al.*, 2000).

Planning, design and management

Communication was identified as a crucial component for integrating scientific research into the planning arena. Strategies for improving this communication included using urban structural units as a unit of study as they translate easily into planning and management (Breuste, Chapter 21); applying the pattern:process metaphor to help communicate how human decisions affect landscape (Musacchio, Chapter 28); improving the translation of scientific papers into a format that is accessible to practitioners so that the information is more widely available (Nilsson and Florgård, Chapter 32); and using the term 'preservation of vegetation' when discussing natural areas in urban ecosystems, as the term is more active than 'remnant natural vegetation' and thus allows a greater dialogue between researchers and practitioners (Florgård, Chapter 22). The concept of Low Impact Urban Design and Development (LIUDD; Eason *et al.*, Chapter 27), and the application of an Urban Ecological Integrity Index (UEII; Cilliers *et al.*, Chapter 6), were also identified as tools for communicating objectives within the planning arena.

Within the planning process itself, there are key phases where there is the greatest opportunity for scientific input. These are decision-making, planning and design (Florgård, Chapter 22), and there are a number of tools that can be used to increase uptake of scientific knowledge, including economic instruments (Eason *et al.*, Chapter 27), policy frameworks (Eason *et al.*, Chapter 27) and strategic plans (Nilsson and Florgård, Chapter 32). However, the outcomes for preserving vegetation are also improved by the project management component of the construction process through both the design and timing of construction activities, and the creation of a workplace where everyone shares the goals of preserving vegetation (Florgård, Chapter 22).

The design of urban ecosystems occurs at many different levels. Preserving remnant vegetation (Florgård, Chapter 22) and encouraging the use of indigenous plants through education (Meurk *et al.*, Chapter 18) or plant signatures (Ignatieva and Stewart, Chapter 23) were identified as a few of the tools available that discourage homogeneous landscape designs and help express a sense of local and national identity within the urban area. At the landscape scale, the use of corridors (Florgård, Chapter 22) and landscape ecological analysis methods (Mörtberg, Chapter 25) were identified as tools available for obtaining ecological outcomes at the landscape scale. The importance of a 'learning by doing' approach was also identified by Snep *et al.* (Chapter 26).

The ongoing management of preserved natural vegetation in urban areas, and the associated biotic assemblages and ecological processes were also discussed throughout this book. In particular, the use of monitoring was identified as an important tool for achieving our objectives. Key elements to include in the design of monitoring projects include replicated reference and control sites (Lehvävirta and Kotze, Chapter 31); the use of broad functional groups rather than specific species (Hochuli et al., Chapter 13); and the potential for invertebrates to reveal important information about the ecological processes at a site (Hochuli et al., Chapter 13; McIntyre and Rango, Chapter 14).

Geographic Information Systems were also identified as an important tool, for many of the same reasons discussed above. These include the opportunities to evaluate planning decisions (Florgård, Chapter 22; Guntenspergen et al., Chapter 29) and to combine biological information across space and time to develop outcomes with a stronger biodiversity gain (Löfvenhaft, Chapter 24).

Education

In terms of increasing awareness of the potential for maintaining biodiversity in cities, the role of urban natural areas in the education process was highlighted by a number of authors (Hochuli et al., Chapter 13; Meurk et al., Chapter 18; Florgård, Chapter 22). The value of urban natural areas was largely due to their proximity to where people live and work, and therefore the opportunity they provide to raise the profile of natural systems within the wider community. That is why areas of natural vegetation in urban ecosystems, even if they are not pristine or of high conservation significance, still offer a valuable contribution to society through the recreational and educational opportunities they provide (McDonnell, 2007).

In summary, as pointed out by Parris (Chapter 34), there are a range of tools available for studies of urban ecology and their utility has been demonstrated. However, rather than trying to move towards a single standardised set of tools, the most successful approach will be to continue applying the tool or approach that is most suitable for addressing specific questions of interest.

Current state of understanding of ecology of cities and towns

As identified in the introductory chapter (McDonnell et al., Chapter 1), one of the goals of this book was to capture the current state of understanding around the ecology of cities and towns. In addition to presenting their own individual research, many of the chapter authors have also summarised the state of knowledge for their particular sub-discipline. One of the strengths of this book is that it is not limited to terrestrial systems, but also includes examples from marine and freshwater ecosystems (Chapman and Underwood, Chapter 4; Chapman et al., Chapter 9; Guntenspergen et al., Chapter 29), with research focuses varying from carbon and nitrogen cycling (Carreiro et al., Chapter 19;

Pouyat *et al.*, Chapter 20) to landscape patterns (Yang and Zhou, Chapter 16; Zipperer and Guntenspergen, Chapter 17), to organisms from invertebrates (Chapman *et al.*, Chapter 9; Hochuli *et al.*, Chapter 13; McIntyre and Rango, Chapter 14; Eisenbeis and Hänel, Chapter 15) to birds and mammals (Catterall, Chapter 8; Nilon, Chapter 10; van der Ree, Chapter 11; Natuhara and Hashimoto, Chapter 12). As discussed by Florgård (Chapter 22), until recently there has been a lack of overlap between the work performed in Europe and that performed in North America. This book is perhaps unique in that it has contributions from different regions around the world including Europe, Asia, Africa, North America, Australia and New Zealand. It is also unique because it explicitly recognises the local comparative approach that has been used by many researchers and encourages the development of a more regional/global comparative approach to develop a greater understanding of the ecology of cities and towns in the future (McDonnell and Hahs, Chapter 5).

Some of the lessons that can be pulled out of these collected chapters are that while generalities can begin to be developed for some species, such as birds (Catterall, Chapter 8), and intertidal and subtidal marine assemblages around Sydney Harbour (Chapman *et al.*, Chapter 9), there are other areas where the generalities do not hold between studies, such as patterns of nutrient cycling between the New York metropolitan area and Louisville urbanisation gradients (Carreiro *et al.*, Chapter 19). It will be through the identification of these knowledge gaps that we can really expand our understanding of the ecology of cities and towns. In some cases, undertaking an explicitly regional/global comparative approach will help to identify and address these knowledge gaps.

Examples of regionally or globally comparative work

While most of the research to date could be considered to be local comparative studies, there are several examples of where researchers have undertaken regional/global comparative studies, or have made suggestions as to how existing research could be expanded to a more global comparative approach. Examples of global comparative studies presented in this book include comparing the applicability of the human ecosystem model developed for Baltimore to the urban areas of Helsinki (Niemelä *et al.*, Chapter 2) and Potchefstroom (Cilliers *et al.*, Chapter 6); comparing the utility of landscape fragmentation theories in terrestrial and marine systems (Chapman and Underwood, Chapter 4); comparing landscape patterns between cities for both vegetation cover (Yang and Jinxing, Chapter 16) and forest patches (Zipperer and Guntenspergen, Chapter 17); comparing nutrient cycling between cities (Carreiro *et al.*, Chapter 19; Pouyat *et al.*, Chapter 20); and comparing the distribution of organisms such as carabid beetles (Niemelä *et al.*, Chapter 2) and birds (Nilon, Chapter 10) between cities. These studies have been invaluable in indentifying where patterns remain constant between cities or ecosystems, and where the effects have been modified by the context in which the study was performed. Examples of potential global comparative projects for future research include a study of bird assemblages across Europe, North America and Australia in patches with similar origins and management histories but different historical and environmental contexts (Nilon, Chapter 10); comparing human pressure on ecosystems by examining the spatial structure of ecosystems, rates of change over time, and quality of change based on urban structural units (Breuste, Chapter 21); comparing biodiversity within and between different spatial scales within a city, and between areas undergoing different types of development (Eason *et al.*, Chapter 27); and comparing the distribution and composition of garden gnomes between urban areas that vary in their history and spatial configuration (Parris, Chapter 34).

Examples of integrating ecological research with planning and management

One of the motivations for undertaking ecological research in urban areas is to improve the design and management of human settlements in order to make them more sustainable and to enhance biodiversity conservation outcomes. Both of these actions will improve the quality of life for people living in cities and towns. Therefore, the second aim of this book was to investigate how ecological research has been successfully integrated into planning and management actions (Section 3). Such integration can occur through several avenues and at various stages during the planning process. For example, Landscape Ecological Assessments (LEA; Mörtberg, Chapter 25) and expert-based models were used early in the planning process to evaluate different planning designs (Eason *et al.*, Chapter 27) and wetland restoration activities (Guntenspergen *et al.*, Chapter 29), thereby providing opportunities to include ecological information in the planning process. The importance of incorporating spatio-temporal data in this process was highlighted by Löfvenhaft (Chapter 24), and the contribution that transdisciplinary research can make to implementing LIUDD in New Zealand has also been illustrated (Eason *et al.*, Chapter 27).

The findings from individual studies can also be incorporated into future designs, as demonstrated by Eisenbeis and Hänel (Chapter 15) who provided recommendations on how to improve the design and regulation of artificial night lighting to minimise the impact on nocturnal insects, and Natuhara and Hashimoto (Chapter 12) who provided examples of how research findings on the distributions of butterflies and mammals could be used to direct landscape designs. Examples were also provided of where specific recommendations had resulted in positive outcomes for biodiversity, such as improving the design of seawall repairs (Chapman *et al.*, Chapter 9), and implementing recommendations for preserving remnant natural vegetation during the construction phase of urban development (Florgård, Chapter 22). Additional examples showed how education and outreach can help achieve ecologically sound planning, by shifting public perceptions about ecological systems, such as challenging the commonly held perception that arthropods are undesirable in urban ecosystems (McIntyre and Rango, Chapter 14).

These examples illustrate the potential role of urban ecological research in improving the planning, management and design of our cities and towns. Some of the challenges around this integration are discussed below in the section on ways to move forward, and elsewhere throughout this chapter.

Current knowledge gaps

Throughout the book, several authors have identified gaps in our current understanding of the ecology of urban ecosystems. These knowledge gaps fall under five major groups: (1) data availability; (2) effects and mechanisms; (3) relationships; (4) monitoring; and (5) tools. These five areas will be addressed individually.

Data availability

The data that are most commonly identified as missing are those that are available for use in GIS or provide basic ecological information to inform studies (e.g. abundance and distribution of organisms, nutrient fluxes, disturbance regimes). The basic data themes for use in GIS are generally limited in developing nations where the resources have not been available to invest in collating and constructing such datasets, although this has partially been addressed by the expansion of free online services such as satellite imagery and Google Maps. GIS data can be quite expensive to obtain, as can the GIS software, which can also require a level of training and investment beyond the current reach of some smaller research organisations. Also, there is generally a lack of geo-referenced and context-specific ecological data (Löfvenhaft, Chapter 24). All of these issues have been considered previously in the discussion of GIS as a research tool.

The second area of limited data availability is basic ecological information (McIntyre and Rango, Chapter 14), especially data with a spatial and temporal component (Löfvenhaft, Chapter 24). This is slowly being rectified as more and more ecological studies are conducted in urban areas. However, the fact that basic ecological data are being collected using a relatively ad hoc approach means that comparable data may not be available for all cities (McDonnell and Hahs, Chapter 5). This has implications for global comparative research, in that it can limit the potential study sites to those cities with appropriate datasets, rather than those cities which best address the question of interest.

Mechanistic understanding of drivers and their impacts

Some of the basic information that is needed to design more ecologically sustainable cities is currently lacking. The effects of roads in urban areas (van der Ree, Chapter 11); how changes in land use affect ecological systems (Hochuli *et al.*, Chapter 13; Snep *et al.*, Chapter 26), particularly wetland and marine ecosystems (Chapman *et al.*, Chapter 9; Guntenspergen *et al.*, Chapter 29), and biogeochemical cycles (Pouyat *et al.*, Chapter 20); the effect of green structures and landscape design on the survival of species (Snep *et al.*, Chapter 26) are all currently lacking. There is also a general lack of knowledge on the effects of infill development compared with spreading development (McIntyre and Rango, Chapter 14), the legacies of historic events compared with current events (Hochuli *et al.*, Chapter 13), and the effects of urbanisation compared with non-urban effects (Pouyat *et al.*, Chapter 20). The last three effects in particular lend themselves to local and global comparative studies, as they require several systems to address the questions adequately.

There is also a general lack of understanding of the mechanisms through which some of these effects take place (Nilon, Chapter 10; Hochuli *et al.*, Chapter 13). For example, the abundance of a species may decline with increasing road density, but this correlation would not reveal the respective roles played by increased pollution due to the vehicular traffic, increased mortality due to vehicle collisions, or decreased genetic fitness due to increased isolation from similar populations. Developing this mechanistic understanding can only be addressed by more in-depth studies. Currently most studies are still collecting the basic ecological information, and thus are not addressing questions at this more sophisticated level. However, there are some areas where our basic understanding has advanced enough for us to begin to investigate mechanisms of actions, as demonstrated by Catterall and colleagues for birds in southern Queensland (Catterall, Chapter 8). This knowledge gap will also be addressed by the inclusion of more specific measures of urbanisation in future studies, as discussed by McDonnell and Hahs (Chapter 5).

Understanding the relationship between pattern and process

Similar to the knowledge gaps surrounding the effects of urbanisation, there is a general lack of understanding of several relationships that are relevant to the ecology of cities and towns. Some of the poorly understood relationships identified within this book include the relationship between species and ecosystem function (Hochuli *et al.*, Chapter 13), key abiotic drivers along urbanisation gradients and their relationship to nutrient cycling (Carreiro *et al.*, Chapter 19) and the direct effects that humans have on biogeochemical cycles (Pouyat *et al.*, Chapter 20). These gaps in our ecological understanding in general have also been discussed by Jones and Lawton (1995), Decker *et al.* (2000) and Kaye *et al.* (2006). There is also a great lack of studies which have successfully integrated the role of humans into their models and research questions, although Loucks (Chapter 33) has identified several areas of research that begin to address these questions using methodologies not covered in the current volume. Several of the frameworks discussed in this book also begin to identify how the role of humans can be incorporated into ecological research, for example by using the human ecosystem framework (Pickett *et al.*, Chapter 3), or the frameworks proposed by Grimm *et al.* (2000) or Alberti *et al.* (2003). Therefore, we do have the potential to address this particular knowledge gap, and such studies should begin to emerge in the future.

Monitoring

Although there is active environmental monitoring of climatic conditions as well as air and water quality in cities and towns, there is relatively little monitoring at fine scales, especially in regard to biodiversity and the status of restoration or design projects. Some of the chapters in this book have identified the importance of evaluating the degree of success of restoration projects (Hochuli *et al.*, Chapter 13), the performance of LIUDD at various spatial scales (Eason *et al.*, Chapter 27) and the effects of soil sealing at different spatial scales (Breuste, Chapter 21). The successful use of monitoring to evaluate the effects of changes in seawall configurations in Sydney Harbour (Chapman *et al.*, Chapter 9) and the potential for using monitoring in conjunction with experimental manipulation of ecosystems (e.g. van der Ree, Chapter 11), suggest that this is an important technique which deserves wider use.

Opportunities and challenges of developing a global comparative approach

Urban ecosystems all share many common features, such as the presence of trees in residential gardens and parks (McIntyre and Rango, Chapter 14), turfgrass lawns (McIntyre and Rango, Chapter 14; Zipperer and Guntenspergen, Chapter 17; Ignatieva and Stewart, Chapter 23), artificial night lighting (Eisenbeis and Hänel, Chapter 15), and similar landscape designs in former colonial cities largely due to shared urban planning structure and landscape architectural styles (Ignatieva and Stewart, Chapter 23). However, cities also differ in their environmental context (McIntyre and Rango, Chapter 14), historical context (Ignatieva and Stewart, Chapter 23) and social and cultural context, such as developed versus developing nations (Cilliers *et al.*, Chapter 6). Understanding how the generalities developed by individual studies in a particular context are modified by the social, cultural, historical or environmental setting is important if we are to apply this knowledge to create ecologically sustainable cities and towns. Comparative research approaches between cities are one way to investigate the fit between patterns and processes identified for one context and their applicability in another context.

As mentioned by McDonnell and Hahs (Chapter 5), many ecological research approaches could be considered to have a local comparative component, whether it is comparing sites in urban and rural landscapes, or evaluating the findings of a study relative to similar studies in the published literature (see also Cole *et al.*, 1991). Indeed, research described in this book used a diversity of comparative approaches that ranged from local comparisons (e.g. along urbanisation gradients studied by Zipperer and Guntenspergen, Chapter 17) to multiple city comparisons (e.g. New York versus Baltimore, Pickett *et al.*, Chapter 3; Carreiro *et al.*, Chapter 19; GLOBENET, Niemelä *et al.*, Chapter 2). Other comparative studies described in the book analyse data from either multiple organisms (e.g. response of birds versus response of butterflies, McIntyre and Rango, Chapter 14) or multiple ecosystems (e.g. aquatic and terrestrial, Chapman *et al.*, Chapter 9; freshwater and marine, Guntenspergen *et al.*, Chapter 29).

Opportunities

As described by McDonnell and Hahs (Chapter 5), the use of the comparative approach at the local scale (i.e. patches within cities or along urbanisation gradients) has made significant contributions to our understanding of the ecology of cities and towns. Comparative studies at the regional and global scale are not as common, but they offer several opportunities to advance our understanding of the ecology of human settlements. First, by including more than one city in the study, it is possible to develop generalities and test how well they hold between cities or between locations within a city. Second, they provide an opportunity to investigate the mechanisms that are driving the observed patterns and processes, and how the historical, environmental and social context of a system may influence the ecology within. A third benefit is the chance to address questions that cannot be investigated using a single city, such as those investigating patterns at the city scale. Examples might be questions related to the ecology of a city (Grimm *et al.*, 2000; Pickett *et al.*, Chapter 3), the metabolism of a city (e.g. the urban footprint; Loucks, Chapter 33), or related to the incremental loss of habitat associated with the construction of roads or other urban development features (van der Ree, Chapter 11). Finally, local, regional and global comparative studies provide an opportunity for greater interactions between researchers, whether they are studying similar systems within different cities (e.g. GLOBENET; Niemelä *et al.*, Chapter 2), or studying different systems within a city (e.g. marine versus terrestrial ecology, Chapman and Underwood, Chapter 4; ecological versus socio-economic systems, Pickett *et al.*, Chapter 3).

Challenges

There are several challenges that accompany the development of regional and global comparative research, which need to be considered and addressed to make the most of the opportunities. These challenges include: (1) the resources required to undertake regional/global comparative studies; (2) the lack of standardised terminology and definitions; (3) the lack of standardised variables and measurement techniques; (4) the lack of common datasets between cities; and (5) the increased need for interdisciplinary interactions. As these challenges are potential barriers to the uptake of regional/global comparative research, we will discuss each of them in a little more detail, including strategies for how they might be overcome.

Establishing regional and global comparative studies may be more expensive and have larger resource requirements than studies conducted on a single system. This can be due to larger data requirements, travel costs between sites, and longer time frames required to acquire and analyse data. These considerations can be particularly relevant when existing data need to be supplemented by the acquisition of field data or standardised spatial datasets. One potential way to work around this may be to establish a network of researchers working in different cities, but using a standardised approach, such as that demonstrated by the GLOBENET project (Niemelä *et al.*, Chapter 2). However, it may still be necessary for the participating researchers to meet in person at key stages in the research project to ensure that the best research output is obtained for the effort. Similarly, if the regional/global comparative research project is being conducted by a group of researchers at a centralised location, the majority of the grant monies would be required for travel and accommodation during data collection, or other costs associated with obtaining the relevant data. For all of these reasons, grant applications for regional/global comparative research projects are likely to have a higher monetary value than those for individual research projects, and the funding opportunities may be more limited.

The lack of a standardised terminology and standardised definitions has been identified several times throughout this book as being a barrier to potential regional/global comparative research (Niemelä *et al.*, Chapter 2; Pickett *et al.*, Chapter 3; Catterall, Chapter 8; van der Ree, Chapter 11; Hochuli *et al.*, Chapter 13; McIntyre and Rango, Chapter 14; Breuste, Chapter 21; Florgård, Chapter 22;

Snep *et al.*, Chapter 26; Wittig, Chapter 30). In particular, authors have high-lighted the use of the term 'urban' (McDonnell and Hahs, Chapter 5; Wittig, Chapter 30), the differences between land cover and land use (Yang and Jinxing, Chapter 16; Breuste, Chapter 21), and differences in the terms used to describe preserved natural vegetation in urban areas and their use by different groups of researchers (Florgård, Chapter 22). Similarly, the terms used by ecologists working on marine ecosystems do not always overlap with the terms used by ecologists working in terrestrial systems (Chapman and Underwood, Chapter 4). This is a challenge in a couple of respects. First, literature searches between disciplines or even between different groups of researchers in the same discip-lines are hampered, as the search terms may have specialised uses within groups of researchers, and thus the results of related studies are not always incorpor-ated (see Chapman and Underwood, Chapter 4). Second, where a single term is used, but the definition varies between researchers, more detail is required to work out how the study outcomes can be integrated. Differing definitions for the terms 'urban' (see Wittig, Chapter 30) and 'soil sealing' (see Breuste, Chapter 21) provide important examples of this. Obtaining a consensus on a standardised terminology and definitions is beyond the scope of this book, and would be quite a challenge because of the large number of researchers using these terms with their own interpretations of what they mean. Therefore, this challenge is per-haps best dealt with using the strategy suggested by Parris (Chapter 34), who recommends that when such terms are used they should be accompanied by an explicit definition which will allow other researchers to interpret their research and outcomes in the most appropriate way.

The lack of standardised variables and measurement techniques is partly related to the previous point. However, it is treated as a separate challenge here, as the strategies for dealing with the selection and measurement of dependent and independent variables, and the potential outcomes of addressing this chal-lenge, are different. The independent (predictor) variables presented in this book have taken several forms, including biotopes (Löfvenhaft, Chapter 24), land-use types (Catterall, Chapter 8), landscape structural units (Breuste, Chapter 21), and several measures of urbanisation (McDonnell and Hahs, Chapter 5; Meurk *et al.*, Chapter 18; Carreiro *et al.*, Chapter 19; Pouyat *et al.*, Chapter 20) or the effects of urbanisation (Chapman *et al.*, Chapter 9; Natuhara and Hashimoto, Chapter 12). This diversity of independent variables is not necessarily a bad thing, as studies using land-use units are testing something quite different from studies using a measure of pollution (Chapman *et al.*, Chapter 9) or urbanisation (McDonnell and Hahs, Chapter 5). Where it does become problematic is when the techniques used to define a particular measure are not standardised between studies, such as the different ways to define biotopes mentioned by Löfvenhaft (Chapter 24).

Addressing this issue might require a group of researchers to meet and reach some form of consensus on how a particular group of regularly used variables will be measured and defined. The dependent (response) variables presented in this book have also taken several forms, depending on the focus of the study, and the tools and resources available for measurements. For example, the response variables have included community measures such as species richness or density (Chapman *et al.*, Chapter 9; Nilon, Chapter 10; Eisenbeis and Hänel, Chapter 15; Löfvenhaft, Chapter 24; Mörtberg, Chapter 25); functional community measures such as trophic structures or functional groups (Catterall, Chapter 8; Hochuli *et al.*, Chapter 13); landscape metrics (Yang and Zhou, Chapter 16; Zipperer and Guntenspergen, Chapter 17) or aspects of nitrogen and carbon cycling such as N-mineralisation (Carreiro *et al.*, Chapter 19; Pouyat *et al.*, Chapter 20). Examples of how the availability of tools or resources has influenced the measures include the different variables obtained from intensive compared with extensive field surveys (Meurk *et al.*, Chapter 18; Pouyat *et al.*, Chapter 20). Strategies for dealing with these different dependent variables are similar to those for dealing with the independent variables. First, selecting the variables which are appropriate for the research question should be the primary consideration (Parris, Chapter 34). Studies should include an explicit definition of how they defined or measured their particular variables. Following this, groups of researchers who regularly study particular variables could meet and try to reach a consensus about how those variables could be captured using a standardised methodology. This final step would be particularly valuable for the emerging area of functional groups, as identified by Catterall (Chapter 8), where the concept is still developing and has not yet been widely implemented.

The lack of common datasets between cities is a challenge to regional and global comparative research, in that existing information will not always be available for the cities of interest, and therefore a degree of additional effort will be required to obtain the necessary data. This challenge may eventually be reduced, as research is conducted in more and more cities, particularly if some of the obstacles related to standardised variables discussed previously can be overcome. In the meantime, unless common datasets are available and are suitable for the research question, this challenge will best be addressed by allocating sufficient monies in grant applications towards collecting appropriate and standardised data.

The final challenge accompanying the development of regional/global comparative research is the need to move towards more interdisciplinary research. This challenge can also be seen as a potential opportunity. However, it is discussed in this section as it has been identified in several chapters in this book as being a potential obstacle, with its own unique strategies for working towards a solution. Comparative ecology can take the form of local comparisons as well as regional and global comparisons between cities (Heal and Grime, 1991). However, even within disciplines, the call for greater attention to the ecology 'of' cities (Niemelä *et al.*, Chapter 2), and the need to develop better mechanistic understandings of ecological systems in urban areas (McIntyre and Rango, Chapter 14), demand the integration of social, economic and ecological systems (Grimm *et al.*, 2000; Pickett *et al.*, 2001; Alberti *et al.*, 2003). Therefore, there are many ways in which local and regional/global comparative ecology can benefit from strong interdisciplinary approaches. Some of the issues which have been identified as hampering interdisciplinary interactions have already been discussed in this section. However, some additional challenges include: the lack of common forums as barriers to communication (Chapman and Underwood, Chapter 4, McIntyre and Rango, Chapter 14); the coarser resolution of our ecological understanding compared with our understanding of social and economic systems (Niemelä *et al.*, Chapter 2); the subtly differing objectives of the research; and the lack of understanding regarding the role that ecologists can take within the realm of planning and decision-making (Nilsson and Florgård, Chapter 32). Addressing these issues will require persistence, as they are likely to require considerable resources (time, money and energy), as evidenced by the two urban Long-Term Ecological Research programmes in the United States (CAP and BES LTER programs). However, as more groups begin to successfully deliver interdisciplinary and transdisciplinary studies, the lessons learnt can filter through to other research groups, and perhaps lead to an increase in the number of integrated studies being published. An example of these lessons is provided by Eason *et al.* (Chapter 27), who found that their transdisciplinary research was improved by regular meetings and work programmes, ongoing interactions and communication between stakeholders and a collaborative learning approach.

Ways forward

In light of these opportunities and challenges, what are the ways of making progress in urban ecological studies over the next 10 to 20 years? The major areas identified throughout this book are: (1) moving towards a more mechanistic understanding of the ecology 'in' and 'of' cities (Catterall, Chapter 8; Hochuli *et al.*, Chapter 13; McIntyre and Rango, Chapter 14; Lehvävirta and Kotze, Chapter 31); (2) incorporating more interdisciplinary knowledge into ecological studies (Pickett *et al.*, Chapter 3; McCarthy, Chapter 7; Eason *et al.*, Chapter 27); (3) developing more broadly applicable generalities than can be used to inform planning and management; (4) changing our thinking about urban environments; and (5) improving the way we report definitions, methodologies and statistical outputs to make the study outcomes more amenable to meta-analyses. These five key areas are discussed briefly below.

Until recently, the level of ecological information for urban areas has been relatively scarce, so many studies have focused on documenting the basic patterns and processes occurring in urban areas. However, with the increasing level of understanding comes the need to change the focus of our research to allow more sophisticated understandings to develop. Part of this shift requires the development of a mechanistic understanding of the relationships between urbanisation and ecological patterns and processes (Shochat *et al.*, 2006; McIntyre and Rango, Chapter 14; Lehvävirta and Kotze, Chapter 31). Some of the ways that this mechanistic understanding can be developed include experimentation (Catterall, Chapter 8; van der Ree, Chapter 11; Hochuli *et al.*, Chapter 13; Pouyat *et al.*, Chapter 20); modelling (McCarthy, Chapter 7; Pouyat *et al.*, Chapter 20) and monitoring (Pouyat *et al.*, Chapter 20; Guntenspergen *et al.*, Chapter 29). The components of strong experimental research are discussed more fully by Catterall (Chapter 8) and Lehvävirta and Kotze (Chapter 31). Comparative studies within and between cities also provide an opportunity to investigate the mechanisms acting in urban areas, and how their influence varies in different systems. The components of strong comparative research largely follow those outlined for experiments.

Cities and towns are composed of complex ecosystems, with many different processes acting to shape the ecology of the city. These include influences from social systems, such as the human population and cultural institutions; economic systems, whether this means the division between developed and developing nations, urban and rural populations, or class hierarchies within an urban system; as well as the ecological systems, relating to the physical and chemical environment, the local climate, and the biota that inhabit these areas (Pickett *et al.*, 2001; Alberti *et al.*, 2003). Therefore, in order to obtain a rich understanding of the relationship between urbanisation and ecological systems, it is important to begin incorporating information from outside the traditional realm of ecology (Pickett *et al.*, Chapter 3; Cilliers *et al.*, Chapter 6; McCarthy, Chapter 7). In doing this, we need to examine the role of the ecologist in the scientific process, and the subsequent decision-making processes. Local, regional and global comparative studies again have a role to play in teasing out the relationships and influences of these different components of urban ecosystems.

The third area we need to address is the development of some broadly applicable generalities regarding the ecology of cities, and how that knowledge can best be integrated into planning, design and management. For example, numerous studies have demonstrated the reduction in stream biota and health if the surrounding watershed is covered by more than 20% impermeable surface (Paul and Meyer, 2001). This knowledge will also be enriched by understanding how those generalities change with changes in the social, historical and environmental contexts in which they are to be applied. Regional and global comparative studies will be particularly valuable in developing that greater understanding of how the context influences the outcomes.

As our study of urban ecology has progressed, it has become clear that there are several areas in which we need to change our thinking. Urbanisation needs to be acknowledged as something different from the classical disturbance hypothesis, as urbanisation events rarely provide opportunities for the system to revert back to a pre-urban state (McIntyre and Rango, Chapter 14). Therefore, the process of urbanisation needs to be acknowledged as a perturbation to a new system state, where the concepts of disturbed and undisturbed are redefined. The concept of remnant primary ecosystems may no longer be as relevant as the concept of recombinant systems (Guntenspergen *et al.*, Chapter 29), and we may need to change our objectives for ecological systems to something that is more realistic in this new environment (Florgård, Chapter 22; Guntenspergen *et al.*, Chapter 29).

The final area in which we can advance our research is through the improvement of how we report the definitions, methodologies and statistics used during our research. Providing explicit definitions for concepts presented in a study, particularly for those concepts that are ambiguous or have multiple interpretations, will allow for better syntheses between studies. Similar benefits can be gained from providing explicit descriptions of methodologies to ensure that the studies can be repeated by other researchers. Finally, the way we present the outcomes of our statistical analyses can be improved to provide better information to those who are reading our research. McCarthy (Chapter 7) and Lehvävirta and Kotze (Chapter 31) both have specific recommendations as to how we can improve our reporting of these analyses.

Conclusion

The purpose of this book is not to provide a prescription for how to conduct comparative research. Rather, it is an exploration of how research has proceeded in the recent past, and how the explicit recognition of the value of comparative studies might capitalise on our current understanding. The process of initiating more regional and global comparative work begins with understanding the nature of the work currently being done at the local scale. This book has provided examples capturing the breadth of research being undertaken on a range of scales (from patches in an urban matrix to urbanisation gradients), organisms (vertebrates, invertebrates, plants), processes (N-mineralisation, litter decomposition), and ecosystems (marine, freshwater, terrestrial). The research has covered a number of geographical regions including Asia, South Africa, Australia, New Zealand, Europe and North America.

We hope that in our discussion of this diversity we have been able to show that diversity does not mean that anything goes, but that different approaches or generalities may be more suitable in different contexts, and therefore need to be examined for context before application. We would still encourage researchers to put forward frameworks or methodologies that worked well so that they can be taken up by other researchers. However, as should happen with all strong science, we would encourage people to examine the idea first, understand how it applies to the specific context, and also explore areas where there might be alternative ways of explaining the outcomes.

The aim of comparative work at any scale is to increase our understanding of how ecological patterns and processes are influenced by the components of urbanisation, with the ultimate goal of increasing conservation outcomes and quality of life for people living in urban areas. We hope that this book has made a contribution towards achieving this ultimate goal.

References

Aber, J. D., McDowell, W. H., Nadelhoffer, K. J. *et al.* (1998). Nitrogen saturation in temperate forest ecosystems: hypotheses revisited. *BioScience* **48**, 921–34.

Able, K. W., Manderson, J. P. and Studholme, A. L. (1999). Habitat quality for shallow water fishes in an urban estuary: the effects of man-made structures on growth. *Marine Ecology Progress Series*, **187**, 227–35.

Adair, R. J. and Groves, R. H. (1998). *Impact of Environmental Weeds on Biodiversity: A Review and Development of a Methodology*. Canberra: Environment Australia.

Adams, C. C. (1935). The relation of general ecology to human ecology. *Ecology* **16**, 316–35.

Adams, C. C. (1938). A note for social-minded ecologists and geographers. *Ecology* **19**, 500–502.

Adams, L. W. and Dove, L. E. (1989). *Wildlife Reserves and Corridors in the Urban Environment: A Guide to Ecological Landscape Planning and Resource Conservation*. Columbia, Maryland: National Institute for Urban Wildlife.

Agenda 21: United Nations (1992). *The Global Partnership for Environment and Development – A Guide to Agenda 21*. Geneva: UNCED.

Ahlén, I. and Nilsson, S. G. (1982). Samband mellan fågelfauna och biotopareal på öar med naturskog i Mälaren och Hjälmaren. *Vår Fågelvärld*, **41**, 161–84. (In Swedish)

Airola, T. M. and Buchholz, K. (1984). Species structure and soil characteristics of five urban sites along the New Jersey Palisades. *Urban Ecology*, **8**, 149–64.

Aizen, M. A. and Feinsinger, P. (1994). Forest fragmentation, pollination, and plant reproduction in a Chaco dry forest, Argentina. *Ecology*, **75**, 330–51.

Akbari, H. and Taha, H. (1992). The impact of trees and white surfaces on residential heating and cooling energy use in four Canadian cities. *Energy*, **17**, 141–9.

Alaruikka, D., Kotze, D. J., Matveinen, K. and Niemela, J. (2002). Carabid beetle and spider assemblages along a forested urban–rural gradient in southern Finland. *Journal of Insect Conservation*, **6**, 195–206.

Alberti, M. (1999). Modeling the urban ecosystem: a conceptual framework. *Environment and Planning B: Planning and Design*, **26**, 605–30.

Alberti, M., Botsford, E. and Cohen, A. (2001). Quantifying the urban gradient: linking urban planning and ecology. In *Avian Ecology and Conservation in an Urbanizing*

World, ed. J.M. Marzluff, R. Bowman and R. Donnelly. Norwell, Massachusetts: Kluwer Academic Publishers, pp. 89–116.

Alberti, M., Marzluff, J.M., Shulenberger, E., Bradley, G., Ryan, C. and Zumbrunnen, C. (2003). Integrating humans into ecology: opportunities and challenges for studying urban ecosystems. *BioScience*, **53**, 1169–79.

Alevizon, W.S. and Gorham, J.C. (1989). Effects of artificial reef deployment on nearby resident fishes. *Bulletin of Marine Science*, **44**, 646–61.

Alihan, M.A. (1964). *Social Ecology: A Critical Analysis*. New York: Cooper Square Publishing.

Allen, E.B., Covington, W. and Falk, D.A. (1997). Developing the conceptual basis for restoration ecology. *Restoration Ecology*, **5**, 275–6.

Allen, T.F.H. and Wyleto, E.P. (1983). A hierarchical model for the complexity of plant communities. *Journal of Theoretical Biology*, **101**, 529–40.

Ambuel, B. and Temple, S.A. (1983). Area-dependent changes in the bird communities and vegetation of southern Wisconsin forests. *Ecology*, **64**, 1057–68.

Amundson, R. and Jenny, H. (1991). The place of humans in the state factor theory of ecosystems and their soils. *Soil Science*, **151**, 99–109.

Anacostia Watershed Restoration Committee (2002). *Working Together to Restore the Anacostia Watershed.* 2001 Annual Report.

Andersen, A.N. (1990). The use of ant communities to evaluate change in Australian terrestrial ecosystems: a review and a recipe. *Proceedings of the Ecological Society of Australia*, **16**, 347–57.

Andersen, A.N. (1997). Functional groups and patterns of organisation in North American ant communities: a comparison with Australia. *Journal of Biogeography*, **24**, 433–60.

Andersen, A.N. (1999). My bioindicator or yours? Making the selection. *Journal of Insect Conservation*, **3**, 1–4.

Anderson, D.R., Burnham, K.P. and Thompson, W.L. (2000). Null hypothesis testing: problems, prevalence, and an alternative. *Journal of Wildlife Management*, **64**, 912–23.

Anderson, J.R., Hardy, E.E., Roach, J.T. and Witmer, R.E. (1976). *A Land Use and Land Cover Classification System for Use with Remote Sensor Data. Professional Paper 964.* Washington, DC: US Geological Survey.

Andrén, H. (1994). Effects of habitat fragmentation on birds and mammals in landscapes with different proportion of suitable habitat: a review. *Oikos*, **71**, 355–66.

Angel, S., Sheppard, S.C. and Civco, D.L. (2005). *The Dynamics of Global Urban Expansion. Transport and Urban Development Department.* Washington DC: The World Bank.

Antrop, M. (2001). The language of landscape ecologists and planners. A comparative content analysis of concepts used in landscape ecology. *Landscape and Urban Planning*, **55**, 163–73.

Aoki, J. (1979). Difference in sensitivities of oribatid families to environmental change by human impacts. *Revue D'Ecologie et de Biologie du Sol*, **16**, 415–22.

Appleyard, D. (1980). Urban trees, urban forests: what do they mean? In *Proceedings of the National Urban Forestry Conference*, Syracuse, 13–16 November 1978. Syracuse: State University of New York College of Environmental Science and Forestry, pp. 138–55.

Arbeitsgruppe Methodik der Biotopkartierung im besiedelten Bereich (1986). Flächendeckende Biotopkartierung im besiedelten Bereich als Grundlage einer ökologisch bzw. am Naturschutz orientierten Planung: Grundprogramm für die Bestandsaufnahme und Gliederung des besiedelten Bereichs und dessen Randzonen. *Natur und Landschaft*, **61**, 371–89.

Arbeitsgruppe Methodik der Biotopkartierung im besiedelten Bereich (1993). Flächendeckende Biotopkartierung im besiedelten Bereich als Grundlage einer am Naturschutz orientierten Planung: Programm für die Bestandsaufnahme, Gliederung und Bewertung des besiedelten Bereichs und dessen Randzonen: Überarbeitete Fassung 1993. *Natur und Landschaft*, **68**, 491–526.

Archambault, P. and Bourget, E. (1996). Scales of coastal heterogeneity and benthic intertidal species richness, diversity and abundance. *Marine Ecology Progress Series*, **136**, 111–21.

Archambault, P., Banwell, K. and Underwood, A. J. (2001). Temporal variation in the structure of intertidal assemblages following the removal of sewage. *Marine Ecology Progress Series*, **222**, 51–62.

Arendt, R., Brabec, E. A., Dodson, H. L., Reid, C. and Yaro, R. D. (1994). *Rural by Design: Maintaining Small Town Character*. Chicago: American Planning Association.

Ariansen, P. (1993). *Miljöfilosofi*. Lund: Nya Doxa.

Arizona Riparian Council (1994). Arizona Riparian Council Fact Sheet, No. 1. Accessed on 24 July 2004. http://azriparian.asu.edu/newsletters/Fact11994.pdf

Arizona Riparian Council (2004). Web page. Accessed on 24 July 2004. http://azriparian.asu.edu/

Arnberger, A. (2006). Recreation use of urban forests: an inter-area comparison. *Urban Forestry and Urban Greening*, **4**, 135–44.

Arnold, C. L. and Gibbons, C. J. (1996). Impervious surface coverage: the emergence of a key environmental indicator. *Journal of the American Planning Association*, **62**, 243–58.

Arnold, T. B. and Potter, D. A. (1987). Impact of high-maintenance lawn-care program on nontarget invertebrates in Kentucky bluegrass turf. *Environmental Entomology*, **16**, 100–5.

Ashton, D. H. (1975). Studies on the litter of *Eucalyptus regnans* F. Muell. *Australian Journal of Botany*, **23**, 399–411.

Ashton, D. H. and Attiwill, P. M. (1994). Tall open forests. In *Australian Vegetation* 2nd edn, ed. R. H. Groves. Cambridge, UK: Cambridge University Press, pp. 157–96.

Askins, R. A., Philbrick, M. J. and Sugeno, D. S. (1987) Relationship between the regional abundance of forest and the composition of forest bird communities. *Biological Conservation*, **39**, 129–52.

Asomani-Boateng, R. (2002). Urban cultivation in Accra: an examination of the nature, practices, problems, potentials and urban planning implications. *Habitat International*, **26**, 591–607.

Astles, K. L. (1993). Patterns of abundance and distribution of species in intertidal rock pools. *Journal of the Marine Biological Association of the United Kingdom*, **73**, 555–69.

Atkinson, I.A.E. and Cameron, E.K. (1993). Human influences on the terrestrial biota and biotic communities of New Zealand. *Trends in Ecology and Evolution*, **8**, 447–51.

Attiwill, P.M. (1994). The disturbance of forest ecosystems: the ecological basis for conservative management. *Forest Ecology and Management*, **63**, 247–300.

Auckland City Council (2000). *Growing Our City Through Liveable Communities 2050*. Auckland: Auckland City Council.

Auckland City Council (2003). *On-site Stormwater Management*. Auckland: Auckland City Council.

Auckland Regional Council (1996). *The Environmental Impacts of Accelerated Erosion and Sedimentation*. Technical Publication 69. Auckland: Auckland Regional Council.

Auckland Regional Council (2000). *Low-impact Design Manual for the Auckland Region*. Technical Publication 124. Auckland: Auckland Regional Council.

Auckland Regional Council (2002). *Auckland Regional Pest Management Strategy 2002–2007*. Auckland: Auckland Regional Council.

Auckland Regional Council (2003a). *A Day in the Life of Auckland Regional Council*. Auckland: Auckland Regional Council.

Auckland Regional Council (2003b). *Stormwater Management Devices: Design Guidelines Manual*. Technical Publication 10. Auckland: Auckland Regional Council.

Auckland Regional Growth Forum (1999). *Auckland Regional Growth Strategy: 2050*. Auckland: Auckland Regional Growth Forum.

Auhagen, A. and Sukopp, H. (1983). Ziel, Begründung und Methoden des Naturschutzes im Rahmen der Stadtentwicklungspolitik von Berlin. *Natur und Landschaft*, **58**, 9–15.

Austin, M.P. and Gaywood, M.J. (1994). Current problems of environmental gradients and species response curves in relation to continuum theory. *Journal of Vegetation Science* **5**, 473–82.

AustRoads (2003). *Road Facts 2000 (with 2003 update)*. Sydney, Australia: AustRoads Incorporated.

AustRoads (2005). *Road Facts 2005*. Sydney, Australia: AustRoads Incorporated.

Avissar, R. (1996). Potential effect of vegetation on the urban thermal environment. *Atmospheric Environment*, **30**, 437–48.

Avondet, J.L., Blair, R.B., Berg, D.J. and Ebbert, M.A. (2003). *Drosophila* (Diptera: Drosophilidae) response to changes in ecological parameters across an urban gradient. *Environmental Entomology*, **32**, 347–58.

AZB (1998). *Arizona Business*, **45**(1). Tempe, AZ: Center for Business Research, Arizona State University College of Business.

Bacchiocchi, F. and Airoldi, L. (2003). Distribution and dynamics of epibiota on hard structures for coastal protection. *Estuarine, Coastal and Shelf Science*, **56**, 1157–66.

Bagnall, R.G. (1979). A study of human impact on an urban forest remnant: Redwood Bush, Tawa, near Wellington, New Zealand. *New Zealand Journal of Botany*, **17**, 117–26.

Baine, M. (2001). Artificial reefs: a review of their design, application, management and performance. *Ocean & Coastal Management*, **44**, 241–59.

Baines, C. (2000). *How to Make a Wildlife Garden*. London: Frances Lincoln.

Baker, H. G. (1974). The evolution of weeds. *Annual Review of Ecology and Systematics*, **5**, 1–24.

Baker, L. A., Brazel, A. J., Selover, N. *et al.* (2002). Urbanization and warming of Phoenix (Arizona, USA): Impacts, feedbacks and mitigation. *Urban Ecosystems*, **6**, 183–203.

Baldwin, A. H. (2004). Restoring complex vegetation in urban settings: the case of tidal freshwater marshes. *Urban Ecosystems*, **7**, 125–38.

Baldwin, A. H. and DeRico, E. F. (1999). The seed bank of a restored tidal freshwater marsh in Washington, DC. *Urban Ecosystems*, **3**, 5–20.

Baldwin, A. H. and Pendleton, F. N. (2003). Interactive effects of animal disturbance and elevation on vegetation of a tidal freshwater marsh. *Estuaries*, **26**, 905–15.

Baldwin, A. H., Egnotovich, M. S. and Clarke, E. (2001). Hydrologic change and vegetation of tidal freshwater marshes: field, greenhouse, and seed-bank experiments. *Wetlands*, **21**, 519–31.

Balfors, B. and Schmidtbauer, J. (2002). Strategic environmental assessment and EU Interreg IIA programmes. In *Nordiske Prosjekt om Strategiske Miljövurderinger (SEA) for Planer og Programmer*, ed. T. Lerstang and E. Plathe. TemaNord 1999:539. Copenhagen: Nordic Council of Ministers.

Balfors, B., Mörtberg, U., Gontier, M. and Brokking, P. (2005). Impacts of region-wide urban development on biodiversity in strategic environmental assessment. *Journal of Environmental Assessment Policy and Management*, **7**, 229–46.

Band, L. E., Patterson, P., Nemani, R. and Running, S. W. (1993). Forest ecosystem processes at the watershed scale: incorporating hillslope hydrology. *Forest Meteorology*, **63**, 93–126.

Band, L. E., Tague, C. L., Brun, S. E., Tenenbaum, D. E. and Fernandes, R. A. (2000). Modeling watersheds as spatial object hierarchies: structure and dynamics. *Transactions in Geographic Information Systems*, **4**, 181–96.

Band, L. E., Tague, C., Groffman, P. and Belt, K. (2001). Forest ecosystem processes at the watershed scale: hydrological and ecological controls of nitrogen export. *Hydrological Processes*, **15**, 2013–28.

Bard, S. M. (1999). Global transport of anthropogenic contaminants and the consequences for the Arctic marine ecosystem. *Marine Pollution Bulletin*, **38**, 356–79.

Baron, J. S. ed. (2002). *Rocky Mountain Futures*. Washington: Island Press.

Barrera-Roldán, A. and Saldívar-Valdés, A. (2002). Proposal and application of a Sustainable Development Index. *Ecological Indicators*, **2**, 251–6.

Barrett, M. E., Walsh, P. M., Malina, J. F. and Charbeneau, R. J. (1998). Performance of vegetative controls for treating highway runoff. *Journal of Environmental Engineering*, **124**, 1121–8.

Basher, L. (2000). Soils and geomorphology of the urban environment. In *Urban Biodiversity and Ecology as a Basis for Holistic Planning and Design*, ed. G. H. Stewart and M. E. Ignatieva. Christchurch: Wickliffe Press, pp. 14–21.

Bastian, O. (2001). Landscape ecology – towards a unified discipline? *Landscape Ecology*, **16**, 757–66.

Bastin, L. and Thomas, C. D. (1999). The distribution of plant species in urban vegetation fragments. *Landscape Ecology*, **14**, 493–507.

Batty, M. (1995). Fractals: new ways of looking at cities. *Nature*, **377**, 574.

Bauer, R. (1993). Untersuchung zur Anlockung von nachtaktiven Insekten durch Beleuchtungseinrichtungen. Unpublished Diploma thesis, Department of Biology, University of Konstanz, Germany.

Baur, B. (1994). Thermal radiation from a city causes extinction of a snail. *Urban Nature Magazine*, **2**, 6–7.

Baxter, J.W., Pickett, S.T.A., Carreiro, M.M. and Dighton, J. (1999). Ectomycorrhizal diversity and community structure in oak forest stands exposed to contrasting anthropogenic impacts. *Canadian Journal of Botany*, **77**, 771–82.

Baxter, J.W., Pickett, S.T.A., Dighton, J. and Carreiro, M.M. (2002). Nitrogen and phosphorus availability in oak forest stands exposed to contrasting anthropogenic impacts. *Soil Biology and Chemistry*, **34**, 623–33.

Beatley, T. (1994). *Habitat Conservation Planning*. Austin, Texas: University of Texas.

Beatley, T. (2000). Preserving biodiversity: challenge for planners. *Journal of the American Planning Association*, **66**, 5–20.

Beauchemin, S. and Simard, R.E. (1999). Soil phosphorus saturation degree: review of some indices and their suitability for P management in Quebec, Canada. *Canadian Journal of Soil Science*, **79**, 615–29.

Beaulac, M.N. and Reckhow, K.H. (1982). An examination of land use – nutrient export relationships. *Water Resources Bulletin*, **18**, 1013–24.

Beca Planning (2001). *District Plan Review: Low-impact Design*. Prepared for the Auckland Regional Council: Auckland, New Zealand.

Beck, M.W. (1997). Inference and generality in ecology: current problems and an experimental solution. *Oikos*, **78**, 265–73.

Begon, M., Harper, J.L. and Townsend, C.R. (1990). *Ecology: Individuals, Populations and Communities*. Oxford: Blackwell Scientific Publications.

Behrents, K.C. (1987). The influence of shelter availability on recruitment and early juvenile survivorship of *Lythrypnus dalli* Gilbert (Pisces: Gobiidae). *Journal of Experimental Marine Biology and Ecology*, **107**, 45–59.

Beijing Statistics Bureau (2003). Statistics of city development. [online]. Beijing, China: Beijing Statistics Bureau. Accessed 23 November 2003. URL: http://www.bjstats. gov.cn/ztlm/jwtj/wz/index.htm

Beissinger, S.R. and Osborne, D.R. (1982). Effects of urbanization on avian community organization. *Condor*, **84**, 75–83.

Belant, J.L., Ickes, S.K. and Seamans, T.W. (1998). Importance of landfills to urban-nesting herring and ring-billed gulls. *Landscape and Urban Planning*, **43**, 11–19.

Bellis, E.D. and Graves, H.B. (1971). Deer mortality on a Pennsylvania interstate highway. *Journal of Wildlife Management*, **35**, 232–7.

Belnap, J., Hawkes, C.V. and Firestone, M.K. (2003). Boundaries in miniature: two examples from soil. *BioScience*, **53**, 739–49.

Benda, L., Poff, N.L., Miller, D. *et al.* (2004). The network dynamics hypothesis: how channel networks structure riverine habitats. *BioScience*, **54**, 413–27.

Bender, E.A., Case, T.J. and Gilpin, M.E. (1984). Perturbation experiments in community ecology. *Ecology*, **65**, 1–13.

Benetin, J., Šoltész, A. and Martoň, J. (1988). Hydrological balance changes in urbanized territory. In *Hydrological Processes and Water Management in Urban Areas. Urban Waters 88*, ed. National Committee for the International Hydrological Programme of UNESCO. Netherlands: UNESCO.

Benn, C. R. and Ellison, S. L. (1998). *La Palma Night-sky Brightness*, Isaac Newton Group (ING) La Palma Technical Note 115, La Palma. http://www.ing.iac.es/Astronomy/observing/manuals/ps/tech_notes/tn115.ps.gz

Bennett, A. F. (1999). *Linkages in the Landscape: The Role of Corridors and Connectivity in Wildlife Conservation*. Cambridge: IUCN, The World Conservation Union.

Bennett, A. F. and van der Ree, R. (2001). Roadside vegetation in Australia: conservation and function of a linear habitat network in rural environments. In *Hedgerows of the World: Their Ecological Functions in Different Landscapes*, ed. C. Barr and S. Petit. UK: IALE, pp. 231–40.

Benson, D. and Howell, J. (1990). *Taken for Granted: The Bushland of Sydney and its Suburbs*. Sydney: Royal Botanic Gardens Sydney/Kangaroo Press.

Bentley, J. M. and Catterall, C. P. (1997). The use of bushland, corridors and linear remnants by birds in south east Queensland, Australia. *Conservation Biology*, **11**, 1173–89.

Berish, C. W., Durbrow, B. R., Harrison, J. E., Jackson, W. A. and Riitter, K. H. (1998). Conducting regional environmental assessments: the southern Appalachian experience. In *Ecosystem Management for Sustainability*, ed. J. D. Peine. New York: Lewis Publishers, pp. 117–66.

Berlekamp, L.-R. (1987). Bodenversiegelung als Faktor der Grundwasserneubildung–Untersuchungen am Beispiel der Stadt Hamburg. *Landschaft + Stadt*, **19**, 129–36.

Bermingham, E. and Moritz, C. (1998). Comparative phylogeography: concepts and applications. *Molecular Ecology*, **7**, 367–9.

Berry, B. J. L., II. (1990). Urbanization. In *The Earth as Transformed by Human Action*, ed. B. L. Turner, W. C. Clark, R. W. Kates, J. F. Richards, J. T. Matthews and W. B. Meyers. New York: Cambridge University Press, pp. 103–20.

Berryman, A. A. (2003). On principles, laws and theory in population ecology. *Oikos*, **103**, 695–701.

Bertness, M. D., Ewanchuk, P. and Silliman, B. R. (2002). Anthropogenic modification of New England salt marsh landscapes. *Proceedings of the National Academy of Science*, **99**, 1395–8.

Bhattacharya, M., Primack, R. and Gerwin, J. (2003). Are roads and railroads barriers to bumblebee movement in a temperate suburban conservation area? *Biological Conservation*, **109**, 37–45.

Bhuju, D. R. and Ohsawa, M. (1998). Effects of nature trails on ground vegetation and understorey colonization of a patchy remnant forest in an urban domain. *Biological Conservation*, **85**, 123–35.

Bhuju, D. R. and Ohsawa, M. (1999). Species dynamics and colonization patterns in an abandoned forest in an urban landscape. *Ecological Research*, **14**, 139–53.

Bhuju, D. R. and Ohsawa, M. (2001). Patch implications in the maintenance of species richness in an isolated forest site. *Biological Conservation*, **98**, 117–25.

Bidwell, S., Attiwill, P. M. and Adams, M. A. (2006). Nitrogen availability and weed invasion in a remnant native woodland in urban Melbourne. *Austral Ecology*, **31**, 262–70.

Birch, G. F. (1996). Sediment-bound metallic contaminants in Sydney's estuaries and adjacent offshore, Australia. *Estuarine, Coastal and Shelf Science*, **42**, 31–44.

Bisgrove, R. (1992). *The Gardens of Gertrude Jekyll*. London, UK: Little, Brown and Company.

Black, P. E. (1991). *Watershed Hydrology*. Englewood Cliffs, New Jersey: Prentice Hall.

Blair, J. M., Parmelee, R. W. and Lavelle, P. (1995). Influence of earthworms on biogeochemistry. In *Earthworm Ecology and Biogeography in North America*, ed. P. F. Hendrix. Boca Raton, FL: CPC Press, pp. 127–58.

Blair, R. B. (1996). Land use and avian species diversity along an urban gradient. *Ecological Applications*, **6**, 506–19.

Blair, R. B. (2001a). Birds and butterflies along urban gradients in two ecoregions of the United States: is urbanization creating a homogenous fauna? In *Biotic Homogenization*, ed. J. L. Lockwood and M. L. McKinney. New York: Kluwer Academic / Plenum Publishers, pp. 33–56.

Blair, R. B. (2001b). Creating a homogeneous avifauna. In *Avian Ecology and Conservation in an Urbanizing World*, ed. J. Marzluff, R. Bowman and R. Donnelly. Boston: Kluwer Academic Publishers, pp. 459–86.

Blair, R. B. and Launer, A. E. (1997). Butterfly diversity and human land use: species assemblages along an urban gradient. *Biological Conservation*, **80**, 113–25.

Blake, J. G. (1991). Nested subsets and the distribution of birds on isolated forest. *Conservation Biology*, **5**, 58–66.

Blake, S., Foster, G. N., Eyre, M. D. and Luff, M. L. (1994). Effects of habitat type and grassland management practices on the body size distribution of carabid beetles. *Pedobiologia*, **38**, 502–12.

Blaustein, A. R., Wake, D. B. and Sousa, W. P. (1994). Amphibian declines: judging stability, persistence and susceptibility of populations to local and global extinctions. *Conservation Biology*, **8**, 60–71.

Blewett, C. M. and Marzluff, J. M. (2005). Effects of urban sprawl on snags and the abundance and productivity of cavity-nesting birds. *Condor*, **107**, 678–93.

Bligh, B. (1980). *Cherish The Earth. The Story of Gardening in Australia*. Sydney: The David Ell Press.

Blockley, D. J. (2007). Effect of wharves on intertidal assemblages on seawalls in Sydney Harbour, Australia. *Marine Environmental Research* **63**, 409–27.

Blomberg, O., Itamies, J. and Kuusela, K. (1978). The influence of weather factors on insect catches in traps equipped with different lamps in northern Finland. *Annales Entomologici Fennici*, **44**, 56–62.

Blood, E. (1994). Prospects for the development of integrated regional models. In *Integrated Regional Models*, ed. P. M. Groffman and G. E. Likens. New York: Chapman and Hall, pp. 145–53.

Blum, P. (1991). Stadtstruktureinheiten als räumliches Bezugssystem für die städtische Umweltplanung. Eine Untersuchung zur Erhebung und Bewertung

umweltbezogener Daten–dargestellt am Beispiel München-Moosbach.
Unpublished diploma thesis, Lehrstuhl für Landschaftsökologie, Technischen
Universität München Weihenstephan.

Blume, H. P. (1992). *Handbuch des Bodenschutzes*, Ecomed Verlags GmbH Landberg-Lech.

Boal, C. W. and Mannan, R. W. (1999). Comparative breeding ecology of Cooper's Hawks
in urban and exurban areas of southeastern Arizona. *Journal of Wildlife
Management*, **63**, 77–84.

Böcker, R. (1985). Bodenversiegelung–Verlust vegetationsbedeckter Flächen in
Ballungsräumen–am Beispiel von Berlin (West). *Landschaft und Stadt*, **17**, 57–61.

Boecklen, W. J. and Gotelli, N. J. (1984). Island biogeographic theory and conservation
practice: species–area or specious-area relationships. *Biological Conservation*,
29, 63–80.

Bohlen, P. J., Groffman, P. M., Fahey, T. J. and Fisk, M. C. (2004). Ecosystem consequences
of exotic earthworm invasion of north temperate forests. *Ecosystems* **7**, 1–12.

Bohm, D. (1996). *On Dialogue*. New York: Routledge.

Bohnsack, J. A. and Sutherland, D. L. (1985). Artificial reef research: a review with
recommendations for future priorities. *Bulletin of Marine Science*, **37**, 11–39.

Bolger, D. T. (2001). Urban birds: population, community, and landscape approaches.
In *Avian Ecology and Conservation in an Urbanizing World*, ed. J. Marzluff, R. Bowman
and R. Donnelly. Boston: Kluwer Academic Publishers, pp. 155–78.

Bolger, D. T. (2002). Habitat fragmentation effects on birds in southern California:
contract to the 'top-down' paradigm. *Studies in Avian Biology*, **25**, 141–57.

Bolger, D. T., Alberts, A. C. and Soule, M. E. (1991). Occurrence patterns of bird
species in habitat fragments: sampling, extinction, and nested species subsets.
The American Naturalist, **137**, 155–66.

Bolger, D. T., Scott, T. A. and Rotenberry, J. (1997). Breeding bird abundance in an
urbanizing landscape in coastal Southern California. *Conservation Biology*,
11, 406–21.

Bolger, D. T., Scott, T. A. and Rotenberry, J. T. (2001). Use of corridor-like landscape
structures by bird and small mammal species. *Biological Conservation*, **102**, 213–24.

Bolger, D. T., Suarez, A. V., Crooks, K. R., Morrison, S. A. and Case, T. J. (2000). Arthropods
in urban habitat fragments in southern California: area, age and edge effects.
Ecological Applications, **10**, 1230–48.

Bollen, K. A., Entwisle, B. and Alderson, A. S. (1993). Macrocomparative research
methods. *Annual Review of Sociology*, **19**, 321–51.

Bonnet, X., Naulleau, G. and Shine, R. (1999). The dangers of leaving home: dispersal
and mortality in snakes. *Biological Conservation*, **89**, 39–50.

Borcard, D. and Legendre, P. (2002). All-scale spatial analysis of ecological data by means
of principal coordinates of neighbour matrices. *Ecological Modelling*, **153**, 51–68.

Borchert, J. R. (1967). American metropolitan evolution. *Geographical Review*, **57**, 301–32.

Bormann, F. H. and Likens, G. E. (1979). *Pattern and Process in a Forested Ecosystem*.
New York: Springer-Verlag.

Bormann, F. H., Balmori, D. and Geballe, G. (2001). *Redesigning the American Lawn.
A Search for Environmental Harmony*. New Haven: Yale University Press.

Bornkamm, R. (1980). Hemerobie und Landschaftsplanung. *Landschaft und Stadt*, **12**, 49–55.

Bornkamm, R., Lee, J. A., and Seaward, M. R. D., eds. (1982). *Urban Ecology: The Second European Ecological Symposium*. Oxford: Blackwell Scientific Publications.

Borowitzka, M. A. and Lethbridge, R. C. (1989). Seagrass epiphytes. In *Biology of Seagrasses*, ed. A. W. D. Larkum, A. J. McComb and S. A. Shepherd. Amsterdam: Elsevier, pp. 458–99.

Botequilha Leitao, A. and Ahern, J. (2002). Applying landscape ecological concepts and metrics in sustainable landscape planning. *Landscape and Urban Planning*, **59**, 65–93.

Botkin, D. B. (1990). *Discordant Harmonies: A New Ecology for the Twenty-first Century*. New York: Oxford University Press.

Botkin, D. B. and Beveridge, C. E. (1997). Cities as environments. *Urban Ecosystems*, **1**, 3–19.

Bowden, J. (1981). The relationship between light- and suction-trap catches of *Chrysoperla carnea* (Stephens) (Neuroptera: Chrysopidae), and the adjustment of light-trap catches to allow for variation in moonlight. *Bulletin of Entomological Research*, **71**, 621–9.

Bowden, J. (1982). An analysis of factors affecting catches of insects in light-traps. *Bulletin of Entomological Research*, **72**, 535–56.

Bowers, J. K. (1995). Innovations in tidal marsh restoration: the Kenilworth Marsh account. *Restoration and Management Notes*, **13**, 155–61.

Bowman, D. M. J. S. (2000). *Australian Rainforests. Islands of Green in a Land of Fire*. Cambridge: Cambridge University Press.

Bowman, R. and Marzluff, J. (2001). Integrating avian ecology into emerging paradigms in urban ecology. In *Avian Ecology and Conservation in an Urbanizing World*, ed. J. Marzluff, R. Bowman and R. Donnelly. Boston: Kluwer Academic Publishers, pp. 569–77.

Boxall, A. B. A. and Maltby, L. (1995). The characterization and toxicity of sediment contaminated with road runoff. *Water Research*, **29**, 2043–50.

Boxall, A. B. A. and Maltby, L. (1997). The effects of motorway runoff on freshwater ecosystems. 3. Toxicant confirmation. *Archives of Environmental Contamination and Toxicology*, **33**, 9–16.

Boyden, S., Millar, S., Newcombe, K. and O'Neill, B. (1981). *The Ecology of a City and its People: The Case of Hong Kong*. Canberra: Australian National University Press.

Bradshaw, A. D. (1987). Comparison: its scope and limits. *The New Phytologist*, **106**, 3–22.

Bradshaw, A. D. (2003). Natural ecosystems in cities: a model for cities as ecosystems. In *Understanding Urban Ecosystems: A New Frontier for Science and Education*, ed. A. R. Berkowitz, C. H. Nilon and K. S. Hollweg. New York: Springer-Verlag, pp. 77–94.

Brady, R. F., Tobias, T., Eagles, P. F. J. *et al.* (1979). A typology for the urban ecosystem and its relationship to larger biogeographical landscape units. *Urban Ecology*, **4**, 11–28.

Brandt, J. (1998). Key concepts and interdisciplinarity in landscape ecology: a summing-up and outlook. In *Key Concepts in Landscape Ecology*, ed. J. W. Dover and R. G. H. Bunce. Preston, UK: IALE, pp. 421–34.

Brazel, A., Selover, N., Vose, R. and Heisler, G. (2000). The tale of two climates – Baltimore and Phoenix urban LTER sites. *Climate Research*, **15**, 123–35.

Breitburg, D. L., Baxter, J. W., Hatfield, C. A. *et al.* (1998). Understanding effects of multiple stressors: ideas and challenges. In *Successes, Limitations, and Frontiers in Ecosystem Science*, ed. M. L. Pace and P. M. Groffman. New York: Springer-Verlag, pp. 416–31.

BRESCO (2000). *The Hockerton Housing Project – Design Lessons for Developers and Clients.* New Practice Profile 119, Energy-Efficient Best Practice Programme. Garston, Watford, UK: Building Research Establishment.

Breuste, J. (1985). Methodische Aspekte der Analyse und Bewertung der urbanen Landschaftsstruktur. In *Institute of Experimental Biology and Ecology, Center of Biological-Ecological Sciences, Slovak Academy of Sciences (Hrsg.) VII. Intern. Symposium über die Problematik der ökologischen Landschaftsforschung*, Panel 1, vol. 10. p. 10.

Breuste, J. (1986). Methodische Ansätze und Problemlösungen bei der Erfassung der urbanen Landschaftsstruktur und ihrer ökologischen und landeskulturellen Bewertung unter Berücksichtigung von Untersuchungen in Halle/Saale. Unpublished dissertation, University of Halle-Wittenberg, Halle.

Breuste, J. (1989). Landschaftsökologische Struktur und Bewertung von Stadtgebieten. *Geographische Berichte*, **131**, 105–16.

Breuste, J. (1995). Kulturlandschaft Stadt und Umland-Wandel und Perspektiven. In *ANL Vision Landschaft 2020*, Laufener Seminarbeiträge 4/95. Laufen/Salzach.

Breuste, J. (1996). Landschaftsschutz–ein Leitbild in urbanen Landschaften. In *50. Deutscher Geographentag Potsdam*, 1995, 1, ed. H.-R. Bork, G. Heinritz and R. Wießner. pp. 134–43.

Breuste, J. (2001). Nutzung als Untersuchungsgegenstand und Raumbezug der Stadtökologie. *Natur und Landschaft*, **33**, 95–100.

Breuste, J. (2004). Decision making, planning and design for the conservation of indigenous vegetation within urban development. *Landscape and Urban Planning*, **68**, 439–52.

Breuste, J. and Böhm, P. (1997). Stadtstrukturtypen der Stadt Leipzig. In *Sozialatlas der Stadt Leipzig*, ed. S. Kabisch, A. Kindler and D. Rink. Leipzig, Karte 4.1.

Breuste, J., Feldmann, H. and Uhlmann, O., eds. (1998). *Urban Ecology*. Berlin: Springer-Verlag.

Breuste, J., Keidel, T., Meinel, G., Münchow, B., Netzband, M. and Schramm, M. (1996). *Erfassung und Bewertung des Versiegelungsgrades befestigter Flächen*. Leipzig. (UFZ-Bericht 12/1996).

Breuste, J., Meurer, M. and Vogt, J. (2002). Stadtökologie – Mehr als nur Natur in der Stadt. In *Geographie heute – für die Welt von morgen*, Gotha/Stuttgart: Leser, Hartmut, Manfred Ehlers, pp. 36–45.

Bridgman, H., Warner, R. and Dodson, J. (1995). *Urban Biophysical Environments*. Melbourne: Oxford University Press.

Briggs, M. K. (1996). *Riparian Ecosystem Recovery in Arid Lands: Strategies and References*. Tucson: The University of Arizona Press.

Briggs, W. R. (2006). Physiology of plant responses to artificial lighting. In *Ecological Consequences of Artificial Night Lighting*, ed. C. Rich and T. Longcore. Covelo, California: Island Press, 389–401.

Brookes, R. (1763). *The Natural History of Vegetables, as well foreign as indigenous*. London.

Brosnan, D. M. and Crumrine, L. L. (1994). Effects of human trampling on marine rocky shore communities. *Journal of Experimental Marine Biology and Ecology*, **177**, 79–97.

Brown, B. J. and Mitchell, R. J. (2001). Competition for pollination: effects of pollen of an invasive plant on seed set of a native congener. *Oecologia*, **129**, 43–9.

Brown, K. S. Jr and Freitas, A. V. L. (2002). Butterfly communities of urban forest fragments in Campinas, São Paulo, Brazil: structure, instability, environmental correlates, and conservation. *Journal of Insect Conservation*, **6**, 217–31.

Bruijn, Z. (1990). Domestic cat *Felis catus* as a predator of bats. *Lutra*, **33**, 30–4.

Brun, S. E. and Band, L. E. (2000). Simulating runoff behaviour in an urbanising watershed. *Computers, Environment and Urban Systems*, **24**, 1.

Brunner, M., Duhme, F., Mück, F., Patsch, J. and Weinisch, F. (1979). Kartierung erhaltenswerter Lebensräume in der Stadt. *Gartenamt*, **28**, 1–8.

Brush, G. S., Lenk, C. and Smith, J. (1980). The natural forests of Maryland: an explanation of the vegetation map of Maryland (with 1:250,000 map). *Ecological Monographs*, **50**, 77–92.

Bucht, E. (1973). *Vegetationen i tio bostadsområden*. Stockholm: Statens institut för byggnadsforskning. (In Swedish)

Buckley, G. P., ed. (1989). *Biological Habitat Reconstruction*. London: Bellhaven Press.

Buddenhagen, C. E., Timmins, S., Owen, D., Champion, P., Nelson, W. and Reid, V. (1998). An overview of weed impacts and trends. In *Department of Conservation Strategic Plan for Managing Weeds*, ed. S. J. Owens. Wellington: Department of Conservation.

Burgess, J., Harrison, C. M. and Limb, M. (1988). People, parks and the urban green: a study of popular meanings and values for open spaces in the city. *Urban Studies*, **25**, 455–73.

Burgess, R. L. and Sharpe, D. M., eds. (1981). *Forest Island Dynamics in Man-dominated Landscapes*, Ecological Studies, Vol. 41. New York: Springer Verlag.

Burghardt, W. (1994). Soils in urban and industrial environments. *Zeitschrift fur Pflanzenernähr und Bodenkonde*, **157**, 205–14.

Burmil, S., Daniel, T. C. and Hetherington, J. D. (1999). Human values and perceptions of water in arid landscapes. *Landscape and Urban Planning*, **44**, 99–109.

Burrows, C. J. (1994a). Fruit types and seed dispersal modes of woody plants in Ahuriri Summit Bush, Port Hills, Western Banks Peninsula, Canterbury, New Zealand. *New Zealand Journal of Botany*, **32**, 169–81.

Burrows, C. J. (1994b). The seeds always know best. *New Zealand Journal of Botany*, **32**, 349–63.

Burrows, S. (1999). Dieback of *Eucalyptus botryoides* in urban forest remnants. Unpublished M.Sc. (Environmental Science) thesis, The University of Sydney.

Cadenasso, M. L., Pickett, S. T. A. and Grove, J. M. (2006). Dimensions of ecosystem complexity: heterogeneity, connectivity, and history. *Ecological Complexity*, **3**, 1–12.

Cadenasso, M. L., Pickett, S. T. A. and Schwarz, K. (2007). Spatial heterogeneity in urban ecosystems: reconceptualizing land cover and a framework for classification. *Frontiers in Ecology and the Environment*, **5**, 80–8.

Cadenasso, M. L., Pickett, S. T. A., Weathers, K. C. *et al.* (2003a). An interdisciplinary and synthetic approach to ecological boundaries. *BioScience*, **53**, 717–22.

Cadenasso, M. L., Pickett, S. T. A., Weathers, K. C. and Jones, C. G. (2003b). A framework for a theory of ecological boundaries. *BioScience*, **53**, 750–8.

Cadenasso, M. L., Traynor, M. M. and Pickett, S. T. A. (1997). Functional location of forest edges: gradients of multiple physical factors. *Canadian Journal of Forest Research*, **27**, 774–82.

Cadwallader, M. (1988). Urban geography and social theory. *Urban Geography*, **9**, 227–51.

Caine, E. A. (1987). Potential effect of floating dock communities on a South Carolina Estuary. *Journal of Experimental Marine Biology and Ecology*, **108**, 83–91.

Cale, P. (1990). The value of road reserves to the avifauna of the central wheatbelt of Western Australia. *Proceedings of the Ecological Society of Australia*, **16**, 359–67.

Callaway, J. C. and Zedler, J. B. (2004). Restoration of urban salt marshes: lessons from southern California. *Urban Ecosystems*, **7**, 107–24.

Callender, E. and Rice, K. C. (2000). The urban environmental gradient: anthropogenic influences on the spatial and temporal distributions of lead and zinc in sediments. *Environmental Science and Technology*, **34**, 232–8.

Cam, E., Nichols, J. D., Sauer, J. E., Hines, J. E. and Flather, C. H. (2000). Relative species richness and community completeness: birds and urbanization in the mid-Atlantic states. *Ecological Applications*, **10**, 1196–210.

Campaign to Protect Rural England, (2003). Night blight! London: Campaign to Protect Rural England. http://www.cpre.org.uk/campaigns/light-pollution/index.htm

Campbell, J. B. (1987). *Introduction to Remote Sensing*. New York: The Guilford Press.

Canaday, C. (1997). Loss of insectivorous birds along a gradient of human impact in Amazonia. *Biological Conservation*, **77**, 63–77.

Capra, F. (1996). *The Web of Life: A New Scientific Understanding of Living Systems*. New York: Anchor Books.

Capra, F. (2002). *The Hidden Connections: Integrating the Biological, Cognitive and Social Dimensions of Life into a Science of Sustainability*. New York: Doubleday.

Caraco, D., Claytor, R. and Zielinski, J. (1998). *Nutrient Loading from Conventional and Innovative Site Development. Final Report*. Ellicott City, MD: Center for Watershed Protection.

Carlton, J. T. (1993). Neoextinctions of marine invertebrates. *American Zoologist*, **33**, 499–509.

Carlton, J. T. and Geller, J. B. (1993). Ecological roulette: the global transport and invasion of nonindigenous marine organisms. *Science*, **261**, 78–82.

Carney, S. E., Byerley, M. B. and Holway, D. A. (2003). Invasive Argentine ants (*Linepithema humile*) do not replace native ants as seed dispersers of *Dendromecon rigida* (Papaveraceae) in California, USA. *Oecologia*, **135**, 576–82.

Carpenter, S. R. (1998). The need for large-scale experiments to assess and predict the response of ecosystems to perturbation. In *Successes, Limitations and Frontiers in*

Ecosystem Science, ed. M. L. Pace and P. M. Groffman. New York: Springer-Verlag, pp. 287–312.

Carpenter, S., Walker, B., Anderies, J. M. and Abel, N. (2001). From metaphor to measurement: resilience of what to what? *Ecosystems*, **4**, 765–81.

Carr, M. H. and Hixon, M. A. (1997). Artificial reefs: the importance of comparisons with natural reefs. *Fisheries*, **22**, 28–33.

Carreiro, M. (2003). Measuring a city's effects on nature. *Sustain*, **8**, 23–31.

Carreiro, M. M. and Tripler, C. (2005). Forest remnants along urban–rural gradients: examining their potential for global change research. *Ecosystems*, **8**, 568–82.

Carreiro, M. M., Howe, K., Parkhurst, D. F. and Pouyat, R. V. (1999). Variation in quality and decomposability of red oak leaf litter along an urban-rural gradient. *Biology and Fertility of Soils*, **30**, 258–68.

Carreiro, M., Sinsabaugh, R., Repert, D. and Parkhurst, D. (2000). Microbial enzyme shifts explain litter decay responses to simulated nitrogen deposition. *Ecology*, **81**, 2359–65.

Cars, G. (1992). *Förhandlingar mellan privata och offentliga aktörer i samhällsbyggandet.* Stockholm: KTH, avd. för Regional Planning.

Carter, E. and Ignatieva, M. (2002). *City of Syracuse Open Space Study: A Contribution to the City of Syracuse Comprehensive Plan.* Syracuse: New York.

Casey, R. E. and Klaine, S. J. (2001). Nutrient attenuation by a riparian wetland during natural and artificial runoff events. *Journal of Environmental Quality*, **30**, 1720–31.

Castilla, J. C. and Duran, L. R. (1985). Human exclusion from the rocky intertidal zone of central Chile: the effects on Concholepas concholepas (Gastropoda). *Oikos*, **45**, 391–9.

Catterall, C. P. (1991). On the importance of watching birds. *Wildlife Australia*, **28**, 3–5.

Catterall, C. P. (2004). Birds, garden plants and suburban bush lots: where good intentions meet unexpected outcomes. In *Urban Wildlife: More than Meets the Eye*, ed. S. Burgin and D. Lunney. Mosman, NSW: Royal Zoological Society of NSW, pp. 21–31.

Catterall, C. P. and Kingston, M. (1993). Human populations, bushland distribution in south eastern Queensland and the implications for birds. In *Birds and Their Habitats: Status and Conservation in Queensland*, ed. C. P. Catterall, P. Driscoll, K. Hulsman and A. Taplin. Brisbane: Queensland Ornithological Society, pp. 105–22.

Catterall, C. P., Green, R. J. and Jones, D. N. (1989). The occurrence of birds in relation to plants in a subtropical city. *Australian Wildlife Research*, **16**, 289–305.

Catterall, C. P., Green, R. J. and Jones, D. N. (1991). Habitat use by birds across a forest–suburb interface in Brisbane: implications for corridors. In *Nature Conservation 2, The Role of Corridors*, ed. D. A. Saunders and R. H. Hobbs. Chipping Norton: Surrey Beatty and Sons, pp. 247–58.

Catterall, C. P., Kanowski, J., Wardell-Johnson, G. *et al.* (2004). Quantifying the biodiversity values of reforestation: perspectives, design issues and outcomes in Australian rainforest landscapes. In *Conservation of Australia's Forest Fauna* 2nd edn, ed. D. Lunney, pp. 359–93.

Catterall, C.P., Kingston, M.B. and Park, K. (1997a). Use of remnant forest habitat by birds during winter in subtropical Australia: patterns and processes. *Pacific Conservation Biology*, **3**, 262–74.

Catterall, C.P., Kingston, M.B., Park, K. and Sewell, S. (1998). Effects of clearing lowland eucalypt forests on a regional bird assemblage. *Biological Conservation*, **84**, 65–81.

Catterall, C.P., Piper, S. and Goodall, K. (2002). Noisy miner irruptions associated with land use by humans in south east Queensland: causes, effects and management implications. In *Landscape Health of Queensland*, ed. A. Franks, J. Playford and A. Shapcott. Brisbane: Proceedings of the Royal Society of Queensland, pp. 117–27.

Catterall, C.P., Storey, R.J. and Kingston, M.B. (1997b). Reality versus rhetoric: a case study monitoring regional deforestation. In *Conservation Outside Nature Reserves*, ed. P. Hale and D. Lamb. Brisbane: Centre for Conservation Biology, University of Queensland, pp. 367–77.

Catton, W. Jr and Dunlap, R.E. (1978). Environmental sociology: A new paradigm. *The American Sociologist*, **13**, 41–9.

CH2MHILL (2002). *Burnaby Mountain Watercourse and Stormwater Management Plan*. Prepared by CH2MHILL consultants for Burnaby Mountain Community Corporation: Vancouver, Canada.

Chaney, R.L., Sterrett, S.B. and Mielke, H.W. (1984). The potential for heavy metal exposure from urban gardens and soils. In *Proceedings of the Symposium on Heavy Metals in Urban Gardens*, ed. J.R. Preer. Washington, DC: University of the District of Columbia Extension Service, pp. 37–84.

Chapin, F.S. III, Matson, P.A. and Mooney, H.A. (2002). *Principles of Terrestrial Ecosystem Ecology*. New York: Springer-Verlag.

Chapman, M.G. (1999). Are there adequate data to assess how well theories of rarity apply to marine invertebrates? *Biodiversity and Conservation*, **8**, 1295–1318.

Chapman, M.G. (2003). Paucity of mobile species on constructed seawalls: effects of urbanization on biodiversity. *Marine Ecology Progress Series*, **264**, 21–9.

Chapman, M.G. and Bulleri, F. (2003). Intertidal seawalls – new features of landscape in intertidal environments. *Landscape and Urban Planning*, **62**, 159–72.

Chapman, M.G. and Clynick, B.G. (2006). Experiments testing the use of waste material in estuaries as habitat for subtidal organisms. *Journal of Experimental Marine Biology and Ecology*, **338**, 164–78.

Chapman, M.G., People, J. and Blockley, D. (2005). Intertidal assemblages associated with natural Corallina turf and invasive mussel beds on seawalls. *Biodiversity and Conservation*, **14**, 1761–76

Chapman, M.G., Underwood, A.J. and Skilleter, G.A. (1995). Variability at different spatial scales between a subtidal assemblage exposed to the discharge of sewage and two control assemblages. *Journal of Experimental Marine Biology and Ecology*, **189**, 103–22.

Chiba, S. (1973). Changes in animals habitats and their retreat in Tokyo. *Natural Science and Museum*, **40**, 69–73.

Chiesura, A. (2004). The role of urban parks for the sustainable city. *Landscape and Urban Planning*, **68**, 129–38

Chikamatsu, M., Natuhara, Y., Mizutani, Y. and Nakamura, A. (2002). Effect of artificial gaps on the butterfly assemblage in urban woods. *Journal of the Japanese Society of Revegetation Technology*, **28**, 97–102. (In Japanese with English abstract)

Chocholousková, Z. and Pysek, P. (2003). Changes in composition and structure of urban flora over 120 years: a case study of the city of Plzeň. *Flora*, **198**, 366–76.

Chow, S. L. (1996). *Statistical Significance: Rationale, Validity and Utility*. London: SAGE Publications.

Christchurch City Council (1999). *Waterways and Wetlands Natural Asset Management Strategy*. Christchurch: Christchurch City Council.

Christchurch City Council (2000). *Waterways and Wetlands Natural Asset Management Strategy*. Vol. 2, *Implementation*. Christchurch: Christchurch City Council.

Christian, C. E. (2001). Consequences of a biological invasion reveal the importance of mutualism for plant communities. *Nature*, **413**, 635–9.

Christie, F. J. and Hochuli, D. F. (2005). Elevated levels of herbivory in urban landscapes: are declines in tree health more than an edge effect? *Ecology and Society*, **10**, 10. http://www.ecologyandsociety.org/vol10/iss1/art10/

Churchill, T. B. (1997). Spiders as ecological indicators: an overview for Australia. *Memoirs of the Museum of Victoria*, **56**, 331–8.

Cilliers, S. S. (1999). Vegetation analysis of urban open spaces in Potchefstroom, North West Province, South Africa. In *African Plants: Biodiversity, Taxonomy and Uses. Proceedings AETFAT Congress, Harare, Zimbabwe*, ed. J. Timberlake and S. Kativu. Kew: Royal Botanic Gardens.

Cilliers, S. S. and Bredenkamp, G. J. (2000). Vegetation of roadside verges on an urbanisation gradient in Potchefstroom, South Africa. *Landscape and Urban Planning*, **46**, 217–39.

Cilliers, S. S., Müller, N. and Drewes, J. E. (2004). Overview on urban nature conservation: situation in the western-grassland biome of South Africa. *Urban Forestry and Urban Greening* **3**, 49–62.

Cilliers, S. S., Schoeman, L. L. and Bredenkamp, G. J. (1998). Wetland plant communities in the Potchefstroom municipal area, North West Province, South Africa. *Bothalia*, **28**, 213–9.

Cilliers, S. S., Van Wyk, E. and Bredenkamp, G. J. (1999). Urban nature conservation: vegetation of natural areas in the Potchefstroom municipal area, North West Province, South Africa. *Koedoe*, **42**, 1–30.

Cincotta, R. P., Wisnewski, J. and Engelman, R. (2000). Human population in the biodiversity hotspots. *Nature*, **404**, 990–2.

Cinzano, P. (2000a). The growth of light pollution in north-eastern Italy from 1960–1995. In *Measuring and Modelling Light Pollution*, ed. P. Cinzano. *Memorie della Societa Astronomica Italiana*, **71**, 159–65.

Cinzano, P. (2000b). The propagation of light pollution in diffusely urbanised areas. In *Measuring and Modelling Light Pollution*, ed. P. Cinzano. *Memorie della Societa Astronomica Italiana*, **71**, 93–112.

Cinzano, P., ed. (2000c). Measuring and modelling light pollution. *Memorie della Societa Astronomica Italiana*, **71**, pp. 279.

Cinzano, P., ed. (2002). *Light Pollution and the Protection of the Night Environment.* Proceedings of the Conference Light Pollution and the Protection of the Night Environment, Venice 2002. Thiene, Italy: Light Pollution and Science Technology Institute.

Cinzano, P., Falchi, F., Elvidge, C. D. and Baugh, K. E. (2000a). The artificial night sky brightness from DMSP satellite Operational Linescan System measurements. *Monthly Notices of the Royal Astronomical Society*, **318**, 641–57.

Cinzano, P., Falchi, F., Elvidge, C. D. and Baugh, K. E. (2000b). Mapping the artificial sky brightness in Europe from DMSP satellite measurements: the situation of the night sky in Italy in the last quarter of century. *Memorie della Societa Astronomica Italiana*, **71**, 1149–57.

Cinzano, P., Falchi, P. and Elvidge, C. D. (2001). The first World Atlas of the artificial night sky brightness. *Monthly Notices of the Royal Astronomical Society*, **328**, 689–707.

City of Lacey (2002). *Critical Area Ordinance – Zero Effect Drainage Discharge.* Chapter 14.31. Thurston County, Washington: City of Lacey.

City of Port Phillip (2003). *Inkerman Oasis Development at the Former Municipal Depot Site, St Kilda: A Joint Venture Residential Development Between the City of Port Phillip and Inkerman Development PTY. Ltd. Sustainable Design Features.* Melbourne: City of Port Phillip.

City of Seattle (2002). *Seattle's Street Edge Alternatives Project.* Accessed on 28 November 2002. http://www.cityofseattle.net/util

Clark, T. E. and Samways, M. J. (1997). Sampling arthropod diversity for urban ecological landscaping in a species-rich southern hemisphere. *Journal of Insect Conservation*, **1**, 221–34.

Clarke, K. R. (1993). Non-parametric multivariate analyses of change in community structure. *Journal of Ecology*, **18**, 117–43.

Clarke, R. D. (1972). The effect of toe clipping on survival in Fowler's toad (*Bufo woodhousei fowleri*). *Copeia*, **1972**, 182–5.

Clay, G. (1973). *Close Up: How to Read the American City.* New York: Praeger Publishers.

Clay, G. (1994). *Real Places: An Unconventional Guide to America's Generic Landscape.* Chicago: University of Chicago Press.

Clements, A. (1983). Suburban development and resultant changes in the vegetation of the bushland of the northern Sydney region. *Australian Journal of Ecology*, **8**, 307–19.

Clergeau, P., Croci, S., Jokimäki, J., Kaisanlahti-Jokimäki, M. and Dinetti, M. (2006). Avifauna homogenization by urbanisation: analysis at different European latitudes. *Biological Conservation*, **127**, 336–44.

Clergeau, P., Savard, J.-P. L., Mennechez, G. and Falardeau, G. (1998). Bird abundance and diversity along an urban–rural gradient: a comparative study between two cities on different continents. *Condor*, **100**, 413–25.

Cleve, K. (1967). Das spektrale Wahrnehmungsvermögen nachts fliegender Schmetterlinge. *Nachrichtenblatt der Bayerischen Entomologen*, **16**, 33–53.

Clevenger, A. P. (1997). *Wildlife Underpass Use by Ungulates and Large Carnivores along Twinned Sections of the Trans-Canada Highway in Banff National Park, 1995–1997.* Canmore, Alberta, Canada: Alberta Environmental Protection, Natural Resources Service.

Clevenger, A. P. and Waltho, N. (1999). Dry drainage culvert use and design considerations for small- and medium-sized mammal movement across a major transportation corridor. In *Proceedings of the Third International Conference on Wildlife Ecology and Transportation*, ed. G. Evink, P. Garrett and A. D. Ziegler. Missoula, Montana, USA: Florida Department of Transportation.

Clevenger, A. P., Chruszcz, B. and Gunson, K. E. (2003). Spatial patterns and factors influencing small vertebrate fauna road-kill aggregations. *Biological Conservation* **109**, 15–26.

Clout, M. N. and Gaze, P. D. (1984). Effects of plantation forestry on birds in New Zealand. *Journal of Applied Ecology*, **21**, 795–815.

Clynick, B. G. (2007). Harbour swimming nets: a novel habitat for seahorses. *Aquatic Conservation*, **17**, 1–10.

Clynick, B. G. (2008). Characteristics of an urban fish assemblage: distribution of fish associated with coastal marinas. *Marine Environmental Research*, **65**, 18–33.

Clynick, B. G., Chapman, M. G. and Underwood, A. J. (2007). Effects of epibiota on assemblages of fish associated with urban structures. *Marine Ecology Progress Series*, **332**, 201–10.

Cochran, W. W. and Graber, R. R. (1958). Attraction of nocturnal migrants by lights on a television tower. *Wilson Bulletin*, **70**, 378–80.

Coe, W. R. (1932). Season of attachment and rate of growth of sedentary marine organisms at the pier of the Scripps Institute of Oceanography, La Jolla, California. *Bulletin of the Scripps Institution of Oceanography*, **3**, 37–86.

Coffman, L. (2000). Low-impact development design: a new paradigm for stormwater management mimicking and restoring the natural hydrologic regime – an alternative stormwater management technology. *Proceedings of the National Conference on Tools for Urban Water Resource Management and Protection*, February 2000, pp. 1–158.

Cohen, J. E. (2003). Human population: the next half century. *Science*, **302**, 1172–5.

Cohen, R. J. and Sullivan, W. T., eds. (2001). *Preserving the Astronomical Sky*. Proceedings of the 196th Symposium of the International Astronomical Union in Conjunction with UNISPACE III at Vienna, Austria, July 12–16, 1999. San Francisco: ASP Conference Series.

Colandini, V., Legret, M., Brosseaud, Y. and Balades, J. D. (1995). Metallic pollution in clogging materials of urban porous pavements. *Water Science and Technology*, **32**, 57–62.

Cole, J., Lovett, G. and Findlay, S., eds. (1991). *Comparative Analysis of Ecosystems: Patterns, Mechanisms and Theories*. New York: Springer-Verlag.

Cole, J. J., Peierls, B. L., Caraco, N. F. and Pace, M. L. (1993). Nitrogen loading of rivers as a human-driven process. In *Humans as Components of Ecosystems: The Ecology of Subtle Human Effects and Populated Areas*, ed. M. J. McDonnell and S. T. A. Pickett. New York: Springer-Verlag, pp. 141–57.

Coleman, M. A. and Connell, S. D. (2001). Weak effects of epibiota on the abundances of fishes associated with pier pilings in Sydney Harbour. *Environmental Biology of Fishes*, **61**, 231–9.

Collins, J.P., Kinzig, A., Grimm, N.B. *et al.* (2000). A new urban ecology. *American Scientist*, **88**, 416–25.

Collins, S.L. (1992). Fire frequency and community heterogeneity in tallgrass prairie vegetation. *Ecology*, **73**, 2001–6.

Congalton, R. and Green, G.K. (1999). *Assessing the Accuracy of Remotely Sensed Data: Principles and Practices*. Boca Raton, Florida: Lewis Publishers.

Connell, J.H. (1972). Community interactions on marine rocky intertidal shores. *Annual Review of Ecology and Systematics*, **3**, 169–92.

Connell, J.H. (1978). Diversity in tropical rainforests and coral reefs. *Science*, **199**, 1302–10.

Connell, J.H. (1983). On the prevalence and relative importance of interspecific competition: evidence from field experiments. *American Naturalist*, **122**, 661–96.

Connell, J.H. and Keough, M.J. (1985). Disturbance and patch dynamics of subtidal marine animals on hard substrata. In *The Ecology of Natural Disturbance and Patch Dynamics*, ed. S.T.A. Pickett and P.S. White. London: Academic Press, pp. 125–51.

Connell, S.D. (2000). Floating pontoons create novel habitats for subtidal epibiota. *Journal of Experimental Marine Biology and Ecology*, **247**, 183–94.

Connell, S.D. (2001a). Urban structures as marine habitats: an experimental comparison of the composition and abundance of subtidal epibiota among pilings, pontoons and rocky reefs. *Marine Environmental Research*, **52**, 115–25.

Connell, S.D. (2001b). Predatory fish do not always affect the early development of epibenthic assemblages. *Journal of Experimental Marine Biology and Ecology*, **260**, 1–12.

Connell, S.D. and Glasby, T.M. (1999). Do urban structures influence local abundance and diversity of subtidal epibiota? A case study from Sydney Harbour, Australia. *Marine Environmental Research*, **47**, 373–87.

Connell, S.D. and Jones, G.P. (1991). The influence of habitat complexity on postrecruitment processes in a temperate reef fish population. *Journal of Experimental Marine Biology and Ecology*, **151**, 271–94.

Connor, E.F. and McCoy, E.D. (1979). The statistics and biology of the species–area relationship. *American Naturalist*, **113**, 791–833.

Connor, E.F., Hafernik, J., Levy, J., Moore, V.L. and Rickman, J.K. (2002). Insect conservation in an urban biodiversity hotspot: the San Francisco Bay Area. *Journal of Insect Conservation*, **6**, 247–59.

Conover, M.R. (1995). What is the urban deer problem and where did it come from? In *Urban Deer: A Manageable Resource*, ed. J. McAninch. St. Louis, MO: North Central Section of The Wildlife Society.

Constant, C. (1994). *The Woodland Cemetery: towards a spiritual landscape*. Stockholm: Byggförlaget.

Coovadia, Y., Dominik, T., Walton, B. and Wulfsohn, T. (1993). How green is my urban development NGO: sustainable development responses from BESG. In *Hidden Faces: Environment, Development, Justice: South Africa and the Global Context*, ed. D. Hallowes. Pietermaritzburg: Earthlife Africa, pp. 156–84.

Coppolillo, P., Gomez, H., Maisels, F. and Wallace, R. (2004). Selection criteria for suites of landscape species as a basis for site-based conservation. *Biological Conservation*, **115**, 419–30.

Costanza, R., d'Arge, R., de Groot, R. *et al.* (1997). The value of the world's ecosystem services and natural capital. *Nature*, **387**, 253–60.

Costermans, L. (1983). *Native Trees and Shrubs of South-eastern Australia*. Sydney: Weldon.

Cousins, A. and Nagpaul, H. (1979). *Urban Life. The Sociology of Cities and Urban Society*. New York: John Wiley and Sons.

Cox, P.A. and Elmqvist, T. (2000). Pollinator extinction in the Pacific Islands. *Conservation Biology*, **14**, 1237–9.

Craig, J.L., Craig, C.J., Murphy, B.D. and Murphy, A.J. (1995). Community involvement for effective conservation: what do the community want? In *Nature Conservation 4: The Role of Networks*, ed. D.A. Saunders, J.L. Craig and E.M. Mittisky. Chipping Norton: Surrey Beatty and Sons, pp. 130–9.

Cranfield, H.J., Carbines, G., Michael, K.P., Dunn, A., Stotter, D.R. and Smith, D.J. (2001). Promising signs of regeneration of blue cod and oyster habitat changed by dredging in Foveaux Strait, southern New Zealand. *New Zealand Journal of Marine and Freshwater Research*, **35**, 897–908.

Crawley, M.J., Brown, S.L., Heard, M.S. and Edwards, G.R. (1999). Invasion-resistance in experimental grassland communities: species richness or species identity? *Ecology Letters*, **2**, 140–8.

Creedy, J. and Wurzbacher, A.D. (2001). The economic value of a forested catchment with timber, water and carbon sequestration benefits. *Ecological Economics*, **38**, 71–83.

Cringan, A.T. (1987). Use of Kulcyznski's similarity indices in analysis of urban avifaunas. In *Integrating Man and Nature in the Metropolitan Environment*, ed. L.W. Adams and D.L. Leedy. Columbia, MD: National Institute for Urban Wildlife.

Crisp, D.J. and Southward, A.J. (1959). The further spread of *Elminius modestus* in the British Isles to 1959. *Journal of the Marine Biological Association of the United Kingdom*, **38**, 429–37.

Cronon, W. (2003). *Changes in the Land: Indians, Colonists, and the Ecology of New England* 20th anniversary edn. New York: Hill and Wang.

Crooks, K.R. and Soule, M.E. (1999). Mesopredator release and avifaunal extinctions in a fragmented system. *Nature*, **400**, 563–6.

Crooks, K.R., Suarez, A.V. and Bolger, D.T. (2004) Avian assemblages along a gradient of urbanization in a highly fragmented landscape. *Biological Conservation*, **115**, 451–62.

Crossland, A. (2005). A national biodiversity hot-spot from the treatment of urban wastewater – the Bromley Oxidation Ponds and Te Huingi Wildlife Refuge, Christchurch. In *Greening the City*, ed. M.I. Dawson. Proceedings of a conference held by the Royal New Zealand Institute of Horticulture, Christchurch, 21–24 October 2003. Christchurch: Caxton Press, pp. 189–96.

Crowe, T. (1996). Different effects of microhabitat fragmentation on patterns of dispersal of an intertidal gastropod in two habitats. *Journal of Experimental Marine Biology and Ecology*, **206**, 83–107.

Crucitti, P., Malori, M. and Rotella, G. (1998). The scorpions of the urban habitat of Rome (Italy). *Urban Ecosystems*, **2**, 163–70.

Cummings, S. L. (1994). Colonisation of a nearshore artificial reef at Boca Raton (Palm Beach County), Florida. *Bulletin of Marine Science*, **55**, 1193–215.

Cunningham, S. A. (2000). Depressed pollination in habitat fragments causes low fruit set. *Proceedings of the Royal Society of London B*, **267**, 1149–52.

Curry, R. J. (1981). *Hydrology of Catchments Draining to the Pauatahanui Inlet. Water and Soil Technical Publication 23*. Wellington: Ministry of Works and Development.

Curtis, J. T. and McIntosh, R. P. (1951). An upland forest continuum in the prairie-forest border region of Wisconsin. *Ecology*, **72**, 476–96.

Cwikowa, A., Grabowski, A., Lesiñski, A. J. and Myxzkowski, S. (1984). Flora and vegetation of the Niepolomice Forest. In *Forest Ecosystems in Industrial Regions*, ed. W. Grodziñski, J. Weiner and P. F. Maycock. New York: Springer-Verlag, pp. 1–11.

Czechowski, W. (1982). Occurrence of carabids (*Coleoptera, Carabidae*) in the urban greenery of Warsaw according to the land utilization and cultivation. *Memorabilia Zoologica*, **39**, 3–108.

Daily, G. C., ed. (1997). *Nature's Services: Societal Dependence on Natural Ecosystems*. Washington, DC: Island Press.

Daily, G. C. and Ellison, K. (2002). *The New Economy of Nature*. Washington, DC: Island Press.

Danermark, B., Ekström, M., Jakobsen, L. and Karlsson, C. (1997). *Att förklara samhället*. Lund: Stuentlitteratur.

Daniels, G. D. and Kirkpatrick, J. B. (2006). Comparing the characteristics of front and back domestic gardens in Hobart, Tasmania, Australia. *Landscape and Urban Planning*, **78**, 344–52.

Danielson, W. R., De Graaf, R. M. and Fuller, T. K. (1997). Rural and suburban forest edges: effect of egg predators and nest predation rates. *Landscape and Urban Planning*, **38**, 25–36.

Danthanarayana, W. (1986). Lunar periodicty of insect flight and migration. In *Insect Flight: Dispersal and Migration*, ed. W. Danthanarayana. Berlin, Heidelberg: Springer, pp. 88–119.

Darnall, M. J. (1983). The American cemetery as picturesque landscape. *Winterthur Portfolio*, **18**, 249–69.

Davies, R. and Christie, J. (2001). Rehabilitating Western Sydney's bushland: processes needed for sustained recovery. *Ecological Management and Restoration*, **2**, 167–78.

Davis, A. and Glick, T. F. (1978). Urban ecosystems and island biogeography. *Environmental Conservation*, **52**, 37–48.

Davis, B. N. K. (1978). Urbanization and the diversity of insects. In *Diversity of Insect Faunas, Symposium of the Royal Entomological Society of London 9*, ed. L. A. Mound and N. Waloff. Oxford: Blackwell, pp. 126–38.

Davis, B. N. K. (1982). Habitat diversity and invertebrates in urban areas. In *Urban Ecology*, ed. R. Bornkamn, J. A. Lee and M. R. D. Seaward. Oxford: Blackwell Scientific Publications, pp. 49–63.

Davis, N. and Van Blaricom, G. R. (1982). Man-made structures on marine sediments: effects on adjacent benthic communities. *Marine Biology*, **70**, 295–303.

Dawson, D. (1994). *Are Habitat Corridors Conduits for Animals and Plants in a Fragmented Landscape? A Review of the Scientific Evidence.* English Nature Research Reports No. 94. Peterborough: English Nature.

Dayton, P. K. (1971). Competition, disturbance, and community organization: the provision and subsequent utilization of space in a rocky intertidal community. *Ecological Monographs,* **41,** 351–89.

De Kimpe, C. D. and Morel, J. (2000). Urban soil management: a growing concern. *Soil Science,* **165,** 31–40.

De Mers, M. N. (1993). Roadside ditches for range expansion of the western harvester ant (*Pogonomyrmex occidentalis* Cresson). *Landscape Ecology,* **8,** 93–102.

Dean, T. A. and Hurd, L. E. (1980). Development in an estuarine fouling community: the influence of early colonists on later arrivals. *Oecologia,* **46,** 295–301.

Debinski, D. M. and Holt, R. D. (2000). A survey and overview of habitat fragmentation experiments. *Conservation Biology,* **14,** 342–55.

Debinski, D. M., Ray, C. and Saveraid, E. H. (2001). Species diversity and the scale of the landscape mosaic: do scales of movement and patch size affect diversity? *Biological Conservation,* **98,** 179–90.

Decker, E. H., Elliott, S., Smith, F. A., Blake, D. R. and Rowland, F. S. (2000). Energy and material flow through the urban ecosystem. *Annual Review of Energy and Environment,* **25,** 685–740.

Deelstra, T. (1998). Towards ecological sustainable cities: strategies, models and tools. In *Urban Ecology,* ed. J. Breuste, H. Feldmann and O. Uhlmann. Berlin: Springer, pp. 17–22.

Del Campillo, M. C., Van der Zee, S. E. A. T. M. and Torrent, J. (1999). Modelling long-term phosphorus leaching and changes in phosphorus fertility in excessively fertilized acid sandy soils. *European Journal of Soil Science,* **50:** 391–9.

Dember, S. (1993). Urban forestry in Beijing. *Unasylva, 173. Urban and Peri-Urban Forestry.* Accessed 13 March 2005. http://www.fao.org/docrep/u9300e/u9300e00.htm

Dennis, J. G. and Ruggiero, M. A. (1996). Biodiversity inventory: building an inventory at scales from local to global. In *Biodiversity in Managed Landscapes,* ed. R. C. Szaro and D. W. Johnston. Oxford: Oxford University Press, pp. 149–56.

Dennis, R. L. H. and Hardy, P. B. (2001). Loss rates of butterfly species with urban development. A test of atlas data and sampling artifacts at a fine scale. *Biodiversity and Conservation,* **10,** 1831–7.

Denys, C. and Schmidt, H. (1998). Insect communities on experimental mugwort (*Artemisia vulgaris* L.) plots along an urban gradient. *Oecologia,* **113,** 266–77.

Department of Environmental Affairs and Tourism (DEAT) (2001). *Sustaining Development in South Africa: An Analytical Review of Progress towards Sustainable Development in South Africa.* Pretoria: DEAT.

Department of the Prime Minister and Cabinet (2003). *Sustainable Development for New Zealand Programme of Action.* Wellington: Department of the Prime Minister and Cabinet.

Derraik, J. G. B. (2002). The pollution of the marine environment by plastic debris: a review. *Marine Pollution Bulletin,* **44,** 842–52.

Develey, P. F. and Stouffer, P. C. (2001). Effects of roads on movements by understorey birds in mixed-species flocks in central Amazonian Brazil. *Conservation Biology*, **15**, 1416–22.

Dewar, D. (1994). Urban planning, shelter strategies and economic development. In *The Economic Reconstruction of South African Cities*, ed. R. Tomlinson, D. Dewar, R. Hunter, J. Robinson and C. Boldogh. Johannesburg: Witwatersrand University Press.

Diamond, J. M. (1996). A-bombs against amphibians. *Nature*, **383**, 386–7.

Diamond, J. M. (1997). *Guns, Gems and Steel: The Fates of Human Societies*. New York: W. W. Norton and Co.

Dickman, C. R. (1986). Habitat utilization and diet of the harvest mouse *Micromys minutus* in an urban environment. *Acta Theriologica*, **31**, 249–56.

Dickman, C. R. (1987). Habitat fragmentation and vertebrate species richness in an urban environment. *Journal of Applied Ecology*, **24**, 337–51.

Didham, R. K. (1998). Altered leaf-litter decomposition rates in tropical forest fragments. *Oecologia*, **116**, 397–406.

Didham, R. K., Hammond, P. M., Lawton, J. H., Eggleton, P. and Stork, N. E. (1998). Beetle species responses to tropical forest fragmentation. *Ecological Monographs*, **68**, 295–323.

Diekelmann, J. and Schuster, R. (1982). *Natural Landscaping: Designing with Native Plant Communities*. New York: McGraw-Hill.

Dinetti, M. (1996). Urban ornithological atlases in Italy. *Acta Ornithologica*, **31**, 15–23.

Dixon, J., Dupuis, A., Lysnar, P., Spoonley, P. and Le Heron, R. (2001). *From Clay Pit to Community: A Study of Medium Density Housing in Ambrico Place, New Lynn*. Report for the Waitakere City Council. Auckland: Massey University and The University of Auckland.

Doering, P. H., Roman, C. T., Beatty, L. L., Keller, A. A. and Oviatt, C. A. (1995). *Water Quality and Habitat Evaluation of Bass Harbor Marsh, Acadia National Park, Maine*. Boston, MA: National Park Service, New England System Support Office. NPS/NESORNR/NRTR/95–31.

Doheny, E. (1999). *Index of Hydrologic Characteristics and Data Resources for the Gwynns Falls Watershed, Baltimore County and Baltimore City, Maryland*. Baltimore, MD: United States Geological Survey, Open-File Report, pp. 99–213.

Donnay, J. P., Barnsley, M. J. and Longley, P. A. (2001). *Remote Sensing and Urban Analysis*. London: Taylor and Francis.

Dorney, J. R., Guntenspergen, G. R., Keough, J. R. and Stearns, F. (1984). Composition and structure of an urban woody plant community. *Urban Ecology*, **8**, 69–90.

Dougherty, A. B. (1992). *Major Uses of Land in the United States. Agricultural Economics Report no. 723*. Washington, DC: Natural Resources and Environment Division, Economic Research Service, US Department of Agriculture.

Douglas, I. (1994). Human settlements. In *Changes in Land Use and Land Cover: A Global Perspective*, ed. W. B. Meyer and B. L. Turner. Cambridge: Cambridge University Press, pp. 149–69.

Dow, D. D. (1977). Indiscriminate interspecific aggression leading to almost sole occupancy of space by a single species of bird. *Emu*, **77**, 115–21.

Dow, K. (2000). Social dimensions of gradients in urban ecosystems. *Urban Ecosystems*, **4**, 255–75.

Downing, J. A. (1991). Comparing apples with oranges: methods of inter-ecosystem comparison. In *Comparative Analyses of Ecosystems: Patterns, Mechanisms, and Theories*, ed. J. Cole, G. Lovett, and S. Findlay. New York: Springer-Verlag, pp. 24–45.

Drayton, B. and Primack, R. B. (1996). Plant species lost in an isolated conservation area in metropolitan Boston from 1894 to 1993. *Conservation Biology*, **10**, 30–9.

Dreistadt, S. H., Dahlsten, D. L. and Frankie, G. W. (1990). Urban forest and insect ecology: complex interactions among trees, insects and people. *BioScience*, **40**, 192–8.

Drewes, J. E. and Cilliers, S. S. (2004). Integration of urban biotope mapping in spatial planning. *Town and Regional Planning*, **47**, 15–29.

Dryzek, J. (1997). *The Politics of the Earth: Environmental Discourses*. Oxford: Oxford University Press.

Duarte, C. M. (1991). Variance and the description of nature. In *Comparative Analysis of Ecosystems: Patterns, Mechanisms and Theories*, ed. J. J. Cole, G. M. Lovett, S. E. G. Findlay. New York: Springer-Verlag, pp. 301–18.

Duffey, E. (1975). The effects of human trampling on the fauna of grassland litter. *Biological Conservation*, **7**, 255–74.

Duhme, F. and Lecke, Th. (1986). Zur Interpretation der Nutzungstypenkarte München. *Landschaft und Stadt*, **18**, 174–85.

Duhme, F. and Pauleit, S. (1992a). Naturschutzprogramm für München: Landschaftsökologisches Rahmenkonzept. *Geographische Rundschau*, **44**, 554–61.

Duhme, F. and Pauleit, S. (1992b). *Structure Type Mapping as a Tool of Spatial-incusive Analysis and Assessment of Environmental Conditions in Munich. Part 1: Objectives and Methodology*. Freising.

Duhme, F. and Pauleit, S. (1994). *Structure Type Mapping as a Tool of Spatial-incusive Analysis and Assessment of Environmental Conditions in Munich. Part 2: Testing the Structure Type Mapping in a Test Area*. Freising.

Duhme, F. and Pauleit, S. (2000). A landscape ecological masterplan for the city of Munich. In *Habitat Creation and Wildlife Conservation in Urban and Post-Industrial Environments*, ed. J. O. Riley and S. E. Page. Chichester: Packard Publishing.

Dunlap, R. E. and Catton, W. Jr (1994). Struggling with human exemptionalism: the rise, decline, and revitalisation of environmental sociology. *The American Sociologist*, **25**, 5–30.

Dunlap, T. R. (1999). *Nature and the English Diaspora. Environment and history in the United States, Canada, Australia, and New Zealand*. Cambridge, UK: Cambridge University Press.

Dwyer, J. F., Nowak, D. J., Noble, M. H. and Sisinni, S. M. (2000). *Connecting People with Ecosystems in the 21st Century: An Assessment of our Nation's Urban Forests*. USDA Forest Service Technical Report PNW-GTR-490.

Dyrberg, T. B. (1997). *The Circular Structure of Power – Politics, Identity, Community*. London and New York: Verso.

Dyring, A.-K. (1982). *Naturmark i utbyggingsområder–Sluttrapport*. Oslo: Norges Landbruksvidenskapelige Forskningsråd rapport nr 420. (In Norwegian)

Dyring, A.-K. (1984). Naturmark i utbyggingsområder. [Summary: Natural Vegetation in Development Areas]. Unpublished doctoral thesis, Institutt for Landskapsarkitektur, the Norwegian Agricultural University. (In Norwegian)

Dyring, A.-K. (1986). *Natur i boligområder*. Oslo: Landbruksforlaget. (In Norwegian)

Eason, C. T. and O'Halloran, K. (2002). Biomarkers in toxicology versus ecological risk assessment. *Toxicology*, **181–2**, 517–21.

Eberhardt, L. L. and Thomas, J. M. (1991). Designing environmental field studies. *Ecological Monographs*, **6**, 53–73.

Eckrich, C. E. and Holmquist, J. G. (2000). Trampling in a seagrass assemblage: direct effects, response of associated fauna, and the role of substrate characteristics. *Marine Ecology Progress Series*, **201**, 199–209.

Egan, D. (1990). Historic initiatives in ecological restoration. *Restoration and Management Notes*, **8**, 83–9.

Egerton, F. N. (1993). The history and present entanglements of some general ecological perspectives. In *Humans as Components of Ecosystems: The Ecology of Subtle Human Effects and Populated Areas*, ed. M. J. McDonnell and S. T. A. Pickett. Berlin: Springer-Verlag, pp. 9–23.

Ehnberg, M. (1991). *Isolerade skogsområden i Esbo*. Esbo, Finland: Esbo stadsplaneringsverks undersökningar och utredningar, B16: 1991. (In Swedish)

Ehrenfeld, D. W. (1976). The conservation of non-resources. *American Scientist*, **64**, 660–8.

Ehrenfeld, J. G. (2000). Evaluating wetlands within an urban context. *Ecological Engineering*, **15**, 253–65.

Ehrenfeld, J. G. (2003). Effects of exotic plant invasions on soil nitrogen cycling processes. *Ecosystems*, **6**, 503–23.

Ehrenfeld, J. G. (2004). The expression of multiple functions in urban forested wetlands. *Wetlands*, **24**, 719–33.

Ehrenfeld, J. G. and Schneider, J. P. (1993). Responses of forested wetland vegetation to perturbations of water chemistry and hydrology. *Wetlands*, **13**, 122–9.

Eisenbeis, G. (2001a). *Künstliches Licht und Lichtverschmutzung – eine Gefahr für die Diversität der Insekten? Verhandlungen Westdeutscher Entomologen Tag 2000*, Dusseldorf: Löbbeche Museum, pp. 31–50.

Eisenbeis, G. (2001b). Künstliches Licht und Insekten: eine vergleichende Studie in Rheinhessen. *Schriftenreihe für Landschaftspflege und Naturschutz*, **67**, 75–100.

Eisenbeis, G. (2006). Artificial night lighting and insects: insects at street lamps in a rural setting in Germany. In *Ecological Consequences of Artificial Night Lighting*, ed. C. Rich and T. Longcore. Covelo, California: Island Press, pp. 281–304.

Eisenbeis, G. and Hassel, F. (2000). Zur Anziehung nachtaktiver Insekten durch Straßenlaternen – eine Studie kommunaler Beleuchtungseinrichtungen in der Agrarlandschaft Rheinhessens. *Natur und Landschaft*, **75**, 145–56.

Ellenberg, H., Weber, H. E., Düll, R. *et al.* (1992). *Zeigerwerte von Pflanzen in Mitteleuropa*, 2nd edn. *Scripta Geobotanica*, **18**, 258.

Elliott, B. (1986). *Victorian Gardens*. Portland, OR: Timber Press.

Ellis, E. C. (2004). Long-term ecological changes in the densely populated rural landscapes of China. In *Ecosystems and Land Use Change*. ed. G. P. Asner, R. S. DeFries and R. H. Houghton, Geophysical Monographs Series Vol. 153. Washington, DC: American Geophysical Union, pp. 303–20.

Ellis, E. C., Li, R. G., Yang, L. Z. and Cheng, X. (2000). Long-term change in village-scale ecosystems in China using landscape and statistical methods. *Ecological Applications*, **10**, 1057–73.

Ellis, E. C., Wang, H., Xiao, H. S. *et al.* (2006). Measuring long-term ecological changes in densely populated landscapes using current and historical high resolution imagery. *Remote Sensing of the Environment*, **100**, 457–73.

Ellis, F. and Sumberg, J. (1998). Food production, urban areas and policy responses. *World Development*, **26**, 213–25.

Elmqvist, T., Colding, J., Barthel, S. *et al.* (2004). The dynamics of social-ecological systems in urban landscapes. *Annals of the New York Academy of Sciences*, **1023**, 308–22.

Elster, J. ed. (1998). *Deliberative Democracy*. Cambridge: Cambridge University Press.

Elton, C. S. (1958). *The Ecology of Invasion by Animals and Plants*. London: Methuen.

Emlen, J. T. (1974). An urban bird community in Tucson, Arizona: derivation, structure, regulation. *Condor*, **76**, 184–97.

Emmanuel, R. (1997). Urban vegetational change as an indicator of demographic trends in cities: the case of Detroit. *Environment and Planning*, **24**, 415–26.

Endres, K.-P. and Schad, W. (1997). *Biologie des Mondes – Mondperiodik und Lebensrhythmen*. Stuttgart, Leipzig: S. Hirzel.

Esler, A. E. (1988a). The naturalisation of plants in urban Auckland, New Zealand. 4. The nature of the naturalised species. *New Zealand Journal of Botany*, **26**, 345–85.

Esler, A. E. (1988b). The naturalisation of plants in urban Auckland, New Zealand. 5. Success of the alien species. *New Zealand Journal of Botany*, **26**, 565–84.

Estes, J. E. (1966). Some applications of aerial infrared imagery. *Annals of the Association of American Geographers*, **56**, 673–82.

Etzioni, A. (1973). Mixed-scanning: a 'third' approach to decision-making. In *A Reader in Planning Theory*, ed. A. Faludi. Oxford: Pergamon Press.

Eversham, B. C., Roy, D. B. and Telfer, M. G. (1996). Urban, industrial and other manmade sites as analogues of natural habitat for Carabidae. *Annali Zoologica Fennici*, **33**, 149–56.

Fábos, J. G. (2004). Greenway planning in the United States: its origins and recent case studies. *Landscape and Urban Planning*, **68**, 321–42.

Facelli, J. M. and Pickett, S. T. A. (1991). Plant litter: its dynamics and effects on plant community structure. *Botanical Review*, **57**, 1–32.

Fagan, W. F., Fortin, M.-J. and Soykan, C. (2003). Integrating edge detection and dynamic modeling in quantitative assessment of ecological boundaries. *BioScience*, **53**, 730–8.

Fahrig, L. (1997). Relative effects of habitat loss and fragmentation on population extinction. *Journal of Wildlife Management*, **61**, 603–10.

Fahrig, L. (2003). Effects of habitat fragmentation on biodiversity. *Annual Review of Ecology, Evolution and Systematics*, **34**, 487–515.

Fahrig, L., Pedlar, J. H., Pope, S. E., Taylor, P. D. and Wegner, J. F. (1995). Effect of road traffic on amphibian density. *Biological Conservation*, **73**, 177–82.

Fairweather, P. G. (1991). A conceptual framework for ecological studies of coastal resources: an example of a tunicate collected for bait on Australian seashores. *Ocean and Shoreline Management*, **15**, 125–42.

Falck, J. (1996). Pre-commercial thinning in urban forests. In *Urban Forestry in the Nordic Countries*. Proceedings of a Nordic workshop on urban forestry, held in Reykjavik, Iceland, 21–24 September 1996, ed. T. B. Randrup and K. Nilsson. Danish Forest and Landscape Research Institute, pp. 28–31.

Falck, J. and Rydberg, D. (1996). *Framtidens skog – att sköta tätortsnära ungskog. Stad and Land nr 139*. Alnarp, Sweden: Movium. (In Swedish)

Falkenmark, M. and Chapman, T. (1989). *Comparative Hydrology: An Ecological Approach to Land and Water Resources*. Paris: UNESCO.

Faludi, A. (1987). *A Decision-Centred View of Environmental Planning*. Oxford: Pergamon Press.

Fanalli, G., Piraino, S., Belmonte, G., Geraci, S. and Boero, F. (1994). Human predation along Apulian rocky coasts (SE Italy): desertification caused by *Lithophaga lithophaga* (Mollusca) fisheries. *Marine Ecology Progress Series*, **110**, 1–8.

Farris, C. N. and Oviatt, C. A. (1999). Changes in metabolic rates under fluctuating salinity regimes for two subtidal estuarine habitats. *Estuaries*, **22**, 126–37.

Faubion, J. D., ed. (2002). *The Essential Works of Foucault, 1954–1984*. Vol. 3, *Power*. London: Penguin.

Faulkner, S. (2004). Urbanization impacts on the structure and function of forested wetlands. *Urban Ecosystems*, **7**, 89–106.

Felson, A. J. and Pickett, S. T. A. (2005). Design experiments: new approaches to studying urban ecosystems. *Frontiers in Ecology and Environment*, **3**, 549–56.

Fernandes, J. P. (2000). Landscape ecology and conservation management – evaluation of alternatives in a highway EIA process. *Environmental Impact Assessment Review*, **20**, 665–80.

Fernández-Juricic, E. (2000). Avifaunal use of wooded streets in an urban landscape. *Conservation Biology*, **14**, 513–21.

Fernández-Juricic, E. and Jokimäki, J. (2001). A habitat island approach to conserving birds in urban landscapes: case studies from southern and northern Europe. *Biodiversity and Conservation*, **10**, 2023–43.

Fidler, F., Burgman, M. A., Cumming, G., Buttrose, R. and Thomason, N. (2006). Impact of criticism of null-hypothesis significance testing on statistical reporting practices in Conservation Biology. *Conservation Biology*, **20**, 1539–44.

Findlay, C. S. and Bourdages, J. (2000). Response time of wetland biodiversity to road construction on adjacent lands. *Conservation Biology*, **14**, 86–94.

Findlay, S. and Jones, C. G. (1990). Exposure of cottonwood plants to ozone alters subsequent leaf decomposition. *Oecologia*, **82**, 248–50.

Findlay, S., Carreiro, M. M., Krischik, V. and Jones, C. G. (1996). Effects of damage to living plants on leaf litter quality. *Ecological Applications*, **6**, 269–75.

Flannery, T. (1999). *The Birth of Sydney*. Melbourne: The Text Publishing Company.

Fleishman, E., Jonsson, B. G. and Sjögren-Gulve, P. (2000). Focal species modeling for biodiversity conservation. *Ecological Bulletins*, **48**, 85–99.

Floerl, O. and Inglis, G. J. (2003). Boat harbour design can exacerbate hull fouling. *Austral Ecology*, **28**, 116–27.

Florgård, C. (1978). *Natur i stad–betydelse, slitage, tålighet, möjligheter att bevara.* Stockholm: Swedish Council for Building Research report BFR T25:1978. (In Swedish)

Florgård, C. (1980). *Att bevara naturmark–kostar det?* Unpublished report to the Swedish Council for Building Research, grant 821437–9. (In Swedish)

Florgård, C. (1981). Naturmark i bebyggelse. [Summary: Natural Vegetation and Development]. Doctoral thesis, Swedish University of Agricultural Sciences, *Landskap*, 64. (In Swedish)

Florgård, C. (1985). Wechselbeziehungen zwischen natürlicher Vegetation und städtischer Bebauung – Ausnutzung vorhandener Vegetation als Mittel ökologischer orientierter Stadtplanung. In *Tagungsbericht 3. Leipiziger Symposium urbane Ökologie.* Leipzig, pp. 325–45. (In German)

Florgård, C. (1991). Natural vegetation as a resource in urban development planning. In *Urban Ecology.* Proceedings of the International Symposium held at Didim, Türkiye, June 5–10 1991, ed. M. A. Öztürk, Ü. Erdem and G. Görk. Izmir, Türkiye: Ege University Press.

Florgård, C. (2000). Long-term changes in indigenous vegetation preserved in urban areas. *Landscape and Urban Planning*, **52**, 101–16.

Florgård, C. ed. (2002). *Indigenous Vegetation Within Urban Development – Ecology and Management of Natural Vegetation Preserved in Urban Areas. Programme and Abstracts.* Uppsala, Sweden: Department of Landscape Planning Ultuna, The Swedish University of Agricultural Sciences.

Florgård, C. (2004) Preservation of indigenous vegetation in urban areas – an introduction. *Landscape and Urban Planning*, **8**, 343–5.

Florgård, C. (2007a). Treatment measures for original natural vegetation preserved in the urban green infrastructure at Järvafältet, Stockholm. In *Globalisation and Landscape Architecture: Issues for Education and Practice International Conference*, 3–6 June 2007. St Petersburg, Russia: St Petersburg State Forest Technical Academy.

Florgård, C. (2007b). Preserved and remnant natural vegetation in cities: a geographically divided field of research. *Landscape Research*, **32**, 79–94.

Florgård, C. (2007c). Preservation of pastures as parts of the urban green infrastructure at Järvafältet, Stockholm: risk of damage caused by man? In *25 Years of Landscape Ecology: Scientific Principles in Practice IALE World Congress*, 8–12 July 2007. Wageningen, The Netherlands.

Florgård, C. and Forsberg, O. (2006). Residents' use of remnant natural vegetation at the residential area of Järvafältet, Stockholm. *Urban Forestry and Urban Greening*, **5**, 83–92.

Florgård, C. and Palm, R. (1980). *Vegetationen i dagvattenhanteringen.* Stockholm: Naturvårdsverket (The Swedish Environment Protection Agency). (In Swedish)

Florgård, C., Andersson, R., Ledin, S., Nord, M. and Rosen, B. (1977). *Naturmark och byggande.* Delrapport 2 från projektet 'Naturmark som resurs i bebyggelseplanering'. Stockholm: Byggforskningsrådet R73:1977. (In Swedish)

Florgård, C., Aspeli, P., Bergholm, J., Ledin, S., Nord, M. and Wallentinus, H.-G. (1984). *Naturmark i bostadsområden. Förändringar i klimat, föroreningssituation, hydrologi, mark och vegetation, orsakade av exploatering och slitage.* Stockholm: Byggforskningsrådet R116:1984. (In Swedish)

Florgård, C., Söderblom, P. and Axelsson, C. (1979). IBM Kista – ett extremt exempel? Abstract p. 168: [The conservation of natural qualities in development areas. IBM Sweden Headquarters as an extreme example on nature preservation]. *Landskap*, **7**, 156–8. (In Swedish)

Flyvbjerg, B. (1998). *Rationality och Power–Democracy in Practice.* Chicago: University of Chicago Press.

Folke, C., Jansson, Å., Larsson, J. and Costanza, R. (1997). Ecosystem appropriation by cities. *Ambio*, **26**, 167–72.

Fong, P. and Zedler, J. B. (2000). Sources, sinks and fluxes of nutrients (N + P) in a small highly modified urban estuary in southern California. *Urban Ecosystems*, **4**, 125–44.

Forbes, S., Cooper, D. and Kendle, A. D. (1997). The history and development of ecological landscape styles. In *Urban Nature Conservation*, ed. A. D. Kendle and S. Forbes. London: E. and F. N. Spon, pp. 69–113.

Force, J. E. and Machlis, G. E. (1997). The human ecosystem. 2. Social indicators in ecosystem management. *Society and Natural Resources*, **10**, 369–82.

Ford, E. D. (2000). *Scientific Method for Ecological Research.* Cambridge: Cambridge University Press.

Foresman, T. W., Pickett, S. T. A. and Zipperer, W. C. (1997). Methods for spatial and temporal land use and land cover assessment for urban ecosystems and application in the greater Baltimore–Chesapeake region. *Urban Ecosystems*, **1**, 201–16.

Forester, J. (1989). *Planning in the Face of Power.* University of California.

Forman, R. T. T. (1995). *Land Mosaics: The Ecology of Landscapes and Regions.* Cambridge: Cambridge University Press.

Forman, R. T. T. (2000). Estimate of the area affected ecologically by the road system in the United States. *Conservation Biology*, **14**, 31–5.

Forman, R. T. T. and Godron, M. (1986). *Landscape Ecology.* New York: John Wiley and Sons.

Forman, R. T. T., Sperling, D., Bissonette, J. A. *et al.* (2002). *Road Ecology: Science and Solutions.* Washington, USA: Island Press.

Forster, B. C. (1983). Some urban measurements from Landsat Data. *Photogrammetric Engineering and Remote Sensing*, **14**, 1693–1707.

Forster, B. C. (1985). An examination of some problems and solutions in monitoring urban areas from satellite platforms. *International Journal of Remote Sensing*, **6**, 139–51.

Foster, D. R. (1993). Land-use history and forest transformations in central New England. In *Humans as Components of Ecosystems*, ed. M. J. McDonnell and S. T. A. Pickett. New York: Springer-Verlag, pp. 91–110.

Fralish, J. S. (2002). Community-based ordination: the problem of data handling and interpretation. *Bulletin of the Ecological Society of America*, **83**, 77–81.

Frank, K. D. (1988). Impact of outdoor lighting on moths: an assessment. *Journal of the Lepidopterists' Society*, **42**, 63–93.

Freeman, C. (1999). Development of a simple method for site survey and assessment in urban areas. *Landscape and Urban Planning*, **44**, 1–11.

Freeman, C. and Buck, O. (2003). Development of an ecological mapping methodology for urban areas in New Zealand. *Landscape and Urban Planning*, **63**, 161–73.

Frey, H. T. (1984). *Expansion of Urban Area in the United States: 1960–1980*. Washington, DC: USDA Economic Research Service Staff Report No. AGES830615.

Friberg, P. (1979). The parklands of Scandinavian cities. In *Nature in Cities. The Natural Environment in the Design and Development of Urban Green Space*, ed. I. Laurie. Chichester, New York: John Wiley and Sons, pp. 327–52.

Friend, J. and Hickling, A. (1997). *Planning Under Pressure – The Strategic Choice Approach*. Oxford: Butterworth-Heinemann.

Frink, C. R. (1991). Estimating nutrient exports to estuaries. *Journal of Environmental Quality*, **20**, 717–24.

Frühauf, M., Diaby, K., Dippmann, S. *et al.* (1993). *Geoökologische Umweltanalyse in der Stadtregion Halle*. Halle: unpublished project report for German Federal Ministry of Research and Technology.

Fry, G. L. A. (2001). Multifunctional landscapes – towards trans-disciplinary research. *Landscape and Urban Planning*, **57**, 159–68.

Fukamachi, K., Oku, H. and Nakashizuka, T. (2001). The change of a satoyama landscape and its causality in Kamiseya, Kyoto Prefecture, Japan between 1970 and 1995. *Landscape Ecology*, **16**, 703–17.

Fuller, R. J., Stuttard, P. and Ray, M. (1989). The distribution of breeding songbirds within mixed coppiced forest in Kent, England, in relation to vegetation age and structure. *Annals Zoologici Fennici*, **26**, 265–75.

Fyson, A. (2000). Angiosperms in acidic waters at pH 3 and below. *Hydrobiologia*, **433**, 129–35.

Gabites, I. and Lucas, R. (1998). *The Native Garden: Design Themes from Wild New Zealand*. Auckland: Random House.

Gabrey, S. W. (1997). Bird and small mammal abundance at four types of waste-management facilities in northeast Ohio. *Landscape and Urban Planning*, **37**, 223–33.

Gabriele, M., Bellet, A., Gallotti, D. and Brunnetti, R. (1999). Sublittoral hard substrate communities of the northern Adriatic Sea. *Cahiers de Biologie Marine*, **40**, 65–76.

Gärdenfors, U., ed. (2000). *Rödlistade arter i Sverige 2000. The 2000 Red List of Swedish Species*. Uppsala: Swedish Threatened Species Unit, Swedish University of Agricultural Sciences.

Garstang, R. H. (1991). Dust and light pollution. *Publications of the Astronomical Society of the Pacific*, **103**, 1109–16.

Gary, M. (2005). *Greening the National Map*. Accessed 13 March 2005. http://www.americanforests.org/downloads/urban_forests/national_map.pdf

Gaston, K. J. (1994). *Rarity*. London: Chapman & Hall.

Gaston, K. J., Smith, R. M., Thompson, K. and Warren, P. H. (2005). Urban domestic gardens (II): experimental tests of methods for increasing biodiversity. *Biodiversity and Conservation*, **14**, 395–413.

Gatz, D. F. (1991). Urban precipitation chemistry: a review and synthesis. *Atmospheric Environment*, **25B**, 1–15.

Geddes, P. (1997). *Cities in Evolution: An Introduction to the Town Planning Movement and the Civics*. London: Routledge.

Geelmuyden, A. K. (1985). *Skjøtsel av naturmark og parkskog i byer*. Institutt for landskapsarkitektur, Norges landbrukshøgskole, Ås-NLH. (In Norwegian)

Geis, A. D. (1974). Effects of urbanization and type of urban development on bird populations. In *Planning and Resource Development Series 28*, ed. J. H. Noyes and D. R. Prpogulske. Amherst: Holdsworth Natural Resource Center, University of Massachusetts, pp. 97–105.

Geneletti, D. (2002). *Ecological Evaluation for Environmental Impact Assessment*. Utrecht: Netherlands Geographical Studies.

GenStat Committee (2002). *GenStat Release 6.1 Reference Manual, Parts 1–3*. Oxford: VSN International.

Germaine, S. S. and Wakeling, B. F. (2001). Lizard species distributions and habitat occupation along an urban gradient in Tucson, Arizona, USA. *Biological Conservation*, **97**, 229–37.

GESAMP (UNEP/IMO/FAO/UNESCO/IEAE/UN Group of Experts on Scientific Aspects of the Management of Pollution) (1994). *Biological Indicators and Their Use in the Measurement of the Condition of the Marine Environment*. London: UNEP.

Getz, L., Cole, L. F. R. and Gates, D. L. (1978). Interstate roadsides as dispersal routes for *Microtus pennsylvanicus*. *Journal of Mammalogy*, **59**, 208–12.

Gibb, H. and Hochuli, D. F. (1999). Nesting analysis of arthropod assemblages in habitat fragments in the Sydney region. In *The Other 99%: The Conservation and Biodiversity of Invertebrates*, ed. W. Ponder and D. Lunney. Mosman, Australia: Royal Zoological Society of NSW, pp. 77–81.

Gibb, H. and Hochuli, D. F. (2002). Habitat fragmentation in an urban environment: large and small fragments support different arthropod assemblages. *Biological Conservation*, **106**, 91–100.

Gibbons, P. and Lindenmayer, D. B. (2002). *Tree Hollows and Wildlife Conservation in Australia*. Collingwood, Victoria: CSIRO Publishing.

Gilbert, O. L. (1989). *The Ecology of Urban Habitats*. London, New York: Chapman and Hall.

Gill, A. M. (1981). Adaptive responses of Australian vascular plant species to fires. In *Fire and the Australian Biota*, ed. A. M. Gill, R. H. Groves and I. R. Noble. Canberra: Australian Academy of Science.

Gilpin, M. E. and Hanski, I. A. (1991). *Metapopulation Dynamics: Empirical and Theoretical Investigations*. London: Academic Press.

Gingrich, S. E. and Diamond, M. L. (2001). Atmospherically derived organic surface films along an urban–rural gradient. *Environmental Science and Technology*, **35**, 4031–7.

Gittleman, J. L. and Luh, H.-L. (1992). On comparing comparative methods. *Annual Review of Ecology and Systematics*, **23**, 383–404.

Given, D. and Meurk, C. (2000). Biodiversity of the urban environment: The importance of indigenous species and the role urban environments can play in their preservation. In *Urban Biodiversity and Ecology as a Basis for Holistic Planning and Design*, ed. G. H. Stewart and M. E. Ignatieva. Christchurch, New Zealand: Lincoln University, Wyckliffe Press, pp. 22–33.

Givnish, T. J. (1987). Comparative studies of leaf form: assessing the relative roles of selective pressures and phylogenetic constraints. *New Phytologist*, **106**, 131–60.

Glasby, T. M. (1998). Estimating spatial variability in developing assemblages of epibiota on subtidal hard substrata. *Marine and Freshwater Research*, **49**, 429–37.

Glasby, T. M. (1999a). Differences between subtidal epibiota on pier pilings and rocky reefs at marinas in Sydney, Australia. *Estuarine, Coastal and Shelf Science*, **48**, 281–90.

Glasby, T. M. (1999b). Interactive effects of shading and proximity to the seafloor on the development of subtidal epibiotic assemblages. *Marine Ecology Progress Series*, **190**, 113–24.

Glasby, T. M. (2000). Surface composition and orientation interact to affect subtidal epibiota. *Journal of Experimental Marine Biology and Ecology*, **248**, 177–90.

Glasby, T. M. and Connell, S. D. (1999). Urban structures as marine habitats. *Ambio*, **28**, 595–8.

Glasby, T. M. and Connell, S. D. (2001). Orientation and position of substrata have large effects on epibiotic assemblages. *Marine Ecology Progress Series*, **214**, 127–35.

Glasby, T. M. and Underwood, A. J. (1996). Sampling to differentiate between pulse and press perturbations. *Environmental Monitoring and Assessment*, **42**, 241–52.

Gleason, H. A. (1917). The structure and development of the plant association. *Bulletin of the Torrey Botanical Club*, **44**, 463–81.

Gloyne, C. C. and Clevenger, A. P. (2001). Cougar *Puma concolor* use of wildlife crossing structures on the Trans-Canada highway in Banff National Park, Alberta. *Wildlife Biology*, **7**, 117–24.

Gobster, P. H. and Westphal, L. M. (2004). The human dimension of urban greenways: planning for recreation and related experiences. *Landscape and Urban Planning*, **68**, 147–65.

Gödde, M., Richarz, N. and Walter, B. (1995). Habitat conservation and development in the city of Düsseldorf, Germany. In *Urban Ecology as the Basis for Urban Planning*, ed. H. Sukopp, M. Numata and A. Huber. The Hague: SPB Academic Publishing, pp. 163–71.

Godefroid, S. (2001). Temporal analysis of the Brussels flora as indicator for changing environmental quality. *Landscape and Urban Planning*, **52**, 203–24.

Godefroid, S. and Koedam, N. (2003). Distribution pattern of the flora in a peri-urban forest: an effect of the city-forest ecotone. *Landscape and Urban Planning*, **65**, 169–85.

Godron, M. and Forman, R. T. T. (1983). Landscape modification and changing ecological characteristics. In *Disturbance and Ecosystems: components of response*, ed. H. A. Mooney and M. Godron. New York: Springer-Verlag, pp. 12–28.

Gold, A. J., DeRagon, W. R., Sullivan, W. M. and LeMunyon, J. L. (1990). Nitrate nitrogen losses to groundwater from rural and suburban land uses. *Soil and Water Conservation*, **45**, 305–10.

Goldberg, E. D. (1995). Emerging problems in the coastal zone for the twenty-first century. *Marine Pollution Bulletin*, **31**, 152–8.

Goldberg, N. A. and Foster, M. S. (2002). Settlement and post-settlement processes limit the abundance of the geniculate coralline alga Calliarthron on subtidal walls. *Journal of Experimental Marine Biology and Ecology*, **278**, 31–45.

Goldsmith, W. (2002). Integrated ecology, geomorphology, and bioengineering for watershed-friendly design. In *Handbook of Water Sensitive Planning and Design*, ed. R. L. France. Boca Raton, New York and Washington: Lewis Publishers, pp. 341–54.

Gomez-Gesteira, M., Decastro, M., Prego, R. and Martins, F. (2002). Influence of the Barrie de la Maza dock on the circulation pattern of the Ria of A Coruna (NW-Spain). *Scientia Marina*, **66**, 337–46.

Gontier, M., Balfors, B. and Mörtberg, U. (2006). Biodiversity in environmental assessment – current practice and tools for prediction. *Environmental Impact Assessment Review*, **26**, 268–86.

Goode, D. (1998). Integration of nature in urban development. In *Urban Ecology*, ed. J. Breuste, H. Feldmann and O. Uhlmann. Berlin: Springer-Verlag, pp. 598–92.

Goryshina, T. K. and Ignatieva, M. E. (2000). *Botanical Excursions around the City*. St Petersburg: Chimisdat.

Gosz, J. R. (1991). Fundamental ecological characteristics of landscape boundaries. In *Ecotones: The Role of Changing Landscape Boundaries in the Management and Restoration of Changing Environments*, ed. M. M. Holland, P. G. Risser and R. J. Naiman. New York: Chapman and Hall, pp. 8–30.

Goto, S., Morioka, T. and Fujita, S. (1999). Evaluation of ecological networks in urban area by habitat analysis of indicator species. *Environmental Information Science*, **13**, 43–8.

Gottberg, C.-J. (1972). Kokemuksia luonnonvaraisen puiston säilyttämisestä Tapiolan alueella rakennusvaiheen yli. *Dendrologian Seuran Tiedoituksia*, **3**, 15–17. (In Finnish)

Gottdiener, M. and Hutchison, R. (2000). *The New Urban Sociology*, 2nd edn. New York: McGraw Hill.

Government of Western Australia (1995). *Urban Bushland Strategy* (Final). Perth: Government of Western Australia, Ministry for Planning.

Graf, W. L. (2001). Damage control: restoring the physical integrity of America's rivers. *Annals of the Association of American Geographers*, **91**, 1–27.

Grahn, P. (1994). Green structures – the importance for health of nature areas and parks. *European Regional Planning*, **56**, 89–112.

Grahn, P. and Stigsdotter, U. A. (2003). Landscape planning and stress. *Urban Forestry and Urban Greening*, **2**, 1–18.

Grandchamp, A.-C., Niemelä, J. and Kotze, J. (2000). The effects of trampling on assemblages of ground beetles (Coleoptera, Carabidae) in urban forests in Helsinki, Finland. *Urban Ecosystems*, **4**, 321–32.

Grant, J. J., Wilson, K. C., Grover, A. and Togstad, H. A. (1982). Early development of Pendleton artificial reef. *Marine Fisheries Review*, **44**, 53–60.

Gray, J. S. (2002). Species richness of marine soft sediments. *Marine Ecology Progress Series*, **244**, 285–97.

Grayson, J. A., Chapman, M. G. and Underwood, A. J. (1999). The assessment of restoration of habitat in urban wetlands. *Landscape and Urban Planning*, **43**, 227–36.

Green, R. H. (1979). *Sampling Design and Statistical Methods for Environmental Biologists*. New York: Wiley.

Green, R. J. and Catterall, C. P. (1998). The effects of forest clearing and regeneration on the fauna of Wivenhoe Park, south east Queensland. *Wildlife Research*, **25**, 677–90.

Gregg, J. W., Jones, C. G. and Dawson, T. E. (2003). Urbanization effects on tree growth in the vicinity of New York City. *Nature*, **424**, 183–7.

Greller, A. M. (1975). Persisting natural vegetation in northern Queens County, New York, with proposals for its conservation. *Environmental Conservation*, **2**, 61–71.

Grey, M. J., Clarke, M. F. and Loyn, R. H. (1997). Initial changes in the avian communities of remnant eucalypt woodlands following a reduction in the abundance of noisy miners. *Wildlife Research*, **24**, 631–48.

Grey, M. J., Clarke, M. F. and Loyn, R. H. (1998). Influence of the noisy miner *Manorina melanocephala* on avian diversity and abundance in remnant grey box woodland. *Pacific Conservation Biology*, **4**, 55–69.

Griffiths, T. (2001). *Forests of Ash: An Environmental History*. Sydney: Cambridge University Press.

Grimbacher, P. and Hughes, L. (2002). Response of ant communities and ant–seed interactions to bush regeneration. *Ecological Management and Restoration*, **3**, 188–99.

Grimm, N. B. and Redman, C. L. (2004). Approaches to the study of urban ecosystems: The case of Central Arizona – Phoenix. *Urban Ecosystems*, **7**, 199–214.

Grimm, N. B., Baker, L. J. and Hope, D. (2003). An ecosystem approach to understanding cities: familiar foundations and uncharted frontiers. In *Understanding Urban Ecosystems: A New Frontier for Science and Education*, ed. A. R. Berkowitz, C. H. Nilon and K. S. Hollweg. New York: Springer-Verlag, pp. 95–114.

Grimm, N. B., Grove, J. M., Pickett, S. T. A. and Redman, C. A. (2000). Integrated approaches to long-term studies of urban ecological systems. *BioScience*, **50**, 571–84.

Grodzinski, W., Weiner, J. and Maycock, P. F., eds. (1984). *Forest Ecosystems in Industrial Regions*. New York: Springer Verlag.

Groffman, P. M. and Crawford, M. K. (2003). Denitrification potential in urban riparian zones. *Journal of Environmental Quality*, **32**, 1144–9.

Groffman, P. M. and Likens, G. E., eds. (1994). *Integrated Regional Models: Interactions between Humans and their Environment*. New York: Chapman and Hall.

Groffman, P. M., Bain, D. J., Band, L. E. (2003). Down by the riverside: urban riparian ecology. *Frontiers in Ecology and Environment*, **1**, 315–21.

Groffman, P. M., Law, N. L., Belt, K. T., Band, L. E. and Fisher, G. T. (2004). Nitrogen fluxes and retention in urban watershed ecosystems. *Ecosystems*, **7**, 393–403.

Groffman, P. M., Pouyat, R. V., Cadenasso, M. C. *et al.* (2006). Land use context and natural soil controls on plant community composition and soil nitrogen and carbon dynamics in urban and rural forests. *Forest Ecology and Management*, **236**, 177–92.

Groffman, P. M., Pouyat, R. V., McDonnell, M. J., Pickett, S. T. A. and Zipperer, W. C. (1995). Carbon pools and trace gas fluxes in urban forest soils. In *Soil Management and Greenhouse Effect*, ed. R. Lal, J. Kimble, E. Levine and B. A. Stewart. Boca Raton: CRC Lewis Publishers, pp. 147–58.

Gross, C. L. and Mackay, D. (1998). Honeybees reduce fitness in the pioneer shrub *Melastoma affine* (Melastomataceae). *Biological Conservation*, **86**, 169–78.

Grossman, G. D., Jones, G. P. and Seaman, W. J. (1997). Do artificial reefs increase regional fish production? A review of existing data. *Fisheries*, **22**, 17–23.

Grove, J. M. and Burch, W. R. Jr (1997). A social ecology approach and application of urban ecosystem and landscape analyses: a case study of Baltimore, Maryland. *Urban Ecosystems*, **1**, 259–75.

Grove, J. M. and Burch, W. Jr (2003). *Using Patch Dynamics to Characterize Social Areas at the Neighbourhood Level in the Baltimore Ecosystem Study*. 18. General Technical Report. South Burlington: USDA Forest Service.

Grove, J. M., Cadenasso, M., Burch, W. R. Jr *et al.* (2006a). Data and methods comparing social structure and vegetation structure of urban neighborhoods in Baltimore, Maryland. *Society and Natural Resources* **19**, 117–36.

Grove, J. M., Cadenasso, M. L., Burch, W. R. Jr *et al.* (in press). The social ecology of prestige: group identity and social status of ecological structure and its implications for urban watershed dynamics in the Baltimore metropolitan region, Baltimore, Maryland. *Society and Natural Resources*.

Grove, J. M., Troy, A. R., O'Neil-Dunne, J. P. M., Burch, W. R. Jr, Cadenasso, M. L. and Pickett, S. T. A. (2006b). Characterization of households and its implications for the vegetation of urban ecosystems. *Ecosystems*, **9**, 578–97.

Grumbine, R. E. (1994). What is ecosystem management? *Conservation Biology*, **8**, 27–38.

Guisan, A. and Zimmermann, N. E. (2000). Predictive habitat distribution models in ecology. *Ecological Modelling* **135**, 147–86.

Gundersen, V., Frivold, L. H., Löfström, I., Jörgensen, B. B., Falck, J. and Öyen, B.-H. (2005). Urban woodland management – the case of 13 major Nordic cities. *Urban Forestry and Urban Greening*, **3**, 189–202.

Gunderson, L. H. and Holling, C. S. (2002). *Panarchy: Understanding Transformations in Human and Natural Systems*. Washington, DC: Island Press.

Guntenspergen, G. R. and Dunn, C. P. (1998). Introduction: long-term ecological sustainability of wetlands in urbanising landscapes. *Urban Ecosystems*, **2**, 187–9.

Guntenspergen, G. R. and Levenson, J. B. (1997). Understorey plant species composition in remnant stands along an urban-to-rural land-use gradient. *Urban Ecosystems*, **1**, 155–69.

Gurevitch, J. and Hedges, L. V. (1993). Meta-analysis: combining the results of independent experiments. In *Design and Analysis of Ecological Experiments*, ed. S. M. Scheiner and J. Gurevitch. New York: Chapman and Hall, pp. 378–98.

Gustavsson, L. and Hansson, L. (1997). Corridors as a conservation tool. *Ecological Bulletins*, **46**, 182–90.

Gustavsson, R. (1986). *Struktur i lövskogslandskap [Summary: Structure in the broadleaved landscape]*. *Stad. and Land, 48*. Alnarp, Sweden: Movium. (In Swedish)

Gutzwiller, K. J. and Barrow, W. C. Jr (2003). Bird communities, roads and development: prospects and constraints of applying empirical models. *Biological Conservation*, **113**, 239–43.

Haas, R., Kraeling, W. and Boulois, R. (1997). Lichtkontamination – UWSF. *Zeitschrift für Umweltchemie Ökotoxikologie*, **9**, 24.

Haase, G. and Richter, H. (1980a). *Entwicklungstendenzen und Aufgabenstellungen in der Landschaftsforschung der DDR*. Geograficky Casopis. pp. 231–47.

Haase, G. and Richter, H. (1980b). *Geographische Landschaftsforschung als Beitrag zur Lösung von Landeskultur- und Umweltproblemen*. Berlin: Sitzungsber eichte der Akademie der Wissenschaften der DDR, pp. 23–51.

Hadidian, J., Sauer, J., Swarth, C. *et al.* (1997). A citywide breeding bird survey for Washington, DC. *Urban Ecosystems*, **1**, 87–102.

Haeckel, E. (1870). Ueber Entwicklungsgang und Aufgabe der Zoologie. Rede gehalten beim Eintritt in die philosophische Facultät zu Jena am 12. Januar 1869. In *Studien über Moneren und andere Protisten*, ed. E. Haeckel. Leipzig: Verlag W. Engelmann, p. 3–20.

Hahs, A.K. and McDonnell, M.J. (2006). Selecting independent measures to quantify Melbourne's urban–rural gradient. *Landscape and Urban Planning*, **78**, 435–48.

Haila, Y. (1988). The multiple faces of ecological theory and data. *Oikos*, **53**, 408–11.

Haila, Y. (1995). *Kestävän kehityksen luontoperusta. Mitä päättäjien tulee tietää ekologiasta?* [*Ecological Basis for Sustainable Development. What Decision-makers Should Know About Ecology*]. Helsinki: Suomen kuntaliitto. (In Finnish)

Haila, Y. (1999). Islands as fragments. In *Maintaining Biodiversity in Forest Fragments*, ed. M.L. Hunter. Cambridge: Cambridge University Press, pp. 234–64.

Haila, Y. (2002). A conceptual genealogy of fragmentation research: from island biogeography to landscape ecology. *Ecological Applications*, **12**, 321–34.

Haila, Y. and Levins, R. (1992). *Humanity and Nature*. London: Pluto Press.

Haila, Y., Hanski, I.K. and Raivio, S. (1993). Turnover of breeding birds in small forest fragments: The 'sampling' colonisation hypothesis corroborated. *Ecology*, **74**, 714–25.

Hair, C.A., Bell, J.D. and Kingsford, M.J. (1994). Effects of position in the water column, vertical movement and shade on settlement of fish to artificial habitats. *Bulletin of Marine Science*, **55**, 434–44.

Hallegraeffe, G., Steffensen, D.A. and Wetherbee, R. (1988). Three estuarine Australian dinoflagellates that can produce paralytic shellfish toxins. *Journal of Plankton Research*, **10**, 533–41.

Halme, E. and Niemelä, J. (1993). Carabid beetles in fragments of coniferous forest. *Annales Zoologici Fennici*, **30**, 17–30.

Halvorsen Thoren, A.-K. and Nyhuus, S. (1993). Grønnstrukturen som overordnet byplaneelement: Hvordan har vi tatt hensyn til natur i by? In: *Planera för en bärkraftig utveckling. 21 nordiska forskare ger sin syn*, ed. B. Kullinger and K. Strömberg. Stockholm: Byggforskningsrådet T26:1993. (In Norwegian)

Hamabata, E. (1980). Changes of herb-layer species composition with urbanisation in secondary oak forests of Musashino plain near Tokyo – studies on the conservation of suburban forest stands 1. *Japanese Journal of Ecology*, **30**, 347–58. (In Japanese with English abstract)

Hammerschlag, R.S., Baldwin, A.H., Krafft, C.C., Hatfield, J.S., Paul, M.M. and Brittingham, K.D. (2003). *Year 3 (2002) Annual Report for the Kingman Monitoring Project*. Laurel, Maryland: US Geological Survey, Patuxent Wildlife Research Center.

Hänel, A. (2001). The situation of light pollution in Germany. In *Preserving the Astronomical Sky*, ed. R. J. Cohen and W. T. Sullivan. Proceedings of the 196th Symposium of the International Astronomical Union in conjunction with UNISPACE III at Vienna, Austria, July 12–16, 1999. San Francisco: ASP Conference Series, pp. 142–6.

Hanks, L. M. and Denno, R. F. (1993). Natural enemies and plant water relations influence the distribution of an armored scale insect. *Ecology*, **74**, 1081–91.

Hansen, A. J. and Urban, D. L. (1992). Avian response to landscape pattern: the role of species' life histories. *Landscape Ecology*, **7**, 163–80.

Hanski, I. (1998). Metapopulation dynamics. *Nature*, **396**, 41–9.

Hanski, I. and Gilpin, M. E. (1997). *Metapopulation Biology: Ecology, Genetics, and Evolution*. San Diego: Academic Press.

Hanski, I. and Gyllenberg, M. (1997). Uniting two general patterns in the distribution of species. *Science*, **275**, 397–400.

Hansson, L. (1979). On the importance of landscape heterogeneity in northern regions for the breeding population densities of homeotherms: a general hypothesis. *Oikos*, **33**, 182–9.

Hardy, P. B. and Dennis, R. L. H. (1999). The impact of urban development on butterflies within a city region. *Biodiversity and Conservation*, **8**, 1261–79.

Harlin, M. M. and Thorne-Miller, B. (1981). Nutrient enrichment of seagrass beds in a Rhode Island coastal lagoon. *Marine Biology*, **65**, 221–9.

Harms, J. (1990). Marine plastic litter as an artificial hard bottom fouling ground. *Helgolander Meeresuntersuchungen*, **44**, 503–6.

Harms, W. B., Knol, W. C. and Roos-Klein Lankhorst, J. (2000). Modelling landscape changes in the Netherlands: the Central City Belt case study. In *Landscape Perspectives of Land Use Changes*, ed. Ü. Mander and R. Jongman. Southampton (UK): WIT, *Advances in Ecological Sciences*, **6**, 1–17.

Harper, K. A. and Macdonald, S. E. (2001). Structure and composition of riparian boreal forest: new methods for analyzing edge influence. *Ecology*, **82**, 649–59.

Harris, C. D. (1956). The pressure of residential-industrial land use. In *Man's Role in Changing the Face of the Earth*, ed. W. L. Thomas, C. O. Sauer, M. Bates and L. Mumford. Chicago, IL: University of Chicago Press, pp. 881–95.

Harris, S. and Raynor, J. M. V. (1986). Models for predicting urban fox (*Vulpes vulpes*) numbers in British UK cities and their application for rabies control. *Journal of Animal Ecology*, **55**, 593–604.

Harris, S. and Smith, G. C. (1987). Demography of two urban fox (*Vulpes vulpes*) populations. *Journal of Applied Ecology*, **24**, 75–86.

Harrison, C., Limb, M. and Burgess, J. (1987). Nature in the city – popular values for a living world. *Journal of Environmental Management*, **25**, 347–62.

Harrison, S. and Bruna, E. (1999). Habitat fragmentation and large-scale conservation: what do we know for sure? *Ecography*, **22**, 225–32.

Harrison, S. and Voller, J. (1998). Connectivity. In *Conservation Biology Principles for Forested Landscapes*, ed. J. Voller and S. Harrison. Vancouver: UBC Press, pp. 76–97.

Hartstack, A.W., Hollingsworth, J.P. and Lindquist, D.A. (1968). A technique for measuring trapping efficiency of electric insect traps. *Journal of Economic Entomology*, **61**, 546–52.

Hasebe, H. and Suzuki, M. (1997). GIS analysis of open space transition in urbanisation process of Edo-Tokyo. *Journal of the Japanese Institute of Landscape Architecture* **60**, 633–8. (In Japanese)

Hashimoto, H., Murakami, K. and Morimoto, Y. (in press). Relative species–area relationship and nestedness pattern of forest birds in urban area of Kyoto City. *Landscape Ecology and Management*, **10**. (In Japanese with English abstract)

Hashimoto, H., Natuhara, Y. and Morimoto, Y. (2005). A habitat model for Great Tits, *Parus major minor*, using a logistic regression model in the urban area of Osaka, Japan. *Landscape and Urban Planning*, **70**, 245–50.

Hashimoto, Y., Kamihogi, A. and Hattori, T. (1994). A study on the conservation of fragmented forests as inhabitant arthropods in the new town, using ant-biodiversity for indicator of arthropods-biodiversity. *Journal of the Japanese Institute of Landscape Architecture*, **57**, 223–8. (In Japanese)

Haskell, D.G., Knupp, A.M. and Schneider, M.C. (2001). Nest predator abundance and urbanization. In *Avian Ecology and Conservation in an Urbanizing World*, ed. J.M. Marzluff, R. Bowman and R. Donnelly. Norwell, Massachusetts: Kluwer Academic Publishers, pp. 243–58.

Hatcher, B., Johennes, R. and Robertson, A. (1989). Review of research relevant to the conservation of shallow tropical marine ecosystems. *Oceanography and Marine Biology Annual Review*, **27**, 337–414.

Hattori, T., Kamihogi, A., Kodate, S., Kumadaki, E., Fujii, T. and Takeda, Y. (1994). A study on the actual conditions of the fragmented forests in flower town and their conservation. *Journal of the Japanese Institute of Landscape Architecture*, **57**, 217–22. (In Japanese)

Hauxwell, J., Cebrian, J. and Valiela, I. (2003). Eelgrass *Zostera marina* loss in temperate estuaries: relationship to land-derived nitrogen loads and effect of light limitation imposed by algae. *Marine Ecology Progress Series*, **247**, 59–73.

Hawkins, J.P. and Roberts, C.M. (1993). Effects of recreational scuba diving on coral reefs: trampling on reef-flat communities. *Journal of Applied Ecology*, **30**, 25–30.

Hawkins, S.J. and Hartnoll, R.G. (1980). A study of the small-scale relationship between species number and area on a rocky shore. *Estuarine and Coastal Marine Science*, **10**, 201–14.

Hawley, A.H. (1944). Ecology and human ecology. *Social Forces*, **2**, 398–405.

Hawley, A.H. (1986). *Human Ecology: a theoretical essay*. Chicago: University of Chicago Press.

Hay, M.E. (1984). Patterns of fish and urchin grazing on Caribbean coral reefs: are previous results typical? *Ecology*, **65**, 446–54.

Haywood, M.D.E., Vance, D.J. and Loneragan, N.R. (1995). Seagrass and algal beds as nursery habitats for tiger prawns (*Penaeus semisulcatus* and *P. esculentus*) in a tropical Australian estuary. *Marine Biology*, **122**, 213–23.

Heal, O.W. and Grime, J.P. (1991). Comparative analysis of ecosystems: past lessons and future directions. In *Comparative Analyses of Ecosystems: Patterns, Mechanisms, and Theories*, ed. J. Cole, G. Lovett and S. Findlay. New York: Springer-Verlag, pp. 7–23.

Healey, P. (1997). *Collaborative Planning – Shaping Places in Fragmented Societies*. London: Macmillan Press Ltd.

Healey, P., Khakee, A., Motte, A. and Needham, B. eds. (1997). *Making Strategic Spatial Plans – Innovation in Europe*. London: UCL Press Limited.

Heath, J. (1974). A century of change in the Lepidoptera. In *The Changing Flora and Fauna of Britain*, ed. D.L. Hawksworth. *Systematics Association Special Volume*, **6**, 275–92.

Heberlein, T.A. and Ericson, G. (2005). Ties to the countryside: Accounting for urbanites' attitudes toward hunting, wolves and wildlife. *Human Dimensions of Wildlife* **10**(3), 213–227.

Heck, K.L., Pennock, J.R., Valentine, J.F., Coen, L.D. and Sklenar, S.L. (2000). Effects of nutrient enrichment and small predator density on seagrass ecosystems: an experimental assessment. *Limnology and Oceanography*, **45**, 1041–57.

Hedblom, M. (2007). Birds and butterflies in Swedish urban and peri-urban habitats: a landscape perspective. *Acta Universitatis Agriculturae Sueciae* **2007**, 60.

Hedgecock, D. (1994). Does variance in reproductive success limit effective population sizes of marine organisms? In *Genetics and Evolution of Aquatic Organisms*, ed. A.R. Beaumont. London, New York: Chapman and Hall, pp. 122–34.

Heilman, G.E., Strittholt, J.R., Slosser, N.C. and Dellasala, D.A. (2002). Forest fragmentation of the conterminous United States: assessing forest intactness through road density and spatial characteristics. *BioScience*, **52**, 411–22.

Heiman, S., Lehvävirta, S., Fritze, H., Kotze, D.J. and O'Hara, B. (2003). The effects of dogs on soil and vegetation in urban spruce (*Picea abies*) dominant woodlands in Helsinki, Finland. In *Environmental Problems and Policies in Growing Urban Areas*. Abstracts from the Maj and Tor Nessling Foundation 4th Environmental Symposium, Hanasaari, Espoo, Finland.

Heino, J. (1974). Finlands statsägda skogar betraktade speciellt ur friluftssynvinkel. *Folia Forestalia*, **223**, 1–47. (In Finnish)

Heinz Centre. (2002). *The State of the Nation's Ecosystems*. The Heinz Centre Indicator Report. Washington, DC: Heinz Centre.

Heliölä, J., Koivula, M. and Niemelä, J. (2001). Distribution of carabid beetles (Coleoptera, Carabidae) across a Boreal forest-clearcut ecotone. *Conservation Biology*, **15**, 370–7.

Helle, P. and Muona, J. (1985). Invertebrate numbers in edges between clear-fellings and mature forests in northern Finland. *Silva Fennica*, **19**, 281–94.

Hercock, M.J. (1997). Appreciating the biodiversity of remnant bushland: an 'architectural' approach. *The Environmentalist*, **17**, 249–58.

Heremaia, C. (2000). *Education Strategy Waterways and Wetlands: Ko te Aratohu Poipoi e whai ake ki te Matauranga a Nga Arawai Repo*. Christchurch: Christchurch City Council.

Herzog, F. and Lausch, A. (2001). Supplementing land-use statistics with landscape metrics: some methodological considerations. *Environmental Monitoring and Assessment*, **72**, 37–50.

Hess, G.R. and Fischer, R.A. (2001). Communicating clearly about conservation corridors. *Landscape and Urban Planning*, **55**, 195–208.

Hesse, M. and Schmitz, S. (1998). Stadtentwicklung im Zeichen von 'Auflösung' und Nachhaltigkeit. *Informationen zur Raumentwicklung* **7/8**, 435–53

Hicks, D.M. (1993). *Sedimentation and Erosion in the Avon-Heathcote Catchment and Estuary*. Miscellaneous Report 27. Christchurch: Freshwater Division, NIWA.

Hicks, D.M. (1994). *Storm Sediment Yields from Basins with Various Land Uses in the Auckland Area*. Technical Publication 151. Auckland: Auckland Regional Council Environment Division.

Hicks, G., ed. (1998). *City Life! A Guide to Bush City*. Wellington, New Zealand: Te Papa Press.

Higgs, E.S. (1997). What is good ecological restoration? *Conservation Biology*, **11**, 338–48.

Higuchi, H., Tsukamoto, Y., Hanawa, S. and Takeda, M. (1982). Relationship between forest areas and the number of bird species. *Strix*, **1**, 70–8. (In Japanese with English abstract)

Hildén, M., Valve, H., Jónsdóttir, S. *et al.* (1998). *EIA and its Application for Policies, Plans and Programmes in Sweden, Finland, Iceland and Norway. TemaNord 1998:567*. Copenhagen: Nordic Council of Ministers.

Hilty, J., Lidicker, W. Jr and Merenleder, A. (2006). *Corridor Ecology: The Science and Practice of Linking Landscapes for Biodiversity Conservation*. USA: Island Press.

Hindson, D. (1994). Global Forum '94 – Contemplating cities and sustainable development. *Muniviro*, **11**, 3–7.

Hitchings, S.P. and Beebee, T.J.C. (1997). Genetic sub-structuring as a result of barriers to gene flow in urban *Rana temporaria* (common frog) populations: implications for biodiversity conservation. *Heredity*, **79**, 117–27.

Hitchmough, J. (1993). The urban bush. *Landscape Design*, July/August 1993, 13–17.

Hiura, I. (1973). *Umi o Wataru Cho [Butterflies from Overseas]*. Tokyo: Soju Shobo. (In Japanese)

Hiura, I. (1976). A consideration on butterfly fauna and its transformation in the lowland of Osaka and Nara, Central Japan. *Shizenshi-Kenkyu, Occasional Papers from the Osaka Museum of Natural History*, **1**, 189–205. (In Japanese)

Hobbs, E. (1988a). Species richness of urban forest patches and implications for urban landscape diversity. *Landscape Ecology*, **1**, 141–52.

Hobbs, E. (1988b). Using ordination to analyze the composition and structure of urban forest islands. *Forest Ecology and Management*, **23**, 139–58.

Hobbs, R. (1997). Future of landscapes and the future landscape ecology. *Landscape and Urban Planning*, **37**, 1–9.

Hobbs, R.J. and Wilson, A.M. (1998). Corridors: theory, practice and the achievement of conservation objectives. In *Key Concepts in Landscape Ecology*, ed. J.W. Dover and R.G.H. Bunce. Preston, UK: IALE, pp. 265–79.

Hochuli, D.F., Gibb, H., Burrows, S.E. and Christie, F.J. (2004). Ecology of Sydney's urban fragments: has fragmentation taken the sting out of insect herbivory? In *Urban Wildlife: More Than Meets the Eye*, ed. S. Burgin and D. Lunney. Mosman, NSW: Royal Zoological Society of NSW, pp. 63–79.

Hoehne, L. M. (1981). The groundlayer vegetation of forest islands in an urban-suburban matrix. In *Forest Island Dynamics in Man-dominated Landscapes*, ed. R. L. Burgess and D. M. Sharpe, *Ecological Studies* Vol. 41. New York: Springer Verlag, pp. 41–54.

Hogan, D. M. (2005). An assessment of riparian wetlands as a function of urbanization in Fairfax County, Virginia. Unpublished Ph.D. dissertation, George Mason University, Fairfax, VA.

Hogsden, K. L. and Hutchinson, T. C. (2004). Butterfly assemblages along a human disturbance gradient in Ontario, Canada. *Canadian Journal of Zoology – Revue Canadienne De Zoologie*, **82**, 739–48.

Hohtola, E. (1978). Differential changes in bird community structure with urbanisation: a study in Central Finland. *Ornis Scandinavica*, **9**, 94–100.

Holland, C. C., Honea, J., Gwin, S. E. and Kentula, M. E. (1995). Wetland degradation and loss in the rapidly urbanizing area of Portland, Oregon. *Wetlands*, **15**, 336–45.

Holling, C. S. (1973). Resilience and stability of ecological systems. *Annual Review of Ecology and Systematics*, **4**, 1–23.

Holling, C. S. (1996). Engineering resilience versus ecological resilience. In *Engineering within Ecological Constraints*, ed. P. Schulze. Washington, DC: National Academy Press, pp. 31–44.

Holloway, M. G. and Connell, S. D. (2002). Why do floating structures create novel habitats for subtidal epibiota? *Marine Ecology Progress Series*, **235**, 43–52.

Holloway, M. G. and Keough, M. J. (2002). An introduced polychaete affects recruitment and larval abundance of sessile invertebrates. *Ecological Applications*, **12**, 1803–23.

Holmgren, J., Joyce, S., Nilsson, M. and Olsson, H. (2000). Estimating stem volume and basal area in forest compartments by combining satellite image data with field data. *Scandinavian Journal of Forest Research*, **15**, 103–11.

Holz, T. W. (2002). *Zero Impact Development: Source Control for Stream Protection*. Presented to the Washington Hydrological Society, 20 November 2002. Seattle, Washington: Washington Hydrological Society.

Homberger, E. (1994). *The Historical Atlas of New York City. A Visual Celebration of Nearly 400 Years of New York's History*. New York, USA: Henry Holt and Company.

Homewood, K., Lambin, E. F., Coast, E. *et al.* (2001). Long-term changes in Serengeti-Mara wildebeest and land cover: pastoralism, population, or policies? *Proceedings of the National Academy of Sciences*, **98**, 12544–9.

Honnay, O., Endels, P., Vereecken, H. and Hermy, M. (1999). The role of patch area and habitat diversity in explaining native plant species richness in disturbed suburban forest patches in northern Belgium. *Diversity and Distributions*, **5**, 129–41.

Hooten, A. J. (1990). Fairfax County, Virginia: a case-study for an ecological-resource inventory program for use by local governments. *Forest Ecology and Management*, **33/34**, 253–69.

Hope, D., Gries, C., Zhu, W. *et al.* (2003). Socioeconomics drive urban plant diversity. *Proceedings of the National Academy of Sciences*, **100**, 8788–92.

Hope, D., Zhu, W., Gries, C. *et al.* (2005). Spatial variation in soil inorganic nitrogen across an arid urban ecosystem. *Urban Ecosystems*, **8**, 251–73.

Hopfenberg, R. and Pimentel, D. (2001). Human population numbers as a function of food supply. *Environment, Development and Sustainability*, **3**, 1–15.

Hornbeck, J. W. and Swank, W. T. (1992). Watershed ecosystem analysis as a basis for multiple-use management of eastern forests. *Ecological Applications*, **2**, 238–47.

Hörnsten, L., ed. (2000). Outdoor recreation in Swedish forests – implications for society and forestry. Doctoral thesis, Acta Universitatis Arboriculturae Suecie, Silvestria 169.

Hörnsten, L. and Dahlin, B. (2000). Managing urban forests in Sweden – from silvicultural recommendations towards a planning concept. In *Outdoor Recreation in Swedish Forests – Implications for Society and Forestry*, ed. L. Hörnsten. Acta Universitatis Arboriculturae Suecie, Silvestria 169.

Hosmer, D. W. and Lemeshow, S. (1989). *Applied Logistic Regression*. New York: John Wiley and Sons.

Hostetler, M. (2001). The importance of multi-scale analyses in avian habitat selection studies in urban environments. In *Avian Ecology and Conservation in an Urbanizing World*, ed. J. M. Marzluff, R. Bowman and R. Donnelly. Norwell, Massachusetts: Kluwer Academic Publishers, pp. 139–54.

Hostetler, M. and Knowles-Yanez, K. (2003). Land use, scale, and bird distributions in the Phoenix metropolitan area. *Landscape and Urban Planning*, **62**, 55–68.

Hotta, M. (1977). Distribution of Taraxacum spp. in Kinki District, Japan. *Bulletin of Osaka Museum of Natural History*, **1**, 117–34. (In Japanese)

Hough, M. (1995). *Cities and Natural Process*. London: Routledge.

Houston, D. R. (1985). Dieback and declines of urban trees. *Journal of Arboriculture*, **11**, 65–72.

Howard, M., Mangold, S. and Mpambane, S. (2002). Water resources. In *The State of the Environment Report 2002 of the North West Province, South Africa*, ed. S. Mangold, M. Kalule-Sabiti and J. Walmsley. Mafikeng: North West Province Department of Agriculture, Conservation and Environment, Chapter 10.

Howard, T. G., Gurevitch, J., Hyatt, L., Carreiro, M. and Lerdau, M. (2004). Forest invasibility in communities in southeastern New York. *Biological Invasions*, **6**, 393–410.

Howarth, R. W., Boyer, E. W., Pabich, W. and Galloway, J. N. (2002). Nitrogen use in the United States from 1961–2000 and potential future trends. *Ambio*, **31**, 88–96.

Howe, R. W. (1984). Local dynamics of bird assemblages in small forest habitat islands in Australia and North America. *Ecology*, **65**, 1585–601.

Howell, J. and Benson, D. (2000). *Sydney's Bushland. More Than Meets the Eye*. Sydney: Royal Botanic Gardens Sydney.

Hsiao, H. S. (1972). *Attraction of Moths to Light and to Infrared Radiation*. San Francisco Press.

Hubbell, S. P. (2001). *The Unified Neutral Theory of Biodiversity and Biogeography*. Princeton: Princeton University Press.

Huber, D. M. and Watson, R. D. (1974). Nitrogen form and plant disease. *Annual Review of Phytopathology*, **12**, 139–65.

Hülbusch, K.-H. (1982). Landschaftsökologie der Stadt. Naturschutz und Landschaftspflege zwischen Erhalten und Gestalten: Referate und Ergebnisse des Deutschen

Naturschutztages 1982 vom 19.–23. Mai 1982 in Kassel. *Jahrbuch für Naturschutz and Landschaftspflege*, **33**, 38–61.

Hull, A. (1996). Strategic planning in Europe: institutional innovation. *Planning Practice and Research*, **11**, 253–65.

Hummel, F. C. (1983). Trees in the evolution of the European landscape. In *Trees in the 21st Century*, based on the first arboricultural conference. Oxford: Academic Publishers, pp. 23–34.

Humphries, R. B. (1979). Dynamics of a breeding frog community. Unpublished Ph.D. thesis, The Australian National University.

Hunsaker, C. T. and Levine, D. A. (1995). Hierarchical approaches to the study of water quality in rivers. *BioScience*, **45**, 193–203.

Huntley, B. J. (1996). Biodiversity conservation in the new South Africa. In *Biodiversity, Science and Development, Towards a New Partnership*, ed. F. Di Castri and T. Younès. Wallingford: CAB International, pp. 282–303.

Huser, B. and Wilson, B. (1996). *Waikato River: Water Quality Monitoring Programme Data Report 1995*. Report 96/8. Hamilton, New Zealand: Environment Waikato.

Huser, B. and Wilson, B. (1997). *Waikato River: Water Quality Monitoring Programme Data Report 1996*. Technical Report 1997/5. Hamilton, New Zealand: Environment Waikato.

Hutchinson, G. E. (1957). Concluding remarks. *Cold Spring Harbor Symposia on Quantitative Biology*, **22**, 415–27.

Iakovoglou, V., Thompson, J., Burras, L. and Kipper, R. (2001). Factors related to tree growth across urban–rural gradients in the Midwest, USA. *Urban Ecosystems*, **5**, 71–85.

Iannuzzi, T. J., Weinstein, M. P., Sellner, K. G. and Barrett, J. C. (1996). Habitat disturbance and marina development: an assessment of ecological effects. 1. Changes in primary production due to dredging and marina construction. *Estuaries*, **19**, 257–71.

Ichinose, T. and Katoh, K. (1994). The factors that influenced bird communities on the fragmented woodlots in the Tokorozawa City, Saitama Prefecture. *Journal of the Japanese Institute of Landscape Architecture*, **57**, 235–40.

Ide, H. and Kameyama, A. (1993). *Landscape Ecology*. Tokyo: Asakura-shoten. (In Japanese)

Idso, C. D., Idso, S. B. and Balling, R. C. (2001). An intensive two-week study of an urban CO_2 dome in Phoenix, Arizona, USA. *Atmospheric Environment*, **35**, 995–1000.

Ignatieva, M., Meurk, C. and Newell, C. (2000). Urban biotopes: the typical and unique habitats of city environments and their natural analogues. In *Urban Biodiversity and Ecology as Basis for Holistic Planning and Design*, ed. G. H. Stewart and M. E. Ignatieva. Lincoln University New Zealand: Wickliffe Press, pp. 46–53.

Imai, C. and Natuhara, Y. (1996). Comparison of butterfly fauna among urban greeneries in and around Osaka City and an application to island biogeography theory. *Japanese Journal of Environmental Entomology and Zoology*, **8**, 23–34. (In Japanese with English abstract)

Ingelög, T., Olsson, M. and Bödvarsson, H. (1977). *Effekter av långvarigt tramp och fordonskörning på mark, vegetation och vissa markdjur i ett äldre tallbestånd.* [Summary: *Effects of Long-term Trampling and Vehicle-driving on Soil, Vegetation and Certain Soil*

Animals of an Old Scots Pine Stand]. Stockholm-Uppsala: Skogshögskolan, avdelningen för skoglig marklära, Rapporter och uppsatser nr 27. (In Finnish)

Inman, J. C. and Parker, G. R. (1978). Decomposition and heavy metal dynamics of forest litter in northwestern Indiana. *Environmental Pollution*, **17**, 34–51.

Inoue, N., Natuhara, Y. and Hashimoto, H. (in press). The effect of percentage of tree cover on breeding performance of great tit (*Parus major*). *Landscape Ecology and Management*, **10**. (In Japanese with English abstract)

IPCC (2001). Climate Change (2001) Impacts, adaptation, and vulnerability. In *Contribution of Working Group II to the Third Assessment Report of the Intergovernmental Panel on Climate Change*, ed. J. J. McCarthy, O. F. Canziani, N. A. Leary, D. J. Dokken and K. S. White. Cambridge: Cambridge University Press.

Ishii, M., Hirowatari, T. and Fujiwara, S. (1995). Species diversity of butterfly communities in 'Mt. Mikusa Coppice for Zephyrus'. *Japanese Journal of Environmental Entomology Zoology*, **7**, 134–46. (In Japanese with English abstract)

Ishitani, M., Kotze, D. J. and Niemelä, J. (2003). Changes in carabid beetle assemblages across an urban–rural gradient in Japan. *Ecography*, **26**, 481–9.

Isobe, S. and Hirayama, T., eds. (1998). *Preserving the Astronomical Windows*. ASP Conference Series, Vol. 139. San Francisco: ASP.

Itoh, S., ed. (2003). *Proposals for the International Competition of Sustainable Urban Systems Design*. Report of the International Gas Union Special Project, proposal Canada, pp. 95–142.

IUCN (International Union for Conservation of Nature and Natural Resources) (2007). IUCN Red List of Threatened Species. http://www.iucnredlist.org

Iwasaki, K. (1995). Comparison of mussel bed community between two intertidal mytilids *Septifier virgatus* and *Hormomya mutabilis*. *Marine Biology*, **123**, 109–19.

Izuta, T. (1998). Ecophysiological responses of Japanese forest tree species to ozone, simulated acid rain and soil acidification. *Journal of Plant Research*, **111**, 471–80.

Jaatinen, E. (1974). Recreational utilization of Helsinki's forests. *Folia Forestalia*, **186**, 1–35.

Jackson, K. T. (1985). *Crabgrass Frontier. The Suburbanisation of the United States*. Oxford, UK: Oxford University Press.

Janzen, D. H. (1983). No park is an island: increase in interference from outside as park size decreases. *Oikos*, **41**, 402–10.

Jamarillo, E., Bertran, C. and Bravo, A. (1992). Community structure of the subtidal macroinfauna in an estuarine mussel bed in southern Chile. *Marine Ecology*, **13**, 317–31.

Jax, K. (1998). Holocoen and ecosystem – on the origin and historical consequences of two concepts. *Journal of the History of Biology*, **31**, 113–42.

Jenerette, G. D. and Wu, J. G. (2001). Analysis and simulation of land-use change in the central Arizona-Phoenix region, USA. *Landscape Ecology*, **16**, 611–26.

Jenkins, V. (1994). *The Lawn. A History of an American Obsession*. Washington and London: Smithsonian Institution Press.

Jenny, H. (1941). *Factors of Soil Formation*. New York: McGraw-Hill Book Co.

Jenny, H. (1961). Derivation of state factor equations of soils and ecosystems. *Soil Science Society America Proceedings*, **25**, 385–8.

Jensen, J. R. (1996). *Introductory Digital Image Processing: A Remote Sensing Perspective*, 2nd edn. New Jersey: Prentice-Hall.

Jensen, J. R. and Cowen, D. C. (1999). Remote sensing of urban/suburban infrastructure and socio-economic attributes. *Photogrammetric Engineering and Remote Sensing*, **65**, 611–22.

Jerzak, L. (2001). Synurbanization of the magpie in the Paleartic. In *Avian Ecology and Conservation in an Urbanizing World*, ed. J. M. Marzluff, R. Bowman and R. Donnelly. Boston: Kluwer Academic, pp. 403–25.

Jim, C. Y. (1998). Impacts of intensive urbanization on trees in Hong Kong. *Environmental Conservation*, **25**, 146–59.

Jim, C. Y. and Lie, H. T. (2001). Species diversity of three major urban forest types in Guangzhou City, China. *Forest Ecology and Management*, **146**, 99–114.

Johnsen, A. M. and VanDruff, L. W. (1987). Summer–winter distribution of introduced bird species and native bird species richness within a complex urban environment. In *Integrating Man and Nature in the Metropolitan Environment*, ed. L. W. Adams and D. L. Leedy. Columbia, MD: National Institute for Urban Wildlife, pp. 123–7.

Johnson, E. A. and Gutsell, S. L. (1994). Fire frequency models, methods and interpretations. *Advances in Ecological Research*, **25**, 239–87.

Johnston, C. A. (1991). Sediment and nutrient retention by freshwater wetlands: effects on surface water quality. *Critical Reviews in Environmental Control*, **21**, 491–565.

Jokimäki, J. (1996). Patterns of bird communities in urban environments. Dissertation. Arctic Centre Report No: 16. Rovaniemi, Finland: University of Lapland.

Jokimäki, J. (1999). Occurrence of breeding bird species in urban parks: effects of park structure and broad-scale variables. *Urban Ecosystems*, **3**, 21–34.

Jokimäki, J. and Suhonen, J. (1998). Distribution and habitat selection of wintering birds in urban environments. *Landscape and Urban Planning*, **39**, 253–263.

Jones, C. G. and Lawton, J. H., eds. (1995). *Linking Species and Ecosystems*. New York: Chapman and Hall.

Jones, J. A., Swanson, F. J., Wemple, B. C. and Snyder, K. U. (2000). Effects of roads on hydrology, geomorphology, and disturbance patches in stream networks. *Conservation Biology*, **14**, 76–85.

Jones, T. H., Thompson, L. J., Lawton, J. H. *et al.* (1998). Impacts of rising atmospheric carbon dioxide on model terrestrial ecosystems. *Science*, **280**, 441–3.

K2M Technologies (2002). *North West Economic Development and Industrialisation Strategy (NWEDIS)*. Unpublished report.

Kabisch, S., Kindler, A. and Rink, D. (1997). *Sozialatlas der Stadt Leipzig 1997*. Leipzig.

Kaerkes, W. M. (1985). *Stadtökologie – Landschaftsökologie der Stadt?* Dokumente and Inform. zur Schweizerischen Orts-, Regional- und Landesplanung, ETH Zürich. Nr. 80/81 (Sondernr. Stadtentwicklung), pp. 36–41.

Kaerkes, W. M. (1987). Zur ökologischen Bedeutung urbaner Freiflächen – dargestellt an Beispielen aus dem mittleren Ruhrgebiet. *Materialien zur Raumordnung*, **XXXV**, Bochum.

Kalnay, E. and Cai, M. (2003). Impact of urbanization and land-use change on climate. *Nature*, **423**, 528–31.

Kamada, M. and Nakagoshi, N. (1996). Landscape structure and the disturbance regime at three rural regions in Hiroshima Prefecture, Japan. *Landscape Ecology*, **11**, 15–25.

Kaplan, S. (1995). The urban forest as a source of psychological well-being. In *Urban Forest Landscapes: Integrating Multidisciplinary Perspectives*, ed. G. A. Bradley. Seattle: University of Washington Press.

Kardell, L. (1974). *Vegetationsslitage i samband med orienteringstävlingar. [Summary: Damage to the Vegetation Caused by Orienteering]*. Research Notes no. 4. Stockholm: Royal College of Forestry, Department of Silviculture. (In Swedish)

Karlson, R. (1978). Predation and space utilization patterns in a marine epifaunal community. *Journal of Experimental Marine Biology and Ecology*, **31**, 225–39.

Karr, J. R., Fausch, K. D., Angermeier, P. L., Yant, P. R. and Sclosser, I. J. (1986). *Assessment of Biological Integrity in Running Waters. A Method and its Rationale*. Champaign, Illinois: Illinois Natural History Survey Special Publication 5.

Kasanko, M., Barredo, J. I., Lavalle, C. *et al.* (2006). Are European cities becoming dispersed? A comparative analysis of 15 European urban areas. *Landscape and Urban Planning*, **77**, 111–130.

Kaule, G. (1975). Kartierung schutzwürdiger Biotope in Bayern. Erfahrungen 1974. *Verhandlungen Gesellschaft für Ökologie* **3**, 257–60.

Kay, A. M. and Keough, M. J. (1981). Occupation of patches in the epifaunal communities on pier pilings and the bivalve *Pinna bicolor* at Edithburgh, South Australia. *Oecologia*, **48**, 123–30.

Kaye, J. P., Groffman, P. M., Grimm, N. B., Baker, L. A. and Pouyat, R. V. (2006). A distinct urban biogeochemistry? *Trends in Ecology and Evolution*, **21**, 192–9.

Käyhkö, N. and Skånes, H. (2006). Change trajectories and key biotopes – assessing landscape dynamics and sustainability. *Landscape and Urban Planning*, **75**, 300–21.

Kearns, C. A., Inouye, D. W. and Waser, N. M. (1998). Endangered mutualisms: the conservation of plant–pollinator interactions. *Annual Review of Ecology and Systematics*, **29**, 83–112.

Keen, P. and Morton, M. S. (1978). *Decision Support Systems: An Organizational Perspective*. Reading, MA: Addison Wesley.

Keilman, N. (2003). The threat of small households. *Nature*, **421**, 489–90.

Keitt, B. S., Wilcox, C., Tershy, B. R., Croll, D. A. and Donlan, C. J. (2002). The effect of feral cats on the population viability of black-vented shearwaters (*Puffinus opisthomelas*) on Natividad Island, Mexico. *Animal Conservation*, **5**, 217–23.

Kelaher, B. P., Chapman, M. G. and Underwood, A. J. (2001). Spatial patterns of diverse macrofaunal assemblages in coralline turf and their associations with environmental variables. *Journal of the Marine Biological Association of the United Kingdom*, **81**, 917–30.

Kelaher, B. P., Underwood, A. J. and Chapman, M. G. (1998). Effect of boardwalks on the semaphore crab *Heloecius cordiformis* in temperate urban mangrove forests. *Journal of Experimental Marine Biology and Ecology*, **227**, 281–300.

Kellert, S. and Wilson, E. O. (1993). *The Biophilia Hypothesis*. Washington, DC: Island Press.

Kellomäki, S. (1973). Tallaamisen vaikutus mustikkatyypin kuusikon pintakasvillisuuteen. [Summary: Ground cover response to trampling in a spruce stand of myrtillus type]. *Silva Fennica*, **7**, 96–113. (In Finnish)

Kellomäki, S. (1977). Deterioration of forest ground cover during trampling. *Silva Fennica*, **11**, 153–61.

Kellomäki, S. and Loikkanen, A. (1982). Metsät. Luonnonolosuhteiden huomioonotaminen uusien asuinalueiden suunnittelussa. [Summary: Utilization of forests in urban planning]. YJK:n julkaisusarjassa 1979 numerolla B 25. (In Finnish)

Kellomäki, S. and Saastamoinen, V.L. (1975). Trampling tolerance of forest vegetation. *Acta Forestalia Fennica*, **147**, 1–22.

Kellomäki, S. and Wuorenrinne, H. (1979). Kaupunkei vaurioitumiseen vaikuttavista tekijöistä. [Summary: On factors effecting deterioration of urban forests]. *Silva Fennica*, **13**, 177–83. (In Finnish)

Kendle, T. and Forbes, S. (1997). *Urban Nature Conservation*. London: Spon.

Kennedy, C. E. J. and Southwood, T. R. E. (1984). The number of species of insects associated with British trees: a re-analysis. *Journal of Animal Ecology*, **53**, 455–78.

Kentula, M. E. and Magee, T. K. (1999). Foreword. Special section on wetlands in an urbanising landscape. *Wetlands*, **19**, 475–6.

Kentula, M. E., Gwin, S. E. and Pierson, S. M. (2004). Tracking changes in wetlands with urbanization: sixteen years of experience in Portland, Oregon, USA. *Wetlands*, **24**, 734–43.

Keough, M. J. (1984). Dynamics of the epifauna of the bivalve *Pinna bicolor*: Interactions among recruitment, predation and competition. *Ecology*, **6**, 677–88.

Keough, M. J. and Jenkins, G. P. (1995). Seagrass meadows and their inhabitants. In *Coastal Marine Ecology of Temperate Australia*, ed. A. J. Underwood and M. G. Chapman. Sydney: UNSW Press, pp. 221–39.

Kerr, J. T. (2001). Butterfly species richness patterns in Canada: energy, heterogeneity, and the potential consequences of climate change. *Conservation Ecology*, **5**, 10. Accessed 7th August 2005. http://www.consecol.org/vol5/iss1/art10

Khakee, A. (2000). *Samhällsplanering*. Lund: Studentlitteratur.

Khan, Z. R., Ampong-Nyarko, K., Chiliswa, P. *et al.* (1997). Intercropping increases parasitism of pests. *Nature*, **388**, 631–2.

Kilham, P. and Hecky, R. E. (1988). Comparative ecology of marine and freshwater phytoplankton. *Limnology and Oceanography*, **33**, 776–95.

Killham, K. (1990). Nitrification in coniferous forest soils. *Plant and Soil*, **128**, 31–44.

Kilpatrick, H. J., LaBonte, A. M. and Seymour, J. T. (2002). A shotgun-archery deer hunt in a residential community: evaluation of hunt strategies and effectiveness. *Wildlife Society Bulletin*, **30**, 478–86.

Kim, K. C. (1993). Biodiversity, conservation and inventory: why insects matter. *Biodiversity and Conservation*, **2**, 191–214.

King, S. A. and Buckney, R. T. (2001). Exotic plants in the soil-stored seed bank of urban bushland. *Australian Journal of Botany*, **49**, 717–20.

King, S. A. and Buckney, R. T. (2002). Invasion of exotic plants in nutrient-enriched urban bushland. *Austral Ecology*, **27**, 573–83.

Kingett Mitchell and Associates (1992). *An Assessment of Stormwater Quality and the Implications for Treatment of Stormwater in the Auckland Region.* Technical Publication 5. Auckland: Auckland Regional Council.

Kingsford, M.J., Underwood, A.J. and Kennelly, S.J. (1991). Humans as predators on rocky reefs in New South Wales, Australia. *Marine Ecology Progress Series*, **72**, 1–14.

Kinney, E.H. and Roman, C.T. (1998). Response of primary producers to nutrient enrichment in a shallow estuary. *Marine Ecology Progress Series*, **163**, 89–98.

Kinzig, A.P. and Grove, J.M. (2001). Urban–suburban ecology. In *Encyclopedia of Biodiversity*, ed. S.A. Levin. San Diego: Academic Press, pp. 733–45.

Kirkpatrick, J.B. (1975). Vegetation change in a suburban coastal reserve. *Australian Geographical Studies*, **13**, 137–53.

Kirkpatrick, J.B. (1986). The viability of bush in cities – ten years of change in an urban grassy woodland. *Australian Journal of Botany*, **34**, 691–708.

Kirkpatrick, J.B. (2004). Vegetation change in an urban grassy woodland 1974–2000. *Australian Journal of Botany*, **52**, 597–608.

Kirkpatrick, J.B., Daniels, G.D. and Zagorski, T. (2007). Explaining variation in front gardens between suburbs of Hobart, Tasmania, Australia. *Landscape and Urban Planning*, **79**, 314–22.

Kitahara, M. and Fujii, K. (1994). Biodiversity and community structure of temperate butterfly species within a gradient of human disturbance: an analysis based on the concept of generalist vs. specialist strategies. *Research on Population Ecology*, **36**, 187–99.

Klausnitzer, B. (1993). *Ökologie der Grosstadtfauna. 2:e bearbeitete Auflage.* Jena and Stuttgart, Germany: Fischer Verlag. (In German)

Klausnitzer, B. and Richter, K. (1983). Presence of an urban gradient demonstrated for carabid associations. *Oecologia*, **59**, 79–82.

Kleinman, P.J.A., Bryant, R.B. and Reid, W.S. (1999). Development of pedotransfer functions to quantify phosphorus saturation of agricultural soils. *Journal of Environmental Quality*, **28**, 2026–30.

Klotz, S. (1990). Species/area and species/inhabitants relations in European cities. In *Urban Ecology: Plants and Plant Communities in Urban Environments*, ed. H. Sukopp, S. Hejný and I. Kowarik. The Hague: SPB Academic Publishing, pp. 99–103.

Klotz, S. and Kühn, I. (2002). Indikatoren des anthropogenen Einflusses auf die Vegetation. *Schriftenreihe für Vegetationskunde*, **38**, 241–6.

Knacker, T., Förster, B., Römbke, B. and Frampton, G.K. (2003). Assessing the effects of plant protection products on organic matter breakdown in arable fields – litter decomposition test systems. *Soil Biology and Biochemistry*, **35**, 1269–87.

Knick, S.T. and Rotenberry, J.T. (2000). Ghosts of habitats past: contribution of landscape change to current habitats used by shrubland birds. *Ecology*, **81**, 220–7.

Knol, W.C. and Verweij, P.J.F.M. (1999). A spatial decision support system for river ecosystems. In *Issues in Landscape Ecology*, ed. J.A. Wiens and M.R. Moss. Proceedings of the Fifth World Congress, International Association for Landscape Ecology, Snowmass Village, CO, USA.

Knopf, J., Wasowski, S., Boring, J. *et al.* (2002). *A Guide to Natural Gardening.* San Francisco: Fog City Press.

Kocher, S. D. and Williams, E. H. (2000). The diversity and abundance of North American butterflies vary with habitat disturbance and geography. *Journal of Biogeography*, **27**, 785–94.

Koenig, J., Shine, R. and Shea, G. (2001). The ecology of an Australian reptile icon: how do blue-tongued lizards (*Tiliqua scincoides*) survive in suburbia? *Wildlife Research*, **28**, 215–27.

Koenig, J., Shine, R. and Shea, G. (2002). The dangers of life in the city: patterns of activity, injury and mortality in suburban lizards (*Tiliqua scincoides*). *Journal of Herpetology*, **36**, 62–8.

Koh, L. P. and Sodhi, N. S. (2004). Importance of reserves, fragments, and parks for butterfly conservation in a tropical urban landscape. *Ecological Applications*, **14**, 1695–708.

Kolligs, D. (2000). Ökologische Auswirkungen künstlicher Lichtquellen auf nachtaktive Insekten, insbesondere Schmetterlinge (Lepidoptera). *Faunistisch-Ökologische Mitteilungen, Suppl.*, **28**, 1–136.

Konstantinov, V. M., Nowicki, W. and Pichurin, A. G. (1996). Recent changes in the avifauna of cities in European Russia and eastern Poland – results of a questionnaire. *Acta Ornithologica*, **31**, 59–66.

Korpela, K. M., Hartig, T., Kaiser, F. and Fuhrer, U. (2001). Restorative experience and self-regulation in favourite places. *Environment and Behavior*, **33**, 572–89.

Kostel-Hughes, F. (1995). The role of soil seed banks and leaf litter in the regeneration of native and exotic tree species in urban forests. Unpublished doctoral dissertation. Bronx, New York: Fordham University.

Kostel-Hughes, F., Young, T. P. and McDonnell, M. J. (1998a). The soil seed bank and its relationship to the aboveground vegetation in deciduous forests in New York City. *Urban Ecosystems*, **2**, 43–59.

Kostel-Hughes, F., Young, T. P. and Carreiro, M. M. (1998b). Forest leaf litter quantity and seedling occurrence along an urban–rural gradient. *Urban Ecosystems*, **2**, 263–78.

Kostof, S. (1992). *The City Assembled. The Elements of Urban Form Through History*. London, UK: Bullfinch Press; Little, Brown and Company.

Kowarik, I. (1983). Flora und Vegetation von Kinderspielplätzen in Berlin (West) – ein Beitrag zur Analyse städtischer Grünflächentypen. *Verhandlungen des Berliner Botanischen Vereins*, Berlin (West), **2**, pp. 3–49.

Kowarik, I. (1990). Some responses of flora and vegetation to urbanization in central Europe. In *Urban Ecology: plants and plant communities in urban environments*, ed. H. Sukopp, S. Hejný and I. Kowarik. The Hague: SPB Academic Publishers, pp. 45–74.

Kramer, H. (1990). Methoden und Ergebnisse der Biotopkartierung Frankfurt am Main. *Courier Forschungsinstitut Senckenberg*, **126**, 23–49.

Kremen, C. and Ricketts, T. (2000). Global perspectives on pollination disruptions. *Conservation Biology*, **14**, 1226–8.

Kremen, C., Colwell, R. K., Erwin, T. L. *et al.* (1993). Terrestrial arthropod assemblages: their use in conservation planning. *Conservation Biology*, **7**, 796–808.

Kruess, A. and Tscharntke, T. (1994). Habitat fragmentation, species loss, and biological control. *Science*, **264**, 1581–4.

Kruess, A. and Tscharntke, T. (2000). Species richness and parasitism in a fragmented landscape: experiments and field studies with insects on *Vicia sepium*. *Oecologia*, **122**, 129–37.

Krugman, P. (1996). *The Self Organizing Economy*. Cambridge: Blackwell.

Kucharik, T.I. and Kakareka, S.V. (1998). An analysis of the condition of peatlands in the urban landscape. In *Urban Ecology*, ed. J. Breuste, H. Feldmann and O. Uhlmann. Berlin: Springer-Verlag, pp. 608–12.

Kuchelmeister, G. and Braatz, S. (1993). Urban forestry revisited. *Unasylva*, **173**, 13–18.

Kuchler, A.W. (1964). *Potential Natural Vegetation of the Conterminous United States*. New York: American Geographical Society.

Kuczera, G.A. (1987). Prediction of water yield reductions following a bushfire in ash–mixed species eucalypt forest. *Journal of Hydrology*, **150**, 433–57.

Kunick, W. (1974). Veränderung von Flora und Vegetation einer Großstadt, dargestellt am Beispiel von Berlin (West). Unpublished dissertation, Technical University Berlin (West).

Kunick, W. (1978). *Stadtbiotopkartierung Berlin-Kreuzberg Nord*. (unpublished). Technical University Berlin.

Kunkel, B.A., Held, D.W. and Potter, D.A. (1999). Impact of halofenozide, imidacloprid and bendiocarb on beneficial invertebrates and predatory activity in turfgrass. *Journal of Economic Entomology*, **92**, 922–30.

Kureck, A. (1996). Das Massenschwärmen der Eintagsfliegen am Rhein. Zur Rückkehr von *Ephoron virgo* (Olivier 1791). *Natur und Landschaft*, **67**, 407–9.

Kurtze, W. (1974). Synökologische und experimentelle Untersuchungen zur Nachtaktivität von Insekten. *Zoologische Jahrbücher Systematik*, **101**, 297–344.

Kuschel, G. (1990). *Beetles in a Suburban Environment: A New Zealand Case Study*. Department of Scientific and Industrial Research, New Zealand.

Kylin, M. (2003). Children's dens. *Children, Youth and Environments*, **13**, Retrieved from http://colorado.edu/journals/cye.

LaDell, T. (1986). A suitable case for trees. *Landscape Design*, December 1986, 28–31.

Lake, P.S. (2001). On the maturing of restoration: linking ecological research and restoration. *Ecological Management and Restoration*, **2**, 110–15.

Lambeck, R.J. (1997). Focal species: a multispecies umbrella for nature conservation. *Conservation Biology*, **11**, 849–56.

Lancaster, R.K. and Rees, W.E. (1979). Bird communities and the structure of urban habitats. *Canadian Journal of Zoology*, **57**, 2358–68.

Landesanstalt für Ökologie, Landschaftsentwicklung und Forstplanung Nordrhein-Westfalen (1989). *Biotopkartierung Nordrhein-Westfalen: Methodik und Arbeitsanleitung zur Kartierung im besiedelten Bereich* (Naturschutz: Praktisch: Beiträge zum Artenschutzprogramm NM: Grundlagen des Biotop- und Artenschutz, No. 31). Recklinghausen.

Landolt, E. (2000). Some results of a floristic inventory within the city of Zurich (1984–1998). *Presalia*, **72**, 441–55.

Landres, P. B., Morgan, P. and Swanson, F. J. (1999). Overview of the use of natural variability concepts in managing ecological systems. *Ecological Applications*, **9**, 1179–88.

Landsberg, H. E. (1981). *The Urban Climate*. International Geophysics Series, Vol. 28. New York: Academic Press.

Landskap (1979). *Landskap No. 7/1979. Special issue: Bevaring av natur i utbyggingsområder. [Summary p. 168: The Conservation of Natural Qualities in Development Areas]*. Guest editor: Trygve Sundt. (In Danish, Norwegian and Swedish)

LaPage, W. F. (1967). Some observations on campground trampling and ground cover response. US Forest Service Research Paper NE-68.

Larsson, T., ed. (2001). Biodiversity evaluation tools for European forests. *Ecological Bulletins*, **50**.

Lasiak, T. (1991). The susceptibility and/or resilience of rocky littoral molluscs to stock depletion by the indigenous coastal people of Transkei, Southern Africa. *Biological Conservation*, **56**, 245–64.

Law, N. L., Band, L. E. and Grove, J. M. (2004). Nutrient input from residential lawn care practices. *Journal of Environmental Management*, **47**, 737–55.

Lawrynowicz, M. (1982). Macro-fungal flora of Lodz. In *Urban Ecology: The Second European Ecological Symposium*, ed. R. Bornkamm, J. A. Lee and M. R. D. Seaward. Oxford: Blackwell Scientific Publications, pp. 41–7.

Lawton, J. (1999). Are there general laws in ecology? *Oikos*, **84**, 177–92.

Le, W. Z. (1994). Study of landscape planning in Shanghai in 1990s. *Chinese Landscape and Gardening*, **10**, 49–52. (In Chinese)

Lee, K. N. (2007). An urbanizing world. In: *State of the World 2007: Our Urban Future*. Washington DC: World Watch Institute, pp. 3–21.

Lehvävirta, S. (1999). Structural elements as barriers against wear in urban woodlands. *Urban Ecosystems*, **3**, 45–56.

Lehvävirta, S. (2005). Urban woodland ecology – methodological perspectives and empirical studies. Unpublished doctoral thesis, University of Helsinki, Department of Biology and Environmental Sciences.

Lehvävirta, S. and Rita, H. (2002). Natural regeneration of trees in urban woodlands. *Journal of Vegetation Science*, **13**, 57–66.

Lehvävirta, S., Kotze, D. J., Niemelä, J., Mäntysaari, M. and O'Hara, R. B. (2006). Effects of fragmentation and trampling on carabid beetle assemblages in urban woodlands in Helsinki, Finland. *Urban Ecosystems*, **9**, 13–26.

Lehvävirta, S., Rita, H. and Koivula, M. (2004). Barriers against wear affect the spatial distribution of tree saplings in urban woodlands. *Urban Forestry and Urban Greening*, **3**, 3–17.

Lemckert, F. (1996). Effects of toe-clipping on the survival and behaviour of the Australian frog *Crinia signifera*. *Amphibia-Reptilia*, **17**, 287–90.

Lepczyk, C. A., Mertig, A. G. and Liu, J. (2003). Landowners and cat predation across rural-to-urban landscapes. *Biological Conservation*, **115**, 191–201.

Lerberg, S. B., Holland, A. F. and Sanger, D. M. (2000). Responses of tidal creek macrobenthic communities to the effects of watershed development. *Estuaries*, **23**, 838–53.

Levenson, J. B. (1981). Woodlots as biogeographic islands in southeastern Wisconsin. In *Forest Island Dynamics in Man-dominated Landscapes*, ed. R. L. Burgess and D. M. Sharpe. New York: Springer-Verlag, pp. 13–40.

Levin, S. A. and Paine, R. T. (1974). Disturbance, patch formation, and community structure. *Proceedings of the National Academy of Science*, **71**, 2744–7.

Levins, R. (1969). Some demographic and genetic consequences of environmental heterogeneity for biological control. *Bulletin of the Entomological Society of America*, **15**, 237–40.

Lewin, R. (1983). Santa Rosalia was a goat. *Science*, **221**, 636–9.

Leykauf, J., Nieber, J., Villwock, G. and Walossek, W. (1989). Der Aufbau eines Datenspeichers für ein Geographisches Informationssystem 'Stadtregion Halle'. *Petermanns Geographische Mitteilung*, **1133**, 245–54.

Li, H. and Wu, J. (2004). Use and misuse of landscape indices. *Landscape Ecology*, **19**, 389–99.

Liddle, M. J. (1997). *Recreation Ecology: The Ecological Impact of Outdoor Recreation and Ecotourism*. London: Chapman Hall.

Likens, G. (1991). Human-accelerated environmental change. *BioScience*, **41**, 130.

Likens, G. E. and Bormann, F. H. (1995). *Biogeochemistry of a Forested Ecosystem*, 2nd edn. New York: Springer-Verlag.

Likens, G. E., Driscoll, C. T. and Buso, D. C. (1996). Long-term effects of acid rain: response and recovery of a forest ecosystem. *Science*, **272**, 244–6.

Lillesand, T. M. and Kiefer, R. W. (1994). *Remote Sensing and Image Interpretation*, 3rd edn. Toronto, Canada: John Wiley and Sons.

Lim, H. C. and Sodhi, N. S. (2004). Responses of avian guilds to urbanisation in a tropical city. *Landscape and Urban Planning*, **66**, 199–215.

Lindblom, C. (1965). *The Intelligence of Democracy – Decision Making Through Mutual Adjustment*. New York: Free Press. London: Collier-Macmillan.

Lindblom, C. (1973). The science of muddling through. In *A Reader in Planning Theory*, ed. A. Faludi. Oxford: Pergamon Press.

Lindegarth, M. and Hoskin, M. G. (2001). Patterns of distribution of macro-fauna in different types of estuarine, soft-sediment habitats adjacent to urban and non-urban areas. *Estuarine, Coastal and Shelf Science*, **52**, 237–47.

Lindegarth, M. and Underwood, A. J. (2002). A manipulative experiment to evaluate predicted changes in intertidal, macro-faunal assemblages after contamination by heavy metals. *Journal of Experimental Marine Biology and Ecology*, **274**, 41–64.

Lindenmayer, D. B. (1996). *Wildlife and Woodchips: Leadbeater's Possum as a Test Case for Sustainable Forestry*. Sydney: University of New South Wales Press.

Lindenmayer, D. B. and Franklin, J. F. (2002). *Conserving Forest Biodiversity: A Comprehensive Multiscaled Approach*. Washington, DC: Island Press.

Lindhagen, A. (1996). An approach to clarifying public preferences about silvicultural systems. *Scandinavian Journal of Forest Research*, **11**, 375–87.

Lintas, C. and Seed, R. (1994). Spatial variation in the fauna associated with *Mytilus edulis* on a wave-exposed rocky shore. *Journal of Molluscan Studies*, **60**, 165–74.

Liow, L. H., Sodhi, N. S. and Elmqvist, T. (2001). Bee diversity along a disturbance
    gradient in tropical forests of south-east Asia. *Journal of Applied Ecology*, **38**, 180–92.

Liptan, T. and Murase, R. K. (2002). Water gardens as stormwater infrastructure
    (Portland, Oregon). In *Handbook of Water Sensitive Planning and Design*, ed.
    R. L. France. Boca Raton, Florida: Lewis Publishers, pp. 125–54.

Liu, C. J., Shen, X. H., Zhou, P. S., Che, S. Q., Zhang, Y. L. and Shen, G. R. (2004). Urban
    forestry in China: status and prospects. *Urban Agriculture Magazine*, **13**, 15–17.
    Accessed 18 March 2006. http://www.ruaf.org/node/385

Liu, J. Y., Zhan, J. Y. and Deng, X. Z. (2005). Spatio-temporal patterns and driving forces of
    urban land expansion in China during the economic reform era. *Ambio*, **34**, 450–5.

Lloyd, S. D., Wong, T. H. F. and Chesterfield, C. J. (2001a). Opportunities and
    impediments to water sensitive urban design in Australia. In *Proceedings of the
    Second South Pacific Stormwater Conference: Rain the Forgotten Resource*. Auckland,
    New Zealand, pp. 302–09.

Lloyd, S. D., Wong, T. H. F. and Chesterfield, C. J. (2002). *Water Sensitive Urban Design –
    A Storm Water Management Perspective*. Monash University, Victoria, Australia:
    Cooperative Research Centre for Catchment Hydrology.

Lloyd, S. D., Wong, T. H. F. and Porter, B. (2001b). The planning and construction of an
    urban stormwater management scheme. *Water Science and Technology*, **45**, 1–10.

Lockwood, J. L. and McKinney, M. L., eds. (2001). *Biotic Homogenization*. New York, USA:
    Kluwer Academic/Plenum Publishers.

Löfvenhaft, K. (2002). Spatial and temporal perspectives on biodiversity for physical
    planning. Examples from Stockholm, Sweden. Unpublished Ph.D. thesis,
    Stockholm University.

Löfvenhaft, K. (2004). Biotope patterns and amphibian distribution as indicators
    in urban landscape planning. *Landscape and Urban Planning*, **68**, 403–27.

Löfvenhaft, K. and Wikberger, C. (2004). Stockholms ekologiska infrastruktur:
    Underlag till fortsatt översilktsplanering-Stockholm 2030. Stockholms
    stadsbyggnadskontor, Stadsbyggnadsexpeditionen (unpublished report).

Löfvenhaft, K., Bjorn, C. and Ihse, M. (2002a). Biotope patterns in urban areas:
    a conceptual model integrating biodiversity issues in spatial planning.
    Landscape and Urban Planning, **58**, 223–40.

Löfvenhaft, K., Runborg, S. and Sjögren-Gulve, P. (2004). Biotope patterns and
    amphibian distribution as assessment tools in urban landscape planning.
    Landscape and Urban Planning, **68**, 403–27.

Löfvenhaft, K., Sjögren-Gulve, P., Norström, M. and Karlström, A. (2002b). Using
    amphibians as reference tool for biodiversity assessments in urban areas:
    significance of geographic isolation and water chemistry. In *Spatial and Temporal
    Perspectives on Biodiversity for Physical Planning. Examples from Stockholm, Sweden*,
    ed. K. Löfvenhaft. Ph.D. thesis, paper no. 2, Stockholm University.

Logan, J. R. and Molotch, H. L. (1987). *Urban Fortunes: The Political Economy of Place*.
    Berkeley: University of California Press.

Lohse, D. P. (1993). The importance of secondary substratum in a rocky intertidal
    community. *Journal of Experimental Marine Biology and Ecology*, **166**, 1–17.

Lonsdale, W.M. and Lane, A.M. (1994). Tourist vehicles as vectors of weed seeds in Kakadu-National-Park, northern Australia. *Biological Conservation*, **69**, 277–83.

Lopez, R.R. (2004). Florida key deer (*Odocoileus virginianus clavium*): effects of urban development and road mortality. In *Species Conservation and Management*, ed. H.R. Akcakaya, M.A. Burgman, O. Kindvall *et al.* Oxford, UK: Oxford University Press, pp. 450–8.

López-Jamar, E., Inglesias, J. and Otero, J.J. (1984). Contribution of infauna and mussel-raft epifauna to demersal fish diets. *Marine Ecology Progress Series*, **15**, 13–18.

Lorenz, K., Preston, C.M., Krumrei, S. and Feger, K.H. (2004). Decomposition of needle/leaf litter from Scots pine, black cherry, common oak and European beech at a conurbation forest site. *European Journal of Forest Research*, **123**, 177–88.

Loucks, O.L. (1994). Sustainability in urban ecosystems: beyond an object of study. In *The Ecological City*, ed. R.H. Platt, R.A. Rowntree, and P.C. Muick. Amherst: The University of Massachusetts Press.

Loucks, O.L. (2001). Social and political metabolism of landscapes: an interdisciplinary challenge. Paper presented at the International Association for Landscape Ecology, Arizona State University, April 27, 2001.

Loudon, J.C. (1830). *Hortus Britannicus: A Catalogue of All the Plants Indigenous, Cultivated in, or Introduced to Britain*. London.

Louv, R. (2005). *Last Child in the Woods: Saving Our Children from Nature Deficit Disorder*. Chapel Hill, North Carolina: Allgonquin Books.

Lövei, G.L. and Sunderland, K.D. (1996). Ecology and behavior of ground beetles (*Coleoptera: Carabidae*). *Annual Review of Entomology*, **41**, 231–56.

Lovett, G.M., Traynor, M.M., Pouyat, R.V., Carreiro, M.M., Zhu, W. and Baxter, J.W. (2000). Atmospheric deposition to oak forests along an urban–rural gradient. *Environmental Science and Technology*, **34**, 4294–300.

Low, T. (2002). *The New Nature*. Melbourne, Australia: Viking.

Lu, D.S. and Weng, Q.H. (2004). Spectral mixture analysis of the urban landscape in Indianapolis with Landsat ETM+ imagery. *Photogrammetric Engineering and Remote Sensing*, **70**, 1053–62.

Luck, M. and Wu, J. (2002). A gradient analysis of urban landscape pattern: a case study from the Phoenix metropolitan region, Arizona, USA. *Landscape Ecology*, **17**, 327–9.

Luck, M.A., Jenerette, G.D., Wu, J.G. and Grimm, N.B. (2001). The urban funnel model and the spatially heterogeneous ecological footprint. *Ecosystems*, **4**, 782–96.

Lüddecke, H. and Amézquita, A. (1999). Assessment of disc clipping on the survival and behaviour of the Andean frog *Hyla labialis*. *Copeia*, **1999**, 824–30.

Ludwig, D. (1993). Environmental sustainability: magic, science, and religion in natural resource management. *Ecological Applications*, **3**, 555–8.

Luginbuhl, C.B. (2001). Why astronomy needs low-pressure sodium lamps. In *Preserving the Astronomical Sky, Proceedings of the 196th Symposium of the International Astronomical Union*, ed. R.J. Cohen and W.T. Sullivan. San Francisco: Astronomical Society of the Pacific, pp. 81–6.

Lui, J., Daily, G.C., Ehrlich, P.R. and Luck, B.W. (2003). Effects of household dynamics on resource consumption and biodiversity. *Nature*, **421**, 530–3.

Luken, J. O. (1990). *Directing Ecological Succession*. New York: Chapman and Hall.

Luniak, M. (1980). An experiment in Poland: Bialoleka Dworska. *Naturop*, **36**, 14.

Luniak, M. (1990). Avifauna of cities in central and eastern Europe: results of an international inquiry. In *Urban Ecological Studies in Central and Eastern Europe*, ed. M. Luniak. Wroclaw: Polish Academy of Sciences, pp. 131–49.

Luniak, M., Muslow, M. and Walasz, K. (1990). Urbanisation of the European blackbird – expansion and adaptations of urban population. In *Urban Ecological Studies in Central and Eastern Europe*, ed. M. Luniak. Wroclaw: Polish Academy of Sciences, pp. 187–99.

Lunt, I. D. (1998). Two hundred years of land use and vegetation change in a remnant coastal woodland in southern Australia. *Australian Journal of Botany*, **46**, 629–47.

Luonto ja kaupinkien asuntoalueet (1984). [*Summary: Nature and urban residential areas* – Finnish-Soviet Scientific and Technological Co-operation]. Rakennuskirja OY, Helsingfors.

Lyle, J. T. (1985). *Design for Human Ecosystems*. New York: Van Nostrand Reinhold.

Lyle, J. T. (1994). *Regenerative Design for Sustainable Development*. New York: John Wiley and Sons.

Lynch, K., Binns, T. and Olofin, E. (2001). Urban agriculture under threat. *Cities*, **18**, 159–71.

Mac Nally, R. and Bennett, A. F. (1997). Species-specific predictions of the impact of habitat fragmentation: local extinction of birds in the box-ironbark forests of central Victoria, Australia. *Biological Conservation*, **82**, 147–55.

Mac Nally, R., Bennett, A. F. and Horrocks, G. (2000). Forecasting the impacts of habitat fragmentation. Evaluation of species-specific predictions of the impact of habitat fragmentation on birds in the box-ironbark forests of central Victoria, Australia. *Biological Conservation*, **95**, 7–29.

MacArthur, R. and MacArthur, J. (1961). On bird species diversity. *Ecology*, **42**, 594–8.

MacArthur, R. H. (1972). *Geographical Ecology: Patterns in the Distribution of Species*. New York: Harper and Row.

MacArthur, R. H. and Wilson, E. O. (1967). *The Theory of Island Biogeography*. New Jersey: Princeton University Press.

Macaskill, J. B., Vant, W. N. and McBride, G. B. (1996). *Hamilton City: Assessment of Effluent Impacts on the Receiving Water*. Report prepared for Hamilton City Council. Hamilton, New Zealand: NIWA.

Machlis, G. E., Force, J. E. and Burch, W. R. Jr (1997). The human ecosystem. 1. The human ecosystem as an organizing concept in ecosystem management. *Society and Natural Resources*, **10**, 347–67.

Mackey, B., Lindenmayer, D., Gill, M., McCarthy, M. and Lindesay, J. (2002). *Wildlife, Fire and Future Climate: A Forest Ecosystem Analysis*. Collingwood, Victoria: CSIRO Publishing.

Madaleno, I. (2000). Urban agriculture in Belém, Brazil. *Cities*, **17**, 73–7.

Madhavan, B. B., Kubo, S., Kurisaki, N. and Sivakumar, T. V. (2001). Appraising the anatomy and spatial growth of the Bangkok Metropolitan area using a vegetation-impervious-soil model through remote sensing. *International Journal of Remote Sensing*, **22**, 789–806.

Mäding, H. (1997). Entwicklungsperspektiven für die Stadt – Trends und Chancen. *Difu-aktuelle Information*, **Dec. 1997**, 1–11.

Magee, T. K., Ernst, T. L., Kentula, M. E. and Dwire, K. A. (1999). Floristic comparison of freshwater wetlands in an urbanizing environment. *Wetlands*, **19**, 517–34.

Magill, A. H., Aber, J. D., Hendricks, J. J., Bowden, R. D., Melillo, J. M. and Steudler, P. A. (1997). Biogeochemical response of forest ecosystems to simulated chronic nitrogen deposition. *Ecological Applications*, **7**, 402–15.

Magura, T., Tóthmérész, B. and Molnár, T. (2004). Changes in carabid beetle assemblages along an urbanization gradient in the city of Debrecen, Hungary. *Landscape Ecology*, **19**, 747–59.

Majer, J. D. (1980). The influence of ants on broadcast and naturally spread seeds in rehabilitated bauxite mines. *Reclamation Review*, **3**, 3–9.

Majer, J. D. (1997). The use of pitfall traps for sampling ants: a critique. *Memoirs of the Museum of Victoria*, **56**, 323–9.

Majer, J. D. and Nichols, O. G. (1998). Long-term recolonization patterns of ants in Western Australian rehabilitated bauxite mines, with reference to use as indicators of restoration success. *Journal of Applied Ecology*, **35**, 161–81.

Major, R. E., Gowing, G. and Kendal, C. E. (1996). Nest predation in Australian urban environments and the role of the pied currawong, *Strepera graculina*. *Australian Journal of Ecology*, **21**, 399–409.

Major, R. E., Smith, D., Cassis, G., Gray, M. R. V. and Colgan, D. J. (1999). Are roadside strips important reservoirs of invertebrate diversity? A comparison of the ant and beetle faunas of roadside strips and large remnant woodlands. *Australian Journal of Zoology*, **47**, 611–24.

Malanson, G. P. (1993). *Riparian Landscapes*. Cambridge, UK: Cambridge University Press.

Malicky, H. (1965). Freilandversuche an Lepidopterenpopulationen mit Hilfe der Jermyschen Lichtfalle, mit Diskussion biozönologischer Gesichtspunkte. *Zeitschrift für Angewandte Entomologie*, **56**, 358–77.

Mallick, S. A., Hocking, G. J. and Driessen, M. M. (1998). Road-kills of the eastern barred bandicoot (*Perameles gunnii*) in Tasmania: an index of abundance. *Wildlife Research*, **25**, 139–46.

Malmivaara, M., Löfström, I. and Vanhaa-Majamaa, I. (2002). Anthropogenic effects on understorey vegetation in Myrtillus type urban forests in southern Finland. *Silva Fennica*, **36**, 367–81.

Mangold, S., Kalule-Sabiti, M. and Walmsley, J., eds. (2002b). *State of the Environment Report 2002, North West Province, South Africa*. Mafikeng: North West Province Department of Agriculture, Conservation and Environment.

Mangold, S., Momberg, M. and Newbery, R. (2002a). Biodiversity and conservation. In *The State of the Environment Report 2002 of the North West Province, South Africa*, ed. S. Mangold, M. Kalule-Sabiti and J. Walmsley. Mafikeng: North West Province Department of Agriculture, Conservation and Environment, Chapter 11.

Mann, R. B. (1988). Ten trends in the continuing renaissance of urban waterfronts. *Landscape and Urban Planning*, **16**, 177–99.

Mansikka, M. (1984). NEKASU. *Luonto kaupungissa – kaupunki luonnossa.* Center for urban and regional studies, Helsinki University of Technology. NEKASU B32. Helsingfors. (In Finnish with English summary)

Manson, F. J., Loneragan, N. R. and Phinn, S. R. (2003). Spatial and temporal variation in distribution of mangroves in Moreton Bay, subtropical Australia: a comparison of pattern metrics and change detection analyses based on aerial photographs. *Estuarine Coastal and Shelf Science*, **57**, 653–66.

Manukau City Council (2003). Accessed January 2003. http://www.manukau.govt.nz/getinfo.htm

Margules, C. R. and Austin, M. P. (1994). Biological models for monitoring species decline: the construction and use of data bases. *Philosophical Transactions of the Royal Society of London on Biological Sciences*, **344**, 69–75.

Marinelli, J., ed. (1994). *Going Native: Biodiversity in Our Own Backyards*. Brooklyn, NY: Brooklyn Botanic Garden publication 140, p. 112.

Marino, P. C. and Landis, D. A. (1996). Effect of landscape structure on parasitoid diversity and parasitism in agroecosystems. *Ecological Applications*, **6**, 276–84.

Markkola, A. M., Ohtonen, R., Tarvainen, O. and Ahonen-Jonnarth, U. (1995). Estimates of fungal biomass in Scots pine stands on an urban pollution gradient. *New Phytologist*, **131**, 139–47.

Marquis, R. J. and Whelan, C. J. (1994). Insectivorous birds increase growth of white oak through consumption of leaf-chewing insects. *Ecology*, **75**, 2007–14.

Marsh, G. P. (1864). *Man and Nature; Or, Physical Geography as Modified by Human Action.* Cambridge, MA: Harvard University Press.

Martel, A. and Chia, F.-S. (1991). Drifting and dispersal of small bivalves and gastropods with direct development. *Journal of Experimental Marine Biology and Ecology*, **150**, 131–47.

Martin, C. A. (2001). Landscape water use in Phoenix, Arizona. *Desert Plants*, **17**, 26–31.

Martin, T. G. and Catterall, C. P. (2001). Do fragmented coastal heathlands have habitat value to birds in eastern Australia? *Wildlife Research*, **28**, 1–15.

Marzluff, J. M. (2001). Worldwide urbanization and its effects on birds. In *Avian Ecology and Conservation in an Urbanizing World*, ed. J. M. Marzluff, R. Bowman and R. Donnelly. Norwell, Massachusetts: Kluwer Academic Publishers, pp. 19–47.

Marzluff, J. M. and Hamel, N. (2001). Land use issues. In *Encyclopaedia of Biodiversity*, Vol. 3. New York: Academic Press, pp. 659–73.

Marzluff, J. M., Bowman, R. and Donnelly, R., eds. (2001). *Avian Ecology and Conservation in an Urbanizing World*. Norwell, Massachusetts: Kluwer Academic Publishers.

Masek, J. G., Lindsay, F. E. and Goward, S. N. (2000). Dynamics of urban growth in the Washington DC metropolitan area, 1973–1996, from Landsat observations. *International Journal of Remote Sensing*, **21**, 3473–86.

Maske, H. A., Havlin, S. and Stanley, H. E. (1995). Modelling urban growth patterns. *Nature*, **377**, 608–12.

Mather, G. and Laurence, C. (1993). *Managing Your Bushland: A Guide for Urban Councils.* Sydney: Total Environment Centre Inc.

Matlack, G. R. (1993a). Microenvironment variation within and among forest edge sites in the eastern United States. *Biological Conservation*, **66**, 185–94.

Matlack, G. R. (1993b). Sociological edge effects: spatial distribution of human impact in suburban forest fragments. *Environmental Management*, **17**, 829–35.

Matson, P. (1990). The use of urban gradients in ecological studies. *Ecology*, **71**, 1231.

Matthews, M. J., O'Connor, S. and Cole, R. S. (1988). Database for the New York State urban wildlife habitat inventory. *Landscape and Urban Planning*, **15**, 23–37.

Mattson, W. J. (1980). Herbivory in relation to plant nitrogen content. *Annual Review of Ecology and Systematics*, **11**, 119–61.

Matunga, H. (2000). Urban ecology, tangata whenua and the colonial city. In *Urban Biodiversity and Ecology as a Basis for Holistic Planning and Design*, ed. G. H. Stewart and M. E. Ignatieva. Christchurch: Wickliffe Press, pp. 65–71.

Maxim Planning Solutions (MPS) (2003). *North West Spatial Development Framework and Zoning Plan*. Unpublished report.

May, J. and Rogerson, C. M. (1995). Poverty and sustainable cities in South Africa: the role of urban cultivation. *Habitat International*, **19**, 165–81.

McAllister, T. L., Overton, M. F. and Brill, E. D. (1996). Cumulative impact of marinas on estuarine water quality. *Environmental Management*, **20**, 385–96.

McBride, J. R. and Jacobs, D. F. (1976). Urban forest development: A case study, Menlo Park, California. *Urban Ecology*, **2**, 1–14.

McCarthy, M. A. (2007). *Bayesian Methods for Ecology*. Cambridge, UK: Cambridge University Press.

McCarthy, M. A. and Burgman, M. A. (1995). Coping with uncertainty in forest wildlife planning. *Forest Ecology and Management*, **74**, 23–36.

McCarthy, M. A. and Lindenmayer, D. B. (1998). Multi-aged mountain ash forest, wildlife conservation and timber harvesting. *Forest Ecology and Management*, **104**, 43–56.

McCarthy, M. A. and Parris, K. M. (2004). Clarifying the effect of toe clipping on frogs with Bayesian statistics. *Journal of Applied Ecology*, **41**, 780–6.

McCarthy, M. A., Gill, A. M. and Bradstock, R. A. (2001). Theoretical fire-interval distributions. *International Journal of Wildland Fire*, **10**, 73–7.

McCarthy, M. A., Gill, A. M. and Lindenmayer, D. B. (1999). Fire regimes in mountain ash forest: evidence from forest age structure, extinction models and wildlife habitat. *Forest Ecology and Management*, **124**, 193–203.

McClure, M. S. (1991). Nitrogen fertilization of hemlock increases susceptibility to hemlock woolly adelgid. *Journal of Arboriculture*, **17**, 227–9.

McConchie, J. A. (1992). Urban hydrology. In *Waters of New Zealand*, ed. M. P. Mosley. Wellington: New Zealand Hydrological Society, pp. 335–63.

McDonald, W. and St Clair, C. C. (2004). Elements that promote highway crossing structure use by small mammals in Banff National Park. *Journal of Applied Ecology*, **41**, 82–93.

McDonald, T., Wale, K. and Bear, V. (2002). Restoring blue gum high forest: lessons from Sheldon Forest. *Ecological Management & Restoration* **3**, 15–26.

McDonnell, M. J. (1988). The challenge of preserving urban natural areas: a forest for New York. *Journal of American Associations of Botanical Gardens*, **3**, 28–31.

McDonnell, M. J. (1997). A paradigm shift. *Urban Ecosystems*, **1**, 85–6.

McDonnell, M. J. (2007). Restoring and managing biodiversity in an urbanizing world filled with tensions. *Environmental Management and Restoration*, **8**, 83–4.

McDonnell, M. J. and Hahs, A. K. (2008). The use of gradient studies in advancing our understanding of the ecology of urbanizing landscapes: Current status and future directions. *Landscape Ecology*, DOI: 10.1007/s10980–008–9253–4.

McDonnell, M. J. and Pickett, S. T. A. (1990). Ecosystem structure and function along urban–rural gradients: an unexploited opportunity for ecology. *Ecology*, **71**, 1232–7.

McDonnell, M. J. and Pickett, S. T. A. (1993a). Introduction: scope and need for an ecology of subtle human effects and populated areas. In *Humans as Components of Ecosystems: The Ecology of Subtle Human Effects and Populated Areas*, ed. M. J. McDonnell and S. T. A. Pickett. Berlin: Springer-Verlag, pp. 1–5.

McDonnell, M. J. and Pickett, S. T. A., eds. (1993b). *Humans as Components of Ecosystems: Subtle Human Effects and the Ecology of Populated Areas*. New York: Springer-Verlag.

McDonnell, M. J. and Stiles, E. W. (1983). The structural complexity of old field vegetation and the recruitment of bird-dispersed plant species. *Oecologia*, **56**, 109–16.

McDonnell, M. J., Pickett, S. T. A., Groffman, P. *et al.* (1997). Ecosystem processes along an urban-to-rural gradient. *Urban Ecosystems*, **1**, 21–36.

McDonnell, M. J., Pickett, S. T. A. and Pouyat, R. V. (1993). The application of the ecological gradient paradigm to the study of urban effects. In *Humans as Components of Ecosystems: The Ecology of Subtle Human Effects and Populated Areas*, ed. M. J. McDonnell and S. T. A. Pickett. New York: Springer-Verlag, pp. 175–89.

McDonnell, M. J., Pickett, S. T. A., Pouyat, R. V. and Zipperer, W. C. (1995). Urban–rural ecological gradients: a new perspective for urban forestry. In *Proceedings of the 7th National Urban Forestry Conference*, ed. C. Kollin. Washington, DC: American Forests, pp. 22–4.

McGeoch, M. A. and Chown, S. L. (1997). Impact of urbanization on a gall-inhabiting Lepidoptera assemblage: the importance of reserves in urban areas. *Biodiversity and Conservation*, **6**, 979–93.

McGuinness, K. A. (1984). Species–area relations of communities on intertidal boulders: testing the null hypothesis. *Journal of Biogeography*, **11**, 439–56.

McGuinness, K. A. and Underwood, A. J. (1986). Habitat structure and the nature of communities on intertidal boulders. *Journal of Experimental Marine Biology and Ecology*, **104**, 97–123.

McHarg, I. (1969). *Design with Nature*. Garden City, New York: Doubleday/The Natural History Press.

McIntyre, N. E. (1999). Influences of urban land use on the frequency of scorpion stings in the Phoenix, Arizona, metropolitan area. *Landscape and Urban Planning*, **45**, 47–55.

McIntyre, N. E. (2000). The ecology of urban arthropods: a review and a call to action. *Annals of the Entomological Society of America*, **93**, 825–35.

McIntyre, N. E. and Hostetler, M. E. (2001). Effects of urban land use on pollinator (Hymenoptera: Apoidea) communities in a desert metropolis. *Basic and Applied Ecology*, **2**, 209–18.

McIntyre, N. E., Knowles-Yanez, K. and Hope, D. (2000). Urban ecology as an interdisciplinary field: differences in the use of 'urban' between the social and natural sciences. *Urban Ecosystems*, **4**, 5–24.

McIntyre, N. E., Rango, J., Fagan, W. F. and Faeth, S. H. (2001). Ground arthropod community structure in a heterogeneous urban environment. *Landscape and Urban Planning*, **52**, 257–74.

McIntyre, S. and Hobbs, R. (1999). A framework for conceptualising human effects on landscapes and its relevance to management and research methods. *Conservation Biology*, **13**, 1282–92.

McKenzie, C. L. Jr (1996). History of oystering in the United States and Canada, featuring the eight great oyster estuaries. *Marine Fisheries Review*, **58**, 1–87.

McKergow, L. (1994). *Urban Stormwater Quality: Pakuranga, Auckland*. Technical Publication 49. Auckland: Auckland Regional Council.

McKinney, M. L. (2002). Urbanization, biodiversity and conservation. *BioScience*, **52**, 883–90.

McKinney, M. L. (2004). Measuring floristic homogenization by non-native plants in North America. *Global Ecology and Biogeography*, **13**, 47–53.

McKinney, M. L. (2006). Urbanization as a major cause of biotic homogenization. *Biological Conservation*, **127**, 247–60.

McNulty, S., Currie, W., Rustad, L. and Fernandez, I. (1998). Nitrogen saturation in temperate forest ecosystems: hypotheses revisited. *Bioscience*, **48**, 921–34.

McPherson, E. G. (1998). Atmospheric carbon dioxide reduction by Sacramento's urban forest. *Journal of Arboriculture*, **24**, 215–23.

McWilliam, W. J. and Brown, R. D. (2001). Effects of housing development on bird species diversity in a forest fragment in Ontario, Canada. *Landscape Research*, **26**, 407–28.

Medley, K. E., McDonnell, M. J. and Pickett, S. T. A. (1995). Forest-landscape structure along an urban-to-rural gradient. *Professional Geographer*, **47**, 159–68.

Meinig, D. W. (1979). Symbolic landscapes. Some idealizations of American communities. In *The Interpretation of Ordinary Landscape*, ed. D. W. Meinig. Oxford, UK: Oxford University Press, pp. 164–92.

Melillo, J. M., Aber, J. D. and Muratore, J. F. (1982). Nitrogen and lignin control of hardwood leaf litter decomposition dynamics. *Ecology*, **63**, 621–6.

Melles, S., Glenn, S. and Martin, K. (2003). Urban bird diversity and landscape complexity: species–environment associations along a multiscale habitat gradient. *Conservation Ecology*, **7**, 5. http://www.consecol.org/vol7/iss1/art5

Mensing, D. M., Galatowitsch, S. M. and Tester, J. R. (1998). Anthropogenic effects on the biodiversity of riparian wetlands of a northern temperate landscape. *Journal of Environmental Management*, **53**, 349–77.

Metroplan (2000). *Southern District Council: Land Development Objectives*. (Including Kerksdorp, Potchefstroom, Maquassi Hills and Ventersdorp) Northwest Province, South Africa. Unpublished report.

Metropolitan Washington Council of Governments (2004). *The Anacostia Watershed Network*. http://www.anacostia.net

Metzger, J. P. (1997). Relationships between landscape structure and tree species diversity in tropical forests of South-East Brazil. *Landscape and Urban Planning*, **37**, 29–35.

Meurk, C. D. (2005). Cities are cultural and ecological keys to biodiverse futures. In *Greening the City*, ed. M. I. Dawson. Proceedings of a conference held by the Royal New Zealand Institute of Horticulture, Christchurch, 21–24 October 2003, Caxton Press, Christchurch, pp. 301–10.

Meurk, C. D. and Buxton, R. P. (1990). What is happening to the natural landscape of Aotearoa? *Proceedings of the New Zealand Grassland Association*, **51**, 35–8.

Meurk, C. D. and Greenep, H. (2003). Practical conservation and restoration of herbaceous vegetation. *Canterbury Botanical Society Journal*, **37**, 99–108.

Meurk, C. D. and Hall, G. M. J. (2000). Biogeography and ecology of urban landscapes. In *Urban Biodiversity and Ecology as a Basis for Holistic Planning and Design*, eds. G. H. Stewart and M. E. Ignatieva. Proceedings of a workshop held at Lincoln University, 28–29, 2000, Lincoln University International Centre for Nature Conservation Publication 1. Christchurch: Wickliffe Press Ltd, pp. 34–45.

Meurk, C. D. and Hall, G. M. J. (2006). Options for enhancing forest biodiversity across New Zealand's managed landscapes based on ecosystem modelling and spatial design. *New Zealand Journal of Ecology*, **30**, 131–46.

Meurk, C. D. and Swaffield, S. R. (2000). A landscape ecological framework for indigenous regeneration in rural New Zealand–Aotearoa. *Landscape and Urban Planning*, **50**, 129–44.

Meyer, T., Kellner, K. and Viljoen, C. (2002). Land transformation and soil quality. In *The State of the Environment Report 2002 of the North West Province, South Africa*, eds. S. Mangold, M. Kalule-Sabiti and J. Walmsley. Mafikeng: North West Province Department of Agriculture, Conservation and Environment, Chapter 9.

Mikkelsen, P. S., Hafliger, M., Ochs, M., Tjell, J. C., Jacobsen, P. and Boller, M. (1996). Experimental assessment of soil and groundwater contamination from two old infiltration systems for road run-off in Switzerland. In *The Science of the Total Environment*, **189/190**, 341–7.

Mikkola, K. (1972). Behavioural and electrophysiological responses of night-flying insects, especially Lepidoptera, to near-ultraviolet and visible light. *Annales Zoologici Fennici*, **9**, 225–54.

Miller, J. R. and Hobbs, R. J. (2002). Conservation where people live and work. *Conservation Biology*, **16**, 330–7.

Miller, J. R., Fraterrigo, J. M., Hobbs, N. T., Theobald, D. and Wiens, J. A. (2001). Urbanization, avian communities, and landscape ecology. In *Avian Ecology and Conservation in an Urbanizing World*, ed. J. Marzluff, R. Bowman and R. Donnelly. Boston: Kluwer Academic Publishers, pp. 117–38.

Miller, J. R., Joyce, L. A., Knight, R. L. and King, R. M. (1996). Forest roads and landscape structure in the southern Rocky Mountains. *Landscape Ecology*, **11**, 115–27.

Millsap, B. A. and Bear, C. (2000). Density and reproduction of burrowing owls along an urban development gradient. *Journal of Wildlife Management*, **64**, 33–41.

Ministerie LNV (1990). *Het Natuurbeleidsplan: regeringsbeslissing*. Ministry of Agriculture, Nature Management and Fisheries. The Hague: SDU.

Ministry for the Environment (2000). *Curbing the Sprawl: Urban Growth Management in the United States. Lessons for New Zealand*. Wellington: Ministry for the Environment.

Ministry for the Environment (2002a). *People + Places + Spaces. A Design Guide for Urban New Zealand*. Wellington, New Zealand: Ministry for the Environment.

Ministry for the Environment (2002b). *Regional Authority Liaison Group 12: National Critical Issues*. Wellington, New Zealand: Ministry for the Environment.

Mintzberg, H. (2000). *The Rise and Fall of Strategic Planning*. New York: Free Press.

Mitchell, G. (2000). Indicators as tools to guide progress on the sustainable development pathway. In *Sustaining Human Settlement: A challenge for the new millenium*, ed. R. J. Lawrence. London: Urban International Press.

Mitsch, W. J. and Gosselink, J. G. (2000). *Wetlands*, 3rd edn. New York: John Wiley and Sons.

Miyashita, T., Shinkai, A. and Chida, T. (1998). The effects of forest fragmentation on web spider communities in urban areas. *Biological Conservation*, **86**, 357–64.

Mizon, B. (2002). *Light Pollution: Responses and Remedies*. Patrick Moore's Practical Astronomy Series. London: Springer.

Molander, B. (1996). *Kunskap i handling*. Göteborg: Daidalos.

Molenaar, J. G., de Jonkers, D. A. and Henkens, R. J. H. G. (1997). Wegverlichting en Natuur. *DWW series Ontsnipperingsreeks deel Ministerie van Verkeer en Waterstaat*, **34**, Delft, Netherlands, p. 292.

Molenaar, J. G., de Jonkers, D. A. and Sanders, M. E. (2000). Road illumination and nature. III. Local influence of road lights on a black-tailed gowit (*Limosa l. limosa*) population. *DWW series Ontsnipperingsreeks deel Ministerie van Verkeer en Waterstaat*, **38A**, Delft, Netherlands, p. 85.

Moller-Jensen, L. (1990). Knowledge-based classification of an urban area using texture and context information in Landsat TM Imagery. *Photogrammetric Engineering and Remote Sensing*, **65**, 899–904.

Molles, M. C. Jr (1978). Fish species diversity on model and natural reef patches: experimental insular biogeography. *Ecological Monographs*, **48**, 289–305.

Molloy, B. P. J. (1995). *Riccarton Bush: Putaringamotu*. Christchurch: Riccarton Bush Trust.

Monteiro, S. M., Chapman, M. G. and Underwood, A. J. (2002). Patches of the ascidian *Pyura stolonifera* (Heller, 1878): structure of habitat and associated intertidal assemblages. *Journal of Experimental Marine Biology and Ecology*, **270**, 171–89.

Moore, M., Gould, P. and Keary, B. S. (2003). Global urbanization and impact on health. *International Journal of Hygiene and Environmental Health*, **206**, 269–78.

Moran, M. (1984). Influence of adjacent land use on understorey vegetation of New York forests. *Urban Ecology*, **8**, 329–40.

Morancho, A. B. (2003). A hedonic valuation of urban green areas. *Landscape and Urban Planning*, **66**, 35–41.

Morgan, J. W. (1998). Patterns of invasion of an urban remnant of a species-rich grassland in southeastern Australia by non-native plant species. *Journal of Vegetation Science*, **9**, 181–90.

Morneau, F., Décarie, R., Pelletier, R., Lambert, D., DesGranges, J.-L. and Savard, J.-P. (1999). Changes in breeding bird richness and abundance in Montreal parks over a period of 15 years. *Landscape and Urban Planning*, **44**, 111–21.

Morrisey, D. J., Underwood, A. J. and Howitt, L. (1996). Effects of copper on the faunas of marine soft-sediments: an experimental field study. *Marine Biology*, **125**, 199–213.

Mörtberg, U. (1996). Biologisk mångfald i Stockholms grönstruktur – fåglar. Inledande landskapsekologisk studie. [Summary: Biodiversity in Stockholm's green infrastructure – birds. Introductory landscape ecology study]. TRITA-AMI LIC 2017. Unpublished licentiate thesis, Royal Swedish University of Technology (KTH), Stockholm. (In Swedish)

Mörtberg, U. M. (1998). Bird species diversity in urban forest remnants: landscape pattern and habitat quality. In *Key Concepts in Landscape Ecology*, ed. R. W. Dover and R. G. H. Bunce. Proceedings of the 1998 European Congress of the International Association for Landscape Ecology, 3rd–5th September 1998, pp. 239–44.

Mörtberg, U. M. (2001). Resident bird species in urban forest remnants: landscape and habitat perspectives. *Landscape Ecology*, **16**, 193–203.

Mörtberg, U. M. (2004). *Landscape Ecological Analysis and Assessment in an Urbanising Environment: Forest Birds as Biodiversity Indicators*. Dissertation, Royal Institute of Technology, Department of Land and Water Resources Engineering, Stockholm.

Mörtberg, U. and Balfors, B. 2007. Biodiversity in urban areas and applications in strategic planning. In *Green Structures in the Sustainable City. Baltic University Urban Forum, Urban Management Guidebook* V, ed. D. Wlodarczyk, pp. 33–38.

Mörtberg, U. and Karlström, A. (2005). Predicting forest grouse distribution taking account of spatial autocorrelation. *Journal for Nature Conservation* **13**, 147–159.

Mörtberg, U. M. and Wallentinus, H.-G. (2000). Red-listed forest bird species in an urban environment: assessment of green space corridors. *Landscape and Urban Planning*, **50**, 215–26.

Mörtberg, U. M., Balfors, B. and Knol, W. C. (2007). Landscape ecological assessment: a tool for integrating biodiversity issues in strategic environmental assessment and planning. *Journal of Environmental Management*, **82**, 457–70.

Moser, C. A. and Scott, W. (1961). *British Towns: A Statistical Study of their Social and Economic Differences*. Edinburgh: Oliver and Boyd.

Muller, N. (1990). Lawns in German cities. A phytosociological comparison. In *Urban Ecology: Plants and Plant Communities in Urban Environments*, ed. H. Sukopp, S. Hejný and I. Kowarik. The Hague: SPB Academic Publishing, pp. 209–22.

Müller, N. and Waldert, R. (1981). Erfassung erhaltenswerter Lebensräume für Pflanzen und Tiere in der Stadt. Augsburg Stadtbiotopkartierung. *Natur und Landschaft*, **56**, 419–29.

Mumme, R. L., Schoech, S. J. and Fitzpatrick, J. W. (2000). Life and death in the fast lane: demographic consequences of road mortality in the Florida Scrub-Jay. *Conservation Biology*, **14**, 501–12.

Münchow, B. and Schramm, M. (1997). Permeable pavements: an appropriate method to reduce stormwater flow in urban sewer systems? In *Urban Ecology*, ed. J. Breuste, H. Feldmann and O. Uhlmann. Leipzig, pp. 183–6.

Munguira, M. L. and Thomas, J. A. (1992). Use of road verges by butterfly and burnet populations, and the effect of roads on adult dispersal and mortality. *Journal of Applied Ecology*, **29**, 316–29.

Murakami, K. and Morimoto, Y. (2000). Landscape ecological study on the woody plant species richness and its conservation in fragmented forest patches in Kyoto City area. *Journal of the Japanese Society of Revegetation Technology*, **25**, 345–50. (In Japanese with English abstract)

Murakami, K., Matsui, R., Maenaka, H. and Morimoto, Y. (2003). Relationship between species composition of Pteridophytes and micro-landform types in fragmented forest patches in Kyoto City area. *Journal of the Japanese Institute of Landscape Architecture*, **66**, 513–16. (In Japanese with English abstract)

Murcia, C. (1995). Edge effects in fragmented forests: implications for conservation. *Trends in Ecology and Evolution*, **10**, 58–62.

Murray, B.G. (2001). Are ecological and evolutionary theories scientific? *Biological Reviews*, **76**, 255–89.

Musacchio, L.R. and Wu, J. (2002). Cities of resilience: integrating ecology into urban planning, policy, design and management. Special session at the 2002 Ecological Society of America Meeting/Society for Ecological Restoration, Tucson, Arizona.

Musacchio, L.R. and Wu, J. (2004). Collaborative landscape-scale ecological research: emerging trends in urban and regional ecology. *Urban Ecosystems*, **7**, 175–8.

Nabhan, G.P. (1997). *Cultures of Habitat: On Nature, Culture and Story*. Washington, DC: Counterpoint.

Nabhan, G.P. (2004). *Cross-pollinators: The Marriage of Science and Poetry*. Minneapolis, MN: Milkweed Editions.

Naess, P. (2001). Urban planning and sustainable development. *European Planning Studies*, **9**, 503–24.

Naiman, R.J. and Décamps, H. (1997). The ecology of interfaces: riparian zones. *Annual Review of Ecology and Systematics*, **28**, 621–58.

Naiman, R.J., Décamps, H and Pollock, M. (1993). The role of riparian corridors in maintaining regional biodiversity. *Ecological Applications*, **3**, 209–12.

Nakagoshi, N. (1995). *Ground Design of Landscape*. Tokyo: Kyoritsu Shuppan. (In Japanese)

Nakamura, A., Morimoto, Y. and Mizutani, Y. (2005). Adaptive management approach to increasing the diversity of a 30-year-old planted forest in an urban area of Japan. *Landscape and Urban Planning*, **70**, 291–300.

Nakamura, N. (1988). *Mori to Tori to (Forests and Birds)*. Nagano: Shinano Mainichi Shinbunsha. (In Japanese)

Narisada, K. and Schreuder, D. (2004). *Light Pollution Handbook*. Astrophysics and Space Science Library. Dordrecht, The Netherlands: Springer.

Nash, R. (1982). *Wilderness and the American Mind*. New Haven: Yale University Press.

Nassauer, J.I. (1995). Culture and changing landscape structure. *Landscape Ecology*, **10**, 229–37.

Nassauer, J.I. (1997). *Placing Nature*. Washington, DC: Island Press.

National Research Council (2002). *Riparian Areas: Functions and Strategies for Management*. Washington, DC: National Academy Press.

Natuhara, Y. (1998). Ant faunae in Osaka City and three other sites in Osaka Prefecture. *Bulletin of Myrmecological Society of Japan*, **22**, 1–5. (In Japanese with English abstract)

Natuhara, Y. (2000). Changes in butterfly assemblage along the urban–forest gradient. *Journal of the Japanese Institute of Landscape Architecture*, **63**, 515–18. (In Japanese with English abstract)

Natuhara, Y. and Imai, C. (1996). Spatial structure of avifauna along urban–rural gradients. *Ecological Research*, **11**, 1–9.

Natuhara, Y. and Imai, C. (1999). Prediction of species richness of breeding birds by landscape-level factors of urban woods in Osaka Prefecture, Japan. *Biodiversity and Conservation*, **8**, 239–53.

Natuhara, Y., Imai, C. and Takahashi, M. (1999). Pattern of land mosaics affecting butterfly assemblage at Mt Ikoma, Osaka, Japan. *Ecological Research*, **14**, 105–18.

Natur mellan hus [Nature Between Houses] (1975). Statens Planverk rapport 32. Stockholm. (In Swedish)

Naturmark i bebyggelsesplanen (1986). *Det norske hageselskap – Planleggingsavdelingen*. [Preserved Natural Vegetation in Local Area Development Planning in Norway] De grönne blad 106. Oslo. (In Norwegian)

Neckles, H. A., Kopp, B. S., Nielsen, M. G. and Guntenspergen, G. R. (2002). Autotrophic responses to nutrient loadings in a Ruppia dominated estuary: current status and future projections. *17th Biennial Conference of the Estuarine Research Federation*, Seattle, WA, 14–18 September 2003. Abstracts. Estuarine Research Federation.

Neckles, H. A., Wetzel, R. L. and Orth, R. J. (1993). Relative effects of nutrient enrichment and grazing on epiphyte-macrophyte (*Zostera marina* L.) dynamics. *Oecologia*, **93**, 285–95.

Neef, E. (1963). Topologische und chronologische Arbeitsweisen in der Landschaftsforschung. *Petermanns Geographische Mitteilungen*, **107**, 249–59.

Neef, E. (1967). *Die theoretischen Grundlagen der Landschaftslehre*. Gotha.

Neef, E., Schmidt, G. and Lauckner, M. (1961). Landschaftsökologische Untersuchungen an verschiedenen Physiotopen in Nordwestsachsen. *Abhandlungen Sächsische Akademie der Wissenschaften zu Leipzig, Math.-nat. Kl.*, **47**, vol. 1.

Neff, K. P. (2002). Plant colonization and vegetation change in a restored tidal freshwater wetland in Washington, DC. Unpublished M.Sc. thesis, University of Maryland, College Park.

Neilson, B. and Cronin, L., eds. (1981). *Estuaries and Nutrients*. Clifton, NJ: Humana.

Netherton, N., Sweig, D., Artemel, J., Hickin, P. and Reed, P. (1978). *Fairfax County, Virginia: A History*. Fairfax County, Virginia: Fairfax County Board of Supervisors.

Neville, L. R., Grove, J. M. and Zipperer, W. (1995). Ecological classification for urban ecosystem management. In *Proceedings of the 7th Annual National Urban Forestry Conference*, September 12–17, New York, ed. C. Kollin. Washington, DC: American Forests, p. 5.

New, T. R. (1993). Angels on a pin: dimensions of the crisis in invertebrate conservation. *American Zoologist*, **33**, 623–30.

New, T. R. (1998). *Invertebrate Surveys for Conservation*. Melbourne: Oxford University Press.

New, T. R. and Sands, D. P. A. (2002). Conservation concerns for butterflies in urban areas of Australia. *Journal of Insect Conservation*, **6**, 207–15.

New Zealand Government (1991). *Resource Management Act*. Wellington: Government Printer.

New Zealand Government (2002). *Local Government Act*. Wellington: GP Legislation.

Newcombe, K.J., Kalma, D. and Aston, A.R. (1978). The metabolism of a city: the case study of Hong Kong. *Ambio*, **7**, 3–15.

Newell, R.C., Seiderer, L.J. and Hitchcock, D.R. (1998). The impact of dredging works in coastal waters: a review of the sensitivity to disturbance and subsequent recovery of biological resources on the sea bed. *Oceanography and Marine Biology Annual Review*, **36**, 127–78.

Newman, P. and Kenworthy, J. (1999). *Sustainability and Cities*. Washington, DC: Island Press.

Nichols, O.G. and Nichols, F.M. (2003). Long-term trends in faunal recolonization after bauxite mining in the Jarrah forest of southwestern Australia. *Restoration Ecology*, **11**, 261–72.

Nielsen, M.G. (2002a). *Water Budget for and Nitrogen Loads to Northeast Creek, Bar Harbor, Maine*. US Geological Survey Water-Resources Investigations Report 02–4000.

Nielsen, M.G. (2002b). *Estimated Quantity of Water in Fractured Bedrock Units on Mt Desert Island, and Estimated Groundwater Use, Recharge, and Dilution of Nitrogen in Septic Waste in the Bar Harbor Area, Maine*. US Geological Survey OFR02–435.

Niemelä, J. (1996). From systematics to conservation – carabidologists do it all. *Annales Zoologici Fennici*, **33**, 1–4.

Niemelä, J. (1999a). Ecology and urban planning. *Biodiversity and Conservation*, **8**, 119–31.

Niemelä, J. (1999b). Is there a need for a theory of urban ecology? *Urban Ecosystems*, **3**, 57–65.

Niemelä, J. and Halme, E. (1998). Effects of forest fragmentation on Carabid assemblages in the urban setting: implications for planning and management. In *Urban Ecology*, ed. J. Breuste, H. Feldmann and O. Uhlmann. Berlin: Springer-Verlag, pp. 692–8.

Niemelä, J. and Spence, J. (1991). Distribution and abundance of an exotic ground beetle (*Carabidae*): a test of community impact. *Oikos*, **62**, 351–9.

Niemelä, J., Kotze, J., Ashworth, A. *et al.* (2000). The search for common anthropogenic impacts on biodiversity: a global network. *Journal of Insect Conservation*, **4**, 3–9.

Niemelä, J., Kotze, D.J., Venn, L. *et al.* (2002). Carabid beetle assemblidges (Coleoptera, Carabidae) across urban–rural gradients: an international comparison. *Landscape Ecology*, **17**, 387–401.

Nilon, C. (1996). Wildlife conservation issues in ecological restoration of urban areas. *Published Abstract* Vol. 79 Madison: Society for Ecological Restoration.

Nilon, C. and Huckstep, S. (1998). Impacts of site disturbance on the small mammal fauna of urban woodlands. In *Urban Ecology*, ed. J. Brueste, H. Feldmann and O. Uhlmann. Berlin: Springer-Verlag.

Nilon, C.H. and Pais, R.C. (1997). Terrestrial vertebrates in urban ecosystems: developing hypotheses for the Gwynns Falls Watershed in Baltimore, Maryland. *Urban Ecosystems*, **1**, 247–57.

Nilon, C.H., Berkowitz, A.R. and Hollweg, K.S. (2003). Introduction: ecosystem understanding is a key to understanding cities. In *Understanding Urban Ecosystems*:

A New Frontier for Science and Education, ed. A. R. Berkowitz, C. H. Nilon and K. S. Hollweg. New York: Springer-Verlag, pp. 1–17.

Nilon, C. H., Long, C. N. and Zipperer, W. C. (1995). Effects of wildland development on forest bird communities. *Landscape and Urban Planning*, **32**, 81–92.

Nilsson, K. (2003). *Planning in a Sustainable Direction: The Art of Conscious Choices.* Stockholm: KTH, The Royal Institute of Technology.

Nishikawa, O. (1951). Geographical landscape and its researches (Carl Troll). *Geographical Review of Japan*, **24**, 172–3.

Nix, H. (1972). The city as a life system? *Proceedings of the Ecological Society of Australia* Vol. 7. Canberra.

Nixon, S. W. (1995). Coastal marine eutrophication: a definition, social causes, and future concerns. *Ophelia*, **41**, 199–219.

Nixon, S. W., Oviatt, C. A., Rodgers, C. and Taylor, R. K. (1971). Mass and metabolism of a mussel bed. *Oecologia*, **8**, 21–30.

NOAA (National Oceanic and Atmospheric Administration) (1985). *Climates of the States*, 3rd edn, Vol. 2. *New York–Wyoming*. Detroit, Michigan: Gale Research Company.

North Shore City Council (1999). *Long Bay Structure Plan: Report on Questionnaire Survey. The Future of Long Bay – Have Your Say.* New Zealand: Policy and Planning Directorate, North Shore City Council.

North Shore City Council (2001). *North Shore City Proposed District Plan. Proposed Variation 64 Long Bay Structure Plan.* New Zealand: North Shore City Council.

North Shore City Council (2002). *Long Bay Is Worth Protecting.* New Zealand: North Shore City Council.

Norton, D. A. and Stafford Smith, M. (1999). Why might roadside mulgas be better mistletoe hosts. *Australian Journal of Ecology*, **24**, 193–8.

Noss, R. F. (1990). Indicators for monitoring biodiversity. *Conservation Biology*, **4**, 355–64.

Noss, R. F. (1993). Wildlife corridors. In *Ecology of Greenways*, ed. D. S. Smith and P. C. Hellmund. Minneapolis: University of Minnesota Press, pp. 43–68.

Noss, R. F., O'Connell, M. A. and Murphy, D. D. (1997). *The Science of Conservation Planning: Habitat Conservation under the Endangered Species Act.* Washington, DC: Island Press.

Nowak, D. J. (1993). Historical vegetation change in Oakland and its implications for urban forest management. *Journal of Arboriculture*, **19**, 313–19.

Nowak, D. J. (1996). Estimating leaf area and leaf biomass of open-grown deciduous urban trees. *Forest Science*, **42**, 504–7.

Nowak, D. J. and Crane, D. E. (2000). The urban forest effects (UFORE) model: quantifying urban forest structure and functions. In *IUFRO Conference Integrated Tools for Natural Resources Inventories in the 21st Century*, General Technical Report NC-212, ed. M. Hansen and T. Burk. St Paul, MN: USDA Forest Service, North Central Research Station, pp. 714–20.

Nowak, D. J. and McBride, J. R. (1991). Comparison of Monterey Pine stress in urban and natural forests. *Journal of Environmental Management*, **32**, 383–95.

Nowak, D. J., Kuroda, M. and Crane, D. E. (2003). Tree mortality rates and tree population projections in Baltimore, Maryland, USA. *Urban Forestry and Urban Greening*, **2**, 139–48.

Nowak, D.J., Nobles, M.H., Sisinni, S.M. and Dwyer, J.F. (2001). Assessing the US urban forest resource. *Journal of Forestry*, **99**, 37–42.

Nowak, D.J., Rowntree, R., McPherson, E.G., Sisinni, S.M., Kerkmann, E. and Stevens, J.C. (1996). Measuring and analysing urban tree cover. *Landscape and Urban Planning*, **36**, 49–57.

Nowinszky, L., Szabó, S., Tóth, G., Ekk, I. and Kiss, M. (1979). The effect of the moon phases and of the intensity of polarized moonlight on the light-trap catches. *Zeitschrift für Angewandte Entomologie*, **88**, 337–53.

Nuckols, M.S. and Connor, E.F. (1995). Do trees in urban or ornamental plantings receive more damage by insects than trees in natural forests? *Ecological Entomology*, **20**, 253–60.

Numata, M. (1976). Methodology of urban ecosystem studies. In *Science for a Better Environment*. Proceedings of the International Congress on the Human Environment, Kyoto, 1975. HESC, Tokyo, pp. 221–8.

Numata, M. (1977). The impact of urbanization on vegetation in Japan. In *Vegetation Science and Environmental Protection*, ed. A. Miyawaki and R. Tüxen. Proceedings of the International Symposium in Tokyo on Protection of the Environment and Excursions on Vegetation Science through Japan, Tokyo: Maruzen Co., pp. 161–71.

Numata, M. (1982). Changes in ecosystem structure and function in Tokyo. In *Urban Ecology*, ed. R. Bornkamm, J.A. Lee and M.R.D. Seaward. Oxford, UK: Blackwell Scientific Publications, pp. 139–47.

Numata, M. (1987) *Urban Ecology*. Tokyo: Iwanami.

Nuygen, W. and Poortvliet, R. (1977). *Gnomes*. New York: Harry N. Abrams, Inc.

Nyhuus, S. and Halvorsen Thorén, A.-K. (1996). *Grønnstrukturens vilkår i kommunal arealplanlegging 1965–1995. Endringer av Grønnstrukturen i noen utvalgte by- og tettstedsområder fra 50-tallet till dag. [Summary: Changes in the urban green structure from 1965–1995 in some Norwegian municipalities]*. Norsk institutt for by- og regionforsking/ MILKOM notat 15/96. Oslo. (In Norwegian)

Nylund, K. (1995). *Det förändrade planeringstänkandet*. Stockholm: Nordplan.

Nylund, M., Nylund, L., Kellomäki, S. and Haapanen, A. (1979). Deterioration of forest ground vegetation and decrease of radial growth of trees on camping sites. *Silva Fennica*, **13**, 343–56.

O'Malley, T. (1999). The lawn in early American landscape and garden design. In *The American Lawn*, ed. G. Teyssot. New York: Princeton. Architectural Press, pp. 65–87.

Ochi, S., Ikegami, Y. and Nakagoshi, N. (2000). Analysing landscape change at patch level on urbanising region. *Journal of the Japanese Institute of Landscape Architecture*, **63**, 775–8.

Odgers, B.M. (1994). Seed banks and vegetation of three contrasting sites in an urban Eucalypt forest reserve. *Australian Journal of Botany*, **42**, 371–82.

Odum, E.P. (1997). *Ecology: A Bridge between Science and Society*. Sunderland, MA: Sinauer.

Odum, W. (1988). Comparative ecology of tidal freshwater and salt marshes. *Annual Review of Ecology and Systematics*, **19**, 147–76.

Odum, W.E., Smith, T.J. III, Hoover, J.K. and McIvor, C.C. (1984). *The Ecology of Tidal Freshwater Marshes of the United States East Coast: A Community Profile*. FWS/OBS-83/17. Washington, DC: US Fish and Wildlife Service.

O'Dwyer, C. and Attiwill, P. M. (1999). A comparative study of habitats of the Golden Sun Moth *Synemon plana* Walker (Lepidoptera: Castniidae): implications for restoration. *Biological Conservation*, **89**, 131–41.

Oertel, A. S. (1998). *Use of Small Eucalypt Forest Remnants by Birds in South East Queensland*. Unpublished B.Sc. thesis, Brisbane: Griffith University.

Office of Regional Planning and Urban Transportation (1995). *Trafik och miljö. Regionala strukturstudier*. Rapport 3. Stockholm, Sweden: Office of Regional Planning and Urban Transportation. (In Swedish)

Official Journal of the European Communities (1993). Convention on biological diversity. *Official Journal*, L **309**/1, 13 December 1993.

Official Journal of the European Communities (2001). Directive 2001/42/EC of the European Parliament and the Council of the 27 June 2001 on the assessment of the effects of certain plans and programmes on the environment. *Official Journal*, L **197**/30, 21 July 2001.

Oguz, D. (2004). Remaining tree species from the indigenous vegetation of Ankara, Turkey. *Landscape and Urban Planning*, **68**, 371–88.

Oke, T. R. (1982). The energetic basis of the urban heat-island. *Quarterly Journal of the Royal Meteorological Society*, **108**, 1–24.

Oke, T. R. (1989). The micrometeorology of the urban forest. *Philosophical Transactions of the Royal Society London B*, **324**, 335–49.

Oke, T. R. (1995). The heat island characteristics of the urban boundary layer: characteristics, causes and effects. In *Wind Climate in Cities*, ed. J. E. Cermak, A. G. Davenport, E. J. Plate and D. X. Viegas. Netherlands: Kluwer Academic Publishers, pp. 81–107.

Oke, T. R., Crowther, J. M., McNaughton, K. G., Monteith, J. L., and Gardiner, B. (1989). The micrometeorology of the urban forest [and discussion]. *Philosophical Transactions of the Royal Society of London. Series B, Biological Science*, **324**, 335–49.

Olabarria, C. and Chapman, M. G. (2001). Comparison of patterns of spatial variation of microgastropods between two contrasting intertidal habitats. *Marine Ecology Progress Series*, **220**, 201–11.

Olff, H. and Ritchie, M. E. (2002). Fragmented nature: consequences for biodiversity. *Landscape and Urban Planning*, **58**, 83–92.

Oliver, I. (2002). An expert panel-based approach to the assessment of vegetation condition within the context of biodiversity conservation. Stage 1: the identification of condition indicators. *Ecological Indicators*, **2**, 223–37.

Olivier, D. F. (1999). Please, more real farmers in our cities! *Faith and Earthkeeping*, **16**, 1–13.

Olsen, M. L., Geelmuyden, A. K. and Dyring, A.-K. (1987). *Naturmark i byströk*. Oslo: Landbruksforlaget. (In Norwegian)

Ønvik Pedersen, Å., Nyhuus, S. Blindheim, T. and Wergeland Krog, O. M. (2004). Implementation of a GIS based management tool for conservation of biodiversity within the municipality of Oslo, Norway. *Landscape and Urban Planning*, **68**, 429–38.

Opdam, P. F. M. (1991). Metapopulation theory and habitat fragmentation: a review of holarctic breeding bird studies. *Landscape Ecology*, **5**, 93–106.

Opdam, P., Foppen, R. and Vos, C. (2002). Bridging the gap between ecology and spatial planning in landscape ecology. *Landscape Ecology*, **16**, 767–79.

Opdam, P., van Dorp, D. and ter Braak, C. J. F. (1984). The effect of isolation on the number of forest birds in small woods in the Netherlands. *Journal of Biogeography*, **11**, 473–8.

Osaka City Greenery Promotion Division (1995). *Osaka City Basic Greenery Plan*. Osaka City.

Ortega, Y. K. and Capen, D. E. (1999). Effects of forest roads on habitat quality for ovenbirds in a forested landscape. *Auk*, **116**, 937–46.

Orth, R. J. and Moore, K. A. (1983). Chesapeake Bay: an unprecedented decline in submerged aquatic vegetation. *Science*, **222**, 51–3.

Osibanjo, O., Bouwman, H., Bashir, N. H. H., Okond'Ahoka, J., Choong Kwet Yve, R. and Onyoyo, H. A. (2002). *Regionally Based Assessment of Persistent Toxic Substances: Sub-Saharan Regional Report*. UNEP Chemicals/GEF. Geneva, Switzerland. http://www.chem.unep.ch.

Overmars, K. P., de Koning, G. H. J. and Veldkamp, A. (2003). Spatial autocorrelation in multi-scale land use models. *Ecological Modelling*, **164**, 257–70.

Owen, S. J. (1998). *Department of Conservation Strategic Plan for Managing Invasive Weeds*. Wellington, New Zealand: Department of Conservation.

Ozanne, C. M. P., Hambler, C., Foggo, A. and Speight, M. R. (1997). The significance of edge effects in the management of forests for invertebrate biodiversity. In *Canopy Arthropods*, ed. N. E. Stork, J. Adis and R. K. Didham. London: Chapman and Hall, pp. 534–50.

Pacione, M. (2003). Urban environmental quality and human wellbeing – a social geographical perspective. *Landscape and Urban Planning*, **65**, 19–30.

Page, B. (2002). Urban agriculture in Cameroon: an anti-politics machine in the making? *Geoforum*, **33**, 41–54.

Paine, R. T. (1979). Disaster, catastrophe, and local persistence of the sea palm *Postelsia palmaeformis*. *Science*, **205**, 685–6.

Paine, R. T. (1994). *Marine Rocky Shores and Community Ecology: An Experimentalist's Perspective*. Oldendorf/Luhe, Germany: Ecology Institute.

Palm, R. (1973). Befintlig vegetation och bebyggelseplanering [Summary: Existing vegetation in building planning]. *Byggmästaren*, **5**, 2–7. (In Swedish)

Palmer, A. R. (2000). Quasireplication and the contract of error: lessons from sex ratios, heritabilities and fluctuating asymmetry. *Annual Review of Ecology and Systematics*, **31**, 441–80.

Palmer, M. A., Ambrose, R. F. and Roff, N. L. (1997). Ecological theory and community restoration ecology. *Restoration Ecology*, **5**, 291–300.

Palumbi, S. R. (1994). Genetic divergence, reproductive isolation, and marine speciation. *Annual Review of Ecology and Systematics*, **25**, 547–72.

Palumbi, S. R. (2003). Population genetics, demographic connectivity, and the design of marine reserves. *Ecological Applications* **13**, S146–S158.

Pandey, S., Taylor, M., Shaver, E. and Lee, B. (2003). Reduction in road runoff contaminants through low-cost treatment well systems. *Proceedings of the 3rd South Pacific Conference on Stormwater, Auckland, 14–16 May 2003*. Auckland: New Zealand Water and Wastes Association.

Paquet, P. (1996). Effects of linear developments on winter movements of gray wolves in the Bow River valley of Banff National Park, Alberta. In *Trends in Addressing Transportation Related Wildlife Mortality*, ed. G. L. Evink, P. Garrett, D. Zeigler and J. Berry. Tallahassee. Florida Department of Transportation and Federal Highway Administration.

Park, K. (1994). Aspects of migration and residency in birds of eucalypt forests in South East Queensland. Unpublished B.Sc. thesis, Brisbane: Griffith University.

Park, R. A., Trehan, M. S., Mausel, P. W. and Howe, R. C. (1989). *The Effects of Sea Level Rise on U. S. Coastal Wetlands and Lowlands*. Indianapolis: HRI Report No. 164.

Park, R. E. and Burgess, E. W. (1967). *The City*. Chicago: University of Chicago Press.

Parker, V. T. and Pickett, S. T. A. (1997). Restoration as an ecosystem process: implications of the modern ecological paradigm. In *Restoration Ecology and Sustainable Development*, ed. K. M. Urbanska, N. R. Webb and P. J. Edwards. Cambridge: Cambridge University Press, pp. 17–32.

Parliamentary Commissioner for the Environment (1998). *The Cities and Their People: New Zealand's Urban Environment*. Wellington, New Zealand: Parliamentary Commissioner for the Environment.

Pärnänen, A., ed. (1979). Erilaisten maankäyttötapojen ja hoitotoimenpitelden ekologiset vaikutukset metsiin – Man and Biosphere (MAB)-seminaari. [Summary: Ecological effects of the different land uses and management practices on boreal forest landscapes – A Man and the Biosphere programme project 2 seminar]. *Silva Fennica*, **13**, 131–76. (In Finnish)

Parody, J. M., Cuthbert, F. J. and Decker, E. H. (2001). The effect of 50 years of landscape change on species richness and community composition. *Global Ecology and Biogeography*, **10**, 305–13.

Parris, K. M. (2006). Urban amphibian assemblages as metacommunities. *Journal of Animal Ecology*, **75**, 757–64.

Parsons, H., French, K and Major, R. E. (2004) The influence of remnant bushland on the composition of suburban bird assemblages in Australia. *Landscape and Urban Planning* **66**, 43–56.

Parsons, H. M. and Major, R. E. (2004). Bird interactions in Sydney gardens: some initial findings of the Birds in Backyards program. In *Urban Wildlife: More than Meets the Eye*, ed. S. Burgin and D. Lunney. Mosman, NSW: Royal Zoological Society of NSW, pp. 211–15.

Partridge, T. R. (1989). Soil seed banks of secondary vegetation on the Port Hills and Banks Peninsula, Canterbury, New Zealand, and their role in succession. *New Zealand Journal of Botany*, **27**, 421–36.

Pastor, J., Aber, J. D., McClaugherty, C. A. and Melillo, J. M. (1984). Aboveground production and N and P cycling along a nitrogen mineralization gradient on Blackhawk Island, Wisconsin. *Ecology*, **65**, 256–68.

Paton, D.C. (1993). Honeybees *Apis mellifera* in the Australian environment: does *Apis mellifera* disrupt or benefit native biota? *BioScience*, **43**, 95–103.

Patten, M.A. and Bolger, D.T. (2003). Variation in top-down control of avian reproductive success across a fragmentation gradient. *Oikos*, **101**, 479–88.

Patterson, B.D. and Atmar, W. (1986). Nested subsets and the structure of insular mammalian faunas and archipelagos. *Biological Journal of the Linnean Society*, **28**, 65–82.

Paul, E.A. and Clark, F.E. (1996). *Soil Microbiology and Biochemistry*. New York, USA: Academic Press.

Paul, M.J. and Meyer, J.L. (2001). Streams in the urban landscape. *Annual Review of Ecology and Systematics*, **32**, 333–65.

Pavao-Zuckerman, M.A. (2003). Soil ecology along an urban to rural gradient in the southern Appalachians. Unpublished Ph.D. Dissertation. Athens, Georgia: University of Georgia.

Pavao-Zuckerman, M.A. and Coleman, D.C. (2005). Decomposition of chestnut oak (*Quercus prinus*) leaves and nitrogen mineralisation in an urban environment. *Biological Fertility Soils*, **41**, 343–9.

Pedroli, B., de Blust, G., van Looy, K. and van Rooij, S. (2002). Setting targets in strategies for river restoration. *Landscape Ecology*, **17**, 5–15.

Peierls, B.L., Caraco, N.F., Pace, M.L. and Cole, J.J. (1991). Human influence on river nitrogen. *Nature*, **350**, 386–7.

Peintinger, M., Bergamini, A. and Schmid, B. (2003). Species–area relationships and nestedness of four taxonomic groups in fragmented wetlands. *Basic and Applied Ecology*, **4**, 385–94.

People, J. (2006). Mussel beds on different types of structures support different macroinvertebrate assemblages. *Austral Ecology*, **31**, 271–81.

Perelman, R. (1979). Nature and urban development on the Cote D'Azur. In *Nature in Cities. The Natural Environment in the Design and Development of Urban Green Space*, ed. I. Laurie. Chichester, New York: John Wiley and Sons, pp. 353–66.

Peterman, R.M. (1990). Statistical power analysis can improve fisheries research and management. *Canadian Journal of Fisheries and Aquatic Sciences*, **47**, 2–15.

Peters, R.H. (1986). The role of prediction in ecology. *Limnology and Oceanography*, **31**, 1143–59.

Peters, R.H. (1991). *A Critique for Ecology*. Cambridge: Cambridge University Press.

Peters, R.H, Armesto, J.J., Boeken, B. *et al.* (1991). On the relevance of comparative ecology to the larger field of ecology. In *Comparative Analyses of Ecosystems: Patterns, Mechanisms, and Theories*, ed. J. Cole, G. Lovett and S. Findlay. New York: Springer-Verlag, pp. 46–63.

Peterson, G., Allen, C.R. and Holling, C.S. (1998). Ecological resilience, biodiversity, and scale. *Ecosystems*, **1**, 6–18.

Pew Oceans Commission (2003). Cleaning coastal waters. In *America's Living Oceans: Charting a Course for Sea Change*. Arlington, VA.: Pew Oceans Commission, pp. 59–72.

Phillips, J.A. and Price, I.R. (2002). How different is Mediterranean *Caulerpa taxifolia* (Caulerpales: Chlorophyta) to other populations of the species? *Marine Ecology Progress Series*, **238**, 61–71.

Pickett, S.T.A. (1989). Space-for-time substitution as an alternative to long-term studies. In *Long-Term Studies in Ecology: Approaches and Alternatives*, ed. G.E. Likens. New York: Springer-Verlag, pp. 110–35.

Pickett, S.T.A. (2003). Why is developing a broad understanding of urban ecosystems important to science and scientists? In *Understanding Urban Ecosystems: A New Frontier for Science and Education*, ed. A.R. Berkowitz, C.H. Nilon and K.S. Hollweg. New York: Springer-Verlag, pp. 58–72.

Pickett, S.T.A. and Cadenasso, M.L. (2002). Ecosystem as a multidimensional concept: meaning, model and metaphor. *Ecosystems*, **5**, 1–10.

Pickett, S.T.A. and Kolasa, J. (1989). Structure of theory in vegetation science. *Vegetation*, **83**, 7–15.

Pickett, S.T.A. and McDonnell, M.J. (1989). Changing perspectives in community dynamics: a theory of successional forces. *Trends in Ecology and Evolution*, **4**, 241–5.

Pickett, S.T.A. and Rogers, K.H. (1997). Patch dynamics: the transformation of landscape structure and function. In *Wildlife and Landscape Ecology*, ed. J.A. Bissonette. New York: Springer-Verlag.

Pickett, S.T.A., Burch, W.R. Jr, Dalton, S.E. and Foresman, T.W. (1997a). Integrated urban ecosystem research. *Urban Ecosystems*, **1**, 183–4.

Pickett, S.T.A., Burch, W.R. Jr, Dalton, S.E. *et al.* (1997b). A conceptual framework for the study of human ecosystems in urban areas. *Urban Ecosystems*, **1**, 185–99.

Pickett, S.T.A., Burch, W.R. Jr and Grove, J.M. (1999a). Interdisciplinary research: maintaining the constructive impulse in a culture of criticism. *Ecosystems*, **2**, 302–7.

Pickett, S.T.A., Burke, I.C., Dale, V.H. *et al.* (1994a). Integrated models of forest ecosystems. In *Integrated Regional Models: Interactions between Humans and their Environment*, ed. P.M. Groffman and G.E. Likens. New York: Chapman and Hall, pp. 120–41.

Pickett, S.T.A., Cadenasso, M.L. and Grove, J.M. (2004). Resilient cities: meaning, models and metaphor for integrating the ecological, socio-economic and planning realms. *Landscape and Urban Planning*, **69**, 369–84.

Pickett, S.T.A., Cadenasso, M.L., Grove, J.M. *et al.* (2001). Urban ecological systems: linking terrestrial ecology, physical, and socioeconomic components of metropolitan areas. *Annual Review of Ecology and Systematics*, **32**, 127–57.

Pickett, S.T.A., Cadenasso, M.L. and Jones, C.G. (2000). Generation of heterogeneity by organisms: creation, maintenance, and transformation. In *Ecological Consequences of Habitat Heterogeneity*, ed. M. Hutchings. New York: Blackwell, pp. 33–52.

Pickett, S.T.A., Kolasa, J. and Jones, C.G. (1994b). *Ecological Understanding: The Nature of Theory and the Theory of Nature*. San Diego: Academic Press.

Pickett, S.T.A., Ostfeld, R.S., Shachak, M. and Likens, G.E., eds. (1997c). *The Ecological Basis of Conservation: Heterogeneity, Ecosystems and Biodiversity*. New York: Chapman and Hall.

Pickett, S.T.A., Parker, V.T. and Fiedler, P.L. (1992). The new paradigm in ecology: implications for conservation biology above the species level. In *Conservation*

Biology: The Theory and Practice of Nature Conservation, Preservation and Management, ed. P. L. Fiedler and S. K. Jain. New York: Chapman and Hall, pp. 65–88.

Pickett, S. T. A., Wu, J. and Cadenasso, M. L. (1999b). Patch dynamics and the ecology of disturbed ground: a framework for synthesis. In *Ecosystems of the World: Ecosystems of Disturbed Ground*, ed. L. R. Walker. Amsterdam: Elsevier Science, pp. 707–22.

Pietsch, J. and Kamith, H. (1991). *Stadtböden. Entwicklungen, Belastungen, Bewertung und Planung*. Taunusstein.

Pimm, S. L. (1991). *The Balance of Nature? Ecological Issues in the Conservation of Species and Communities*. Chicago: University of Chicago Press.

Piper, S. D. and Catterall, C. P. (2003). A particular case and a general pattern: hyperaggressive behaviour by one species may mediate avifaunal decreases in fragmented Australian forests. *Oikos*, **101**, 602–14.

Piper, S. D. and Catterall, C. P. (2004). Effects of edge type and nest height on predation of artificial nests within subtropical Australian eucalypt forests. *Forest Ecology and Management*, **203**, 361–72.

Pirnat, J. (2000). Conservation and management of forest patches and corridors in suburban landscapes. *Landscape and Urban Planning*, **52**, 135–43.

Plant, L. (1996). Brisbane's urban forests. Past influence, current trends and future need. *Trees and Natural Resources*, **30**, 6–8.

Poiani, K. A., Richter, B. D., Anderson, M. G. and Richter, H. E. (2000). Biodiversity conservation at multiple scales: functional sites, landscapes and networks. *Bioscience*, **50**, 133–46.

Policy Co-ordination and Advisory Services (PCAS). (2003). *National Spatial Development Perspective*. Pretoria: Government Printer.

Pollan, M. (1991). *Second Nature: A Gardener's Education*. New York: Dell Publishing.

Pollard, D. A. (1989). Artificial habitats for fisheries enhancement in the Australian region. *Marine Fisheries Review*, **51**, 11–26.

Pollard, E. and Yates, T. J. (1993). *Monitoring Butterflies for Ecology and Conservation*. London: Chapman and Hall.

Port, G. R. and Thompson, J. R. (1980). Outbreaks of insect herbivores on plants along motorways in the United Kingdom. *Journal of Applied Ecology*, **17**, 649–56.

Porter, E. E., Forschner, B. R. and Blair, R. B. (2001). Woody vegetation and canopy fragmentation along a forest-to-urban gradient. *Urban Ecosystems*, **5**, 131–51.

Posch, T., Hron, J. and Wuchterl, G. (2002). Wieviele Sterne sehen wir noch? *Sterne und Weltraum*, **41**, 62–63. http://www.astro.uni.vie.ac.at/~scw

Postel, S. (1999). *Pillar of Sand*. London: W. W. Norton and Company.

Potchefstroom University (PU) (2000). *North West Province Integrated Rural Development Strategy*. Unpublished report.

Pote, D. H., Daniel, T. C., Nichols, D. J. *et al.* (1999). Relationship between phosphorus levels in three Ultisols and phosphorus concentrations in runoff. *Journal of Environmental Quality*, **28**, 170–5.

Potter, D. A. and Braman, S. K. (1991). Ecology and management of turfgrass insects. *Annual Review of Entomology*, **36**, 383–406.

Potter, D.A., Bridges, B.L. and Gordon, F.C. (1985). Effect of N fertilization on earthworm and microarthropod populations in Kentucky bluegrass turf. *Agronomy Journal*, **77**, 367–72.

Pouyat, R.V. (1991). The urban–rural gradient: an opportunity to better understand human impacts on forest soils. In *Proceedings of Society of American Foresters 1990 Annual Convention, July 27–August 1, 1990*, Washington, DC, Bethesda, MD: Society of American Foresters, pp. 212–18.

Pouyat, R.V. (1992). Soil characteristics and litter dynamics in mixed deciduous forests along an urban rural gradient. Unpublished doctoral dissertation, Rutgers University, New Brunswick, New Jersey.

Pouyat, R.V. and Carreiro, M.M. (2003). Controls on mass loss and nitrogen dynamics of oak leaf litter along an urban–rural land-use gradient. *Oecologia*, **135**, 288–98.

Pouyat, R.V. and Effland, W.R. (1999). The investigation and classification of humanly modified soils in the Baltimore Ecosystem Study. In *Classification, Correlation, and Management of Anthropogenic Soils, Proceedings – Nevada and California, September 21–October 2, 1998*, ed. J.M. Kimble, R.J. Ahrens and R.B. Bryant. Lincoln, Nebraska: USDA Natural Resource Conservation Service, National Survey Centre, pp. 141–54.

Pouyat, R.V. and McDonnell, M.J. (1991). Heavy metal accumulation in forest soils along an urban–rural gradient in southern New York, USA. *Water, Air and Soil Pollution*, **57–58**, 797–807.

Pouyat, R.V., Belt, K., Pataki, D., Groffman, P.M., Hom J. and Band, L. (2007a). Effects of urban land-use change on biogeochemical cycles. In *Terrestrial Ecosystems in a Changing World*, ed. P. Canadell, D. Pataki and L. Pitelka. Berlin, Heidelberg, New York: Springer, pp. 45–58.

Pouyat, R.V., Groffman, P.M., Russell-Anneli, J. and Yesilonis, I. (2003). Soil carbon in urban forest ecosystems. In *Potential of United States Forest Soils to Sequester Carbon and Mitigate the Greenhouse Effect*, ed. R. Lal, J. Kimble, R.F. Follett and R. Birdsey. New Jersey: CRC Press, pp. 347–62.

Pouyat, R.V., McDonnell, M.J. and Pickett, S.T.A. (1995b). Soil characteristics of oak stands along an urban–rural land use gradient. *Journal Environmental Quality*, **24**, 516–26.

Pouyat, R.V., McDonnell, M.J. and Pickett, S.T.A. (1996). Litter and nitrogen dynamics in oak stands along an urban–rural gradient. *Urban Ecosystems*, **1**, 117–31.

Pouyat, R.V., McDonnell, M.J. and Pickett S.T.A. (1997). Litter decomposition and nitrogen mineralization in oak stands along an urban–rural land use gradient. *Urban Ecosystems*, **1**, 117–31.

Pouyat, R.V., McDonnell, M.J., Pickett, S.T.A. *et al.* (1995a). Carbon and nitrogen dynamics in oak stands along an urban-rural gradient. In *Carbon Forms and Functions in Forest Soils*, ed. J.M. Kelly and W.W. McFee. Madison, Wisconsin: Soil Science Society of America, pp. 569–87.

Pouyat, R.V., Parmelee, R.W. and Carreiro, M.M. (1994). Environmental effects of forest soil-invertebrates and fungal densities in oak stands along an urban–rural land use gradient. *Pedobiologia*, **38**, 385–99.

Pouyat, R. V., Yesilonis, I. D. and Nowak, D. J. (2006). Carbon storage by urban soils in the USA. *Journal Environmental Quality*, **35**, 1566–75.

Pouyat, R. V., Yesilonis, I. and Russell-Anelli, J. (2007b). Soil chemical and physical properties that differentiate urban land-use and cover types. *Soil Science Society America Journal*, **71**, 1010–19.

Povey, A. and Keough, M. J. (1991). Effects of trampling on animal and plant populations on rocky shores. *Oikos*, **61**, 355–68.

Pratt, J. R. (1994). Artificial habitats and ecosystem restoration: managing for the future. *Bulletin of Marine Science*, **55**, 268–75.

Probst, J. R. and Crow, T. R. (1991). Integrating biological diversity and resource management. *Journal of Forestry*, **89**, 12–17.

Profous, G. V. (1992). Trees and urban forestry in Beijing, China. *Journal of Arboriculture*. **18**, 145–53.

Pudlo, R. J., Beattie, A. J. and Culver, D. C. (1980). Population consequences of changes in an ant–seed mutualism in *Sanguinaria canadensis*. *Oecologia*, **46**, 32–7.

Pulliam, H. R. (1988). Sources, sinks and population regulation. *American Naturalist*, **132**, 652–61.

Putter, J. (2004). *Vegetation Dynamics of Urban Open Spaces Subjected to Different Anthropogenic Influences*. Unpublished report for Magister Scientae, North-West University (Potchefstroom Campus), South Africa.

Pyšek, P. (1989). On the richness of Central European urban flora. *Preslia*, **61**, 329–34.

Pyšek, P. (1993). Factors affecting the diversity of flora and vegetation in central European settlements. *Vegetatio*, **106**, 89–100.

Quinn, G. P. and Keogh, M. J. (2002). *Experimental Design and Data Analysis for Biologists*. Cambridge: Cambridge University Press.

Rainio, J. and Niemelä, J. (2003). Ground beetles (*Coleoptera: Carabidae*) as bioindicators. *Biodiversity and Conservation*, **12**, 489–506.

Ramirez, J. (1995). Skapande mening. Avhandling 13:1, Stockholm: Nordplan.

Rango, J. J. (2002). *Influences of Priority Effects, Nutrients and Urbanization on Creosote Bush Arthropod Communities*. Unpublished Ph.D. dissertation, Arizona State University.

Ranney, J. W., Bruner, M. C. and Levenson, J. B. (1981). The importance of edge in the structure and dynamics of forest islands. In *Forest Island Dynamics in Man-Dominated Landscapes*, ed. R. L. Burgess and D. M. Sharpe. New York: Springer-Verlag, pp. 67–96.

Ranta, P. (2001). Changes in urban lichen diversity after a fall in sulphur dioxide levels in the city of Tampere, SW Finland. *Annales Botanici Fennici*, **38**, 295–304.

Ranta, P., Tanskanen, A. and Siitonen, M. (1997). Vascular plants of the city of Vantaa, S Finland – urban ecology, biodiversity and conservation. *Lutukka*, **13**, 67–87. (In Finnish with English summary)

Rapoport, E. H. (1993). The process of plant colonization in small settlements and large cities. In *Humans as Components of Ecosystems: the ecology of subtle human effects and populated areas*, ed. M. J. McDonnell and S. T. A. Pickett. New York: Springer-Verlag, pp. 190–207.

Reader, T. and Hochuli, D. F. (2003). Understanding gregariousness in a larval lepidopteran: the roles of host plant, predation and microclimate. *Ecological Entomology*, **28**, 729–37.

Reaser, J. K. and Dexter, R. E. (1996). *Rana pretiosa* (spotted frog). Toe clipping effects. *Herpetological Review*, **27**, 195–6.

Rebele, F. (1994). Urban ecology and special features of urban ecosystems. *Global Ecology and Biogeography Letters*, **4**, 173–87.

Reckhow, K. H., Beaulac, M. N. and Simpson, J. T. (1980). *Modeling Phosphorus Loading and Lake Response Under Uncertainty: A Manual and Compilation of Export Coefficients*. US EPA/440/ 5-80/011, Washington, DC: US Environmental Protection Agency.

Reddy, K. R., Kadlec, R. H., Flaig, E. and Gale, P. M. (1999). Phosphorus retention in streams and wetlands: a review. *Critical Reviews in Environmental Science and Technology*, **29**, 83–146.

Reichard, S. H. and White, P. S. (2001). Horticulture as a pathway of invasive plant introductions in the United States. *Bioscience*, **51**, 103–13.

Reichholf, J. (1989). *Siedlungsraum – Zur Ökologie von Dorf, Stadt und Straße*. Munich: Steinbachs Biotopführer, Mosaik, p. 222.

Reidl, K. (1992). Flora und Vegetation als Grundlage für den Naturschutz in der Stadt. Teil 1: Methodik und Ergebnisse der Kartierung am Beispiel Essen. *Naturschutz und Landschaftsplanung*, **4**, 136–41.

Reijnen, R., Foppen, R., Terbraak, C. and Thissen, J. (1995). The effects of car traffic on breeding bird populations in woodland. III. Reduction of density in relation to the proximity of main roads. *Journal of Applied Ecology*, **32**, 187–202.

Reijnen, R., Foppen, R. and Veenbas, G. (1997). Disturbance by traffic of breeding birds: evaluation of the effect and considerations in planning and managing road corridors. *Biodiversity and Conservation*, **6**, 567–81.

Reimer, A. A. (1976). Description of a *Tetraclita stalactifera panamensis* community on a rocky intertidal Pacific shore of Panama. *Marine Biology*, **35**, 225–38.

Reinelt, L., Horner, R. and Azous, A. (1999). Impacts of urbanization on palustrine (depressional freshwater) wetlands – research and management in the Puget Sound region. *Urban Ecosystems*, **2**, 219–36.

Rempel, R. (2003). Patch Analyst 3.0 [online]. Centre for Northern Forest Ecosystem Research, Lakehead University Campus, Thunder Bay, Ontario. Accessed 23 November 2003. http://flash.lakeheadu.ca/~rrempel/patch/

Reynaud, P. A. and Thiolouse, J. (2000). Identification of birds as biological markers along a neotropical urban–rural gradient (Cayenne, French Guiana), using co-inertia analysis. *Journal of Environmental Management*, **59**, 121–40.

Ribera, I., Dolédec, S., Downie, I. S. and Foster, G. N. (2001). Effect of land disturbance and stress on species traits of ground beetle assemblages. *Ecology*, **82**, 1112–29.

Rich, C. and Longcore, T., eds. (2006). *Ecological Consequences of Artificial Night Lighting*. Covelo, CA: Island Press.

Richards, J. F. (1990). Land transformation. In *The Earth as Transformed by Human Action*, ed. B. L. Turner, W. C. Clark, R. W. Kates, J. F. Richards, K. T. Matthew and W. V. Meyer. Cambridge: Cambridge University Press with Clark University, pp. 163–78.

Richards, N. A., Mallett, J. R., Simpson, R. J. and Macie, E. A. (1984). Residential greenspace and vegetation in mature City: Syracuse, New York. *Urban Ecology*, **8**, 99–125.

Richardson, C. J. (1985). Mechanisms controlling phosphorus retention capacity in freshwater wetlands. *Science*, **228**, 1424–7.

Richter, H. (1984). Land-use and land transformation. *GeoJournal*, **8**, 67–74.

Richter, H. (1989). Die Stellung der Flächennutzung in der Territorialstruktur. *Geographische Berichte*, **131**, 91–103.

Richter, H. and Kugler, H. (1972). Landeskultur und landeskultureller Zustand des Territoriums. Soz. Gesellschaft und Territorium in der DDR. *Wissenschaftliche Abhandlungen Geographische Gesellschaft der DDR*, **9**, 33–46.

Ricketts, T. and Imhoff, M. (2003). Biodiversity, urban areas and agriculture: locating priority ecoregions for conservation. *Conservation Ecology*, **8**, 1. [online] http://www.consecol.org/vol8/iss2/art1

Rickman, J. K. and Connor, E. F. (2003). The effect of urbanization on the quality of remnant habitats for leaf-mining Lepidoptera on *Quercus agrifolia*. *Ecography*, **26**, 777–87.

Ridd, M. K. (1995). Exploring a V–I–S (Vegetation–Impervious Surface–Soil) model for urban ecosystem analysis through remote sensing: comparative anatomy for cities. *International Journal of Remote Sensing*, **16**, 2165–85.

Riegel, K. W. (1973). Light pollution: outdoor lighting is a growing threat to astronomy. *Science*, **179**, 1285–91.

Rieley, J. O. and Page, S. O. (1995). Survey, mapping and evaluation of green space in the federal territory of Kuala Lumpur, Malaysia. In *Urban Ecology as the Basis of Urban Planning*, ed. H. Sukopp, M. Numata and A. Huber. The Hague, The Netherlands: SPB Academic Publishing, pp. 173–83.

Riley, S. P. D., Sauvagot, R. M., Fuller, T. K. *et al.* (2003). Effects of urbanization and habitat fragmentation on bobcats and coyotes in southern California. *Conservation Biology*, **17**, 566–76.

Rilov, G. and Benayahu, Y. (1998). Vertical artificial structures as an alternative habitat for coral reef fishes in disturbed environments. *Marine Environmental Research*, **45**, 431–51.

Rilov, G. and Benayahu, Y. (2000). Fish assemblage on natural versus vertical artificial reefs: the rehabilitation perspective. *Marine Biology*, **136**, 931–42.

Roberts, D. C. (2001). Using the development of an Environmental Management System to develop and promote a more holistic understanding of urban ecosystems in Durban, South Africa. In *Understanding Urban Ecosystems: a new frontier for science and education*, ed. A. R. Berkowitz, C. H. Nilon and K. S. Hollweg. New York: Springer, pp. 384–98.

Roberts, R. D. and Forrest, B. M. (1999). Minimal impact from long-term dredge spoil disposal at a dispersive site in Tasman Bay, New Zealand. *New Zealand Journal of Marine and Freshwater Research*, **33**, 623–33.

Robertson, A. I. and Duke, N. C. (1987). Mangroves as nursery sites: comparisons of the abundance and species composition of fish and crustaceans in mangroves and other nearshore habitats in tropical Australia. *Marine Biology*, **96**, 193–205.

Robertson, D.P. and Hull, R.B. (2001). Beyond biology: toward a more public ecology for conservation. *Conservation Biology*, **15**, 970–9.

Robertson, G.P., Coleman, D.C., Bledsoe, C.S. and Sollins, P., eds. (1999). *Standard Soil Methods for Long-Term Ecological Research*. New York: Oxford University Press.

Robien, A., Striebel, T. and Herrmann, R. (1997). Modelling of dissolved and particle-bound pollutants in urban street runoff. *Water Science and Technology*, **36**, 77–82.

Robinson, G.R. and Handel, S.N. (2000). Directing spatial patterns of recruitment during an experimental urban woodland reclamation. *Ecological Applications*, **10**, 174–88.

Robinson, H.S. and Robinson, P.J.M. (1950). Some notes on the observed behaviour of Lepidoptera in flight in the vicinity of light-sources together with a description of a light-trap designed to take entomological samples. *Entomologist's Gazette*, **1**, 3–20.

Robinson, N. (1993). Place and plant design: plant signatures. *The Landscape*, Autumn, 26–8.

Rogers, E. (2001). *Landscape Design. A Cultural and Architectural History*. New York, USA: Harry N. Abrams Inc.

Rogers, G.F. and Rowntree, R.A. (1988). Intensive surveys of structure and change in urban natural areas. *Landscape and Urban Planning*, **15**, 59–78.

Rohrlich F. (1987). *From Paradox to Reality: Our Basic Concepts of the Physical World*. Cambridge: Cambridge University Press.

Rohweder, J.J., Fox, T.J., Guntenspergen, G.R., Nielsen, M.G. and Neckles, H.A. (2004). *Acadia National Park Nutrient Load and Estuarine Response Decision Support System. User's Manual*. Final Report to the National Park System, Acadia National Park.

Roman, C.T., Jaworski, N., Short, F.T., Findlay, S. and Warren, R.S. (2000). Estuaries of the northeastern United States: habitat and land use signatures. *Estuaries*, **23**, 743–64.

Romesburg, H.C. (1981). Wildlife science: gaining reliable knowledge. *Journal of Wildlife Management*, **45**, 293–313.

Rooker, J.R., Dokken, Q.R., Pattengill, C.V. and Holt, G.J. (1997). Fish assemblages on artificial and natural reefs in the Flower Garden Banks National Marine Sanctuary, USA. *Coral Reefs*, **16**, 83–92.

Rose, S. and Fairweather, P.G. (1997). Changes in floristic composition of urban bushland invaded by *Pittosporum undulatum* in northern Sydney, Australia. *Australian Journal of Botany*, **45**, 123–49.

Rosen, P.C. and Lowe, C.H. (1994). Highway mortality of snakes in the Sonoran desert of southern Arizona. *Biological Conservation*, **68**, 143–8.

Rosengren, C. (1979). Luonnonkasvillisuus asuntoalueilla. [Summary: Natural vegetation within housing areas]. *Silva Fennica*, **13**, 166–9. (In Finnish)

Ross, D.J., Johnson, C.R. and Hewitt, C.L. (2002). Impact of introduced seastars *Asterias amurensis* on survivorship of juvenile commercial scallops *Fluvia ternicosta*. *Marine Ecology Progress Series*, **241**, 99–112.

Roubik, D.W. (2000). Pollination system stability in tropical America. *Conservation Biology*, **14**, 1235–6.

Rudd, H., Vala, J. and Schaefer, V. (2002). Importance of backyard habitat in a comprehensive biodiversity conservation strategy: a connectivity analysis of urban green spaces. *Restoration Ecology*, **10**, 368–75.

Rudnicky, J.L. and McDonnell, M.J. (1989). Forty-eight years of canopy change in a hardwood-hemlock forest in New York City. *Bulletin of the Torrey Botanical Club*, **116**, 52–64.

Ruiz, G.M., Carlton, J.T., Grosholz, E.D. and Hines, A.H. (1997). Global invasions of marine and estuarine habitats by non-indigenous species: mechanisms, extent and consequences. *American Zoologist*, **37**, 621–32.

Ruszczyk, A. (1996). Spatial patterns in pupal mortality in urban palm caterpillars. *Oecologia*, **107**, 356–63.

Ryan, P.G. and Moloney, C.L. (1993). Marine litter keeps increasing. *Nature*, **361**, 23.

Rydberg, D. (1998). Urban forestry in Sweden: silvicultural aspects focusing on young forests. Unpublished doctoral thesis, Acta Universitatis Agriculturae Sueciae, Silvestria 73.

Rydberg, D. and Falck, J. (1998). Designing the urban forest of tomorrow: pre-commercial thinning adapted for use in urban areas in Sweden. *Arboricultural Journal*, **22**, 147–71.

Rydberg, D. and Falck, J. (2000). Urban forestry from a silvicultural perspective: a review. *Landscape and Urban Planning*, **47**, 1–18.

Saastamoinen, O. and Sievänen, T. (1981). Keravan ja Rovaniemen lähimetsien ulkoilukäutön ajallinen vaihtelu. [Summary: Time patterns of recreation in urban forests in two Finnish towns]. *Folia Forestalia*, **473**, 1–24. (In Finnish)

Sala, O.A., Jackson, R.B., Mooney, H.A. and Howarth, R.W., eds. (2000). *Methods in Ecosystem Science*. New York: Springer.

Salmon, W.C., ed. (1994). *Logic, Language, and the Structure of Scientific Theories*. Pittsburgh: University of Pittsburgh Press.

Samways, M.J. (1992). Some comparative insect conservation issues of north temperate, tropical and south temperate landscapes. *Agriculture, Ecosystems and Environment*, **40**, 137–54.

Samways, M.J. and Steytler, N.S. (1996). Dragonfly (Odonata) distribution patterns in urban and forest landscapes, and recommendations for riparian management. *Biological Conservation*, **78**, 279–88.

Sanders, R.A. (1984). Some determinants of urban forest structure. *Urban Ecology*, **8**, 13–24.

Sanderson, J.C. (1990). A preliminary survey of the distribution of the introduced macroalga, *Undaria pinnatifida* (Harvey) Suringer on the east coast of Tasmania, Australia. *Botanica Marina*, **33**, 153–7.

Sand-Jensen, K. and Borum, J. (1991). Interactions among phytoplankton, periphyton, and macrophytes in temperate freshwaters and estuaries. *Aquatic Botany*, **41**, 137–75.

Sands, D.P.A., Scott, S.E. and Moffatt, R. (1997). The threatened Richmond Birdwing Butterfly (*Ornithoptera richmondia* Gray): a community conservation project. *Memoirs of the Museum of Victoria*, **56**, 449–53.

Santas, P. (1986). Soil communities along a gradient of urbanisation. *Revue d'Ecologie et de Biologie du Sol*, **23**, 367–80.

Santelman, M.V. and Larson, K.L. (2004). Foreword. Special section on sustaining multiple functions in urban wetlands. *Wetlands*, **24**, 717–18.

Saunders, D.A. and Hobbs, R.J. (1991). The role of corridors in conservation: what do we know and where do we go? In *Nature Conservation 2: The Role of Corridors*, ed. D.A. Saunders and R.J. Hobbs. Chipping Norton, New South Wales: Surrey Beatty and Sons, pp. 421–7.

Saunders, D.A., Craig, J.L. and Mattiske, E.M., eds. (1995). *Nature Conservation 4: The Role of Networks*. Chipping Norton, New South Wales, Australia: Surrey Beatty and Sons.

Saunders, D.A., Hobbs, R.J. and Margules, C.R. (1991). Biological consequences of ecosystem fragmentation: a review. *Conservation Biology*, **5**, 18–32.

Sauvajot, R.M., Buechner, M., Kamradt, D.A. and Shonewald, C.M. (1998). Patterns of human disturbance and response by small mammals and birds in chaparral near urban development. *Urban Ecosystems*, **2**, 279–97.

Sawyers, C., Pesch, B. and Keim, J., eds. (1990). *Gardening with Wildflowers and Native Plants*. Brooklyn, New York: Brooklyn Botanic Garden publication 119.

Schacht, H. (1981). Erfassung schutzwürdiger und entwicklungsfähiger Landschaftsteile und Elemente in Wien, Vol. 1/2, Wien.

Schacht, W. and Witt, T. (1986). Warum nachtaktive Insekten künstliche Lichtquellen anfliegen (Insecta). *Zeitschrift für Entomologi.e.*, **7**, 121–8.

Schanowski, A. and Späth, V. (1994). *Überbelichtet – Vorschläge für eine umweltfreundliche Außenbeleuchtung*. Kornwestheim: Naturschutzbund Deutschland Kornwestheim.

Schantz, P. (2002). Lagtillämpning och konsekvenser. In *Nationalstadsparken ett experiment i hållbar utveckling*, ed. L. Holm and P. Schantz. Stockholm: FORMAS, pp. 213–37. (In Swedish)

Scheibe, M. (2003). Über den Einfluss von Straßenbeleuchtung auf aquatische Insekten (Ephemeroptera, Plecoptera, Trichoptera, Diptera: Simuliidae, Chironomidae, Empididae). *Natur und Landschaft*, **78**, 264–7.

Scheibe, M.A. (1999). Über die Attraktivität von Straßenbeleuchtungen auf Insekten aus nahegelegenen Gewässern unter Berücksichtigung unterschiedlicher UV-Emission der Lampen. *Natur und Landschaft*, **74**, 144–6.

Scheibe, M.A. (2000). Quantitative Aspekte der Anziehungskraft von Straßenbeleuchtungen auf die Emergenz aus nahegelegenen Gewässern (Ephemeroptera, Plecoptera, Trichoptera, Diptera: Simuliidae, Chironomidae, Empididae) unter Berücksichtigung der spektralen Emission verschiedener Lichtquellen. Unpublished Ph.D. thesis, Universität Mainz.

Scheltema, R.S. (1971). Larval dispersal as a means of genetic exchange between geographically separated populations of shallow-water benthic marine gastropods. *Biological Bulletin of the Marine Biological Laboratory, Woods Hole*, **140**, 284–322.

Scheu, S. and Parkinson, D. (1994). Effects of earthworms on nutrient dynamics, carbon turnover and microorganisms in soils from cool temperate forests of the Canadian Rocky Mountains – laboratory studies. *Applied Soil Ecology*, **1**, 113–25.

Schiller, A. and Horn, S. P. (1997). Wildlife conservation in urban greenways of the mid-southeastern United States. *Urban Ecosystems*, **1**, 103–16.

Schlesinger, W. H. and Andrews, J. A. (2000). Soil respiration and the global carbon cycle. *Biogeochemistry*, **48**, 7–20.

Schmid, J. A. (1975). *Urban Vegetation. A Review and Chicago Case Study*. The University of Chicago, Department of Geography, Research Paper No. 161.

Schmid, J. A. (1994). Wetlands in the urban landscape of the United States. In *The Ecological City: Preserving and Restoring Urban Biodiversity*, ed. R. H. Platt, R. A. Rowntree and P. C. Muick. Amherst: The University of Massachusetts Press, pp. 106–33.

Schmidt, F. L. (1996). Statistical significance testing and cumulative knowledge in psychology: implications for training researchers. *Psychological Methods*, **1**, 115–29.

Schmidt, H. (1985). Umgestaltungsprozesse räumlicher Stadtstrukturen. Hall. *Jahrbuch für Geowissenschaft, Gotha/Leipzig*, **10**, 103–114.

Schmiedel, J. (2001). Auswirkungen von künstlichen Lichtquellen auf die Tierwelt – ein Überblick. *Schriftenreihe Landschaftspflege und Naturschutz*, **67**, 19–51.

Scholes, R. J. and Biggs, R. (2005). A biodiversity intactness index. *Nature* **434**, 45–9.

Schön, D. (1983). *The Reflective Practitioner: How Professionals Think in Action*. London: Arena.

Schönfelder, G. (1988). Aufgaben, Inhalte und Formen landschaftsökologischer Karten städtischer Verdichtungen – ein Beitrag zur Stadtkartographie. *Petermann Geographische Mitteilungen*, **132**, 47–59.

Schowengerdt, R. A. (1997). *Remote Sensing: Models and Methods for Image Processing*, 2nd edn. San Diego: Academic Press.

Schrader, F. (1985). Zu arealen, vertikalen und zeitlichen Merkmalen der Flächennutzung und zur flächennutzungsbezogenen Analyse und Diagnose von Naturressourcen- und Natureffekt-Beziehungen agrarisch-forstlicher Landschaften bei Potsdam. Dispp. (B) Potsdam 1985.

Schreier, H. and Brown. S. (2002). Scaling issues in watershed assessments. *Water Policy*, **3**, 475–89.

Schueler, T. R. (1987). *Controlling Urban Runoff: A Practical Manual for Planning and Designing Urban BMPs*. Washington, DC: Department of Environmental Programs, Metropolitan Washington Council of Governments.

Schueler, T. R. (1994). The importance of imperviousness. *Watershed Protection Techniques*, **1**, 100–11.

Schulz, A. (1982). Der KÖH-Wert, Modell einer komplexen, planungsrelevanten Zustandserfassung. *Informationen zur Raumentwicklung*, pp. 847–63.

Schwabe, C., Viljoen, J. and O'Donovan, M. (2001). *SA Environmental Indicator Project, Special Review: Social Issues*. Pretoria: HSRC.

Schwartz, M. W., Thorne, J. H. and Viers, J. H. (2006). Biotic homogenizations of the California flora in urban and urbanizing regions. *Biological Conservation*, **127**, 282–91.

Schwirian, K. P. (1974). *Comparative Urban Structure: Studies in the Ecology of Cities*. Lexington, MA: D. C. Heath and Co.

Scott, J. M., Heglund, P. J., Morrison, M. L. *et al.*, eds. (2002). *Predicting Species Occurrences: Issues of Accuracy and Scale*. Washington, DC: Island Press.

Seabrook, W. A. and Dettmann, E. B. (1996). Roads as activity corridors for cane toads in Australia. *Journal of Wildlife Management*, **60**, 363–8.

Seastedt, T. R. (1984). The role of microarthropods in decomposition and mineralisation processes. *Annual Review of Entomology*, **29**, 25–46.

Seed, R. and Suchanek, T. H. (1992). Population and community ecology of Mytilus. In *The Mussel Mytilus: Ecology, Physiology, Genetics and Culture*, ed. E. M. Gosling. Amsterdam: Elsevier, pp. 87–169.

Sernander, R. (1926). *Stockholms natur*. Uppsala: Almqvist and Wiksell. (In Swedish)

Serveiss, V. B., Bowen, J. L., Dow, D. and Valiela, I. (2004). Using ecological risk principles to identify the major anthropogenic stressor in the Waquoit Bay Watershed, Cape Cod, Massachusetts. *Environmental Management*, **33**, 730–40.

Sewell, S. and Catterall, C. P. (1998). Bushland modification and styles of urban development: their impacts on birds in south east Queensland. *Wildlife Research*, **25**, 41–64.

Sfriso, A., Pavoni, B., Marcomini, A. and Orio, A. A. (1992). Macroalgae, nutrient cycles, and pollutants in the Lagoon of Venice. *Estuaries*, **15**, 517–28.

Shaffer, P. W., Kentula, M. E. and Gwin, S. E. (1999). Characterization of wetland hydrology using hydrogeomorphic classification. *Wetlands*, **19**, 490–504.

Shanks, A. L., Grantham, B. A. and Carr, M. H. (2003). Propagule dispersal distance and the size and spacing of marine reserves. *Ecological Applications*, **13**, S159–69.

Shannon, M. A. (2002). Theoretical approaches to understanding intersectoral policy integration. Paper presented at the Finland COST Action meeting (European Forest Institute). http://www.metla.fi/eu/cost/e19/shannon.pdf

Sharpe, D. M., Stearns, F., Leitner, L. A. and Dorney, J. R. (1986). Fate of natural vegetation during urban development of rural landscapes in southeastern Wisconsin. *Urban Ecology*, **9**, 267–87.

Shaw, W. W., Harris, L. K. and Livingston, M. (1998). Vegetative characteristics of urban land covers in metropolitan Tucson. *Urban Ecosystems*, **2**, 65–73.

Shaver, E. (2000). *Low Impact Design Manual for the Auckland Region*. Auckland, New Zealand: Auckland Regional Council Technical Publication 124. Available online at http://www.arc.govt.nz/env/water/stormwater-publications.crm.

Shipley, B. (2000). *Cause and Correlation in Biology*. Cambridge, UK: Cambridge University Press.

Shirley-Smith, C. L. (2002). Integrated water management as a tool for sustainable urban regeneration. In *The Sustainable City 11: Urban Regeneration and Sustainability*, ed. C. A. Brebbie, J. F. Martin-Duque and L. C. Wadhwa. WIT Press: Boston, pp. 117–31.

Shochat, E., Stefanov, W. L., Whitehouse, M. E. A. and Faeth, S. H. (2004). Spider diversity in the greater Phoenix area: the influence of human modification to habitat structure and productivity. *Ecological Applications*, **14**, 268–80.

Shochat, E., Warren, P. S., Faeth, S. H., McIntyre, N. E. and Hope, D. (2006). From patterns to emerging processes in mechanistic urban ecology. *Trends in Ecology and Evolution*, **21**, 186–91.

Short, F. T. and Burdick, D. M. (1996). Quantifying eelgrass habitat loss in relation to housing development and nitrogen loading in Waquoit Bay, Massachusetts. *Estuaries*, **19**, 730–9.

Short, F. T., Burdick, D. M. and Kaldy, J. E. (1995). Mesocosm experiments quantify the effects of eutrophication on eelgrass, *Zostera marina*. *Limnology and Oceanography*, **40**, 740–9.

Shrader-Frechette, K. S. and McCoy, E. D. (1993). *Method in Ecology: strategies for conservation*. Cambridge, UK: Cambridge University Press.

Shukuroglou, P. and McCarthy, M. A. (2006). Modelling the occurence of rainbow lorikeets (*Trichoglossus haematodus*) in Melbourne. *Austral Ecology*, **31**, 240–53.

Shuttleworth, C. M. (2001). Traffic related mortality in a red squirrel (*Sciurus vulgaris*) population receiving supplemental feeding. *Urban Ecosystems*, **5**, 109–18.

Sieverts, T. (1998a). Die Stadt in der Zweiten Moderne, eine europäische Perspektive. *Informationen zur Raumentwicklung* 7/8, 455–73.

Sieverts, T. (1998b). *Zwischenstadt: zwischen Ort und Welt, Raum und Zeit, Stadt und Land*, 2nd edn. Braunschweig/Wiesbaden.

Simberloff, D. (1981). Community effects of introduced species. In *Biotic Crises in Ecological and Evolutionary Time*, ed. M. H. Nitecki. New York: Academic Press, pp. 53–82.

Simberloff, D. (1998). Flagships, umbrellas, and keystones: is single-species management passe in the landscape era? *Biological Conservation*, **83**, 247–57.

Simberloff, D. S. and Abele, L. G. (1976). Island biogeography theory and conservation practice. *Science*, **121**, 285–6.

Simberloff, D., Farr, J. A., Cox, J. and Mehlman, D. W. (1992). Movement corridors: conservation bargains or poor investments? *Conservation Biology*, **6**, 493–504.

Simcock, R. (2004). *Use the Right Soil to Get the Stormwater Treatment You Want*. Proceedings of the New Zealand Water and Wastes Association Stormwater Conference, Rotorua, New Zealand, 6–7 May, 2004.

Simons, T. (1979). Arkkitehdit ja metsänhoitajat Suomen metsäisen maiseman muotoilijoina. [Summary: The role of architects and foresters in shaping the forest landscape in Finland]. *Silva Fennica*, **13**, 170–76. (In Finnish)

Singh, A. K., Gupta, H. K., Gupta, K. *et al.* (2007). A comparative study of air pollution in Indian cities. *Bulletin of Environmental Contamination and Toxicology*, **78**, 411–16.

Sismondo, S. (2000). Island biogeography and the multiple domains of models. *Biology and Philosophy*, **15**, 239–58.

Sixma, J. J. (2000). *Impact of Outdoor Lighting on Man and Nature*. Advisory Report of the Dutch Health Council. The Hague, Netherlands, p. 46.

Sjögren-Gulve, P. and Ray, C. (1996). Using logistic regression to model metapopulation dynamics: large-scale forestry extirpates the pool frog. In *Metapopulations and Wildlife Conservation*, ed. D. R. McCullough. Washington, DC: Island Press, pp. 111–37.

Sjöström, U. (1985). *Låna varandras glasögon – om energiproduktion och människors villkor*. Stockholm: Stockholms Universitet, Pedagogiska Institutionen.

Skånes, H. (1996). Landscape Changes and Grassland Dynamics. Retrospective studies based on aerial photographs and old cadastral maps during 200 years in south Sweden. Unpublished Ph.D. thesis, Stockholm University.

Slabbekoorn, H. and Peet, M. (2003). Birds sing at a higher pitch in urban noise. *Nature*, **424**, 267–8.

Slip, D. J. and Shine, R. (1988). Habitat use, movements and activity patterns of free-ranging diamond pythons, *Morelia* s. *spilota* (Serpentes: Boidae): a radiotelemetric study. *Australian Wildlife Research*, **15**, 515–31.

Small, C. (2001). Estimation of vegetation abundance by spectral mixture analysis. *International Journal of Remote Sensing*, **22**, 1305–34.

Small, C. (2002). Multitemporal analysis of urban reflectance. *Remote Sensing of Environment*, **81**, 427–42.

Small, E. C., Sadler, J. P. and Telfer, M. G. (2003). Carabid beetle assemblages on urban derelict sites in Birmingham, UK. *Journal of Insect Conservation*, **6**, 233–46.

Smith, D. S. and Hellmund, P. C. (1993). *Ecology of Greenways*. Minneapolis: University of Minnesota Press.

Smith, J. and Nasr, J. (1992). Urban agriculture for sustainable cities: using wastes and idle land and water bodies as resources. *Environment and Urbanization*, **4**, 141–52.

Smith, J.-P, Theron, P. D., Cilliers, S. S. and Maboeta, M. (2004). The influence of urbanisation on the process of soil organic matter breakdown. Poster delivered at the XIVth International Colloquium on Soil Biology and Ecology, Mont Saint Aignan, France.

Smith, R. B. and Woodgate, P. (1985). Appraisal of fire damage for timber salvage by remote sensing in mountain ash forests. *Australian Forestry*, **48**, 252–63.

Smith, R. M., Gaston, K. J., Warren, P. H. and Thompson, K. (2005). Urban domestic gardens (V): relationships between land cover composition, housing and landscape. *Landscape Ecology*, **20**, 235–53.

Snape, D. (2002). *The Australian Garden: Designing with Australian Plants*. Hawthorn, Vic.: Bloomings Books.

Snelder, T. and Trueman, S. (1995). *The Environmental Impacts of Urban Stormwater Runoff*. Technical Publication 53. Auckland: Auckland Regional Council.

Snep, R. P. H. (in preparation). Biodiversity conservation at business sites: a multifunctional land use example. Wageningen University, the Netherlands.

Snep, R. P. H., Kwak, R. G. M. and Kramer, H. (2005). *The Ecology of the Urban Landscape Mapped: A Pilot-study of the Use of High-resolution Satellite Images for the Description of Urban Nature and Urban Green*. Alterra report 1108. Alterra, Wageningen UR. (In Dutch)

Snep, R. P. H., Kwak, R. G. M., Timmermans, H. and Timmermans, W. (2001). *Landscape Ecological Analysis in the Port of Rotterdam: LARCH-scenario Studies on the Potential for Nature of Derelict Land and Industrial Verges*. Alterra report 231. Alterra, Wageningen. (In Dutch)

Snep, R. P. H., Opdam, P. F. M., Baveco, J. M. *et al.* (2006). How peri-urban design can strengthen animal populations within cities: a modeling approach. *Biological Conservation*, **127**, 345–55.

Snyder, C. D., Young, J. A., Villela, R. and Lemarié, D. P. (2003). Influences of upland and riparian land-use patterns on stream biotic integrity. *Landscape Ecology*, **18**, 647–64.

Soh, M. C. K., Sodhi, N. S., Seoh, R. K. H. and Brook, B. W. (2002). Nest site selection of the house crow (*Corvus splendens*), an urban invasive bird species in Singapore and implications for its management. *Landscape and Urban Planning*, **59**, 217–26.

Somaschini, A., Ardizzone, G. D. and Gravina, M. F. (1997). Long-term changes in the structure of a polychaete community on artificial habitats. *Bulletin of Marine Science*, **60**, 460–6.

Song, I. J., Hong, S. K., Kim, H. O., Byun, B. and Gin, Y. (2005). The pattern of landscape patches and invasion of naturalized plants in developed areas of urban Seoul. *Landscape and Urban Planning*, **70**, 205–19.

Soule, M. E., Bolger, D. T., Alberts, A. C., Wright, J., Sorice, M. and Hill, S. (1988). Reconstructed dynamics of rapid extinctions of chaparral-requiring birds in urban habitat islands. *Conservation Biology*, **2**, 75–92.

Sousa, W. P. (1979a). Disturbance in marine intertidal boulder fields: the nonequilibrium maintenance of species diversity. *Ecology*, **60**, 1225–39.

Sousa, W. P. (1979b). Experimental investigations of disturbance and ecological succession in a rocky intertidal algal community. *Ecological Monographs*, **49**, 227–54.

Sousa, W. P. (1985). Disturbance and patch dynamics on rocky intertidal shores. In *The Ecology of Natural Disturbance and Patch Dynamics*, ed. S. T. A. Pickett and P. S. White. London: Academic Press, pp. 101–24.

South Africa Ministry of Agriculture and Land Affairs (2001). *White Paper on Spatial Planning and Land Use Management*. Pretoria: Government Printer.

South Africa Ministry of Agriculture and Land Affairs (2002). *Land Use Management Bill*. Pretoria: Government Printer.

South Africa Office of the President (2000). *Local Government: Municipal Systems Act*, No. 32 of 2000. Pretoria: Government Printer.

Souza, O. F. F. and Brown, V. K. (1994). Effects of habitat fragmentation on Amazon termite communities. *Journal of Tropical Ecology*, **10**, 197–206.

Speight, M. R., Hails, R. S., Gilbert, M. and Foggo, A. (1998). Horse chestnut scale (*Pulvinaria regalis*) (Homoptera: Coccidae) and urban host tree environment. *Ecology*, **79**, 1503–13.

Spence, J. R. and Spence, D. H. (1988). Of ground-beetles and men: introduced species and the synanthropic fauna of western Canada. *Memoirs of the Entomological Society of Canada*, **144**, 151–68.

Spirn, A. W. (1998). *The Language of Landscape*. New Haven: Yale University Press.

St Clair, C. C. (2003). Comparative permeability of roads, rivers, and meadows to songbirds in Banff National Park. *Conservation Biology*, **17**, 1151–60.

Stadsbyggnadskontoret (1997). *Nationalstadsparkens ekologiska infrastruktur. Underlag till fördjupning av översiktsplanen för Stockholms del av nationalstadspark Ulriksdal-Haga-Brunnsviken-Djurgården*. Rapport SBK 1997:8. Stockholms stad.

Stadsbyggnadskontoret (2002). *Sociotopkarta för parker och andra friytor i Stockholms innerstad – om metoden, dialogen och resultatet*. Stockholms Stad.

Stadt Berlin, ed. (1996). *Umweltatlas Berlin*. Berlin.

Stadt Halle/Saale, Dezernat für Umwelt und Naturschutz, ed. (1994). *Landschaftsplan der Stadt Halle/Saale – Vorentwurf*. Halle.

Standards New Zealand (2001). *Subdivision for People and the Environment*. Standards New Zealand SNZHB44: 2001. Wellington: Hutcheson, Bowman and Stuart.

Statham, M. and Statham, H. L. (1997). Movements and habits of brushtail possums (*Trichosurus vulpecula* Kerr) in an urban area. *Wildlife Research*, **24**, 715–26.

Stauss, M. (1995). *List of Vascular Plant Species at Kenilworth Marsh, Washington, DC*. Laurel, Maryland: US Geological Survey, Patuxent Wildlife Research Center.

Stearns, F. and T. Montag, eds. (1974). *The Urban Ecosystem: A Holistic Approach*. Stroudsburg: Dowden, Hutchinson and Ross, Inc.

Stefanov, W., Ramsey, M. and Christensen, P. (2001). Monitoring urban land cover change: an expert system approach to land cover classification of semiarid to arid urban centers. *Remote Sensing of the Environment*, **77**, 173–85.

Steffan-Dewenter, I. and Tschartntke, T. (2002). Insect communities and biotic interactions on fragmented calcareous grasslands – a mini review. *Biological Conservation*, **104**, 275–84.

Stein, S. (1997). *Planting Noah's Garden. Further Adventures in Backyard Ecology*. Boston, New York: Houghton Mifflin Company.

Steinberg, D. A., Pouyat, R. V., Parmelee, R. W. and Groffman, P. M. (1997). Earthworm abundance and nitrogen mineralization rates along an urban–rural land use gradient. *Soil Biology and Biogeochemistry*, **29**, 427–30.

Steiner, F. (2000). *The Living Landscape*, 2nd edn. New York: McGraw-Hill.

Steiner, F. (2002). *Human Ecology*. Washington, DC: Island Press.

Stenhouse, R. (2001). Management of urban remnant bushlands by the community and local government. *Australian Journal of Environmental Management*, **8**, 37–47.

Stenhouse, R. (2004a). Fragmentation and internal disturbance of native vegetation reserves in the Perth Metropolitan Area, Western Australia. *Landscape and Urban Planning*, **68**, 389–401.

Stenhouse, R. (2004b). Local government conservation and management of native vegetation in urban Australia. *Environmental Management*, **34**, 209–22.

Stewart, G. H., Ignatieva, M. E., Meurk, C. D. and Earl, R. D. (2004). The re-emergence of indigenous forest in an urban environment, Christchurch, New Zealand. *Urban Forestry and Urban Greening*, **2**, 149–58.

Stiles, J. H. and Jones, R. H. (1998). Distribution of the red imported fire ant, *Solenopsis invicta*, in road and powerline habitats. *Landscape Ecology*, **13**, 335–46.

Strategic Environmental Focus (SEF) (2003). *North West Biodiversity Site Inventory and Database Development*. Unpublished report.

Strayer, D. L. (1991). Comparative ecology and undiscovered public knowledge. In *Comparative Analyses of Ecosystems: Patterns, Mechanisms, and Theories*, ed. J. Cole, G. Lovett and S. Findlay. New York: Springer-Verlag, pp. 3–6.

Streever, W. J. (1998). Kooragang wetland rehabilitation project: opportunities and constraints in an urban wetland rehabilitation project. *Urban Ecosystems*, **2**, 205–18.

Strongman, T. (1998). The use of native plants in Canterbury gardens from Raoul until the present. In *Etienne Raoul and Canterbury Botany 1840–1996*, ed. C. J. Burrows. Christchurch: Canterbury Botanical Society and Manuka Press, pp. 73–7.

Suarez, A. V., Bolger, D. T. and Case, T. J. (1998). The effects of fragmentation and invasion on the native ant community in coastal southern California. *Ecology*, **79**, 2041–56.

Sugiura, T. (1974). Theory and methods of landscape ecology. *Annals of the Tohoku Geographical Association*, **26**, 137–48. (In Japanese)

Sukopp, H. (1998). Urban ecology: scientific and practical aspects. In *Urban Ecology*, ed. J. Breuste, H. Feldmann and O. Uhlmann. Berlin: Springer-Verlag, pp. 3–16.

Sukopp, H. (2002). On the early history of urban ecology in Europe. *Preslia*, **74**, 373–93.

Sukopp, H. (2003). Flora and vegetation reflecting the urban history of Berlin. *Die Erde*, **134**, 295–316.

Sukopp, H. (2004). Human-caused impact on preserved vegetation. *Landscape and Urban Planning*, **68**, 347–55.

Sukopp, H. and Numata, M. (1995). Foreword. In *Urban Ecology as the Basis for Urban Planning*, ed. H. Sukopp, M. Numata and A. Huber. The Hague: SPB Academic Publishing, p. vii.

Sukopp, H. and Trepl, L. (1990). *Naturschutz in Großstädten*. TU Berlin (unpublished).

Sukopp, H. and Weiler, P. (1986). Biotopkartierung im besiedelten Bereich der Bundesrepublik Deutschland. *Landschaft und Stadt*, **18**, 25–38.

Sukopp, H. and Weiler, S. (1988). Biotope mapping and nature conservation strategies in urban areas of the Federal Republic of Germany. *Landscape and Urban Planning*, **15**, 39–58.

Sukopp, H. and Wurzel, A. (2003). The effects of climate change on the vegetation of Central European cities. *Urban Habitats*, **1**, 3–25.

Sukopp, H., Blume, H. P. and Kunick, W. (1979a). The soil, flora and vegetation of Berlin's wastelands. In *Nature in Cities*, ed. I. C. Laurie. Chichester: John Wiley, pp. 115–32.

Sukopp, H., Hejný, S. and Kowarik, I., eds. (1990). *Urban Ecology: plants and plant communities in urban environments*. The Hague: SPB Publishing.

Sukopp, H., Kunick, W. and Schneider, Ch. (1979b). Biotopkartierung in der Stadt. *Natur und Landschaft*, **54**, 66–8.

Sukopp, H., Kunick, W. and Schneider, Ch. (1980). Biotopkartierung im besiedelten Bereich von Berlin (West) Teil II: Zur Methodik von Geländearbeit. *Garten und Landschaft*, **7**, 565–69.

Sukopp, H., Numata, M. and Huber, A., eds. (1995). *Urban Ecology as the Basis of Urban Planning*. The Hague, The Netherlands: SPB Academic Publishing.

Sullivan, W. (1984). Our endangered night sky. *Sky and Telescope*, **67**, 412.

Suter, G. W. (2001). Applicability of indicator monitoring to ecological risk assessment. *Ecological Indicators*, **1**, 101–12.

Sutherland, J. P. (1980). The fouling community at Beaufort, North Carolina: a study in stability. *American Naturalist*, **118**, 500–19.

Svensson, S., Svensson, M. and Tjernberg, M. (1999). *Svensk Fågelatlas*. Stockholm: Sveriges Ornitologiska Förening. (In Swedish)

Swift, M. J., Heal, O. W. and Anderson, J. M. (1979). Decomposition in terrestrial ecosystems. *Studies in Ecology*, **5**. Berkeley and Los Angeles, California, USA: University of California Press.

Sydney Coastal Councils Group (1998). *Sydney Regional Coastal Management Strategy.* Sydney, Australia: Sydney Coastal Council Inc.

Syphax, S. W. and Hammerschlag, R. S. (1995). The reconstruction of Kenilworth Marsh, the last tidal marsh in Washington, DC Park. *Science*, **15**, 15–19.

Szlavecz, K., Placella, S., Pouyat, R. V., Groffman, P. M., Csuzdi, C. and Yesilonis, I. D. (2006). Invasive earthworms and N-cycling in remnant forest patches. *Applied Soil Ecology*, **32**, 54–62.

Tabacchi, E., Planty-Tabacchi, A. M. and Décamps, O. (1990). Continuity and discontinuity of the riparian vegetation along a fluvial corridor. *Landscape Ecology*, **5**, 9–20.

Taha, H. (1997). Modeling impacts of increased urban vegetation on ozone air quality in the South Coast Air Basin. *Atmospheric Environment*, **30**, 3430–2.

Takeuchi, K. (1975). A method of land evaluation in landscape ecology. *Applied Phytosociology*, **5**, 1–60. (In Japanese)

Takeuchi, K. (1991). *Chiiki no seitaigaku* (Ecology in Region). Tokyo: Asakura Shoten. (In Japanese)

Tamm, C. O. (1991). *Nitrogen in Terrestrial Ecosystems.* New York, NY: Springer-Verlag.

Tansley, A. G. (1935). The use and abuse of vegetational concepts and terms. *Ecology*, **16**, 284–307.

Taoda, H. (1973). Bryo-meter, an instrument for measuring the phytotoxic air pollution. *Hikobia*, **6**, 224–8.

Taylor, D. I., Nixon, S. W., Granter, S. L., Buckley, B. A., McMahon, J. P. and Lin, H.-J. (1995). Responses of coastal lagoon plant communities to different forms of nutrient enrichment – a mesocosm experiment. *Aquatic Botany*, **52**, 19–34.

Taylor, L. R., French, R. A. and Woiwod, I. P. (1978). The Rothamsted insect survey and the urbanisation of land in Great Britain. In *Perspectives in Urban Entomology*, ed. G. W. Frankie and C. S. Koehler. London: Academic Press, pp. 31–65.

Ter Braak, C. J. F. and Prentice, I. C. (1988). A theory of gradient analysis. *Advances in Ecological Research*, **18**, 271–317.

Teyssot, G. (1999). The American lawn: surface of everyday life. In *The American Lawn*, ed. G. Teyssot. New York: Princeton Architectural Press, pp. 1–39.

Thacker, C. (1979). *The History of Gardens.* Berkeley and Los Angeles, California: University of California Press.

The Green Building Partnership. (2004). Accessed 12 May 2004. http://www.60lgreenbuilding.com.

Theobald, D. M. (2000). Fragmentation by inholdings and exurban development. In *Forest Fragmentation in the Southern Rocky Mountains*, ed. R. L. Knight, F. H. Smith, S. W. Buskirk, W. H. Romme, and W. L. Baker. Boulder, CO: University Press of Colorado, pp. 155–74.

Theobald, D. M. (2004). Placing exurban land-use change in a human modification framework. *Frontiers in Ecology and Environment*, **2**, 139–44.

Theobald, D. M., Hobbs, N. T., Bearly, T., Zack, J. A., Schenk, T. and Riebsame, W. E. (2000). Incorporating biological information in local land-use decision making: designing a system for conservation planning. *Landscape Ecology*, **15**, 35–45.

Thibault, P. A. and Zipperer, W. C. (1994). Temporal changes of wetlands within an urbanizing agricultural landscape. *Landscape and Urban Planning*, **28**, 245–51.

Thompson, G. G. and Withers, P. C. (2003). Effect of species richness and relative abundance on the shape of the species accumulation curve. *Austral Ecology*, **28**, 355–60.

Thompson, K., Austin, K. C., Smith, R. M., Warren, P. H., Angold, P. G. and Gaston, K. J. (2003). Urban domestic gardens (I): putting small-scale plant diversity in context. *Journal of Vegetation Science*, **14**, 71–8.

Thompson, R. C., Crowe, T. P. and Hawkins, S. J. (2002). Rocky intertidal communities: past environmental changes, present status and predictions for the next 25 years. *Environmental Conservation*, **29**, 168–91.

Thompson, R. C., Wilson, B. J., Tobin, M. L., Hill, A. S. and Hawkins, S. J. (1996). Biologically generated habitat provision and diversity of rocky shore organisms at a hierarchy of spatial scales. *Journal of Experimental Marine Biology and Ecology*, **202**, 73–84.

Thomson, J. D. (2001). Using pollination deficits to infer pollinator declines: can theory guide us? *Conservation Ecology*, **5**, 6. http://www.consecol.org/vol5/iss1/art6/

Thorson, G. (1950). Reproduction and larval ecology of marine bottom invertebrates. *Biological Reviews*, **25**, 1–45.

Tian, G. (1998). Effect of soil degradation on leaf decomposition and nutrient release under humid tropical conditions. *Soil Science*, **163**, 897–906.

Tibbetts, J. (2002). Coastal cities: Living on the edge. *Environmental Health Perspectives*, **110**, A674–81.

Tigas, L. A., van Vuren, D. H. and Sauvajot, R. M. (2002). Behavioral responses of bobcats and coyotes to habitat fragmentation and corridors in an urban environment. *Biological Conservation*, **108**, 299–306.

Tilman, D. (1982). *Resource Competition and Community Structure*. Princeton: Princeton University Press.

Tilman, D. (2001). Functional diversity. In *Encyclopaedia of Biodiversity*, Vol. 3. New York: Academic Press, pp. 109–20.

Timmermans, W. (2001). *Wildlife and the City: Urbanisation as an Instrument for Wildlife Policy*. Best, The Netherlands: Aeneas, Technical Publishers.

Timmermans, W. and Snep, R. P. H. (2001). Ecological models and urban wildlife. In *Ecosystems and Sustainable Development III*, ed. Y. Villacampa, C. A. Brebbia and J. L. Usó. Proceedings of ECOsud Conference, Southampton, WIT, 2001. *Advances in Ecological Science* **10**, 205–16.

Timmermans, W. and Snep, R. P. H. (2003). Combining urban development and wildlife overpasses together in one multi-functional and multi-level building across highways – innovative nature concepts in highly urbanised areas. In *Ecosystems and Sustainable Development III*. (Proceedings ECOsud conference), ed. Y. Villacampa, C. A. Brebbia and J. L. Usó. Southampton: WIT.

Tiroler Landesumweltanwalt (ed.) (2003). *Die Helle Not. Künstliche Lichtquellen: ein unterschätztes Naturschutzproblem*, 2nd edn. Innsbruck, Wien, Austria: Tiroler Landesumweltanwalt.

Titman, W. (1994). *Special Places; Special People. The Hidden Curriculum of School Grounds*. Dorking, UK: WWF UK and Learning through Landscapes.

Tladi, B., Baloyi, T. and Marfo, C. (2002b). Settlement and land use patterns. In *The State of the Environment Report 2002 of the North West Province, South Africa*, ed. S. Mangold, M. Kalule-Sabiti and J. Walmsley. Mafikeng: North West Province Department of Agriculture, Conservation and Environment, Chapter 6.

Tladi, B., Baloyi, T. and Van Boom, E. (2002a). The social environment. In *The State of the Environment Report 2002 of the North West Province, South Africa*, ed. S. Mangold, M. Kalule-Sabiti and J. Walmsley. Mafikeng: North West Province Department of Agriculture, Conservation and Environment, Chapter 3.

Tobias, W. (1996). Sommernächtliches 'Schneetreiben' am Main. Zum Phänomen des Massenfluges von Eintagsfliegen. *Natur und Museum (Frankfurt/M.)*, **126**, 37–54.

Tonteri, T. and Haila, Y. (1990). Plants in a boreal city: ecological characteristics of vegetation in Helsinki and its surroundings, southern Finland. *Annales Botanici Fennici*, **27**, 337–52.

Torrens, P. M. (2003). Cellular automata and multi-agent systems as planning support tools. In *Planning Support Systems in Practice*, ed. S. Geertman and J. Stillwell. New York: Springer, pp 205–22.

Toyama, M. and Nakagoshi, N. (1994). A study on structure of urban greenery spaces and inhabitant ants. *Journal of the Japanese Society of Revegetation Technology*, **20**, 13–20. (In Japanese with English abstract)

Trepl, L. (1984). Flora und vegetation. *Landschaftsentwicklung und Umweltforschung*, **23**, 52–69.

Trepl, L. (1995). Towards a theory of urban biocoenoses. In *Urban Ecology as the Basis for Urban Planning*, ed. H. Sukopp, M. Numata and A. Huber. The Hague: SPB Academic Publishing, pp. 3–21.

Trocmé, M., Cahill, S., de Vries, J. G. et al., eds. (2002). *COST 341. Habitat Fragmentation due to Transportation Infrastructure. The European Review*. Luxembourg: Office for Official Publications of the European Communities.

Trombulak, S. C. and Frissell, C. A. (2000). Review of ecological effects of roads on terrestrial and aquatic communities. *Conservation Biology*, **14**, 18–30.

Trowbridge, A. V. (1998). Start or join an ecocircle. *Land*, 10–12.

Tsamenyi, M., Rose, G. and Castle, A. (2003). International marine conservation law and its implementation in Australia. In *Conserving Marine Environments: Out of Sight, Out of Mind*, ed. P. Hutchings and D. Lunney. Sydney, Australia: Royal Zoological Society of New South Wales, pp. 1–17.

Tupper, M. and Hunte, W. (1998). Predictability of fish assemblages on artificial and natural reefs in Barbados. *Bulletin of Marine Science*, **62**, 919–35.

Turner, B. L. II, Clark, W. C., Kates, R. W., Richards, J. F., Mathews, J. T. and Meyer, W. B., eds. (1990). *The Earth as Transformed by Human Action: Global and Regional Changes in the Biosphere over the Past 300 Years*. New York, USA: Cambridge University Press and Clark University.

Turner, I. M. (1996). Species loss in fragments of tropical rain forest: a review of the evidence. *Journal of Applied Ecology*, **33**, 200–9.

Turner, W. R. (2003). Citywide biological monitoring as a tool for ecology and conservation in urban landscapes: the case of the Tucson bird count. *Landscape and Urban Planning*, **65**, 149–66.

Tylka, D. L., Schaefer, J. M., and Adams, L. W. (1987). Guidelines for implementing urban wildlife programs under state conservation agency administration. In *Integrating Man and Nature in the Metropolitan Environment*, ed. L. W. Adams and D. L. Leedy. Columbia, MD: National Institute for Urban Wildlife, pp. 199–206.

Tyrväinen, L. (1997). The amenity value of the urban forest: an application of the hedonic pricing method. *Landscape and Urban Planning*, **37**, 211–22.

Tyrväinen, L. (2001). Use and valuation of urban forest amenities in Finland. *Journal of Environmental Management*, **62**, 75–92.

Tyrväinen, L. and Miettinen, A. (2000). Property prices and urban forest amenities. *Journal of Environmental Economics and Management*, **39**, 205–23.

Tyrväinen, L. and Väänänen (1998). The economic value of urban forest amenities: an application of the contingent valuation method. *Landscape and Urban Planning*, **43**, 105–18.

Tyrväinen, L., Silvennoinen, H. and Kolehmainen, O. (2003). Ecological and aesthetic values in urban forest management. *Urban Forestry and Urban Greening*, **1**, 135–49.

Udvardy, M. F. D. (1959). Notes on the ecological concepts of habitat, biotope and niche. *Ecology*, **40**, 725–8.

Ulack, R., Raitz, K. and Pauer, G. (1998). *Atlas of Kentucky*. Lexington, KY: The University Press of Kentucky.

Ulrich, R. S. (1986). Human responses to vegetation and landscapes. *Landscape and Urban Planning*, **13**, 29–44.

UN (1997). *Urban and Rural Areas (1996)*. New York: United Nations Publications.

UNCED (1992). Convention on Biological Diversity. United Nations Conference on Environment and Development, Rio de Janeiro, Brazil, June 1992. New York: United Nations Department of Public Information.

Underwood, A. J. (1989). The analysis of stress in natural populations. *Biological Journal of the Linnean Society*, **37**, 51–78.

Underwood, A. J. (1990). Experiments in ecology and management: their logics, functions and interpretations. *Australian Journal of Ecology*, **15**, 365–89.

Underwood, A. J. (1991). The logic of ecological experiments: a case history from studies of the distribution of macro-algae on rocky intertidal shores. *Journal of the Marine Biological Association of the United Kingdom*, **71**, 841–66.

Underwood, A. J. (1992). Beyond BACI: the detection of environmental impacts on populations in the real, but variable, world. *Journal of Experimental Marine Biology and Ecology*, **161**, 145–78.

Underwood, A. J. (1995a). Ecological research and (and research into) environmental management. *Ecological Applications*, **5**, 232–47.

Underwood, A. J. (1995b). Toxicological testing in laboratories is not ecological testing of toxicology. *Human and Ecological Risk Assessment*, **1**, 178–82.

Underwood, A. J. (1996). Detection, interpretation, prediction and management of environmental disturbances: some roles for experimental marine ecology. *Journal of Experimental Marine Biology and Ecology*, **200**, 1–27.

Underwood, A. J. (1997). *Experiments in Ecology: Their Logical Design and Interpretation Using Analysis of Variance*. Cambridge, UK: Cambridge University Press.

Underwood, A. J. (2000). Trying to detect impacts in marine habitats: comparisons with suitable reference areas. In *Statistics in Ecotoxicology*, ed. T. Sparks. Chichester, England: John Wiley & Sons Ltd., pp. 279–308.

Underwood, A. J. and Chapman, M. G. (1999). The environment: an ideas paper on environmental issues for DUAP's forum 'Sydney Harbour Planning Strategy'. In *Sydney Harbour Planning Strategy Forum. Background Report*. Sydney: Department of Urban Affairs and Planning, pp. 1–14.

Underwood, A. J. and Peterson, C. H. (1988). Towards an ecological framework for investigating pollution. *Marine Ecology Progress Series*, **46**, 227–34.

Underwood, A. J. and Petraitis, P. S. (1993). Structure of intertidal assemblages in different localities: how can local processes be compared? In *Species Diversity in Ecological Communities: historical and geographical perspectives*, ed. R. E. Ricklefs and D. Schluter. Chicago: University of Chicago Press, pp. 39–51.

UNEP (1995). *Global Biodiversity Assessment. Summary for Policy-makers*. Cambridge, UK: Cambridge University Press.

United Nations (1993). *Agenda 21 – the United Nations Programme of Action from Rio*. UN Department of Public Information. New York: United Nations.

United Nations (2004). *World Urbanization Prospects: The 2003 Revision*. United Nations Department of Economic and Social Affairs, Population Division Report no. E.04. XIII.6. New York, NY: United Nations.

United Nations Population Fund. (1996). *The State of World Population 1996. Changing Places: Population, Development and the Urban Future*. UNFPA.

Upmanis, H., Eliasson, I. and Lindqvist, S. (2000). The influence of green areas on nocturnal temperatures in a high latitude city (Göteborg, Sweden). *International Journal of Climatology*, **18**, 681–700.

Urban Bushland Council (1999). *Managing our Bushland*. Proceedings of a conference about the protection and management of urban bushland. Perth: Urban Bushland Council.

URS (2001). *Roading Stormwater Pollution Strategy*. Technical document prepared for Ecowater Solutions. Auckland: URS New Zealand.

US Bureau of the Census (2000). http://www.census.gov/population/cen2000/phc-t29/tab03a.pdf

US Bureau of the Census (2001). http://www.census.gov

US Environmental Protection Agency (1997). *An Environmental Characterization of the District of Columbia: A Scientific Foundation for Setting an Environmental Agenda*. EPA 903-R-97-027. Philadelphia, PA: US Environmental Protection Agency Region 3.

USDA (2000). *1997 National Resources Inventory*. United States Department of Agriculture, Natural Resources Conservation Service.

Vähä-Piikkiö, I., Kurtto, A. and Hahkala, V. (2004). Species number, historical elements and protection of threatened species in the flora of Helsinki, Finland. *Landscape and Urban Planning*, **68**, 357–70.

Vale, T. R. and Vale, G. R. (1976). Suburban bird populations in west-central California. *Journal of Biogeography*, **3**, 157–65.

Valiela, I., Collins, G., Kremer, J. *et al.* (1997). Nitrogen loading from coastal watersheds to receiving estuaries: new method and application. *Ecological Applications*, **7**, 358–80.

Valiela, I., Foreman, K., LaMontagne, M. *et al.* (1992). Couplings of watersheds and coastal waters: sources and consequences of nutrient enrichment in Waquoit Bay, Massachusetts. *Estuaries*, **15**, 443–57.

Valiela, I., Tomasky, G., Hauxwell, J. *et al.* 2000. Operationalizing sustainability: Management and risk assessment of land-derived nitrogen loads to estuaries. *Ecological Applications*, **10**, 1006–23.

Van Cleve, K., Chapin, C. T. III, Dyrness, C. T. and Viereck, L. A. (1991). Element cycling in Taiga forests: state factor control. *BioScience*, **41**, 78–88.

Van den Berg, A. E. (2003). Personal need for structure and landscape preference. In *Human Decision-making and Environmental Perception: Understanding and Assisting Human Decision-making in Real Life Settings*, ed. L. Hendrickx, W. Jager and L. Steg. Liber Amoricum for Charles Vlek. Groningen: Rijksuniversiteit Groningen.

Van den Berg, J., Rebe, M., De Bruyn, J. and Van Hamburg, H. (2001). Developing habitat management systems for graminaceous stem borers in South Africa. *Insect Science and its Application*, **21**, 381–8.

van der Ree, R. and Bennett, A. F. (2001). Woodland remnants along roadsides – a reflection of pre-European structure in temperate woodlands? *Ecological Management and Restoration*, **2**, 226–8.

van der Ree, R. and Bennett, A. F. (2003). Home range of the Squirrel Glider *Petaurus norfolcensis* in a network of linear habitats. *Journal of Zoology*, **259**, 327–36.

van der Ree, R. and McCarthy, M. A. (2005). Quantifying the effects of urbanisation on the persistence of indigenous mammals in Melbourne, Australia. *Animal Conservation*, **8**, 309–19.

van der Zee, D. and Zonneveld, I. S. (2001). *Landscape Ecology Applied in Land Evaluation, Development and Conservation. Some Worldwide Selected Examples*. ITC publication no. 81, IALE publication MM-1. Enschede, The Netherlands.

van der Zee, F. F., Wiertz, J., ter Braak, C. J. F. and van Apeldoorn, R. (1992). Landscape change as a possible cause of badger *Meles meles* L. decline in The Netherlands. *Biological Conservation*, **61**, 17–22.

Van Kamp, I., Leidelmeijer, K., Marsman, G. and De Hollander, A. (2003). Urban environmental quality and human well-being: towards a conceptual framework and demarcation of concepts; a literature study. *Landscape and Urban Planning*, **65**, 5–18.

van Roon, M. R. (2005). Emerging approaches to urban ecosystem management: the potential of low impact urban design and development principles. *Journal of Environmental Assessment, Policy and Management*, **7**, 1–24.

van Roon, M. R. and Knight, S. J. (2003). The role of aquatic ecosystem sustainability in shaping distribution and form of urbanisation and dairy farming. *Proceedings of the Farming Land Use Dynamics: Integrating Knowledge on Spatial Dynamics in Socio-economic and Environmental Systems for Spatial Planning in Western Urbanised Countries Conference, Utrecht University, Netherlands 16–18 April, 2003*.

van Roon, M. R. and Knight, S. J. (2004). *Ecological Context of Development: New Zealand Perspectives*. Melbourne: Oxford University Press.

van Roon, M. R. and Moore, S. (2004). Proving low impact design and development will deliver biodiversity gains. *Proceedings of the New Zealand Water and Wastes Association Stormwater Conference,* Rotorua, New Zealand, 6–7 May, 2004.

van Roon, M. R. and van Roon, H. T. (2005). *Low Impact Urban Design and Development Principles for Assessment of Planning, Policy and Development Outcomes*. Working Paper 051. Auckland: Centre for Urban Ecosystem Sustainability and Department of Planning, University of Auckland.

van Wagner, C. E. (1978). Age-class distribution and the forest fire cycle. *Canadian Journal of Forest Research,* **8**, 220–7.

Van Wyk, E., Cilliers, S. S. and Bredenkamp, G. J. (1997). Vegetation studies of fragmented hills in the Klerksdorp municipal area, North West Province. *Suid-Afrikaanse Tydskrif vir Natuurwetenskap en Tegnologie,* **16**, 74–85. (In Afrikaans)

Van Wyk, E., Cilliers, S. S. and Bredenkamp, G. J. (2000). Vegetation analysis of wetlands in the Klerksdorp Municipal Area, North West Province, South Africa. *South African Journal of Botany,* **66**, 52–62.

Van Wyk, J. K. (2003). Environmental security in South Africa: a prognosis for regional security. In *Human Impact on Environment and Sustainable Development in Africa*, ed. M. Darkoh and A. Rwomire. Burlington: Ashgate, pp. 75–97.

VanDruff, L. W., Bolen, E. G. and San Julian, G. E. (1994). Management of urban wildlife. In *Research and Management Techniques for Wildlife and Habitats*, ed. T. A. Bookhout. Bethesda: The Wildlife Society, pp. 507–30.

Vannote, R. L., Minshall, G. W., Cummins, K. W., Sedell, J. R. and Cushing, C. E. (1980). The river continuum concept. *Canadian Journal of Fisheries and Aquatic Sciences,* **37**, 130–7.

Vårdprogram för naturmarken i Hagaparken (1995). [Maintenance Program for Natural Vegetation at the Hagaparken, Stockholm] Del 1: Beskrivning mål och åtgärder. Stockholm: Statens fastighetsverk. (In Swedish)

Veblen, T. T. and Stewart, G. H. (1982). The effects of introduced wild animals on New Zealand forests. *Annals of the Association of American Geographers,* **72**, 372–97.

Vega, S. J. and Rust, M. K. (2001). The Argentine ant: a significant invasive species in agricultural, urban and natural environments. *Sociobiology,* **37**, 3–25.

Venn, S. J., Kotze, D. J. and Niemelä, J. (2003). Urbanization effects on carabid diversity in boreal forests. *European Journal of Entomology,* **100**, 73–80.

Vepsäläinen, K. and Spence, J. R. (2000). Generalization in ecology and evolutionary biology: from hypothesis to paradigm. *Biology and Philosophy,* **15**, 211–38.

Vermeulen, H. J. W. (1994). Corridor function of a road verge for dispersal of stenotopic heathland ground beetles carabidae. *Biological Conservation,* **69**, 339–49.

Viana, M., Maenhaut, W., ten Brink, H. M. *et al.* (2007). Comparative analysis of organic and elemental carbon concentrations in carbonaceous aerosols in three European cities. *Atmospheric Environment,* **41**, 5972–83.

Vigar, G., Healey, P., Hull, A. and Davoudi, S. (2000). *Planning, Governance and Spatial Strategy in Britain: An Institutionalist Analysis*. London: Macmillan Press.

Vincent, A. V. (1998). Seahorses under siege. *Nature Australia*, **25**, 57–63.

Vitousek, P. M. and Howarth, R. W. (1991). Nitrogen limitation on land and sea: how can it occur? *Biogeochemistry*, **13**, 87–115.

Vitousek, P. M. and Matson, P. A. (1991). Gradient analysis of ecosystems. In *Comparative Analysis of Ecosystems: Patterns, Mechanisms and Theories*, ed. J. J. Cole, G. M. Lovett and S. E. G. Findlay. New York: Springer-Verlag, pp. 287–98.

Vitousek, P. M., Aber, J. D., Howarth, G. E. *et al.* (1997a). Human alteration of the global nitrogen cycle: sources and consequences. *Ecological Applications*, **7**, 737–50.

Vitousek, P. M., Mooney, H. A., Lubchenco, J. and Melillo, J. M. (1997b). Human domination of Earth's ecosystems. *Science*, **227**, 494–9.

Vitousek, P. M., Van Cleve, K., Balakrishnan, N. and Mueller-Dombois, D. (1983). Soil development and nitrogen turnover on recent volcanic substrates in Hawaii. *Biotropica*, **15**, 268–74.

Vizyova, A. (1986). Urban woodlots as islands for land vertebrates: a preliminary attempt on estimating the barrier effects of urban structural units. *Ecologia*, **5**, 407–19.

Vogelmann, J. E. (1995). Assessment of forest fragmentation in southern New England using remote sensing and geographic information systems technology. *Conservation Biology*, **9**, 439–49.

Vogelmann, J. E., Howard, S. M., Yang, L., Larson, C. R., Wylie, B. K. and Van Driel, N. (2001). Completion of the 1990s National Land Cover Data set for the conterminous United States from Landsat Thematic Mapper data and ancillary data sources. *Photogrammetric Engineering and Remote Sensing*, **67**, 650–62.

Vos, C. C., Verboom, J., Opdam, P. F. M. and ter Braak, C. J. (2001). Toward ecologically scaled landscape indices. *American Naturalist*, **157**, 24–41.

Vuorisalo, T., Andersson, H., Hugg, T., Lahtinen, H., Laaksonen, H. and Lehikonein, E. (2003). Urban development from an avian perspective: causes of hooded crow (*Corvus corone cornix*) urbanisation in two Finnish cities. *Landscape and Urban Planning*, **62**, 69–87.

Wackernagel, M. and Rees, W. E. (1996). *Our Ecological Footprint*. Gabriola Island, BC: New Society Publishers.

Wackernagel, M. and Yount, J. D. (1998). The ecological footprint: an indicator of progress toward regional sustainability. *Environmental Monitoring and Assessment*, **51**, 511–29.

Wade, P. R. (2000). Bayesian methods in conservation biology. *Conservation Biology*, **14**, 1308–16.

Walbridge, M. R. (1993). Functions and values of forested wetlands in the southern United States. *Journal of Forestry*, **91**, 15–19.

Walbridge, M. R. (1997). Urban ecosystems. *Urban Ecosystems*, **1**, 1–2.

Walbridge, M. R. and Struthers, J. P. (1993). Phosphorus retention in non-tidal Palustrine forested wetlands of the mid-Atlantic region. *Wetlands*, **13**, 84–94.

Walker, D. I., Laketelich, R. J., Bastyan, G. and McComb, A. J. (1989). Effect of boat moorings on seagrass beds near Perth, Western Australia. *Aquatic Botany*, **36**, 69–77.

Walker, H. J., ed. (1988). *Artificial Structures and Shorelines*. Los Angeles: Kluwer Academic Publishers.

References 693

Walmsley, D. and Mangold, S. (2002). Overall recommendations for implementation and management. In *The State of the Environment Report 2002 of the North West Province, South Africa*, ed. S. Mangold, M. Kalule-Sabiti and J. Walmsley. Mafikeng: North West Province Department of Agriculture, Conservations and Environment, Chapter 18.

Walters, C. J. and Holling, C. S. (1990). Large scale management experiments and learning by doing. *Ecology*, **71**, 2060–8.

Wang, W.-X. and Xu, Z.-Z. (1997). Larval swimming and postlarval drifting behavior in the infaunal bivalve *Sinonovacula constricta*. *Marine Ecology Progress Series*, **148**, 71–81.

Wang, Y. and Zhang, X. (1999). Land cover change of metropolitan Chicago area from 1972 to 1997 and the impact to natural communities in the region. Presented at *GeoInformatics99*, University of Michigan, Ann Arbor, Michigan, 19–21 June 1999.

Ward, P. (1968). Origin of the avifauna of urban and suburban Singapore. *Ibis*, **110**, 239–55.

Wardle, P. (1991). *Vegetation of New Zealand*. Cambridge: Cambridge University Press.

Warren, M. S. (1987). The ecology and conservation of the heath fritillary butterfly, *Mellicta athalia*. III. Population dynamics and the effect of habitat management. *Journal of Applied Ecology*, **24**, 499–513.

Warren-Rhodes, K. and Koenig, A. (2001). Escalating trends in the urban metabolism of Hong Kong: 1971–1997. *Ambio*, **30**, 429–38.

Wasowski, S. and Wasowski, A. (2002). *Gardening with Prairie Plants: How to Create Beautiful Native Landscapes*. Minneapolis: University of Minnesota Press.

Watmough, S. A., Hutchinson, T. C. and Sager, E. P. S. (1998). Changes in tree ring chemistry in sugar maple (*Acer saccharum*) along an urban–rural gradient in southern Ontario. *Environmental Pollution*, **101**, 381–90.

Watson, D. M. (2002). A conceptual framework for studying species composition in fragments, islands and other patchy ecosystems. *Journal of Biogeography*, **29**, 823–34.

Watson, F. G. R., Vertessy, R. A. and Grayson, R. B. (1999). Large-scale modelling of forest hydrological processes and their long-term effect on water yield. *Hydrological Processes*, **13**, 689–700.

Watson, V. J., Loucks, O. L. and Wojner, W. (1981). The impact of urbanization on seasonal hydrologic and nutrient budgets of a small North American watershed. *Hydrobiologia*, **77**, 87–96.

Watt, A. S. (1947). Pattern and process in the plant community. *Journal of Ecology*, **35**, 1–22.

Weeks, J. R. (2003). Using remote sensing and Geographic Information Systems to identify the underlying properties of urban environments. In *New Forms of Urbanisation: Beyond the Urban–rural Dichotomy*, ed. T. Champion and G. Hugo. Aldershot, UK: Ashgate Publishing Co.

Weeks, J. R., Larson, D., Stow, D. A. and Rashed, T. (2003). Contrast or continuum: the creation and application of an urban gradient index using remotely sensed imagery and GIS. Prepared for the Annual Meeting of the Population Association of America, Minneapolis, May 2003. Unpublished. http://geography.sdsu.edu/Research/Projects/Aftweb/Publications/Contrast-or-Continuum.pdf

Weigmann, G. (1982). The colonization of ruderal biotopes in the city of Berlin by arthropods. In *Urban Ecology: The Second European Ecological Symposium*, ed.

R. Bornkamm, J. A. Lee and M. R. D. Seaward. Oxford: Blackwell Scientific Publications, pp. 75–82.

Weiner, J. (1995). On the practice of ecology. *Journal of Ecology*, **83**, 153–8.

Weis, J. S. and Weis, P. (2002). Contamination of saltmarsh sediments and biota by CCA treated wood walkways. *Marine Pollution Bulletin*, **44**, 504–10.

Wendt, P. H., Knott, D. M. and Van Doilah, R. F. (1989). Community structure of the sessile biota on five artificial reefs of different ages. *Bulletin of Marine Science*, **44**, 1106–22.

Weng, Y.-C. (2007). Spatiotemporal changes of landscape pattern in response to urbanization. *Landscape and Urban Planning*, **81**, 341–53.

Werner, P. (1999). Why biotope mapping in populated areas? *Deinsea*, **5**, 9–26.

Wessolek, G. and Facklam, M. (1997). Standorteigenschaften und Wasserhaushalt von versiegelten Flächen. *Zeitschrift Pflanzenernährung Bodenkunde*, **160**, 41–6.

Westerdahl, M. (1996). Den svenska skogskyrkogården – en bild från norr till söder. *Stad and Land* nr 136. Alnarp, Sweden: Movium. (In Swedish)

White, C. S. and McDonnell, M. J. (1988). Nitrogen cycling processes and soil characteristics in an urban versus rural forest. *Biogeochemistry*, **5**, 243–62.

White, J. G., Antos, M. J., Fitzsimons, J. A. and Palmer, G. C. (2005). Non-uniform bird assemblages in urban environments: the influence of streetscape vegetation. *Landscape and Urban Planning*, **71**, 123–35.

White, M. A., Nemani, R. R., Thornton, P. E. and Running, S. W. (2002). Satellite evidence of phenological differences between urbanized and rural areas of the eastern United States deciduous broadleaf forest. *Ecosystems*, **5**, 260–77.

Whitney, G. G. and Adams, S. D. (1980). Man as a maker of new plant communities. *Journal of Applied Ecology*, **17**, 431–48.

Whittaker, R. H. (1967). Gradient analysis of vegetation. *Biological Review*, **42**, 207–64.

Whorff, J. S., Whorff, L. L. and Sweet, M. H. (1995). Spatial variation in an algal turf community with respect to substratum slope and wave height. *Journal of the Marine Biological Association of the United Kingdom*, **75**, 429–44.

Wickop, E. (1997). Environmental quality targets for urban structural units in Leipzig with a view to sustainable urban development. In *Urban Ecology*, ed. J. Breuste, H. Feldmann and O. Uhlmann. Leipzig, pp. 49–54.

Wilcock, R. J. (1994). Organic pollutants in sediment of Manukau Harbour. In *Proceedings of the First AgResearch / Landcare Research Pesticides Residue Workshop*, ed. L Boul and J. Aislabie. Lincoln, New Zealand, pp. 39–45.

Wilkie, D., Shaw, E., Rotberg, F., Morelli, G. and Auzel, P. (2000). Roads, development, and conservation in the Congo Basin. *Conservation Biology*, **4**, 1614–22.

Williams, B. K. (1997). Logic and science in wildlife biology. *Journal of Wildlife Management*, **61**, 1007–15.

Williams, C. B. (1936). The influence of moonlight on the activity of certain nocturnal insects, particularly of the family Noctuidae, as indicated by a light trap. *Philosophical Transactions of the Royal Society of London, Series B*, **226**, 357–89.

Williams, M. (1993). An exceptionally powerful biotic factor. In *Humans as Components of Ecosystems: The Ecology of Subtle Human Effects and Populated Areas*, ed. M. J. McDonnell and S. T. A. Pickett. New York: Springer-Verlag, pp. 24–39.

Williams, N. S. G., McDonnell, M. J., Phelan, G. K., Keim, L. D. and van der Ree, R. (2006). Range expansion due to urbanisation: increased food resources attract Grey-headed Flying-foxes (*Pteropus poliocephalus*) to Melbourne. *Austral Ecology*, **31**, 190-8.

Williams, N. S. G., Morgan, J. W., McDonnell, M. J. and McCarthy, M. A. (2005). Plant traits and local extinctions in natural grasslands along an urban-rural gradient. *Journal of Ecology*, **93**, 1203-13.

Williams, P. A. and Karl, B. (1996). Fleshy fruit of indigenous and adventive plants in the diet of birds in forest remnants, Nelson, New Zealand. *New Zealand Journal of Ecology*, **20**, 127-45.

Williamson, I. and Bull, C. M. (1996). Population ecology of the Australian frog *Crinia signifera*: adults and juveniles. *Wildlife Research*, **23**, 249-66.

Williamson, R. B. (1991). *Urban Run-off Data Book, A Manual for the Preliminary Evaluation of Urban Stormwater Impacts on Water Quality*. Water Quality Centre Publication 20. New Zealand: Ecosystems Division, NIWA.

Williamson, R. D. and DeGraaf, R. M. (1980). Habitat associations of ten bird species in Washington, DC. *Urban Ecology*, **5**, 125-36.

Willis, E. O. (1979). The composition of avian communities in remanescent woodlots in southern Brazil. *Papeis Avulsos de Zoologia* (Sao Paulo), **33**, 1-25.

Wilson, K.-J. (2002). *The Flight of the Huia*. Christchurch, New Zealand: Canterbury University Press.

Wilson, R. S., Heislers, S. and Poore, G. C. B. (1998). Changes in benthic communities in Port Phillip Bay, Australia, between 1969 and 1995. *Marine and Freshwater Research*, **49**, 847-61.

Wiltshire, E. (1994). The flora of Hyde Park and Kensington Gardens, 1988-1993. *London Naturalist*, **73**, 37-60.

Wirén, E. (1998). *Planering för säkerhets skull*. Lund: Studentlitteratur.

With, K. A., Gardner, R. H. and Turner, M. G. (1997). Landscape connectivity and population distributions in heterogeneous environments. *Oikos*, **78**, 151-69.

Wittig, R. (1998). Urban development and the integration of nature: reality or fiction? In *Urban Ecology*, ed. J. Breuste, H. Feldmann and O. Uhlmann. Berlin: Springer, pp. 593-9.

Wittig, R. (2002). *Siedlungsvegetation*. Stuttgart: Ulmer.

Wittig, R. and Schreiber, K.-F. (1983). A quick method for assessing the importance of open spaces in towns for urban nature conservation. *Biological Conservation*, **26**, 57-64.

Wittig, R. and Sukopp, H. (1993). Was ist Stadtökologie? In *Stadtökologie*, ed. H. Sukopp and R. Wittig. Stuttgart: Gustav Fischer Verlag, pp. 1-9.

Wittig, R. and Sukopp, H. (1998). Was ist Stadtökologie? In *Stadtökologie*, ed. H. Sukopp and R. Wittig, 2nd edn. Stuttgart: Fischer, pp. 1-9.

Wittig, R., Diesing, D. and Gödde, M. (1985). Urbanophob - Urbanoneutral - Urbanophil. Das Verhalten der Arten gegenüber dem Lebensraum Stadt. *Flora*, **177**, 265-82.

Wolf, K. L. (2003). Freeway roadside management: the urban forest beyond the white line. *Journal of Arboriculture*, **29**, 127-36.

Wolter, C. (2001). Conservation of fish species diversity in navigable waterways. *Landscape and Urban Planning*, **53**, 135–44.

Wong, F., Harner, T., Liu, Q. T. and Diamond, M. L. (2004). Using experimental and forest soils to investigate the uptake of polycyclic aromatic hydrocarbons (PAHs) along an urban–rural gradient. *Environmental Pollution*, **129**, 387–98.

Wood, B. C. and Pullin, A. S. (2002). Persistence of species in a fragmented urban landscape: the importance of dispersal ability and habitat availability for grassland butterflies. *Biodiversity and Conservation*, **11**, 1451–68.

Wood, J., Low, A. B., Donaldson, J. S. and Rebelo, A. G. (1994). Threats to plant species diversity through urbanisation and habitat fragmentation in the Cape Metropolitan Area, South Africa. In *Strelitzia 1. Botanical Diversity in Southern Africa*, ed. B. J. Huntley. Proceedings of a conference on the conservation and utilisation of Southern African botanical diversity. Pretoria: National Botanical Institute.

Woodell, S. (1979). The flora of walls and pavings. In *Nature in Cities*, ed. I. Laurie. Chichester, New York, Brisbane, Toronto: John Wiley and Sons, pp. 135–57.

Woodward, S. M. (1990). Population density and home range characteristics of woodchucks, *Marmota monax*, at expressway interchanges. *Canadian Field Naturalist*, **104**, 421–8.

Wootton, J. T. (1998). Effects of disturbance on species diversity: a multitrophic perspective. *The American Naturalist*, **152**, 803–25.

World Bank (1984). *World Development Report*. Oxford, UK: Oxford University Press.

Worster, D. (1977). *Nature's Economy: A History of Ecological Ideas*. New York: Cambridge University Press.

Worth, C. B. and Muller, J. (1979). Captures of large moths by an ultraviolet light trap. *Journal of the Lepidopterists' Society*, **33**, 261–4.

Wratten, S. D., Hochuli, D. F., Gurr, G. M., Tylianakis, J. and Scarratt, S. L. (2007). Conservation, biodiversity and integrated pest management. In *Perspectives In Ecological Theory and Integrated Pest Management*, ed. Kogan M. and Jepson P. Cambridge, UK: Cambridge University Press, pp. 223–45.

Wright, J. P., Jones, C. G. and Flecker, A. S. (2002). An ecosystem engineer, the beaver, increases species richness at the landscape scale. *Oecologia*, **132**, 96–101.

Wrigley, J. W. (2003). *Australian Native Plants: Cultivation, Use in Landscaping and Propagation*. Frenchs Forest, NSW: Reed New Holland.

Wu, C. and Murray, A. T. (2003). Estimate impervious surface distribution by spectral mixture analysis. *Remote Sensing of Environment*, **84**, 493–505.

Wu, J. (2004). Effects of changing scale on landscape pattern analysis: scaling relations. *Landscape Ecology*, **19**, 125–38.

Wu, J. and David, J. L. (2002). A spatially explicit hierarchical approach to modeling complex ecological systems: theory and applications. *Ecological Modelling*, **153**, 7–26.

Wu, J. and Loucks, O. L. (1995). From balance of nature to hierarchical patch dynamics: a paradigm shift in ecology. *Quarterly Review of Biology*, **70**, 439–66.

Wu, J. and Vankat, J. L. (1995). Island biogeography, theory and applications. In *Encyclopedia of Environmental Biology*, Vol. 2, F–N, ed. W. A Nierenberg (F–N). San Diego: Academic Press, pp. 371–9.

Wu, J., David, J. L. and Jenerette, G. D. (2003). Linking land use change with ecosystem processes: a hierarchical patch dynamics model. In *Integrated Land Use and Environmental Models*, ed. S. Guhathakurta. Berlin: Springer, pp. 99–119.

Wu, J., Shen, W., Sun, W. and Tueller, P. T. (2002). Empirical patterns of the effects of changing scale on landscape metrics. *Landscape Ecology*, **17**, 761–82.

Wuorenrinne, H. (1978). Metsä urbaanin paineen puristuksessa [Summary: The forest under urban pressure]. Espoo, Finland: Espoo yleiskaavaosasto. Ympäristönhoito/metsät. Perusselvitys 13.5.1978. (In Finnish)

Wyatt, B. K., Greatorex-Davies, N. G., Bunce, R. G. H., Fuller, R. M. and Hill, M. O. (1994). *Comparison of Land Cover Definitions. Countryside 1990 Series*, Vol. 3. London: Department of the Environment.

Yabe, K., Yoshida, K. and Kaneko, M. (1998). Effects of urbanisation on the flora of open space in Sapporo City. *Journal of the Japanese Institute of Landscape Architecture* **61**, 571–6. (In Japanese with English abstract)

Yahner, R. H. (1988). Changes in wildlife communities near edges. *Conservation Biology*, **2**, 333–9.

Yamada, K., Elith, J., McCarthy, M. and Zerger, A. (2003). Eliciting and integrating expert knowledge for wildlife habitat modelling. *Ecological Modelling*, **165**, 251–64.

Yan, L. Z. (1998). Introducing the sustainable development of urban afforestation in Shanghai in the 21st century. *Chinese Landscape and Gardening*, **14**, 44–6 (in Chinese).

Yapp, G. A. (1986). Aspects of population, recreation, and management of the Australian coastal zone. *Coastal Zone Management Journal*, **14**, 47–66.

Yaro, R. D. and Hiss, T. (1996). *A Region at Risk. The 3rd Regional Plan for the New York–New Jersey–Connecticut Metropolitan Area*. New York: Regional Plan Association, Covelo, CA: Island Press.

Yli-Pelkonen, V. and Niemelä, J. (2005). Linking ecological and social systems in cities: urban planning in Finland as a case study. *Biodiversity and Conservation*, **14**, 1947–67.

Yokohari, M. and Fukuhara, M. (1988). Analysis of mixed land use in urban fringe using Landsat TM data. *Journal of the Japanese Institute of Landscape Architecture*, **51**, 335–40. (In Japanese with English abstract)

Yokoyama, S. (1995). *Keikan seitaigaku* (Landscape Ecology). Tokyo: Kokin Shoin. (In Japanese).

Young, B. M. and Harvey, L. E. (1996). A spatial analysis of the relationship between mangrove (*Avicennia marina* var. *australasica*) physiognomy and sediment accretion in the Hauraki Plains, New Zealand. *Estuarine, Coastal and Shelf Science*, **42**, 231–46.

Young, C. H. and Jarvis, P. J. (2001). Measuring urban habitat fragmentation: an example from the Black Country, UK. *Landscape Ecology*, **16**, 643–58.

Yui, A., Natuhara, Y., Murakami, K. and Morimoto, Y. (2001). Factors influence the species richness of ants in urban woods. *Journal of the Japanese Society of Revegetation Technology*, **27**, 78–83. (In Japanese with English abstract)

Zabel, J. and Tscharntke, T. (1998). Does fragmentation of Urtica habitats affect phytophagous and predatory insects differentially? *Oecologia*, **116**, 419–25.

Zak, D. R. and Grigal, D. F. (1991). Nitrogen mineralization, nitrification and denitrification in upland and wetland ecosystems. *Oecologia*, **88**, 189–96.

Zanders, J., McLeod, M. and Thornburrow, D. (2002). Urban soil implications for on-site stormwater mitigation. Hamilton, New Zealand: Presentation to NIWA.

Zanette, L., Doyle, P. and Tremont, S. M. (2000). Food shortage in small fragments: evidence from an area-sensitive Passerine. *Ecology*, **81**, 1654–66.

Zanette, L. R. S., Martins, R. P. and Ribeiro, S. P. (2005). Effects of urbanization on Neotropical wasp and bee assemblages in a Brazilian metropolis. *Landscape and Urban Planning*, **71**, 105–21.

Zedler, J. B. (1988). Salt marsh restoration: lessons for California. In *Rehabilitating Damaged Ecosystems*, Vol. 1, ed. J. Cairns. Boca Raton, California: CRC Press, pp. 123–38.

Zedler, J. B. (1993). Lessons on preventing overexploitations. *Ecological Applications*, **3**, 577–8.

Zedler, J. B. (2003). Wetlands at your service: reducing impacts of agriculture at the watershed scale. *Frontiers in Ecology and the Environment*, **2**, 65–72.

Zedler, J. B., Fellows, M. Q. and Trnka, S. (1998). Wastelands to wetlands: links between habitat protection and ecosystem science. In *Successes, Limitations and Frontiers in Ecosystem Science*, ed. M. L. Pace and P. M. Groffman. New York: Springer-Verlag, pp. 69–112.

Zerbe, S., Maurer, U., Schmitz, S. and Sukopp, H. (2003). Biodiversity in Berlin and its potential for nature conservation. *Landscape and Urban Planning*, **62**, 139–48.

Zettler, J. A., Spira, T. P. and Allen, C. R. (2001). Ant–seed mutualisms: can red imported fire ants sour the relationship? *Biological Conservation*, **101**, 249–53.

Zhu, L., Qian, G., Su, Y., Sun, Y. and Dai, Z. (1986). Analysis of the house rodent community succession and the relation to the housing structure in Tancqiao, Shanghai, China. *Acta Theriologica Sinica*, **6**, 147–54.

Zhu, W. and Carreiro, M. M. (1999). Chemoautotrophic nitrification in acidic forest soils along an urban-to-rural transect. *Soil Biology and Biochemistry*, **31**, 1091–100.

Zhu, W. and Carreiro, M. M. (2004a). Temporal and spatial variations in nitrogen cycling in deciduous forest ecosystems along an urban–rural gradient. *Soil Biology and Biochemistry*, **36**, 267–78.

Zhu, W. and Carreiro, M. M. (2004b). Soluble organic nitrogen and microbial nitrogen dynamics in deciduous forest soils: neglected segments of the nitrogen cycle. *Soil Biology and Biochemistry*, **36**, 279–88.

Zipperer, W. C. (2002). Species composition and structure of regenerated and remnant forest patches within an urban landscape. *Urban Ecosystems*, **6**, 271–90.

Zipperer, W. C. and Pickett, S. T. A. (2001). Urban ecology: patterns of population growth and ecological effects. In *Encyclopedia of Life Science*. London: Nature Publishing Group, p. 6. http//www.els.net

Zipperer, W. C. and Zipperer, C. E. (1992). Vegetation responses to changes in design and management of an urban park. *Landscape and Urban Planning*, **22**, 1–10.

Zipperer, W. C., Burgess, R. L. and Nyland, R. D. (1990). Patterns of deforestation and reforestation in different landscape types in central New York. *Forest Ecology and Management*, **36**, 103–17.

Zipperer, W. C., Foresman, T. W., Sisinni, S. M. and Pouyat, R. V. (1997). Urban tree cover: an ecological perspective. *Urban Ecosystems*, **1**, 229–46.

Zipperer, W. C., Grove, J. M. and Neville, L. R. (1995). Ecosystem management in urban environments. In *Proceedings of the 7th Annual National Urban Forestry Conference, September 12–17, New York*, ed. C. Kollin. Washington, DC: American Forests, p 9.

Zipperer, W. C., Wu, J. G., Pouyat, R. V. and Pickett, S. T. A. (2000). The application of ecological principles to urban and urbanizing landscapes. *Ecological Applications*, **10**, 685–8.

Ziska, L. H. and George, K. (2007). Establishment and persistence of common ragweed (*Ambrosia artemisiifolia* L.) in disturbed soil as a function of an urban–rural macro-environment. *Global Change Biology*, **13**, 266–74.

Ziska, L. H., Bunce, J. A. and Goins, E. W. (2004). Characterization of an urban–rural CO_2/temperature gradient and associated changes in initial plant productivity during secondary succession. *Oecologia*, **139**, 454–8.

Zonneveld, I. S. (1989). The land unit – a fundamental concept in landscape ecology and its applications. *Landscape Ecology*, **3**, 67–89.

Zube, E. H. (1982). An exploration of southwest landscape images. *Landscape Journal*, **1**, 31–40.

Zuylen, G. van (1994). *The Garden. Visions of Paradise*. London, UK: Thames and Hudson.

Index

700